History of Biblical Exegesis

Editors

Mark W. Elliott (Dingwall, UK / Toronto, CA)
Jennie Grillo (Notre Dame, IN)
Michael Legaspi (Yonkers, NY)
David Lincicum (Notre Dame, IN)
Benjamin Schliesser (Bern, CH)

6

Revelation's New Jerusalem
in Late Antiquity

Edited by

Nathan Betz, Anthony Dupont,
and Johan Leemans

Mohr Siebeck

Nathan Betz, born 1976; MA in Liberal Arts from St. John's College (Annapolis); MSt in Patristic Theology from the University of Oxford; ReMa in Theology from KU Leuven; PhD in Theology from KU Leuven; currently research fellow at the Beyond Canon Centre, University of Regensburg.
orcid.org/0000-0002-6852-333X

Anthony Dupont, born 1979; MA in Philosophy, in Religious Studies, and in Theology from KU Leuven; PhD in Theology from KU Leuven; currently research professor at KU Leuven.
orcid.org/0000-0003-4967-7541

Johan Leemans, born 1965; MA in Ancient History, in Religious Studies, and in Theology; PhD in Theology from KU Leuven; currently Professor for Christianity in Late Antiquity (Greek Patristics) at the Faculty of Theology and Religious Studies at KU Leuven.
orcid.org/0000-0003-1378-7028

ISBN 978-3-16-162376-9 / eISBN 978-3-16-162628-9
DOI 10.1628/978-3-16-162628-9

ISSN 2748–0313 / eISSN 2748–0321 (History of Biblical Exegesis)

The Deutsche Nationalbibliothek lists this publication in the Deutsche Nationalbibliographie; detailed bibliographic data are available at *https://dnb.de*.

© 2023 Mohr Siebeck Tübingen, Germany. www.mohrsiebeck.com

This book may not be reproduced, in whole or in part, in any form (beyond that permitted by copyright law) without the publisher's written permission. This applies particularly to reproductions, translations and storage and processing in electronic systems.

The book was typeset by Martin Fischer in Tübingen using Minion typeface, printed on non-aging paper by Laupp & Göbel in Gomaringen, and bound by Buchbinderei Nädele in Nehren.

Printed in Germany.

Table of Contents

Nathan Betz, Anthony Dupont, Johan Leemans
General Introduction: The New Jerusalem – More Than the World
to Come 1

Part 1

Studies on Specific Authors, Works, and Corpora

Nathan Betz
Not Just Millennialists: Some Second-Century Greek Interpretations
of Revelation's Holy City 9

Martina Vercesi
Tracking the New Jerusalem in North African Christianity
through the Fourth Century 35

Konrad Huber
In hoc regno: On the Geographical Localization of the New Jerusalem
in Victorinus of Petovium 57

Antti Laato
The Heavenly Jerusalem and the Jewish Remnant in the Book of Isaiah:
The Changing Interpretation of Eusebius of Caesarea 71

Alessandro Capone
Revelation 20 and 21 and the New Jerusalem According
to Ambrosiaster and Jerome 93

Anni Maria Laato
The Heavenly Jerusalem According to Two Fourth-Century
Female Pilgrims 107

Tobias Nicklas
From the Heavenly Jerusalem to the City of Christ:
Revelation and the Visio Pauli 123

Mark W. Elliott
New Jerusalem as the "Flipside" to the Last Judgment
in Primasius, Bede, and Beatus 137

Francis X. Gumerlock
Two Early Medieval Hiberno-Latin Texts on the New Jerusalem:
Introduction, Transcription, and Translation 153

Ian Boxall
Imagining the Celestial City: Visual Reception of Patristic Exegetical
Traditions in the Carolingian, Beatus, and Anglo-Norman Apocalypses ... 173

Part 2

Topical Studies

Joseph Verheyden and Mathieu Cuijpers
Heaven on Earth: Some Noteworthy Greek and Roman Parallels
to Revelation 21:2 197

T. C. Schmidt
Stones of Stumbling: The Petrographic Scandal of the New Jerusalem
in Origen and His Eastern Inheritors 217

Mateusz Kusio
The Walls of the New Jerusalem: Jewish Context and Patristic Reception .. 229

Armin F. Bergmeier
Representing the Heavenly Jerusalem: Encounters with the Divine
in Images and Spaces in Late Antiquity 263

Mark Edwards
Where Is the New Jerusalem? 287

List of Contributors 305
Index of References 307
Index of Modern Authors 327
Index of Historical Figures 331
Index of Places 333
Index of Subjects 335

Abbreviations

ANF	*The Ante-Nicene Fathers.* Edited by Alexander Roberts and James Donaldson. 1885–1887. 10 vols. Repr., Peabody, MA: Hendrickson, 1994.
CCCM	Corpus Christianorum: Continuatio Mediaevalis
CCSG	Corpus Christianorum: Series Graeca
CCSL	Corpus Christianorum: Series Latina
CPG	*Clavis Patrum Graecorum.* Edited by Maurice Geerard. 5 vols. Turnhout: Brepols, 1974–1987
CPL	*Clavis Patrum Latinorum.* Edited by Eligius Dekkers. 2nd ed.
CSCO	*Corpus Scriptorum Christianorum Orientalium.* Edited by Jean-Baptiste Chabot et al. Paris, 1903
CSEL	Corpus Scriptorum Ecclesiasticorum Latinorum
FC	Fathers of the Church
GCS	Die griechischen christlichen Schriftsteller der ersten [drei] Jahrhunderte
LCL	Loeb Classical Library
NPNF	*A Select Library of the Nicene and Post-Nicene Fathers of the Christian Church.* 2 series (14 vols. each). Edited by Philip Schaff et al. 1887–1994. Repr., Peabody, MA: Hendrickson, 1994.
PG	Patrologia Graeca [= *Patrologiae Cursus Completus:* Series Graeca]. Edited by Jacques-Paul Migne. 162 vols. Paris, 1857–1886
PL	Patrologia Latina [= *Patrologiae Cursus Completus:* Series Latina]. Edited by Jacques-Paul Migne. 217 vols. Paris, 1844–1864
SC	Sources Chrétiennes
WUNT	Wissenschaftliche Untersuchungen zum Neuen Testament

General Introduction:
The New Jerusalem – More Than the World to Come

One of the most iconic paintings in Belgian art history is the *Mystic Lamb*, also called the *Ghent Altarpiece*, a religious polyptych by brothers Hubert and Jan van Eyck that was probably completed around 1432. The central panel shows the adoration of the *Agnus Dei* situated in Heavenly Jerusalem. Depicted as a beautiful Gothic city, the latter is seen amidst wondrous natural beauty, angels overhung with jewels, and elongated processions of saints, martyrs, confessors, judges, kings, knights, and pilgrims on their way to the heavenly city.

By this introduction, we do not intend to engage in product placement and advertise our patrimony – though Belgium does reward its visitors richly. Rather, we merely wish to point out that this masterpiece of European art expresses a profoundly human question about life after death, which in Christianity has frequently developed into a fascination with the New Jerusalem that is described in the last book of the New Testament. It is a colorful image in which theology, liturgy, and architecture are intimately intertwined, an idea that was prepared throughout the whole of the Bible and Judeo-Christian culture, and a concept that enjoyed a rich reception history in the first centuries of Christianity. The latter – its early Christian reception – is the subject of the present volume.

While the New Jerusalem has not always or even mainly been interpreted as an image of the afterlife – something that will become increasingly evident throughout this volume – it is along eschatological lines that the image has often been imagined throughout history and until today. Humanity has never ceased to construe images of life after death, especially within what one might today call "religious" contexts. Late antique Christianity is no exception, and it has been a fertile breeding ground for reflections about the life to come and of our journey towards it. How should the otherworld – both the world above and the world below, both "heaven" and "hell" – be understood? Likewise, Christians of the first millennium grappled with intricate questions about body, soul, and resurrection. These questions and their answers found expression both in literary and pictorial artistry, not least in the imaginative representations of an enticing heavenly abode and a dreadful underworld. Drawing on pagan and Jewish forbears, the result of the late antique Christian creativity was a multitude of images, portrayals, pictures, metaphors, and stories that together shaped how the ancients conceived of the afterlife.[1] The early church's hope for eschatological redemption – and the fear of eternal punishment with which it was always accompanied – proved too great to be subsumed under a single image. Two examples may illustrate this multifarious creativity.

The first, a well-known example, originates from the *Passion of Perpetua and Felicity (Passio Perpetuae)*. In her first vision, Perpetua sees a great ladder that reaches into heaven. Upon climbing it, she arrives in an expansive paradise-like garden. At the center of the garden a man with white hair is seated surrounded by a multitude clothed in white robes. Seeing her, the man welcomes Perpetua and offers her a piece of cheese. Perpetua receives it with open hands and eats it as all those present say "Amen." At this point, she awakes from her vision.[2] Later in the text, we read of a vision that Saturus, one of Perpetua's companions, receives. In continuity with Perpetua's vision, Saturus describes the martyrs' postmortem fate, for again, the martyrs are brought to a spacious garden in the middle of which a white-haired man is seated. The description of how Saturus and Perpetua are welcomed and integrated into this heavenly community is much more elaborate and detailed. Remarkably, at the entrance of the garden they encounter a bishop, Optatus, and a learned presbyter, Aspasius, who ask them to intervene and heal a breach that had occurred between them. Here one may read between the lines a reflection on the position of martyrs and confessors in the community and their role over against bishops and presbyters, proof of how this-wordly concerns could find themselves squarely in the middle of narrations of the world to come.[3]

The second example is taken from the *Vision of Dorotheus*, a fourth-century poem in dactylic hexameters that is preserved in the first folios of Bodmer Papyrus 29.[4] Dorotheus receives his heavenly vision while sitting in the imperi-

---

[1] From the wealth of scholarship on this topic, of fundamental importance still are the articles in the *Reallexikon für Antike und Christentum* 17 (1996): Carsten Colpe, Ernst Dassmann, Joseph Engemann, Paul Habermehl, Karl Hoheisel, "Jenseits (Jenseitsvorstellungen)," 246–407; Colpe et al., "Jenseitsfahrt I (Himmelfahrt)," 407–66; Colpe, "Jenseitsfahrt II (Unterwelts- oder Höllenfahrt)," 466–89; Colpe and Habermehl, "Jenseitsreise (Reise durch das Jenseits)," 490–543. See further Ra'anan S. Boustan, Annette Yoshiko Reed, ed., *Heavenly Realms and Earthly Realities in Late Antique Religions* (Cambridge: Cambridge University Press, 2004); Tobias Nicklas, Joseph Verheyden, Erik M. M. Eynikel, Florentino Garcia Martinez, ed., *Other Worlds and Their Relation to This World: Early Jewish and Ancient Christian Traditions*, Supplements to the Journal for the Study of Judaism 143 (Leiden: Brill, 2010); Walter Ameling, ed., *Topographie des Jenseits. Studien zur Geschichte des Todes in Kaiserzeit und Spätantike*, Altertumswissenschaftliches Kolloquium 21 (Stuttgart: Franz Steiner Verlag, 2011).

[2] *Passio Perpetuae* 4. Jacqueline Amat, ed., *Passion de Perpétue et de Félicité suivi des Actes*, Sources Chrétiennes 417 (Paris: Cerf, 1996), 112–17.

[3] *Passio Perpetuae* 11–13. Amat, *Passion* (cf. note 2), 142–53.

[4] A. H. M. Kessels and Pieter Willem van der Horst, "The Vision of Dorotheus (Pap. Bodmer 29): Edited with Introduction, Translation and Notes," *Vigiliae Christianae* 41 (1987): 313–59. The most recent contribution (with updated bibliography) is Joseph Verheyden, "When Heaven

al palace. In his vision he is transported to God's celestial palace, which in this text is presented as an imperial court. Dorotheus is invited to join the ranks of the angels and become the gatekeeper of the palace – a post for which he receives new attire befitting his honorable new position. Growing overconfident, he leaves his place at the gate to explore what is inside the palace. As punishment for this transgression, Christ subjects him to whipping. Dorotheus now bleeding profusely, Christ and the angel Gabriel stop flogging him and, on their intercession, God agrees that Dorotheus should be allowed to return to his place at the gate. His blood is washed away and after his baptism he embraces Andreas (from *andreia* – courage) as his new name. Having taken up his former position at the gate, he fares well and wins the admiration of many. Once again, however, he grows overconfident and asks God for a more important position. The request is denied and the vision ends.

At least two interpretations of this text – and not mutually exclusive ones – present themselves. On a more individual level, it may be read as a poem written by a troubled soul who, enduring an existential crisis, is projecting his fears of what may go wrong into the afterlife.[5] One may connect these fears with the dangers of persecution and the challenge to remain loyal to the Christian faith, though this is not a necessary connection.[6] On the level of the text's discourse – its setting within the imperial palace, Dorotheus' role as gatekeeper, and so forth – it may also be interpreted as a sign of how successfully the Roman government exercised control over its inhabitants – even in their dreams and visions – or, reversely, as a sign of how Christians saw themselves within the new imperial ideology.[7]

Whichever interpretation one favors, just like the text of the *Passion of Perpetua and Felicity*, the *Vision of Dorotheus* illustrates how images of heaven, of the afterlife, are often inspired by and serve the interests of individuals or groups in the here and now. *Jenseits* and *Diesseits* are communicating vessels. In looking at the

---

Turns into Hell: The Vision of Dorotheus and the Strange World of Human Imagination," in Ameling, *Topographie des Jenseits* (cf. note 1), 123–41.

[5] Joseph Verheyden, "When Heaven Turns into Hell" (cf. note 4), 140, formulates it as follows: "Rather than being persecution literature or hagiography, this is a very personal account of an existential crisis and how it was finally overcome. ... This is the highly imaginative account of a man who at one point of his life, whether for a particular reason or led by a particular event, comes to realize in a most dramatic way that all he has done was wrong, that his 'stay in heaven', which he naturally anticipated to happen one day, was not assured at all, and that God and Christ personally will take care that he gets what he deserves. It is the account of a nightmare ...."

[6] Kessels and van der Horst, "The Vision of Dorotheus" (cf. note 4), 316 defends it; Verheyden, "When Heaven Turns into Hell" (cf. note 4), 139–40 points to many difficulties against this interpretation, most notably that God, Christ, and Gabriel, in afflicting Dorotheus, are in fact working *against* him.

[7] Christopher Kelly, "Empire Building," in Glen Bowersock, Peter Brown, Oleg Grabar, ed., *Late Antiquity: A Guide to the Postclassical World* (Cambridge, MA: Harvard University Press, 1999), 170–96, 181–82.

images of the afterlife that late antique Christians held, construed, and expressed, it is interesting to try to see what agendas and whose interests are being served. With this in mind, we now turn towards the theme of this anthology.

The collection of early Christian writings known as the New Testament arguably was the most extensive and, as time went by, authoritative source that provided late antique Christians with many potent and multivalent images of the hereafter. Think of Lazarus resting at Abraham's bosom and the rich man being cast in the torments of Hades (Lk 16:23), or the Father's house with its many abodes or mansions (John 14:2). More threatening is Matthew's depiction of the last judgement: all the nations will be gathered before the Son of Man, who, sitting on a glorious throne, will separate them as a shepherd distinguishes sheep from goats (Matt 25:31–46). Paul writes that he was caught up to the third heaven (2 Cor 12:2–4), suggesting that there is more than one heaven and that they are not inaccessible to humans. The *Letter to the Hebrews* speaks of the reward of a promised land, indeed a heavenly country (Heb 11:9, 16). These and many more images from their Holy Writ provided Christians with abundant resources to develop in literary and pictorial artistry a concept of heaven that would become deeply ingrained into the collective memory of Christianity for centuries to come.

Fittingly, the ultimate chapters of the last book of the New Testament offer a most extensive description of what future existence of the righteous might be. Indeed, Rev 21–22 describes in great detail a heavenly city, the New Jerusalem as seen by John the Seer. He saw "a new heaven and a new earth," and he saw "the holy city, a new Jerusalem, coming down out of heaven from God" (Rev 21:1–2). It is called a dwelling place where God Himself will dwell with his people (21:3). Christ, seated upon a throne (cf. 20:11–14; 22:1), speaks words of consolation and promise but also of threat and punishment (21:5–8). Next, an angel comes forward and shows the Seer the holy city Jerusalem coming down of heaven from God (21:10). The city is described in great detail throughout the remainder of the chapter and the next: its form, its measure, its walls and gates, its river of life and great street, its tree of life. There is no day or night, as the glory of God illumines it. His throne and that of the Lamb are also in the city, and there his servants will worship him and behold his face (21:15–22:6). The pericope ends with the words of admonishment and promise that the angel who had shown the city to the Seer utters to him (22:6–21).

Revelation 21–22 is obviously an extraordinary text, rife with imagery and opening up very different ways of interpretation in addition to the well-known eschatological approaches. One of the most recognizable figures in the Christian tradition, this extravagantly portrayed city of the New Jerusalem was appropriated by Christians throughout the late-antique period to represent an array of meanings and to support various priorities. Thus, Revelation's New Jerusalem has been taken to signify *inter alia* the believer's soul, the universal church, various ecclesiastical buildings, the present life of virtue, the future messianic reign, the coming reward of the just, and the consummated union of the virtuous with Christ in eternity. Besides Rev 21–22 *stricto sensu*, for a full appraisal of the image of the New Jerusalem, adjacent and related material must be taken into consideration. We think here in particular of accounts of the spiritual Jerusalem that emerge from a rich network of biblical, classical, and apocalyptic texts that ancient authors draw on in connection with the New Jerusalem. Examples of such sources include Paul's "Jerusalem above" pericope (Gal 4:26), the "heavenly Jerusalem" passage of Heb 12:21–22, representations of a renewed Jerusalem in the Psalter and the Prophets, Virgil's *Eclogue* 4, the Sibylline oracles, Plato's ideal city, and so forth. Treatments of the New Jerusalem inspired by non-textual ancient sources should not be forgotten either. The reception of these patristic notions of the New Jerusalem has had a direct, profound, and enduring influence on the idea of the holy city in both the West and East in many contexts and leaves a legacy that continues to shape our culture to this very day, as, once again, the *Ghent Altarpiece* demonstrates.

Surprisingly enough, to date a thorough and synthetic survey of the late antique reception of the image of the New Jerusalem of Rev 21–22 and its adjacent imagery, in textual and material culture, does not yet exist. Some decades ago Clementina Mazzucco made some forays in this field,[8] and very recently, two doctoral dissertations have marked noteworthy progress on the topic. Martina Vercesi analyzed the reception of, among other things, the image of the New Jerusalem image in Christian literature from North Africa up to the end of the fourth century,[9] and Nathan Betz provided an exhaustive survey of the same topic in the literature of the first Christian centuries (Latin and Greek) up to the dawn of the Constantinian era.[10] To move more quickly beyond this present state of the art, a symposium was organized (online, due to COVID restrictions) in Leuven on September, 30, 2020. The title of the symposium was "New Jerusalem: Conceptions of Revelation's Holy City in Late Antique Christianity." This book brings together substantially revised versions of a selection of peer-reviewed

---

[8] Clementina Mazzucco, Egidio Pietrella, "Il rapporto tra la concezione del millennio dei primi autori cristiani e l'Apocalisse di Giovanni," *Augustinianum* 18 (1978): 29–45; Clementina Mazzucco, "La Gerusalemme celeste dell''Apocalisse' nei Padri," in *'La dimora di Dio con gli uomini': Immagini della Gerusalemme celeste dal III al XIV secolo (Ap XXI,3)*, ed. Maria Louisa Gatti Perer (Milan: Vita e Pensiero, 1983): 49–75.

[9] Martina Vercesi, "'Quale Regnum Exinde Iustorum! Qualis Civitas Nova Hierusalem!': Revelation 19–21 in the Exegesis of the Christian Communities of Roman Africa from the II to the IV Century" (PhD dissertation, University of St Andrews, 2021).

[10] Nathan Betz, "City of Gods: The New Jerusalem of John's Revelation in Early Christianity (through ca. 313)" (PhD dissertation, KU Leuven, 2022). See also, from the same author, "'The city is the people': The New Jerusalem of Rev. 21–22 in Origen and His Predecessors," *Annali di Storia dell'Esegesi* 39, no. 2 (2022): 313–46 and "The New Jerusalem: A Metaphor for Deification in the Commentaries on Revelation by Oecumenius and Andrew of Caesarea," *Ephemerides Theologicae Lovanienses* 96, no. 1 (2020): 1–39.

papers delivered on that occasion. Some contributions were not presented at the conference but were offered afterwards; these also underwent peer review.

The fifteen contributions in the present volume reveal different facets of the manifold reception history of the concept of the New Jerusalem: Possible Jewish, Greek, and Roman sources are pointed out. Fascinating corpora such as the *Visio Pauli*, fourth-century female pilgrim narratives, and early medieval Hiberno-Latin documents are unlocked. Specific authors (Origen, Victorinus of Petovium, Eusebius of Caesarea, Ambrosiaster, Jerome, Primasius, Bede, Beatus, etc.) are featured. Larger geographical or language-centered collections of sources such as second-century Greek, early North African, and later texts representing the Oriental Christianity are studied. Non-literary questions are also explored – Where is the New Jerusalem situated? What is there to say of its famous walls and precious stones? How can the divine be experienced in places and images? How is the New Jerusalem and its authoritative interpretations depicted in medieval illuminations? Though contributors were given maximal freedom in developing a smaller or broader topic in the way they thought most fruitful, some obvious foci of interest had been defined to strengthen the coherence of the current anthology. These five foci may be summarized as follows: (1) the various late antique Christian interpretations of the New Jerusalem, (2) the theological, ethical, ecclesiological, and political priorities it has been enlisted to support, (3) the sources upon which these interpretations and appropriations were based, (4) early artistic developments of the image, and (5) the motivations of the actors involved. The geographical and chronological delimitations are those of the Roman Empire during the (very) long Late Antiquity, running from ca. AD 100 to ca. 800, and sometimes even later and further afield. This book does not have the ambition to speak the final word on the subject but aims rather to stimulate further research by offering more steppingstones towards this overall synthesis.

Special acknowledgements are given to the Fonds Wetenschappelijk Onderzoek – Vlaanderen (FWO) for its support of the doctoral research project "The New Jerusalem: The History of a Biblical Image in Late Antique Christianity (ca. 150–600)" and to the KU Leuven BOF-funded interdisciplinary research project "Longing for Perfection. Living the Perfect Life in Late Antiquity – A Journey between Ideal and Reality" (nr. 3H170345). We are also grateful to Sarah Mullen for her expert editorial support.

Nathan Betz, Anthony Dupont, Johan Leemans

Part 1

Studies on Specific Authors, Works, and Corpora

Not Just Millennialists

Some Second-Century Greek Interpretations of Revelation's Holy City*

Nathan Betz

Introduction

In this contribution, I set out to correct an enduring misconception. Since the nineteenth century, there has been a persisting impression that chiliasm, or millennialism,[1] was the dominant eschatological outlook of the second-century church. Accordingly, an assumption has prevailed that the New Jerusalem, elaborately described in Rev 21 and 22, was held by most in the second century to be a basically millennial phenomenon – that is to say, it was the earthly city from which Christ, at his return, would reign on earth during his thousand-year kingdom prior to the final judgment and end of all things.[2]

Adolf von Harnack, perhaps the single most influential scholar of early Christianity since the nineteenth century, confirmed and broadly disseminated this opinion. In 1878, he noted in the widely referred-to *Encyclopedia Britannica*

---

* For their stimulating questions and comments on an early draft of this contribution, I am grateful to the participants in the "New Jerusalem: Conceptions of Revelation's Holy City in Late Antique Christianity" symposium in Leuven (September 30, 2020). I am thankful also to my doctoral supervisors, Johan Leemans and Anthony Dupont, for their insights and challenges that helped improve the present contribution. This work is part of a greater doctoral project that was graciously funded by the Flemish Research Foundation.

[1] By the Latin-derived *millennialism* and its corresponding Greek term *chiliasm,* I mean in this contribution the belief that Christ will one day return to earth to set up a physical kingdom, centered in Jerusalem, which will endure for a thousand years prior to the end of all things. On the definition of millennialism in the context of early Christianity, see Charles E. Hill, *Regnum Caelorum: Patterns of Millennial Thought in Early Christianity*, 2nd ed. (Grand Rapids, MI: Eerdmans, 2001), 1–8.

[2] Clementina Mazzucco has observed the same tendency amongst modern scholars, specifically tracing the impression within the French literature: Clementina Mazzucco, "La Gerusalemme celeste dell' 'Apocalisse' nei Padri," in *'La dimora di Dio con gli uomini': Immagini della Gerusalemme celeste dal III al XIV secolo (Ap XXI,3),* ed. Maria Louisa Gatti Perer (Milan: Vita e Pensiero, 1983): 49–75, at 49–50. Hill's monograph *Regnum Caelorum* (cf. note 1) has shown carefully and conclusively that Christians in the first two Christian centuries were not monolithically chiliast.

that Justin Martyr's acceptance of the teaching made chiliasm "a necessary part of complete orthodoxy." That Justin, a Hellenic philosopher, would accept this teaching, complete with the restoration of the city of Jerusalem mentioned in John's Revelation, provides what Harnack calls "the strongest proof that these enthusiastic expectations were inseparably bound up with the Christian faith down to the middle of the second century."[3] Harnack's characterization of millennialism and its renewed Jerusalem continued to be printed in *Britannica* deep into the twentieth century. At first sight, the ancient record appears to confirm Harnack's judgment. Origen railed against the chiliastic interpretation of the future Jerusalem in *On First Principles (De principiis)*, giving the impression that he is fighting singlehandedly against a dominant eschatological error.[4] Indeed, Robert Louis Wilken, in his well-known work *The Land Called Holy: Palestine in Christian History and Thought*, goes so far as to state categorically that Origen was the first to launch an alternative to chiliasm.[5] Origen's student Eusebius, too, seems to think that second-century Christianity was in general benighted by chiliastic convictions.[6]

In the following pages, I will demonstrate that for as long as Christians have been writing about the book of Revelation, their thinking on the New Jerusalem has been in important respects far from univocal. From the first part of the second century, evidence points to a variety of early perspectives regarding the identity, significance, and temporal appearance of the New Jerusalem. In reviewing this evidence, I uncover some of the earliest surviving Greek roots of Christian reflection on the biblical figure and call attention to key elements of these interpretations that subsequent Christian traditions would variously repudiate and develop. The resulting picture will, I hope, shake the casual yet persistent impression amongst scholars of early Christianity that the New Jerusalem of Revelation, especially in its second-century interpretations, was viewed dominantly, or even monolithically, through the lens of chiliasm and literalism.[7]

The structure of this contribution is simple. First, I will highlight how two early authorities – Justin Martyr and Irenaeus of Lyons – forthrightly discuss the

---

[3] Adolf von Harnack, "Millennium," in *Encyclopedia Britannica*, 9th ed. (New York, 1878), 16:316.

[4] Origen, *De princ.* 2.11.3. Text and translation: John Behr, ed. and trans., *Origen: On First Principles*, 2 vols. (Oxford: Oxford University Press, 2017).

[5] Robert Louis Wilken, *The Land Called Holy: Palestine in Christian History and Thought* (New Haven: Yale University Press, 1992), 64, 65, 70, 78. In an earlier article, however, Wilken writes about Origen's influence with greater circumspection: Robert Louis Wilken, "Early Christian Chiliasm, Jewish Messianism, and the Idea of the Holy Land," *Harvard Theological Review* 79, nos. 1–3 (1986): 298–307.

[6] E.g. Eusebius, *Historia ecclesiastica* 3, where he identifies Cerinthus as a literalist interpreter of the coming kingdom (3.28) and repeatedly questions the value and provenance of Revelation (e.g. 3.24.18; 3.25.2, 4; see also 7.25.22).

[7] Charles E. Hill, in *Regnum Caelorum* (cf. note 1), has done much the same for early Christian teaching on the millennium in general.

diversity of early Christian thought concerning the New Jerusalem. Second, I will provide some case studies that represent this early hermeneutical diversity; specifically, I will visit key texts pertaining to the New Jerusalem from Papias of Hierapolis, Justin Martyr, Melito of Sardis, Irenaeus of Lyons, and Clement of Alexandria – authors who are not only geographically representative but are among the period's most authoritative voices. Third, I will compare how the highlighted authors interpret the significance of the New Jerusalem, observing some of the overall patterns of thought that emerge among them. Finally, I will indicate how these sometimes competing, sometimes complementary conceptions of Revelation's New Jerusalem were received amongst Greek-speaking Christians in subsequent centuries.

1 Early Witness to Competing Perspectives

From the earliest years following the writing, or at least acceptance, of the book of Revelation, a diversity of thought concerning its New Jerusalem seems to have existed amongst Christians. Both Justin and Irenaeus speak about at least two ancient and "orthodox" Christian perspectives on the millennium and the renewed Jerusalem.[8] Of these competing views, Justin writes:

> I have declared to you earlier that, with many others, I feel that such an event will take place. I did, however, point out that there are many pure and pious Christians who do not share our opinion. Moreover, I also informed you that there are some who are called Christians, but in reality are godless and impious heretics, whose doctrines are entirely blasphemous, atheistic, and senseless. ... I, and all other wholeheartedly orthodox Christians, feel certain that there will be a resurrection of the flesh, followed by a thousand years in the rebuilt, embellished, and enlarged city of Jerusalem, as was announced by the prophets Ezekiel, Isaiah and the others.[9]

Here, Justin, in a debate that happened as early as the mid-130s, identifies three well-formed perspectives on the question of whether the faithful will gather with Christ in Jerusalem upon his return. The first, held by himself and "all

---

[8] Justin, *Dialogue with Trypho* (*Dialogus cum Tryphone*) 80.1.
[9] Justin, *Dial.* 80.2–3, 5: ὡμολόγησα οὖν σοι καὶ πρότερον ὅτι ἐγὼ μὲν καὶ ἄλλοι πολλοὶ ταῦτα φρονοῦμεν, ὡς καὶ πάντως ἐπίστασθε τοῦτο γενησόμενον· πολλοὺς δ' αὖ καὶ τῶν τῆς καθαρᾶς καὶ εὐσεβοῦς ὄντων Χριστιανῶν γνώμης τοῦτο μὴ γνωρίζειν ἐσήμανά σοι. τοὺς γὰρ λεγομένους μὲν Χριστιανούς, ὄντας δὲ ἀθέους καὶ ἀσεβεῖς αἱρεσιώτας, ὅτι κατὰ πάντα βλάσφημα καὶ ἄθεα καὶ ἀνόητα διδάσκουσιν, ἐδήλωσά σοι. ... ἐγὼ δέ, καὶ εἴ τινές εἰσιν ὀρθογνώμονες κατὰ πάντα Χριστιανοί, καὶ σαρκὸς ἀνάστασιν γενήσεσθαι ἐπιστά πάντα Χριστιανοί, καὶ σαρκὸς ἀνάστασιν γενήσεσθαι ἐπιστάμεθα καὶ χίλια ἔτη ἐν Ἰερουσαλὴμ οἰκοδομηθείσῃ καὶ κοσμηθείσῃ καὶ πλατυνθείσῃ, ὡς οἱ προφῆται Ἰεζεκιὴλ καὶ Ἡσαίας καὶ οἱ ἄλλοι ὁμολογοῦσιν. Text: Miroslav Marcovich, ed., *Justin. Dialogus cum Tryphone* (Berlin: de Gruyter, 1997). Translation: Michael Slusser, Thomas B. Falls, trans., *Justin. Dialogue with Trypho*, Selections from FC 3 (Washington, DC: Catholic University of America Press, 2003).

other wholeheartedly orthodox [ὀρθογνώμονες] Christians" maintains that such a gathering will take place. To support this position, he produces prophetic evidence from Isaiah, Ezekiel, and John's Revelation. The second, also held by orthodox Christians, did not maintain a belief in a millennial gathering in Jerusalem. The third, a view that Justin does not consider to be authentically Christian, is what might now be called a generically "gnostic" view.[10] Irenaeus, too, identifies these three same perspectives – the fully orthodox (chiliasts), the less orthodox (the non-chiliasts who nevertheless *putantur recte credidisse*), and the heretics (the gnostics).[11] Like Justin, he counts himself within the first group.[12] No more need be said except to underscore the general orthodoxy of the two perspectives on the coming Jerusalem that both Justin and Irenaeus mention.

This testimony, originating in the case of Justin from as early as the 130s and certainly no later than 160 or so, demonstrates that, already within the first half or even third of the second century, at least two major perspectives on the New Jerusalem had currency in so-called "orthodox" Christian circles: the literal chiliastic perspective, held by the authors themselves, and another non-literal perspective, about which authors appear to tell us little. This much alone, even before we proceed to investigate several representative surviving interpretations of the New Jerusalem is enough to dislodge the assumption that early Christians adhered monolithically and necessarily to a physical and literal interpretation of Revelation's New Jerusalem.

2 Case Studies

Several case studies representing the broad sweep of second-century Greek Christianity bear this out. These I have selected for their demonstrable and more-or-less straightforward reliance on John's Revelation. I will proceed chronologically, from the earliest to the latest, which is to say, from Papias of Hierapolis and Justin Martyr, who are active in the first half of the century and represent Asia and Rome respectively, to Melito of Sardis, writing in the 160s in Asia, to Irenaeus and Clement of Alexandria, whose works date to the 180s

---

[10] At *Dial.* 35.6 Justin indicates that these are various sorts of non-Christian sects, naming the Marcionites, Valentinians, and Basilidians. Their perspectives on the millennial Jerusalem, since they were not considered authentically Christian by most either at that time or subsequently, will not enter into this contribution.

[11] Since this gnostic perspective shows little evidence of being influenced by the Revelation of John, I leave it out of this contribution.

[12] Irenaeus, *Against Heresies (Adversus haereses)* 5.32.1–2 (the chiliasts); 5.31.1, 5.35.1–2 (the non-chiliasts); 5.31.1 (the gnostics). Text: Adelin Rousseau, Louis Doutreleau, and Charles Mercier, ed., *Irénée. Contre les hérésies: Livre 5*, SC 153 (Paris: Cerf, 1969). Translation: *ANF* 1, modified.

and 190s and represent Asia, Rome, and Gaul in the case of the former, and Alexandria in the case of the latter. Together, these small studies form a survey of second-century Greek material that represents most of the century and many of the church's most influential geographical centers. As such, it may be considered a representative study.

2.1 Papias of Hierapolis and His Presbyterial Tradition

Perhaps the most famous early proponent of chiliasm is Papias of Hierapolis. While his work is fragmentary, it is of great importance to this study. His main work, *Exposition of the Sayings of the Lord*, was probably completed sometime between 120 and 140.[13] According to Irenaeus, Papias heard John the Revelator himself.[14] Eusebius reports the same.[15] Furthermore, as someone who received much of what he knew via yet earlier oral tradition, we potentially have in Papias testimony of very early thinking on the New Jerusalem – perhaps stretching back to the author of Revelation himself.[16]

Irenaeus, the earliest preserver of any Papian fragments, details the Hierapolitan's highly physicalist anticipation of the kingdom to come. Importantly, Irenaeus indicates that Papias's view comes from sources yet older than Papias himself.[17] Eusebius, too, records Papias as saying that "after the resurrection of the dead there will be a period of a thousand years when the kingdom of Christ will be set up in material form on this earth."[18] John of Dara, a ninth-century ecclesiastic, confirms Papias's belief in the millennial residence of the just in Jerusalem.[19] If what Eusebius and John of Dara say is true – and certainly Irenaeus's record confirms their reliability – what we have in Papias, a hearer of John himself, is likely a very early belief in the literally restored Jerusalem during the millennium.

Intriguingly, however, the ancient record suggests that Papias's view was not merely literalist. Anastasius of Sinai, a monk and priest active in the late seventh century, was convinced that Papias adhered to a "spiritual" interpretation of early sayings about paradise and indeed referred such sayings "to the church of

---

[13] Michael W. Holmes, *The Apostolic Fathers: Greek Texts and English Translations*, 3rd ed. (Grand Rapids, MI: Baker Academic, 2007), 722. All text and translations quoted in this section are from this volume.

[14] Irenaeus, *Haer.* 5.33.4.

[15] Eusebius confirms this (*Church History* [*Hist. eccl.*] 3.39.1) in the same context of challenging the apostolicity of Revelation (*Hist. eccl.* 3.39.5).

[16] Eusebius, *Hist. eccl.* 3.39.8, 11.

[17] Irenaeus, *Haer.* 5.33.3–5.

[18] Eusebius, *Hist. eccl.* 3.39.12. Luke J. Stevens has argued that Eusebius did not know Papias's work at first hand and relied instead on Irenaeus and others for his knowledge of Papias's thoughts. Luke J. Stevens, "Did Eusebius Read Papias?" *Journal of Theological Studies* 70, no. 1 (2019): 163–83, at 170–71.

[19] John of Dara, *On the Resurrection of Bodies* 2.13.

Christ."[20] As we shall see, a late contemporary of Papias, Justin of Rome, certainly adhered to such a teaching, and Anastasius actually names Justin as a spiritualizing interpreter in the same passage. Anastasius further names Irenaeus, who of course quotes Papias at length when enlarging on his own partially spiritual interpretation of paradise and Revelation's eschatological city.[21] In Papias then, we seem to have a tradition of chiliasm that was open to a complementary spiritual interpretation of the New Jerusalem.

In *Against Heresies,* Irenaeus quotes the tradition that Papias preserves[22] in order to describe the eternal state of the righteous not during but *after* the millennial kingdom. Concerning the new heaven and new earth in which man is to flourish in his incorruptible state, Irenaeus gives us Papias's tradition:

And as the presbyters say, Then those who are deemed worthy of an abode in heaven shall go there, others shall enjoy the delights of paradise, and others shall possess the splendor of the city; for everywhere God [Lat. *Deus;* Gk. Σωτὴρ] shall be seen according as they who see Him shall be worthy. [They say, moreover], that there is this distinction between the habitation of those who produce an hundred-fold, and that of those who produce sixty-fold, and that of those who produce thirty-fold: for the first will be taken up into the heavens, the second will dwell in paradise, the last will inhabit the city; and that was on this account the Lord declared, "In My Father's house are many mansions" [John 14:2].[23]

This passage indicates that Papias, or at least the tradition he cites, points to a spiritual mode of existence following the millennium in which "the city" features prominently, and which is blessed, along with paradise and heaven, with the *visio Dei.* As Irenaeus also quotes Papias as reporting shortly thereafter, the city represents part of the *telos* of the process of salvation that the righteous undergo prior to the millennium and the eschaton – a process whereby they ascend gradually to the Father:

The presbyters, the disciples of the apostles, affirm that this is the gradation and arrangement of those who are being saved and that they advance by such steps, and ascend

---

[20] Anastasius of Sinai, *Considerations on the Hexameron* 1.

[21] Anastasius of Sinai, *Considerations on the Hexameron* 1.7.

[22] That this passage from Irenaeus is ultimately from Papias is amply demonstrated by Joseph Barber Lightfoot, *Essays on the Work Entitled Supernatural Religion* (London: Macmillan, 1889), 194–98. Against Lightfoot, see Charles E. Hill, *The Johannine Corpus in the Early Church* (Oxford: Oxford University Press, 2004), 111, who maintains that a positive identification cannot be made. Stephen C. Carlson categorizes it simply as a "potential citation." Carlson, *Exposition of Dominical Oracles: The Fragments, Testimonia, and Reception of a Second-Century Commentator,* Oxford Early Christian Texts (Oxford: Oxford University Press, 2021), 296–99.

[23] Irenaeus, *Haer.* 5.36.1: *Et quemadmodum Presbyteri dicunt, tunc qui digni fuerint caelorum conuersatione illuc transibunt, id est in caelos, alii autem paradisi deliciis utentur, alii autem speciositatem ciuitatis possidebunt, ubique autem Deus uidebitur, quemadmodum et digni erunt uidentes eum. Esse autem distantiam hanc habitationis eorum qui centum fructificauerunt et eorum qui sexaginta et eorum qui triginta, quorum quidam in caelum assumentur, alii in paradiso conuersabuntur, alii in ciuitate inhabitabunt: et propter hoc dixisse Dominum multas esse apud Patrem mansiones.*

through the Spirit to the Son, and through the Son to the Father, the Son finally yielding his work to the Father, as it is also said by the apostle: "For he must reign until he puts all enemies under his feet" [1 Cor 15:25].[24]

This, Irenaeus tells us – presumably making explicit the line of thought passed to him via Papias – will take place after the times of the kingdom. The kingdom ultimately results in all things being subdued to God, "that God may be all in all."[25]

While Papias's fragmentary record presents difficulties, it seems likely that he would have adhered to a chiliastic interpretation of John's New Jerusalem. At the same time, his focus on the New Jerusalem as a locus of the *visio dei* and the place that the city has in the process of advance on the part of those who are being saved following the millennium suggests that his eschatology, while chiliastic, must also be understood in richly spiritual terms and that he cannot be reduced to the chiliastic caricature that Eusebius paints of him.[26]

2.2 Justin Martyr

Whether Justin, who may have been active in Ephesus in addition to Rome, knew the writings of Papias, also active in Asia, is unknown. In any event, this Roman citizen originally hailing from Flavia Neapolis in Samaria writes in the 150s or early 160s about a debate with one Trypho, a Jew, that likely happened in the mid to late 130s.[27] This, of course, was a highly fraught period of Jerusalemite history. In around AD 130 the Emperor Hadrian had personally visited this city famous for rebellion – and razed by Titus in AD 70 – and rebuilt it as a Roman colony and military garrison. Dedicating it to Jupiter, he renamed Jerusalem "Aelia Capitolina" after his own family. The local Jewish response to these developments, the Bar Kokhba revolt (132–136), attracted a fierce Roman backlash that included Hadrian's expulsion of the Jews from Jerusalem in around 135. This event Justin mentions at least three times in the course of the debate.[28] These events alone, to say nothing of the larger question of ancient Hebrew prophecies

---

[24] Irenaeus, *Haer.* 5.36.2: *Hanc esse adordinationem et dispositionem eorum qui saluantur dicunt Presbyteri Apostolorum discipuli, et per huiusmodi gradus proficere, et per Spiritum quidem [<ad]> Filium, per Filium autem ascendere ad Patrem. Filio deinceps cedente Patri opus suum, quemadmodum et [ab] Apostolo dictum est: Quoniam oportet regnare eum, quoadusque ponat omnes inimicos sub pedibus eius.*

[25] Irenaeus, *Haer.* 5.36.2, quoting 1 Cor 15:27–28. Already here we see several roots of Origen's thinking of the New Jerusalem as consummation. While Origen rejects the chiliasm, he nevertheless appropriates a crucial part of the millennialist interpretation of the New Jerusalem (*Princ.* 2.11.2; 3.6.3; *Commentary on the Song of Songs* [*Commentarius in Canticum*] Prol. 84.15–85.27 [GCS 33]).

[26] Eusebius, *Hist. eccl.* 3.39.12–13.

[27] See Adalbert G. Hamman, "Essai de chronologie de la vie et des œuvres de Justin," *Augustinianum* 35, no. 1 (1995): 231–39.

[28] Justin, *Dial.* 16.2; 92.2; 108.3.

concerning Jerusalem, would have made the question of a renewed Jerusalem a pressing issue, one of intense interest both to Trypho the Jew and Justin the Samaria-born Roman Christian.

No surprise, then, that Justin is questioned on the topic by Trypho:

> Tell me truthfully, do you really believe that this place Jerusalem shall be rebuilt, and do you actually expect that you Christians will one day congregate there to live joyfully with Christ, together with the patriarchs, the prophets, the saints of our race, or even those who became proselytes before your Christ arrived?[29]

Justin replies that he does, going on to state that after the resurrection of the flesh, there will be "a thousand years in the rebuilt, embellished, and enlarged city of Jerusalem."[30] This, Justin points out, was confirmed by "a man among us named John, one of Christ's apostles, [who] received a revelation and foretold that the followers of Christ would dwell in Jerusalem for a thousand years" – this preceding the "universal and ... everlasting resurrection" and the ensuing judgment.[31]

Justin here seems to situate John's New Jerusalem within the millennium described in Rev 20:4–6. Accordingly, he describes it in the rich physical terms used in Isa 65:17–25, which he quotes in full and takes as a prophecy of the millennium in particular.[32] He also assigns the tree of life, mentioned in the same Isa 65 passage, to this millennial Jerusalem, understanding Isaiah's phrase "the days of the tree of life" as referring to the "period of the thousand years" in symbolic language.[33] A strict reading of Revelation, of course, assigns the tree of life to the New Jerusalem that arrives in the new heaven and new earth, not the millennium prior to the final resurrection (Rev 22:2, 13; cf. 2:9).

Yet at the same time, Justin elsewhere employs the *qualia* of this millennial New Jerusalem – immortality, incorruptibility, and painlessness – to describe the rest of the just in the kingdom of God *following* the millennium as well.[34] Crucially, he also uses the term "Jerusalem" to designate not merely the saints'

---

[29] Justin, *Dial.* 80.1: εἰπὲ δέ μοι, ἀληθῶς ὑμεῖς ἀνοικοδομηθῆναι τὸν τόπον Ἰερουσαλὴμ τοῦτον ὁμολογεῖτε, καὶ συναχθήσεσθαι τὸν λαὸν ὑμῶν καὶ εὐφρανθῆναι σὺν τῷ Χριστῷ, ἅμα τοῖς πατριάρχαις καὶ τοῖς προφήταις καὶ τοῖς ἀπὸ τοῦ ἡμετέρου γένους ἢ καὶ τῶν προσηλύτων γενομένων πρὶν ἐλθεῖν ὑμῶν τὸν Χριστόν, προσδοκᾶτε, ἤ, ἵνα δόξῃς περικρατεῖν ἡμῶν ἐν ταῖς ζητήσεσι, πρὸς τὸ ταῦτα ὁμολογεῖν ἐχώρησας;

[30] Justin, *Dial.* 80.5: ἐγὼ δέ, καὶ εἴ τινές εἰσιν ὀρθογνώμονες κατὰ πάντα Χριστιανοί, καὶ σαρκὸς ἀνάστασιν γενήσεσθαι ἐπιστάμεθα καὶ χίλια ἔτη ἐν Ἰερουσαλὴμ οἰκοδομηθείσῃ καὶ κοσμηθείσῃ καὶ πλατυνθείσῃ, ὡς οἱ προφῆται Ἰεζεκιὴλ καὶ Ἡσαΐας καὶ οἱ ἄλλοι ὁμολογοῦσιν.

[31] Justin, *Dial.* 81.4: καὶ ἔπειτα καὶ παρ' ἡμῖν ἀνήρ τις, ᾧ ὄνομα Ἰωάννης, εἷς τῶν ἀποστόλων τοῦ Χριστοῦ, ἐν ἀποκαλύψει γενομένῃ αὐτῷ χίλια ἔτη ποιήσειν ἐν Ἰερουσαλὴμ τοὺς τῷ ἡμετέρῳ Χριστῷ πιστεύσαντας προεφήτευσε, καὶ μετὰ ταῦτα τὴν καθολικὴν καί, συνελόντι φάναι, αἰωνίαν ὁμοθυμαδὸν ἅμα πάντων ἀνάστασιν γενήσεσθαι καὶ κρίσιν.

[32] Justin, *Dial.* 82.1–2.

[33] Justin, *Dial.* 82.3.

[34] Justin, *Dial.* 45.4; 46.7; 69.7; 117.3.

millennial habitation but their eternal state.[35] Thus, Justin seems to see the New Jerusalem as beginning in a renewed, rebuilt physical Jerusalem in the millennium following the resurrection of the just, then continuing into a final and eternal Jerusalem. In other words, he sees the New Jerusalem as being a two-stage affair: the millennial kingdom of Christ described in Rev 20 and the postmillennial kingdom of God depicted in Rev 21–22. Even so, in his description of the millennial Jerusalem, Justin appears to import ideas from the New Jerusalem of Rev 21–22 into the Jerusalem of Rev 20.

There are two additional points that must be considered in light of Justin's New Jerusalem idea. First, in his account of this postmillennial Jerusalem, Justin identifies the just in their eternal state as somehow angelic as being the sons of God.[36] This, of course, is also the case in the description of the New Jerusalem in Revelation that stands behind Justin's account (Rev 21:7). The text he actually quotes is Luke 20:35–36, where Christ speaks of the saints as "equal to the angels" and "sons of God." Elsewhere, Justin enlarges on what he means by "sons of God" when he discusses Ps 82 (81 LXX), which names the saints not only as "sons of God" but also as "gods."[37] Certainly the inhabitants of the renewed Jerusalem will participate in immortality and incorruptibility, key attributes of deified individuals in early Christianity.[38] While Justin is among the first to point to the deified status of the just in the final Jerusalem, we will soon see that he is by no means the last.

Second, we must bear in mind the extended discussion of the vision of God that Justin provides early in the dialogue. There, he closely associates the *visio Dei* with the reward and final state of the just – indeed, as the final end of human life, as the Platonists had long taught.[39] In Justin's mind, the vision of God, while attainable in this life by pure souls, is properly and fully to be contemplated in the reward of the eternal New Jerusalem, and perhaps in the millennial reward of the New Jerusalem as well.[40]

---

[35] Justin, *Dial.* 113.4–5; 138.3. This eternal state is elsewhere indicated at 24.2; 25.1; 26.1; 76.4. See Oskar Skarsaune, *The Proof from Prophecy: A Study in Justin Martyr's Proof-Text Tradition* (Leiden: Brill, 1987), 403. Leslie William Barnard also remarks on this eschatological chronology in *Justin Martyr: His Life and Thought* (Cambridge: Cambridge University Press, 1967), 163–66.

[36] Justin, *Dial.* 81.4.

[37] Justin, *Dial.* 124.1–2, 4. Psalm 82 is oft used by early Christian authors to support the divine sonship and deification of believers in Christ. Carl Mosser, "The Earliest Patristic Interpretations of Psalm 82, Jewish Antecedents, and the Origin of Christian Deification," *Journal of Theological Studies* 56, no. 1 (2005): 30–74.

[38] Jules Gross, *The Divinization of the Christian According to the Greek Fathers,* trans. Paul A. Onica (Anaheim: A&C Press, 2002), 350.

[39] Justin, *Dial* 3.7–4.7.

[40] The *visio Dei,* of course, had long been considered tantamount to deification, or union with God, in both Christian and Hellenistic thought. Hans Boersma, *Seeing God: The Beatific Vision in Christian Tradition* (Grand Rapids, MI: Eerdmans, 2018), 45–75.

This in turn suggests that Justin's Jerusalem-centered eschatology, far from being bolted on to his theology as an afterthought, is integral to it. Indeed, the stated goal of the dialogue is transparently to convince Jews that "the crucified Jesus Christ ... is indeed the new law, the new covenant, and the expectation of those who, from every nation, have awaited the blessings of God."[41] Further, it is to convince the unbelieving that those who believe in Christ, irrespective of their nation, "are the true spiritual Israel and the descendants of Judah, Jacob, Isaac, and Abraham, who, though uncircumcised, was approved by God because of his faith and was called the father of many nations."[42] Central to Justin's burden in this dialogue, then, is demonstrating how the physical race of Israel with its physical Jerusalem in Judea has been supplanted spiritually by the new Israel, the church of Christ.[43] Since the old Israel had the old Jerusalem, Justin seems to imply, the new Israel must have a new Zion or Jerusalem.[44] Admission into this new Israel and ultimately its New Jerusalem is through a new covenant that replaces the old,[45] that is, through repentance and baptism, a new circumcision that supersedes the ritual circumcision of the flesh.[46] This should not be read to mean, of course, that the Jews are in any way precluded from receiving an inheritance on the "Mountain of God."[47] Indeed, he opens the door wide: should they but acknowledge Jesus as the Messiah, they, with the redeemed from among the nations, would fulfill the prophecy of Isaiah and "be called a city sought after."[48] Indeed, "those circumcised persons who approach Him with faith in their hearts and a prayer on their lips for His blessings will be welcomed and blessed by Him."[49] It is in this way that the Jews receive salvation in precisely the same way that the nations do and may hope to dwell with Christ and their Jewish forefathers in a rebuilt Jerusalem once Christ returns.[50]

Justin's view of the New Jerusalem is therefore central to his theology and is deeply integrated with his Hellenistic and Jewish milieu. As such, it plays a role throughout his corpus, especially the *Dialogue*. While it is essentially an eschatological reality, it has its existence already in the present age as the Christian faithful, the church. Then, in the millennium following Christ's return, "the rebuilt, embellished, and enlarged city of Jerusalem" will be jointly inhabited by Christ and the just. Yet it also has an existence after the millennium, when the

---

[41] Justin, *Dial.* 11.4.

[42] Justin, *Dial.* 11.5.

[43] See, for instance, Justin, *Dial.* 63.5; 64; 122.6; 123.6–7, 9.

[44] Justin, *Dial.* 22.11, 24; 80–81.

[45] Justin, *Dial.* 67.9–10.

[46] Justin, *Dial.* 43.1–2; 44.4; 47.

[47] Justin, *Dial.* 25.6, where Justin has just quoted Isa 64:10–11, and *Dial.* 80–81.

[48] Justin, *Dial.* 26.3, quoting Isa 62:12. See also *Dial.* 95.3 and 142.2–3.

[49] Justin, *Dial.* 33.2. Justin takes pains to display a special compassion for the Jews and their plight at *Dial.* 108.3. See also *Dial.* 120.

[50] Justin, *Dial.* 80.1–2.

just become equal to angels, are called the sons of God, and delight in the end of their salvation, the vision of God. In any case, in Justin the New Jerusalem stands at the endpoint of the Christian and ecclesial experience and as such is an early example of a pattern that carries throughout the remainder of the century.

2.3 Melito of Sardis

Of the earliest fathers whose perspective on John's New Jerusalem would seem to have gone missing, the case of Melito of Sardis is among the more regrettable. Bishop of one of the cities directly addressed by John in Revelation in the late mid-second century (cf. Rev 3:1–5), Melito, like Papias and the proto-Montanists associated with Philadelphia, was presumably witness to the earliest Asian Johannine tradition. Certainly, the Sardian was intimately familiar with the book – intimately enough to have authored a now-lost treatise entitled *On the Devil and the Revelation of John*.[51] Indeed, he draws on its language several times in his only full surviving work, *On Pascha (De Pascha)* (ca. 160–170),[52] once even quoting an opening verse of Revelation's New Jerusalem pericope.[53] That said, his surviving corpus would at first appear scant with regard to his understanding of the New Jerusalem itself.

Even so, relevant surviving material allows us, in light of his certain deep familiarity with the text, to get a glimpse of his conception of it.[54] As mentioned, Melito borrows material from early in Revelation's New Jerusalem pericope when he says of Christ that "He is the Alpha and the Omega; he is beginning and end, beginning inexpressible and end incomprehensible," a loose but recognizable appropriation of Rev 21:6.[55] In Rev 21, of course, those titles of Christ occur following the famous description of the holy city descending out of heaven as a bride adorned for her husband in v. 2 and immediately prefacing the detailed description of the city proper that begins at v. 7.

Another helpful entry point is Melito's use of Paul's language from Gal 4:26. Melito writes that while "the Jerusalem below was precious, ... it is worthless now because of the Jerusalem above."[56] Here Melito contrasts two Jerusalems – the Jerusalem below (ἡ κάτω Ἰερουσαλήμ), which refers to the Jews and their former earthly capital, and the Jerusalem above (ἡ ἄνω Ἰερουσαλήμ), which is

---

[51] Eusebius, *Hist. eccl.* 4.26.2; Jerome, *On Illustrious Men (De viris illustribus)* 24.
[52] Stuart George Hall, ed., trans., *Melito of Sardis* On Pascha *and Fragments,* Oxford Early Christian Texts (Oxford: Clarendon, 1979), xi–xii.
[53] Melito, *Pasch.* 105 quotes Rev 21:6 and Rev 1:8. Text and translation: *Melito of Sardis* On Pascha *and Fragments* (cf. note 52), with the editor's corrections from "Melito *Peri Pascha*: Corrections and Revisions," *Journal of Theological Studies* 64, no. 1 (2013): 105–10.
[54] I provide a much fuller treatment of Melito's idea of the New Jerusalem in Nathan Betz, "Reconstructing Melito of Sardis's Lost Interpretation of Revelation's New Jerusalem," *Vigiliae Christianae* 77, no. 5 (2023): 522–542.
[55] Melito, *Pasch.* 105.
[56] Melito, *Pasch.* 45.

the "true" Jerusalem and people of God, the church.[57] Is this "Jerusalem above" in fact the New Jerusalem? Certainly, as we shall see, both Irenaeus and Clement (who knew *On Pascha* well enough to emulate it) will use the term to label the New Jerusalem when quoting Rev 21.

In any event, while "Jerusalem above" is strictly a Pauline expression, one might try to look at it through a Johannine lens, especially since Melito is known to have written a book on Revelation. Central to Melito's *On Pascha* is the understanding that the paschal lamb as slaughtered by the children of Israel in Egypt referred forward to Christ, and the children of Israel themselves were a type of the church. As he states, God called Israel and instituted the Passover because he saw in them "the image of the future thing." Indeed, in these things, as well as in the law as given by God on Sinai, God "[saw] the pattern and the material and the reality" of the "heavenly things" that were to come.[58] Those heavenly things were, by Melito's lights, nothing less than Christ himself and his church.[59] In the fullness of time, these models and mere images gave way to "the truly real things."[60] Once the "really precious things" had been revealed,[61] the preciousness of things like the original Passover lamb was removed "on account of the spotless Son … [and] because of the Christ above [τὸν ἄνω Χριστόν]."[62] This was true also of the Jews' sacred city. Three times in this poem Melito mentions the physical city of Jerusalem, and all three times it is a metonym for the people of Israel.[63] Whereas the old and "lawless" Israel did not live up to their God-given name in that they "did not see God," the church as the new Israel will behold God.[64] As Christ tells the church (in the words of Melito), "I am your salvation, I am your resurrection, I am your king. I will raise you up by my right hand; I am leading you up to the heights of heaven; *there I will show you the Father from ages past*."[65] The vision of God is, of course, central to John's account of the New Jerusalem, as it had been for Papias and Justin, and will be seen to be to others.[66]

---

[57] Melito, *Pasch.* 40–43.
[58] Melito, *Pasch.* 38–39.
[59] Melito, *Pasch.* 39–43.
[60] Melito, *Pasch.* 43.
[61] Melito, *Pasch.* 43.
[62] Melito, *Pasch.* 44.
[63] Melito, *Pasch.* 72; 93; 94. See also *Frag.* 11 (line 5).
[64] Melito, *Pasch.* 81–82, emphasis added: Ὦ Ἰσραὴλ παράνομε, τί τοῦτο ἀπηργάσω τὸ καινὸν ἀδίκημα, καινοῖς ἐμβαλών σου τὸν κύριον πάθεσιν, τὸν δεσπότην σου, τὸν πλάσαντά σε, τὸν ποιήσαντά σε, τὸν τιμήσαντά σε, τὸν Ἰσραὴλ καλέσαντά; σὺ δὲ Ἰσραὴλ οὐχ εὑρέθης· οὐ γὰρ εἶδες τὸν θεόν, οὐκ ἐνόησας τὸν κύριον·
[65] Melito, *Pasch.* 103, emphasis added: ἐγὼ τὸ πάσχα τῆς σωτηρίας, ἐγὼ ὁ ἀμνὸς ὁ ὑπὲρ ὑμῶν σφαγείς, ἐγὼ τὸ λύτρον ὑμῶν, ἐγὼ ἡ ζωὴ ὑμῶν, ἐγὼ τὸ φῶς ὑμῶν, ἐγὼ ἡ σωτηρία ὑμῶν, ἐγὼ ἡ ἀνάστασις ὑμῶν, ἐγὼ ὁ βασιλεὺς ὑμῶν· ἐγὼ ὑμᾶς ἀναστήσω διὰ τῆς ἐμῆς δεξιᾶς· ἐγὼ ὑμᾶς ἀνάγω εἰς τὰ ὑψηλὰ τῶν οὐρανῶν· ἐκεῖ ὑμῖν δείξω τὸν ἀπ' αἰώνων πατέρα.
[66] Rev 22:3–4. In the New Jerusalem, the slaves of God will serve him and "see his face" – ὄψονται τὸ πρόσωπον αὐτοῦ.

In this light, Melito's mentions of Christ as "architect of Jerusalem" and "builder of Jerusalem" in a separate fragment makes a great deal of sense.[67] If Abraham awaited a city whose architect and builder was God, and this city is not the earthly Jerusalem below but rather the church as the Jerusalem above, we have yet another point supporting an ecclesiological reading of Jerusalem that could inform Melito's putative understanding of John's New Jerusalem. Just as Christ is the one who, having attained "the heights of heaven,"[68] is the saints' salvation and leads them too "up to the heights of heaven"[69] so, too, could this Jerusalem be populated by the people of the church, who in the fragment cited above are called "the just and heavenly people."[70] This ecclesiological reading comports well with the fact that we have no textual evidence to suggest that Melito would have interpreted the New Jerusalem, nor indeed any part of Revelation, after a millenarian fashion – which fact alone suggests that Melito was among that group of Christians whom Justin and Irenaeus pointed out as not adhering to a millennial eschatology of Jerusalem.[71]

It thus dawns how Melito may well have interpreted the New Jerusalem elsewhere in his now-lost corpus, such as in his treatise *On the Devil and the Revelation of John*. Here is the evidence before us. First, that Melito was aware of the New Jerusalem pericope of Revelation is certain, since he quotes several of the titles of Christ that are unique to it and is known to have written a treatise on the book of Revelation. Second, Melito's view of the Jerusalem above was substantially supersessionist and ecclesiological – Jerusalem above is in fact the church today. Third, Melito implicitly transfers the possibility of the vision of God from the Jews to the Christian church, which church is rewarded with the vision of God after being led above to Jerusalem by Christ. Fourth, this might be confirmed by *New Fragment* 2, where he refers to Christ as the architect and builder of Jerusalem and would seem to link this Jerusalem with the just, who expect a heavenly existence. Finally, since Melito cannot on the basis of surviving evidence be classified as a chiliast, he would not have maintained a millennialist interpretation of the New Jerusalem. The evidence leads us to conclude that Melito most likely adopted a heavily ecclesiological interpretation of the New Jerusalem, one in which the church as the "Jerusalem above" in the present age becomes in some way the heavenly New Jerusalem in the next. There, the just will presumably enjoy their celestial reward with Christ and, as the true Israel,

---

[67] Melito, *New Fragment* 2.18–19.
[68] Melito, *Pasch.* 70; 99; 104.
[69] Melito, *Pasch.* 103.
[70] Melito, *New Fragment* 2.1.
[71] Justin, *Dial.* 80.2. Hill gives a brief genealogy of the erroneous association of Melito with chiliasm. Hill finds its root in von Harnack and a misreading of Gennadius's attribution of chiliasm to an unknown sect of *Melitani* at *Eccl. Dogm.* 55 (Hill, *Regnum Caelorum* [cf. note 1], 103–7).

behold God. As will become apparent, this interpretation presages what we will find in Clement, who knew and emulated Melito's *De Pascha*.[72]

2.4 Irenaeus of Lyons

Justin's influence is unmistakable in Irenaeus's treatment of the New Jerusalem.[73] Even so, in his lengthy and more systematic discussion of the topic, Irenaeus surfaces important points that are either not present or are not easily discernable in the writings of his purported teacher.

Irenaeus's first substantial mention of an eschatological Jerusalem comes in Book Four. It is a compact description of the glorious state of the lovers of God in the age to come. Immediately apparent are such familiar *topoi* as the kingdom, the vision of God, and the glorification of its inhabitants:

[W]hen [the law] is read by the Christians, it is a treasure ... showing forth the wisdom of God and declaring His dispensations with regard to man, and forming the kingdom of Christ beforehand, and preaching by anticipation the inheritance of the holy Jerusalem, and proclaiming beforehand that the man who loves God shall arrive at such excellency as even to see God, and hear His word, and from the hearing of His discourse be glorified to such an extent, that others cannot behold the glory of his countenance.[74]

Difficult to discern in this passage is the exact identification of "the holy Jerusalem." Whether Irenaeus is here identifying it with the age of the kingdom, or with the eternal state that follows the kingdom (Justin already tells us that Jerusalem figures prominently in both) is unclear. Even so, in Book Five, he explicitly develops both these aspects of the eschatological Jerusalem and helpfully contrasts them. The renewed Jerusalem of the kingdom age he covers from 5.30.4 to 5.35.2 and again briefly at 5.36.3. His discussion of the New Jerusalem proper begins at 5.35.2 and continues to 5.36.3, that is, to the conclusion of the entire treatise. Pervading these accounts is an idea of advance, or progress, and perfection, a theme central to Irenaeus's soteriology and theology more broadly and one that is only negligibly emphasized in Justin.[75]

---

[72] Eusebius, *Hist. eccl.* 4.26.4; cf. 6.13.9.

[73] On Justin's certain influence on Irenaeus, see, in addition to *Haer.* 4.6.2, where Irenaeus names and quotes Justin as an intellectual antecedent as regards recapitulative soteriology: Irenaeus M. C. Steenberg, "Tracing the Irenaean Legacy," in *Irenaeus: Life, Scripture, Legacy*, ed. Sara Parvis and Paul Foster (Minneapolis: Fortress, 2012), 199–211, at 202, 252–53.

[74] Irenaeus, *Haer.* 4.26.1: *A Christianis uero cum legitur, thesaurus est ... ostendens sapientiam Dei, et eas quae sunt erga hominem dispositiones eius manifestans, et Christi regnum praeformans, et hereditatem sanctae Hierusalem praeeuangelizans, et praenuntians quoniam in tantum homo diligens Deum proficiet, ut etiam uideat Deum et audiat sermonem eius, et ex auditu loquelae eius in tantum glorificabitur, uti reliqui non possint intendere in faciem gloriae eius.*

[75] Where it is especially present in Justin is in the context of being perfected so as to receive the vision of God (*Dial.* 3.7–4.7).

First, let us look at Irenaeus's elucidation of the renewed Jerusalem of the kingdom age. Relying heavily on texts of Ezekiel, Isaiah, 2 Baruch, Daniel, and the presbyterial tradition of Papias discussed above, Irenaeus espouses a view of Jerusalem during the time of the kingdom that is not far different from the Justinian and Papian positions: following the conclusion of the present age, Christ will return to initiate his kingdom and restore the earthly Jerusalem to its rightful place as his administrative center during the *tempora regni* – the times of the kingdom – that is, the "hallowed seventh day."[76] During that time, those worthy from the church of the gentiles[77] will be physically resurrected to inherit and inhabit this city, thus allowing them to receive their reward and reign as sons of God on the earth and in the flesh.[78] It is during the times of the kingdom, whether in Jerusalem or in the renewed earth more broadly (Irenaeus here calls it the "Father's kingdom"), that the returning Christ will fulfill the promise of Matt 26:29 and drink the fruit of the vine anew with the now-glorified sons of God.[79] This Jerusalem and the earth of which it is the center exhibits supernatural fecundity, something Irenaeus describes by way of a famed quotation from Papias.[80] As to the earthly Jerusalem proper, Irenaeus draws on Isa 54:11–14 to describe the foundations, ramparts, gates, and wall – all made of precious stones.[81] Death itself will be suspended.[82] These prophecies concerning this earthly Jerusalem, Irenaeus stresses, must not be allegorized.[83] They must refer to a physical reality that will exist on the present earth in the age to come.

Crucially, it is in the renewed Jerusalem during the kingdom times that the worthy "gradually grow accustomed to containing God [*capere Deum*]" and "grow stronger by their vision of the Lord."[84] Indeed, it is in this eschatological earthly Jerusalem that "the righteous are disciplined beforehand for incorruption and prepared for salvation."[85] Or, as he puts it not long thereafter, it is then and there that the righteous flourish in order that they "may be capable of receiving the glory of the Father."[86]

Just as he is concluding his discourse on the millennial Jerusalem, Irenaeus makes a sharp distinction between it and the "Jerusalem above," which follows

---

[76] Irenaeus, *Haer.* 5.35.2; 5.34.4.
[77] Irenaeus, *Haer.* 5.32.1; 5.34.1, 3–4.
[78] Irenaeus, *Haer.* 5.32.1.
[79] Irenaeus, *Haer.* 5.33.1.
[80] Irenaeus, *Haer.* 5.33.3–4. For a discussion of this fragment from Papias and its analogs in early Jewish and Christian apocalyptic, see Stephen C. Carlson, "Eschatological Viticulture in 1 Enoch, 2 Baruch, and the Presbyters of Papias," *Vigiliae Christianae* 71, no. 1 (2017): 37–58.
[81] Irenaeus, *Haer.* 5.34.4.
[82] Irenaeus, *Haer.* 5.34.4.
[83] Irenaeus, *Haer.* 5.35.1–2, *passim*.
[84] Irenaeus, *Haer.* 5.32.1; 5.35.1.
[85] Irenaeus, *Haer.* 5.35.2.
[86] Irenaeus, *Haer.* 5.35.2.

upon the kingdom with its earthly Jerusalem.[87] At 5.35.2 he appeals to the New Jerusalem of Rev 21 while labeling it with the terminology of Paul – "Jerusalem above" (Gal 4:26) – and the Epistle to the Hebrews – "heavenly Jerusalem" (Heb 12:22). Quoting Rev 21:1–6, Irenaeus identifies this *heavenly* Jerusalem with the "holy city, New Jerusalem, coming down from heaven, as a bride adorned for her husband."[88] This New Jerusalem, he stresses, is in fact the archetypal Jerusalem upon which the millennial Jerusalem is patterned.[89] Whereas the Jerusalem of the age of the kingdom is of the *current* earth, the Jerusalem that appears "after the times of the kingdom" belongs to the *new* earth. It is into this truly *New Jerusalem* that the saints are inducted and in which they are fully saved, receiving there "the glory of the Father" to the highest possible degree:[90]

> When these things, therefore, pass away above the earth, John, the Lord's disciple, says that the New Jerusalem above shall [then] descend, as a bride adorned for her husband; and that this is the tabernacle of God, in which God will dwell with men. Of this Jerusalem the former is an image – that Jerusalem of the former earth in which the righteous are disciplined beforehand for incorruption and prepared for salvation. ... [W]hen all things are made new, [man] shall truly dwell in the city of God. For it is said, "He who sits on the throne said, 'Behold, I make all things new'" [Rev 21:5].[91]

Once again, in connection with the New Jerusalem of the new earth, Irenaeus relies on the presbyterial fragment preserved by Papias and reproduced above. Making sense of it in Irenaeus's usage is not easy. Though this passage could perhaps be read as applying to the times of the kingdom – advance being a key feature of that Jerusalem – the passage falls after Irenaeus's pivot away from the times of the kingdom to the archetypal, eternal Jerusalem, which is manifested after the times of the kingdom and in which the saints continue their progress.

If my reading is correct, Irenaeus's use of the term "New Jerusalem" comprehends the entire new creation that follows the general resurrection and the consummation of the old creation. Crucial to keep in mind is that, for Irenaeus, the substance and essence of the old creation is maintained even as it is

---

[87] Jean Daniélou also observes this: "Irenaeus makes an explicit distinction between the earthly rebuilding of Jerusalem during the millennial reign and the manifestation of the heavenly Jerusalem after the judgment and the new creation." Jean Daniélou, *The Theology of Jewish Christianity,* John Austin Baker, trans. (London: Darton, Longman & Todd, 1964), 388.

[88] Irenaeus, *Haer.* 5.35.2.

[89] A similar thought is found in Irenaeus's *Demonstration of the Apostolic Teaching* 26, 29.

[90] Irenaeus, *Haer.* 5.35.2.

[91] Irenaeus, *Haer.* 5.35.2. *His itaque praetereuntibus, super terram nouam superiorem Hierusalem ait Domini discipulus Johannes descendere, quemadmodum sponsam ornatam uiro suo, et hoc esse tabernaculum Dei in quo inhabitabit Deus cum hominibus. Huius Hierusalem imago illa quae in priori terra Hierusalem, in qua iusti praemeditantur incorruptelam et parantur in salute. ... [D]einde omnibus renouatis, uere in ciuitate habitabit Dei. Dixit enim, inquit, sedens super thronum: Ecce noua facio omnia.*

refashioned as the new.⁹² Hence, presumably, the Jerusalem of the kingdom period, a physical city on earth, will continue its existence as a city in the new creation on the new earth as well. Irenaeus makes this clear in 5.36.1–2, where he again adduces Papias's sources to show that this new creation consists of three degrees or stations (*gradus*, τάξεις) through which man, even in the consummation, continues to advance even after the kingdom. In each of these stations, human beings "perpetually hold fresh converse with God" (*semper nove confabulans Deo*) – and, according to the degree of their relative worthiness, delight in the vision of God.⁹³ This existence, however, is not static. On the contrary, the blessed ascend from one *gradus* to the next, with the worthiest receiving an abode in heaven. Those still increasing in worthiness enjoy the delights of paradise. The least advanced, by contrast, "shall possess the splendor of the city," this presumably is the renewed vestige of the millennial Jerusalem. Thus do the people of God advance from one stage to another: from the city, to paradise, to heaven itself. Again drawing on the Papian tradition, Irenaeus explains that each of these stages represents one of the abodes (*mansiones*, μοναί) referred to by the Lord in John 14:2 – "In my Father's house are many abodes" – and corresponds to those who bear fruit thirty-fold, sixty-fold, and a hundred-fold respectively in Matt 13:8 and Mark 4:20. Such, Irenaeus tells us, is what the disciples of the apostles themselves describe as "the graduation and arrangement of those who are saved" (*adordinationem et dispositionem eorum qui salvantur*).⁹⁴ It is in this way, Irenaeus continues, again citing Papias's tradition, that the inhabitants of the new creation make another triadic ascent – "through the Spirit to the Son, and through the Son to the Father."⁹⁵ This, Irenaeus elsewhere leads us to believe, is an ascent that continues for eternity.⁹⁶ So much for the eschatological Jerusalems.

On now to the ecclesiological Jerusalem. Though he does not emphasize it, Irenaeus indicates that he considered the New Jerusalem to represent the church. This is hinted at in Book Five, where the church of the gentiles is repeatedly observed to have become the principle, and perhaps the only, recipient of Israel's

---

⁹² Irenaeus, *Haer.* 5.36.1.
⁹³ Irenaeus, *Haer.* 5.36.1–2.
⁹⁴ Irenaeus, *Haer.* 5.36.2.
⁹⁵ Irenaeus, *Haer.* 5.36.2.
⁹⁶ Irenaeus, *Haer.* 4.11.2: "God also is truly perfect in all things, Himself equal and similar to Himself, as He is all light, and all mind, and all substance, and the fount of all good; but man receives advancement and increase towards God. For as God is always the same, so also man, when found in God, shall always go on towards God. For neither does God at any time cease to confer benefits upon, or to enrich man; nor does man ever cease from receiving the benefits, and being enriched by God." *Et Deus quidem perfectus in omnibus, ipse sibi aequalis et similis, totus cum sit lumen et totus mens et totus substantia et fons omnium bonorum, homo uero profectum percipiens et augmentum ad Deum. Quemadmodum enim Deus semper idem est, sic et homo in Deo inuentus semper proficiet ad Deum. Neque enim Deus cessat aliquando in benefaciendo et locupletando hominem, neque homo cessat beneficium accipere et ditari a Deo.*

prophetic promises during the kingdom.⁹⁷ Irenaeus indicates the same in his *Demonstration of the Apostolic Teaching (Epideixis tou apostolikou kērygmatos)*, where he implies that the church today is the "Jerusalem above" of Gal 4:26, a title which of course he elsewhere applies to the New Jerusalem of Rev 21.⁹⁸ To Irenaeus's thinking, both the church and the inhabitants of the millennial Jerusalem are instantiations of the eternal and archetypal New Jerusalem that emerges in the consummation.

Along with Justin, Irenaeus associates the heavenly, or new, Jerusalem with the sons of God.⁹⁹ Like Justin, he makes use of Ps 82 in connection with the *topos* of the sons of God.¹⁰⁰ When he deals specifically with the New Jerusalem of Rev 21, he sets forth above all a mystical interpretation of it, namely, an eternal reality in which the salvation for which man was destined and prepared is perfected. As noted above, Irenaeus frequently populates the renewed Jerusalem with the glorified sons of God. Even the structure of Book Five bears this out. At its very outset, Irenaeus introduces deification as the final end both of God's creation of humankind and of the incarnation of the Logos, a thought most clearly visible in his use of the so called "exchange formula": the Word became what we are so that we might become even what he is himself.¹⁰¹ Then, upon arriving at the very conclusion of the book, he speaks of the saints' acquisition of God's glory, their advance from the Spirit to the Son to the Father, their full vision of God, and the consummation of their salvation, all of which is experienced in the reality that he describes as the city of God, the Jerusalem above, the New Jerusalem. Summing up the prophecies of John, the Old Testament prophets, Paul, and the Lord himself that he has made use of throughout his discussion of the New Jerusalem, Irenaeus concludes Book 5 thus:

In all these things, and by them all, the same God the Father is manifested, who fashioned man, and gave promise of the inheritance of the earth to the fathers, who brought it [the creature] forth [from bondage] at the resurrection of the just, and fulfils the promises for the kingdom of His Son; subsequently bestowing in a paternal manner "those things which neither the eye has seen, nor the ear has heard, nor has arisen within the heart of man" [1 Cor 2:9], for there is the one Son, who accomplished His Father's will; and one human race also in which the mysteries of God are wrought, "which the angels desire to look into" [1 Pet 1:12]; and they are not able to search out the Wisdom of God, by means of which His handiwork, conformed to and incorporated with His Son [*conformatum et*

---

⁹⁷ Irenaeus, *Haer.* 5.32.2.

⁹⁸ Irenaeus, *Epid.* 94. While Irenaeus does not there say outright that the church is the Jerusalem above, he states that she is the "barren one" of Isa 54:1, which Paul labels "Jerusalem above" in Gal 4:26. He also identifies the church with Jerusalem and Israel at *Epid.* 26, 29.

⁹⁹ The connection between Jerusalem and the sons of God is a very old one, appearing in Isa 54 and derivatively in Gal 4, to name but two pertinent sources directly linked to the New Jerusalem of Rev 21.

¹⁰⁰ Irenaeus, *Haer.* 3.6.1; 5.36.3; cf. 5.32.1.

¹⁰¹ Irenaeus, *Haer.* 5 prologue; cf. 4.1.1.

concorporatum Filio], is brought to perfection; that His offspring, the first-begotten Word, should descend to the creature, that is, to what had been molded, and that it should be contained [*capiatur*] by Him; and, on the other hand, the creature should contain [*capiat*] the Word, and ascend to Him, passing beyond the angels, and be made after the image and likeness of God [Gen 1:26].[102]

With these words, Irenaeus both summarizes the rich soteriological potential that lay within the tradition of teaching on the New Jerusalem that he had received and develops, and brings to an end his entire treatise.

2.5 Clement of Alexandria

Writing immediately after Irenaeus had completed Book Five, Clement (ca. 150–ca. 215) becomes the first Alexandrian whose thoughts on the city of Rev 21 and 22 survive. Standing at the end of the second century, Clement would have been aware of both the chiliastic and amillennial approaches to the New Jerusalem that continued to coexist in the apostolic church.[103] An amillennialist himself – he nowhere supports a literal, much less a chiliastic reading of the New Jerusalem[104] – Clement's thought chimes in many ways with the authors discussed above while also showing great originality.

Not surprisingly, his reading of the holy city has a pronounced eschatological orientation. In the *Instructor* (*Paedagogus*), a book written for new converts, Clement tells us that at the time of our regeneration, we received the good news that we would enjoy "the Jerusalem above."[105] There we will partake of Christ the Word as heavenly food and drink of him as the fountain of life – possible

---

[102] Irenaeus, *Haer.* 5.36.3: *Et in omnibus his et per omnia idem Deus Pater ostenditur, qui plasmauit hominem et hereditatem terrae promisit patribus, qui eduxit illam in resurrectione iustorum et promissiones adimplet in Filii sui regnum, postea praestans illa paternaliter 'quae neque oculus uidit neque auris audiuit neque in cor hominis ascendit.' Etenim unus Filius, qui uoluntatem Patris perfecit, et unum genus humanum, in quo perficiuntur mysteria Dei, quem concupiscunt angeli uidere, non praeualentes inuestigare Sapientiam Dei per quam plasma eius conformatum et concorporatum Filio perficitur, ut progenies eius primogenitus Uerbum descendat in facturam, hoc est in plasma, et capiatur ab eo, et factura iterum capiat Uerbum et ascendat ad eum, supergrediens angelos et fiens secundum imaginem et similitudinem Dei.*

[103] Eusebius affirms that Clement, for instance, knew and sought to preserve Melito and Irenaeus among others (*Hist. eccl.* 6.13.9). Henry Chadwick has argued that Clement knew Justin: *Early Christian Thought and the Classical Tradition: Studies in Justin, Clement, and Origen* (Oxford: Oxford University Press, 1966), 40. Lloyd G. Patterson makes a good case that Clement would have interacted deeply with Irenaeus's *Against Heresies* and through it knew the fragments of Papias that Irenaeus preserves: "The Divine Became Human: Irenaean Themes in Clement of Alexandria," *Studia Patristica* 31 (1997): 497–516.

[104] Clement, *Extracts from the Prophets* (*Eclogae Propheticae*) 57.4, quoted in Brian E. Daley, *The Hope of the Early Church: A Handbook of Patristic Eschatology* (Cambridge: Cambridge University Press, 1991), 45.

[105] Clement, *Paed.* 1.6.45. Text: Marguerite Harl, Henri-Irénée Marrou, Claude Mondésert and Chantal Matray, ed., *Clément d'Alexandrie. Le pédagogue,* 3 vols., SC 70, 108, 158 (Paris: Cerf, 1:1960; 2:1965; 3:1970). Translation: *ANF* 2, with modifications.

allusions to Rev 21:1–2, where the blessed enjoy the fruit of the tree of life and water from the river of life.[106] We will also become angels and see the divine promises "face to face,"[107] and having become perfect, we will know and see God, even becoming gods.[108] Piloting us all along this journey to the "haven of heaven" and the contemplation of God is none other than Christ himself,[109] whose steps we follow to attain salvation and to be transformed from earth-born men to heavenly men who fully realize within themselves the image and likeness of God.[110] Only thus may we attain eternal beatitude and gain admittance into the "city of truth."[111]

A great part of the journey to this heavenly Jerusalem therefore consists in the attainment and practice of virtue. This – the ethical dimension of the city – is probably Clement's greatest contribution to the interpretation of the New Jerusalem. In Book Two of the *Instructor*, Clement employs the New Jerusalem image not just as the goal of the life of virtue, but as the very attainment of virtue. Criticizing the "excessive fondness for jewels and gold ornaments"[112] that the women of Clement's Alexandria displayed, the teacher enjoins his readers to let go their childish delight in precious stones and pearls.[113] Instead of decking themselves in these, they ought rather to adorn themselves "with the sacred jewel, the Word of God, whom the Scripture has somewhere called a pearl, the pure and pellucid Jesus ... by whom the water-regenerated flesh becomes precious."[114] Pointing to the Scripture, the Alexandrian directs his readers' attention to Revelation:

We have accepted ... that the "Jerusalem above" [Gal 4:26] is walled with holy stones; and we allow that the twelve gates of the heavenly city [οὐρανοπόλεως], by being likened to precious stones, indicate the everywhere-visible grace of the apostolic voice. For colors are assigned to costly stones, and these [colors] are precious while the other parts remain of earthy material. Symbolically, it is with these [stones], as is meet, that the city of the saints, which is spiritually built, is walled. By that brilliancy of stones, therefore, is meant the inimitable brilliancy of the spirit, the purity and holiness of being.[115]

---

[106] Clement, *Paed.* 1.6.45.
[107] Clement, *Paed.* 1.6.36.
[108] Clement, *Paed.* 1.6.26, in the second instance quoting Ps 82:6, a verse used in similar fashion by Justin and Irenaeus. Clement views the eternal vision of God as the *telos* of human life (*Stromata* 7.3.13).
[109] Clement, *Paed.* 1.7.54; cf. *Exhortation to the Greeks (Protrepticus)* 12.118.
[110] Clement, *Paed.* 1.12.98.
[111] Clement, *Paed.* 2.8.65.
[112] Clement, *Paed.* 2.12 section heading.
[113] Clement, *Paed.* 2.12.118.
[114] Clement, *Paed.* 2.12.118.
[115] Clement, *Paed.* 2.12.119: Λίθοις δὲ ἁγίοις τὴν ἄνω Ἰερουσαλὴμ τετειχίσθαι παρειλήφαμεν, καὶ τὰς δώδεκα τῆς οὐρανοπόλεως πύλας τιμίοις ἀπεικασμένας λίθοις τὸ περίοπτον τῆς ἀποστολικῆς [φωνῆς] αἰνίττεσθαι χάριτος ἐκδεχόμεθα. Ἐπὶ γὰρ τῶν λίθων τῶν πολυτελῶν αἱ χρόαι τετάχαται, τίμιαι δὲ αὗται, τὰ δ' ἄλλα ὕλη γεώδης καταλείπονται. Συμβολικῶς τούτοις

This earliest known exegesis of Rev 21:11–21, however brief, is notable for its specifically ethical reading of the passage. This is conveyed especially in Clement's emphasis on the spiritual meaning of colors. Color, Clement maintains, is what makes an otherwise common stone precious; the earthly substance (ὕλη γεώδης) itself has little special value by itself. That the stones of the New Jerusalem are not merely earthly but heavenly is manifest by the fact that they bear color, and it is this heavenliness that elevates the value of the earthly stone, that is, of the human nature. But, one wonders, what exactly is this heavenly "color"? Each regenerate human, Clement tells us in answer, ought to bear within their material being an "inimitable brilliancy of the spirit." This resplendency of spirit, or "color," he explains, is the purity and holiness that each advancing Christian ought to carry in addition their human nature. These spiritual qualities and their corresponding way of life, not material gems and stones, are the "material" with which Christians ought to adorn themselves. By mixing the heavenly brilliance with their own earthly nature by means of the virtuous life, humans, led by the example of the apostles and their way of life, constitute an "ouranopolis" – a city both human and heavenly – here and now.[116] And since Christ is the precious stone, the pearl, that we must put on – recall that he introduced this section noting that fact – we must conclude that the attainment of virtue is in fact a putting on of Christ, the precious stone *par excellence*, containing as he does both the earthly nature and the colors, or brilliancy, of the divine life.

Clement does not only employ the New Jerusalem to enjoin his hearers to virtue and the mystical union that it entails; as a good Hellenistic Christian well-grounded in Scripture, he also uses it to describe the end of the attainment of true knowledge. Book Four of the *Miscellanies (Stromata)* provides an example of how the heavenly Jerusalem illustrates this. There, he expands upon the final end of one who is on the way to advanced knowledge of the Logos. Such a person – Clement calls him a "gnostic" – is someone who, according to Plato's thought, "contemplates the unseen God" and consequently "lives as a god among men." Clement lays special stress on the fact that, as Plato notes, "gods frequent cities."[117] As true gods, advanced Christians orient themselves toward

εἰκότως τειχίζεται τῶν ἁγίων ἡ πόλις πνευματικῶς οἰκοδομουμένη. Πρὸς τὸ ἄνθος τῶν λίθων τὸ ἀμίμητον τὸ ἄνθος τοῦ πνεύματος τὸ ἀκήρατον καὶ ἅγιον τῆς οὐσίας νενοήκασιν.

[116] From here, it is a short step to the teaching that subsequent generations of exegetes would offer regarding the stones of the New Jerusalem. Origen writes of the precious stones of the New Jerusalem as virtues (*Homilies on Ezekiel [Homiliae in Ezechielem]* 3.1–3), and others write that the twelve stones of the New Jerusalem represent the virtues of the twelve apostles, and by extension, of all who are of the faith and are sanctified (e. g., Victorinus, *Commentary on Revelation [Explanatio in Apocalypsin]* 21.6; Andrew of Caesarea, *Commentary on Revelation [Comm. Apoc.]* 23.67; Bede the Venerable, *Explanation of Revelation [Expl. Apoc.]* 3.37). Early roots of this teaching may be found in Hermas's *Shepherd* (i.e., Similitude 9 [92]), a text that Clement appreciated and cited frequently. For a development of "Ouranopolis" as a *topos*, see Verheyden's and Cuijpers's contribution to this volume.

[117] Clement, *Strom.* 4.25.155, quoting Plato, *Sophist* 216C. Text: Ludwig Früchtel, Otto Stählin,

inhabiting a city of their own – the paradigmatic city in heaven for which the likes of Abraham and Plato had yearned.[118] Considering themselves strangers and sojourners in the body, true gnostics fix their hope nowhere below but rather on their abode (μονή) with God in heaven.[119] "But I shall pray the Spirit of Christ," he prays in a sudden expression of his own hope, "to wing me to my Jerusalem."[120] In this way the Jerusalem above is revealed to be heaven itself.[121] Hinted at in Irenaeus's quotation of Papias's tradition, and perhaps implied before that in the New Testament,[122] this idea seems to emerge clearly within the Christian tradition only with Clement. While the tripartite reward in the eschaton is present with Clement – with humans being assigned a degree of glory in proportion to their knowledge of God and advancing to perfection through saving and purging knowledge by stages (μοναί) – a city plays no named role in it.[123]

Even so, heaven is not so much a location to which one goes but rather a reality into which one enters and which one even becomes. For not only does the gnostic contemplate heaven and the divine things, Clement writes, but by contemplating them she leaves earth and carnal things and has thus already "become heaven": "the soul of the gnostic, that of the man who has applied himself to the contemplation of heaven and divine things, and in this way has become an Israelite, 'heaven.'"[124] Indeed, for the gnostic, "the future is already present."[125] This comports well with Clement's earlier teaching for the newly converted, where he enjoins them to add divine virtues to their human nature thus to become constituent parts of the New Jerusalem. It is both by putting on the divine virtues in one's manner of living and by contemplating the heavenly realities as one advances in knowledge that one becomes the holy city that John saw descending from heaven. By having imitated God and become gods, human persons fulfill in body and soul the image and likeness in which God created them.[126]

If individuals become Jerusalem, what of those individuals considered collectively as a whole? While the Jerusalem above is a paradigm for the just city on earth generally,[127] it is a paradigm for the church particularly. Just as a city is

---

and Ursula Treu, ed., *Clemens Alexandrinus,* vols. 2, 3rd ed., and 3, 2nd ed., GCS 52(15), 17 (Berlin: Akademie, 2:1960; 3:1970). Translation: *ANF* 2, modified.

[118] Clement, *Strom.* 4.26.172, alluding to Plato, *Republic (Resp.)* 592A–B.
[119] Clement, *Strom.* 4.26.166, alluding to John 14:2.
[120] Clement, *Strom.* 4.26.172, alluding to Plato, *Resp.* 592A–B.
[121] Cf. Clement, *Strom.* 1.1.
[122] Gal 4:26; Phil 3:20; Heb 12:22–3; Rev 21:2.
[123] Clement, *Strom.* 6.13–15; 7.10.56; see also *Ecl.* 56–57.
[124] Clement, *Strom.* 4.26.169: καὶ οὐρανὸν τὴν τοῦ γνωστικοῦ ψυχὴν τὴν οὐρανοῦ καὶ τῶν θείων θέαν ἐπανῃρημένου καὶ ταύτῃ Ἰσραηλίτην γεγονέναι.
[125] Clement, *Strom.* 7.7.1.
[126] Clement, *Strom.* 4.26.171; 6.14.116, both alluding to Gen 1:26.
[127] Clement, *Strom.* 4.26.172; *Adumbrations (Adumbrationes in epistulas canonicas)* 1 Pet. 1:3.

governed by the law, Clement reasons, the church is governed by the divine Logos who calls, instructs, and brings to full knowledge those who accept his ministrations. As a consequence, Clement calls the church "a city on earth impregnable." The church turns out to be a reification on this earth of the heavenly Jerusalem of which true gnostics have within their own lifetimes become citizens.[128] Not relegated to the eschaton in heaven, it exists already in the church, a "product of the divine will on the earth as in heaven."[129] It is in, for, and unto this Jerusalem that the Christian is to be tutored in the present age.[130]

To conclude, we may summarize Clement in four points. First, Clement connects the New Jerusalem both with the ethical instruction and mystical development of which the New Jerusalem is both pinnacle and destination. Second, Clement makes clear that the New Jerusalem, while it is descriptive of the eschatological state of the saints in the age to come, is also descriptive of those who are becoming perfected as true gnostics. Third, Clement takes the New Jerusalem as a figure of the church in the present age. Finally, in becoming Jerusalem, the gnostic and the church have become divine. Along the way, we have seen how Clement receives and develops a number of important scriptural passages and images in his treatment of the New Jerusalem. In sum, the New Jerusalem represents for Clement a condensed symbol containing the whole of both the Christian existence and Clement's own theology.

Conclusions

At the beginning of this contribution, I highlighted the common misconception amongst some theologians that the earliest conceptions of the New Jerusalem of Revelation were chiliastic. Against this, I presented evidence from Justin and Irenaeus that orthodox Christians during their times were in fact divided on the topic and that both chiliastic and non-chiliastic understandings held sway in the church's first full century. Via a number of representative case studies of the Greek theologians of the second century – theologians representing Asia, Rome, Gaul, and Alexandria – it emerged that whereas some took the New Jerusalem of Rev 21 to be in some way descriptive of the prophecies of the rebuilt Jerusalem, these named the final and eternal state that post-dated the millennium to be the New Jerusalem. This new and true Jerusalem, while it still had a material manifestation and was inhabited by embodied human beings, bears a greater mystical

---

[128] Clement, *Strom.* 4.26.172.
[129] Clement, *Strom.* 4.26.172.
[130] Oleh Kindiy, "Approximating Church and School in Clement of Alexandria's *Stromateis* VII," in *The Seventh Book of the "Stromateis": Proceedings of the Colloquium on Clement of Alexandria (Olomouc, October 21–23, 2010)*, ed. Matyáš Havrda, Vit Hušek, and Jana Plátová (Leiden: Brill, 2012), 291–98, at 292.

and spiritual emphasis than the restored earthly Jerusalem of the millennium that precedes it. Indeed, it stands to reason that their double eschaton features a double Jerusalem, both of which draw on the imagery of Revelation's New Jerusalem. At the same time, there is clear evidence that these chiliastic authors also thought of the church in the present age as in some way being an early appearance of the New Jerusalem. In the long run, the chiliastic use of the New Jerusalem fades into the background in the authoritative teaching of the ancient church. In the medium term, however, it remains viable in the Latin West as evidenced by the writings of Tertullian, Victorinus, Lactantius, and even the young Augustine. So also amongst the Greek theologians, and not only in teachers such as Nepos of Arsinoe, Dionysius of Alexandria's theological sparring partner in the mid-third century; Hippolytus and Methodius also preserve the remnants of the chiliastic tradition.

What, then, of those early Christians who, according to Justin and Irenaeus, dispensed with a millennium while keeping a New Jerusalem? In this contribution, we reviewed the perspectives of such unimpeachably orthodox non-chiliastic Christians as Melito of Sardis and Clement of Alexandria, who reject a literal millennium yet, like many of the millennialists, discover the New Jerusalem to have already begun in the present age in the form of the church, and, again like the millennialists, anticipate its full manifestation at the consummation. Setting off in a novel individualizing direction, Hippolytus advances a christological interpretation in his Old Testament commentaries, and before long, all of these interpretations were enfolded in one way or another into Origen's conception of the New Jerusalem.[131] Likewise, it was from this tradition that several generations of theologians distilled the essence of what was to become the church's authoritative view of the Heavenly Jerusalem in centuries to come, both in the East and the West.

In this contribution, I have demonstrated how, *contra* von Harnack, who insisted that an early belief in the millennium and its New Jerusalem was a *sine qua non* of second-century orthodox Christianity, second-century Greek thinking on the New Jerusalem was in fact far more diverse while at the same time displaying a stable core of teaching common to all authors regardless of their views on the millennium. If we were to distill all second-century Greek teaching on the New Jerusalem reviewed in this contribution – chiliastic and amillennialist – into the broad commonalities that were received into subsequent generations regardless of the stand on the millennium, it would be something like the following:

---

[131] For a fuller development of Origen's reading of Revelation's New Jerusalem, see Nathan Betz, "'The city is the people': The New Jerusalem of Rev. 21–22 in Origen and His Predecessors," *Annali di Storia dell'Esegesi* 39, no. 2 (2022): 313–46.

1. As to time, its initial appearance is in the present age in the church and her members, and its full appearance is in the consummation.
2. As to its significance, it is broadly recognized to be a metaphor or symbol of the closest possible intimacy between God and humans, the result of God having become incarnate and humans having become divine.
3. As such, the New Jerusalem, or the reality it represents, is the fulfillment of the divine image and likeness according to which mankind was originally fashioned and the *telos* of all history.
4. It is the locus of the vision of God.
5. It is the true end of the sons of God, that is, of all those who have lived virtuously, have become divine, and bear the divine glory.
6. There are degrees of blessedness enjoyed by those who inhabit the New Jerusalem in proportion to their worthiness, and in some cases, progress or approach toward greater knowledge of and intimacy with God.
7. As to its role in the teaching life of the church and the virtuous life of its members, the New Jerusalem comes to become both an incitement to, and a model of, the life of virtue.

These elements form some of the key lineaments of thinking on the New Jerusalem that will develop within the church, East and West, millennial and amillennial, throughout the remainder of late antiquity. Some authors or traditions will stress, de-emphasize, or augment certain of these ideas or certain Scriptures based upon their specific priorities. But the core, despite having arisen out of an initial diversity, remains remarkably stable throughout late antiquity.[132]

---

[132] A full exploration of the New Jerusalem in all Christian sources through the early fourth century may be found in Nathan Betz, *City of Gods: The New Jerusalem of John's Revelation in Early Christianity (through ca. 313)* (PhD dissertation, KU Leuven, 2022). For a study on the later development of the New Jerusalem *topos* in the first surviving patristic Greek commentaries on Revelation can be found in Nathan Betz, "The New Jerusalem: A Metaphor for Deification in the Commentaries on Revelation by Oecumenius and Andrew of Caesarea," *Ephemerides Theologicae Lovanienses* 96, no. 1 (2020): 1–39.

Tracking the New Jerusalem in North African Christianity through the Fourth Century*

Martina Vercesi

Introduction

For a book whose status was so troubled in the Eastern church, Revelation seems to have become fairly popular in Latin Christianity by the early third century. Already at the start of the century, Tertullian had made much use of the text, and in the second half of the century, Victorinus of Petovium (modern-day Ptuj, Slovenia) had dedicated a commentary to Revelation.[1] Moreover, in the North African region starting with Tertullian, Revelation played a key role not only in the works of the church fathers, but also in martyrdom literature.[2]

This study will focus on the reception of Revelation's New Jerusalem (Rev 21–22) from the beginning of North African Christianity until the end of the fourth century, with the purpose of examining how Christian authors interpreted it, and how the references to the New Jerusalem shaped their exegesis. In other words, what was the role of the holy city in the North African authors' literary production?[3]

---

* This contribution derives from the research I conducted for my dissertation: "'Quale Regnum Exinde Iustorum! Qualis Civitas Nova Hierusalem!': Revelation 19–21 in the Exegesis of the Christian Communities of Roman Africa from the II to the IV Century," PhD dissertation, University of St Andrews, 2021.

[1] Brief insights on the interpretation of the book of Revelation in ancient Christian literature may be found in Martin Meiser, "Before Canonisation: Early Attestation of Revelation," in *Book of the Seven Seals: The Peculiarity of Revelation, Its Manuscripts, Attestation, and Transmission*, ed. Thomas J. Kraus and Michael Sommer, WUNT 363 (Tübingen: Mohr Siebeck, 2016), 137–58 and Craig R. Koester, *Revelation: A New Translation with Introduction and Commentary*, The Yale Anchor Bible Commentaries (London: Yale University Press, 2015), 29–39.

[2] T. W. Mackay, "Early Christian Exegesis of the Apocalypse," *Studia Biblica* 3 (1978): 257–63, at 257.

[3] For a brief account on the various interpretations of Rev 21–22 see Judith Kovacs and Christopher Rowland, *Revelation: The Apocalypse of Jesus Christ*, Blackwell Bible Commentaries (Malden: Blackwell, 2004), 220–46. Clementina Mazzucco investigates the interpretations of the New Jerusalem in ancient Christian literature in "La Gerusalemme celeste dell''Apocalisse' nei Padri," in *"La dimora di Dio con gli uomini" (Ap XXI,3): Immagini della Gerusalemme celeste dal III al XIV secolo*, ed. Maria Louisa Gatti Perer (Milan: Vita e Pensiero, 1983), 49–75. As I have outlined in "Intimations of Revelation 19–21 in the Early North African Christian

Without approaching the analysis of the literary context of the New Jerusalem in John's Apocalypse, which is not the purpose of this contribution, it is necessary here to simply note the fact that its coming marks the renewal of the world that takes place after the return of Jesus (ch. 19), the millennium, and the final defeat of the devil (ch. 20).[4] The eschatological restoration that is fulfilled in Rev 21:1, "Then I saw a new heaven and a new earth,"[5] and the New Jerusalem "coming down out of heaven" (Rev 21:2) constitute the end of all history (which began with Genesis).[6]

It is also worth noting a methodological premise: as stressed by Clementina Mazzucco, "one must realize that the fathers' interpretations of chapters 21 and 22 must be contextualized in the interpretation of the rest of the book. Within Revelation itself, the final chapters appear connected with the others, through a whole series of references."[7] This aspect pertains to one of the fundamental

---

Communities," *Open Theology* 7 (2017): 413–425, at 413, the studies on the reception of Revelation in the North African communities primarily concentrate on specific authors instead of proposing a big picture.

[4] For some bibliographical notes on Revelation's New Jerusalem, see Craig R. Koester, "Revelation's Vision of New Jerusalem: God's Life-Giving Reign for the World," *Word & World* 40, no. 2 (2020): 112–19; Andreas Hoeck, *The Descent of the New Jerusalem: A Discourse Analysis of Rev 21:1–22:5*, European University Studies (Frankfurt: Lang, 2003); Jan A. Rand, "The New Jerusalem as Pinnacle of Salvation: Text (Rev 21:1–22:5) and Intertext," *Neotestamentica* 38, no. 2 (2004): 275–302; Jörg Frey, "The New Jerusalem Text in Its Historical and Traditio-Historical Context," in *The Dead Sea Scrolls Fifty Years After Their Discovery: Proceedings of the Jerusalem Congress, July 20–25, 1997*, ed. Lawrence H. Schiffman, Emanuel Tov, and James C. VanderKam (Jerusalem: Israel Exploration Society, 2000), 800–16; José A. Filho, "A Nova Jerusalém: um estudo de Apocalipse 21,9–22,9," *Estudos biblicos* 101 (2009): 81–92; Francesco Contreras Molina, "La nuova Gerusalemme, città aperta," in *Apokalypsis: percorsi nell'Apocalisse in onore di Ugo Vanni*, ed. Elena Bosetti and Angelo Colacrai (Assisi: Cittadella editrice, 2005), 621–45; Josef Wohlmuth, "Das Neue Jerusalem als Topos der Eschatologie," *Internationale katholische Zeitschrift Communio* 38, no. 1 (2009): 44–56. See also the bibliography provided by David A. Aune, *Revelation 17–22*, Word Biblical Commentary 52c (Nashville: Nelson, 2008), 1108–09 and 1133–35.

[5] All the English quotations of the Bible come from the English Standard Version.

[6] On this concept see Külli Tõniste, *The Ending of the Canon: A Canonical and Intertextual Reading of Revelation 21–22* (London: Bloomsbury, 2016) and Ugo Vanni, *Apocalisse di Giovanni*, vol. 2, ed. Luca Pedroli (Assisi: Cittadella editrice, 2018), 651.

[7] Mazzucco, "La Gerusalemme celeste" (cf. note 3), 52–53 (my translation). See a comment by Kovacs and Rowland for some connected themes in Revelation itself and in other NT books: "Coming at the end of the book, Rev 21 draws together themes from throughout the book: for example, in 21:5 the command to John to 'write' recalls the beginning in 1:19, and the title 'Alpha and Omega' recalls 1:8; 'those who conquer' in 21:7 echoes the promises of the messages in Rev 2–3 (2:7, 11, 17, 26; 3:5, 12, 21), and the end of sorrow and thirst in 21:4, 6 recalls promises to those 'robed in white' in 7:16. As we saw in the Introduction (see above, 5–6), the Apocalypse shares themes with many other New Testament books. Here the end of death in 21:4 echoes 1 Cor 15:26, and the heavenly Jerusalem is alluded to briefly in both Gal 4:26 and Heb 12:22. The Apocalypse reflects the ambivalence evident throughout the Bible towards Zion (Jerusalem) as both a focus of hope and a place of rebellion (evident from Rev 11:8)." (Kovacs and Rowland, *Revelation* [cf. note 3], 221).

features of the book of Revelation itself; the various images that recur in the entire book provide the reader with the hermeneutical keys to understand it.[8] Thus, the analysis will also take into consideration other references that appear to connect with the New Jerusalem.

1 Tertullian

The first author encountered is Tertullian (Quintus Septimius Florens Tertullianus), who inaugurated Christian theology in the Latin tradition.[9] Tertullian was a prolific writer but not all his works have survived.[10] Among these lost works, the treatise *On the hope of the faithful (De spe fidelium)* might have been essential for this study, since Jerome's account indicates that it treated the millenarian theme.[11]

---

[8] Michael Labahn and Outi Lehtipuu stress: "Understanding the book of Revelation means understanding its imagery. This puzzling book contains a fascinating world of pictures and images – every chapter and every page of it is filled with different kinds of images coming from different traditions and developing different sorts of meaning …. On the whole, the book of Revelation largely develops its story by the use of different kinds of imagery. Therefore, understanding the imagery of Revelation is crucial for understanding how this prophetic book develops its meaning. Furthermore, regarding the reception history of revelation, it is important to know how interpreters of the book have understood themselves and the world they live in the light of such imagery." Michael Labahn and Outi Lehtipuu, ed., *Imagery in the Book of Revelation*, Contributions to Biblical Exegesis and Theology 60 (Leuven: Peeters, 2011), 78. See also Kenneth A. Strand, *Interpreting the Book of Revelation: Hermeneutical Guidelines, with Brief Introduction to Literary Analysis* (Worthington: Ann Arbor, 1976), 19–20.

[9] Kovacs and Rowland dedicated a brief comment on the reception of Rev 21 in Tertullian: "According to Tertullian, the kingdom is at first an earthly kingdom for a thousand years; after this it becomes a heavenly kingdom (*Against Marcion* 3.24). Unlike many other interpreters, he takes account of the negative note in verses like 21:8 and 27. The eight categories of sinners are not pagans, he says, but fallen Christians (*Concerning Flight in Persecution* 7)." (Kovacs and Rowland, *Revelation*, 223 [cf. note 3]). See also Mazzucco, "La Gerusalemme celeste" (cf. note 3), 55 and the recent article of Anni M. Laato which treats precisely this matter: "The New Jerusalem in Tertullian," in *Understanding the Spiritual Meaning of Jerusalem in Three Abrahamic Religions*, ed. Antti Laato, Studies on the Children of Abraham 6 (Leiden: Brill, 2019), 125–34.

[10] "We know of forty-two treatises, composed by Tertullian between 195 and 220 C.E., eleven of them being lost." Charles Kannengiesser, *Handbook of Patristic Exegesis: The Bible in Ancient Christianity* (Leiden: Brill, 2004), 368. See also Geoffrey D. Dunn, *Tertullian*, The Early Church Fathers (New York: Routledge, 2004), 7.

[11] Jerome, *De viris illustribus* 18 and *Commentariorum in Ezechielem libri XVI* 11.36. The same Tertullian refers to his treatise in *Adversus Marcionem* 3.24. Millenarianism (from the Latin *mille*), or chiliasm (from the Greek χίλιοι) was a belief widespread in the early Christian communities. It maintains that before the end of the world, there would be a kingdom of one thousand years on the earth only for the righteous. This was not a single movement, since it presented diversifications and different use of sources, among which Rev 20 certainly had a role. On this topic see Clementina Mazzucco, "Il millenarismo cristiano delle origini (II–III sec.)," in *"Millennium": l'attesa della fine nei primi secoli cristiani: Atti delle III giornate patristiche torinesi, Torino 23–24 ottobre 2000*, ed. Renato Uglione (Torino: CELID, 2002), 145–82.

The first reference to the New Jerusalem appears in one of the earliest treatises written by Tertullian, *On Shows (De spectaculis)*, which is commonly dated to the year 197, or between that year and 200.[12] In this paraenetic work, Tertullian condemns the Roman shows in their different forms, explaining why Christians should not attend this kind of entertainment. The reference to the New Jerusalem of the book of Revelation is found at the very end. In the last chapter, Tertullian sharply describes what is the real and great spectacle for the Christians: the parousia and the last judgment in which they will be the real spectators of the terrible sufferings and damnation of others. There is no exact quotation of Revelation. However, its imagery can be recognized:

> But what a spectacle is that fast-approaching advent of our Lord, now owned by all, now highly exalted, now a triumphant one! What that exultation of the angelic hosts! What the glory of the rising saints! What the kingdom of the just thereafter! What the city New Jerusalem![13]

This series of exclamations narrates the events in a chronological way, mirroring the same succession in Revelation: the coming of the millennial kingdom (Rev 20:4.6), the rising saints (Rev 20:4.6), the new city Jerusalem (Rev 21:2, 10). The provenance of the reference to the New Jerusalem in this eschatological context is debated; scholars disagree on the sources that lay behind these words. Although this passage is usually employed to explicate Tertullian's adherence to millenarianism, it is worth remembering that Revelation was not the only biblical text interpreted in that direction.[14] This is the reason why some scholars proposed

---

[12] Tertullian, *Les spectacles (De spectaculis): Introduction, texte critique, traduction et commentaire*, ed. Marie Turcan, SC 332 (Paris: Cerf, 1986), 43 (discussion at pages 37–45). See also Tertullian, *Opere catechetiche: gli spettacoli, la preghiera, il battesimo, la pazienza, la penitenza, alla moglie, l'eleganza femminile*, ed. Sara Matteoli et al., Scrittori cristiani dell'Africa romana (Roma: Città nuova, 2008), 17. Other references in Tertullian to Rev 21–22 which, however, are not useful for this discussion are *De resurrectione carnis* 58.3 (Rev 21:4); *Marc.* 4.11.9 (Rev 21:5); 1.29.4 (Rev 21:6); *De pudicitia* 19.8 (Rev 21:7); *De fuga in persecutione* 7.2, 9.3, *Pud.* 19.7–8, and *Scorpiace* 12.1 (Rev 21:8); *De monogamia* 5.2 and *Marc.* 1.29.4 (Rev 22:13); *Marc.* 2.10.6 and *Pud.* 19.9 (Rev 22:14); *Marc.* 2.5.1 and *Pud.* 19.9 (Rev 22:15); *Adversus Hermogenem* 22.5 (Rev 22:18–19).

[13] Tertullian, *De spectaculis* 30.1: *Quale autem spectaculum in proximo est aduentus domini iam indubitati, iam superbi, iam triumphantis! Quae illa exultatio angelorum, quae gloria resurgentium sanctorum! Quale regnum exinde iustorum! Qualis ciuitas noua hierusalem!* Eligius Dekkers et al., ed., *Tertullianus. Opera I. Opera Catholica*, CCSL 1 (Turnhout: Brepols, 1954); translation from *ANF* 3, 138–39. An analysis of this passage with emphasis on the millenarian background can be found in Carlo Tibiletti, "Inizi del millenarismo di Tertulliano," in *Annali della Facoltà di Lettere e Filosofia della Università di Macerata 1* (Napoli: Libreria scientifica, 1968), 201–3. See also Laato, "The New Jerusalem" (cf. note 9), 127 and Emanuele Castorina, ed., *Tertulliani. De spectaculis: Introduzione, testo critico, commento e traduzione* (Florence: La nuova Italia, 1961), 382–95.

[14] See the chapter dedicated to millenarianism in Jean Daniélou, *La teologia del giudeo-cristianesimo* (Bologna: EDB, 2016), 427–58, and Mazzucco, "Il millenarismo cristiano" (cf. note 11), 155–62.

that this series of events does not come from Revelation but from other sources.[15] Nevertheless, as others have argued, it is more than likely that the reference to the eschatological city came from Revelation; indeed, one can recognize here the same pattern of the events narrated in John's Revelation.[16] Furthermore, in the description of the same events in Tertullian's *Against Marcion (Adversus Marcionem)*, Tertullian indicates his biblical sources in an unambiguous statement. The passage related to the New Jerusalem is found in ch. 24 of the third book,[17] whose topic is the Marcionite Christology and Tertullian's demonstration that Christ was previously announced by the Old Testament. As far as the return of Christ is concerned, Tertullian states:

> But we do confess that a kingdom is promised to us upon the earth, although before heaven, only in another state of existence: inasmuch as it will be after the resurrection for a thousand years in the divinely-built city of Jerusalem, let down from heaven, which the apostle also calls our mother from above: and, while declaring that our *politeuma*, or citizenship, is in heaven, he predicates of it that it is really a city in heaven. This both Ezekiel had knowledge of and the Apostle John beheld. And the word of the new prophecy which is a part of our belief, attests how it foretold that there would be for a sign a picture of this very city exhibited.[18]

Again, the events here respect the order of Revelation: the resurrection of the thousand years (Rev 20:4–6) and the New Jerusalem coming down from heaven (Rev 21:2, 10). Further, Tertullian mentions the sources he uses: Ezekiel and the Apostle John. This passage is generally taken as evidence for the millenarianism of Tertullian,[19] even though some scholars have tried to downplay this

---

[15] See Turcan in *Les spectacles* (cf. note 12), 318, and Jerónimo Leal, *La antropología de Tertuliano. Estudio de los tratados polémicos de los años 207–212 d.C.* (Roma: Institutum Patristicum Augustinianum, 2001), 163–64.

[16] Antonio Delrio, "Il millenarismo di Tertulliano," *Augustinianum* 43, no. 2 (2003): 365–96, at 372.

[17] René Braun proposes to date this treatise to around 207/208. René Braun, *Tertullien. Contre Marcion: Tome III*, SC 399 (Paris: Cerf, 1994), 9–10.

[18] Tertullian, *Marc.* 3.24.3–4: *Nam et confitemur in terra nobis regnum promissum, sed ante caelum, sed alio statu, utpote post resurrectionem in mille annos in ciuitate diuini operis hierusalem caelo delatum, quam et apostolus matrem nostram sursum designat. Et politeuma nostrum, id est municipatum, in caelis esse pronuntians, alicui utique caelesti ciuitati eum deputat. Hanc et Ezechiel nouit, et apostolus Ioannes uidit et qui apud fidem nostram est nouae prophetiae sermo testatur, ut etiam effigiem ciuitatis ante repraesentationem eius conspectui futuram in signo praedicarit.* Emil Kroymann et al., ed., CCSL 1 (Turnhout: Brepols, 1954); translation from *ANF* 3, 569. For comment on this passage see: Tibiletti, "Inizio del millenarismo" (cf. note 11), 196–98; Laato, "The New Jerusalem" (cf. note 9), 127–29; and Claudio Moreschini, ed., *Tertulliano. Opere Dottrinali I: Contro Marcione. Libri I–III*, Scrittori cristiani dell'Africa romana (Roma: Città Nuova, 2014), 259–60.

[19] See Carlo Nardi, *Il millenarismo. Testi dei secoli I–II* (Bologna: Edizioni Dehoniane Bologna, 1995), 219. Laato stresses: "The most interesting and most discussed passage in Adv Marc 3,24, the only preserved passage in which Tertullian combines the New Jerusalem with millennialistic ideas." Laato, "The New Jerusalem" (cf. note 9), 127–28.

feature.[20] However, it seems that as far as Revelation is concerned, there is a clear reference to chs. 20 and 21, as in the last chapter of Tertullian's *Shows* examined above.[21] Thus, although references to the New Jerusalem are mixed with other sources, and taking into account the probable influence of the New Prophecy on Tertullian,[22] it seems at least arguable that the coming of the holy city represents, for this author, the eschatological reward promised by God which, after the millennium, will inaugurate the heavenly kingdom.

In this regard, another reference is visible in *Antidote to the Scorpion's Sting (Scorpiace)*, a reflection on martyrdom dated to around the persecutory measures of the proconsul Scapula.[23]

Then to every conqueror the Spirit promises now the tree of life, and exemption from the second death, now the hidden manna with the stone of glistening whiteness, and the name unknown (to every man save him that receives it): now power to rule with a rod of iron, and the brightness of the morning star; now the being clothed in a white raiment, and not having the name blotted out of the book of life, and being made in the temple of God a pillar with the inscription on it of the name of God and of the Lord, and of the heavenly Jerusalem; now a sitting with the Lord on his throne – which once was persistently refused to the sons of Zebedee.[24]

Here, the name of the "heavenly Jerusalem" (*hierusalem caelestis*) is written on conquerors, who are the martyrs (as Tertullian makes clear slightly after: "Who, pray, are these so blessed conquerors, but martyrs in the strict sense of the word?"). Anni Maria Laato stresses that Tertullian is probably referring to Heb 12:22–23 since the expression *caelestis* never occurs in Revelation.[25] This

---

[20] Paolo Siniscalco, "L'escatologia di Tertulliano: tra Rivelazione scritturale e dati razionali, 'psicologici,' naturali," *Annali di storia dell'esegesi* 17, no. 1 (2000): 83–84.

[21] Nevertheless, one must point out that these two references are to be considered allusions, since Tertullian does not quote the exact text.

[22] In the passage of Tertullian, *Marc.*, examined above, there is the allusion to the city of the New Prophecy: *et qui apud fidem nostram est novae prophetiae sermo testatur*. On the influence of the Montanist movement see Christine Trevett, *Montanism: Gender, Authority and the New Prophecy* (Cambridge: Cambridge University Press, 1996), 66–76 and 95–100. Laato efficiently explains the concerns around this matter: "We have too little precise information pertaining to the eschatological beliefs of the New Prophecy movement to evaluate with certainty to what degree Tertullian was influenced by them in his teaching on the New Jerusalem." Laato, "The New Jerusalem" (cf. note 9), 134.

[23] Thus, around 212: Pietro Podolak, *Introduzione a Tertulliano*, Letteratura Cristiana Antiqua (Brescia: Morcelliana, 2006), 72. An earlier date has been proposed by Timothy D. Barnes: "Tertullian's *Scorpiace*," *Journal of Theological Studies* 20 (1969): 105–32.

[24] Tertullian, *Scorp.* 12.8: *Exinde uictoribus quibusque promittit nunc arborem uitae et mortis ueniam secundae, nunc latens manna cum calculo candido et nomine ignoto, nunc ferreae uirgae potestatem et stellae matutinae claritatem, nunc albam uestiri nec deleri de libro uitae et columnam fieri in dei templo in nomine dei et domini et hierusalem caelestis inscriptam, nunc residere cum domino in throno eius, quod aliquando zebedaei filiis negabatur*. August Reifferscheid and Georg Wissowa, ed., *Tertullianus. Opera II. Opera montanistica*, CCSL 2 (Turnhout: Brepols, 1954); translation from *ANF* 3, 1125.

[25] Laato, "The New Jerusalem" (cf. note 9), 126–27.

explanation is possible, but it is also worth observing that the passage presents a huge number of references to Revelation – for example the reference to the tree of life (Rev 2:7), the second death (Rev 2:10), and the name unknown (Rev 2:17). Consequently, I suggest that this reference could allude to Rev 3:12 and is viewed as a reward of martyrdom.[26] Finally, all the references to the book of Revelation outlined here should be contextualized in the whole corpus of Tertullian's writings in which the eschatological theme plays a central role.[27] The passages examined made clear that the New Jerusalem of Revelation in Tertullian is always present in an eschatological context, in the description of the future events for Christians, and the advent of this city constitutes the glorious fulfilment of the Christians' life.

2 *De Montibus Sina et Sion*

Another significant text is *On the Mountains Sinai and Zion (De montibus Sina et Sion)*,[28] which was written in Roman Africa[29] between the end of the second century and the second half of the third century[30]. This homily is part of the so-called "Pseudo-Cyprianic" writings, a collection of works attributed to the bishop of Carthage but composed anonymously. Scholars have proposed various descriptions of the author of *De montibus*. According to Jean Daniélou, this work was written by a Jew who knew Hebrew but whose knowledge of Latin

---

[26] For this insight, see the comment in *Tertulliano. Opere montaniste,* vol. 4/1, Giovanna Azzali Bernardelli et al., ed., Scrittori cristiani dell'Africa romana (Roma: Città Nuova, 2011), 242–45.

[27] Jaroslav Pelikan, "The Eschatology of Tertullian," *Church History* 21, no. 2 (1952): 108–22. On this matter, Eric Osborn provides some observations in *Tertullian: First Theologian of the West* (Cambridge: Cambridge University Press, 2001), 214–24.

[28] For a brief note on Revelation's New Jerusalem in this work: Mazzucco, "La Gerusalemme celeste" (cf. note 3), 66–67.

[29] This position is no longer discussed: Clara Burini, ed., *Pseudo Cipriano. I due monti Sinai e Sion: De duobus montibus*, Biblioteca Patristica (Fiesole: Nardini, 1994), 18–21. I will mostly refer to the study of Burini and that of Anni Maria Laato, *Jews and Christians in De duobus montibus Sina et Sion: An Approach to Early Latin Adversus Iudaeos Literature* (Åbo: Åbo Akademi University Press, 1998), which are the most recent studies and which provide a rich bibliography.

[30] The dating of this work is still controversial. Cf. Burini for a survey of the various positions (*I due monti Sinai e Sion* [cf. note 29], 21–27). She expresses the preference for the second half of the third century ("con estensione alla prima metà del quarto," 23), while Anni Maria Laato writes, "I suggest a date in the time of Tertullian, in any case not later than the mid-third century" (*Jews and Christians* [cf. note 29], 168). See the discussion about date and place in *Jews and Christians*, 19–22 and a survey of previous research at pages 2–4. Recently, Dominique Cerbelaud proposed an early date, arguing that there is no reason to date this writing after the 220s: "Thèmes de la polémique chrétienne contre le judaïsme au IIIe siècle: le *De montibus Sina et Sion*," *Revue des Sciences philosophiques et théologiques* 91, no. 4 (2007): 726.

was limited.³¹ Clara Burini has rejected this opinion, claiming that the Jewish-Christian origin of the author is not demonstrable.³²

The scope of this treatise is to prove that Christ has fulfilled the prophecies described in the Old Testament. This argumentation is developed through the typological antithesis of the two mountains: Sinai, which represents the Old Testament, and Zion, which represents the New Testament.³³ In ch. 9 the author explains the significance of the new law using the image of the cross, which has a fundamental role since it represents the new covenant that brings fulfillment to the prophecies announced in the Old Testament.³⁴ As Burini has highlighted: "Christ's passion-death constitutes the decisive concept of *De montibus*' Christology."³⁵

Jesus's sacrifice on the cross returns in ch. 10 in association with the New Jerusalem as it is described in the book of Revelation:

> Nailed onto a tree the flesh let out a word of the Lord saying: "Eli, Eli" and the earlier mentioned spiritual prophet's word was fulfilled: "Out of Zion shall go forth the law and the word of the Lord from Jerusalem" [Isa. 2:3]. Jerusalem is a new city that comes down from heaven, it is made square by four Gospels, it has twelve foundations in twelve prophets and twelve gates in twelve apostles: on the basis of their announcement about Christ they will enter this holy and new city, that is the spiritual Church.³⁶

Here, the following references to Revelation can be recognized:

- The descent of Jerusalem from heaven (Rev 21:2, 10)
- The city's square shape (Rev 21:16)
- Its twelve foundations in twelve prophets and its twelve gates in twelve apostles (Rev 21:12, 14b).³⁷

In this passage, the author of the treatise links the vision of the New Jerusalem of Rev 21 with the last breath of Jesus on the cross. As suggested by Burini, this

---

³¹ Jean Daniélou, *Les origines du christianisme latin* (Paris: Les Éditions du Cerf, 1978), 56.

³² Burini in *I due monti Sinai e Sion* (cf. note 29), 17; see also the discussion at pages 14–17 and 26–27. Laato argues: "The author is thus a mild and theological representative of *Adversus Iudaeos* literature." *Jews and Christians* (cf. note 29), 169. See also the conclusion at pages 168–69, and a preliminary discussion at 29–35.

³³ Insights on the method of interpretation are offered by Laato, *Jews and Christians* (cf. note 29), 58–73, and Burini in *I due monti Sina e Sion* (cf. note 29), 89–111.

³⁴ Burini in *I due monti Sina e Sion* (cf. note 29), 72–73.

³⁵ Burini in *I due monti Sina e Sion* (cf. note 29), 77–78 (my translation).

³⁶ Pseudo Cyprian, *Mont.* 10.1: *Caro ligno confixa emisit uerbum dominicum dicens: Heli, heli et adinpletum est propheticum spiritale ante dictum: de Sion exiet lex, et uerbum Domini ab Hierusalem; de caelo descendentem nouam ciuitatem, quadratam per quattuor euangelia, habens duodecim fundamenta duodecim prophetarum et duodecim portas duodecim apostolorum: per quorum adnuntiationem christiani in hanc ciuitatem sanctam et nouam introierunt, quae spiritalis est ecclesia.* Translation from Laato, *Jews and Christians* (cf. note 29), 179.

³⁷ See Burini in *I due monti Sina e Sion* (cf. note 29), 269–70, and Laato, *Jews and Christians* (cf. note 29), 155–56.

new city "is the city of the eschatological time, the 'spiritual church' where the highest promise of the kingdom of heavens' eternity is realized."[38] Burini also emphasizes the spiritual nature of the church, which is opposed to the earthly world. However, rather than the prominence of the spiritual features of this city (outlined more in the parable of the vineyard in chs. 14–15),[39] here the eschatological characteristic stands out.[40] In ch. 4 of *De montibus* Jesus's death is located at the six thousandth year.[41] This is not enough to confirm that the author shares a millenarian view,[42] however with Jesus's death at this stage, it is evident that his sacrifice inaugurated the seventh millennium, the cosmic overturning. This connection is also suggested by the vision of the New Jerusalem in the moment of Jesus's last breath. As Patricio de Navascués has suggested, an apocalyptic view can be recognized in this text; this worldview is the same present in the first Christian generation which introduces the "mystery of the cross and resurrection of Christ, which breaks history in order to renew it definitively."[43] The cross is, therefore, a turning point not only in the life of Jesus, but it becomes an anticipation of the destiny of the Christian communities, which, in commemorating the crucifixion, celebrate the event of the recapitulation of history. Therefore, it is possible to recognize the link that the author establishes between the cross and the descent of the New Jerusalem – the latter of which in the text of Revelation is the apocalyptic end which occurs after the final battle between the powers of God and those of the antichrist. It is just here where one can begin to glimpse thoughts that fit well into the Christian martyrdom literature, in which the martyr gains the highest eschatological reward precisely because he or she repeats, in a most painful death, the sacrifice of Christ.[44]

---

[38] Burini in *I due monti Sina e Sion* (cf. note 29), 88 (my translation). Of the same opinion is also Mazzucco, "La Gerusalemme celeste" (cf. note 3), 67.

[39] Laato, *Jews and Christians* (cf. note 29), 154–55. See also Burini in *I due monti Sina e Sion* (cf. note 29), 281–97.

[40] Laato: "Two special features of Pseudo-Cyprian's view of the Church are conspicuous here: first, its immediate contact with and dependence on the crucified Christ and second, its eschatological character." *Jews and Christians* (cf. note 29), 158.

[41] Pseudo Cyprian, *Mont.* 4.3: *Hic ergo numerus XLVI passionem declarat, eo quod sexto millesimo anno hora sexta passus, resurgens a mortuis quadragesimo die in caelis ascendit*. Burini has emphasized that the phrase *sexto millesimo anno* refers to an exact date, not to the sixth millennium. Although she is probably right about the linguistic issue, I think here the accent is more on the theological meaning, rather than the numerical one. *I due monti Sina e Sion* (cf. note 29), 79–80.

[42] See the observations of Daniélou who claims that in this text one can find references to the millenarianism movement. Daniélou, *Les origins* (cf. note 31), 50–51. See also Laato who shares this vision at *Jews and Christians* (cf. note 29), 66–67. Patricio de Navascués proposes allusions to Tyconius's theology in "*De montibus Sina et Sion*: judíos, magos y mártires entre apocalíptica y donatismo," *Vetera Christianorum* 37, no. 2 (2000): 307–11.

[43] De Navascués, "*De montibus Sina et Sion*" (cf. note 42), 279–80.

[44] Laato: "The eschatological orientation is apparent above all in the narrative of the New Jerusalem, but also in the characterization of the Church as heavenly, spiritual and holy and the

3 Passio Perpetuae et Felicitatis

In this regard, a passage of the *Passion of Perpetua and Felicity (Passio Perpetuae et Felicitatis)* is instructive. This account narrates the martyrdom of a group of Christians which took place in Carthage on the seventh of March 203.[45] Though no direct quotations of Revelation are to be found in the text, this Passion is constellated by references to the book. Indeed, an allusion to the New Jerusalem is found precisely in the context of the martyrs' rewards, specifically when Saturus, one of the Christians about to be martyred, dreams of what he and the others would experience after their death in the arena. His description of the place where he would arrive with his companions recalls the description of Revelation's New Jerusalem (Rev 21:18): "And we came near a place, whose walls seemed to have been built out of light. And before the door of that place stood four angels, who clothed those who entered in white robes."[46] If the allusion to the New Jerusalem can indeed be identified here, one can say that the holy city represents, in the martyrs' dreams, the highest eschatological reward that the saints gain following their sacrifice.[47]

4 Lactantius

At the beginning of the third century, between 304 and 311,[48] Lactantius (Lucius Caecilius Firmianus Lactantius) composed the *Divine Institutes (Divinarum institutionum libri VII)*, an apology in seven books. This huge work presents a

---

flesh of the Christians as spiritual and immortal. The Christians shall acquire the land promised to them in heaven in times to come (11.1). The hope of Christians is to live forever in eternity with their emperor and king. Both of these themes, dependence on Christ and the heavenly reward, are present in the martyrdoms and are cited as ground for standing firm in the face of persecution." *Jews and Christians* (cf. note 29), 158.

[45] This date is the subject of a majority consensus. See Jacqueline Amat, *Passion de Perpétue et de Félicité, suivi des Actes*, SC 417 (Paris: Cerf, 1996), 19–22. A discussion is also provided in Thomas J. Heffernan, ed., *The Passion of Perpetua and Felicity* (Oxford: Oxford University Press, 2012), 60–78.

[46] *Passio* 12.1: *Et uenimus prope locum, cuius loci parietes tales erant quasi de luce aedificati; et ante ostium loci illius angeli quattuor stabant, qui introeuntes uestierunt stolas candidas.* Text and translation are from Éric Rebillard, *Greek and Latin Narratives about the Ancient Martyrs*, Oxford Early Christian Texts (Oxford: Oxford University Press, 2019).

[47] The references to the book of Revelation and the New Jerusalem are also found in other martyrdom accounts of the North Africa tradition. See Mazzucco, "La Gerusalemme celeste" (cf. note 3), 70. On this matter, relevant is the contribution of Remo Cacitti: "Vae tibi saeculum. Il contrasto fra regno e cosmo nelle visioni dei martiri paleocristiani d'Africa," in *Il Dio mortale: teologie politiche tra antico e contemporaneo*, ed. Paolo Bettiolo and Giovanni Filoramo (Brescia: Morcelliana, 2002), 163–92.

[48] For a brief overview of other authors' proposals see Elizabeth DePalma Digeser, "Lactantius and Constantine's Letter to Arles: Dating the *Divine Institutes*," *Journal of Early Christian*

unique characteristic with regard to the author's aim. Because Lactantius wanted to be understandable to his pagan readership, he often used pagan sources instead of Christian ones.[49] As he makes clear in 7.25.1 (after having narrated the events of the millennial kingdom) he deliberately decides not to rely on *sacra scriptura*.[50] Full quotations of the Bible, even regarding the New Jerusalem, should therefore not be expected in this work.

Nevertheless, references to the New Jerusalem are found in chapters 24–26 of the seventh book of the *Divine Institutes (De vita beata)*, in which Lactantius describes the last events of the world. Lactantius's millenarian theme shows various influences.[51] From Julius Africanus and Hippolytus he adopted the conviction that the end was less than two hundred years away. He shows pagan influences in his description of the golden age – which Lactantius, opposite the classical

---

Studies 2, no. 1 (1994): 44. Stefan Freund claims: "Aus den genannten Erwägungen ergibt sich für die Arbeit am siebten Buch eine maximale Zeitspanne von 305/306 bis 310, höchstens Anfang 311." Stefan Freund, *Laktanz, Divinae Institutiones Buch 7: De vita beata: Einleitung, Text, Übersetzung* (Berlin: De Gruyter, 2009), 5.

[49] Anthony J. Bowen and Peter D. A. Garnsey: "He makes heavy use of non-Christian authorities, both human and divine, and relatively rarely cites Scriptures." *Lactantius: Divine Institutes*, trans. Anthony J. Bowen and Peter D. A. Garnsey (Liverpool: Liverpool University Press, 2011), 14. A comment on this matter is provided at pages 14–21. See also Anthony P. Coleman, *Lactantius the Theologian: Lactantius and the Doctrine of Providence*, Gorgias Studies in Early Christianity and Patristics 68 (Piscataway: Gorgias, 2017), 37–54; Robert Maxwell Ogilvie, *The Library of Lactantius* (Oxford: Clarendon, 1978), 7–110. Jeremy M. Schott offers a detailed study on Hermetica, Apollo, Sibylline Oracles, and Hystaspes the Median sage: "Vera Religio and Falsae Religiones: Lactantius's Divine Institutes," in *Christianity, Empire, and the Making of Religion in Late Antiquity*, ed. Jeremy M. Schott (Philadelphia: University of Pennsylvania Press, 2008), 84–96. For a bibliography on the Sibylline Oracles see Andreas Lehnardt, *Bibliographie zu den Jüdischen Schriften aus hellenistisch-römischer Zeit*, Jüdische Schriften aus hellenistisch-römischer Zeit 6, no. 2 (Gütersloh: Gerd Mohn, 1999). On Lactantius's use of the oracular literature, see Oliver Nicholson, "Broadening the Roman Mind: Foreign Prophets in the Apologetic of Lactantius," *Studia Patristica* 36 (2001): 364–74. On the use of Latin poets, see Alain Goulon, "Les citations des poètes latins dans l'oeuvre de Lactance," in *Lactance et son temps. Recherches actuelles. Actes du IVᵉ colloque d'études historique et patristiques, Chantilly, 21–23 septembre 1976*, ed. Jacques Fontaine and Michel Perrin (Paris: Beauchesne, 1978), 107–56 (he offers a table with the number of quotes for each author at 113). On the same topic, see Vinzenz Buchheit, "Cicero Inspiratus: Vergilius Propheta? Zur Wertung paganer Autoren bei Laktanz," *Hermes* 118 (1990): 357–72.

[50] Lactantius, *Inst.* 7.25: *Haec sunt quae a prophetis futura dicuntur; quorum testimonia et uerba ponere opus esse non duxi, quoniam esset infinitum nec tantam rerum multitudinem mensura libri caperet tam multis uno spiritu similia dicentibus, simulque ne fastidium legentibus fieret, si ex omnibus collecta et translata congererem, praeterea ut ea ipsa quae dicerem non nostris, sed alienis potissimum litteris confirmarem doceremque non modo apud nos, uerum etiam apud eos ipsos qui nos insectantur, ueritatem con signatam teneri, quam recusent agnoscere.* Eberhard Heck and Antonie Wlosok, ed., *Lactantius. Divinarum Institutionum: liber VII* (Berlin: De Gruyter, 2011). Translation from Bowen and Garnsey, *Lactantius: Divine Institutes* (cf. note 49).

[51] This has been characterised as materialistic: Daniélou, "La typologie millénariste de la semaine," *Vigiliae Christianae* 2, no. 1 (1948): 14–16. See also Manlio Simonetti, "Il *millenarismo* in Occidente: Commodiano e Lattanzio," Annali di storia dell'esegesi 15 (1998): 181–189, at 186–87.

Latin tradition, placed at the *end* of the history of the world (as opposed to at its beginning). He also shows some familiarity with Irenaeus's concept of the seven millennia.[52] As Franz Cumont has stressed, there are other influences on Lactantius as well, including the eschatology of the Hellenistic Magians, one of whom was Hystaspes.[53] Despite the presence of other influences, scholars agree on the importance recognizing the influence of the book of Revelation when it comes to understanding Lactantius's chiliasm.[54] Table 1 shows the events narrated in book seven of the *Divine Institutes* and its parallels in the book of Revelation:

Table 1. Thematic parallels between Lactantius's *Divine Institutes* 7 and Rev 19–21

Divine Institutes 7	Rev 19–21
19 The second coming of Christ	19 The second coming of Christ
20 The first resurrection only for Christians	20:4–6 The first resurrection for martyrs
22–23 The soul and resurrection in the pagan tradition	n/a
24.2 The millennial kingdom 24.5 The devil bound 24.6 The holy city on the earth 24.7–14 The golden age	20:4–6 The millennial kingdom 20:1–3 The devil bound 21:2 The holy city on the earth (with description 21:9–27)
25 When does the end take place?	n/a
26.1 The final battle 26.5 The renewal of the world 26.6 The second resurrection, judgment, and punishment	20:7–9 The final battle 21:1 The renewal of the world 20:15 / 21:8 Judgment and punishment

---

[52] Irenaeus, *Adversus haereses* 5.28.3. As Daniélou has emphasized, the concept of the seven millennia is not derived from the Asian tradition, but comes from Irenaeus. This tradition is then found in Lactantius. Daniélou, *La teologia* (cf. note 14), 453–54. Coleman also observed: "Here we discover that the rhetorician follows the millennialist path pioneered by Irenaeus, Justin and Tertullian." Coleman, *Lactantius the Theologian* (cf. note 49), 227.

[53] For a detailed comment about Hystaspes's influence on Lactantius, see Franz Cumont, "La fin du monde selon les mages occidentaux," *Revue de l'histoire des religions* 103 (1931): 68–93. For the relationship between Lactantius and Hystaspes, see also Joseph Bidez and Franz Cumont, *Les mages hellénisés. Zoroastre, Ostanès et Hystaspe d'après la tradition grecque* (Paris: Les Belles Lettres, 1938), 215–22.

[54] See Valentí Fàbrega, "Die chiliastische Lehre des Laktanz. Methodische und theologische Voraussetzungen und religionsgeschichtlicher Hintergrund," *Jahrbuch für Antike und Christentum* 17 (1974): 126–46, at 136, and Hedwig W. A. Van Rooijen-Dijkman, *De vita beata: Het zevende boek van de Divinae Institutiones van Lactantius: analyse en bronnenonderzoek* (Assen: Van Gorcum, 1967), 102. Insight on the New Jerusalem in Lactantius can be found in Mazzucco, "La Gerusalemme celeste" (cf. note 3), 56.

Although the order of the events is sometimes slightly different, Lactantius for the most part adheres to Revelation's timeline. In this light, the mention of the holy city may well refer to the New Jerusalem of Rev 21, even if not all scholars agree:[55] "After God's coming the just will gather from all over the world, and after his judgment the holy city will be set up at the center of earth, and God himself will dwell in it with the just in control."[56] The mention is not followed by the description of the city as Rev 21 presents it; instead, Lactantius takes inspiration from the notion of the Golden Age (7.24.7–14),[57] which should not surprise us considering the author's particular use of sources. At the end of 7.24, however, we find a reference to Rev 21:24 ("By its light will the nations walk, and the kings of the earth will bring their glory into it, and its gates will never be shut by day, and there will be no night there"):[58]

People will thus live lives of great peace and plenty, and will reign side by side with God; kings of nations will come from the ends of the earth with offerings and gifts to honour and adore the great king, and his name will be known and revered by all people under heaven and by all kings with dominion on earth.[59]

Lactantius, being influenced by the pagan audience to whom he decided to address the *Divine Institutes*, chose not to rely openly on biblical texts. However,

---

[55] Freund in *Laktanz. Divinae Institutiones Buch 7* (cf. note 48), 551. See also Jan Dochhorn's brief comment: "The righteous, meanwhile, will dwell with God in the holy city described in Rev 21–22." Jan Dochhorn, "Laktanz und die Apocalypse. Eine Untersuchung zu *Inst.* 7.15–26," in *Ancient Christian Interpretations of "Violent Texts" in the Apocalypse*, ed. Joseph Verheyden, Tobias Nicklas, and Andreas Merkt (Göttingen: Vandenhoeck & Ruprecht, 2011), 157 (my translation). From the opposite point of view, Simonetti argues that since Lactantius nowhere mentions the descent of the New Jerusalem and he explicitly quotes Revelation only once, it is possible to suggest that the author took the description of the millennium from the "traditional Cerinthus-Papias-Justin-Irenaeus line." Simonetti, "Il millenarismo in Occidente" (cf. note 51), 187 (my translation).

[56] Lactantius, *Inst.* 7.24.6: *Post ciuis adventum congregabuntur iusti ex omni terra peractoque iudicio civitas sancta constituetur in medio terrae, in qua ipse conditor deus cum iustis dominantibus commoretur. Quam civitas sancta constituetur in medio terrae, in qua ipse conditor deus cum iustis dominantibus commoretur.* The same event is described in the *Epitome divinarum institutionum* 67.3.

[57] For an exhaustive comment on the sources, see Freund in *Laktanz. Divinae Institutiones Buch 7* (cf. note 48), 551–65. See also Fàbrega, "Die chiliastische Lehre," 142–45; Domenico Ciarlo, "Salvezza ed escatologia in Lattanzio," in *Pagani e cristiani alla ricerca della salvezza (secoli I–III): XXXIV Incontro di Studiosi dell'Antichità Cristiana, Roma, 5–7 maggio 2005*, Studia ephemeridis Augustinianum 96 (Roma: Institutum Patristicum Augustinianum, 2006), 562–65.

[58] See Freund, *Laktanz. Divinae Institutiones Buch 7* (cf. note 48), 565 and Dochhorn, "Laktanz und die Apocalypse" (cf. note 55), 157.

[59] Lactantius, *Inst.* 7.24.15: *Uiuent itaque homines tranquillissimama et copiosissimam vitam et regnabunt cum deo pariter, reges gentium ueniet a finibus terrae cum donis ac muneribus, ut adorent et honorificent regem magnum, cuius nomen erit praeclarum ac uenerabile universis nationibus quae sub caelo erunt et regibus qui dominabuntur in terra.* Translation by Bowen and Garnsey, *Lactantius: Divine Institutes* (cf. note 49), 436.

the reader can in fact recognize Christian sources hidden in the work, such as Revelation in the present case. Although Lactantius does not quote biblical sources, his references to John's Apocalypse strongly inform his narrative of eschatological events. In this light, even though the New Jerusalem of Revelation is not named, the "holy city" may be fairly read as representing John's city in its "descent from heaven."

5 Commodian

Another author who mentions the New Jerusalem in his description of the last events is Commodian (Commodianus). Although his origin remains a *vexata quaestio*,[60] it is likely that he spent a large part of his life in North Africa where he composed his two writings: the *Instructions (Instructiones)* and the *Song of Apology (Carmen apologeticum)*.[61] Both works present a narration of the last events that is interwoven with millenarian notions that Commodian draws from Revelation and other sources taken from the Jewish apocalyptic world.[62]

In *Carmen*, Commodian alludes to the series of events found in Revelation, and mentions the first resurrection, which he places at the end of the sixth "millennium."[63] In this work, although some references to Revelation can be found, there is no mention of the New Jerusalem as such. Commodian's main inspiration from the Revelation is its chronological series of eschatological events as well several notions to which he alludes.

---

[60] See scholars' proposals up to the 1990s in Eberhard Heck, "Commodianus," in *Die Literatur des Umbruchs: Von der römischen zur christlichen Literatur, 117 bis 284 n. Chr.*, ed. Klaus Sallmann, Handbuch der lateinischen Literatur der Antike 4 (Munich: Beck, 1997), 630–31. For bibliography on Commodian, see N. Castrillo Benito, "Commodiano, primer poeta de la Cristiandad. Estudio del vocalismo, con un apendice bibliografico sobre el autor y sus obras," *Revista Agustiniana* 30 (1989), 44–55.

[61] We are not sure which work comes first, since they seem contemporary. Simonetti, "Il millenarismo in Occidente" (cf. note 51), 182.

[62] Mazzucco, "La Gerusalemme celeste" (cf. note 3), 55–56. On Commodian's millenarianism see Simonetti, "Il millenarismo in Occidente" (cf. note 51), 182–85; Pier Luigi Ciceri, "Il regno millenario in Commodiano," *Athenaeum* 2 (1914): 195–203, in which the author examines the relationship between the works of Commodian, Revelation, and other sources; and Christoph Schubert, "Apokalypse auf Römisch? Inkulturation und Exotismus christlich-jüdischer Endzeitvorstellungen bei Commodian," in *Von Zeitenwenden und Zeitenenden: Reflexion und Konstruktion von Endzeiten und Epochenwenden im Spannungsfeld von Antike und Christentum*, ed. Stefan Freund, Meike Rühl, and Christoph Schubert, Palingenesia 103 (Stuttgart: Steiner, 2015), 180–82.

[63] Commodian, *Carm.* 791–792: *Sex milibus annis prouenient ista repletis, quo tempore nos ipsos spero iam in litore portus. Tunc homo resurget solis in agone reductus et gaudet in deo reminiscens, quid fuit ante; qui, sicut audiuit fragilis in pristina carne, cum sit incorruptus, recognoscit ante promissa.* Antonio Salvatore, ed., *Commodianus. Carmen apologeticum* (Torino: Società Editrice Internazionale, 1977), 96.

It is rather in the *Instructiones* that the New Jerusalem plainly appears. Commodian dedicates the last three chapters of the first book – called *De saeculi istius fine* (1.44), *De resurrectione prima* (1.45), and *De die iudicii* (1.46) respectively – to eschatological events. The New Jerusalem is described in the second of these:[64]

From heaven will descend the city in the first resurrection; this is what we may tell of such a celestial fabric. We shall arise again to him, who have been devoted to him. And they shall be incorruptible, even already living without death. And neither will there be any grief nor any groaning in that city. They shall come also who overcame cruel martyrdom under Antichrist, and they themselves marrying, beget for a thousand years. There are prepared all the revenues of the earth, because the earth renewed without end pours forth abundantly. Therein are no rains; no cold comes into the golden camp. No sieges as now, nor rapines. Nor does that city crave the light of a lamp. It shines from its founder. Moreover him it obeys: in breadth 12,000 furlongs and length and depth. It levels its foundation in the earth, but it raises its head to heaven. In the city before the doors, moreover, sun and moon shall shine. He who is evil is hedged up in torment, for the sake of the nourishment of the righteous. But from the thousand years God will destroy all those evils.[65]

Commodian narrates the event differently than does Revelation, as he locates the New Jerusalem within the millennium; the new city, in fact, comes at the same moment as the first resurrection: "From heaven will descend the city in the first resurrection." Johannes Stettner has examined this particular feature, claiming that one should not see it as a contradiction, but rather as a special interpretation.[66] The link between the two events, indeed, is present in the chiliastic tradition.[67] Indeed, Lactantius, as seen above, adopts a similar construction.[68]

---

[64] For a very detailed analysis of the reception of Revelation in *Instr.* 1.44 see Johannes Stettner, *Veränderte Endzeitvorstellungen: Die Rezeption der Offenbarung des Johannes beim ersten christlich-lateinischen Dichter Commodian,* WUNT II 504 (Tübingen: Mohr Siebeck, 2019), 18–103.

[65] Commodian, *Instr.* 1.44: *De caelo descendit ciuitas in anastase prima. / Et quod referamus de fabrica tanta caeleste? / Resurgimus illi, qui fuimus illi deuoti, / et incorrupti erint iam tunc sine morte uiuentes, / sed nec dolor ullus nec gemitus erit in illa. / Uenturi sunt illi quoque, sub antechristo qui uincunt / robusta mar[tyr]ia, et ipsi toto tempore uiuunt / recipiunt que bona, quoniam mala passi fuere, / et generant ipsi per annos mille nubentes. / Conparantur ibi tota uectigalia terrae, / terra quia nimium fundit sine fine nouata. / Inibi non pluuiam, non frigus in aurea castra, / obsidiae nullae, sicut nunc, neque rapinae. / Nec lucernae lumen desiderat ciuitas illa: / ex auctore suo lucet, nec nox ibi paret. / Per duodecim milia stadia lata, longa, sic alta; / radicem in terra, sed caput cum caelo peraequat; / in urbem pro foribus autem sol aut luna lucebit. / Malus in angore saeptus propter iustos alendos / Ab annis autem mille deus omnia portat.* Josef Martin, ed., *Commodianus. Instructiones,* CCSL 128 (Turnhout: Brepols, 1960). Translation from *ANF* 4, 387.

[66] Stettner, *Veränderte Endzeitvorstellungen* (cf. note 64), 30.

[67] Stettner notes that this connection already appeared in Victorinus, who mentions the descent of the city in the first resurrection. *Veränderte Endzeitvorstellungen* (cf. note 64), 31 and discussion at 29–31.

[68] Stettner, *Veränderte Endzeitvorstellungen* (cf. note 64), 33–36.

Other traits taken from Revelation are present in the present passage as well:

- Line 5: "And neither will there be any grief nor any groaning in that city" (cf. Rev 21:4)
- Lines 14–15, 18: "Nor does that city crave the light of a lamp. It shines from its founder. In the city before the doors, moreover, sun and moon shall shine" (cf. Rev 21:23, 25)
- Line 16: "in breadth 12,000 furlongs and length and depth" (cf. Rev 21:16)

It is established that Commodian alludes to ch. 21 as he describes the awaited city. However, he combines his description with other elements from Revelation also, as well as with elements from other traditions. For instance, those who are to be resurrected are described as the faithful, which brings to mind the resurrection of Rev 20:4–6. The company of the resurrected is also composed of those "who overcame cruel martyrdom under Antichrist" – possibly an explicit reference to Rev 20:4, where the martyrs are those who participate in the first resurrection. As regards sources other than Revelation, Commodian's mention of the resurrected saints' begetting of children shows similarity with the Old Testament Pseudepigrapha (1 Enoch 10:18–19); likewise, the motif of the earth's fertility has its origin in both classical literature describing the Golden Age and in the Jewish and chiliastic traditions (Virgil, *Ecl.* 4; Amos 9:14; Irenaeus, *Haer.* 5.33.3).

6 Tyconius

The present analysis of the interpretation of Revelation's New Jerusalem in North Africa ends with Tyconius, a theologian who lived in the last part of the fourth century and who inaugurates the series of commentaries on the book of Revelation that emerged in North Africa. The monograph by Traugott Hahn, *Tyconius-Studies: ein Beitrag zur Kirchen- und Dogmengeschichte des 4. Jahrhunderts*,[69] published at the very beginning of the twentieth century, set the tone for many subsequent studies of Tyconius when the author indicates that one should focus on the Donatist theologian's affinities with Augustine. However, as Jesse A. Hoover has noticed, this connection was not always observed by ancient commentators, many of whom expressed negative judgments concerning Tyconius's adherence to the Donatist movement.[70] In any case, it is likely best to

---

[69] Traugott Hahn, *Tyconius-Studien: ein Beitrag zur Kirchen- und Dogmengeschichte des 4. Jahrhunderts,* Studien zur Geschichte der Theologie und der Kirche 6, no. 2 (Leipzig: Dieterich, 1900).

[70] "Modern academic assessments have tended to emphasize Tyconius' precarious place within the Donatist communion and formative influence on Augustine's own developing eschatology (not to mention ecclesiology). Ancient commentators on Tyconius' Revelation commentary, on the other hand, made no such allowances. For them ... Tyconius always remained

analyze Tyconius's interpretation of Revelation in its own right. Furthermore, while some scholars have labeled Tyconius's exegesis as "anti-millenarian," I am not convinced that the label really applies, as I will demonstrate below.[71]

In order to better understand the interpretation of the New Jerusalem in Tyconius's literary production, some premises are necessary. First, Tyconius's conception of eschatological events is closely linked to his thoughts about the church; indeed, the church is in many respects the focus of his commentary on Revelation *(Expositio Apocalypseos)*.[72] Second, Tyconius makes clear that he believes that the schism that the church was undergoing at the time – that between the so-called Donatists and the Catholics – would soon be at an end, at which point there would be a final purification of the church.[73] Indeed, the precarious and very real situation of the North African Christian communities at the end of the fourth century strongly influences his view of eschatological events and therefore his exegesis of Revelation; one can understand with little difficulty why the church occupies such a prominent place in the commentary. It is not too much to say that Tyconius's interpretation can be identified only if we place ourselves in his time and situation, that is, during the period in which the persecuted and conflicted church was, in his view, approaching the end times.[74]

The commentary, which does not survive intact, has had to be reconstructed through later authors who quoted it (e.g. Primasius of Hadrumetum, Caesarius of Arles, the venerable Bede, and Beatus of Liébana).[75] Besides these quotations and allusions, some fragments from the commentary have survived, namely the

---

first and foremost a Donatist." Jesse A. Hoover, *The Donatist Church in an Apocalyptic Age* (Oxford: Oxford University Press, 2018), 35.

[71] Paula Fredriksen has defined it as "typological, anti-apocalyptic exegesis of Revelation." "Tyconius and the End of the World," *Revue des Études Augustiniennes* 28, no. 1/2 (1982): 59–75, at 60.

[72] David Robinson writes: "From beginning to end, Tyconius's exposition of Revelation is centered on the church, especially its experience of spiritual warfare and tribulation throughout history." David C. Robinson, intro. and notes, Francis X. Gumerlock, trans., *Tyconius of Carthage. Exposition of the Apocalypse* (Washington, DC: The Catholic University of America Press, 2017), 15.

[73] See his comment on Rev 10:7.

[74] Ian Boxall argues: "Tyconius offered a reading of Revelation as essentially the story of the Church, its trials and tumults as well as its joys, played out symbolically in John's dramatic and colourful visions." Ian Boxall, "The Apocalypse Unveiled: Reflections on the Reception History of Revelation," *The Expository Times* 125, no. 6 (2014): 261–71, at 265.

[75] See Roger Gryson, "Les commentaires patristiques latins de l'Apocalypse," *Revue théologique de Louvain* 28 (1997): 305–37; Kenneth B. Steinhauser, *The Apocalypse Commentary of Tyconius: A History of its Reception and Influence*, European University Studies (Frankfurt am Main; Bern; New York: Lang, 1987); and Paola Marone, "La continuità esegetica che caratterizza le opere di Ticonio ovvero l'applicazione delle 'Regole' nel 'Commento all'Apocalisse'," *Studi e Materiali di Storia delle Religioni* 67 (2001): 253–70, at 255–56. In 2011 Gryson published the critical edition of the reconstructed commentary of Tyconius: *Tyconii Afri Expositio apocalypseos: Accedunt eiusdem expositionis a quodam retractatae Fragmenta Taurinensia*, CCSL 107A (Turnhout: Brepols, 2011).

so-called Turin fragments, which retain his comments on 2:18–4:1 and 7:16–12:6,[76] and the Budapest Fragments, which contain his commentary on Rev 6:6–13.[77]

Modern studies on Tyconius's interpretation of Revelation emphasize how the hermeneutical processes he adopted can be understandable if one considers the method present in another of Tyconius's works, the *Book of Rules (Liber regularum)*.[78] In the *Book of Rules,* Tyconius examines seven rules[79] which, as Charles Kannengiesser characterizes them, are "structural principles, which belong to the very core of scriptural literature ... and make the whole of Scripture become intelligible."[80]

The fifth rule in particular is important. In this rule, called "On Times" *(De temporibus)*, Tyconius claims that the numbers do not have a significance *per se,* but must be understood as symbols:

> Moreover, just as the whole time is reckoned in the first part of any time period, so also the last hour is reckoned as a whole day, or what is left of a thousand years is reckoned as a thousand years. The world's age is six days, i.e., of these 1000 years, the Lord was born, suffered and rose again. Similarly what is left of the 1000 years is called the thousand years of the first resurrection. For just as what was left of the sixth day of the week, i.e., three hours, is reckoned as a whole day – one of the three that the Lord was in the tomb – so what is left of the greater sixth day on which the church rose from the dead is reckoned as a whole day, i.e., 1000 years.[81]

---

[76] Francesco Lo Bue, *The Turin Fragments of Tyconius' Commentary on Revelation*, Texts and Studies: Contributions to Biblical and Patristic Literature, Second Series (Cambridge: Cambridge University Press, 2009).

[77] Roger Gryson, "Fragments inedits du commentaire de Tyconius sur l'Apocalypse," *Revue Bénédictine* 107 (1997): 189–226; László Mezey, "Un fragment de codex de la première époque carolingienne (Ticonius in Apocalypsin?)," in *Miscellanea codicologica F. Masai dicata MCMLXXIX*, vol. 1, ed. François Masai et al., Les publications de scriptorium 8 (Ghent: Story-Scientia, 1979), 41–50.

[78] F.C. Burkitt, *The Book of Rules of Tyconius*, Texts and Studies 3, pt. 1 (Cambridge, 1894); Jean-Marc Vercruysse, *Tyconius. Le livre des règles* (Paris: Cerf, 2004); Pamela Bright, *The Book of Rules of Tyconius: Its Purpose and Inner Logic*, Christianity and Judaism in Antiquity (Notre Dame: University of Notre Dame Press, 1988); David C. Robinson, *The Mystic Rules of Scripture: Tyconius of Carthage's Keys and Windows to the Apocalypse* (PhD dissertation, University of St Michael's College, 2010).

[79] For a detailed study of this writing see Palma Camastra, *Il liber regularum di Ticonio: contributo alla lettura* (Roma: Vivereln, 1998) and Vercruysse, *Tyconius* (cf. note 78).

[80] Charles Kannengiesser, "Quintilian, Tyconius and Augustine," *Illinois Classical Studies* 19 (1994): 239–52, at 247.

[81] Tyconius, *Reg.* 5.3: *Sicut autem in prima parte cuiusque temporis totum tempus est, ita et nouissima hora totus dies est, aut reliquiae mille annorum mille anni sunt. Sex dies sunt mundi aetas, id est sex milia annorum. In reliquiis sexti diei, id est M annorum, natus est Dominus, passus et resurrexit. Itidem reliquiae M annorum dictae sunt mille anni primae resurrectionis. Sicut enim reliquiae sextae feriae, id est très horae, totus dies est, unus ex tribus sepulturae Domini, ita reliquiae sexti diei maioris quo surrexit Ecclesia totus dies est, id est M anni.* Vercruysse, *Tyconius* (cf. note 78). Translation from William S. Babcock, trans., *Tyconius. The Book of Rules*, Texts and Translations 31 (Atlanta: Scholars Press, 1989).

Key to observe here is Tyconius' mention of the church as a hermeneutical key according to which interpret the book of Revelation. Through the use of the synecdoche, Tyconius explains to the readers that this is the time of the one-thousand-year resurrection (Rev 20:4). Moreover, Tyconius places the events of history in the cosmic week, arguing that humanity is currently experiencing the sixth millennium. Since other authors had already proposed this calculation, Tyconius's proposal contributes little that is original.[82] What is important to underline, however, is that Tyconius here speaks about the first resurrection, which, as he understands it, is happening right now in the church. This means that the sixth millennium is not yet fulfilled.

In a subsequent passage, Tyconius clarifies the role of the cosmic week in his interpretation of the time of the church. The seven days, he writes, are the first seven thousand years (*Et VII dies primi VII anni sunt*). This he established on the fact that the Lord worked for six days and rested on the seventh (*sex diebus operatus est Dominus 'et requievit ab omnibus operibus suis die septimo'*).[83] Via a citation of John 5:17 – "Jesus answered them, 'My Father is working until now, and I am working'" – Tyconius concludes that just as this world was created for six days, so too the spiritual world – that is to say, the church – was created for six thousand years. The church, like this world, will end on the seventh "day," which God blesses and makes eternal.[84] The first resurrection of Revelation is thus explained as an event that is currently taking place in the present time, that is, during the sixth millennium. The history of the church is inserted in the cosmic week, according to which the seventh and final day will be the seventh millennium. Hence, the eschatological fateful day, as of the time of Tyconius's writing, had not yet happened.

In his commentary on Revelation, Tyconius interprets the millennium as the time of the church, and it is achieved for the righteous through baptism ("This is the first resurrection, indeed in which we rise through baptism").[85] The one thousand years predicted in Revelation should not be regarded as a future event because it is still part of the sixth millennium in which Jesus died and rose. Nevertheless, this does not mean no future events are predicted, as Tyconius makes clear in his interpretation of the final part of Rev 20, where the last judgment is described.

An ecclesiological interpretation permeates his depiction of the New Jerusalem, which he identifies as the church:

---

[82] Lactantius and Commodian, for example.
[83] Tyconius, *Reg.* 5.6.
[84] Tyconius, *Reg.* 5.6: *Sicut enim mundum istum sex diebus operatus est, ita mundum spiritalem, qui est Ecclesia, per sex milia annos operatur, cessaturus die septimo quem benedixit fecitque aeternum.*
[85] Tyconius, *Exp. Apoc.* 7.19–22. The Latin is from Gryson, *Tyconius* (cf. note 75); the English translation comes from Gumerlock, *Tyconius* (cf. note 72).

He calls this "Jerusalem" the church, by recapitulating from the passion of Christ up to the day on which she rises and, having triumphed with Christ, she is crowned in glory. He mixes each time together, now the present, now the future, and declares more fully when she is taken with great glory by Christ and is separated from every incursion of evil people.[86]

The times are mixed: the New Jerusalem is the church of today, but also that of the future. Tyconius still refers to the separation as something which is not yet happened. In fact, he concludes ch. 21 by stating, "He describes the church of the future time when, with the wicked already separated from the midst, only the good will reign with Christ."[87]

In summary, the dual trend of interpreting Tyconius as both anti-millenarian and as being in continuity with Augustine does not seem to result in an accurate interpretation of this author's exegesis. It is true that Tyconius is speaking about the church of his time; but at the same time he does not neglect the church's future aspect. The harsh times in which Tyconius lived and wrote influenced his thoughts and are reflected in them. In sum, he sees the New Jerusalem as the true church of today – the "Donatist" one – and the church of the future, itself the eschatological reward.

Conclusion

This essay has focused on the exegesis of the New Jerusalem in the early Christian communities of Roman Africa. Beginning with Tertullian, a strong eschatological emphasis has characterized reflections on the holy city. However, it has also been interpreted in light of Christian martyrdom and Jesus's own sacrifice, and has also been commented on in an ecclesiological register. Moreover, Revelation's New Jerusalem has also be interpreted as having millenarian traits derived from classical sources and Jewish literature.

These reflections give opportunity to introduce new elements into ongoing research on the reception of the New Jerusalem in early Christian communities. For example, it would be interesting to explore the exegesis that is present in interpretations from other parts of the Roman empire. A comparison between the "Western" and "Eastern" receptions could also provide new insights into similarities and differences between various conceptions of Revelation. Finally, this research has surfaced some questions that are in need of further investigation.

---

[86] Tyconius, *Exp. Apoc.* 7.31: *Hanc Ierusalem ecclesiam dicit, recapitulando a Christi passione usque in diem quo resurgat et cum Christo inuicta coronetur in gloria. Miscet utrumque tempus, nunc presens, nunc futurum, et cum quanta gloria suscipiatur a Christo et separata sit ab omni malorum incursu plenius declarat.*

[87] Tyconius, *Exp. Apoc.* 7.48: *Futuri temporis describit ecclesiam, quando iam malis de medio segregatis soli cum Christo boni regnabunt.*

In particular, is Tyconius the real representative of the "end of eschatology" in North African communities as some scholars suggest? Could other chiliastic or strongly eschatological influenced exegesis of the New Jerusalem be recovered in North African Christian communities? Further research into the matter might provide new answers to old questions.

In hoc regno

On the Geographical Localization of the New Jerusalem in Victorinus of Petovium

Konrad Huber

Introduction

Victorinus of Petovium wrote a Latin commentary on the Revelation of John in around AD 260. The bishop of the Roman colony of Poetovio, to whom numerous other commentaries – no longer extant – are attributed,[1] is often regarded as the founder of Latin biblical exegesis.[2] His commentary on John's Apocalypse is the oldest preserved Latin-language commentary on the Bible and at the same time the oldest commentary on the book of Revelation.[3] Traces of reception of John's Apocalypse are tangible much earlier[4] and selective interpretation of individu-

---

[1] Jerome, *Vir. ill.* 74, lists commentaries on the Old Testament books of Genesis, Exodus, Leviticus, Isaiah, Ezekiel, Habakkuk, Qoheleth, and Song of Songs in addition to John's Revelation, elsewhere explicitly also a commentary on the Gospel of Matthew. Cf. Jerome, *Orig. Hom. Luc.* prol. (*PL* 26:220); *Comm. Matt.* prol. (*PL* 26:20).

[2] So e.g. Antonie Wlosok, "Victorinus von Pettau," in *Restauration und Erneuerung: Die lateinische Literatur von 284 bis 374 n.Chr.*, ed. Reinhart Herzog, vol. 5 of *Handbuch der lateinischen Literatur der Antike*, ed. Reinhart Herzog and Peter Lebrecht Schmidt, series 8 of *Handbuch der Altertumswissenschaft* (Munich: Beck, 1989), 410–15, at 413.

[3] The oldest surviving Christian commentary on a biblical book is the commentary on Daniel by Hippolytus of Rome.

[4] Tobias Nicklas, "Rezeption und Nicht-Rezeption der Offenbarung des Johannes durch antike christliche Apokalypsen," in *Tot sacramenta quot verba: Zur Kommentierung der Apokalypse von den Anfängen bis ins 12. Jahrhundert*, ed. Konrad Huber, Rainer Klotz, and Christoph Winterer (Münster: Aschendorff, 2014), 1–27, discusses text passages from Did. 16, Mart. Ascen. Isa. 6–11, Herm. Vis., 5 Ezra, 6 Ezra, and Sib. Or. Martin Karrer, *Johannesoffenbarung: Teilband 1: Offb 1,1–5,14*, Evangelisch-Katholischer Kommentar zum Neuen Testament 24/1 (Ostfildern: Patmos; Göttingen: Vandenhoeck & Ruprecht, 2017), 108–14, also refers to Papias of Hierapolis, Melito of Sardis, Marcion, Justin, the letter of the churches of Vienne and Lyons, Theophilus of Antioch, and to the non-Christian author Lucian. Cf. also Martine Dulaey, *Victorin de Poetovio: Premier exégète latin*, 2 vols., Collection des Études Augustiniennes: Série Antiquité 139 and 140 (Paris: Institut d'Études Augustiniennes, 1993), I:129–47; Charles E. Hill, "The Interpretation of the Book of Revelation in Early Christianity," in *The Oxford Handbook of the Book of Revelation*, ed. Craig R. Koester (Oxford: Oxford University Press, 2020), 395–411, at 395–407.

al passages is found in Origen and Methodius,[5] but longer commentaries on the book of Revelation, though they are not strictly such, can only be found in Irenaeus of Lyons, in the fifth book of his writing *Against Heresies*.[6] A commentary by Hippolytus of Rome mentioned in Jerome[7] has been lost except for fragments, and only isolated sections of the contents of this work, presumably written in Greek, can be reconstructed from other early Christian writings.[8] In view of this source situation, the commentary on Revelation by Victorinus of Petovium is not only of great importance and interest with regard to the last book of the New Testament canon in general, but also concerning the question of the reception and early interpretation of the vision of the New Jerusalem coming down from heaven described in Rev 21:1–22:5.

1 The New Jerusalem, the First Resurrection, and the Millennial Reign

In Victorinus's commentary on Revelation (*Explanatio in Apocalypsin*), the relatively extensive remarks on the New Jerusalem, which nevertheless bring the work to an unexpectedly abrupt conclusion, are in remarkably close connection with the sections of the text immediately preceding them, namely, his brief comments on the vision of Christ in Rev 19:11–21 and his interpretation of the vision of the millennial reign and the final judgment in Rev 20:1–15. These three sections of the commentary form a literary and thematic unit.[9] This is indicated by the events being continuously linked to the coming of the Lord (*aduentus domini*).[10] The reference in *Expl. Apoc.* 20.2 and 21.1 to the New Jerusalem, the "holy

---

[5] In Origen's case mainly in his commentary on the Gospel of John, in Methodius's case in his *Symposium*. Origen apparently did not carry out his intention, expressed in *Comm. Matt.* 49 (*PG* 13:1673–74), to write a commentary on the Revelation of John.

[6] Irenaeus, *Haer.* 5.28–36.

[7] Jerome, *Vir. ill.* 61.

[8] Cf. Pierre Prigent, "Hippolyte, commentateur de l'Apocalypse," *Theologische Zeitschrift* 28 (1972): 391–412; Pierre Prigent and Ralph Stehly, "Les fragments du De Apocalypsi d'Hippolyte," *Theologische Zeitschrift* 29 (1973): 313–33.

[9] Cf. Martin Hasitschka, "Ankunft des Herrn, erste Auferstehung und tausendjähriges Reich. Die Schlussabschnitte im Apokalypsekommentar von Victorinus von Pettau und die Hinzufügung des Hieronymus," in *Ancient Christian Interpretations of "Violent Texts" in the Apocalypse*, ed. Joseph Verheyden, Tobias Nicklas, and Andreas Merkt, Novum Testamentum et Orbis Antiquus/Studien zur Umwelt des Neuen Testaments 92 (Göttingen: Vandenhoeck & Ruprecht, 2011), 118–32, at 118.

[10] Cf. Victorinus, *Expl. Apoc.* 19; 20.1; 21.2, 5. The coincidence of the coming of the Lord with the end of the reign of the antichrist and the beginning of the reign of the saints is already emphasized in *Expl. Apoc.* 14.3: *in aduentum domini, consummationem regni Antichristi et adapertionem regni sanctorum* ("at the coming of the Lord, the end of the reign of antichrist, and the appearance of the reign of the saints"). The passages of Victorinus's commentary on Revelation are counted according to the text edition by Martine Dulaey, *Victorin*

city" (Rev 21:2), already appearing in the time of the "first resurrection" and continuing during the duration of the millennial reign of the faithful Christians with Christ (cf. Rev 20:5–6),[11] indicates this close linking and at the same time gives a possible reason for it. Subsequently, it is often difficult to decide whether Victorinus is speaking of the millennial reign or of the heavenly Jerusalem; this suggests, though not with absolute certainty, that these two realities are simply identical for him. This has consequences for the already disputed assessment of how Victorinus is to be positioned in relation to chiliastic ideas in general, as well as for the assumption that he potentially shaped such ideas quite specifically.[12]

Victorinus directs his attention to the "reign of the saints" (*regnum sanctorum*) for the first time in the final sections of his commentary when he refers to Christ riding on a white horse in Rev 19:11 and thus to the coming of the Lord. Indicated in this he sees not only the destruction of "all the nations," but also the beginning of the reign of Christ (*dominum nostrum ... aduenientem ad regnandum*). The reign of the saints thereby initiated, however, will – indeed must – come to an end again after the judgment and the renewed release of Satan (*Expl. Apoc.* 19; cf. Rev 20:7–10). Without saying so, Victorinus already conveys the impression that this interim reign is to be understood as taking place in an eschatological but earthly, this-worldly realm.

The duration of this reign – a thousand years – and its equation with what John's Apocalypse calls the first resurrection (Rev 20:5) is communicated by Victorinus in his interpretation of Rev 20 (*Expl. Apoc.* 20.1). There, he also makes a connection between the first resurrection and the vision of those one hundred and forty-four thousand (cf. Rev 7:1–8) who stand on Mount Zion together with

---

de Poetovio: Sur l'Apocalypse suivi du Fragment Chronologique et de La Construction du Monde: Introduction, texte critique, traduction, commentaire et index, SC 423 (Paris: Cerf, 1997). The critical edition by Roger Gryson, *Victorini Poetovionensis Explanatio in Apocalypsin una cum recensione Hieronymi, Tractatus de fabrica mundi, Fragmentum de vita Christi*, CCSL 5 (Turnhout: Brepols, 2017), from which the Latin quotations are taken, has recently introduced a counting system which, unlike Dulaey, is based on the manuscript tradition. It is remarkable that the entire commentary on Rev 19–22 is grouped under a single section, section A V,1–133. The references to Jerome's version are based on Gryson's text edition. The English translation of Victorinus's texts is my own. For English translations see also William C. Weinrich, *Revelation*, Ancient Christian Commentary on Scripture: New Testament 12 (Downers Grove: InterVarsity Press, 2005), 307, 333–34, 363–64, 384–86; *ANF* 7, 339–60.

[11] Victorinus, *Expl. Apoc.* 20.2: "At this same first resurrection will also be that future, splendid city expressed through this writing"; *In hac eadem prima resurrectione et ciuitas futura et speciosa per hanc scripturam expressa est. Expl. Apoc.* 21.1: "Therefore in the reign and in the first resurrection, the holy city will appear ..."; *In regno ergo et in prima resurrectione exhibetur 'ciuitas sancta'...* .

[12] Dulaey, *Victorin de Poetovio: Premier exégète latin* (cf. note 4), I:219, 264–67, speaks of a chiliasm of a very special stripe and describes it as candid, spiritual, theological, and biblical ("un millénarisme d'une couleur très particulière," 219; "son millénarisme est candide ... spirituel, théologique et scripturaire," 266). See also Giancarlo Pani, "L'Apocalisse e il millenarismo di Vittorino di Petovio," *Studi e materiali di storia religioni* 68 (2002): 43–69.

the Lamb, i. e. with Christ, in Rev 14:1–5. As already in *Expl. Apoc.* 7, Victorinus understands the one hundred and forty-four thousand as people of Jewish ethnicity who will come to faith in Christ "in the last time" (*in nouissimo tempore*) on account of the proclamation of the prophet Elijah (cf. *Expl. Apoc.* 12.4). Admittedly, the phrase "in the last time," which is encountered frequently in the commentary is used altogether too vaguely to clearly establish that it refers only to the specific eschatological period of time which precedes the time (*tempus*) or the reign (*regnum*) of the antichrist (cf. Rev 20:7–10).[13] However, this circumstance does not diminish the idea of a reality that can still be experienced here on the earth. This is confirmed by the reference to a first and a last resurrection that Victorinus makes relating to his claim that the trumpets mentioned in 1 Thess 4:15–17 are to be distinguished from those of 1 Cor 15:52:[14] He refers to the fact that those who are raised from the dead in the course of the first resurrection will reign together with Christ for a thousand years "over the world" and thus "over all the nations" (*Expl. Apoc.* 20.2: *surgere in prima resurrectione et regnare cum Christo super orbem super gentes uniuersas*). The reference to Mount Zion, which the reference back to Rev 14:1–5 opens up indirectly (it does not actually name it), is, however, realized only later and with reference to prophetic quotations relevant in this regard (cf. *Expl. Apoc.* 21.3 and Isa 4:5).

When Victorinus speaks of this reign and the first resurrection in *Expl. Apoc.* 21.1, he ties them in with this very idea. And it is the period of the first resurrection thus outlined in which he also locates the appearance of the New Jerusalem. By means of fragmentary quotations from Rev 21:1–22:5, specific features of this heavenly city are emphasized: the preciousness of the building materials of the quadrangular complex (precious stones, gold, and crystal), the abundance of life that can be experienced in it (stream, spring, and tree of life), and its unsurpassable glory which needs no sun because the Lamb, Christ, is himself its light. The eclectically descriptive summary concludes in *Expl. Apoc.* 21.2 by referring to the twelve gates of the city, each consisting of a single pearl, which are always open. Only at the very end of his account, in *Expl. Apoc.* 21.6, will Victorinus again refer to the stones that differ in type and color and the gates that are always open, and together with the foundation stones of the city, which are only mentioned at this point, he will read them as an allegory of the people and the diversity of their faith, and of the apostles and the grace given through them respectively. "In this place" (*hoc loco*), one will see God face to face; and those – Victorinus concludes – who rule "in this reign" (*in hoc regno*) "will judge the world" (cf. 1 Cor 6:2).

---

[13] See Victorinus, *Expl. Apoc.* 7; 14.1; 20.1; cf. on the other hand *Expl. Apoc.* 19.
[14] Cf. Dulaey, *Victorin de Poetovio: Premier exégète latin* (cf. note 4), I:211–12; according to Dulaey, Victorinus is the first chiliast who clearly states the doctrine of the two resurrections. Cf. Pani, "L'Apocalisse" (cf. note 12), 55–56.

In *Expl. Apoc.* 21.6 the equation of the "holy city" (*ciuitas sancta*) descending from heaven with "this reign" (*hoc regnum*), i.e. the equation of the New Jerusalem with the millennial reign of the Christians with Christ, is more a casual suggestion than an inevitable conclusion. This equation, however, has already been developed by Victorinus in the preceding sections and has been unfolded in several stages, finishing with *Expl. Apoc.* 21.3 by means of a complex chain of argumentation alongside a colorful collage of scriptural quotations and allusions. Already in *Expl. Apoc.* 21.2, a passage that must be discussed in more detail, the "city" (*ciuitas*), described as surpassing all imagination in its size and outshining the sun in its brightness, is associated with a very specific area (*regio*) on the one hand and with the dominion exercised by the Lord at his coming (*dominabitur ... in aduentum Domini*) on the other. Genesis 13:14–15 and Gen 15:18, the land promise to Abraham, as well as Ps 72(71):8 are cited as scriptural evidence in this regard, linked, and evaluated accordingly.

From there, Victorinus can subsequently relate prophetic promises from other parts of Scripture to the New Jerusalem of Rev 21:2: about Jerusalem and Zion (Isa 4:5, 6; 60:1, 19–20), about the city like a fortress above the peaks of the mountains (Ps 72[71]:16), and about the stone that has become a great mountain, filling the whole earth and symbolizing that other kingdom that will endure forever, which the saints of the Most High will receive as a kingdom (Dan 2:31–45; 7:18). Terminologically as well as in terms of content, in *Expl. Apoc.* 21.3 the trail is laid from the city (*ciuitas*) to the kingdom or reign (*regnum*), and at the same time the immeasurable greatness and strength of this eschatological reign is emphasized.

Almost stereotypically, one after the other, *Expl. Apoc.* 21.4–6 strings together references to various other promises throughout Scripture, which Victorinus understands to refer to this eschatological reign and which will be fulfilled in it. After a *huius regni* at the beginning of the list, the phrase *in hoc regno* acts as introduction to most sentences, five times altogether, while *in eodem regno* and *de hoc regno* appear once each, besides *ibi, in hoc, hic* and *hoc loco*. Some of the scriptural references proper are only introduced by keywords; in some cases, they only unfold their full potential in their own wider context.

Christ's reign until the final subjugation of all God-opposing enemies, as it is discussed in 1 Cor 15:25 in the context of 1 Cor 15:20–28, the apostle Paul's description of the course of eschatological events, thus means nothing other than the very reign which is also spoken of at the end of John's Apocalypse (*Expl. Apoc.* 21.4). A combination of Ps 60(59):8 and Ps 48(47):9 is referred to as the saying of the saints who will belong to that reign (*Expl. Apoc.* 21.4), with the *exultaui* ("I have rejoiced") of Ps 60(59) originally being part of a God-speech that names Shechem, the vale of Succoth, Gilead, Manasseh, Ephraim, Judah, Moab, Edom, and the land of the Philistines as areas of his victorious exercise of dominion (Ps 60[59]:8–10), and the postscript *quemadmodum audiuimus* ("as we have heard") from Ps 48(47) echoing a hymn of praise to the God of Israel who scatters the enemy armies and makes the city on Mount Zion stand forever. According to Victorinus, all those Christians who are steadfast in their faith will rejoice in this reign when they stand before God's throne on the sea of glass[15] and sing the song of Moses and the Lamb (*Expl. Apoc.* 21.4).

Those who have left everything in following Jesus now (*nunc*) receive the hundredfold reward predicted in Matt 19:29 (par. Mark 10:30) and are promised eternal life for the future (*in futurum*).[16] Martyrs and those persecuted for Christ's sake receive the consolation promised to mourners in Matt 5:4 (cf. also Luke 16:25): besides "heavenly treasures" in general, also "crowns," i.e. participation in Christ's exercise of dominion, in particular (*Expl. Apoc.* 21.5). And by invoking several other biblical texts – Joel 2:25, Isa 60:17, Isa 60:5, Isa 61:6, and Isa 25:6-7 are brought into play one after the other – Victorinus describes the abundance marking life in this reign as the divine gift of a creation protected from destruction (*Expl. Apoc.* 21.5). The fact that there is also talk of drinking wine (Isa 25:6) provides the link for finally taking up Jesus's prophecy during the last supper, expressing the conviction that at his announcement of drinking of the fruit of the vine with his own only in a future reign (Matt 26:29) "the Lord made mention of this reign" (*de hoc regno meminit dominus*) – the very reign which is intended and described in the final vision of John's Revelation (*Expl. Apoc.* 21.6).

Even if much of this remains undefined and figurative-allegorical, Victorinus's remarks nevertheless give the impression that the eschatological participation of the saints in the reign spoken of here also has concrete, this-worldly dimensions. It is certainly chiliastic from a temporal point of view, insofar as the New Jerusalem in Victorinus's interpretation means nothing other than the millennial reign of the Christians with Christ. The extent to which this is meant to denote an earthly reality of spatial extent and localizable nature must probably remain a matter of dispute. But even in Victorinus's explanations mentioned so far, a spatial dimension has already come to light repeatedly and can be perceived as a consistently weighted aspect not only on the lexical level.[17] This is the direction taken by Victorinus's remarkable and widely discussed statement in *Expl. Apoc.* 21.2 on the geographical location and extent of the "city" (*ciuitas*) seen in Rev 21, which, although again standing in a biblical context of promise, can ultimately only be understood in concrete terms.

---

[15] Their standing on the sea of glass is allegorically related to baptism by Victorinus.

[16] The temporal differentiation evident in Matt 19:29 should also be considered here: The *nunc* is then to be referred to the time of the millennial reign, the eternal life (*uita aeterna*) only to the time afterwards, the time of the second resurrection.

[17] The fact that the "city of the saints" (*ciuitas sanctorum*), Jerusalem, is permanently referred to as "reign" (*regnum*) contributes to this, as does the imagery used in the prophetic texts alluded to.

2 The Geographical Localization of the Holy City

As already noted, in *Expl. Apoc.* 21.2 Victorinus refers to the unimaginable dimensions of the New Jerusalem and locates it in a very specific area (*regio*) described with geographical detail. The text at this point reads as follows:

> By the way, city is spoken of as the entire region of the eastern provinces promised to the patriarch Abraham. Look up, he says, into the heaven from the place in which you are now standing, that is, from the great river Euphrates to the river of Egypt; all the land, which you see, I will give it to you and to your seed. Then the Holy Spirit says: It will be ruled from sea to sea, that is, from the Red Sea, which is in Arabia, to the Sea of the North, which is the Sea of Phoenicia, and to the ends of the earth – these are the land parts of greater Syria.[18]

Accordingly, the city corresponds to the entire territory of the "eastern provinces," which was already promised by God to the patriarch Abraham. Parts of Gen 13:14–15 and Gen 15:18, the two land promises given to Abraham by God (cf. Sir 44:21), are explicitly quoted and combined. Gen 13:14–15 mentions all four directions in which Abraham is to look from his position; and everything as far as his eye can reach is promised to him and his descendants by God as a land possession. In Victorinus, however, God's invitation to Abraham reads in a strikingly different way, probably because it is a reference to the Jerusalem descending from heaven (Rev 21:2, 10): *aspice in caelo!* The patriarch is to "look up into the heaven"[19] in order to be able to see what territory he will receive. The promise becomes tangible only if God's speech in Gen 15:18 is taken into account, where the great river Euphrates[20] and the river of Egypt, the Nile, are named to designate the boundaries of the territory promised to Abraham as an inheritance. Thereby, a very specific region on earth is outlined, and the *prouinciarum orientalium regio* – the terms *regio* and *prouincia* lead us to expect this anyway – becomes a geographically definite location.

And in the same way it continues. With reference to a word inspired by the Holy Spirit from Ps 72(71):8, an almost all-encompassing dominion is first outlined from one sea to the other and to the ends of the earth. In the context of Ps 72(71) this is the dominion of the messianically connoted king who reigns

---

[18] *Ceterum dicitur ciuitas omnis illa prouinciarum orientalium regio promissa patriarchae Abrahae. Aspice, inquit, in caelo a loco in quo modo tu stas, id est a flumine magno Eufrate, usque ad flumen Aegypti; omnem terram quam tu aspicis, tibi dabo illam et semini tuo. Deinde spiritus sanctus ait: Dominabitur a mari usque ad mare, id est a mari Rubro, quod est Arabiae, usque ad mare Aquilonis, quod est mare Fenicis, et usque ad fines terrae, – sunt Siriae maioris partes.*

[19] Victorinus also uses the verb *aspicere* ("to look up") in the quotation from Gen 13:15. The formulation perhaps also contains an allusion to the promise of descendants in Gen 15:5: *suspice caelum* ("look toward heaven").

[20] The fact that the Euphrates is mentioned first in *Expl. Apoc.* 21.2 is perhaps also due to the annotated context of the book of Revelation (cf. Rev 9:14; 16:12).

in justice over Israel.[21] This very territory is then identified by Victorinus as the region between the Red or Arabian Sea and the Sea of the North or the Phoenician Sea and is called "the land parts of greater Syria." If the biblical promises may still be read and understood in a figurative, metaphorical sense, Victorinus's *Siriae maioris partes* ("the land parts of greater Syria") in line with the *prouinciarum orientalium regio* ("the region of the eastern provinces") cannot: in this passage at least, the idea of a geographically definite realm must be assumed.[22] Victorinus speaks of "all these provinces," administrative units of the Roman Empire, in the concluding sentence of *Expl. Apoc.* 21.2 (*has igitur prouincias uniuersas*) and assumes that this entire area will be levelled and purified at the eschatological coming of the Lord (cf. Isa 62:10; 4:4) and subsequently will be ablaze with heavenly glory (cf. Isa 4:5–6; *Expl. Apoc.* 21.3).

Victorinus's interpretation of the vision of the New Jerusalem here and in the following sections is probably influenced decisively by Irenaeus of Lyons and his explanations in *Haer.* 5.[23] Not only do they, on a fundamental level, share the expectation of an eschatological earthly reign of the righteous in a New Jerusalem (e. g. *Haer.* 5.32.1; 5.35.1), but also, a number of strikingly corresponding details suggest an influence of Irenaeus on Victorinus. Thus, like Victorinus in *Expl. Apoc.* 19 (cf. 21.2), Irenaeus also speaks of the fact that chosen ones from among the nations will then be in the service of the saints (*Haer.* 5.35.1).[24] The goods of

---

[21] If one reads the psalm messianically, Victorinus's combination of quotations indirectly suggests the idea of a joint regency of Christ and the people of God from the descendants of Abraham.

[22] The term *Siria maior* is not otherwise familiar as a technical term. Galen speaks of Συρία ἡ μεγάλη or ἡ μεγάλη Συρία (*magna Syria*) in *De simplicium medicamentorum temperamentis ac facultatibus* 6.22 (Karl Gottlob Kühn, ΚΛΑΥΔΙΟΥ ΓΑΛΗΝΟΥ ΑΠΑΝΤΑ / *Claudii Galeni Opera Omnia: Tomus XI*, Medicorum Graecorum Opera quae exstant 11 [Leipzig: Libraria Car. Cnoblochii, 1826], 821.13–14; in the same passage there is also talk of ἡ κοίλη Συρία) and in *De antidotis* 2 (Karl Gottlob Kühn, ΚΛΑΥΔΙΟΥ ΓΑΛΗΝΟΥ ΑΠΑΝΤΑ / *Claudii Galeni Opera Omnia: Tomus XIV*, Medicorum Graecorum Opera quae exstant 14 [Leipzig: Libraria Car. Cnoblochii, 1827], 8.15; named there in addition to Palestine), although it is unclear to which region he refers (I am indebted to Prof. Hartmut Leppin [Frankfurt am Main] for this hint). In Strabo, *Geographica* 16.2.2 (Stefan Radt, *Strabons Geographika: Band 4: Buch XIV–XVII: Text und Übersetzung* [Göttingen: Vandenhoeck & Ruprecht, 2005], 308), the term ἡ Συρία ὅλη (*tota Syria*), which is admittedly different in meaning, is found. According to Maria Veronese, by *Siria maior* Victorinus simply means a larger area: "Vittorino con *Syria maior* intende evidentamente riferirsi al territorio più ampio" (Maria Veronese, *Vittorino di Petovio: Opere*, Corpus Scriptorum Ecclesiae Aquileiensis 2 [Rome: Città Nuova, 2002], 233–382, at 313), bordered by the Taurus, Arabia, Egypt and the Euphrates. Cf. Pani, "L'Apocalisse" (cf. note 12), 59.

[23] Cf. on this also Dulaey, *Victorin de Poetovio: Premier exégète latin* (cf. note 4), I:265 and II:133 note 106, 107, and 113. For text and translation cf. Norbert Brox, *Irenäus von Lyon: Adversus Haereses / Gegen die Häresien: Fünfter Teilband*, Fontes Christiani 8/5 (Freiburg im Breisgau: Herder, 2001); *ANF* 1.

[24] The idea is biblically based on Isa 60:10; 61:5; Ps 72(71):11. Cf. Martin Hasitschka, "Die Vision von der tausendjährigen Herrschaft (Offb 20,4–6) und ihre Interpretation durch Viktorin von Pettau," in *Tot sacramenta quot verba: Zur Kommentierung der Apokalypse von*

the millennial reign (*Expl. Apoc.* 21.5) are comparably dealt with by Irenaeus in *Haer.* 5.32.1. The idea of the preservation of creation that Victorinus mentions in *Expl. Apoc.* 21.5 can be found in a similar vein in Irenaeus in *Haer.* 5.33.3 and 5.36.3. It is Irenaeus who already connects the prophecy of the "first resurrection of the righteous" (Rev 20:5–6) with the Lord's Supper prophecy in Matt 26:29 (*Haer.* 5.36.3; cf. Victorinus, *Expl. Apoc.* 21.6). And when Victorinus, extending the Lord's Supper prophecy, describes the drinking of wine in the future reign as something that will be multiplied "ten times, a thousand times, to greater things and better things" (*decies millies ad maiora et meliora, Expl. Apoc.* 21.6), he thus offers a clear echo of Irenaeus's more detailed description in *Haer.* 5.33.3–4 where this phrase is explicitly attributed to Papias of Hierapolis as a supposedly traditional word of the Lord.[25] Further, this closeness to Irenaeus is particularly clear in Victorinus's connection with the land promises to Abraham and his referring to Abraham's inheritance. As with Victorinus, the same combination of Gen 13:14–15 and Gen 15:18 is found in Irenaeus when he addresses the reality of the life of the descendant(s) of Abraham, i. e. the church, at the resurrection of the righteous in *Haer.* 5.32.2.[26] For Irenaeus too, the inheritance that is promised and provided for them by God is a real, topographical realm, nothing other than the earth. However, Irenaeus neither goes beyond the biblical promise in defining a geographical area, nor does he refer to Ps 72(71):8 or, subsequently, to the provinces or parts of "greater Syria."

The essential difference between Irenaeus and Victorinus – at the same time a specific feature of the bishop of Petovium – lies in the latter's obvious identification of the millennial reign with the new, heavenly Jerusalem of Rev 21–22, something by no means indicated in the text of John's Apocalypse itself. Irenaeus expects the reign of the righteous to transpire after the resurrection; this, he maintains, is the beginning of immortality and constitutes a phase of growing accustomed to the vision of God on a renewed earth promised by God as a result of the appearance of the Lord. While all this can be explicitly connected with promises for Zion and the prophecy of a new Jerusalem, Irenaeus distinguishes from this earthly reign the "upper Jerusalem" (*sursum* or *superior Jerusalem*, cf. Gal 4:26) which only subsequently comes down from heaven to earth. It is there, in this "Jerusalem above," that the everlasting encounter with God actually takes place.[27] Ideas of a millennial intermediate reign of the resurrected on earth and in

---

den Anfängen bis ins 12. Jahrhundert, ed. Konrad Huber, Rainer Klotz, and Christoph Winterer (Münster: Aschendorff, 2014), 121–34, at 125–26.

[25] Cf. also 2 Bar. 29:5. For more details see Hasitschka, "Vision" (cf. note 24), 131–33; cf. also Hasitschka, "Ankunft" (cf. note 9), 125–28.

[26] The call to look up to heaven, however, remains specific to Victorinus. Irenaeus quotes Gen 13:14 as *respice sursum oculis et vide* ("lift up your eyes and look").

[27] Cf. Irenaeus, *Haer.* 5.35.2; 5.36.1. With reference to John 14:2, Irenaeus differentiates in *Haer.* 5.36.1–2 heaven (*caelum*), paradise (*paradisum*), and the city (*ciuitas*) for the mode of

a new or renewed Jerusalem can be found in a comparable way already in Justin and Tertullian and can probably also be assumed for Papias.[28] However, a hasty equation of this reign with the heavenly Jerusalem of John's Apocalypse is not given there either. If, by contrast, Victorinus mixes up the levels of imagination and draws together the respective dimensions, then his already strikingly concrete geographical localization of the millennial reign (*regnum*) inevitably also results in an equally concrete earthly localization of the heavenly city (*ciuitas*).

Similarly concrete and equally chiliastic statements are only occasionally found in Victorinus's work outside the final chapters. In *Expl. Apoc.* 1.5, for example, Victorinus refers to Ps 132(131):7 in his interpreting the feet of Christ who resembles a Son of Man (Rev 1:15) as an allegory of the apostles who prove themselves in the proclamation of Christ after Easter. In a first step, Victorinus takes the quoted Psalm text "Let us worship where his feet have stood!" as a reference to that place where "his [Christ's] feet," i.e. the apostles, "as the first stood and established the church," namely, Judea. In a second step, he connects with it the eschatological expectation that it will be there in Judea, too, that one day "all the saints will come together and worship their God."[29] Judea as the eschatological gathering place of God's people is also mentioned in *Expl. Apoc.*

---

existence in the one eternal God-view as different areas of residence of the perfected according to their merit.

[28] Cf. Justin, *Dial.* 40.4; 80.5; 81.1–4; 85.7; Tertullian, *Marc.* 3.24; Irenaeus, *Haer.* 5.33.3–4; Eusebius, *Hist. eccl.* 3.39.12. Cf. e.g. Karrer, *Johannesoffenbarung* (cf. note 4), 111–13, who calls Papias and Justin the progenitors of the ecclesiastical chiliasm ("die Stammväter des großkirchlichen Chiliasmus," 113), which Irenaeus transmitted to the next centuries. Cf. for example Giancarlo Pani, "Il millenarismo: Papia, Giustino e Ireneo," *Annali di storia dell'esegesi* 15 (1998): 53–84; Manlio Simonetti, "Il millenarismo cristiano dal I al V secolo," *Annali di storia dell'esegesi* 15 (1998): 7–20; Charles E. Hill, *Regnum caelorum: Patterns of Millennial Thought in Early Christianity*, 2nd ed. (Grand Rapids: Eerdmans, 2001). Jerome, *Vir. ill.* 18, calls the doctrine he rejected as erroneous a "Jewish" view (*hic dicitur mille annorum Judaicam edidisse* δευτέρωσιν) and attributes it, besides Papias and Irenaeus, also to Apollinaris, Tertullian, Victorinus of Petovium, and Lactantius (in the prologue to Victorinus's commentary on Revelation he also names the Egyptian bishop Nepos [prol. 8], at the end in H 5.125 also the heretic Cerinthus). Cf. also Eusebius, *Hist. eccl.* 3.28.1–5; 7.24.1–3; 7.25.1–3, who also refers to Dionysius of Alexandria.

[29] Victorinus, *Expl. Apoc.* 1.5: "Let us worship where his feet have stood, because where they as the first stood and established the church, that is Judea, there all the saints will come together and worship their God"; *Adoremus ubi steterunt pedes eius, quoniam ubi illi primi steterunt et ecclesiam confirmauerunt, id est iudeam, ibi omnes sancti conuenturi sunt et deum suum adoraturi*. Jerome not only sticks with the concrete localization in his version, but even makes it clearer with his linguistic correction: *id est in Iudea* ("that is in Judea"). Cf. on the passage also Konrad Huber, "Aspekte der Apokalypse-Interpretation des Victorinus von Pettau am Beispiel der Christusvision in Offb 1," in *Ancient Christian Interpretations of "Violent Texts" in the Apocalypse*, ed. Joseph Verheyden, Tobias Nicklas, and Andreas Merkt, Novum Testamentum et Orbis Antiquus/Studien zur Umwelt des Neuen Testaments 92 (Göttingen: Vandenhoeck & Ruprecht, 2011), 94–117, at 110. Dulaey, *Victorin de Poetovio: Premier exégète latin* (cf. note 4), I:196 and II:97 notes 43 and 44, refers to the Jewish roots of this tradition and its dissemination especially in chiliastically oriented circles.

12.4, in this instance with reference to Matt 24:16, a passage from Jesus's end-time discourse in which, in view of the imminent great tribulation, the inhabitants of Judea are called upon to flee to the mountains. Victorinus relates this passage to the flight of the heavenly woman from the dragon to a place prepared for her in the wilderness, which is described in Rev 12:6, 14: the Christians gathered one day in Judea in anticipation of the Lord's coming will be nourished in that *locus*, in that place of retreat *in montibus*, "for three years and six months away from the face of the devil."[30] Provided that these two passages in Victorinus's commentary on Revelation are informed by chiliastic ideas and are to be assessed in precisely this vein, a concrete earthly location is given also with regard to the abode of God's people in the last days. At the same time, however, a remarkable limitation to Judea only is to be noted in comparison to the final chapters where the area outlined comprises all the provinces of greater Syria.

Much uncertainty remains in determining what Victorinus of Petovium actually understands by the millennial reign and the heavenly city of Jerusalem and which ideas he sees realized in them.[31] However, as far as their explicit and unique geographical localization is concerned, Jerome, in the prologue to his revision of Victorinus's commentary on Revelation from AD 398,[32] is right to judge: That "excellent man" (*egregius uir*) "took some things literally" (*secundum litteram senserit*) in his interpretation (prol. 6 and 13).[33] If one shares Jerome's

---

[30] Victorinus, *Expl. Apoc.* 12.4: "The rest of the twofold people he will find there at the coming of our Lord Jesus Christ. The Lord Christ himself also says in the gospel: Then those who are in Judea shall flee to the mountains, that is, however many will have been gathered in Judea, they shall go to that 'place' which 'they have prepared so that they will be nourished there for three years and six months' away from the face of the devil"; *Ceterum populum binum inueniet ibi in aduentum domini nostri Iesu Christi. Ipse quoque Dominus Christus in euangelio ait: Tunc qui in Iudea sunt fugiant in montibus, id est quotquot in Iudea collecti fuerint, eant in illum 'locum' quem 'paratum habent ut nutriantur ibi triennio et mensibus sex' a facie diaboli.* Here, too, Jerome does not correct the concrete geographical location.

[31] According to Hasitschka, "Vision" (cf. note 24), 132, Victorinus conveys both this-worldly and other-worldly ideas concerning the millennial reign beginning with the parousia of Jesus and the city coming from God, without always clearly delimiting them from each other. Cf. also Hasitschka, "Ankunft" (cf. note 9), 127. Differently, e. g. Karrer, *Johannesoffenbarung* (cf. note 4), 121, according to whom Victorinus even intensified the sensual chiliasm of Irenaeus.

[32] On the question of dating, cf. Martine Dulaey, "Jérôme 'éditeur' du Commentaire sur l'Apocalypse de Victorin de Poetovio," *Revue des Études Augustiniennes* 37 (1991): 199–236, at 203–7 and 216. See also Alessandro Capone's contribution to this volume.

[33] Cf. H 5.33–35: *nam mille annorum regnum non arbitror esse terrenum* ("For I do not consider the reign of the thousand years to be earthly"); H 5.124–125: *ergo audiendi non sunt qui mille annorum regnum terrenum esse confirmant* ("Therefore, one should not listen to those who claim that the reign of the thousand years will be earthly"). Jerome often speaks of a literal understanding when it is specifically a matter of rejecting chiliastic views; cf. Dulaey, "Jérôme, 'éditeur'" (cf. note 32), 202 note 10. Jerome also interprets the number one thousand allegorically: the number ten signifies the ten commandments, and the number one hundred signifies the crown of virginity (H 5.40–44). – In contrast, Hasitschka, "Vision" (cf. note 24), 133, describes Jerome's criticism as not entirely accurate. Similarly already Carmelo Curti, "Il

conviction that the millennial reign is not an earthly, this-worldly reign,[34] it is precisely the aspect of the topographically all too definite location that must be perceived as problematic and assessed as untenable. In the end, it is irrelevant that in view of the spatial extent mentioned by Victorinus, the literal understanding that he is reproached with concerns the dimensions of the promised land and cannot actually refer to the twelve thousand stadia measured in Rev 21:16 for the length, width and height of the city, dimensions of about two thousand four hundred kilometers each, which in area alone exceeds the entire *Imperium Romanum*. As is well known, Jerome replaces Victorinus's commentary in *Expl. Apoc.* 21 with an addition from his own pen that includes a few of Victorinus's passages, but that, with its consistently allegorizing, spiritualizing and individually ethicizing reading, basically offers a completely independent interpretation.[35] The explanations on the localization of *regnum* and *ciuitas* are completely omitted. However, although Jerome speaks of having successively corrected also the rest of Victorinus's commentary on Revelation where ignorance had led to the introduction of errors by copyists (prol. 13–15), he has not corrected the two topographical concretizations in *Expl. Apoc.* 1.5 and 12.4. Rather, he seems to have (at the least) ignored them – if he did not simply overlook them in the course of the probably very rapid editing – and he obviously (still) considered the reference to Judea to be innocuous.[36]

---

regno millenario in Vittorino di Petovio," *Augustinianum* 18 (1978): 419–33; according to Curti, in summary, the millennial reign in Victorinus's conception is characterized by a softening of the materialistic colors, by the valorization of spiritual goods, and, above all, by the presence of allegorical interpretations.

[34] Eusebius expresses the comparable view that with such an understanding, the statements made mysteriously in images are misunderstood (*Hist. eccl.* 3.39.12). On Jerome's overall ambivalent attitude towards chiliasm and its development, cf. e. g. Martine Dulaey, "Jérôme, Victorin de Poetovia et le millénarisme," in *Jérôme entre l'Occident et l'Orient: XVIe centenaire du départ de saint Jérôme de Rome et de son installation à Bethléem. Actes des Colloque de Chantilly (septembre 1986)*, ed. Yves-Marie Duval (Paris: Études Augustiniennes, 1988), 83–98. Carmelo Curti, "Girolamo e il millenarismo di Vittorino di Petovio," *Annali di storia dell'esegesi* 15 (1998): 191–203, distinguishes a first, moderate period (AD 387–398) from a second, clearly polemical antichiliastic period (AD 406–416).

[35] Cf. e. g. Capone in this volume; Dulaey, "Jérôme, 'éditeur'" (cf. note 32), 207–17; Hasitschka, "Ankunft" (cf. note 9), 129–32.

[36] Cf. also Dulaey, "Jérôme, 'éditeur'" (cf. note 32), 235. Nevertheless, alongside Tertullian, Lactantius, Julius Africanus, and Commodianus, Victorinus was also condemned for his chiliastic views in the *Decretum Gelasianum* (sixth century), and his works were rejected in total as apocryphal (*opuscula Victorini Petabionensis apocrypha*).

Summary

The commentary on Revelation by Victorinus of Petovium opens up a thoroughly independent approach to understanding the vision of the New Jerusalem descending from heaven in Rev 21:1–22:5. Remarkable characteristics set it apart from its sources and predecessors and would also seem to put it in tension with the text of Revelation itself regarding decisive aspects.

Victorinus addresses the vision of the New Jerusalem as a genuine part of the larger time and event framework which, according to his understanding, begins with the coming (*aduentus*) of the Lord indicated in Rev 19:11. As far as can be seen, he identifies the New Jerusalem with the millennial reign of the faithful Christians that will begin with the eschatological coming of Christ, and ultimately conflates these two realms. When he speaks of this reign (*regnum*), he obviously also speaks of the holy city (*ciuitas sancta*). If for him there is another reign after that, then he remains silent about it.

In traditional manner and with reference to a wide range of passages, Victorinus understands the millennial reign as a time of fulfillment of manifold Old and New Testament promises for the righteous in the course and for the duration of the first resurrection. The reference to several elements of the city's furnishings that frames his interpretation still remains entirely on a figurative-allegorical level, and perhaps, indeed very probably, a largely spiritual understanding can be assumed regarding the aforementioned goods and living conditions that this city or reign promises. Yet, the topographically connoted terminology that is present throughout and, in particular, the localization that Victorinus specifies on several occasions inevitably make us think of the millennial reign and thus also of the New Jerusalem as an earthly, this-worldly realm, and as a result also make us assume that at least some of the promises addressed will be realized, despite a certain apparent inconsistency, in an earthly-sensual way.

By outlining a very specific area in the dimensions of the promised land and moreover explicitly identifying it with the area of the eastern provinces and the land parts of greater Syria, Victorinus bestows a tangible geographical location and remarkable concreteness in the present world on the New Jerusalem expected for the end times. In this concreteness, Victorinus goes beyond earlier chiliastic ideas in an almost entirely singular way.

The Heavenly Jerusalem and the Jewish Remnant in the Book of Isaiah

The Changing Interpretation of Eusebius of Caesarea*

Antti Laato

Introduction

This contribution focuses on how Eusebius related the idea of the Heavenly Jerusalem to the texts of the book of Isaiah, especially to Isa 2:1–4 and Isa 1:8–9, which, in his writings, are closely interlinked.[1] I will illustrate how Eusebius's view on the Heavenly Jerusalem changed as witnessed in his writings. In addition, I also offer some remarks on earlier Christian traditions that influenced Eusebius's view when he interpreted the Heavenly Jerusalem in relation to the texts of the book of Isaiah.

It must be said at the outset that Eusebius's idea of the Heavenly Jerusalem was not directly linked with Rev 21–22, the subject of the present volume. However, there are two other New Testament texts, Gal 4:26 and Heb 12:22–24, which contain an idea of a heavenly city of Jerusalem with which Christians have a spiritual contact.[2] These two texts were used by Eusebius in his writings when he speaks

---

* I would like to thank Nathan Betz and those experts who evaluated this contribution in the peer review process. In the editing process of the volume, Nathan Betz and myself have noticed that we completely and independently agree that Eusebius's assessment in *Life of Constantine* (*Vita Constantini*) 3.33, according to which the Holy Sepulchre is the new Jerusalem, was not related to the image of Rev 21–22 but to the theology of the prophets, especially to the book of Isaiah. This essay is related to a research project that I lead called "Isaiah between Judeo-Christian Borderlines." This project, which has received financial support from the Polin Institute (2022–2024) and from the Academy of Finland (2022–2026), focuses on the early Christian and Jewish reception history of Isaiah. The preliminary thesis of the project is that early Christian Isaiah exegesis considered Jewish reception historical topics by adopting, modifying, challenging, and refuting them but later developed its own discourses with strong anti-Jewish statements.

[1] Concerning Eusebius's life and works see e.g., Aaron P. Johnson, *Eusebius*, Understanding Classics (London: I. B. Tauris, 2014). See further important political and theological contributions to Eusebius's works in Sabrina Inowlocki and Claudio Zamagni, ed., *Reconsidering Eusebius: Collected Papers on Literary, Historical, and Theological Issues*, Supplements to Vigiliae Christianae 107 (Leiden: Brill, 2011).

[2] See, for example, Hans Dieter Betz, *Galatians: A Commentary on Paul's Letter to the*

about the Heavenly Jerusalem in relation to the book of Isaiah. An interesting variation on the heavenly mount of Zion in Heb 12:22–24 is Heb 13:14, where apparently the same heavenly city is referred to but is characterized with the words "the city that is to come." Thus, according to the theology of Hebrews "the heavenly Jerusalem" is the "Jerusalem to come."[3] The writer of Hebrews combined Old Testament prophetic expectations of the coming glory of Jerusalem with an idea that the heavenly Jerusalem[4] exists and is ready to come down in the eschatological end-time. An important prophetic text, which in the later reception history was understood as a reference to the heavenly Jerusalem, is Isa 2:1–4.

1 The Heavenly Jerusalem and Isaiah Texts in Eusebius's *Commentary on Isaiah*

It is significant that Eusebius rarely uses the book of Revelation in his writings. This is not to say that he would have rejected the book entirely; rather, he regarded it as belonging to those texts that did not have unanimous authority among Christians.[5] From his *Church History* (*Historia ecclesiastica*)[6] it is also

---

Churches in Galatia, Hermeneia (Philadelphia: Fortress, 1979), 246; Bianca Kühnel, *From the Earthly to the Heavenly Jerusalem: Representations of the Holy City in Christian Art of the First Millennium*, Römische Quartalschrift für Christliche Altertumskunde und Kirchengeschichte Supplementheft 42 (Freiburg: Herder, 1987), 49–59; Judith Kovacs and Christopher Rowland, *Revelation: The Apocalypse of Jesus Christ*, Blackwell Bible Commentaries (Malden, MA: Blackwell, 2004), 220–21.

[3] See the general lines of development of the spiritual meaning of Jerusalem in Antti Laato, "Understanding the Spiritual Meaning of Jerusalem: A Religious Historical and Theological Overview," in *Understanding the Spiritual Meaning of Jerusalem in Three Abrahamic Religions*, ed. Antti Laato, Studies on the Children of Abraham 6 (Leiden: Brill, 2019), 3–40.

[4] When exactly the idea of the Heavenly Jerusalem was developed and whether it was originally a Christian innovation is discussed among scholars. See Rivka Nir, *The Destruction of Jerusalem and the Idea of Redemption in the Syriac Apocalypse of Baruch*, Early Judaism and its Literature 20 (Leiden: Brill, 2003), 26; Mark Verman, "Earthly and Heavenly Jerusalem in Philo and Paul: A Tale of Two Cities," in *With Letters of Light: Studies in the Dead Sea Scrolls, Early Jewish Apocalypticism, Magic, and Mysticism in Honor of Rachel Elior*, ed. Andrei A. Orlov, and Daphna V. Arbel, Ekstasis 2 (Berlin: De Gruyter, 2010), 133–56; and contributions in Markus Bockmuehl and Guy Stroumsa, *Paradise in Antiquity: Jewish and Christian Views* (Cambridge: Cambridge University Press, 2013).

[5] Concerning the authority of the book of Revelation in early Christianity, see especially Tobias Nicklas, "Revelation and the New Testament Canon," in *The Oxford Handbook of the Book of Revelation*, ed. Craig R. Koester (Oxford: Oxford University Press, 2020). Nicklas notes that the scriptural authority of Revelation was discussed in the Eastern Church in particular, which is where Eusebius was active. On this see also Bruce M. Metzger, *The Canon of the New Testament: Its Origin, Development, and Significance* (Oxford: Clarendon, 1988), 201–28.

[6] For the text of *Hist. eccl.*, I use Gustave Bardy, ed., *Eusebius. Histoire ecclésiastique: Tome 1, Livres I–IV*, SC 31 (Paris: Cerf, 1952); *Histoire ecclésiastique: Tome 2, Livres V–VII*, SC 41 (Paris: Cerf, 1994); *Histoire ecclésiastique: Tome 3, Livres VIII–X et Les martyrs en Palestine*, SC 55 (Paris: Cerf, 1958); Gustave Bardy and Pierre Périchon, ed., *Histoire ecclésiastique: Tome 4,*

Table 1. Gal 4:26 and Heb 12:22–24 in Eusebius's *Commentary on Isaiah*. This list records all passages of Eusebius's *Commentary* in which the author makes reference to the Heavenly Jerusalem. Passages that contain the longer quotation from Heb 12:22–24 are marked in **bold**. I have also included the Isaiah text that Eusebius interprets. (*CI* = Ziegler's edition; A = Armstrong's translation).

Isaiah text interpreted	Gal 4:26	Heb 12:22–24
Isa 2:1–4	*CI* 15–17; A 11–12	*CI* 15–17; A 11–12
Isa 4:2–3		*CI* 26–27; A 20
Isa 8:16–18		***CI* 59–60; A 46**
Isa 18:7		***CI* 123–124; A 94**
Isa 19:23–25		*CI* 135–137; A 104
Isa 22:1		***CI* 143–144; A 110**
Isa 24:21–23		*CI* 159–161; A 123
Isa 25:6–8		***CI* 162–164; A 125**
Isa 26:1		*CI* 166; A 127
Isa 26:2–8a		*CI* 166–167; A 127
Isa 30:25–26		*CI* 199–201; A 154
Isa 35:9–10		*CI* 230; A 177–178
Isa 49:11	*CI* 312–313; A 244	***CI* 312–313; A 244**
Isa 51:11		*CI* 234; A 254
Isa 57:12–14		*CI* 353–354; A 277–278
Isa 60:21	*CI* 378; A 296	*CI* 378; A 296
Isa 65:8–9		***CI* 393–394; A 309**
Isa 66:18–20		*CI* 406–407; A 319
Isa 66:23		*CI* 409–410; A 320
Isa 66:23		***CI* 409–410; A 321** ("myriads of angels")

apparent that Eusebius characterized it as being quite difficult to interpret. He was familiar with many of the problematic theological statements that originated from Revelation.[7] Instead of using Revelation, Eusebius based his ideas of the Heavenly Jerusalem on two other New Testament texts: Gal 4:26 and Heb 12:22–24. These two texts are regularly quoted and referred to in Eusebius's works, particularly in his *Commentary on Isaiah* (*Commentarius in Isaiam*),[8] when he

---

Introduction, SC 73 (Paris: Cerf, 1987). I use the English translation from Roy J. Deferarri, *Eusebius. Ecclesiastical History*, 2 vols., FC 19 and 29 (Washington, DC: Catholic University of America Press, 2005).

[7] This becomes clear when Eusebius deals with Cerinthus's problematic teaching related to Revelation and quotes Dionysius of Alexandria's text concerning it (*Hist. eccl.* 3.27; 7.25). For Eusebius's view on the book of Revelation, see further Robert M. Grant, *Eusebius as Church Historian* (Oxford: Clarendon, 1980), 126–37.

[8] The text for this work that I use is Joseph Ziegler, ed., *Eusebius Werke 9: Der Jesajakommentar*, GCS (Berlin: De Gruyter, 1975) and the English translation used is that found in Jonathan J. Armstrong, trans., Joel C. Elowsky, ed., *Eusebius. Commentary on Isaiah*, Ancient Christian Texts (Downers Grove, IL: InterVarsity Press, 2013).

writes about the Heavenly Jerusalem. He never uses Rev 21–22 as a scriptural basis for the Heavenly Jerusalem. In Table 1, I list those passages in *Comm. Isa.* where Gal 4:26 and especially Heb 12:22–24 are quoted.

In this contribution I concentrate on four of Eusebius's writings. The first is his *General Elementary Introduction* (*Generalis elementaria introductio*) 6–9, which is known also as the *Extracts from the Prophets* (*Eclogae propheticae*) 1–4.[9] It was written at the time of great persecutions (ca. 303). The second text is *The Demonstration of the Gospel* (*Demonstratio evangelica*) which was written soon after the Edict of Milan (313).[10] The third work is Eusebius's *Commentary on Isaiah*, which was completed around the time of the Council of Nicaea (ca. 325).[11] I end this contribution by discussing the famous passage of *The Life of Constantine* (*Vita Constantini*) 3.25–40.[12] *Vit. Const.* is Eusebius's last work, and one that remained uncompleted when he died in 339. With regard to this last work, I will demonstrate the ways in which *Vit. Const.* 3.25–40 is dependent on ideas and themes presented by Eusebius in his *Comm. Isa.*[13]

2 Eclogae propheticae

In *Ecl. proph.* Eusebius begins the interpretation of Isa 2:1–4 by showing how the new law, not identical with that of Moses, was proclaimed to all peoples and nations from Jerusalem. The new people of God consist of those who have been called according to Isa 65:1–2 (*Ecl. proph.* 173). This latter Isaianic text was

---

[9] I use the text in Thomas Gaisford, ed., *Eusebii Pamphili Episcopii Caesariensis: Eclogae Propheticae* (Oxford: Oxford University Press, 1842), 169–74. See further important characterizations of *Ecl. proph.* in Aaron P. Johnson, "Eusebius the Educator: The Context of the *General Elementary Introduction*," in Inowlocki and Zamagni, *Reconsidering Eusebius* (cf. note 1), 99–118; Sébastien Morlet, "Origen as an Exegetical Source in Eusebius' Prophetic Extracts," in *Eusebius of Caesarea: Tradition and Innovations*, ed. Aaron P. Johnson and Jeremy Schott, Hellenic Studies Series 60 (Washington, DC: Center for Hellenic Studies, 2013).

[10] The text edition used is Ivar A. Heikel, ed., *Eusebius Werke. Band 6. Die Demonstratio Evangelica*. GCS (Leipzig: Hinrichs, 1913); the English translation is from William J. Ferrar, trans., *The Proof of the Gospel, Being the Demonstratio Evangelica of Eusebius of Caesarea*, vols. 1–2 (London: SPCK; New York: Macmillan, 1920). References to *Dem. ev.* are made with page numbers of Heikel's edition.

[11] For edition and translation used in this chapter, see above.

[12] For the text of *Vit. Const.*, I use Friedhelm Winkelmann, ed., *Eusebius Werke. Band 1. Teil 1. Das Leben des Kaisers Konstantin* (Berlin: De Gruyter, 2011); the translation used is from Averil Cameron and Stuart G. Hall, *Eusebius: Life of Constantine*, Clarendon Ancient History Series (Oxford: Clarendon, 1999).

[13] Concerning the date of these works, see especially Andrew Carriker, *The Library of Eusebius of Caesarea*, Vigiliae Christianae Supplements 67 (Leiden: Brill, 2003), 37–45; see also Michael J. Hollerich, *Eusebius of Caesarea's* Commentary on Isaiah: *Christian Exegesis in the Age of Constantine*, Oxford Early Christian Studies (Oxford: Clarendon, 1999), 57–61. Hollerich has also made a detailed analysis of Eusebius's way of seeking self-definition of the Christian "state" in the Constantinian empire.

interpreted already by Paul (Rom 10:20) as referring to the people whom God invites into the new covenant with Christ instead of the Jewish people who had rejected their own messiah, Jesus Christ. Eusebius contrasts the prophecy of Isa 2:1–4 with the situation of the earthly Jerusalem, which was laid waste according to the words of Jesus (Matt 23:38) and the words of Isaiah (Isa 1:8, 10–17, 21–25). In *Ecl. proph.* 172–173 Eusebius relates the interpretation of Isa 2:1–4 to Gal 4:26 by emphasizing that the Christians have come into this heavenly Jerusalem (Isa 2:3) and heard the words of the new covenant. In this way Eusebius contrasts the Heavenly Jerusalem with the earthly Jerusalem in Palestine. Peter Walker and Robert Wilken have analyzed Eusebius's theology before 325. While they based their interpretation mainly on *Dem. ev.* and other later writings of Eusebius, it seems to me that the results can also be used to understand *Ecl. proph.* Eusebius emphasized the spiritual aspect of Christianity that is not restricted to any local place. Rather, the gospel is a universal message for the whole world and thus every human being everywhere has the possibility of coming into a relationship with God without travelling to one specific corner of the world, namely, to that corner where Jerusalem is situated. Eusebius's spiritual interpretation of the Heavenly Jerusalem can be compared with that of Origen.[14]

While Eusebius's dependence on Origen's spiritual interpretation does seem clear in this early work of Eusebius, Walker and Wilken's analyses must be complemented by emphasizing that Eusebius's spiritual interpretation of Isa 2:1–4 did not exclude the more literal fulfilment of the prophecy. Eusebius notes that the Isaianic prophecy will be fulfilled in the "second coming of Christ" more finally and literally (*Ecl. proph.* 173). Eusebius's eschatological interpretation of Isa 2:1–4 went hand in hand with the wording of Isa 2:1, according to which the prophetic vision will be fulfilled in "the coming days" or "in the eschatological period." Eusebius's emphasis on the literal and more final fulfilment of Isa 2:1–4 and Gal 4:26 in the second coming of Christ is similar to an idea of Irenaeus,[15] who argues against Gnostics that the heavenly Jerusalem mentioned in Gal 4:26 and Rev 21 (together with Isaianic texts Isa 49:16; 65:17–18) will be realized in the world in a very concrete way when the heavenly Jerusalem will descend (*Haer.* 5.35.2).[16] Irenaeus's text has been compared with Tertullian's, who also

---

[14] See Peter W. L. Walker, *Holy City, Holy Places? Christian Attitudes to Jerusalem and the Holy Land in the Fourth Century* (Oxford: Clarendon, 1990), 51–92; Robert L. Wilken, *The Land Called Holy: Palestine in Christian History and Thought* (New Haven: Yale University Press, 1992), 65–100.

[15] Concerning Eusebius's dependence on Irenaeus's works, particularly *Haer.*, see especially Carriker, *Library of Eusebius* (cf. note 13), 217–19.

[16] It is worth noting that Irenaeus interprets Isa 2:3–4 in *Haer.* 4.34.4 and *Epid.* 86 as referring to the way in which the gospel was proclaimed among nations by apostles who went out from Jerusalem. These passages do not contain any reference to the nations having a connection to the Heavenly Jerusalem. However, Isa 2:1–4 emphasizes that nations will actively come to Mount Zion, and therefore these two passages of Irenaeus cannot be regarded as being in disharmony

emphasizes the concrete fulfilment of Gal 4:26 in the eschatological time in his text *Against Marcion* (*Adversus Marcionem*) 3.24 but connects it to his chiliastic interpretation.[17] While it is clear that we cannot find any support from Eusebius's writings for a chiliastic interpretation similar to that of Tertullian, it is, nonetheless, significant that Irenaeus's interpretation does not contain a clear chiliastic emphasis. Exegetical analysis of Rev 21–22 indicates that the vision of the new, heavenly Jerusalem that will come down to the earth is placed after the so-called kingdom of a thousand years (Rev 20:1–6), as well as after the resurrection and the creation of the new heaven and earth (Rev 21:1; cf. Isa 65:17). This being the case, according to Revelation's theology, eternal life will be lived out in the new city of Jerusalem on earth once the earth has been created anew. Therefore, Tertullian's way of using the texts of Rev 21–22 to describe his chiliastic interpretation is exegetically an innovation, and we have good reason to ask whether Irenaeus (who knew the Johannine tradition well)[18] presents another interpretation. I am keen to follow Smith's idea that Irenaeus's interpretation of Rev 21–22 should be related to his recapitulation theology indicating that the concrete fulfilment of the descent of the heavenly Jerusalem will take place at the second coming of Jesus and not during the chiliastic period.[19] In this respect Eusebius's view in *Ecl. proph.* that the descent of the heavenly Jerusalem will take place at the second coming of Christ is similar to that of Irenaeus.[20]

Eusebius's *The Martyrs of Palestine* (*De martyribus Palaestinae*), which has been integrated into the manuscripts of *Hist. eccl.*, and was possibly once an integral part of the earlier version of the work prior to the Edict of Milan, is from about the same time as *Ecl. proph.*[21] In that work Eusebius recounts a story of

---

with *Haer.* 5.35.2. See the texts in Adelin Rousseau, ed., *Contre les hérésies. Livre 4, T. 2, texte et traduction*, SC 100 (Paris: Cerf, 1965) ; Adelin Rousseau, Charles Mercier, and Louis Doutreleau, ed., *Irénée de Lyon: Contre les hérésies Livre V Tome 2*, SC 153 (Paris: Cerf, 1969); and Adelin Rousseau, ed., *Irénée de Lyon: Démonstration de la prédication apostolique*, SC 406 (Paris: Cerf, 1995).

[17] Concerning Tertullian's chiliastic interpretation, see Anni Maria Laato, "The New Jerusalem in Tertullian," in A. Laato, *Understanding the Spiritual Meaning* (cf. note 3), 125–34.

[18] See especially Bernhard Mutschler, *Irenäus als johanneischer Theologe: Studien zur Schriftauslegung bei Irenäus von Lyon*, Studien und Texte zu Antike und Christentum 21 (Tübingen: Mohr Siebeck, 2004). See also Jackson Lashier, *Irenaeus on the Trinity*, Vigiliae Christianae Supplements 127 (Leiden: Brill, 2014). Lashier emphasizes the role of the Fourth Gospel in Irenaeus's christology. With the same emphasis, see also Stephen O. Presley, "Irenaeus and the Exegetical Roots of Trinitarian Theology," in *Irenaeus: Life, Scripture, Legacy,* ed. Sara Parvis and Paul Foster (Minneapolis: Fortress, 2012), 165–72.

[19] For this aspect of Irenaeus's, theology see especially Christopher R. Smith, "Chiliasm and Recapitulation in the Theology of Irenaeus," *Vigiliae Christianae* 48 (1994): 313–31.

[20] The picture that Eusebius gives of Irenaeus in several places of *Hist. eccl.*, especially Book 5, is very positive. It would be an important topic for further research to examine in what way Irenaeus's exegetical reasoning has influenced Eusebius's theology.

[21] Concerning different possibilities for interpreting the end of *Hist. eccl.*, see Andrew Louth, "The Date of Eusebius' *Historia Ecclesiastica*," *Journal of Theological Studies* 41 (1990): 111–23; Richard Burgess, "The Dates and Editions of Eusebius' *Chronici Canones* and *Historia*

Pamphilus and his companions. Eusebius refers to an unnamed Christian who was tortured, and who, when he was asked the name of the country he came from, answered "that Jerusalem was his city – meaning, to be sure, that one of which it was said by Paul, 'But the Jerusalem that is above is free, which is our mother' and, 'You are come unto Mount Zion, and unto the city of the living God, the heavenly Jerusalem.'" Further, Eusebius recounts that the Christian martyr, when asked where that city was, "philosophized" about the location of Jerusalem, stating "it was the country of the Christians alone. For, said he also, none others save they alone had a share in it, and it lay towards the East and the light itself and the sun."[22] The location of the city in the direction of the rising sun indicates that it exists already (in heaven) and will appear in the future (on earth).[23]

Summing up, in his early work *Ecl. proph.* Eusebius interprets Isa 2:1–4 as Christians having a connection to the Heavenly Jerusalem through faith (as Paul writes in Gal 4:26) but that they will enter the city in the coming eschatological era when the Heavenly Jerusalem descends to earth.

3 *Demonstratio evangelica*

In *Dem. ev.* Eusebius gives detailed analyses of the book of Isaiah in several places. I focus here on Eusebius's interpretation of Isa 1–4 in particular because it is related to the idea of the Heavenly Jerusalem in Gal 4:26. In *Dem. ev.* 67–75 he compares "the actual Jerusalem and figurative Jerusalem" with each other (*Dem. ev.* 75) when referring to Isa 4:2–3. This comparison of Eusebius's begins already in *Dem. ev.* 67. There he deals with nations who have heard the gospel of Jesus: "And they will worship Him not in Jerusalem below, which is in Palestine, but each from his own place, and all who are in the isles of Gentiles."[24]

Ecclesiastica," *Journal of Theological Studies* 48 (1997): 471–504; Johnson, *Eusebius* (cf. note 1), 104–12; James Corke-Webster, *Eusebius and Empire: Constructing Church and Rome in the Ecclesiastical History* (Cambridge: Cambridge University Press, 2019) and literature referred to within.

[22] *Mart. Pal.* 11. The text used is from Eduard Schwartz, ed., *Eusebius Werke. Band 2. Teil 2. Die Kirchengeschichte. Die Bücher VI bis X; Über die Märtyrer in Palästina*, GCS (Leipzig: Hinrichs, 1908), 907–50. The English translation used is Hugh J. Lawlor and John E. L. Oulton, *Eusebius: The Ecclesiastical History and the Martyrs of Palestine. Volume 1: Translation* (New York: MacMillan, 1927), esp. 385–86.

[23] The Hebrew language indicates this time-related speaking of the "east" nicely when the Hebrew word *qedem* means not only the "east" but also "the past time." This means that the event that will become real must first come up behind the horizon in the east and its future will be behind the observer's (oriented toward the east; Job 23:8–9) back in the west. This means that the Christian martyr confesses that the heavenly Jerusalem is already a reality through faith and, therefore, the city has become "visible" in the east.

[24] This emphatic contrast between the earthly Jerusalem and the heavenly Jerusalem is apparently taken from Origen's writings. See Wilken, *Land* (cf. note 14), 65–100.

This can be regarded as an indirect reference to Gal 4:26 as also noted in Ivar Heikel's edition.[25] The typical feature in Eusebius's way of interpreting Isa 1–4 is to distinguish between the passages of doom and those of salvation. All the passages of doom are interpreted as referring to the Jewish people, while references to salvation, especially Isa 2:1–4 and 4:2–6, are seen to be about the Christian church. Before quoting Isa 2:2–3, Eusebius introduces the biblical text with the following statement (*Dem. ev.* 73): "While in addition to this they tell of the coming of a new Mount, and the manifesting of another House of God, besides the one in Jerusalem."

This introduction aptly indicates that Eusebius's main emphasis in *Dem. ev.* is still the idea that Isa 2:2–4 will be fulfilled figuratively. An interesting detail in Eusebius's interpretation of Isaiah 1–4 is that he introduces Paul's teaching on the remnant in Rom 9–11. He quotes Rom 11:27–29 (where reference is made to Isa 1:9) and Rom 11:1–5 and emphasizes the "remnant" of the Jewish people (*Dem. ev.* 68–69) in a similar way as, for example, Justin Martyr (see *1 Apol.* 53.7; cf. *Dial.* 55.3; 140.3). The interpretation of Isa 1:7–9 (text given in italics in the translation below) and its reference to the remnant of the Jewish people is expressed in the following way in *Dem. ev.* 70:

For the daughter of Zion (by whom was meant the worship celebrated on Mount Zion) from the time of the coming of our Savior has been left *as a tent in a vineyard, as a hut in a garden of cucumbers*, or as anything that is more desolate than these. And *strangers devour the land before their eyes*, now exacting tax and tribute, and now appropriating for themselves the land which belonged of old to Jews. Yea, and the beauteous Temple of their mother-city was laid low, *being cast down by alien peoples*, and their *cities were burnt with fire*, and Jerusalem became truly *a besieged city*. But since, when all this happened, the choir of the Apostles, and those of the Hebrews who believed in Christ, were preserved from among them as a fruitful seed, and going through every race of men in the world, filled every city and place and country with the seed of Christianity and Israel, so that like corn springing from it, the churches which are founded in our Savior's name have come into being, the divine prophet naturally adds to his previous threats against them: "*We should have been as Sodom, and we should have been like unto Gomorrah*." Which the holy Apostle in the Epistle to the Romans more clearly defines and interprets.[26]

---

[25] Cf. note 10.

[26] "ἥ τε γὰρ θυγάτηρ Σιών" (αὕτη δὲ ἦν ἡ ἐπὶ ὄρους τοῦ καλουμένου Σιὼν ἐπιτελουμένη θρησκεία) ἀπὸ τῆς Ἰησοῦ τοῦ σωτῆρος ἡμῶν παρουσίας ἐγκαταλέλειπται "ὡς σκηνὴ ἐν ἀμπελῶνι καὶ ὡς ὀπωροφυλάκιον ἐν σικυηράτῳ", καὶ εἴ τι τούτων ἐρημότερον "τήν τε χώραν αὐτῶν ἀλλότριοι ἐνώπιον αὐτῶν κατεσθίουσι", τοτὲ μὲν δασμοὺς καὶ φόρους αὐτοὺς εἰσπραττόμενοι, τοτὲ δὲ ἴδιον ἑαυτῶν κτῆμα τὴν πάλαι τῶν Ἰουδαίων γῆν πεποιημένοι· ἀλλὰ καὶ τὸ ἱερὸν τὸ εὐπρεπὲς τῆς μητροπόλεως αὐτῶν ἠρείπωται "κατεστραμμένον ὑπὸ λαῶν ἀλλοτρίων", "αἵ τε πόλεις" αὐτῶν "πυρίκαυστοι" γεγόνασι, καὶ γέγονεν Ἰερουσαλὴμ ἀληθῶς "πόλις πολιορχουμένη". Ἀλλ' ἐπεὶ τούτων περὶ αὐτοὺς συμβεβηκότων ὁ τῶν ἀποστόλων χορὸς οἵ τε ἐξ Ἑβραίων εἰς τὸν Χριστὸν πεπιστευκότες γονίμου δίκην σπέρματος ἐξ αὐτῶν ἐκείνων διεφυλάχθησαν, καθ' ὅλης τε τῆς οἰκουμένης καὶ εἰς πᾶν γένος ἀνθρώπων διελθόντες πᾶσαν πόλιν καὶ τόπον καὶ χώραν τοῦ οἰκείου καὶ Ἰσραηλιτικοῦ σπόρου κατέπλησαν, ὥστε ἐξ αὐτῶν στάχυς τὰς ἐπ' ὀνόματος τοῦ σωτῆρος ἡμῶν ὑποστάσας ἐκκλησίας φῦναι, εἰκότως ὁ

This text is striking because Eusebius emphasizes that the right remnant is "the worship celebrated on Mount Zion." In Eusebius's time, an interesting tradition that had been established in Christianity was that a Jewish-Christian remnant had stayed on Mount Zion. According to Eusebius's *Onomasticon*, Golgotha is situated "in Aelia[27] by the northern parts of Mount Zion."[28] This indicates that in *Dem. ev.*, Eusebius relates the righteous remnant of the Jewish people locally to the (Christian) Mount Zion. Later in *Dem. ev.* 131 Eusebius writes:

> And the evidence of the Acts of the Apostles goes to show that there were many myriads of Jews who believed Him to be the Christ of God foretold by the prophets. And history also assures us that there was a very important Christian Church in Jerusalem, composed of Jews, which existed until the siege of the city under Hadrian. The bishops, too, who stand first in the line of succession there are said to have been Jews, whose names are still remembered by the inhabitants.[29]

According to this statement, an important Christian church existed in Jerusalem and Hadrian would have found it. Eusebius apparently regarded this tradition as reliable because he enumerates a long list of circumcised (Jewish-Christian) bishops in Jerusalem (*Hist. eccl.* 4.5), indicating that knowledge of the existence of the Jewish-Christian congregation in Jerusalem had been received from an older tradition. Eusebius is not alone in this. This tradition appears in other Christian sources too and, interestingly, it has been related to Isa 1:7–9. Epiphanius writes in *Weight and Measurements* 14 about the destruction of Jerusalem and the small church that was built on Zion and that Hadrian found there. Epiphanius refers to Isa 1:8 when he describes this church "like a booth in a vineyard" and states that it existed in Zion until the time of Maximona the bishop and Constantine.[30] Epiphanius refers to this small church being one of the seven synagogues that

---

θεῖος προφήτης ἐπιλέγει ταῖς προαποφανθείσαις κατ' αὐτῶν ἀπειλαῖς "εἰ μὴ χύριος Σαβαὼθ· ἐγκατέλιπεν ἡμῖν σπέρμα, ὡς Σόδομα ἂν ἐγενήθημεν καὶ ὡς Γόμορρα ἂν ὡμοιώθημεν". ὅπερ συναγαγὼν ἐπὶ τὸ σαφὲς ἑρμηνεύει ἐν τῇ πρὸς Ῥωμαίους ἐπιστολῇ ὁ ἱερὸς ἀπόστολος·

[27] Aelia is the Roman name for Jerusalem that was in use after the Bar-Kochba war.

[28] Text: Erich Klostermann, ed., *Eusebius Werke. Band 3. Teil 1. Das Onomastikon der biblischen Ortsnamen,* GCS (Leipzig: Hinrich, 1904); Stefan Timm, ed., *Eusebius Werke. Dritter Band. Erster Teil, Das Onomastikon der biblischen Ortsnamen: Kritische Neuausgabe des griechischen Textes mit der lateinischen Fassung des Hieronymus,* GCS (Berlin: de Guyter, 2017). See also Greveille S. P. Freeman-Grenville, Rupert L. Chapman III, and Joan E. Taylor, *Palestine in the Fourth Century* A.D.: *The Onomasticon by Eusebius of Caesarea* (Jerusalem: Carta, 2003).

[29] μαρτυρεῖ δὲ καὶ ἡ τῶν Πράξεων τῶν ἀποστόλων γραφή, ὅτι πολλαὶ μυριάδες ἦσαν Ἰουδαίων ἀνδρῶν πεπεισμένων αὐτὸν εἶναι τὸν Χριστὸν τοῦ θεοῦ, τὸν ὑπὸ τῶν προφητῶν κατηγγελμένον. καὶ ἡ ἱστορία δὲ κατέχει ὡς καὶ μεγίστη τις ἦν ἐκκλησία Χριστοῦ ἐν τοῖς Ἱεροσολύμοις ἀπὸ Ἰουδαίων συγκροτουμένη μέχρι τῶν χρόνων τῆς κατ' Ἀδριανὸν πολιορκίας. λέγονται γοῦν οἱ πρῶτοι κατὰ διαδοχὴν προστάντες αὐτόθι ἐπίσκοποι Ἰουδαῖοι γεγονέναι, ὧν καὶ τὰ ὀνόματα εἰσέτι νῦν παρὰ τοῖς ἐγχωρίοις μνημονεύεται.

[30] James Elmer Dean, *Epiphanius' Treatise on Weights and Measures: The Syriac Version,* Studies in Ancient Oriental Civilizations 11 (Chicago: University of Chicago Press, 1935), 30. See also Renan Baker, "Epiphanius, *On Weights and Measures* 14: Hadrian's Journey to the East and the Rebuilding of Jerusalem," *Zeitschrift für Papyrologie und Epigraphik* 182 (2012): 157–167.

once stood on Zion. This idea of the synagogue that stood on Mount Zion can also be found in another source from the time of Eusebius, in the itinerary of the Bordeaux pilgrim: "Seven synagogues were there once, but only one is left – the rest have been ploughed and sown, as was said by the prophet Isaiah."[31] Again, we find a reference to Isa 1:8–9.[32] The memory that the Jewish-Christian remnant once existed on Mount Zion is also documented in Egeria's pilgrimage narrative when she writes that on Zion is the place "where once after the Lord's passion a crowd had gathered with the apostles" and also refers to the church (or synagogue) that once existed there (*Itinerarium Egeriae* 42.3).[33] All these references indicate that there was a widespread and established tradition at the time of Eusebius that the Jewish-Christian remnant had its congregation on Mount Zion. Eusebius refers to this remnant when he interprets Isa 1:8–9 in the Pauline way as referring to the Jewish remnant inside the Christian church.

To summarize, in his *Dem. ev.* Eusebius continues the outline of *Ecl. proph.* and compares the heavenly and earthly Jerusalems when he interprets Isa 2:1–4. An interesting detail in Eusebius's interpretation is that he refers to a remnant of a Jewish-Christian group that existed on Mount Zion (based on Isa 1:8–9) – a tradition that is well attested in other fourth century Christian sources.

4 *Commentarius in Isaiam*

Eusebius's interpretation of Isa 2:2–4 and Isa 1:8–9 in *Dem. ev.* followed the basic idea in Paul's letters to the Galatians (4:26) and to the Romans (10:27–29; 11:1–5) that the Christian church is the fulfilment of the promised glory of Mount Zion, where a remnant is also left among the Jewish people who will inherit promises given to the Jewish people in the Old Testament/Hebrew Bible. However, in

---

[31] Text from Paul Geyer, Otto Cuntz, Ezio Franceschini, Robert Weber, Ludwig Bieler, Jean Fraipont, François Glorie, ed., *Itineraria et alia geographica*, CCSL 175 (Turnhout: Brepols, 1965), 1–26. Concerning the Bordeaux pilgrim see Herbert Donner, *Pilgerfahrt ins Heilige Land: Die ältesten Berichte christlicher Palästinapilger (4.-7. Jahrhundert)* (Stuttgart: Katholisches Bibelwerk, 1979), 36–68; see the English translation in John Wilkinson, *Egeria's Travels to the Holy Land* (Jerusalem: Ariel, 1981), 158; see also Anne McGowan and Paul F. Bradshaw, *The Pilgrimage of Egeria: A New Translation of the* Itinerarium Egeriae *with Introduction and Commentary* (Collegeville: Liturgical Press Academic, 2018), 202 and Aubrey Stewart, *Itinerary from Bordeaux to Jerusalem: 'The Bordeaux Pilgrim' (333 A.D.)* (London: Adelphi, 1887), 23.

[32] In addition to Isa 1:8–9 the text of Mic 3:12 was also alluded to. It is very possible that the two texts were combined because both could be explained as referring to the destruction of the Second Temple after which there was the same prophecy of a universal "church" (i.e., Isa 2:1–4 and Mic 4:1–5). The combination of Isa 1:8–9 and Mic 3:12 can also be found in Cyril of Jerusalem's *Catechetical Lecture* 16.18. On this, see further Donner, *Pilgerfahrt ins Heilige Land* (cf. note 31), 58 n. 91.

[33] The translation is from McGowan and Bradshaw, *Pilgrimage of Egeria* (cf. note 31), 184–85. Concerning Egeria's pilgrimage, see Anni Maria Laato's approach elsewhere in this volume.

Eusebius's *Commentary on Isaiah* the interpretation of these two passages has changed in a remarkable way. Earlier, Isa 1:8–9 had signified the remnant of the Jewish people, but in *Comm. Isa.* 7, the interpretation is significantly different. In this passage, Eusebius relates the metaphor of the "vineyard" in Isa 1:8–9 to Isa 5:2–7 and interprets it entirely in negative terms:

In light of the statement above – "They have forsaken the Lord and provoked to anger the Holy One of Israel" – it could also be said that they will be abandoned. The verse that says that they have been abandoned like a booth in a vineyard signifies their complete lack of fruitfulness.[34]

The booth is interpreted as referring to the Temple (so also the interpretation of Isa 5:2–7 in *Comm. Isa.* 29–31, where the tower built in the midst of the vineyard signifies the Temple), which now stands in the middle of ruined land (*Comm. Isa.* 7):

We should note that when the entire nation is understood to be the vineyard, then the booth that was set up in the middle of all would be the temple in Jerusalem. Thus, the guard watches over the vineyard as from a lookout tower. But since "instead of a cluster of grapes it produced thorns," he then prophesies that the city and the temple will be abandoned. He says, like a booth in a vineyard, and like a garden-watcher's hut in a cucumber field because the practices they called virtuous did not yield quality bunches of grapes, but it was not quite late summer at that point. Such was the temporary and corporeal worship according to "the law of Moses."[35]

Later in *Comm. Isa.* 86–87, when he interprets Isa 11:11, Eusebius returns to the interpretation of Isa 1:9 and quotes Rom 11:5. Eusebius emphasizes, however, that these texts speak only about past historical events and, moreover, that they have been "fulfilled through his [Christ's] disciples and apostles." Eusebius no longer speaks about the Jewish-Christian remnant on Mount Zion; rather, he emphasizes that the gospel was preached first to Jews and then to gentiles and that the ultimate goal was that there would be only one church that is "no longer divided or separated from one another as before."

Eusebius's new emphases are also clearly visible in his interpretation of Isa 2:2–4. First, he relates the fulfilment of Isa 2:2–4 to the *pax Romana* (*Comm. Isa.* 14–15) by emphasizing that the prophecy predicts that the gospel will be

---

[34] Ἐπεὶ αὐτοὶ πρότεροι ἐγκατέλιπον τὸν κύριον καὶ παρώργισαν τὸν ἅγιον τοῦ Ἰσραήλ, εἰκότως ἐγκαταλειφθήσεσθαι λέγονται. τὸ δέ· ὡς σκηνὴ ἐν ἀμπελῶνι καταλείπεσθαι, σημαίνει τὴν παντελῆ αὐτῶν ἀκαρπίαν.

[35] τοῦ γάρ τοι παντὸς ἔθνους δίκην ἀμπελῶνος συνεστῶτος, ὥσπέρ τις σκηνὴν μέση τοῦ παντὸς ὁ ἐν τῇ Ἱερουσαλὴμ νεὼς ἵδρυτο, ἔνθεν τε ὡς ἀπὸ σκοπῆς ὁ φρουρὸς τὸν ἀμπελῶνα ἐπεσκόπει, ἐπεὶ δέ ἀντὶ σταφυλῆς ἐποίησεν ἀκάνθας, ἀκόλουθον καὶ τὴν πόλιν καὶ τὸν νεὼν ἐγκαταλειφθήσεσθαι θεσπίζει, ὡς σκηνὴ ἐν ἀμπελῶνι, ἀλλὰ καὶ ὡς ὀπωροφυλάκιον ἐν σικυηράτῳ φησὶ διὰ τὸ οὐχ ὅπως τὰς κατ' ἀρετὴν πράξεις ὀνομαζομένας σταφυλὴν τὴν ὡς καρποῖς τιμιωτέραν μὴ φέρειν, ἀλλὰ μηδὲ τὴν καλουμένην ὀπώραν. τοιαύτη δέ τις ἦν ἡ πρόσκαιρος καὶ σωματικὴ κατὰ τὸν Μωσέως νόμον λατρεία.

preached to every nation and that peoples will live in harmony and peace. He states that these things have been already fulfilled now:

> These things were fulfilled right after the coming of our Savior Jesus Christ. And that no one could find the same stable and peaceful state of affairs as existed in prior times under the Roman rule following the times of our Savior, we may see with our own eyes. There were civil relations between nations. There was peace everywhere, in the country as well as in the cities, when the new law and the evangelical word ruled over the lands of the Jews and over Zion itself.[36]

Eusebius relates the outcome of Christianity and its victory to the Roman rule and the peace that was established over all the world. This wonderful change, according to Eusebius, "we may see with our own eyes."

Second, Eusebius states that a significant change occurs in history when the Savior hears and answers the prayers of his church. He identifies the house of God in Isa 2:2–4 with the Christian church and relates it to the vision of Daniel according to which "a stone was cut out from the mountain without human hands," destroying the statue symbolizing the evil power (Dan 2:45).[37] This introduces a new era in the world when everyone will understand "that the phrase 'the house of God shall be on the tops of the mountains' reminds us that our Savior hears the prayers of his church."[38] This change in history is also seen in Eusebius's way of illustrating *Hist. eccl.*, books 8–10, for the church under persecution had lately become the dominant religion in the Roman Empire.

Third, Eusebius has not abandoned the idea that Isa 2:2–4 is related to Gal 4:26. He writes of the deeper meaning of Isa 2:2–4, which "the high and heavenly and angelic word of God and the divine apostle of the 'heavenly' Zion teaches that it is 'the Jerusalem above, which is the mother of us all.'"[39] While in *Dem. ev.* it is *expressis verbis* emphasized that the heavenly and earthly Jerusalem should be distinguished from each other, in *Comm. Isa.* there is a new idea – namely, that the heavenly Zion has invaded the earthly Zion:

> The Christ could very well be this evangelical law, who relocated from the "heavenly" Zion above and set up shop in the Zion on the earth, where the death of the Savior at the hands of men and his resurrection from the dead took place. For once the mysteries and precepts of the new covenant came to power, they advanced throughout the entire world. This same law and the new preaching of the evangelical word to all nations educated those

---

[36] *Comm. Isa.* 15 (Armstrong, *Commentary* 10): ἄντικρυς δὲ καὶ ταῦτα ἐπληροῦτο μετὰ τὴν τοῦ σωτῆρος ἡμῶν Ἰησοῦ Χριστοῦ παρουσίαν· οὐκ ἄν οὖν εὕροι τις ἐν τοῖς πρὸ τούτου χρόνοις τὴν αὐτὴν καιρῶν εὐσταθῆ καὶ εἰρηναίαν κατάστασιν, ὁποίαν ἐπὶ τῆς Ῥωμαίων ἀρχῆς μετὰ τοὺς τοῦ σωτῆρος ἡμῶν χρόνους ὀφθαλμοῖς ὁρῶμεν, ἐπιμιξίας οὔσης τῶν ἐθνῶν καὶ εἰρήνης ἁπανταχοῦ κατ' ἀγρούς καὶ κατὰ πόλεις, ὡς τὸν καινὸν νόμον καὶ τὸν εὐαγγελικὸν λόγον ἀρξάμενον ἀπὸ τῆς τῶν Ἰουδαίων χώρας καὶ ἀπ' αὐτῆς τῆς Σιών.

[37] In Cyprian's *Ad Quirinium testimonia adversus Iudaeos* 2.16–18, Isa 2:2–4 is also related to the destruction of the evil power by a stone in Dan 2.

[38] *Comm. Isa.* 16 (Armstrong, *Commentary* 11).

[39] *Comm. Isa.* 16 (Armstrong, *Commentary* 11–12).

who welcomed it in what concerns the mountain and the house of God, and it taught the nations, saying: Come, let us go up to the mountain of the Lord and to the house of the God of Jacob.[40]

Eusebius interprets the "Constantinian shift"[41] in his *Hist. eccl.* too, stating that the victory of Christianity over the pagan world (and Judaism) became visible in the course of history:

> This means literally that, in the end, after his theophany and after the preaching of the evangelical law to the nations, the nations were deemed worthy to partake of the deepest peace. It also speaks of the word that Christ gave that they shall beat their daggers into plows and their spears into pruning hooks and that war will no longer be taught, although training for war used to be compulsory and was practiced in the country as well as in the cities from the children on up because of the fear of hostile uprisings.[42]

It is significant to see how, in his earlier days, Eusebius followed the older Jewish-Christian tradition and interpreted Isa 1:8–9 as a critical exhortative text toward Jews, which emphasized the existence of a Jewish-Christian minority in the church – a trend that Paul, a Jew, used in his letters to illustrate that a small Jewish remnant had been preserved (Rom 9–11).[43] After the Constantinian shift, however, Eusebius took a small sidewise step away from this Jewish-Christian tradition and related Isa 1:8–9 to Isa 5:1–7, emphasizing the total rejection of the Jewish people. This small step for Eusebius represented a giant leap for

---

[40] *Comm. Isa.* 16 (Armstrong, *Commentary* 12): Εἴη δ' ἂν οὗτος ὁ Χριστοῦ νόμος εὐαγγελικὸς ὁ ἄνωθεν ὁρμηθείς ἐκ Σιὼν τῆς ἐπουρανίου καὶ ἐκ ταύτης δὲ τῆς ἐπὶ γῆς Σιών, ἐν ᾗ ὁ ὑπ' ἀνθρώπων θάνατος τοῦ σωτῆρος καὶ ἡ ἐκ νεκρῶν ἀνάστασις αὐτοῦ, τά τε τῆς καινῆς διαθήκης μυστήρια καὶ παραγγέλματα ἀρχὴν λαβόντα προῆλθον εἰς πᾶσαν τὴν οἰκουμένην. αὐτός δὴ οὗτος ὁ νόμος καὶ ὁ καινός τοῦ εὐαγγελικοῦ λόγου κηρυχθεὶς πᾶσι τοῖς ἔθνεσιν ἐπαίδευσεν τοὺς ὑποδεξαμένους αὐτὸν τὰ περὶ τοῦ ὄρους τοῦ θεοῦ καὶ τοῦ οἴκου, ἐδίδαξέν τε τὰ ἔθνη λέγων· Δεῦτε καὶ ἀναβῶμεν εἰς τὸ ὄρος κυρίου καὶ εἰς τὸν οἶκον τοῦ θεοῦ Ἰακώβ.

[41] I used the term "Constantinian shift" in this contribution not as referring to an instantaneous moment in history but as referring to the church's changing status in the Roman empire, which status developed gradually after the Edict of Milan (AD 313).

[42] *Comm. Isa.* 17 (Armstrong, *Commentary* 12): καὶ πρὸς λέξιν δὲ ταῦτα τέλους ἠξιοῦτο μετὰ τὴν αὐτοῦ θεοφάνειαν καὶ μετὰ τὸν κηρυχθέντα τοῖς ἔθνεσιν εὐαγγελικὸν νόμον διαλαβούσης εἰρήνης βαθυτάτης τὰ ἔθνη, ὃ δὴ καὶ σημαίνει τὸν Χριστὸν ἐδίδου ὁ λόγος φήσας συγκόψειν τὰς μαχαίρας αὐτῶν εἰς ἄροτρα καὶ τὰς ζιβύνας αὐτῶν εἰς δρέπανα καὶ μηκέτι διδάσκεσθαι τὰ πολεμικά, ἃ δὴ καὶ πρότερον ἦσαν ἀναγκαῖα καὶ ἐκ παίδων κατ' ἀγρούς καὶ κατὰ πόλεις ἠσκοῦντο διὰ τὸν ἀπὸ τῶν πλησιοχώρων πολεμίων φόβον.

[43] I have earlier argued that Justin Martyr preserved New Testament trends allowing the existence of a Jewish-Christian minority inside the church. See Antti Laato, "Justin Martyr Encounters Judaism," in *Encounters of the Children of Abraham from Ancient to Modern Times*, ed. Antti Laato and Pekka Lindqvist, Studies on the Children of Abraham 1 (Leiden: Brill, 2010), 97–123; Antti Laato, "Jewish Believers in Jesus and the Mosaic Law: The Opinion of Justin Martyr," in *The Challenge of the Mosaic Torah in Judaism, Christianity, and Islam*, ed. Antti Laato, Studies on the Children of Abraham 7 (Leiden: Brill, 2020), 115–42; Antti Laato, "Abraham in Justin Martyr's Dialogue," in *Religious Polemics and Encounters in Late Antiquity: Boundaries, Conversions and Persuasion*, ed. Timo Nisula, Anni Maria Laato, and Pablo Irizar, Studies on the Children of Abraham 8 (Leiden: Brill, 2021), 1–26.

Christianity, which now oriented itself more firmly in line with its anti-Jewish trends. In this new anti-Jewish trend, intra-Jewish criticism of the New Testament was reinterpreted by introducing a consequent polemical anti-Jewish confrontation that aimed at justifying a rejection of the Jewish people. In this new misleading understanding, all critical prophecies in the book of Isaiah were interpreted as referring to the Jews – an interpretive tendency that was developed from the intra-Jewish criticism of the New Testament.[44]

To sum up this section, in *Comm. Isa.* Eusebius has clearly sharpened his criticism against Judaism. This becomes evident when he no longer interprets Isa 1:8–9 after a Pauline fashion, according to which the emphasis was on the Jewish-Christian minority who had the right to exist inside the Christian church. Eusebius abandoned this interpretation and related the interpretation of Isa 1:8–9 to Isa 5:1–7, emphasizing, without reservation, the doom aspect against Judaism.

5 *Vita Constantini*

Eusebius's final and uncompleted work, *The Life of Constantine*, gives us the opportunity to see how he had to re-evaluate his earlier thought about the importance of holy places. Earlier he had criticized Judaism for being bound to holy places, arguing that the essence of Christianity was spiritual. Instead of depending on local places as the Jews did, Eusebius reasons, Christians had a vital relation to the Heavenly Jerusalem.[45] The establishment of the new Christian center in Palestine after the building of the Holy Sepulchre, however, triggered a re-examination of this thinking. The famous and oft-quoted passage stating that Constantinian Jerusalem is the new city promised in the prophetic writings is *Vit. Const.* 3.33:

---

[44] The question of the position of the Jewish-Christian group in the early church is difficult and multifaceted, and attitudes varied among early Christian theologians. For this see Oskar Skarsaune and Reidar Hvalvik, ed., *Jewish Believers in Jesus: The Early Centuries* (Peabody: Hendrickson, 2007). I have touched on this very problem in several articles and recognized that, in broad terms, the development of Jewish-Christian groups went through three significant transformations: (1) In early Judaism there were intra-Jewish confrontations between different Jewish groups (a good example of this is the Qumran writings), and the first Jewish-Christian groups inherited this concept when they discussed the messiahship of Jesus of Nazareth. (2) This intra-Jewish confrontation later developed into inter-religious confrontation in different early Christian texts while some texts continued to preserve an idea about Jewish-Christian groups that could follow the Mosaic Torah (e.g., Justin Martyr). (3) The Constantinian shift radically changed this multifaceted situation and the inter-religious confrontation, featuring strong anti-Jewish elements, was normalized in the church.

[45] This has been emphasized especially by Walker, *Holy City, Holy Places* (cf. note 14), 51–130 and Wilken, *Land* (cf. note 14), 65–100.

New Jerusalem was built at the very Testimony to the Savior, facing the famous Jerusalem of old, which after the bloody murder of the Lord had been overthrown in utter devastation, and paid the penalty of its wicked inhabitants. Opposite this then the Emperor erected the victory of the Savior over death with rich and abundant munificence, this being perhaps that *fresh new Jerusalem proclaimed in prophetic oracles*, about which long speeches recite innumerable praises as they utter words of divine inspiration.[46]

The text contains a significant mention that the Holy Sepulchre was constructed according to "the predictions of prophets."[47] To which prophetic texts does Eusebius refer here? Apparently, Eusebius had in mind the many works in which he used prophetic texts to demonstrate the validity of the message of the gospel. However, because he wrote the commentary on Isaiah in particular, and because it is also generally accepted that this writing contains many allusions to the new world order inaugurated by the Constantinian shift, I investigate the ways in which Eusebius's *Commentary on Isaiah* gives support for the ideas he presented in *Vit. Const.* 3.25–40.

The following correspondences can be found. First, the text states that Constantine's building of the Holy Sepulchre was called the "new Jerusalem" or "fresh new Jerusalem" (*Vit. Const.* 3.33). In Winkelmann's edition these terms have been compared with references to Rev 3:12 and 21:2.[48] While the term "New Jerusalem" is used in the book of Revelation, it is not at all clear whether Eusebius adopted this term from that particular New Testament writing. As we have already noted, Eusebius very rarely refers to the book of Revelation in his writings. Therefore, my proposal is that Eusebius's *Comm. Isa.* is behind the term "new Jerusalem" in *Vit. Const.* In Table 2, the terms "new Jerusalem" or "new Zion" in *Comm. Isa.* are listed (see Table 2).

This list indicates clearly that the terms "new Jerusalem" and "new Zion" are parallel expressions for Eusebius. Because Eusebius never quotes Rev 21–22 in *Comm. Isa.* but does use Heb 12:22–24 and Gal 4:26, it seems more probable that he relates the term "new Jerusalem" to the prophetic predictions made in the book of Isaiah. It is therefore likely Isaiah, not Revelation, to which Eusebius

---

[46] Emphasis added. καὶ δὴ κατ' αὐτὸ τὸ σωτήριον μαρτύριον ἡ νέα κατεσκευάζετο Ἰερουσαλήμ, ἀντιπρόσωπος τῇ πάλαι βοωμένῃ, ἣ μετὰ τὴν κυριοκτόνον μιαιφονίαν ἐρημιᾶς ἐπ' ἔσχατα περιτραπεῖσα δίκην ἔτισε δυσσεβῶν οἰκητόρων. ταύτης δ' οὖν ἄντικρυς βασιλεὺς τὴν κατὰ τοῦ θανάτου σωτήριον νίκην πλουσίαις καὶ δαψιλέσιν ἀνύψου φιλοτιμίαις, τάχα που ταύτην οὖσαν τὴν διὰ προφητικῶν θεσπισμάτων κεκηρυγμένην καινὴν καὶ νέαν Ἰερουσαλήμ, ἧς πέρι μακροὶ λόγοι μυρία δι' ἐνθέου πνεύματος θεσπίζοντες ἀνυμνοῦσι.

[47] For discussion on how the architecture of the Holy Sepulchre conveys meaning, see Jordan J. Ryan, *From the Passion to the Church of the Holy Sepulchre: Memories of Jesus in Place, Pilgrimage, and Early Holy Sites over the First Three Centuries* (London: Bloomsbury, T&T Clark, 2021), 99–134. See further Kühnel, *From the Earthly to the Heavenly Jerusalem* (cf. note 2), 63–111, where the Mosaic of D. Pudentiana in Rome is discussed in relationship to Constantine's Holy Sepulchre; see also Armin Bergmeier's contribution to the present volume.

[48] A reference to Rev 21–22 is also made in Wilken, *Land* (cf. note 14), 96–97; see also Cameron and Hall's commentary in their translation *Life of Constantine* (cf. note 12), 284–85.

Table 2. "New Jerusalem" and "New Zion" in *Commentary on Isaiah* (*CI* = Ziegler's edition; A = Armstrong's translation).

Isaiah text interpreted	"New Jerusalem"	"New Zion"
Isa 32:7–8	*CI* 208–209; A 160–161	*CI* 208–209; A 160–161
Isa 49:17		*CI* 314; A 246
Isa 52:8		*CI* 331; A 259
Isa 54:12	*CI* 342–343; A 268	
Isa 60:1–2	*CI* 368–370; A 290	
Isa 60:4	*CI* 371; A 291	
Isa 60:18	*CI* 377; A 296	
Isa 62:5–6	*CI* 383–384; A 301	
Isa 66:10–11	*CI* 403–404; A 316	
Isa 66:12–13	*CI* 404; A 316	*CI* 404; A 316

refers in *Vit. Const.* 3.33 when he writes "fresh new Jerusalem proclaimed in prophetic oracles."[49] This being the case, we can establish that the term "new Jerusalem" is closely related to Eusebius's way of interpreting the book of Isaiah, and not Rev 21–22 as scholars have suggested.

Second, we have already noted how Eusebius's attitude towards the Jewish-Christian minority changed from *Dem. ev.* to *Comm. Isa.*, and this change becomes especially visible in his interpretation of Isa 1:7–9. In *Vit. Const.* 3.33 Eusebius continues his anti-Jewish programme by emphasizing how the Holy Sepulchre was built as a new landmark in Jerusalem and witnesses against Jewish murderous actions against the Savior, Jesus Christ. When interpreting Isa 2:1–4, the focus of this contribution, Eusebius writes:

> The mountain of God may be understood in various ways. Like the Jewish people who read the Scriptures literally, one could assume that it is the land of Palestine. But according to the deeper meaning, according to the final word, the high and heavenly and angelic word of God and the divine apostle of the "heavenly" Zion teaches that it is "the Jerusalem above, which is the mother of us all." This mountain was not manifest to the men of old, but the divine Spirit prophesies that it will be manifest to all nations in the last days, when Christ would "appear to put away sin."[50]

---

[49] There were certainly other Old Testament texts that Eusebius probably had in mind. For example, Ezek 40–48 seems to loom behind the description – a topic that I cannot deal with in this contribution. Worth noting also is Zeph 3:8 (LXX), containing the word *martyrion*, which has been related to the Holy Sepulchre.

[50] *Comm. Isa.* 16 (Armstrong, *Commentary*, 11–12): τὸ δὲ ὄρος τοῦ θεοῦ κατὰ διαφόρους ἐξακούεται τρόπους· σωματικώτερον μὲν ὡς ἂν ὑπολάβοιεν Ἰουδαῖοι τὸ ἐπὶ τῆς Παλαιστίνης χώρας, κατὰ διάνοιαν δὲ ὁ ὑψηλός καὶ ἐπουράνιος τοῦ θεοῦ λόγος εὐαγγελικός, κατὰ τρίτον δὲ λόγον ὁ θεῖος Ἀπόστολος Σιὼν ἐπουράνιον εἶναι διδάσκει καὶ τὴν ἄνω Ἰερουσαλήμ, ἥν τινα εἶναι μητέρα πάντων ἡμῶν. οὐκ ἦν δὲ ἄρα τοῖς παλαιοῖς ἀνθρώποις ἐμφανὲς τὸ ὄρος τοῦτο, πλὴν θεσπίζει τὸ θεῖον πνεῦμα ἐμφανὲς αὐτὸ γενήσεσθαι πᾶσιν τοῖς ἔθνεσιν ἐν ταῖς ἐσχάταις ἡμέραις, ὅτε Χριστὸς εἰς ἀθέτησιν τῶν ἁμαρτιῶν πεφανέρωται.

It seems clear that in *Vit. Const.* Eusebius continues to express his anti-Jewish programme. When explaining Isa 51:1–2, Eusebius heavily criticizes Jews because of their disbelief and subsequently presents the reason for this criticism: Jews have not accepted the divine revelation of "the only-begotten Word of God." The words of Isa 51:1–2 lead Eusebius to write about the grave of the Savior:

> And it seems that in this verse, the word foreshadows that very "rock" that welcomed the body of the Savior, in which "Joseph" dug the grave "for his own new tomb" ... Therefore, because of what I have done for Abraham, you should not give up hope that from this rock, which you yourselves hewed, there will come a prospect of salvation for all people. And this prospect is in no way inferior to the promise that was spoken to Abraham, and I will give this prospect to all nations because of the grace of the aforesaid rock. And so then, the rock represents the grave "that Joseph had hewn for a tomb" as well as the Christ himself, whom the divine apostle knew to call a rock when he said: "And the rock was Christ."[51]

Eusebius's way of relating the memory of the Savior's grave to the disbelief of the Jews illustrates well the contrast he presents in *Vit. Const.* 3.33 when he writes that the "new Jerusalem" is "facing the famous Jerusalem of old, which after the bloody murder of the Lord had been overthrown in utter devastation, and paid the penalty of its wicked inhabitants."[52]

Third, Constantine built the Holy Sepulchre as a symbol for the victory of the Savior's resurrection:[53]

> This then was the shrine which the Emperor raised as a manifest testimony of the Savior's resurrection, embellishing the whole with rich imperial decoration. He adorned it with untold beauties in innumerable dedications of gold and silver and precious stones set in various materials. In view of their size, number and variety, to describe in detail the skilled craftsmanship which went into their manufacture would be beyond the scope of the present work.[54]

---

[51] *Comm. Isa.* 321 (Armstrong, *Commentary*, 251): ἔοικε δὲ διὰ τούτων ὁ λόγος αἰνίττεσθαι αὐτὴν ἐκείνην τὴν τὸ σῶμα τοῦ σωτῆρος ὑποδεξαμένην πέτραν, ἐν ᾗ ὁ Ἰωσὴφ τὸ σπήλαιον ὤρυξεν ἐν τῷ καινῷ αὐτοῦ μνημείῳ ... ὥσπερ οὖν ἐπὶ τοῦ Ἀβραὰμ πεποίηκα, οὕτω μὴ ἀπογινώσκετε, ὡς καὶ ἀπὸ τῆς πέτρας ταύτης, ἣν ὑμεῖς αὐτοὶ ἐλατομήσατε, ἔσται τις ἐλπὶς ἅπασιν ἀνθρώποις σωτηρίας, ὡς μὴ ἀπολειφθῆναι τῆς πρὸς τὸν Ἀβραὰμ ἐπαγγελίας, τὴν δοθησομένην ἅπασι τοῖς ἔθνεσιν ἐξ ἐμοῦ διὰ τῆς εἰρημένης πέτρας χάριν, ἣν μὲν οὖν πέτρα καὶ τὸ σπήλαιον, ὁ ἐλατόμησεν ὁ Ἰωσὴφ εἰς μνημεῖον, ἀλλὰ καὶ τὸν Χριστὸν αὐτὸν οἶδεν ὁ θεῖος Ἀπόστολος πέτραν ὀνομάζειν λέγων· ἡ δὲ πέτρα ἦν ὁ Χριστός.

[52] Christians left the temple area with no buildings and in this way demonstrated that Jesus's words about the disbelief of Jews were effective (Matt 24:2): "You see all these, do you not? Truly I tell you, not one stone will be left here upon another; all will be thrown down." For this see especially Günter Stemberger, *Jews and Christians in the Holy Land: Palestine in the Fourth Century* (Edinburgh: T&T Clark, 2000), 51–55, 201–6.

[53] Scholars (Wilken, *Land* [cf. note 14], 88–90; Cameron and Hall, *Life of Constantine* [cf. note 12], 275–76) have emphasized that Eusebius's account in *Vit. Const.* 3.25–28 (excavation of the Holy Sepulchre) refers to efforts to find the holy tomb and every detail is accounted with great respect for the sacrality of the place. There is some evidence that the place of the tomb of Jesus was memorized in the Christian tradition before Constantine. For this see Ryan, *From the Passion* (cf. note 47), 19–97.

[54] *Vit. Const.* 3.40: Τόνδε μὲν οὖν τὸν νεὼν σωτηρίου ἀναστάσεως ἐναργὲς ἀνίστη μαρτύριον

In his *Praise of Constantine* (*De laudibus Constantini*) 9.16 Eusebius similarly emphasizes the Holy Sepulchre as the monument of the Lord's victory over death. In his *Commentary*, Eusebius, while interpreting Isa 65:19–20, combines the heavenly Jerusalem and the idea of resurrection.[55] This is an additional piece of evidence that the Holy Sepulchre and the prophetic prediction about the Heavenly Jerusalem were interconnected in Eusebius's understanding.

Fourth, Eusebius emphasizes how Constantine built the Holy Sepulchre to honor the apostles symbolically:[56]

> Facing these as the chief point of the whole was the hemisphere attached to the highest part of the royal house, ringed with twelve columns to match the number of the Apostles of the Savior, their tops decorated with great bowls made of silver, which the Emperor himself had presented to his God as a superb offering.[57]

According to Eusebius's description, the Holy Sepulchre illustrates the presence of the twelve apostles through its "twelve columns." This description corresponds to Eusebius's interpretations of the spiritual church in his commentary. Illustrative is Eusebius's interpretation of Isa 49:17 where his anti-Jewish sentiments also become visible (this corresponds well to his description of the Holy Sepulchre in *Vit. Const.*):

> Then, since in a short time the church of the nations came about after the disappearance of the religious government that had been present among the Jews, he continues on to say: *And soon you will be built by those by whom you were destroyed*. For just as the Jews were responsible for its destruction, so again they became the builders of the new structure – the apostles of our Savior and the disciples and evangelists, through whom the church of God was raised up from the nations. And these are in fact the ones who demolished the Jewish self-chosen form of worship (as the apostle teaches when he says: "But if I build up again those things which I tore down") who constructed the new Zion according to the government of the gospel. But, there are others besides them, whom the text identifies as those who made Zion desolate, and they certainly did not build it up, and so the text says concerning them: And those who made you desolate will go forth from you. One should not be amazed that the word was fulfilled in a spiritual and historical sense when, after the formation of the church of the nations, the entire nation of

---

βασιλεύς, πλούσια καὶ βασιλικῇ κατασκευῇ τὸν σύμπαντα καταφαιδρύνας, ἐκόσμει δ' αὐτὸν ἀδιηγήτοις κάλλεσι πλείστων ὅσων ἀναθημάτων, χρυσοῦ καὶ ἀργύρου καὶ λίθων πολυτελῶν ἐν διαλλαττούσαις ὕλαις, ὧν τὴν κατὰ μέρος ἐπισκευὴν φιλοτέχνως εἰργασμένην μεγέθει τε καὶ πλήθει καὶ ποικιλίαις οὐ σχολὴ νῦν ἐπεξιέναι τῷ λόγῳ.

[55] *Comm. Isa.* 397–98 (Armstrong, *Commentary*, 311).

[56] In his *Catechetical Lectures*, Cyril of Jerusalem often exhort catechumens to visit holy places. He relates the resurrection of the Savior to the witnesses of the twelve apostles (*Cat. hom.* 4.12) and may have been thinking about the architectural structure of the Holy Sepulchre.

[57] *Vit. Const.* 3.38: τούτων δ' ἄντικρυς τὸ κεφάλαιον τοῦ παντὸς ἡμισφαίριον ἦν ἐπ' ἄκρου τοῦ βασιλείου οἴκου τεταγμένον, ὃ δὴ δυοκαίδεκα κίονες ἐστεφάνουν, τοῖς τοῦ σωτῆρος ἀποστόλοις ἰσάριθμοι, κρατῆρσι μεγίστοις ἐξ ἀργύρου πεποιημένοις τὰς κορυφὰς κοσμούμενοι, οὓς δὴ βασιλεὺς αὐτὸς ἀνάθημα κάλλιστον ἐδωρεῖτο τῷ αὐτοῦ θεῷ.

the Jews and the physical city situated in Palestine were cast aside, and so their religious government came to nothing.[58]

Even more illustrative is Eusebius's interpretation of Isa 54:11–12, which describes the new Jerusalem, where the apostles are regarded as important foundational stones of the church (Isa 54:12):

> He compares them with lapis lazuli because lapis lazuli resembles the color of *heaven*. And their government is *heavenly* and angelic, as Paul teaches when he says: "But our commonwealth is in *heaven*." And there is the verse in the prophet Ezekiel that says: "Under the throne of God, as lapis lazuli." Therefore, "all the prophets and the apostles" were the "foundation" of the godly commonwealth, firm and "steadfast," and portrayed as lapis lazuli because they administer the "government of *heaven*" and because they "bear the image of the man of *heaven*." For this reason, the text reads: *And I will lay your foundations in lapis lazuli*. And the battlements of this temple and of the new Jerusalem are of jasper stone or Carthaginian stone, according to Symmachus, and this stone is special and translucent. Such were those in the church who defended the faith with spiritual armaments, standing as champions of the godly commonwealth and able "to demolish every proud obstacle to the knowledge of God" and to expose every false word spoken against the truth.[59]

In this quotation Eusebius speaks about "the new Jerusalem" (as in *Vit. Const.* 3.33) and "the temple" (as in *Vit. Const.* 3.40) indicating that the Holy Sepulchre

---

[58] *Comm. Isa.* 314 (Armstrong, *Commentary*, 246): Εἶτ ἐπειδήπερ ἐν βραχεῖ χρόνῳ ἡ ἐξ ἐθνῶν ἐκκλησία συνέστη μετὰ τὴν ἀπόπτωσιν τοῦ παρὰ Ἰουδαίοις θεοσεβοῦς πολιτεύματος, ἐπιλέγει ἑξῆς· καὶ ταχὺ οἰκοδομηθήσῃ ὑφ' ὧν καθῃρέθης· ὥσπερ γὰρ Ἰουδαῖοι τῆς καθαιρέσεως αὐτῆς γεγόνασιν αἴτιοι, οὕτω πάλιν ἐξ αὐτῶν ἦσαν οἱ τῆς νέας οἰκοδομῆς ἐργάται, οἱ ἀπόστολοι δηλαδὴ τοῦ σωτῆρος ἡμῶν, μαθηταί τε καὶ εὐαγγελισταί, δι' ὧν ἡ ἐξ ἐθνῶν ἐκκλησία τοῦ θεοῦ ἀνεγήγερται. καὶ αὐτοὶ δὲ οὗτοι τὴν Ἰουδαϊκὴν ἐθελοθρησκείαν καθελόντες, ὡς ὁ Παῦλος διδάσκει λέγων· "εἰ γὰρ ἃ κατέλυσα ταῦτα πάλιν οἰκοδομῶ", τὴν νέαν Σιὼν κατὰ τὴν εὐαγγελικὴν συνεστήσαντο πολιτείαν, ἕτεροι δὲ παρὰ τούτους δηλοῦνται ἑξῆς οἱ ἐρημώσαντες μὲν τὴν Σιών, οὐ μὴν καὶ οἰκοδομήσαντες αὐτήν, περὶ ὧν εἴρηται· καὶ οἱ ἐρημώσαντές σε ἐκ σοῦ ἐξελεύσονται. θαυμάσαι δέ ἐστιν, ὅπως πρὸς τῇ διανοίᾳ καὶ κατὰ τὴν ἱστορίαν ὁ λόγος ἐπληροῦτο τοῦ παντὸς Ἰουδαίων ἔθνους μετὰ τὴν σύστασιν τῆς ἐξ ἐθνῶν ἐκκλησίας ἀποβλήτου γενομένου καὶ τῆς αἰσθητῆς πόλεως τῆς κατὰ Παλαιστίνην κειμένης πρὸς τῷ καὶ τοῦ θεοσεβοῦς πολιτεύματος ἐκπεσεῖν.

[59] *Comm. Isa.* 342 (Armstrong, *Commentary*, 268): σαπφείρῳ δὲ αὐτοὺς ἀπεικάζει διὰ τὸ ἐοικέναι τῷ οὐρανίῳ χρώματι τὸν σάπφειρον. καὶ τούτων δὲ τὴν πολιτείαν οὐράνιον γεγονέναι καὶ ἀγγελικήν, ὡς διδάσκει λέγων ὁ Παῦλος· "ἡμῶν δὲ τὸ πολίτευμα ἐν οὐρανοῖς ὑπάρχει", εἴρηται δὲ καὶ παρὰ τῷ προφήτῃ Ἰεζεκιὴλ ὁ τόπος ὁ ὑπὸ τὸν θρόνον τοῦ θεοῦ ὡς σάπφειρος. οὗτοι δὴ οὖν οἱ προφῆται πάντες καὶ οἱ ἀπόστολοι θεμέλιοί τινες ἦσαν τοῦ θεοσεβοῦς πολιτεύματος εὐπαγεῖς καὶ ἑδραῖοι σαπφείροις ἀφωμοιωμένοι διὰ τὸ οὐράνιον πολίτευμα καὶ διὰ τὸ φορεῖν "τὴν εἰκόνα τοῦ ἐπουρανίου". διὸ εἴρηται· καὶ θήσω τὰ θεμέλιά σου σάπφειρον. καὶ αἱ ἐπάλξεις δὲ τῆς νέας ταύτης καὶ καινῆς Ἱερουσαλὴμ ἴασπις ἦν λίθος, ἢ καρχηδόνιος κατὰ τὸν Σύμμαχον, ἐξαίρετός τις ἦν καὶ διαφανής. τοιοῦτοι δ' ἂν εἶεν οἱ ἐν τῇ ἐκκλησίᾳ τοῦ θεοῦ λογικῇ παρασκευῇ τὴν πίστιν ὠχυρωμένοι ὥσπερ προμαχῶνες ὄντες τοῦ θεοσεβοῦς πολιτεύματος διὰ τὸ δύνασθαι "πᾶν ὕψωμα ἐπαιρόμενον κατὰ τῆς γνώσεως τοῦ θεοῦ" καθαιρεῖν καὶ διελέγχειν πάντα ψευδῆ λόγον τὸν τῆς ἀληθείας πολέμιον. I have in the English translation emphasized the words pertaining to heaven because in my fifth comparative detail below, I emphasize the open-air structure of the Holy Sepulchre.

illustrates the concrete manifestation of the spiritual church, which has a close connection to the heavenly Jerusalem as Eusebius described it in his commentary on Isa 54:12. In the quotation from *Comm. Isa.*, Eusebius compares the apostles to a firm and steadfast foundation used for expensive lapis lazuli stones. According to *Vit. Const.* 3.38, the twelve columns were built up in the Holy Sepulchre and these as symbols for the twelve apostles. Eusebius's way of describing the expensive building materials of the Holy Sepulchre in *Vit. Const.* 3.34–40 corresponds well to the precious stones, which, according to Isa 54:11–12, will be used for the New Jerusalem.

Fifth, Eusebius emphasizes the open-air structure of the Holy Sepulchre and the orientation of the basilica, which faced the rising sun:

> He then went on to a very large space wide open to the fresh air, which was decorated with a pavement of light-colored stone on the ground, and enclosed on three sides by long surrounding colonnades. On the side opposite the cave, which looked towards the rising sun, was connected the royal temple, an extraordinary structure raised to an immense height and very extensive in length and breadth.[60]

The architectural form of this open-air structure has been discussed among scholars, and the main question has been if the tomb of the Savior was covered by the dome (later known as Anastasis). There is no need to solve this problem in this contribution.[61] The fact is that there was an open-air courtyard between the basilica and the tomb of the Savior. Could this open-air structure symbolize the idea that the new Jerusalem has a direct contact to the Heavenly Jerusalem? We have seen that in *Comm. Isa.* Eusebius emphasizes the many ways in which the Christian congregation has a direct connection to the Heavenly Jerusalem. In his interpretation of the new Jerusalem in Isa 54:11–12 (quoted above) in particular, Eusebius uses the word "heaven" four times and "heavenly" once. Because the Holy Sepulchre is notably the monument of the resurrection which, according to Eusebius, opens a new relationship between God and Christians, such an open-air structure around the holy tomb can be interpreted as the heaven being open to all through the resurrection of the Savior. I have already noted how Eusebius retold the story of the Palestinian martyr who speculated how the heavenly Jerusalem was situated in the east, "towards the rising sun." Against

---

[60] *Vit. Const.* 3.35–36: διέβαινε δ' ἑξῆς ἐπὶ παμμεγέθη χῶρον εἰς καθαρὸν αἰθέρα ἀναπεπταμένον, ὅν δὴ λίθος λαμπρὸς κατεστρωμένος ἐπ' ἐδάφους ἐκόσμει, μακροῖς περιδρόμοις στοῶν ἐκ τριπλεύρου περιεχόμενον. τῷ γὰρ καταντικρὺ πλευρῷ τοῦ ἄντρου, ὃ δὴ πρὸς ἀνίσχοντα ἥλιον ἑώρα, ὁ βασίλειος συνῆπτο νεώς, ἔργον ἐξαίσιον εἰς ὕψος ἄπειρον ἠρμένον μήκους τε καὶ πλάτους ἐπὶ πλεῖστον εὐρυνόμενον·

[61] For the opinion that Anastasia was built later, see Charles Coüasnon, *The Church of the Holy Sepulchre in Jerusalem*, The Schweich Lectures of the British Academy, 1972 (London: British Academy, 1974), 14–17, 21–23. Note, however, the arguments in Vered Shalev-Hurvitz, *Holy Sites Encircled: The Early Byzantine Concentric Church of Jerusalem*, Oxford Studies in Byzantium (Oxford: Oxford University Press, 2015), 43–77. See also Ryan, *From the Passion* (cf. note 47), 117–19.

this background "the royal temple," which was "raised to immense height," and the tomb itself, which looked towards the east where the heavenly Jerusalem was situated, would indicate that the architectural structures of the Holy Sepulchre, according to Eusebius, are related to the New Jerusalem, that is, the Heavenly Jerusalem.

Sixth, in his *Vit. Const.* Eusebius emphasizes Constantine's willingness to give offerings to God by building a precious church (or temple) in Jerusalem (see *Vit. Const.* 3.38, 40 quoted above). Because the Holy Sepulchre was purposed to be a replica of the Heavenly Jerusalem, Constantine's offerings can be regarded as corresponding to what Eusebius writes about the Heavenly Jerusalem at the end of his commentary when he interprets Isa 66:18–20 as follows:

> Therefore, just as those who prescribed the worship in the earthly Jerusalem according to the bodily law then practiced these things, so in accord with the earthly example shall those who ascend into the heavenly Jerusalem come with their own fruits. And each will offer the most excellent fruit-bearing gifts in his life.[62]

Because the Holy Sepulchre is called the "New Jerusalem" and is, therefore, a symbol of the Heavenly Jerusalem, it is justified to emphasize Constantine's precious presents to the church.

Conclusions

This essay is a contribution toward understanding Eusebius's way of interpreting the book of Isaiah, especially Isa 2:1–4, and it illustrates well that which took place in the Constantinian shift when Christianity suddenly gained political power. As scholars have rightly noted previously, Eusebius changed his mind concerning the holiness of Christian places after the Constantinian shift. While scholars have emphasized that the Holy Sepulchre, called the New Jerusalem, was related to the image of Rev 21–22, I have argued here that Eusebius related the Holy Sepulchre to the theology of the prophets, especially to the book of Isaiah.

Eusebius had to re-evaluate his attitudes towards holy places, and in so doing, his criticism towards Judaism (and towards Jewish-Christian groups) intensified. This is evident in his way of interpreting Isa 1:8–9. Earlier, Eusebius had followed the Pauline exegesis presented in Rom 9–11, according to which Isa 1:8–9 witnessed to the Jewish-Christian remnant who also inherited all prophetic promises. Subsequently, however, Eusebius more or less actively forgot Paul's exegesis.

---

[62] *Comm. Isa.* 408 (Armstrong, *Commentary*, 319): ὥσπερ οὖν τότε κατὰ τὸν σωματικὸν νόμον ἐπὶ τῆς ἐπιγείου Ἱερονσαλήμ ταυτ' ἔπραττον οἱ τὴν λατρείαν ἐπιτελοῦντες, τὸν αὐτὸν τρόπον κατὰ τὸ ἐπὶ γῆς παράδειγμα οἱ εἰς τὴν ἐπουράνιον Ἱερονσαλὴμ ἀνιόντες ἥξουσι μετὰ τῶν οἰκείων καρπῶν, καὶ ὧν ἕκαστος ἐν τῇ ψυχῇ ἐπικομίζεται δώρων ἐκ τῆς τῶν ἀρετῶν καρποφορίας.

After the Constantinian shift, Eusebius's interpretation of these two passages from Isaiah seem to express a black and white alternative: Judaism will die, Christianity will prosper. In *Ecl. proph.* and *Dem. ev.,* Eusebius continued to follow an old Jewish-Christian parenesis toward Jews, which was deeply rooted in intra-Jewish debates concerning the messianic status of Jesus of Nazareth. In that debate, Isa 1:8–9 was employed to exhort the Jewish people to grasp what had taken place in history when Jerusalem and its city were destroyed.[63] After the Constantinian shift, a new politically justified trend began to dominate in Eusebius's interpretation. Jerusalem had become a Christian city and the fulfilment of Isaiah's prophecies was at hand. Therefore, Jews had to choose. There was no longer an alternative remnant of Judaism, that is, Christian Judaism in which the Mosaic Torah could be followed; only Christianity and Judaism remained. In the former the Mosaic Torah was interpreted christologically; in the latter the instructions of the Mosaic Torah were followed. Therefore, Eusebius no longer spoke about the remnant of the Jewish people when interpreting Isa 1:8–9. Everything in the New Jerusalem witnessed the victory of the Christian church over paganism and Judaism. It is remarkable how evasive a move Eusebius made in his interpretations. Perhaps it seems an almost insignificant of scriptural exegesis. Its influence, however, has been enormous, for it eliminated the possibility that a Jewish-Christian group could continue to exist within the church.

---

[63] Of course, Eusebius's treatment of Jews in these earlier works is not objective. See further Jörg Ulrich, *Euseb von Caesarea und die Juden: Studien zur Rolle der Juden in der Theologie des Eusebius von Caesarea*, Patristische Texte und Studien 49 (Berlin: De Gruyter, 1999); Eduard Iricinschi, "Good Hebrew, Bad Hebrew: Christians as *Triton Genos* in Eusebius' Apologetic Writings," in Inowlocki and Zamagni, *Reconsidering Eusebius* (cf. note 1), 69–86.

Revelation 20 and 21 and the New Jerusalem According to Ambrosiaster and Jerome*

Alessandro Capone

> Debitum ergo reddis,
> non largiris indebitum
> (Ambrose, *De Nabuthae historia* 12.53)

Introduction

As is well known, Jerome very likely oversaw the revision of Victorinus of Petovium's *Commentary on the Apocalypse* in the spring of 398.[1] As he himself declares, he made corrections to Victorinus's text with respect to the millennialist interpretation, literal explanations, and the various errors that were brought into it due to the inexperience of text copyists. Indeed, in the prologue Jerome declares that he immediately reread the books of the ancient authors and from them obtained information about the millennial reign that he incorporated into his recension of Victorinus's *Commentary*.[2]

In the present contribution, I will focus on the ending that Jerome added to Victorinus's text in order to explain Rev 20 and 21. It is in this passage that Jerome provides an allegorical interpretation that replaces the millenarian one proposed by Victorinus.[3] Instead of seeking to treat Jerome's interpretation of

---

* I would like to thank Rita Bennett for helping to improve my English and Andrew Cain and Nathan Betz for some helpful tips.

[1] See Martine Dulaey, "Jérôme 'éditeur' du *Commentaire sur l'Apocalypse* de Victorin de Poetovio," *Revue des études augustiniennes* 37, no. 2 (1991): 203–7. See also Carmelo Curti, "Girolamo e il millenarismo di Vittorino di Petovio," *Annali di Storia dell'Esegesi* 15, no. 1 (1998): 195, who considers the dating, based on the reference to Jerome's disease, not unlikely. As will be seen below, however, this dating of Jerome's revision may now be made with much greater certainty.

[2] Cf. Jerome, *Expl. Apoc.* Prol. (Roger Gryson, ed., *Victorini Poetovionensis Explanatio in Apocalypsin una cum recensione Hieronymi*, CCSL 5 [Turnhout: Brepols, 2017], 109): *Et quia me litteris obtestatus es, nolui differre, sed ne spernerem precantem, maiorum statim libros reuolui et quod in eorum commentariis de mille annorum regno repperi Victorini opusculis sociaui, ablatis inde quae ipse secundum litteram senserit*.

[3] On Victorinus's millennialism, which appears moderate and open to the influences of Alexandrian thought, see Carmelo Curti, "Il regno millenario in Vittorino di Petovio,"

Rev 20–21 exhaustively, I will highlight three points that will shed particular light on Jerome's approach. Specifically, I will focus on (1) the sources that might have informed Jerome's interpretation, (2) an identical interpretation of the New Jerusalem that Jerome offers elsewhere in his *corpus,* and (3) polemical references that Jerome makes with reference to the exegesis of Revelation that was proposed by Ambrosiaster.

1 The Number One Thousand

In introducing his interpretation of chapters 20 and 21 of Revelation, Jerome immediately clarifies that the millennial kingdom described in the text is not an earthly kingdom or, if it is, that it has an end. Jerome thereby makes clear that his interpretation of these chapters stands in stark contrast both to that of Victorinus, whose commentary he was correcting, and to that of Ambrosiaster, whose views on the New Jerusalem were well known to Jerome.[4] The thousand-year kingdom of Rev 20:6–7, Jerome writes, reflects the number of Christian perfection. The number one thousand, he reasons, is the product of ten – which indicates the Decalogue[5] – and one hundred – which represents the crown of virginity.[6] This interpretation of the number one hundred, so necessary to his

---

Augustinianum 18 (1978): 419–33. See also Konrad Huber's contribution to the present volume. On the history of the patristic exegesis of Revelation, see Clementina Mazzucco, "La Gerusalemme celeste dell' 'Apocalisse' nei Padri," in *'La dimora di Dio con gli uomini' (Ap 21,3): immagini della Gerusalemme celeste dal III al XIV secolo,* ed. Maria Louisa Gatti Perer (Milan: Vita e Pensiero, 1983), 49–75; Roger Gryson, "Les commentaires patristiques latins de l'Apocalypse (à suivre)," *Revue théologique de Louvain* 28, no. 3 (1997): 305–37; and Roger Gryson, "Les commentaires patristiques latins de l'Apocalypse (suite et fin)," *Revue théologique de Louvain* 28, no. 4 (1997): 484–502.

[4] Cf. Jerome, *Expl. Apoc.* 5 (Gryson, *Explanatio* [cf. note 2], 253): *Nam mille annorum regnum non arbitror esse terrenum, aut si ita sentiendum est, completis annis mille regnare desinunt.* Cf. in parallel Victorinus's text and Jerome's revision: Victorinus, *Expl. Apoc.* 5 (252): *Coccineum autem diabolum includi et omnes angelos eius refugas in tartarum gehennae in aduentum domini nemo ignoret <et> post mille annos dimitti propter gentes quae seruiuerint Antichristo, ut ipsae solae pereant, quia sic meruerunt, dein fieri catholice iudicium;* Jerome, *Expl. Apoc.* 5 (253): *"Mille anni" in quibus alligatus est Satanas isti sunt ab aduentu primo Christi usque ad terminum saeculi, mille autem dicti eo loquendi modo quo pars significatur a toto, sicut est illud* uerbi quod mandauit in mille generationes, *dum non sunt mille.* Even for Ambrosiaster the millennial reign is earthly, as evidenced by the insistence on the adverb *hic*: Ambrosiaster, *Comm. Matt. frag.* 2.9, 10, 12 (Alessandra Pollastri, ed., *Ambrosiaster. Frammenti esegetici su Matteo,* Biblioteca patristica 50 [Bologna: Edizioni Dehoniane, 2014] 224, 226, 234, 236 and notes).

[5] See Alessandro Capone, "Numeri e simboli nell'esegesi geronimiana dei Salmi," *Rivista di Cultura Classica e Medioevale* 59, no. 1 (2017): 164–72.

[6] Cf. Jerome, *Expl. Apoc.* 5 (*Explanatio* [cf. note 2], 253–255): *Denarius numerus decalogum significat, centenarius uirginitatis coronam ostendit.* On the symbolism of the number one hundred see Heinz Meyer, Rudolf Suntrup, *Lexikon der mittelalterlichen Zahlenbedeutungen,* Münstersche Mittelalter-Schriften (Munich: Wilhelm Fink, 1987), coll. 792–793.

view of the millennium, finds a significant parallel in his *Aduersus Iovinianum* 1.3 (AD 393) with reference to the parable of the sower (Matt 13:8).[7]

This passage from *Aduersus Iovinianum* is significant for our inquiry for at least two reasons. First, it allows us to place Jerome's interpretation of the three numbers mentioned in the parable of the sower – one hundred, sixty, and thirty – within contemporary Latin culture. This is clearly demonstrated by the finger-based computing system in use in imperial Rome to which Jerome refers.[8] His understanding of the millennium, therefore, does not seem influenced, even in its symbolic value, by the Greek tradition. Second, it suggests linking not only the texts but also the contexts of Bethlehem, where Jerome was writing in 398, and Rome, where *Aduersus Iovinianum* was addressed a few years earlier in 393. Consequently, it is possible to discern a connection between the direct or indirect recipients of Jerome's controversy in both 393 and 398. In other words, the elements of affinity between the two Hieronymian texts in question – *De explanatione Apocalypsis prologus* and *Aduersus Iovinianum* 1.3 – suggest that Jerome is arguing, albeit a few years later, with a certain literalist exegetical tendency surrounding the interpretation of the number one thousand that was still active in Rome at the time that he revised Victorinus's *Commentary* on Revelation.

---

[7] Jerome, *Jov.* 1.3 (*PL* 23:223B–224A): *Centesimus et sexagesimus et tricesimus fructus quanquam de una terra, et de una semente nascatur, tamen multum differt in numero. Triginta referuntur ad nuptias. Nam et ipsa digitorum coniunctio, quasi molli se complexans osculo, et foederans, maritum pingit et coniugem. Sexaginta uero ad uiduas, eo quod in angustia et tribulatione sunt positae. Unde et superiori digito deprimuntur; quantoque maior est difficultas expertae quondam uoluptatis illecebris abstinere, tanto maius est praemium. Porro centesimus numerus (diligenter, quaeso, lector, attende) de sinistra transfertur ad dexteram, et iisdem quidem digitis, sed non eum manu, quibus in laeua nuptae significantur et uiduae, circulum faciens, exprimit uirginitatis coronam.* Cf. Jerome, *Epist.* 49.2 (Isidorus Hilberg, ed., *Sancti Hieronymi Eusebii epistulae* [Vindobonae, Lipsiae: F. Tempsky, G. Freytag, 1910], 353–54): note that this letter addressed to Pammachius in 393 quotes the long passage from the *Aduersus Iovinianum* in response to accusations of the excessive, almost Manichean, praise of virginity by Jerome over marriage: see Andrew Cain, *The Letters of Jerome: Asceticism, Biblical Exegesis, and the Construction of Christian Authority in Late Antiquity* (Oxford: Oxford University Press, 2009), 137. Cf. also *Epist.* 107.13 (Hilberg, *Epistulae*, 304): *Sit in gremio auiae, quae repetat in nepte, quidquid praemisit in filia, quae longo usu didicit nutrire, docere, seruare uirgines, in cuius corona centenarii cotidie numeri castitas texitur; Epist.* 123.8 (p. 82): *Nam cum in semente terrae bonae centesimum et sexagesimum et tricesimum fructum euangelia doceant et centenarius pro uirginitatis corona primum gradum teneat, sexagenarius pro labore uiduarum in secundo sit numero, tricenarius foedera nuptiarum ipsa digitorum coniunctione testetur, digamia in quo erit numero?* On this type of interpretation and on other Hieronymian passages see Antonio Quacquarelli, *Il triplice frutto della vita cristiana: 100, 60 e 30 (Matteo XIII – 8, nelle diverse interpretazioni)* (Roma: Edipuglia, 1953), 43–47.

[8] See Quacquarelli, *Il triplice frutto* (cf. note 7), 37–42; Henri-Irénée Marrou, "L'évangile de vérité et la diffusion du comput digital dans l'antiquité," *Vigiliae Christianae* 12, no. 2 (1958): 98–103 (= Henri-Irénée Marrou, *Christiana tempora: Mélanges d'histoire, d'archéologie, d'épigraphie et de patristique*, Collection de l'École Française de Rome 35 [Rome: École française de Rome, 1978], 331–36).

Writing just two weeks before Easter 398 (April 18) – and thus around the same time as he was writing his *Commentary on the Apocalypse* – Jerome in *Commentary on Matthew* 2.13.23 refers back explicitly to *Aduersus Iovinianum* and proposes the same numerological interpretation, albeit in a more succinct way.[9] In fact, Jerome wrote his *Commentary on Matthew* at the request of Eusebius of Cremona, who would have left the monastery of Bethlehem, accompanied by Jerome's brother Paulinus, and who wanted to bring the commissioned writing to Rome. On two occasions in this work, Jerome alludes to the poor health he had experienced in the three months leading up to his writing the Matthew commentary: he hopes to be able to complete his work *si autem mihi uita longior fuerit*[10] and hints at the possibility of commenting more extensively on the book of *Exodus si uita comes fuerit*.[11] Tellingly, Jerome makes a similar comment at the end of the prologue to the *Commentary on the Apocalypse*: *Si uita nobis comes fuerit et dominus sanitatem dederit, tibi nostrum in hoc uolumine potissimum sudabit ingenium, Anatoli carissime*.[12] These data, combined with the common numerological interpretation adduced above and presented for the first time in *Aduersus Iovinianum*, lead us to realize two things. On the one hand, they indicate that the *Commentary on the Apocalypse* and the *Commentary on Matthew* were composed at roughly the same time and could therefore share similar content; on the other hand, they reasonably suggest once again that Jerome

---

[9] Jerome, *Comm. Matt.* 2.13.23 (David Hurst and Marcus Adriaen, ed., *Sancti Hieronymi Presbyteri. Commentariorum in Mathaeum libri iv*, CCSL 77 [Turnhout: Brepols, 1969], 106): *Primum ergo debemus audire, deinde intelligere, et post intelligentiam fructus reddere doctrinarum et facere uel centesimum fructum uel sexagesimum atque tricesimum; de quibus plenius in libro contra Iouinianum diximus et nunc breuiter perstringimus, centesimum fructum uirginibus, sexagesimum uiduis et continentibus, tricesimum sancto matrimonio deputantes.* See the notes *ad locum* in Daniela Scardia, ed., *Girolamo. Commento a Matteo* (Roma: Città Nuova, 2022), 290–291. Note that there was a millennial interpretation of the numbers one hundred, sixty, and thirty in the parable of the sower: cf. Irenaeus, *Haer.* 5.36.1–2 (Adelin Rousseau, Louis Doutreleau, and Charles Mercier, ed., *Contre les hérésies. Livre 5: édition critique d'après les versions arménienne et latine*, SC 153 [Paris: Cerf, 1969], 456–58): Καθὼς οἱ πρεσβύτεροι λέγουσι, τότε οἱ μὲν καταξιωθέντες τῆς ἐν οὐρανῷ διατριβῆς ἐκεῖσε χωρήσουσιν, οἱ δὲ τῆς τοῦ παραδείσου τρυφῆς ἀπολαύσουσιν, οἱ δὲ τὴν καλλονὴν καὶ τὴν λαμπρότητα τῆς πόλεως καθέξουσιν, σὺν πᾶσι τοῖς περὶ αὐτὴν ἀγαθοῖς ἐπιχορηγουμένοις ὑπὸ τοῦ Θεοῦ, πανταχοῦ δὲ ὁ Σωτὴρ ὁραθήσεται, καθὼς ἄξιοι ἔσονται οἱ ὁρῶντες αὐτόν. Εἶναι δὲ τὴν διαστολὴν ταύτην τῆς οἰκήσεως τῶν τὰ ἑκατὸν καρποφορούντων καὶ τῶν τὰ ἑξήκοντα καὶ τῶν τὰ τριάκοντα, ὧν οἱ μὲν εἰς τοὺς οὐρανοὺς ἀναληφθήσονται, οἱ δὲ ἐν τῷ παραδείσῳ διατρίψουσιν, οἱ δὲ τὴν πόλιν κατοικήσουσιν.

[10] Jerome, *Comm. Matt.* praef. (Hurst and Adriaen, *Commentariorum* [cf. note 9], 5); see the notes *ad locum* in Scardia, *Commento* (cf. note 9), 74.

[11] Jerome, *Comm. Matt.* 4.26.1–2 (Hurst and Adriaen, *Commentariorum* [cf. note 9], 245); see the notes *ad locum* in Scardia, *Commento* (cf. note 9), 567.

[12] Jerome, *Expl. Apoc.* Prol. (Gryson, *Explanatio* [cf. note 2], 109). On Anatolius, of whom almost nothing is known, see Dulaey, "Jérôme 'éditeur'" (cf. note 1), 201. Alfons Fürst, *Hieronymus: Askese und Wissenschaft in der Spätantike* (Freiburg i. Br.: Herder, 2003), 155.

intends to specifically address Rome, which, as indicated above, was the intended destination of his *Commentary on Matthew*.

Jerome seems to be aware of the interpretation attested in the work of the anonymous author known as "Ambrosiaster." Indeed, we observe Ambrosiaster using Matt 13:8 and 23 together with other scriptural passages (e. g. Ps 1 and 1 Cor 15:52–53) according to a millennialist perspective, this in order to distinguish three categories of men in relation to their eschatological fate. These three categories are the righteous, the wicked, and the sinners.[13] We find this interpretation explicitly in his explanation of 1 Cor 15:41 and implied in the fragment *De tribus mensuris* of Ambrosiaster's *Commentary on Matthew*.[14] Ambrosiaster presents the anthropological and eschatological tripartition in *Quaestio* 110 as well, when he comments on Ps 1:5.[15]

By providing in his recension of Victorinus's *Commentary* a symbolic interpretation of the number one thousand – one based, as we have seen, on a unique aspect of Latin counting culture – in opposition to a literal interpretation of the number, Jerome is able to distance himself from Victorinus's eschatological reading of Revelation and to introduce a spiritual reading of Alexandrian origin.[16] According to this allegorical reading, the thousand years of the devil's captivity, represents how Christ's priests have killed impure actions and thoughts in

---

[13] See Emanuele Di Santo, *L'apologetica dell'Ambrosiaster. Cristiani, pagani e giudei nella Roma tardoantica*, Studia Ephemeridis Augustinianum 112 (Rome: Institutum Patristicum Augustinianum, 2008), 396–99. On the eschatological vision of Ambrosiaster with particular reference to his *Commentary on Matthew*, see Pollastri, *Frammenti* (cf. note 4), 102–35.

[14] Cf. Ambrosiaster, *Comm. 1 Cor.* 15.41 (Heinrich J. Vogels, ed., *Ambrosiastri qui dicitur Commentarius in Epistulas Paulinas* pars secunda, *in epistulas ad Corinthios* [Vienna: Hoelder, Pichler, Tempsky, 1968], 179–80): *Unius naturae comparatione utitur ad indiscretae substantiae reddendam rationem, quia sicut sol et luna et stellae, cum sint unius quidem naturae, diversae tamen claritatis sunt, ita et homines, cum sint unius generis, merito tamen dissimiles erunt in gloria, ut claritati solis illorum dignitas exaequetur, qui centesimum numerum habent, qui ut perfecti essent primi gradus aemuli fuerunt, de quibus dictum est:* tunc iusti fulgebunt sicut sol in regno patris sui. *Lunari autem claritati hi conparandi sunt, qui sexagesimum numerum bonis operibus mercati sunt, ut secundi gradus meritum haberent. Stellis autem clarioribus eorum merita comparanda sunt, qui tricesimum numerum, tertii gradus dignitatem iustis laboribus quaesiverunt.* Cf. also Ambrosiaster *Comm. Matt. frag.* 4 (Pollastri, *Frammenti* [cf. note 4], 254) and the notes *ad locum*.

[15] Cf. Ambrosiast. *Quaest.* 110.17 (Alexander Souter, ed., *Pseudo-Augustini quaestiones veteris et novi testamenti CXXVII*, [Vienna: F. Tempsky, 1908], 276–77): *In hoc psalmo tria genera hominum significat: impiorum et peccatorum et iustorum, quo ordine coeptus est error. sed impii ab his alieni sunt, quia sub dei decreto, sicut dixi, uiuere noluerunt; peccatores autem sub dei lege agentes ante tribunal Christi sistendi sunt segregati a iustis, ut acceptae legis praestent rationem, emendandi in quibus operam non dederunt, ut plus haberent laudis quam uituperationis; iusti uero ualde propensiores in exercitio implendae legis inuenti remunerandi sunt.* See Alessandra Pollastri, "Escatologia e Scrittura nell'Ambrosiaster," *Annali di Storia dell'Esegesi* 17, no. 1 (2000): 117.

[16] See Dulaey, "Jérôme 'éditeur'" (cf. note 1). For Victorinus's interpretation of the New Jerusalem, see the contribution of Konrad Huber to the present volume.

their hearts, thereby chaining up the devil. Those who are prey to the heretics, however, have abandoned the virginity of both heart and body and allow the devil free rein. For Jerome, the period of a thousand years is not a chronological indication; rather, it is a number that indicates that the number of saints is complete.[17]

2 The Description of the Holy City

Having dispensed with the literal interpretation of the millennium, Jerome can dwell on the description of the city that is presented in Rev 21:16–21 and explain the symbolic value of some of its details.

One among these details is the city's square shape.[18] Traditionally, the square is a symbol of stability. Philo, for instance, understands the square with reference to fair argumentation, equality, justice, and perfection.[19] Origen, too, considers it

---

[17] Cf. Jerome, *Expl. Apoc.* 5 (Gryson, *Explanatio* [cf. note 2], 255–57): *Qui enim uirginitatis integrum seruauerit qui enim uirginitatis integrum seruauerit propositum et decalogi fideliter praecepta impleuerit et impuros mores uel impuras cogitationes intra cordis cubiculum iugulauerit, ne ne dominentur ei, iste uere sacerdos est Christi et millenarium numerum perficiens integre creditur regnare cum Christo et recte apud eum ligatus est diabolus. Qui uero uitiis et dogmatibus hereticorum irretitus est, in eo solutus est diabolus. Sed quia completis mille annis dicit eum solui, completo perfectorum sanctorum numero, in quibus corpore et corde uirginitas regnat ....*

[18] Jerome, *Expl. Apoc.* 5 (Gryson, *Explanatio* [cf. note 2], 259): "*Ciuitatem quadratam*" *sanctorum adunatam turbam ostendit, in quibus nullo modo fides fluctuare potuit, sicut ad Noe praecipitur ut ex quadratis lignis faceret arcam, quae diluuii posset impetus ferre.*

[19] Cf. Philo, *Plant.* 121–122 (Leopold Cohn and Paul Wendland, ed., *Philonis Alexandrini opera quae supersunt*, vol. 2 [Berlin: Reimer, 1897], 157): Πρεσβύτατός τε αὖ τετραγώνων ὁ ἀριθμὸς ὢν ἐν ὀρθαῖς γωνίαις, ὡς τὸ κατὰ γεωμετρίαν δηλοῖ σχῆμα, ἐξετάζεται· αἱ δ᾽ εἰσὶν ὀρθότητος λόγου σαφῆ δείγματα, πηγὴ δὲ ἀέναος ἀρετῶν ὁ ὀρθὸς λόγος. ἀνάγκη μέντοι τὰς τοῦ τετραγώνου πλευρὰς ἴσας εἶναι· δικαιοσύνην δὲ ἰσότης τὴν ἔξαρχον καὶ ἡγεμονίδα τῶν ἀρετῶν ἔτεκεν· ὥστε ἰσότητος καὶ δικαιοσύνης καὶ πάσης ἀρετῆς χωρὶς τῶν ἄλλων ἐπιδείκνυται τὸν ἀριθμὸν εἶναι σύμβολον; Philo, *Opif.* 49–50 (Leopold Cohn, ed., *Philonis Alexandrini opera quae supersunt*, vol. 1, [Berlin: Reimer, 1896], 16):"Ἔστι δὲ καὶ δύναμις ἄλλη τετράδος λεχθῆναί τε καὶ νοηθῆναι θαυμασιωτάτη. πρώτη γὰρ αὕτη τὴν τοῦ στερεοῦ φύσιν ἔδειξε, τῶν πρὸ αὐτῆς ἀριθμῶν τοῖς ἀσωμάτοις ἀνακειμένων· κατὰ μὲν γὰρ τὸ ἓν τάττεται τὸ λεγόμενον ἐν γεωμετρίᾳ σημεῖον, κατὰ δὲ τὰ δύο γραμμή, διότι ῥύσει μὲν ἑνὸς δυάς, ῥύσει δὲ σημείου συνίσταται γραμμή· γραμμὴ δ᾽ ἐστὶ μῆκος ἀπλατές· πλάτους δὲ προσγενομένου γίνεται ἐπιφάνεια, ἣ τέτακται κατὰ τριάδα· ἐπιφανείᾳ δὲ πρὸς τὴν τοῦ στερεοῦ φύσιν ἑνὸς δεῖ τοῦ βάθους, ὃ προστεθὲν τριάδι γίνεται τετράς. ὅθεν καὶ μέγα χρῆμα συμβέβηκεν εἶναι τὸν ἀριθμὸν τοῦτον, ὃς ἐκ τῆς ἀσωμάτου καὶ νοητῆς οὐσίας ἤγαγεν εἰς ἔννοιαν ἡμᾶς τριχῇ διαστατοῦ σώματος τοῦ φύσει πρώτου αἰσθητοῦ. ὁ δὲ μὴ συνεὶς τὸ λεγόμενον ἔκ τινος παιδιᾶς εἴσεται πάνυ συνήθους. οἱ καρυατίζοντες εἰώθασι τρία ἐν ἐπιπέδῳ κάρυα προτιθέντες ἐπιφέρειν ἕν, σχῆμα πυραμοειδὲς ἀπογεννῶντες· τὸ μὲν οὖν ἐν ἐπιπέδῳ τρίγωνον ἵσταται μέχρι τριάδος, τὸ δ᾽ ἐπιτεθὲν τετράδα μὲν ἐν ἀριθμοῖς, ἐν δὲ σχήμασι πυραμίδα γεννᾷ, στερεὸν ἤδη σῶμα; Philo, *Vit. Mos.* 128 (Leopold Cohn and Paul Wendland, ed., *Philonis Alexandrini opera quae supersunt*, vol. 4 [Berlin: Reimer, 1902], 230): Σχῆμα δ᾽ ἀπένειμεν ὁ τεχνίτης τετράγωνον τῷ λογείῳ πάνυ καλῶς αἰνιττόμενος, ὡς χρὴ καὶ τὸν τῆς φύσεως λόγον καὶ τὸν τοῦ ἀνθρώπου βεβηκέναι πάντῃ καὶ κατὰ μηδ᾽ ὁτιοῦν κραδαίνεσθαι. παρὸ καὶ τὰς εἰρημένας δύο ἀρετὰς προσεκλήρωσεν

a symbol of security and strength and in that sense interprets the square beams of Noah's ark.[20] Jerome's own interpretation appears to be indebted directly to an Origenian explanation, which is in turn inserted into a previous tradition. Importantly, Jerome mentions a similar type of explanation in *Epistle* 46, written in the spring of 386.[21] There, the interpretation of the square city as the assembled multitude of saints – here Jerome refers to Heb 12:22–23 – may therefore be identified as a premise of Jerome's exegesis.

Jerome then goes on to comment on Rev 21:19–20, where it is said that the city is adorned with all kinds of precious stones. These stones Jerome interprets according to a spiritual interpretation.[22] The possible Origenian roots of this

---

αὐτῷ, δηλωσίν τε καὶ ἀλήθειαν· ὅ τε γὰρ τῆς φύσεως λόγος ἀληθὴς καὶ δηλωτικὸς πάντων ὅ τε τοῦ σοφοῦ μιμούμενος ἐκεῖνον ὀφείλει προσηκόντως ἀψευδέστατός τε εἶναι τιμῶν ἀλήθειαν καὶ μηδὲν φθόνῳ συσκιάζειν, ὧν ἡ μήνυσις ὠφελήσει τοὺς ἀναδιδαχθέντας.

[20] Cf. Origen, *Hom. Gen.* 2.4 (Willem A. Baerhens, ed., *Origenes. Homilien zum Hexateuch in Rufins Übersetzung*. Erster Teil, *Die Homilien zu Genesis, Exodus und Leviticus* (Leipzig: Hinrichs'sche Buchhandlung, 1920], 32): *Quadratum est quod nulla vacillat ex parte, sed quocumque verteris, fida et solida stabilitate consistit*; Origen, *Frag. Cor.* 16.1.3.16–20 (Francesco Pieri, ed., *Origene. Esegesi paolina. i testi frammentari*, vol 14/4 [Roma: Città nuova, 2009], 84–86): Εἰ θέλεις ἀληθινὸν ναὸν τοῦ Θεοῦ μαθεῖν, ζήτει λίθους ζῶντας καὶ καθαροὺς λελατομημένους, ὑπὸ τοῦ λόγου βεβληκότας, καὶ ἑστῶτας τετραγώνους, μηδὲν ἔχοντας ἄστατον μηδὲ κυλιόμενον· εἰ γὰρ καὶ λίθοι ἅγιοι κυλίονται ἐπὶ τῆς γῆς, ἀλλ' οἱ λατόμοι οὐκ ἐῶσιν αὐτοὺς μέχρι τέλους κυλίεσθαι.

[21] Cf. Jerome, *Epist.* 46.6 (Hilberg, *Epistulae* [cf. note 7], 335–36): *Nec statim potes dicere sanctam dici Hierusalem caelestem, quae futura est, et Aegyptum et Sodomam eam, quae conruit, appellari, quia de futura dicitur, quod bestia, quae ascensura est de abysso, faciat aduersus duos prophetas bellum et uincat illos et occidat et corpora eorum iaceant in plateis ciuitatis magnae. de qua ciuitate et in fine eiusdem libri scribitur*: *et ciuitas in quadrato posita est et longitudo eius et latitudo tanta est, quanta et altitudo. et mensus est ciuitatem de harundine per stadia duodecim milia. longitudo et latitudo et altitudo eius aequalia sunt. et mensus est muros eius centum quadraginta quattuor cubitorum mensura hominis, quae est angeli. et erat structura muri eius ex lapide iaspide, ipsa uero ciuitas auro mundo et cetera*. *ubi quadrum est, nec longitudo nec latitudo appellari potest. et quae est ista mensura, ut tanta sit longitudo et latitudo, quanta et altitudo eius, et muri de lapide iaspide et tota ciuitas de auro mundo et fundamenta et plateae eius de lapidibus pretiosis et duodecim portae fulgentes margaritis?* It is now common opinion that the letter was written by Jerome and not by Paula and Eustochium. On the dating of this letter see Pierre Nautin, "La Lettre de Paule et Eustochium à Marcelle (Jérôme, *Ep.* 46)," *Augustinianum* 24 (1984): 441–48. See also Neil Adkin, "The Letter of Paula and Eustochium to Marcella: Some Notes," *Maia* 51 (1999): 97–110.

[22] Jerome, *Expl. Apoc.* 5 (Gryson, *Explanatio* [cf. note 2], 259–61): *"Pretiosos lapides" fortes in persecutione uiros ostendit, qui nec tempestate persecutorum moueri nec impetu pluuiae a uera fide dissolui potuerunt; propterea "auro mundo" sociantur, ex quibus regis magni ciuitas decoratur. "Platea" uero eorum ostenditur corda ab omnibus mundata sordibus, ubi deambulet dominus. "Flumen" uero "uitae" spiritalis natiuitatis currere gratiam ostendit. "Lignum uitae ex utraque ripa" Christi secundum carnem ostendit aduentum, quem uenturum et passurum uetus lex praedixit et euangelio manifestatur. "Fructus" uero "duodecim per singulos menses" duodecim apostolorum diuersae gratiae ostenduntur, quas ab uno ligno crucis suscipientes populos fame consumptos uerbi dei praedicatione satiarunt. Et quia dicit "in ciuitate solem non esse necessarium," euidenter ostendit creatorem luminum inmaculatum fulgere in medio eius, cuius splendorem nullus poterit sensus cogitare nec lingua proloqui.*

spiritual interpretation have already been highlighted by Martine Dulaey, who notes that it focuses, as is typical of allegorical exegesis, on the details of the biblical text. Even so, it is useful to recall Victorinus's text, which is limited, at least in the first instance, to summarizing the characteristics of the city described in Revelation.[23]

A comparison of these two passages – Jerome's *Expl. Apoc.* 5 and Victorinus's *Expl. Apoc.* 5 – reveals two significant divergences between their respective explanations. The first concerns the concept of "kingdom," which Victorinus, in line with the millennialist tradition, considers on the basis of various scriptural passages to be a real and definite period of chronological time – a concept, as we have seen, that was rejected by Jerome. The second difference concerns the notion of "first resurrection" that Victorinus defines on the basis of two Pauline parallels (1 Thess 4:15–17 and 1 Cor 15:52). This notion and these passages will return in Ambrosiaster's exegesis. In this first resurrection, the manifestation of the holy city takes place as is described in Revelation: namely, that all who have reigned with Christ – whether they are those Jews who at the end of time have believed in the gospel due to the preaching of Elijah or those whom the Spirit proved to be virgins in body and tongue – will rise again.[24]

According to Rev 21:21–25 the holy city has twelve gates, three on each side, each of which is made of a single pearl and will never be closed. For these verses, too, Jerome again in contrast with Victorinus offers a spiritual interpretation. For Jerome, the four sides represent four virtues in relation to one another, namely prudence, fortitude, justice, and temperance.[25] In addition to the parallels to

---

[23] Victorinus, *Expl. Apoc.* 5 (Gryson, *Explanatio* [cf. note 2], 258): *In regno ergo et in prima resurrectione exhibetur "ciuitas sancta," quam dicit "descensuram de caelo" quadratam, differentium et preciositatis et coloris et generis lapidum circumdatam, "auro mundo," id est dilucido, "similem." "Cristallo" inquit "plateam" eius stratam; flumen uitae per medium effluens et uitae fontes aquarum; lignum uitae in circuitu per singulos menses faciens fructus differentes. Lumen ibi solis non esse propter eminentiorem gloriam; "agnus" enim, inquit, id est deus, "lux ei<u>s est."*

[24] Cf. Victorinus, *Expl. Apoc.* 5 (Gryson, *Explanatio* [cf. note 2], 254): *De hac resurrectione ait*: *Et uidi agnum stantem et cum eo centum quadraginta quatuor milia, id est cum Christo stantes, eos scilicet qui ex Iudeis in nouissimo tempore sunt credituri per praedicationem Heliae, quos non solum testatur spiritus corpore uirgineo, sed et lingua.*

[25] Jerome, *Expl. Apoc.* 5 (Gryson, *Explanatio* [cf. note 2], 263–65): *Quattuor arbitror esse uirtutes, prudentiam fortitudinem iustitiam temperantiam, quae inuicem sibi haerent et, dum mutuo miscentur, duodenarium efficiunt numerum. "Portae" uero "duodecim" apostolorum esse credimus numerum, qui in quattuor uirtutibus ut pretiosae margaritae fulgentes iter sanctis – lumen doctrinae suae – manifestantes ad ciuitatem sanctorum ingredi faciunt, ut de conuersatione eorum angelorum laetetur chorus. "Non posse claudi portas": euidenter ostenditur nulla contradicentium tempestate apostolorum doctrinam superari. Etiam fluctus gentium et hereticorum insana superstitione dum ad fidem ueram furiunt, superatae eorum spumae dissoluuntur, quia petra Christus est, a quo et per quem ecclesia fundata nullis fluctibus insanientium hominum superatur. Ergo audiendi non sunt qui mille annorum regnum terrenum esse confirmant, qui cum Cerintho heretico sentiunt.* Cf. Victorinus, *Expl. Apoc.* 5 (Gryson, *Explanatio* [cf. note 2], 258–60).

these passages that Dulaey finds in Jerome's pre-398 *corpus,* one must note a passage from a letter addressed to Pammachius that dates from the beginning of 398 (*Epist.* 66) and also incorporates the concept of the connection of the four virtues.[26] This, incidentally, might further confirm 398 as the year in which Jerome revised Victorinus's commentary. We may also note that *Epist.* 66 proposes relations with Rome, much like his *Commentary on the Apocalypse* seems to.

Building on this interpretation, Jerome goes on to explain that the twelve gates are like the apostles who, making the light of their doctrine shine like precious stones in the four virtues, show the saints the way to enter the holy city.[27] Furthermore, he interprets the fact that the city gates cannot be closed as a demonstration that the doctrine of the apostles will not be overturned by a storm of opponents, even if the waves of pagans and heretics rage against the true faith. In this final passage, it is also interesting to note an affinity with the conclusion of the contemporary *Commentary on Matthew*: *Usque ad consummationem saeculi cum discipulis se futurum esse promittit et illos ostendit semper esse uicturos et se numquam a credentibus recessurum.*[28] This passage, although not entirely perspicuous, seems clearer in the light of what Jerome affirms in his commentary on the final chapters of Revelation, since the victory over heretics and pagans is assured by the presence of Christ, on whose rock the church is founded.

3 Ambrosiaster and the Holy City

Ambrosiaster's adherence to millennialism is known, according to a tradition that runs through part of patristic production, to be especially Western.[29] At the same time, however, Ambrosiaster demonstrates a predilection for chronological

---

[26] Cf. Jerome, *Epist.* 66.3 (Hilberg, *Epistulae* [cf. note 7], 649): *Quattuor uirtutes describunt stoici ita sibi inuicem nexas et mutuo cohaerentes, ut, qui unam non habuerit, omnibus careat: prudentiam, iustitiam, fortitudinem, temperantiam. has omnes sic habetis singuli, ut tamen emineatis in singulis.* See Pierre Nautin, "La date de la mort de Pauline, de l'épître 66 de Jérôme et de l'épître 13 de Paulin de Nole," *Augustinianum* 18 (1978): 547–50. Cf. also Jerome, *Epist.* 64.20 (Hilberg, *Epistulae* [cf. note 7], 611) of 397: *Hoc autem rationale duplex, apertum et absconditum, simplex et musticum, duodecim in se lapides habens et quattuor ordines, quas quattuor puto esse uirtutes: prudentiam, fortitudinem, iustitiam, temperantiam, quae sibi haerent inuicem et, dum mutuo miscentur, duodenarium numerum efficiunt, uel quattuor euangelia, quae in apocalypsi describuntur plena oculis et domini luce radiantia mundum inluminant, in uno quattuor et in quattuor singula; unde et δήλωσις et ἀλήθεια, id est doctrina et ueritas, in pectore sacerdotis est.*

[27] See Meyer and Suntrup, *Lexikon* (cf. note 6), coll. 623–24.

[28] Jerome, *Comm. Matt.* 4.28.20 (Hurst and Adriaen, *Commentariorum* [cf. note 9], 283).

[29] See Manlio Simonetti, "Il millenarismo cristiano dal I al V secolo," and "Il millenarismo in Occidente," *Annali di Storia dell'Esegesi* 15, no. 1 (1998): 7–20 and 181–89.

developments and rejects the materialistic aspects of chiliasm.[30] This may be seen in the anonymous exegete's interpretation of 1 Cor 15:52 and Rev 20:3–7[31].

As has been noted above, Victorinus juxtaposes these same verses – 1 Cor 15:52 and Rev 20:3–7 – and interprets them in a millenarian key. Thanks to the Pauline reference to the last trumpet and to 1 Thess 4:15–17,[32] Victorinus distinguishes two resurrections, identified with the first and second trumpet respectively. In the first resurrection, that is, in the millennium, the Lord will reign, the antichrist will be imprisoned, and the righteous will be raised to immortality and will be transformed and showered with glory. In the second resurrection, that is, in the final judgment, those who have not risen in the first resurrection and have not reigned with Christ in the millennium will rise again. These, of course, are the ungodly, the sinners, and the guilty of all kinds.[33]

Closely related are notions found in several fragments of Ambrosiaster's *Commentary on Matthew*. In fragment 13, he presents what will happen at the end of the seventh millennium: the devil will be freed from prison and a war will begin against the saints together with Gog and Magog, who will then be annihilated.[34] However, it is above all in fragment 15 that he takes into consideration 1 Cor 15:52 and Rev 20:5, referring to some who interpret the first resurrection in reference to baptism on the basis of Col 3:1. To these Ambrosiaster counterpoises the

---

[30] See Di Santo, *L'apologetica* (cf. note 13), 190.

[31] Cf. Ambrosiaster *Comm. 1 Cor* 15.52 (Vogels [cf. note 14], 183–84): *In novissima tuba. Ideo novissima tuba, quia postremum bellum geretur adversus daemones et principes ac potestates et ipsum diabolum. hoc enim fiet post annos mille, quibus hic regnabit salvator extincto Antichristo, cum Satanas dimittetur de carcere suo ad seducendas gentes Gog et Magog, qui sunt daemones, ut pugnent adversus castra sanctorum. nec enim temporales homines poterunt adversum aeternos dimicare.*

[32] On these verses in Ambrosiaster see Pollastri, *Frammenti* (cf. note 4), 86–89.

[33] Cf. Victorinus, *Expl. Apoc.* 5 (Gryson, *Explanatio* [cf. note 2], 254–56): *In hac eadem prima resurrectione et ciuitas futura et speciosa per hanc scripturam expressa est. Hanc primam resurrectionem et Paulus ad ecclesiam Macedoniam ita dixit:* Hoc enim uobis ita dicimus, inquit, in uerbo dei quia ipse dominus suscitaturus in tuba dei descendet de caelo, et mortui in Christo stabunt primi, deinde nos qui uiuimus simul rapiemur cum eis in nubibus in obuiam domino <in aera et ita semper cum domino> erimus. *Audiuimus dici tubam, obseruandum est <quod> alio loco apostolus aliam tubam nominat. Ait ergo ad Corinthios:* In nouissima tuba mortui surgent, immortales fient, *et nos mutabimur. Mortuos quidem immortales ad poenas sustinendas surgituros dixit, nos autem mutari et gloria contegi manifestum est. Ubi esse ergo audiuimus nouissimam tubam, intelligere debemus et primam; haec autem sunt duae resurrectiones. Quotquot ergo non anticipauerint surgere in prima resurrectione et regnare cum Christo super orbem super gentes uniuersas, surgent in nouissima tuba post annos mille, id est in nouissima resurrectione, inter impios et peccatores et uarii generis commissores. Merito adiecit dicendo:* Beatus et sanctus qui habet partem in prima anastase, ad hu<n>c mors secunda non habet potestatem. Mors autem secunda castigatio est in infernum. See Pollastri, "Escatologia," (cf. note 15), 126–29, where it is emphasized how the anonymous exegete echoes both Victorinus's thought and terminology.

[34] Cf. Ambrosiaster, *Comm. Matt. frag.* 13 (Pollastri, *Frammenti* [cf. note 4], 236): see Pollastri, "Escatologia" (cf. note 15), 116–17. Cf. also Ambrosiaster, *Comm. Matt. frag.* 14 (Pollastri, *Frammenti* [cf. note 4], 238).

interpretation that the resurrection takes place through faith and not by sight and consequently the resurrection has to be understood in a real sense.

It is interesting to present in parallel this passage from fragment 15 of Ambrosiaster's *Commentary on Matthew*, a relevant passage from Tyconius's *Commentary on the Apocalypse*, and a corresponding passage from Jerome's revision of Victorinus's *Commentary on the Apocalypse*:

Table 1. Corresponding passages from Ambrosiaster, Tyconius, and Jerome.

Ambrosiaster, *Commentary on Matthew* 15 (Pollastri, *Frammenti*, 242)	Tyconius, *Commentary on Revelation* 7.20 (Gryson, *Expositio*, 220)[35]	Jerome, *Commentary on Revelation* 5 (Gryson, *Explantio*, 253–55)
Quamquam aliquibus "prima resurrectio" in baptismate facta uideatur, quia dicit apostolus "Si conresurrexistis cum Christo" et cetera; in baptismate enim "terrenus homo" deponitur et "caelestis" adsumitur, mori enim uidetur "in baptismo" et resurgere cum renascitur. Sed "per fidem non per speciem," quia hoc in spe habet, "non quod" iam "acciperit." Illa enim resurrectio iam uera non in uerbo sed in re, non quae speretur sed quae iam sit, "prima" et in dignitate et in numero, quia congruum est primum sanctos resurgere et regrare cum Christo.[36]	Ut ostenderet qui sunt isti mille anni, "haec est," inquit, "resurrectio prima," utique qua resurgimus per baptismum, sicut apostolus dicit: "Si consurrexistis cum Christo, quae sursum sunt quaerite," et iterum: "Tamquam ex mortuis uiuentes." Peccatum enim mors est, sicut idem dicit apostolus: "Cum essetis mortui delictis et peccatis uestris." Sicut prima mors in hac est uita per peccata, ita et prima resurrectio in hac est uita per remissionem peccatorum.	Quod autem ait "haec resurrectio prima est," duae sunt resurrectiones, sed prima resurrectio nunc est animarum per fidem, quae non permittit homines transire ad mortem secundam. De hac resurrectione dicit apostolus: Si resurrexistis cum Christo, quae sursum sunt quaerite.

These texts clearly show that Ambrosiaster's polemical allusion finds significant confirmation in Tyconius and Jerome. The importance of this observation takes on special significance if we consider the fact that they seem to be the only ones in which the first resurrection of Rev 20:5 is associated with baptism in Col 3:1.[37]

---

[35] Roger Gryson, ed., *Tyconii Afri Expositio Apocalypseos*, CCSL 107A (Turnhout: Brepols, 2011).

[36] See Pollastri, *Frammenti* (cf. note 4), 156–57 and 318.

[37] See Pollastri, "Escatologia" (cf. note 15), 116–17; Pollastri, *Frammenti* (cf. note 4), 156. See also Emanuela Prinzivalli, "L'Apocalisse tra Ticonio e Agostino," in *L'Apocalisse nel Medioevo. Atti del convegno internazionale dell'Università degli studi di Milano e della Società Internazionale per lo Studio del Medioevo Latino (S. I. S. M. E. L), Gargnano sul Garda, 18–20 maggio*

It is also relevant to note how the interpretation of Rev 20:5 of Ambrosiaster's *Commentary on Matthew* is placed in the context of the anti-Arian polemic, as shown by the closing of fragment 15,[38] on the basis of 1 Cor 15:24.[39] *Quaestio* 97 is also framed in an anti-Arian light. There, Ambrosiaster briefly recalls some verses of Revelation (20:6; 21:22–23). The anonymous exegete understands the passages of Revelation in the sense of proving that the Father and the Son have the same divinity, without this questioning the uniqueness of God.[40]

Finally, in *Quaestio* 112, Ambrosiaster interprets the walls of Jerusalem in Ps 50:28 with reference to the church and its construction by means of holy men, this on the basis of Rev 21:10–12.[41] In Ambrosiaster's interpretation, which he bases on Psalm 50, "church" here is understood in a spiritual sense, for the church is where spiritual sacrifice is offered that is pleasing to God – an offering that is therefore superior to the Jewish one. This type of explanation fits well into Ambrosiaster's millenarian trend, which, on the one hand, is part of a tradition attested in the West and, on the other hand, shuns the more concrete and naive aspects of millenarian teaching.[42]

2009, ed. Rossana E. Guglielmetti (Florence: Sismel. Edizioni del Galluzzo, 2011), 95–115 at 101–2. It is evident that, if Ambrosiaster's reference were also to Jerome, relevant consequences would arise concerning the chronology of the anonymous exegete; this, however, falls outside the scope of this contribution. Furthermore, we also note that, according to Dulaey, "Jérôme 'éditeur'" (cf. note 1), 221, Tyconius's work would be known outside Africa only after 426; which would be a further reason to regard Ambrosiaster's polemical allusion as referring to Jerome's text.

[38] Ambrosiaster, *Comm. Matt.* 15 (Pollastri, *Frammenti* [cf. note 4], 242): *Tradere autem est 'regnum Deo et Patri' post finem sub nomine 'Dei et Patris regnare' Filium, ut regnum sub Dei nomine sit non sub Christi, quia iam cognitum erit de Deo Deum esse Christum, ut sub uno nomine regnet Pater et Filius in saecula saeculorum.* See Pollastri, "Escatologia" (cf. note 15), 118.

[39] On this Pauline text in Ambrosiaster's exegesis, see Pollastri, *Frammenti* (cf. note 4), 173–77.

[40] Ambrosiaster, *Quaest.* 97.4 (Souter, *Quaestiones* [cf. note 15], 174): *Nam spiritus dicitur dei, idem spiritus dicitur et Christi; ecclesia dicitur dei, dicitur et Christi; adoratur deus, adoratur et Christus; seruitur deo, seruitur et Christo; sancti dicuntur sacerdotes dei, dicuntur et sacerdotes Christi; templum ciuitatis sanctae dicitur deus, similiter et Christus; lumine dei inlustrari dicitur ciuitas sancta, eodem modo et Christi; sedes dei est, nec non et Christi; iudex deus est, est et Christus, quia Eseias profeta in throno maiestatis Christum uidit sedentem dominum sabaoth, quod Arrii non negant.* See Alessandra Pollastri, "L'*Apocalisse* nell'Ambrosiaster: una lettura millenarista nella Roma del IV secolo?" in *Apokalypsis: Percorsi nell'Apocalisse di Giovanni in onore di Ugo Vanni,* ed. Elena Bosetti and Angelo Colacrai (Assisi: Cittadella, 2005): 203–733 at 722–23; Di Santo, *L'apologetica* (cf. note 13), 312–13.

[41] Ambrosiaster, *Quaest.* 112.28 (Souter, *Quaestiones* [cf. note 15], 297): *Et adiecit: et aedificentur muri Hierusalem. Quid est ut dicat: 'et aedificentur muri Hierusalem'? Numquid destructi fuerant? Sed muros Hierusalem dicens ecclesiam significat per fidem, quae in Christo disposita erat, construendam, cuius muri sancti esse homines intelleguntur docente nos Apocalypsi Iohannis apostoli. Quia et Hierusalem ciuitas et muri eius dei serui sunt intellegendi. Sciens ergo per Christum rex Dauid promissum, quod futurum erat ad liberationem seruorum dei, orat ut impleatur, id est, ut per fidem aedificetur ecclesia et liberentur sperantes de hac fide salutem.* See Pollastri, "L'*Apocalisse* nell'Ambrosiaster" (cf. note 40), 725.

[42] See Pollastri, *Frammenti* (cf. note 4), 156.

Conclusions

Commenting on Matt 27:52–53, Jerome observes that *sancta ciuitas* mentioned there can refer to both the heavenly Jerusalem and the earthly Jerusalem – even if elsewhere he had proscribed this double interpretation[43] – and specifies that the resurrection mentioned in these verses is not a general resurrection.[44] Because there is no hint of polemic in this passage, it is safe to conclude that Jerome was unfamiliar with Ambrosiaster's *Commentary on Matthew*,[45] where the author interprets Matt 27:52–53 as referring to a general resurrection. Indeed, if Jerome were aware of Ambrosiaster's teaching, he would surely have addressed it. After all, we know that in the spring of 398, in addition to composing *Commentary on Matthew* and revising Victorinus's *Commentary on the Apocalypse*, he had received an anonymous text on the interpretation of Melchizedek as a figure of the Holy Spirit – one that was later identified with Ambrosiaster's *Quaestio* 109 – the refutation of which occupies Jerome's *Epistle* 73.[46]

It seems legitimate, then, to place Jerome's reflection on the heavenly Jerusalem in this context. It is very likely driven by the political motifs coming from Rome, where at the end of the fourth century Ambrosiaster, too, was reflecting on the same theme in the millenarian exegetic tradition, albeit in a more evolved form. It is therefore from Rome, a city characterized by cultural and religious multiplicity and by a variety of soteriological needs, that the call comes to Bethlehem

---

[43] Cf. Jerome, *Epist.* 46.7 (Hilberg, *Epistulae* [cf. note 7], 337–38): *Et quid necesse est plura conquirere, cum post passionem et resurrectionem domini Mattheus euangelista commemoret: et petrae scissae sunt et sepulchra aperta et plurima corpora dormientium sanctorum surrexerunt. Et egredientes de sepulchris post resurrectionem suam ingressi sunt sanctam ciuitatem et apparuerunt multis? Nec statim Hierosolyma caelestis, ut plerique ridicule arbitrantur, in hoc loco intellegitur, cum signum nullum esse potuerit apud homines domini resurgentis, si corpora sanctorum in caelesti Hierusalem uisa sunt.* Cf. also *Epist.* 60.3 (p. 551): *Ante Christum Abraham apud inferos; post Christum latro in paradiso. Et idcirco in resurrectione eius multa dormientium corpora surrexerunt et uisa sunt in caelesti Hierusalem.*

[44] Cf. Jerome, *Comm. Matt.* 4.27.52–53 (Hurst and Adriaen *Commentariorum* [cf. note 9], 275–76): *Et multa corpora sanctorum qui dormierunt surrexerunt et exeuntes de monumentis post resurrectionem eius uenerunt in sanctam ciuitatem et apparuerunt multis. Quomodo Lazarus mortuus resurrexit sic et multa corpora sanctorum resurrexerunt ut Dominum ostenderent resurgentem. Et tamen cum monumenta aperta sint non ante resurrexerunt quam Dominus resurgeret ut esset primogenitus resurrectionis ex mortuis. Sanctam autem ciuitatem in qua uisi sunt resurgentes aut Hierusalem caelestem intellegamus aut hanc terrenam quae ante sancta fuerat. Sicut et Matheus appellatur publicanus non quo et apostolus adhuc permaneat publicanus sed quo pristinum uocabulum teneat, sancta appellabatur ciuitas Hierusalem propter templum et Sancta sanctorum et ob distinctionem aliarum urbium in quibus idola colebantur. Quando uero dicitur: apparuerunt multis, Ostentateur non generalis fuisse resurrectio quae omnibus appareret, sed specialis ad plurimos ut hi uiderent qui cernere merebantur.*

[45] A detailed study on the relationship between these two commentaries on Matthew goes beyond the present study but could perhaps offer some important insights.

[46] On the points of contact between Jerome, *Epist.* 73 and *Expl. Apoc.* Prol., see Dulaey, "Jerome 'editeur'" (cf. note 1), 202–4, 206, 215, 234.

for a new hermeneutic proposal of the heavenly Jerusalem. In this new interpretation, it is possible to re-evaluate Origenian exegetical learning, towards which the Latin-language exegesis was traditionally sceptical.

The Heavenly Jerusalem According to Two Fourth-Century Female Pilgrims

Anni Maria Laato

Introduction

In this contribution, I explore how the idea of the Heavenly Jerusalem is dealt with in texts connected to two Christian pilgrims: Paula of Bethlehem and Egeria.[1] Both visited the city of Jerusalem in the 380s. After their respective visits, Paula stayed in Bethlehem and founded a monastery, while Egeria probably returned home to Spain.[2] Both wrote texts about their visits – Paula a letter and Egeria a travel diary.[3] Helpfully, Jerome describes Paula's life and views. In their writings, Paula and Egeria offer two different perspectives on the understanding of the idea of the Heavenly Jerusalem. Paula gives both literal and spiritual interpretations of biblical texts that refer to the Heavenly Jerusalem, above all Rev 21–22. Egeria, for her part, while she does not use the expression "Heavenly Jerusalem" or quote Revelation, she does describe liturgical practices of her time that may reflect the idea of the connection between the heavenly and the earthly Jerusalem.[4] At the time of Egeria's visit, Cyril, bishop of Jerusalem, taught that

---

[1] On Paula of Bethlehem, see Anni Maria Laato, "What Makes the Holy Land Holy? A Debate between Paula, Eustochium, and Marcella (Jerome, *Ep.* 46)," in *Holy Places and Cult*, ed. Cornelis de Vos and Erkki Koskenniemi, Studies in the Reception History of the Bible 5 (Winona Lake: Eisenbrauns, 2014), 169–199. On Egeria, see John Wilkinson, *Egeria's Travels to the Holy Land: Newly Translated with Supporting Documents and Notes*, rev. ed. (Jerusalem: Ariel, 1981); Anne McGowan and Paul F. Bradshaw, *The Pilgrimage of Egeria: A New Translation of the Itinerarium Egeriae with Introduction and Commentary* (Collegeville, MN: Liturgical Press, 2018).

[2] Egeria probably came from Hispania and intended to return there; since her travel diary ends in Constantinople, however, we do not know whether she was able to return to Hispania. *Itinerarium Egeriae* 23.9–10; McGowan and Bradshaw, *The Pilgrimage of Egeria* (cf. note 1), 20–21.

[3] Editions: Egeria's *Itinerarium*: Pierre Maraval, ed., *Égérie: Journal de voyage (Itinéraire) et Lettre sur la Bienheureuse Égérie*, SC 296 (Paris: Cerf, 1997); Paula's letter: Isidorus Hilberg, ed., XLVI. *Paulae et Eustochiae ad Marcellam*, CSEL54 (Vienna: Tempsky, 1910).

[4] For the liturgical connection between the earthly and the Heavenly Jerusalem, see Serafim Seppälä, "Liturgical Representations of Jerusalem in Eastern Christian Traditions," in *Understanding the Spiritual Meaning of Jerusalem in Three Abrahamic Religions,* ed. Antti Laato, Studies on the Children of Abraham 6 (Leiden: Brill, 2019), 139–60.

the liturgy of the church on earth has its counterpart in the liturgy celebrated in the Heavenly Jerusalem.[5]

The question of the relation between the heavenly and the earthly Jerusalem was actualized during the fourth century by the increase in numbers of pilgrims to the Holy Land.[6] By the time of Paula's and Egeria's visits, pilgrimage to Jerusalem was already an established practice. The earlier development of these pilgrimages had been swift and spontaneous, and it was only toward the end of the fourth century that the theological motives behind such pilgrimages began to come under discussion. There were three Christian positions on pilgrimage to the Holy Land at that time: some argued for it, some criticized it, and perhaps the greatest number showed no interest in it. One of the criticisms levelled against pilgrimage to Jerusalem was that the true home of Christians was the Heavenly Jerusalem, not the earthly, and, moreover, that God does not dwell in particular places.[7] Jerome, for instance, said that there was no better access to the Heavenly Jerusalem from the earthly Jerusalem than from anywhere else, and used the Britons, as well as monks from Egypt, Mesopotamia, Pontus, Cappadocia, and Armenia, as examples of Christians who had never seen Jerusalem, yet for whom the door of Paradise still opened.[8]

Before the time of Constantine, biblical passages about the Heavenly Jerusalem (such as Gal 4:26, Heb 12:22, and Rev 21–22) were often understood as referring to the heavenly church, the city that awaits Christians after their death.[9] The old millennialistic interpretations of the Heavenly Jerusalem, in which the biblical passages about the Heavenly Jerusalem descending to the earth were interpreted more or less literally, also continued to flourish.[10] Once it became possible – and indeed often recommended – for Christians to travel to the earthly Jerusalem, new questions arose. If the Heavenly Jerusalem was all that mattered, what then

---

[5] Cyril of Jerusalem, *Cat.* 18.26. For the development of Jerusalemite liturgy and Cyril's role in it, see Jan Willem Drijvers, *Cyril of Jerusalem: Bishop and City*, Supplements to Vigiliae Christianae 72 (Leiden: Brill, 2004), 72–75.

[6] For the development of Christian pilgrimage to the Holy Land, see e.g. Brouria Bitton-Ashkelony, *Encountering the Sacred: The Debate on Christian Pilgrimage in Late Antiquity* (Berkeley, CA: University of California Press, 2005); Georgia Frank, *The Memory of the Eyes: Pilgrims to Living Saints in Christian Late Antiquity* (Berkeley: University of California Press, 2000); Edward David Hunt, *Holy Land Pilgrimage in the Later Roman Empire: AD 312–460* (Oxford: Clarendon, 1982); Laato, "What Makes" (cf. note 1).

[7] Cf. Acts 17:24; John 4:21–23; Gregory of Nyssa, *Ep.* 2; Jerome, *Ep.* 58.3; Laato, "What Makes" (cf. note 1), 169–70; Robert L. Wilken, *The Land Called Holy: Palestine in Christian History and Thought* (New Haven: Yale University Press, 1992), 91–92.

[8] Jerome, *Ep.* 58.3.

[9] See Anni Maria Laato, "The New Jerusalem in Tertullian," in *Understanding the Spiritual Meaning of Jerusalem*, 125–34. For instance, Origen emphasized the spiritual understanding of the concept of the Heavenly Jerusalem. Wilken, *The Land* (cf. note 7), 70–72.

[10] See e.g. Justin Martyr, *Dial.* 80–81; Irenaeus, *Haer.* 5.33–36; Tertullian, *Marc.* 3.24; Wilken, *The Land* (cf. note 7), 70, 76–78; Laato, "The New Jerusalem in Tertullian" (cf. note 9), 127–28.

was the point of going to the earthly Jerusalem? What kind of relationship was there between the Christian city of Jerusalem – the Heavenly Jerusalem understood as the church – and the promised Heavenly Jerusalem descending to earth? Was the earthly Jerusalem still a holy city?

In this essay, I explore how Paula and Egeria dealt with these questions and how their texts shed light on the development of the understanding of the Heavenly Jerusalem in the context of pilgrimage. I also look at two theologians by whom they were probably influenced: Paula's mentor, Jerome, and Cyril of Jerusalem, who was bishop of Jerusalem from 350 to 386, that is, during Egeria's visit. By the end of this essay, it will have be shown that in the minds of the early pilgrims the understandings of the Heavenly Jerusalem were connected to the earthly Jerusalem, but the emphases varied.

1   Paula of Bethlehem: Literal and Spiritual Interpretation of Jerusalem

Paula was a noblewoman from Rome who, together with her daughter, Eustochium, followed Jerome, teacher and spiritual advisor, to the Holy Land, made a grand tour there, and eventually settled in a monastery in Bethlehem in 386. Jerome dedicated several of his biblical commentaries to them, and many of his letters to them are preserved. Thus, when studying Paula's views, it is valid to look at Jerome's thoughts as well.

Before reading what Jerome has to say, it is good to remember that he liked to play with multiple meanings of words. When he writes "Jerusalem," he does not always intend one meaning alone but often has two in mind. So, in the preface to his translation of *On the Holy Spirit (De Spiritu Sancto)* by Didymus the Blind (which he dedicated both to his brother Paulinus as well as to Paula and Eustochium), he writes about his leaving Rome ("Babylon") for Jerusalem in 385. Indeed, he writes that he resumed his civic rights and returned to Jerusalem – *illico ego, velut postliminio, Jerosolyman sum reversus*. As he had not previously been to Jerusalem and enjoyed no civic rights there, Jerusalem in this context must have meant both the earthly city (because that is where he actually went) and his spiritual home (because as a Christian he had civic rights there according to passages of scripture like as Phil 3:20).[11]

After Paula's death, Jerome wrote about her life in letter 108. There he describes at length Paula's pilgrimage to Jerusalem and the Holy Land. In this letter too, literal and spiritual interpretations of Jerusalem are interwoven. Jerome praises Paula's coming to Jerusalem, but nonetheless emphasizes that the physical location was not her final goal. In relating Paula's visit to Mount Zion, he quotes

---

[11] See Jerome, *Ep.* 58.2–3.

Ps 86(87):1-2 and compares the gates of Jerusalem of their own time (which he describes as having been smashed "into dust and ashes") to the Jerusalem prophesied in the psalm. He thinks that "the gates of Jerusalem" in this psalm refer to the church (he alludes to Matt 16:18) and to the Heavenly Jerusalem (he alludes to Rev 22) and not to the earthly Jerusalem of any era:

> David had long ago taken this city by storm and rebuilt it. Of the city that was stormed it is written: "Woe to you, city of Ariel (in other words 'lion of God' for it was once the most powerful city) which David has taken by storm" [2 Sam 5:7-9], while of the city that has been rebuilt it is said: "Its foundations are on the holy mountains; the Lord loves the gates of Zion more than all the dwellings of Jacob" [Ps 86:1-2]. He does not mean those gates we see today, smashed into dust and ashes, but the gates against which hell cannot prevail, through which the crowds of believers enter to reach Christ.[12]

The city of Jerusalem is not the only spatial image Jerome uses when talking about Paula's life and death. He writes that in leaving Rome, Paula left "Babylon" and "Chaldea" and no longer longed for "the fleshpots of Egypt" (cf. Jer 51:1, 6; Ex 16:3). Instead, she became "a fellow citizen of the Savior,"[13] an expression referring to the citizenship of heaven contained in Rev 21:3 and in Phil 3:20. According to Jerome, when Paula was on her deathbed, she quoted several passages from the Psalter that employ spatial images to indicate that she would go to "the house of the Lord" (Ps 26:8; 84:1-2, 10) and to "the land of the living" (Ps 27:13).[14] When consoling Paula's daughter Eustochium after her mother's death, Jerome says that Paula had gone to "the city of the Lord of hosts, the city of our God" (Ps 48:8). In the sense of "a place where Christians go after death," these expressions are, thus, synonymous with the Heavenly Jerusalem.

Paula herself takes up the interpretation of the New Jerusalem descending from above (Rev 21). In the letter by Paula that is preserved as number 46 among Jerome's letters,[15] she talks about four Jerusalems, or Jerusalem at four stages: the Jerusalem in the Old Testament, the Jerusalem at Jesus's time, the Jerusalem of her own time, and the New Jerusalem found in Rev 21-22. For Paula, these Jerusalems were interconnected; even so, she maintained that each had its own specific quality.

---

[12] Jerome, *Ep.* 108.9: *hanc urbem quondam expugnauit et aedificauit Dauid. de expugnata scribitur: uae tibi, ciuitas Arihel – id est "leo dei" et quondam fortissima – quam expugnauit Dauid; de ea, quae aedificata est: fundamenta eius in montibus sanctis; diligit dominus portas Sion super omnia tabernacula Iacob, non eas portas, quas hodie cernimus in fauillam et cinerem dissolutas, sed portas, quibus infernus non praeualet, per quas credentium ad Christum ingreditur multitude.* Text: Isidorus Hilberg, ed., *Sancti Hieronymi Epistula CVIII*, CSEL 54 (Vienna: Tempsky, 1910). Translation: Carolinne White, trans., *Lives of Roman Christian Women* (London: Penguin, 2010), 81.

[13] Jerome, *Ep.* 108.31.

[14] For Jerome's spiritual interpretation of the land of the living or Promised Land, see Wilken, *The Land* (cf. note 7), 129-30.

[15] On the authorship, see Laato, "What Makes" (cf. note 1), 174-77.

The question in *Letter* 46 is whether or not the Christians should undertake pilgrimages to Jerusalem. The addressee of the letter, Marcella of Rome, saw no point in such journeys, and Paula tried to convince her to change her mind.[16] In her argumentation for a visit to Jerusalem, Paula starts with the question of the holiness of Jerusalem. For her, it is clear that Jerusalem was a holy city at the time of the Old Testament. It was a city in which people from the whole world gathered and from whence they spread out to the whole world. She maintains that the Old Testament characters and events prefigured events that would later transpire in New Testament times and that the Old Testament contained prophecies about these events. So, for example, the building of the temple on a threshing floor of the non-Israelite Araunah the Jebusite points to the church being raised among the nations rather than in Israel. Another example of a fulfilled prophecy is the first Adam, who was buried at Golgotha, as an image of the second Adam, whose blood washed away the sin of the first Adam.[17] A third example is the peace of Jerusalem during the time of Solomon, which prefigured the peace of Christ.

There is an overlap in Paula's discussion about the holiness of the Jerusalem at the time of Jesus vis-à-vis that of the Jerusalem of her own time. Jerusalem is holy because it is the city where Jesus stood (Ps 132:7 Vulg.), because "the evangelists and all the Scriptures speak of Jerusalem as the holy city," and because "the psalmist commands us to worship the Lord 'at his footstool.'"[18] The holiness of Jerusalem is, ultimately, based on the fact that it is the city in which Christ lived and died. Paula maintains, therefore, not only that the Heavenly Jerusalem may be called holy, but that the earthly, Christian, Jerusalem may be too. The geographical Jerusalem of Paula's own time is holier than it was prior because it is the place that the sepulcher of Jesus is to be found. The letter ends with Paula's reason for staying in the Holy Land: it is the place where she found Christ. She quotes the Song of Songs and writes, "Wounded with the Savior's shaft, we shall say one to another: 'I have found Him whom my soul loves; I will hold Him and will not let Him go [Song 3:4].'"[19]

---

[16] For Marcella of Rome, see Silvia Letsch-Brunner, *Marcella Discipula et Magistra: Auf den Spuren einer römischen Christin des 4. Jahrhunderts*, Beihefte zur Zeitschrift fur die neutestamentliche Wissenschaft 91 (Berlin: De Gruyter, 1998), esp. 180–86.

[17] For this tradition, see Laato, "What Makes" (cf. note 1), 180–81; Joachim Jeremias, *Golgotha* (Leipzig: Pfeiffer, 1926), 35.

[18] *Ep.* 46.7.

[19] In a letter to Eustochium, Jerome quotes the same biblical passage (Song 3:4), combines it with Song 6:9, and interprets these verses in the light of Gal 4:26 about the Heavenly Jerusalem, the mother church. He compares Martha and Mary, and writes: "Now that you have put aside the burden of worldly worries, you must sit down at the Lord's feet and say, 'I have found him whom my soul was seeking; I will hold on to him and not let him go' [Song 3:4]. And he will reply, 'My dove, my perfect one, is my only one; she is the darling of her mother, chosen by the one who gave birth to her' [Song 6:9], in other words the Heavenly Jerusalem." (*Ep.* 22.24). Translation: White, *Lives of Roman Christian Women* (cf. note 12), 130.

Paula starts her exposition of Rev 21:16–18 with Marcella's (supposed) claim that "the great city where the prophets were killed" (Rev 11:8) refers to the earthly Jerusalem and cannot therefore be considered holy:

> But you may say, "How come we read in the Revelation of John: 'The beast of that ascends out of the abyss will kill them (no doubt meaning the prophets) and their dead bodies will lie in the streets of the great city that spiritually is called Sodom and Egypt, and where also their Lord was crucified' [Rev 11:7–8]? For if," you say, "the great city in which the Lord was crucified is Jerusalem and if the place of his crucifixion is spiritually called Sodom and Egypt, then as the Lord was crucified at Jerusalem, Jerusalem must be Sodom and Egypt."[20]

Paula, persuaded that Holy Scripture cannot contradict itself, retorts gently that a few lines earlier in the same book, Jerusalem was called holy (Rev 11:1–2); therefore, Sodom and Egypt in this text cannot refer to Jerusalem. A few lines further down, she writes,

> If Revelation was written long after the Lord's passion and in it the holy city is called Jerusalem, how then can it be called spiritually Sodom and Egypt? For you cannot immediately say that the Jerusalem that is called holy is the heavenly one which is in the future, while the one that is called Sodom and Egypt is the one that has fallen down, for it is the Jerusalem to come that is referred to in the description of "the beast that will ascend out of the abyss and will make war against two prophets and will kill them, and their bodies will lie in the streets of the great city" [Rev 11:7–8].[21]

As a proof that the passage about the Heavenly Jerusalem must be understood spiritually and not literally, Paula quotes the description of the Heavenly Jerusalem in Rev 21:16–18. She states that the details have to be understood spiritually, as it would be absurd to think that the measurements and other descriptions of the city could be understood literally:

> At the end of this book the city is described in the following way: "The city is square and its length is the same as its height; and he measured the city with the reed, twelve thousand furlongs. Its length and the breadth and height are equal. He also measured its walls which were a hundred and forty-four cubits according to the measure of man, which is that of an angel. And its wall was of jasper and the city was of pure gold" [Rev 21:16–18] – and

---

[20] *Ep.* 46.6: *Sed dicis: "quomodo in Apocalypsi Iohannis legimus: et occident illos – haud dubium quin prophetas – bestia, quae ascendit ex abysso, et corpora eorum in plateis ciuitatis magnae, quae uocatur spiritaliter Sodoma et Aegyptus, ubi et dominus eorum crucifixus est? si enim,"* ais, *"ciuitas magna, in qua crucifixus est dominus, spiritaliter Sodoma appellatur et Aegyptus, ergo Hierusalem Sodoma est et Aegyptus, in qua crucifixus est dominus."* Translation: White, *Lives of Roman Christian Women* (cf. note 12), 170–71.

[21] *Ep.* 46.6: *Si enim Apocalypsis multo post passionem domini scripta est a Iohanne et in ea Hierusalem sancta ciuitas appellatur, quomodo rursum spiritaliter Sodoma uocatur et Aegyptus? Nec statim potes dicere sanctam dici Hierusalem caelestem, quae future est, et Aegyptum et Sodomam eam, quae conruit, appellari, quia de futura dicitur, quod bestia, quae ascensura est de abysso, faciat aduersus duos prophetas bellum et uincat illos et occidat et corpora eorum iacent in plateis ciuitatis magnae.*

so on. Now where there is a square one cannot distinguish between length and breadth. And what kind of measurement is it to say that the length and the breadth are equal to the height? How can there be walls of jasper or a whole city of pure gold and its foundations and streets made of precious stones, with twelve gates sparkling with pearls? As these facts cannot be taken literally (for in fact it is absurd to talk of a city having a height of twelve thousand furlongs as well as being that long and wide), each fact must be given a spiritual interpretation.[22]

Paula ends her discussion about the Heavenly Jerusalem with an interesting detail. She wants to prove false an interpretation of the verse that rested on the crucifixion narrative: "The tombs also were opened, and many bodies of the saints who had fallen asleep were raised. After his resurrection they came out of the tombs and entered the holy city and appeared to many" (Matt 27:52–53 NRSV). She states that while some claim that this text refers to the Heavenly Jerusalem, this would be absurd since "the apparition there of the bodies of the saints could be no sign to men of the Lord's rising".[23]

To understand Paula's strong words about the absurdity of a literal interpretation of Rev 21, it is important to pay attention to what her teacher, Jerome, said about the same passage. Paula, it turns out, is not alone in calling a literal interpretation of the golden Heavenly Jerusalem absurd. In his *Commentary on Isaiah*, dedicated to Paula and Eustochium and containing several references to them, as well as in his *Commentary on Ezekiel*, which is dedicated to Eustochium alone, Jerome repeatedly deals with Rev 21.[24] Jerome is adamant in his criticism of millennialistic and literal interpretations of the Heavenly Jerusalem descending to the earth. He admits that his spiritual interpretation goes against a long list of earlier theologians.[25] In one passage he says that "very many people" are waiting for a golden Jerusalem adorned with jewels from heaven and a future kingdom that will last for a thousand years. Jerome says that these people err, and he refers to them as "Jews and Judaizers."[26] In interpreting Rev 21, Jerome

---

[22] *Ep.* 46.6–7: *De qua ciuitate et in fine eiusdem libri scribitur: et ciuitas in quadrato posita est et longitudo eius et latitudo tanta est, quanta et altitudo. et mensus est ciuitatem de harundine per stadia duodecim milia. longitudo et latitudo et altitudo eius aequalia sunt. et mensus est muros eius centum quadraginta quattuor cubitorum mensura hominis, quae est angeli. et erat structura muri eius ex lapide iaspide, ipsa uero ciuitas auro mundo et cetera. ubi quadrum est, nec longitudo nec latitudo appellari potest. et quae est ista mensura, ut tanta sit longitudo et latitudo, quanta et altitudo eius, et muri de lapide iaspide et tota ciuitas de auro mundo et fundamenta et plateae eius de lapidibus pretiosis et duodecim portae fulgentes margaritis? Cum ergo haec non possint carnaliter accipi – absurdum quippe est per duodecim milia stadiorum tantam ciuitatis longitudinem et latitudinem, quantam et altitudinem praedicari – spiritaliter intellegenda sunt singula.*

[23] *Ep.* 46.7.

[24] Jerome, *Comm. Isa.* 10.17; 15.7; 17.2; 17.8; 18.1; Jerome, *Comm. Ezech.* 48.30.

[25] Jerome, *Comm. Isa.* 18.1; Jerome, *Comm. Ezech.* 11.36. On the topic of earlier interpretations in the Greek tradition, see especially Nathan Betz's contribution to this volume.

[26] Jerome, *Comm. Isa.* 17.2.

gives detailed information of the jewels, the gates and the walls, and says that this must be understood spiritually as meaning the church and eternal life.[27] In this context, he quotes the same verse quoted by Paula on her deathbed: "The one who will have merited the right to enter this city says while rejoicing in the Lord, 'As we have heard, so we have seen in the city of the Lord of virtues, in the city of our God, God has founded it forever' (Ps 48:8)."

Curiously enough, Jerome expresses very different views on this topic as well. In his letter to Paulinus, where he rather surprisingly argues against pilgrimage to Jerusalem, he emphasizes, in a similar manner, the spiritual understanding of a Heavenly Jerusalem. In this letter, he emphasizes that access to the Heavenly Jerusalem is as easy from Britain as it is from the earthly Jerusalem, thus indicating that some others thought that visiting the earthly Jerusalem was to be preferred.[28] He quotes the very same passages – Rev 22:1 and Gal 4:26 – as Paula. To dissuade Paulinus from coming to Jerusalem, he says that the city one should seek is actually the Heavenly Jerusalem and, moreover, that Christians themselves are the true temple of the Lord. He writes,

> What is praiseworthy is not to have been at Jerusalem but to have lived a good life while there. The city which we are to praise and to seek is not that which has slain the prophets [Matt 23:37] and shed the blood of Christ, but that which is made glad by the streams of the river [Ps 46:4; Rev 22:1], which is set upon a mountain and so cannot be hid [Matt 5:14], which the apostle declares to be a mother of the saints [Gal 4:26] and in which he rejoices to have his citizenship with the righteous [Phil 3:20].[29]

> Those who say "the temple of the Lord, the temple of the Lord" [Jer 7:4] should give ear to the words of the apostle: "you are the temple of the Lord" [2 Cor 6:16], and the Holy Ghost "dwells in you" [Rom 8:11]. Access to the courts of heaven is as easy from Britain as it is from Jerusalem; for "the kingdom of God is within you" [Luke 17:21].[30]

In sum, the texts of Paula and Jerome, both of whom lived in Bethlehem, show that in their time, both literal and spiritual interpretations of the Heavenly Jerusalem in Rev 21–22 existed. They, however, rejected a literal interpretation of the promises of the Heavenly Jerusalem descending from above as absurd and understood these biblical texts as referring to the church and the life to come. In their interpretations, Jerusalem was understood as the church, which has its

---

[27] Jerome, *Comm. Isa.* 15.10; 17.8.

[28] Jerome, *Ep.* 58.3.

[29] Jerome, *Ep.* 58.2: *Non Hierosolymis fuisse, sed Hierosolymis bene vixisse laudandum est. illa, illa expectanda est ciuitas, non quae occidit prophetas et Christi sanguinem fudit, sed quam fluminis impetus laetificat, quae in monte sita celari non potest, quam matrem sanctorum apostolos clamitat, in qua municipatum cum iustis habere laetatur.* Text: Isidorus Hilberg, ed., CSEL 54 (Vienna: Tempsky, 1910). Translation: W. H. Fremantle, G. Lewis and W. G. Martley, *St Jerome: Letters and Select Works*, NPNF[2] 6 (Buffalo, NY: Christian Literature Publishing Co., 1893).

[30] Jerome, *Ep.* 58.3: *Qui dicunt: templum domini, templum domini, templum domini, audiant ab apostolo: uos estis templum dei et spiritus sanctus habitat in uobis. et de Hierosolymis et de Britannia aequaliter patet aula caelestis; regnum enim dei intra nos est.*

celestial counterpart in heaven. In Paula's epitaph (*Ep.* 108) Jerome uses several spatial images connected with the idea of a Heavenly Jerusalem as a place where Christians go after death: she is now in God's city, in the house of the Lord, and in the land of the living.

Important from the point of view of pilgrimage, as Jan Willem Drijvers has noted, is that the holy sites are less important for Jerome and Gregory of Nyssa than they are, for example, for Cyril of Jerusalem.[31] For Paula, Golgotha and the sepulcher of Jesus are the foundation for the holiness of Jerusalem and the reason for her staying in the Holy Land but, nonetheless, she still feels compelled to argue for pilgrimage to Jerusalem.

2 Egeria: The Importance of Topography and Liturgy

Egeria is famous for her *Itinerarium*, a pilgrimage diary in which she describes her journey to the Holy Land, Egypt, and Mesopotamia in the 380s.[32] This work is not preserved in its entirety, but those parts that we do have contain important notations about liturgical life in Jerusalem during her three-year visit there. The character of Egeria's text is more a description of places and events than a meditation on theological questions. Despite this, it opens interesting perspectives on the idea of a Heavenly Jerusalem.

For Egeria, Jerusalem is holy at all times – during Old Testament times, New Testament times, and her own time – and she often uses the epithet "holy" about biblical sites.[33] The present question, however, is whether anything may be said about the new or Heavenly Jerusalem in the light of her text. If so, the thought must be so self-evident that she did not have to spell it out; indeed, she often omits what she thinks is clear for her readers.[34] In their commentary on Egeria's work, Anne McGowan and Paul Bradshaw suggest that her way of using the Scripture is entirely at the literal level and without any hint of typological or allegorical exegesis.[35] I do not entirely agree. Having participated in liturgical life in Jerusalem for three years and having listened to the homilies delivered there, Egeria was no doubt aware of spiritual exegesis, even if she does not recount these interpretations in her book. She says, for instance, that when teaching the catechumens, the bishop always explained biblical texts first literally and then spiritually.[36] On many occasions she states that the reason for her journey

---

[31] Drijvers, *Cyril* (cf. note 5), 155.
[32] See notes 1–3 above.
[33] In this, she is reminiscent of Cyril of Jerusalem. See Drijvers, *Cyril* (cf. note 5), 154.
[34] E. g. details in liturgy. See McGowan and Bradshaw, *The Pilgrimage of Egeria* (cf. note 1), 69.
[35] McGowan and Bradshaw, *The Pilgrimage of Egeria* (cf. note 1), 13.
[36] Egeria, *Itin.*46.3.

to Jerusalem was prayer, that is, her spiritual life, and thus she is not merely reporting on what she sees. It is, therefore, natural to assume that Egeria was not interested only in the practices she describes but also in the ideas behind them. Thus, we are justified in looking at what the theologians she might have heard actually taught about the Heavenly Jerusalem, in particular Cyril of Jerusalem.[37]

When preaching to the catechumens in Jerusalem, Cyril often talked about the city of Jerusalem and its places. He also promoted the practice of processions to different holy places and the celebration of the liturgy at corresponding biblical sites. For instance, the Jerusalem Christians gathered every Sunday morning at the site of the resurrection to hear the Gospel passage about the resurrection read and explained.[38] For Cyril, the church buildings, the city of Jerusalem, as well as the land itself, were all holy places. Golgotha, he writes, is the center of the world.[39] Cyril, of course, also maintained that the church is called Jerusalem. He even addresses his audience as "Jerusalem": "Rejoice, O Jerusalem, and keep high festival, all you that love Jesus; for He is risen. Rejoice, all you that mourned before [cf. Isa 66:10]."[40]

In Cyril's sacred topography, because of the holy places and what had happened there, the earthly Jerusalem reflects the Heavenly Jerusalem, and the Heavenly Jerusalem can be experienced through the earthly.[41] He reminds his listeners that the church carries the image of the Jerusalem above and refers them to Gal 4:26–27. The Heavenly Jerusalem has a counterpart on the earth – the church:

> For this [*ecclesia*] is the peculiar name of this Holy Church, the mother of us all, which is the spouse of our Lord Jesus Christ, the Only-begotten Son of God, for it is written, "as Christ also loved the Church and gave Himself for it" [Eph 5:25], and all the rest, and is a figure and copy of Jerusalem which is above, which is free, and the mother of us all; which before was barren, but now has many children [Gal 4:26–27].[42]

In the final pages of his *Catecheses*, Cyril writes about the New Jerusalem.[43] It is important to note that he has added the word "new" in his quotation of Isa

---

[37] For the discussion about the role of Cyril and other bishops of Jerusalem in developing the liturgy, see Drijvers, *Cyril* (cf. note 5), 72–73.

[38] Cyril, *Cat.* 18.33. For the stational services, see McGowan and Bradshaw, *The Pilgrimage of Egeria* (cf. note 1), 70.

[39] Cyril, *Cat.* 13.28.

[40] Cyril, *Cat.* 14.1.

[41] For this idea, see Drijvers, *Cyril* (cf. note 5), 154–55.

[42] Cyril, *Cat.* 18.26: τοῦτο γὰρ ἰδικὸν ὄνομα τυγχάνει τῆς ἁγίας ταύτης καὶ μητρὸς ἡμῶν ἁπάντων. ἥτις νύμφη μέν ἐστι τοῦ κυρίου ἡμῶν Ἰησοῦ Χριστοῦ, τοῦ μονογενοῦς υἱοῦ τοῦ θεοῦ, (γέγραπται γάρ· καθὼς καὶ ὁ Χριστὸς ἠγάπησε τὴν ἐκκλησίαν καὶ ἑαυτὸν παρέδωκεν ὑπὲρ αὐτῆς, καὶ ὅλα τὰ ἑξῆς,) τύπον δὲ ἔχει καὶ μίμημα τῆς ἄνω Ἰερουσαλήμ, ἥτις ἐλευθέρα ἐστὶ καὶ μήτηρ πάντων ἡμῶν, ἡ πρότερον μὲν στεῖρα, νῦν δὲ πολύτεκνος. Text: Wilhelm C. Reischl and Joseph Rupp, ed., *Cyrilli Hierosolymarum archiepiscopi opera quae supersunt omnia*, 2 vols. (Hildesheim: Olms, 1967). Translation: Edwin Hamilton Gifford, *NPNF*[2] 7 (Buffalo, NY: Christian Literature Publishing Co., 1894).

[43] Cyril, *Cat.* 18.34.

60:1. Cyril is addressing the catechumens who are about to be baptized and he identifies the New Jerusalem and Zion as the church:

> And within a little while you shall hear that excellent lesson which says, "Shine, shine, O thou new Jerusalem; for your light has come" [cf. Isa 60:1].[44] Of *this* Jerusalem the prophet has said, "And afterwards you shall be called the city of righteousness, Zion, the faithful mother of cities" [cf. Isa 1:26] because of "the law which went forth out of Zion, and the word of the Lord from Jerusalem" [Isa 2:3], which word has from hence been showered forth on the whole world. To her [Zion] the Prophet also says concerning you, "Lift up your eyes round about, and behold your children gathered together" [cf. Isa 60:4]; and she answers, saying, "Who are these that fly as a cloud, and as doves with their young ones to me?" [cf. Isa 60:8] (clouds because of their spiritual nature, and doves, from their purity). And again, she says, "Who knows such things? Or who has seen it thus? Did ever a land bring forth in one day? Or was ever a nation born all at once? For as soon as Zion travailed, she brought forth her children" [cf. Isa 66:8]. And all things shall be filled with joy unspeakable because of the Lord who said, "Behold, I create Jerusalem a rejoicing, and her people a joy" [cf. Isa 65:18].[45]

Cyril's use of the concept "Heavenly Jerusalem" concept in this passage is based on Isa 60:1, however with his own addition of "new". For him, the biblical background of the idea of the Heavenly Jerusalem is Gal 4:26–27, which he quotes, and similar passages such as Heb 12:12. Even if he does not accept the Revelation of John as Scripture, he may still have been influenced by its use of this concept.[46]

Cyril's teaching in which the liturgy-celebrating church in the earthly Jerusalem is connected with the liturgy-celebrating church in the Heavenly Jerusalem forms a background for the liturgical practices Egeria describes. It is not possible to define how aware she was of the theological thinking behind the different liturgical practices; I suggest, however, that this motivated her in her writing, at least to some degree. Egeria mentions neither Rev 21–22 nor the concept of the Heavenly Jerusalem but rather focusses on describing the Jerusalem of her day and the liturgical life there. She carefully describes the holy topography of Jerusalem and the continuous prayer taking place in the churches of Jerusalem,

---

[44] Isa 60:1 became one of the texts read at Epiphany very early. See Michael Margoni-Kögler, *Die Perikopen im Gottesdienst bei Augustinus* (Vienna: Österreichische Akademie der Wissenschaften, 2010), 75–77.

[45] Cyril, *Cat.* 18.34, italics mine. καὶ μετ' οὐ πολὺ τῆς ἀγαθῆς ἀναγνώσεως ἀκούσεσθε λεγούσης· φωτίζου, ἡ νέα Ἰερουσαλήμ· ἥκει γάρ σου τὸ φῶς. περὶ ἧς Ἰερουσαλὴμ ὁ προφήτης εἴρηκε· καὶ μετὰ ταῦτα κληθήσῃ πόλις δικαιοσύνης, μητρόπολις πιστὴ Σιών, διὰ τὸν ἐκ Σιὼν ἐξελθόντα νόμον καὶ λόγον κυρίου τὸν ἐξ Ἱερουσαλήμ, ὃς ἐντεῦθεν εἰς ἅπασαν τὴν οἰκουμένην ἐξώμβρησεν. Πρὸς ἣν καὶ ὁ προφήτης περὶ ὑμῶν φησιν· ἆρον κύκλῳ τοὺς ὀφθαλμούς σου καὶ ἴδε συνηγμένα τὰ τέκνα σου. ἡ δὲ ἀποκρίνεται λέγουσα· τίνες οἵδε ὡς νεφέλαι πέτανται καὶ ὡς περιστεραὶ σὺν νεοσσοῖς ἐπ' ἐμέ; νεφέλαι διὰ τὸ πνευματικόν, καὶ περιστεραὶ διὰ τὸ ἀκέραιον. καὶ πάλιν· τίς οἶδε τοιαῦτα; ἢ τίς ἑώρακεν οὕτως; εἰ ὤδινε γῆ ἐν μιᾷ ἡμέρᾳ, καὶ ἐτέχθη ἔθνος εἰς ἅπαξ; ὅτι ὤδινε καὶ ἔτεκε Σιὼν τὰ παιδία αὐτῆς. χαρᾶς δὲ ἀνεκλαλήτου τὰ πάντα πληρωθήσεται, διὰ τὸν εἰπόντα κύριον· ὅτι ἰδοὺ ἐγὼ ποιῶ Ἱερουσαλὴμ ἀγαλλίαμα καὶ τὸν λαόν μου εὐφροσύνην.

[46] Cf. Antti Laato's article on Eusebius in this volume.

thanks to the multitude of pilgrims and Christian monastics who made it possible to have services every day, even at night.[47]

The idea of a connection between the heavenly and earthly liturgies was well known in Egeria's times. In the New Testament already, the continuous liturgy on earth was already connected with the liturgy in the Jerusalem above (Heb 12:22; Rev 4:1–11). This connection is also visible in, for example, the martyr texts.[48] It was natural to develop the idea that the liturgy and prayer in the earthly Christian Jerusalem had its counterpart in the Heavenly Jerusalem.[49] In the visual arts at almost the time of Egeria's visit, the connection between the Heavenly Jerusalem and the church on earth is depicted in the oldest surviving Christian apse mosaics, specifically in the early-fifth-century church Santa Pudenziana in Rome.[50] There, the splendid buildings of the Heavenly Jerusalem are depicted behind the enthroned Christ, while the lower part depicts the church and the apostles. The identification of the city as the Heavenly Jerusalem is clear: the gemmed cross rises from a hill representing Golgotha, but the cross is the cross of Christ's second coming and the arrival of the New Jerusalem of Rev 21. In the sky the four living creatures from Rev 4:7–8 are depicted. The image of the Lamb of God was lost in a baroque restoration.[51]

In the second part of her *Itinerarium*, Egeria focusses on describing the liturgical events that took place in the *Martyrium* and the *Anastasis,* which, together with the surrounding courtyards, formed the Church of the Holy Sepulchre that was originally constructed by Constantine in 335.[52] Other churches were also built by him on places commemorating the life events of Jesus, such as the Church of the Nativity in Bethlehem and Eleona on the Mount of Olives. The new sacred topography expressed both continuity and discontinuity with the Old Testament as well as with the old Jerusalem.[53] This is seen in particular in how the center of

---

[47] This continuous prayer is presented in a table in McGowan and Bradshaw, *The Pilgrimage of Egeria* (cf. note 1), 73.

[48] See e.g. *Passio Perpetuae et Felicitatis* 12.

[49] See Seppälä, "Liturgical Presentation of Jerusalem" (cf. note 4), 139, 145, 160.

[50] For the Heavenly Jerusalem in the mosaic in Santa Pudenziana, see Armin Bergmeier in this volume; Hugo Brandenburg, *Ancient Churches of Rome from the Fourth to the Seventh Century*, Bibliothèque de l'antiquité tardive 8 (Turnhout: Brepols, 2005), 139–42; Ann Marie Yasin, "Sacred Space and Visual Art," in *The Oxford Handbook of Late Antiquity*, ed. Scott Fitzgerald Johnson (Oxford: Oxford University Press, 2012), 936–58, esp. 949–50; Wendy Pullan, "Jerusalem from Alpha to Omega in the Santa Pudenziana Mosaic," in *The Real and Ideal Jerusalem in Jewish, Christian, and Islamic Art: Studies in Honor of Bezalel Narkiss on the Occasion of his Seventieth Birthday*, ed. Bianca Kühnel (Jerusalem: Center for Jewish Art, Hebrew University of Jerusalem, 1998), 405–17; Fredric W. Schlatter, "Interpreting the Mosaic of Santa Pudenziana," in *Vigiliae Christianae* 46 (1992), 276–95.

[51] Robin M. Jensen, *The Cross: History, Art, and Controversy* (Cambridge, MA: Harvard University Press, 2017), 102–3.

[52] See Eusebius, *Vit. Const.* 3.33 and Wilken, *The Land* (cf. note 7), 40–46.

[53] Eusebius, *Vit. Const.* 33. For Eusebius's New Jerusalem, see Wilken, *The Land* (cf. note 7), 82–83; Antti Laato in this volume.

Jerusalem shifted from the temple to the Church of the Holy Sepulchre.[54] Cyril claimed that Golgotha – not the temple, as the Jews had thought – was the center of the world, and the Byzantine map, the so-called Madaba Map, shows the same idea visually. The *Anastasis,* the chapel on the site of Jesus' resurrection, had taken the place of the Holy of Holies.[55] That the Holy Sepulchre had somehow taken on the role of the temple also becomes apparent through the fact that in Constantinian Jerusalem, the temple area was left unbuilt. This was done partly to show that in the Christian Jerusalem, as in the heavenly one, there was no need for a temple, because Christ himself is the temple, and partly to show that Jesus's words in Matt 24:15 had been fulfilled.[56]

This shift from the temple to the Holy Sepulchre is seen in Egeria's description of the festival of *Encaenia.*[57] This name was originally used for the feast of the dedication of Solomon's Temple; as Egeria reports, however, in her time it was celebrated on the day of the dedication of *Martyrium,* the Constantinian basilica. She connects the dedication of the *Martyrium* with that of Solomon's Temple, thus making a clear parallel between the temple and the Church of the Holy Sepulchre. This connection is confirmed by the liturgical texts chosen for this feast day in the Armenian Lectionary. In this lectionary, which describes liturgical life in Jerusalem in the fifth century, texts about the temple of Jerusalem are applied to the Holy Sepulchre.[58]

Another feast where the Gospel reading in Egeria's text and in the Armenian Lectionary actualizes the connection between the earthly temple and its Christian counterpart is *Hypapante*, celebrated forty days after Epiphany to commemorate the presentation of Jesus in the temple.[59] The presentation of Jesus was, in fact, not celebrated precisely where it had originally taken place – namely, in the temple area – but rather in the *Anastasis.* The choice of the Holy Sepulchre over the temple area symbolizes that in the minds of the Christians, the places of the crucifixion and the resurrection of Christ had taken on the role that the temple had once had. One interesting detail in the celebration of these feast days may hint at a connection between the earthy Jerusalem and the Heavenly Jerusalem

---

[54] For this topic, see Wilken, *The Land* (cf. note 7), 93–97.

[55] Eusebius, *Vit. Const.* 3.28; Wilkinson, *Egeria's Travels* (cf. note 1), 38.

[56] It is notable that many of the liturgical practices Egeria describes have their roots in temple service (blessings, Eucharist as offering, praise, and the bishop going alone inside the sepulcher of Jesus). See Seppälä, "Liturgical presentation of Jerusalem," 139–60. For the Christian interpretations of the fact that the temple area was left unbuilt, see Günter Stemberger, *Jews and Christians in the Holy Land: Palestine in the Fourth Century* (Edinburgh: T&T Clark, 2000), 201–6.

[57] McGowan and Bradshaw, *The Pilgrimage of Egeria* (cf. note 1), 82.

[58] The antiphon is Ps 64 ("To you, God, hymns are due, in Zion, and to you are presented prayers in Jerusalem"), the Hallelujah Psalm is Ps 147 ("Praise the Lord, Jerusalem"), and the Gospel reading is John 10:22–42. For the lectionary, see Nicholas Denysenko, "The Hypapante Feast in Fourth to Eighth Century Jerusalem," *Studia Liturgica* 37 (2007): 73–97.

[59] See Denysenko, "The Hypapante Feast" (cf. note 58), 73–75.

described in Revelation: Egeria states that on major feast days, the churches were lavishly decorated with gold, gems, and other precious materials,[60] reminiscent of the description of the Heavenly Jerusalem in Rev 21:10–21.

We must, of course, be careful not to read too much into Egeria's text. After all, she never names the Heavenly Jerusalem in her work. However, when read in connection with the promotor of Jerusalemite liturgy of that time, Cyril of Jerusalem, we can at least suggest that the continuous liturgical practice that Egeria describes was not developed for practical and pedagogical reasons alone, but rather was understood as a counterpart to the continuous prayer in the Heavenly Jerusalem. Not only did the Christian sacred topography express how the new (earthly) Jerusalem formed a counterpart for the old, but the Christian liturgical life expressed a connection between the church on earth and the church above, that is, the Heavenly Jerusalem. Therefore, precisely in Egeria's description of the churches and the liturgy in Jerusalem, connections with the concept of the Heavenly Jerusalem may be seen.

Conclusions

These two pilgrims, Paula and Egeria, actualize how the earlier focus on the Heavenly Jerusalem – as opposed to the earthly Jerusalem – changed when it became possible to undertake pilgrimages to the Holy Land. The transformation of the earthly Jerusalem into a Christian city with churches, monasteries, and liturgical processions made it necessary to rethink what was understood by the concept of the Heavenly Jerusalem.

Both Paula and Egeria express the idea that there is, in a unique way, access to the sacred through the holy places in Jerusalem. Both emphasized the role of the Holy Scriptures in opening up a proper understanding of the places in question. Differences in the emphases of these two pilgrims, however, remain. For Paula, and perhaps even more for her teacher, Jerome, the Heavenly Jerusalem is ultimately universal and not dependent on the earthly Jerusalem. Despite this, they both still considered it important to promote pilgrimages to the earthly Jerusalem, and Paula in particular put forward compelling arguments for the uniqueness of the city. Paula and Jerome strongly dismissed all literal and millennialistic interpretations of the biblical texts about the Heavenly Jerusalem and interpreted Rev 21–22 spiritually as referring to the church and to the afterlife.

Egeria, for her part, seems to share Cyril of Jerusalem's focus on the holy sites in Jerusalem and the liturgical action there.[61] She is equally interested in and happy about the holy sites in all the places she has visited, but Jerusalem

---

[60] Egeria, *Itin.* 25.8.
[61] See Drijvers, *Cyril* (cf. note 5), 155.

takes on a special role in her text. Egeria's text describes the Christian sacred topography as well as Christian liturgy and continuous prayer, which, at least in later theology, were understood as being connected with the liturgy in the Heavenly Jerusalem.[62] Her text can be interpreted as expressing the thought that the continuous praise and the liturgy on earth, as well as the holy sites where it takes place, can be seen as a counterpart to the Heavenly Jerusalem.

---

[62] See Seppälä, "Liturgical Presentations of Jerusalem" (cf. note 4), *passim*.

From the Heavenly Jerusalem to the City of Christ

Revelation and the Visio Pauli

Tobias Nicklas

Introduction

While many early Christian apocalyptic writings (such as Didache 16, the Apocalypse of Peter, the Ascension of Isaiah, the Shepherd of Hermas, 6 Ezra, or the Christian Sibylline Oracles) do not show clear signs of a literary relationship with Revelation,[1] the Apocalypse of Paul is different. This text made use of Revelation[2] and was extremely effective in doing so. The text, originally written in Greek, became highly influential in its Latin translation[3] called the *Visio Pauli*, which may have inspired Dante's *Divine Comedy*, though only indirectly.[4] We also know of Arabic, Armenian, Coptic, Georgian, and Syriac versions of the Apocalypse of Paul, in addition to several translations into vernacular medieval

---

[1] See the discussion in Tobias Nicklas, "Rezeption und Nicht-Rezeption der Offenbarung des Johannes durch antike christliche Apokalypsen," in *Christian Apocrypha. Receptions of the New Testament in Ancient Christian Apocrypha*, ed. Jean-Michel Roessli and Tobias Nicklas, Novum Testamentum Patristicum 26 (Göttingen: Vandenhoeck & Ruprecht, 2014), 325–48. The situation is more complicated with the *Apocalypse of Thomas*, where we have only vague traces of reception (see Tobias Nicklas, "Die apokryphe *Thomasapokalypse* und ihre Rezeption der Offenbarung des Johannes," in *Die Johannesapokalypse: Kontexte – Konzepte – Rezeption*, ed. Jörg Frey, James A. Kelhoffer, and Franz Tóth, WUNT 287 [Tübingen: Mohr Siebeck, 2012], 683–708), while 5 Ezra shows a somewhat critical (or at least distanced) rewriting of Revelation's vision of the eschatological people (see the detailed assessment by Veronika Hirschberger, *Ringen um Israel: Intertextuelle Perspektiven auf das 5. Buch Esra*, Studies on Early Christian Apocrypha 14 [Leuven: Peeters, 2018], 174–241).

[2] For a full overview and discussion of parallels, see Claudio Zamagni, "L'Apocalypse de Paul et l'Apocalypse Johannique: Questions intertextuelles autour d'un apocryphe," in Zamagni, *Recherches sur le Nouveau Testament et les apocryphes chrétiens* (Rimini: Guaraldi, 2017), 313–24.

[3] Lenka Jiroušková, *Die 'Visio Pauli': Wege und Wandlungen einer orientalischen Apokryphe im lateinischen Mittelalter*, Mittellateinische Texte und Studien 34 (Leiden: Brill, 2006), 37–149, mentions 115 Latin manuscripts.

[4] A rather skeptical view regarding the *Visio Pauli*'s influence on Dante is offered by Gerhard Regn, "Die Apokalypse im Irdischen Paradies: Offenbarung, Allegorie und Dichtung in Dantes Commedia," in *Autorschaft und Autorisierungsstrategien in apokalyptischen Texten*, ed. Jörg Frey, Michael R. Jost, Franz Tóth, WUNT 426 (Tübingen: Mohr Siebeck, 2019), 391–412.

languages.⁵ Contrary to earlier conclusions that it could be dated to the second or third century AD, there is good evidence that the original Apocalypse of Paul was produced around the turn of the fourth to the fifth century AD.⁶

The focus of this paper on the *Visio Pauli*, the Latin version(s) of the Apocalypse of Paul, is two-fold. First, I will analyze its use and development of Revelation's description of the Heavenly Jerusalem. Second, I will try to understand *to what extent* and *why* the *Visio Pauli*'s City of Christ is, in many aspects, different from Revelation's Heavenly Jerusalem. Working with this text, however, requires an awareness of a severe methodological problem. The *Visio Pauli* has always been a "living text," meaning that an "earliest recoverable" version of the text is impossible to reconstruct. That is why I must be very careful regarding which text I use. Because it is viewed as its most archaic version I will use the text of the *Visio Pauli* as it is preserved in the ninth century Codex Paris (P: Nouv. acq. lat. 1631; Bibliothèque nationale de France, Paris) as the focus of this study.⁷ Because the scope of this essay does not allow for a complete overview of all existing versions, I will concentrate on the longer Latin texts edited by Silverstein and Hilhorst.⁸ I will set aside important accounts like the Greek version edited by Constantin von Tischendorf,⁹ the Coptic version, whose impact has recently been brought to the forefront of scholarly attention by Lautaro Roig Lanzillotta,¹⁰ and others.

---

[5] Regarding the *Visio Pauli*'s influence in Medieval Latin, early Czech and German versions see Jiroušková, *Visio Pauli* (cf. note 3). For an overview of editions of the different versions see Jan N. Bremmer, "Bibliography of the *Visio Pauli* and the Gnostic *Apocalypse of Paul*," in *The Visio Pauli and the Gnostic Apocalypse of Paul*, ed. Jan N. Bremmer and Istvan Czachesz, Studies on Early Christian Apocrypha 9 (Leuven: Peeters, 2007), 211–36; and Claude Carozzi, *Eschatologie et l'au delà. Recherches sur l'Apocalypse de Paul* (Aix-en-Provence: Presses universitaires de Provence, 1994), 301–3.

[6] The most up-to-date discussion of introductory issues is offered by Jan N. Bremmer, "The Apocalypse of Paul," in *Early New Testament Apocrypha*, ed. J. Christopher Edwards, Ancient Literature for New Testament Studies 9 (Grand Rapids, MI: Eerdmans, 2022), 427–45.

[7] For a description of this manuscript, see Theodore Silverstein and Anthony Hilhorst, ed., *Apocalypse of Paul: A New Critical Edition of Three Long Latin Versions*, Cahiers d'Orientalisme 21 (Geneva: Patrick Cramer, 1997), 23–28. Latin texts quoted follow this edition (including their sometimes incorrect or incorrect sounding Latin); translations are mine.

[8] See the more detailed descriptions of the manuscripts in Silverstein and Hilhorst, *Apocalypse of Paul* (cf. note 7), 23–26. I will not be able to check all these texts regarding every detail. Finally, I have left out the Middle German fragment Vienna (discussed by Silverstein and Hilhorst, *Apocalypse of Paul*, 36–37) for the time being.

[9] *Apocalypses Apocryphae Mosis, Esdrae, Pauli, Iohannis, item Mariae Dormitio, additis evangeliorum et actuum apocryphorum supplementis,* ed. Constantin von Tischendorf (repr. Hildesheim: Olms, 1966), 34–39.

[10] Edition and translation: Ernest A. Wallis Budge, *Miscellaneous Texts in the Dialect of Upper Egypt: Edited with English Translations* (London: British Museum, 1915) 534–74 and 1043–84. For a first discussion of this version see Lautaro Roig Lanzillotta, "The Coptic *Apocalypse of Paul* in Ms Or 7023," in Bremmer and Czachesz, *Visio Pauli and the Gnostic Apocalypse of Paul* (cf. note 5), 158–97. A new critical edition, translation, and commentary on this text was unavailable at the time this contribution was prepared: Roig Lanzillotta and Jacques van der Vliet,

Besides P, I will concentrate on the following manuscripts of Silverstein and Hilhorst's L[1,3] recension: St G is manuscript St Gall MS 317 (ninth century AD); Esc is Codex a.II.3 from the Real Biblioteca del Monasterio El Escorial (tenth century AD); and Arnh is Codex 6, Stichting Arnhemse Openbare en Gelderse Wetenschappelijke Bibliotheek, Arnhem, the Netherlands (fifteenth and early sixteenth century AD). In addition, I will take a look into the (much shorter) L² manuscripts edited by Silverstein and Hilhorst: F is Codex 362 from the Österreichische Nationalbibliothek Vienna (early fourteenth century AD), Gz is Codex 856 of the Universitätsbibliothek Graz, Austria (fifteenth century AD), and Z is Codex C 101 of the Zentralbibliothek Zürich (1470).

I am, of course, also aware that Revelation's text is not exactly identical to those that the critical editions portray. We will, however, quickly see that this poses little problem for the task at hand since the *Visio Pauli* does not include word-for-word quotations but echoes motifs from Revelation (and puts them in new contexts). This relationship is the reason why it is valid to compare the different accounts of the *Visio Pauli* with the critical text of Revelation and consult other translations only where it is required for the argument.

1 The City of Christ in the *Visio Pauli* and Revelation's Heavenly Jerusalem

The long version of the *Visio Pauli* can be divided into the following sections:[11] after an introduction detailing the miraculous rediscovery of the book (1–2), paragraphs 3–10 describe different parts of the cosmos complaining to God about humanity's manifold sins and transgressions. After this, a lengthy section is devoted to the souls of the righteous and the sinful describing their death and beyond (11–18). Only after this is Paul taken to the third heaven (19) where he visits paradise (20), hears words that a human being is not allowed to say (21; cf. 2 Cor 12:4), and is then taken down to the promised land, which is obviously located in the first heaven (21). While Revelation concentrates on a description of the holy city (and does not speak about its surroundings), the *Visio Pauli* situates its City of Christ within the promised land which, with the city as its most important feature, is described broadly in paragraphs 21–30. After this, Paul is brought to the hellish places for which the *Visio Pauli* is most well-known (31).

---

ed., *The Apocalypse of Paul (Visio Pauli) in Sahidic Coptic,* Vigiliae Christianae Supplements 178 (Leiden: Brill, 2023).

[11] I follow the division of the text offered by Silverstein and Hilhorst (cf. note 7).

1.1 The Promised Land (21–22)

Even though it has not mentioned the City of Christ, paragraph 21 already sets the scene in which the city is placed. At the first gate of heaven, Paul sees Oceanus and envisions a country that is seven times brighter than silver.[12] His *angelus interpres* names it the "promised land."[13] According to the angel, this promised land is a hidden place where the souls of the righteous are sent between the time of their death and final judgment. When Paul asks whether this country will become visible after a certain period of time, the angel points to Christ's second coming as a marker. Even though the following description of the things to come echoes Revelation, the *Visio Pauli* puts them in a different order. According to Revelation, the Millennium (together with the first resurrection) comes first (see Rev 20:4–6). After this, the final victory over Satan (Rev 20:7–10) takes place, followed by the final judgment (Rev 20:11–15), and lastly, a new creation into which the Heavenly Jerusalem descends (Rev 21).[14] The *Visio Pauli*'s belief about the end times consists of nearly the same components; however, their different order changes their function, at least partially. A first resurrection, reserved for only some witnesses of Jesus (see Rev 20:4), is no longer necessary. Instead, after death, all souls go to a place prepared for them as a kind of in-between state.[15] The souls of the righteous go on living in the paradise of the promised land while the souls of the sinners are sent to hellish places. When Christ comes with all his holy ones (cf. 2 Thess 1:10) for his parousia, the first earth is dissolved by God's powerful commands. After this, the Millennium starts in the promised land. Revelation's scene of the binding of the dragon for one thousand years (Rev 20:2; cf. 20:7) no longer plays a role.[16]

---

[12] P: *illic autem terra clarior argento septiaes*. The other witnesses of L^{1,3} offer comparable texts. Esc stresses the difference to "this world" with the variation *ibi autem erat terra illa clarior argento septies uius mundi*. The motif does not occur in the somewhat shorter § 21 in the witnesses of L^2.

[13] P: *terra reprimissionis*. Interestingly, the text connects the idea of the land being promised with Matthew's third Beatitude (Matt 5:5): "Blessed are the meek, for they will inherit the earth." Arnh offers a slight, but important variation by speaking about the *locus promissionis* (which, of course, cuts the relation to the quote that follows of Matt 5:5 using *terra*). The motif does not yet occur in the L^2 witnesses.

[14] Regarding Revelation's idea of the "new creation" see Tobias Nicklas, "Schöpfung und Vollendung in der Offenbarung des Johannes," in *Theologies of Creation in Early Judaism and Ancient Christianity: In Honour of Hans Klein*, ed. Tobias Nicklas and Korinna Zamfir, Deuterocanonical and Cognate Literature Studies 6 (Berlin: de Gruyter, 2010), 389–414.

[15] Regarding ideas of such an intermediate state after death (and before the final judgment) called *refrigerium* see the overview by Dagmar Hofmann, "Der 'Ort der Erfrischung': Refrigerium in der frühchristlichen Literatur und Grabkultur," in *Topographie des Jenseits: Studien zur Geschichte des Todes in Kaiserzeit und Spätantike*, ed. Walter Ameling, Altertumswissenschaftliches Kolloquium 21 (Stuttgart: Franz Steiner, 2011), 103–22.

[16] The motif is, of course, logically problematic as the question arises as to why the dragon is now free again after one thousand years – only to be defeated again.

Two passages clearly echo Revelation and make it clear that the last chapters of Revelation form the basis for the following descriptions:[17]

VisPl P   *Tunc sentencia dei dissoluitur terra prima* (= St G)
VisPl Esc   *iussu dei dissolbetur terra prima*
VisPl Arnh   *tunc precepto dei deficiet terra ista*
Rev 21:1b   ὁ γὰρ πρῶτος οὐρανὸς καὶ ἡ πρώτη γῆ ἀπῆλθαν καὶ ἡ θάλασσα οὐκ ἔστιν ἔτι.

The second passage reads as follows:

VisPl P   *et regnabit* [Christ] *super illos* [the saints] *mille annos*
VisPl St G   *et ... regnabit Christus super illos mille annis*
VisPl Esc   *et regnauit Christus super eam [i.e. terram]*
VisPl Arnh   *et regnabit cum eis Christus annis mille*[18]
Rev 20:4   καὶ ἐβασίλευσαν μετὰ τοῦ Χριστοῦ χίλια ἔτη
Rev 20:6   καὶ βασιλεύσουσιν μετ' αὐτοῦ [τὰ] χίλια ἔτη

These descriptions not only show that images from Revelation form a backdrop for the following scenes, but they also make clear to what extent details change. The text, which has just led its readers (alongside Paul) to the third heaven and below, showing them the origins of Oceanus, is no longer interested in the destruction of the heavens and the sea. Instead, it concentrates on the earth. At the same time, it describes a millennium where Christ rules *over* the righteous ones – and not *with* them. It is only in the Arnh version where Christ rules "with them" (*cum eis*), meaning together with "all righteous" (*omnes iustos*), who are mentioned in the sentence before.[19] Such a relationship between Christ and his followers differs from that which is described in Revelation and has significant ecclesiological impact.[20] Neither Paul's influential idea of the *ekklesia* as Christ's body (see 1 Cor 12:12–31a; Rom 12:4–5),[21] nor Revelation's image of the New Jerusalem (and its inhabitants) as Christ's bride (see Rev 21:2, 9; cf. also 19:7),[22] find a place in the theological construct of the *Visio Pauli*.

---

[17] The passage is missing in the manuscripts of L².
[18] The motif does not occur in the manuscripts of L².
[19] Interestingly, P, St G and Esc speak about *omnes sanctos*, another slight difference (which allows a closer connection to 2 Thess 1:10).
[20] Regarding the ecclesiological impact of hopes for an eschatological co-rule of Christ's followers (or at least some of them) see Hanna Roose, *Eschatologische Mitherrschaft. Entwicklungslinien einer urchristlichen Erwartung*, Novum Testamentum et Orbis Antiquus 54 (Göttingen: Vandenhoeck & Ruprecht; Fribourg: Academic Press, 2004), 317.
[21] For the background and development of this and related images see Matthias Walter, *Gemeinde als Leib Christi: Untersuchungen zum Corpus Paulinum und zu den 'Apostolischen Vätern'*, Novum Testamentum et Orbis Antiquus 49 (Fribourg: Universitätsverlag; Göttingen: Vandenhoeck & Ruprecht, 2001).
[22] See, however, the somewhat random sentence in Esc § 22: *Hec que nunc uides nubtialis est locus* (referring to the City of Christ).

After this, paragraph 22 describes the promised land by combining references to biblical texts (e.g. Exod 3:8: "milk and honey" and Matt 5:6) and images of an almost "Land of Cockaigne," meaning a paradise. We read of palm trees, an incredible abundance of fruit, date palms, gigantic grapevines full of innumerable grapes, and much more.[23] At least one passage is influenced by Revelation's description of the holy city. The text describes a river of milk and honey with banks that grow trees bearing manifold fruit:[24]

VisPl P	*Et erant al litus fluminis ipsius arbores plantate plene fructibus. Vna quoque autem arbor erat adferens fructos xii in anno uarios et diuersos fructos abentes.*
VisPl St G	*Et erant in litore illius fluminis arbores plantate plene fructibus. Vnaqueque arbor erat afferens fructus duodecies in annum uarios et diuersos.*
VisPl Esc	*Et erat ad litus fluminis arbores plantate plena fructibus. Vna quoque arbor afferebat xii fructus in anno barios et diuersos.*
VisPl Arnh	*Et fuerunt ad labium fluuii illius arbores inserte plene fructibus, singule arbores afferentes per annum xii^m fructus bonos et alia promiscua.*
Rev 22:2	ἐν μέσῳ τῆς πλατείας αὐτῆς καὶ τοῦ ποταμοῦ ἐντεῦθεν καὶ ἐκεῖθεν ξύλον ζωῆς ποιοῦν καρποὺς δώδεκα, κατὰ μῆνα ἕκαστον ἀποδιδοῦν τὸν καρπὸν αὐτοῦ.[25]

Interestingly, the text of the L^2 manuscripts does not offer this same parallel to Rev 22:2, but only speaks about a river of milk and honey. Here, I only quote F (which has minor variants compared with Gz and Z):

VisPl F	*Et fluuius lacteus et melleus currebat per eam [i.e. terram; TN] et palme pulcherrime in ripa stabant ex diuersis coloribus.*

While the imagery of $L^{1,3}$ texts may also be influenced by Ezek 47:12,[26] the clear overlaps with Revelation (including the idea of trees bearing fruit twelve times a year) are obviously closer. With these parallels in mind, the differences are noticeable as well. Revelation's river (which does not consist of milk and honey, but of the "water of life" [22:1]) flows out of God's throne and into the city, whereas the *Visio Pauli* describes a river running through the country.[27] Perhaps even more interesting may be the following change: stressing the impact of "life"

---

[23] The closest parallel seems to be Papias's description of the millennium quoted by Irenaeus of Lyons, *Adversus haereses* 5.33.3–4; but see also Lactantius, *Divinarum institutionum libri VII* 7.24.

[24] I do not offer corrections of the partly incorrect Latin given in some passages.

[25] The passage is text-critically uncertain.

[26] See also the note in Silverstein and Hilhorst, *Apocalypse of Paul* (cf. note 7), 116–17.

[27] As the City of Christ is situated on an island, the river cannot come out of the city (if we presume that the image wants to follow a certain logic).

(22:1; 22:2) and the idea that the leaves of the tree(s) (22:2[28]) are for the healing of the nations, Revelation indicates that these passages should be understood as *images* that refer to a deeper reality. Instead, the *Visio Pauli* is simply interested in describing the over-abundance of God's gifts for those who are worthy.[29] However, when Paul asks whether these are God's only promises to the faithful, the angel speaks about others that are seven times greater. Paul is led to another place[30] and told: "This is the Acherousian Lake where the City of Christ is, but not everyone is allowed to enter the city."[31] This is a striking combination of motifs from the Apocalypse of Peter 14 (which, like the *Visio Pauli*, speaks about a baptism in the Acherousian Lake)[32] and Revelation's idea that not everyone can enter the Heavenly Jerusalem (Rev 21:27; 22:15). While the restrictions documented in Revelation seem to address everyone and give a chance for most righteous believers to enter the city, the *Visio Pauli*'s criteria for entering the city are somewhat difficult to interpret. In *Visio Pauli*, the promised land is reserved for those who are married but remain chaste, while entrance to the City of Christ is reserved for an even greater elite group of people. P reads: *Virginibus autem et esurientibus et sicientibus ius[t]iciam et adfligentibus se [pro]pter nomen domini, dabit deus maiora his septiaes*.[33] This can be understood in two ways. The first possibility is that someone must meet *one* of the above criteria, either living a pure life or hungering and thirsting for justice (see Matt 5:6). The second option is that the entrance to the city is *only* for persons who lived a chaste life and, (maybe as a result) hungered and thirsted for justice. Although the final passages of paragraph 22 seem to allow entrance to the city even to repentant sinners

---

[28] The text is transmitted in two different forms – the singular is certainly the (preferable) *lectio difficilior*.

[29] § 22 P [in the mouth of the angel]: *quoniam dominus deus abu[n]dans fluenter presta do[na] condignes*. The texts of the other L[1,3] manuscripts show only slight variations, perhaps Arnh showing less significance on the abundance of gifts with the sentence *quoniam ... diues dominus tribuens bona dignis suis*. The motif does not occur in the L[2] manuscripts.

[30] This place is probably part of the same country. According to P, Esc and Arnh, Paul sees another river there (which sounds a bit strange as this river is later called the Acherousian Lake). St G, however, has just "white water": *Aqua candida uidi desuper lacum*.

[31] § 22 P: *Haec est Aceriosus lacus ubi est ciuitas Christi, sed non omnis homo permitetur ingredi in ciuitatem illam*. The texts of the other L[1,3] manuscripts show slight variations mainly in the spelling of "Acherousian"; only Arnh identifies the city as Jerusalem (*... in ciuitatem que est Ierusalem*). The motif does not occur in L[2] manuscripts.

[32] For other Christian writings that use this motif (plus its background in Greco-Roman literature) see T. J. Kraus, "Acherousia und Elysion: Anmerkungen im Hinblick auf deren Verwendung auch im christlichen Kontext," *Mnemosyne* 56 (2003): 145–63.

[33] All other manuscripts of L[1,3] offer texts where a chaste life is understood as the first condition for entering the City of Christ (St G: *Virginum autem ...*; Esc: *set serbantium castitas uirginum ...*; Arnh: *Qui obseruauerunt uirginitatem castitatis sue ...*). In the text of Arnh, the second solution is most clear. Interestingly, the shorter texts of L[2] speak about the righteous or the righteous and elect who enter the place (F and Z: *huc ueniunt iusti*; Gr: *huc ueniunt iusti et electi*).

doing penance, I support the second interpretation: everything that follows makes the most sense if it is addressed to people who remained celibate for at least the final part of their lives. While the souls of most righteous believers will be placed in a transitional state in the promised land, only a few are allowed to enter the City of Christ: those who were formerly celibate. These requirements represent a radical difference from Revelation's Heavenly Jerusalem where these criteria do not play a role.

1.2 The City of Christ

Paragraph 23 finally leads readers into the City of Christ. There, three thousand angels sing while Paul crosses the Acherousian Lake on a golden ship, leading him to the City of Christ. The outward description of the city is, again, heavily influenced by Revelation's Heavenly Jerusalem, but also deviates from it. First, for both the cities in Revelation and the *Visio Pauli*, the number twelve plays a significant role. Revelation's Heavenly Jerusalem, however, consists of one large, high wall with twelve gates and twelve angels at each gate (Rev 21:12), in addition to twelve foundation stones (Rev 21:14). On the other hand, the long account of the *Visio Pauli* describes a city with twelve walls, twelve towers, and twelve gates (23). Revelation, again, connects the image of the twelve gates with the twelve tribes of Israel (Rev 21:12), and the image of the cornerstones with the names of the twelve apostles (Rev 21:14). This is the city for the people of God, which, according to Revelation, will always be connected with Israel.[34] Both features are absent in the *Visio Pauli*, and it shows no interest in the tribes of Israel.[35] Instead, it describes the city as "completely golden,"[36] a motif which corresponds to Revelation 21:18, where the city is said to be made of "pure gold" (cf. also 21:21).[37] In addition, St G, Esc, and Arnh mention the additional theme of the city's incredible brightness.[38] This may be based on Rev 21:23–24: contrary to the City of Christ, the Heavenly Jerusalem does not need the sun or moon because it is

---

[34] For further information regarding the role of Israel in the book of Revelation, see K. Müller, "Noch einmal Einhundertvierundvierzigtausend: Anmerkungen zur judenchristlichen Kompetenz des Verfassers der Johannesapokalypse," in *Mächtige Bilder: Zeit- und Wirkungsgeschichte der Johannesoffenbarung*, ed. Bernhard Heininger, Stuttgarter Bibelstudien 225 (Stuttgart: Katholisches Bibelwerk, 2011), 132–66.

[35] Of course, it mentions figures of Israel's history, but even does not mention Jews in its hellish places.

[36] § 23 P, St G: *erat tota aurea*. Esc differs slightly by offering the words *et erat ciuitas illa tota aurea*; Arnh: *et tota terra erat aurea*. This motif does not occur in the L² manuscripts which speak about an extraordinarily beautiful city (F, Gr, Z: *in ciuitatem pulchram nimis*).

[37] It would be appealing to compare both Revelation's Heavenly Jerusalem and the City of Christ in the *Visio Pauli* with Lucian of Samosata's "Golden city" in his *Vera Historia*. Unfortunately, this must be done in another paper.

[38] ApcPl Arnh: *erat lumen eius super lumen huius mundi, lucens super numerum et modum*. See the comparable passages in St G and Esc. F, Gr and Z have the somewhat shorter *et lux clarior luce priori* (Gr: *priori luce*).

illuminated by the glory of God and the Lamb. Even though the City of Christ still awaits Christ's parousia and his continuous presence, its glory seems to resemble Christ's glory even now.[39] In addition, Revelation's outward description of the city is much more complex than that of the *Visio Pauli*. Again, Revelation encourages the fantasy and imagination of its readers with the help of apparent contradictions and an extraordinary variety of details. The Heavenly Jerusalem shines like a precious gem and as a crystal-clear jasper (Rev 21:11), its walls are built of jasper, and the city (including its streets) is not just made of "pure gold" but also appears "like pure glass" (Rev 21:18, 21). It continues with a highly complex list of the different jewels embellishing the city's cornerstones (Rev 21:19–20) and describes the city's gates as pearls (Rev 21:21). All this serves to describe the key idea that Revelation's city is "filled with God's glory" (Rev 21:11). The *Visio Pauli* is not interested in these sorts of details. Its city has twelve gates of "great beauty"[40] and is surrounded by four rivers:[41] the river Pison[42] flowing with honey, the river Euphrates flowing with milk, the river Gihon[43] flowing with oil, and the river Tigris flowing with wine.[44] Finally, both cities are of immense dimensions. While Revelation describes the angel using a golden measuring rod to measure its length, breadth, and height (twelve thousand stadia) plus the height of its walls (one hundred and forty-four thousand cubits),[45] the *Visio Pauli* is mainly interested in the space between the different walls (one stadium surrounding each wall).[46] In other words, even if the City of Christ in the *Visio Pauli* resembles Revelation's Heavenly Jerusalem quite closely, the *Visio Pauli* emphasizes very different aspects than Revelation does. Both cities are big and immensely beautiful, but Revelation offers a highly symbolic description, an almost ideal implementation of the old idea of God's dwelling both in his holy place (now without a temple; cf. Rev 21:22) and among his people.[47] The *Visio*

---

[39] Or is this motif, which creates a certain logical inconsistency, simply needed to demonstrate that Paul's City of Christ is more or less identical to Revelation's Heavenly Jerusalem?

[40] § 23 P *pulcritudine magna*; St G and Esc: *ornate omnem pulchritudinem*; Arnh: *ornate in ea per omnem pulchritudinem*. The motif does not occur in the L² manuscripts.

[41] Regarding the Old Testament background of this description see Jacques T.A.G.M. van Ruiten, "The Four Rivers of Eden in the Apocalypse of Paul (Visio Pauli): The Intertextual Relationship of Genesis 2.10–4 and the Apocalypse of Paul 23," in Bremmer and Czachesz, *Visio Pauli and the Gnostic Apocalypse of Paul* (cf. note 5), 50–76.

[42] The texts read *Fison* (P, St G, Esc) and *Phison* (Arnh).

[43] The texts read *Gion* (P, St G), *Yeon* (Esc) and *Geon* (Arnh).

[44] The motif is even attested in the L² manuscripts.

[45] Again, the text plays with the number twelve here.

[46] P: *singuli muri abebant inter se singula stadia in circuito* – St G, Esc and Arnh offer the same in slight variation. The motif does not occur in the L² parallels.

[47] A competent discussion of Revelation's shekhinah theology is offered by Franz Tóth, "Die Schechina-Theologie in der Johannesapokalypse," in *Das Geheimnis der Gegenwart Gottes: Zur Schechina-Vorstellung in Judentum und Christentum*, ed. Bernd Janowski and Enno E. Popkes, WUNT 318 (Tübingen: Mohr Siebeck, 2014), 257–304.

Pauli, however, designs a country and a city where all kinds of (vegetarian) food and drink are available in abundance. Unfortunately, meat and sex are still forbidden.

Contrary to everything we read in Revelation, the afterlife in the *Visio Pauli*'s City of Christ is arranged according to a strict hierarchy. This is made even clearer in the paragraphs to come. Even though the following passages do not offer much that can be counted as reception of the book of Revelation, the framework set up in paragraphs 21–23 can be understood as important aspects of change compared to Revelation's Heavenly Jerusalem. Paragraph 24, for example, offers a lengthy description of men sitting in big trees in front of the city's doors.[48] Interestingly, the trees do not bear fruit, but only leaves (perhaps expressing that the men sitting on them also did not bear fruit in their own lives). When Paul asks about these men, the text's focus becomes clear. Even though these people lived a life of fasting and abstinence, their pride and arrogance[49] towards others (St G speaks explicitly about people for whom they opened the door of the monastery)[50] hindered them from entering the City of Christ after their death. Now their trees do penance instead of them, and they can hope to be allowed into the city when "the eternal king Christ enters it with his holy ones."[51] But even then, they will be less valued than those who humbled themselves and served God throughout their lives.

After this, Paul visits the four rivers around the city (§ 25–28). The text's underlying monastic ideals become even clearer now: the river of honey is called the "way of the prophets"[52] and is reserved for each person who "because of God has not done his own will" (25).[53] At the river of milk, Paul meets the innocent children slaughtered by Herod (see Matt 2:16), and this is the place for those who remained chaste and pure during their lifetime (26).[54] The river of wine is reserved for Abraham, Isaac, Jacob, Lot, Job, and all of the others who showed charity and hospitality:

27 VisPl P and St G *quoniam seruasti(s) humanitatem et susceptionem peregrinorum*[55]

---

[48] The whole paragraph lacks in Esc, but is extant in the L² manuscripts.

[49] P, St G and Arnh speak about an "arrogant heart" (P, St G: *cor superbum*; Arnh: *superbum ... cor*). The motif of *superbia* plays a role throughout the paragraph (even in the L² manuscripts).

[50] St G: *aperiebant ianuam monasterii*. See, however, P (*aperiebant*) and Arnh (*aperiebant ianuam domus sue* [!]).

[51] P: *quando ingreditur com sanctis suis rex aeternus Christus*. Slight variations in St G and Arnh – the passage is not extant in Esc.

[52] P and St G: *uia prophetarum*. The passage is not extant in Esc. Arnh reads *chorus prophetarum*.

[53] P: *non facit propriam uoluntatem suam propter deum*.

[54] P: *omnes qui seruiunt castitatem cum puritatem*. Slight variations among the L¹,³ manuscripts.

[55] Slight variations in Esc and Arnh.

The question of whether the recipients of this hospitality are "strangers" or, more explicitly, "pilgrims"[56] depends upon the interpretation of the term *peregrinorum*. In the latter case, the text's monastic context is stressed even more. Finally, the river of oil is for those without pride, who have devoted their lives whole-heartedly to God (28).[57] The theme of "pride" or "arrogance" (*superbia*) mentioned previously in paragraph 24 is presented again.[58] The text's ideals seem at least partly formulated from the perspective of a late antique monastic context. In addition, everyone in the City of Christ is male – the text does not mention any women in the promised land.

The following paragraphs make the differences to Revelation's Heavenly Jerusalem even clearer. Revelation's images of a Heavenly Jerusalem describe a utopia written from the perspective of a world in which the souls of those who were slaughtered for the word of God cry out to God and ask him for justice (Rev 6:9–10). Even if they are clothed in white garments and asked to wait a little longer (Rev 6:11), the reader of Revelation must wait until the end of the book to find out about God's final judgment and his new creation. Revelation's holy city, the New Jerusalem, possessing God's glory, comes down from heaven (Rev 21:10–11). It does not seem to contain any houses or quarters, and its inhabitants understandably do not do anything but look into God's face (Rev 22:4).[59] The idea that beholding God's face may be possible is, as far as I can tell, the decisive change between the first and the new creations. Even if the text goes on to speak about the kings of the earth who bring their glory into the city (Rev 21:24), Revelation's Heavenly Jerusalem seems to be a space in which social distinctions between the city's inhabitants no longer play a role. While sinners are not able to enter the city (Rev 21:26–27),[60] everyone inside may participate in an unbroken relationship with God and the Lamb.

In the *Visio Pauli*, the situation is completely different. While Revelation's Heavenly Jerusalem has only one huge wall, the City of Christ consists of twelve, and only now, in paragraph 29, it becomes clear as to why. When Paul recognizes that the twelfth wall is higher than the others, he asks whether there is any wall

---

[56] See, for example, the translation by Hugo Duensing and Aurelio de Santos Otero, Apokalypse des Paulus, in *Neutestamentliche Apokryphen II: Apostolisches, Apokalypsen und Verwandtes*, ed. Edgar Hennecke and Wilhelm Schneemelcher (Tübingen: Mohr Siebeck, 1997), 644–75, esp. 660.

[57] P: *histi sunt qui deuouerunt se deo ex toto corde, non abentes in se superbia*.

[58] The text of Esc differs here from the other $L^{1,3}$ manuscripts and reads only *qui dederunt se deo ex toto corde suo*.

[59] Regarding the theological impact of this image see Tobias Nicklas, "Gott und Identität: Das Gottesbild der Johannesoffenbarung und ihre Identitätskonstruktion," in *Die Johannesapokalypse: Geschichte – Theologie – Rezeption*, ed. Christina Hoegen-Rohls, Uta Poplutz, and Michael Sommer, WUNT (Tübingen: Mohr Siebeck, 2024, forthcoming).

[60] But see the promises of undeserved grace in Rev 22:17, 21.

in the City of Christ that is more "honorable" than this.[61] The angel's answer is clear: "The second is better than the first, and the third better than the second, as each of them outmatches the other until the twelfth."[62] Paul then asks: "And why, Lord, does each of them outmatch the other in glory?"[63] The angel's response makes the text's pragmatics even stronger: every bit of slander, jealousy, and pride that people have within themselves diminishes their glory within the City of Christ. All this results in a hierarchy of the afterlife based in honor and shame, symbolized by the city's twelve walls. Interestingly, at the top of this hierarchy, we find simple-minded believers full of goodness and compassionate hearts,[64] people who are not overly interested in intellectual study, but who are devout believers, concentrating on God's commands.[65] In other words, this is a text pleading against an intellectual understanding of God's instructions. Placing humble minds on the top of its otherworldly hierarchy may help to rightly align worldly hierarchies because any kind of critical or intellectual discourse can be easily disavowed as a sign of *superbia* (and thus sin).[66] A good believer must do what God asks; he – the text is not interested in women – should not even go so far as considering the fact that it may not always be easy to find out what God *really* desires.

1.3 Liturgy in the City of Christ

Finally, in the middle of the city, Paul recognizes a large and very high altar showing that there is still a distinction between life in the city (an intermediate state following death) and life after the parousia, (bodily resurrection and final judgment). This city, called "Jerusalem," (P) or even "Heavenly Jerusalem,"[67]

---

[61] P: *precedens in honore huic loco.* St G, Esc and Arnh with slight variations.

[62] P: *est secundus melior primo, similiter tercius secondo, quia unus unum precedet usque ad xiimo murum.* St G is even more explicit: *Est secundus melior, est tertius et pretiosior illo. Unus unum precedit in gloriam usque ad duodecimum murum* (see also, with slight variations, Esc and Arnh). The motif does not occur in the L² manuscripts.

[63] P: *Ob quare, domine, unus alium precedet in gloriam.* This passage is not extant in Esc, and much shorter in Arnh (*ob quam rem*).

[64] P: *qui bonitatem et intellectum habent cordis.* St G/Esc: *qui bonitatem et innocentiam (h)abent et intellectum cordis*; Arnh: *qui bonitatem et innocenciam in se habent et intellectum cordis.*

[65] P: *semetipsos stultos fecerunt propter dominum deum, neque scientes scripturas, ne[que] psalmos plures, sed uni[us] cappituli memores de preceptis dei* (slight variations in St G, Esc and Arnh).

[66] The seer of Revelation is, of course, also highly aggressive towards different-minded people (and especially toward women like the prophetess of Thyatira whom he calls Jezebel [2:20]). At the same time I would regard him as an early Christian intellectual. For a fuller argument see Tobias Nicklas, "Crazy Guy or Intellectual Leader? The Seer of Revelation and his Role for the Communities of Asia Minor," in *The Rise of the Christian Intellectual*, ed. Lewis Ayres and H. Clifton Ward, Arbeiten zur Kirchengeschichte 139 (Berlin: de Gruyter, 2020), 7–24.

[67] Esc: *ciuitas Ierusalem celestis*; cf. also Arnh. There is a lacuna in St G; and we should be reminded that Arnh has already identified the city with Jerusalem in § 22. The whole passage is lacking in the L² manuscripts.

does not have the throne of God and the Lamb in the center; both remain in the seventh heaven. Instead, David chants "Hallelujah" with a voice that fills the holy city. But even though neither God or Christ are present, the worship offered in the City of Christ – including the psalms – mirrors what is happening in the seventh heaven. This is important because what is taking place in heaven should also take place on earth.[68] Only one small, logical step is needed, and those who are celibate can interpret their own sacrifice in a different way: they are doing almost exactly what is already going on in the City of Christ *and even more so* in the seventh heaven. The innermost part of the City of Christ describes the ideal earthly worship as one that is connected to heavenly realities. This thesis is made even more plausible in paragraph 30 in a discussion of the term "Hallelujah," which the angel translates as "Let us praise him all together!" This interpretation leads to a (very worldly) problem where a person who does not sing the psalms along with the others is called a sinner.[69]

Interestingly, this passage (which for modern readers may appear anticlimactic) is the final section of the description of the City of Christ in the *Visio Pauli*. After this, Paul is led to hellish places.

2 Conclusion: A New Holy City and Its Function

Looking at only a few accounts of the *Visio Pauli* has shown us how difficult it is to deal with a "living text." If we only had the L^2 manuscripts, it would be impossible to see the clear influence of Revelation's Heavenly Jerusalem on the extracanonical writing's City of Christ. Only the $L^{1,3}$ texts show clear allusions to themes from Revelation. Passages referring to the Heavenly Jerusalem and describing the millennium – certainly influenced by later chiliastic interpretations of Revelation's millennium – play an important role for the portrayal of the promised land. Revelation is never actually quoted verbatim, and we never know for sure whether the author (or redactors or translators) of the *Visio Pauli* had access to a written text of Revelation or if they were merely influenced by images mediated by cultural memory. In any case, Revelation is influential for what follows. However, a close comparison with Revelation reveals that a few key things change. As Paul visits the City of Christ *before* the parousia and the end times, the city he envisions is not yet the dwelling place of God and the Lamb. It is called "Jerusalem," but does not have the features of Revelation's

---

[68] See the text offered by P: *Quia Christus filius dei sedet ad dexteram patris suii et hic Dauid psallet ante eum in vii.mo celo. Et sicut ita et fiunt in celis, ita et in terries similiter, quia non licet sine Dauid ostiam offerre deo, sed necesse est ut psallat Dauid in hora oblacionis corporis et sanguinis Christi. Quemadmodum in celis perficitus, ita et in terra.*

[69] $L^{1,3}$ manuscripts see exceptions for very old and demented participants in the liturgy, while L^2 texts simply call it a big sin not to participate in the community's "Hallelujah."

Heavenly Jerusalem. It is no longer explicitly connected to Israel, the people of God. It does not represent the bride of Christ, as it does in Revelation, and it is certainly not open to every believer. Instead, it is reserved for a small, pure group of elites and structured along a strict hierarchy defined by the fulfilment of chaste living. Interestingly, the highest level of closeness to the holy center of the city is reserved for devout and humble minds who do not study Scripture, but simply follow what are presented as God's commands. Revelation's utopian Jerusalem situated in the end times is turned into a mixture of a vegetarian *Land of Cockaigne* and a heavenly monastery (distanced from the rest of the world by huge walls). Those living in this city do not find fulfillment by meeting with God directly. Instead, their lives center around a liturgy that follows a heavenly model and, at the same time, is a perfect example of worship for the world they inhabit. This combination serves a clear purpose: these types of religious hierarchies silence any kind of critical intellectual debate by placing the "good" and "simple-minded" at the top. In relation to the world outside of this context, the text stabilizes monastic elite thinking and enforces ideals of virginity and chastity.

New Jerusalem as the "Flipside" to the Last Judgment in Primasius, Bede, and Beatus

Mark W. Elliott

Introduction

"New Jerusalem" is a place and a state of being in contradistinction or opposition to an event ("last judgment"). It might of course be conducive of consequences, although not described. Yet as a place of "rest," it is an end in itself. The correspondence between the place of good news and safety and the event of ultimate doom is of course not totally symmetrical. Chapter 21 of the Apocalypse provides a vision of peace (to play with the etymology of "Jerusalem") and provides an oasis or a sabbath amidst a good deal of chaotic and restless imagery in John's vision, not only in ch. 20.

The New Jerusalem is the Heavenly Jerusalem. That means that while it transcends the old or earthly Jerusalem, it did not supersede it in the sense of rendering it otiose. In what follows I will discuss the idea of the new or heavenly Jerusalem in the history of Christian thought before turning to consider how three first-millennium commentators on Apocalypse 21 made sense of that vision and came to understand "Jerusalem" in ways that were diverse and distinct but also commonly ecclesiological.

1 Jerusalem: Below and Above

First of all, the precise significance of the contrast of "Jerusalem below/present-day Jerusalem" (as per Gal 4:26) needs to be understood. Jerusalem had little political status in the first millennium. It was "other" and far away from western Europe – good for holy sites and relics and for the buttressing of a faith that was essentially the faith of the martyrs preserved as remembered from pre-Constantinian times.[1] Yet for the purposes of spiritual resourcing, Jerusalem's holy

---

[1] Klaus Thraede, "Jerusalem II (Sinnbild)," *Reallexikon für Antike und Christentum 17* (1996), 718–64 at 730: "In diesem Sinn hat Clemens auch Phil. 3,20 in Verbindung mit Gal 2,20 zu nutzen versucht: Ich lebe aber, obwohl ich noch im Fleische bin, als wandelte ich schon im

sites would be conserved by the civil authorities, in marked contrast to how the Roman remains in Rome herself would be allowed to be re-purposed or simply to crumble, since there was little worthy enough to be remembered. Hence as the Pope grew politically powerful, Rome was a city of the present. Accordingly, the Emperor was able to depose Pope Martin I in 653 but not Pope Sergius in 687.

Carolingian rulers were thus naturally suspicious of the present Rome's pretensions and for that reason tended to lionise Jerusalem in a way that its imagined spiritual status dwarfed its political actuality. Significantly the Patriarch of Jerusalem sent the key of the Holy Sepulchre Church to Charlemagne in 800 at his coronation in Rome. So while Rome became progressively identified as the earthly seat of the Pope as head of the Western church, the Emperor's vocation was one of ruling over an empire cast as a "city of peace," a spiritual though earthly extension of the "Jerusalem" purchased by Christ, and one that belonged to the past and to future realities, not only of this age, which was simply an age one had to pass through.[2] "Charlemagne was to rule the earth as *gubernator* on behalf of Christ."[3] His kingdom was to mirror the heavenly Jerusalem.

For Augustine the heavenly city has its feet firmly on earth in the shape of believers and their communities, and so it is not the case that the heavenly city needs to be "mirrored" in the church on earth in any particular physical location. The city, also known as "the heavenly Jerusalem," has what one might call its "center of gravity" in heaven.[4] With Augustine "the Jerusalem descended from skies" was not any place on earth, but was the pilgrim church, the *ecclesia in via*. It had no physical location. Likewise, Gregory the Great considered the new Jerusalem to be some "higher place where angels and men dwell together."[5]

However by the time of the Carolingians, the physical and geographical Jerusalem as the holiest place on earth was viewed as being well on the way

---

Himmel ... schon jetzt gleichsam als Bürger der Himmelsstadt (*strom.* 4,12,6)" – see Karl Ludwig Schmidt, "Jerusalem als Urbild und Abbild" in *Eranos Jahrbuch* 18 (1950) (Zürich: Rhein Verlag): 207–48.

[2] On this period see especially Chris Wickham, *The Inheritance of Rome: A History of Europe from 400 to 1000* (London: Allen Lane; Penguin Books, 2009).

[3] See: Johannes Spörl, "Die *Civitate Dei* im Geschichtsdenken Ottos von Freising" in *La Ciudad de Dios* 167, no. 2 (1956): 577–97.

[4] Gustave Bardy, "Jérusalem," *Dictionnaire de spiritualité* 8 (Paris: Beauchesne, 1974), 944–58 at 949: "On remarquera que ce n'est pas l'Église terrestre qui est l'image de la cité céleste. Celle-ci est exile et pérégrine en une partie de ses membres et aspire après le jour où il lui sera donné de les réunir à la société angélique: 'civitas Dei peregrinans in hoc saeculo' (XV,20,1)." Cf. Johannes van Oort, *Jerusalem and Babylon: A Study into Augustine's "City of God" and the Sources of His Doctrine of the Two Cities* (Leiden: Brill, 1991), esp. 161–67. Also, Donald X. Burt, "Cain's City: Augustine's Reflections on the Origins of the Civil Society (Book XV 1–8)," in *Augustinus:* De civitate dei, ed. Christoph Horn (Berlin: Akademie Verlag, 1997), 195–210.

[5] Robert Konrad, "Das himmlische und das irdische Jerusalem im mittelalterlichen Denken," in *Speculum Historiale: Geschichte im Spiegel von Geschichtsschreibung und Geschichtsdeutung: Festschrift für Joahnnes Spörl aus Anlass seines 60. Geburtstages,* ed. Clemens Bauer, Laetitia Boehm, Max Müller (Freiburg: Alber, 1965), 523–540 at 528.

to becoming joined with the heavenly one; as at least a visual aid it reminded the *corpus Christianorum* of the heavenly version, with symbolic, quasi-iconic power. This "realised eschatological" presence would remove any need for an eschatological millennium. Jerusalem was small in terms of nature but large in terms of grace.

There was hence a challenge to Augustine's merely virtual or intellectual understanding of Jerusalem as *visio pacis*. The earthly realm or *realia* of the Empire was the one that mirrored the even more real heavenly *polis*. But increasingly some of that power was channelled through holy sites. By the turn of the millennium when the church came up with the idea of pilgrimage to its holy sites as an extended form of penance, its spiritual importance became fixed.

However as Rome came to assert itself as a *holy* city in the present, Jerusalem became more and more *the* place of pilgrimage, and Jerome's old warning against pilgrimages to the City went unheeded.[6] The verse Ezek 5:5 ("Thus says the Lord Jehovah: 'This Jerusalem have I placed in the midst of the nations, and raised about her the countries'") was popular in the collective imagination.[7] With a nod to the work of Thomas O'Loughlin, David Jenkins concludes: "By the seventh century Jerusalem was an accepted liturgical motif as the place where God was to be met." There are liturgical resonances in the *De locis sanctis* of Adomnan Abelard that saw Zion as *caput regni Christi*; Peter the Venerable regarded the tomb of Christ as the heart of the world.[8] Despite trade maps around 1000 still not showing Jerusalem as central, by 1095 Urban II was sure to proclaim in a sermon that Jerusalem was the center of the earth: and the poet Gilon of Paris from the first decade of the following century in his *Monumentum de Bello Sacro*, describing the campaign to recapture Jerusalem, claimed: "He fights for the twofold kingdom, since he seeks each Jerusalem, battling in one that he might live in the other."[9] Just as Christ went up to a hostile Jerusalem before ascending to heaven, so too must the penitential pilgrim. The movement of the pilgrim church began to circle back "home" to Zion in its march to the future. Bernard of Clairvaux could write:

Hail then, holy city, sanctified by the Most High for his own tabernacle in order that such a generation might be saved in and through you! Hail, city of the Great King, source of so many joyous and unheard of marvels! Hail mistress of nations and queen of provinces,

---

[6] G. Waitz, ed., *Ottonis et Rahewini Gesta Frederici I imperatoris* lib IV, Monumenta Germaniae Historica 46 (Hannover: 1912), 320, on Lam 4:12: *vere Hierusalem erat mater nostra Romana ecclesia*.

[7] Robert Konrad, "Das himmlische und das irdische Jerusalem" (cf. footnote 5), 532.

[8] Peter the Venerable, *Sermon* 2 (PL 189:978).

[9] Urban II: *Hierusalem umbilicus est terrarum, terra prae caeteris fructifera, quasi alter paradisus deliciarum* (at PL 155:672). Gilon: *Pugnat pro duplici regno, quia quaerit utramque Jherusalem, decertat in hac ut uiuat in illa* (at PL 155:991). Both quoted in Emelien Lamirande, "Jérusalem céleste," in *Dictionnaire de spiritualité* 8 (Paris: Beauchesne, 1974), 944–58 at 949.

heritage of patriarchs, mother of apostles and prophets, source of the faith and glory of the Christian people! ... Hail promised land, source of milk and honey for your ancient inheritance, now become the source of healing grace and vital sustenance for the whole earth![10]

As we have seen, Augustine had already established that Christians on earth were only citizens of God through their being co-citizens with angels (*De civitate Dei* 11.7.24), and hence having a heavenly identity in the *patria*, so as to reinforce the church as earthly and *en route*. Much later, in the thirteenth century with Robert Grosseteste this idea is still prominent:

> Paul calls the church "Jerusalem," for she is the vision of peace. And in this name she unites not only the church militant but also the church triumphant with the desire to show through this union of the militant with the triumphant that the militant is free, or else it would not have been united with the triumphant one that is free. For the church whether militant or triumphant is above; but she with her body yet below has her conversation above, knowing these things which are above, not on earth.[11]

Yet monks were already enjoying angelic life, at least according to Bernard of Clairvaux, for whom the angels were brides of Christ. Monks at Clairvaux could even be said to be "in Jerusalem" as in the case of Philip, canon of Leicester whom Bernard excused from travelling on further to the Holy Land: residence even at the mother house at Cîteaux would do just as well as making it to the Levantine Jerusalem. Verses such as Rev 21:2, 9–10,[12] full of nuptial celebration, were popular, ones which Augustine had hardly cited. Unlike Augustine, Bernard equated the bride with the city and joined the love for the community to love for Christ.[13]

---

[10] Bernard of Clairvaux, *De laude novae militiae* 5 (Jean Leclercq and Henri-Maria Rochais, ed., *Bernardi opera*, vol. 3 [Rome: Editiones Cistercienses, 1963], 213–239: *Salve civitas Regis magni, ex qua nova et iucunda mundo miracula nullis paene ab initio defuere temporibus. Salve domina gentium, princeps provinciarum, Patriarcharum possessio, Prophetarum mater et Apostolorum, initiatrix fidei, gloria populi christiani .... Salve terra promissionis, quae olim fluens lac et mel tuis dumtaxat habitatoribus, nunc universo orbi remedia salutis, vitae porrigis alimenta Terra.* English quoted in Sylvia Schein, *Gateway to the Heavenly City: Crusader Jerusalem and the Catholic West (1099–1187)* (London: Taylor & Francis, 2016), 6.

[11] Robert Grosseteste, *Expositio in epistolam Sancti Pauli ad Galatas* 4.35 (James McEvoy and Laura Rizzerio, ed., CCCM 130 [1995]): *uocat autem ecclesiam Hierosolymam, quia ipsa est pacis uisio; et adunat in hoc nomine non solum ecclesiam militantem sed simul cum ea triumphantem, uolens per unitionem militantis cum triumphante ostendere militantem liberam, alioquin non esset unita cum triumphante libera. Ostenditur itaque ecclesia militans libera tam ex libertate noui testamenti significati per liberam quam ex eius unitione cum triumphante libera. Ecclesia autem tam militans quam triumphans sursum est; sed haec, corpore adhuc deorsum conuersatione autem sursum, sapiens ea quae sursum sunt; non quae super terram.*

[12] "Then came one of the seven angels who had the seven bowls full of the seven last plagues, and spoke to me, saying, 'Come, I will show you the Bride, the wife of the Lamb.' And in the Spirit he carried me away to a great, high mountain, and showed me the holy city Jerusalem coming down out of heaven from God" (NRSV).

[13] Elsewhere Bernard adds (*Sermones super Cantica canticorum* 55.2) the idea that the "Jerusalem of prophecy are those living religiously in this world, who imitate the manners of the Jerusalem above by honest and ordered lives according to their strength" – *Puto enim hoc*

There is a mirroring of earthly and heavenly that is almost sacramental. However, on this matter Thomas Aquinas was more cautious than Bernard and Grosseteste.

> The mother by whom we are born is the Church militant; or that mother into whose sons we are born, is the Church triumphant. Thus we are born in the present Church militant so that we might arrive at the triumphant. Expounding this way, our mother is described in four ways – by sublimity, when it says "above," second, by name when it says Jerusalem, third by freedom when it says she is free, and fourth by fertility, when it says "our mother."[14]

For Thomas, the church might well best be seen as in two parts: those in heaven who constitute the church as triumphant, and those below who have yet to get there, and are the church as militant. There is no Platonic idealist or strongly realist personification of the church here: the church exists only as her members *do* (fight). A Christian is not born in heaven, but, oriented teleologically, is on the way to it. The Old Testament is universalised to stand for all law and all legal systems past and present, which have their place, but making those laws cosmic and eternal may dangerously lead to pride. This is not intended by Thomas to contrast the classes of Jews and Gentiles (*pace* John Riches[15]) but to distinguish, almost separate the orders of nature and grace, even if Thomas reckons "the Jews" to be among those who are wilfully stuck in the natural order.

2 The Exegetical Foundation in the Later First Millennium

This paper however, will not venture into the second millennium; the above is sufficient to see where the concepts ended up. More time needs spending on the second half of the first millennium, to which we now turn. In recent attempts to focus on texts rather than on ideas and personalities, Kevin Poole's long essay in *A Companion to the Premodern Apocalypse*[16] is excellent but has to cover all the

---

loco [Soph. I, 12] *prophetam Jerusalem nomine designasse illos qui in hoc saeculo vitam ducunt religiosam, mores supernae Jerusalem conversatione honesta et ordinata pro viribus imitantes....* Quoted in Colin Morris, *The Sepulchre of Christ and the Medieval West* (Oxford: Oxford University Press, 2005), 178.

[14] Aquinas *Super ad Galatas* C4.L8, 264: ... *vel illam per quam generamur, quae est Ecclesia militans; vel illam matrem in cuius filios generamur, quae est Ecclesia triumphans. I Petr. I, 3: regeneravit nos in spem vivam, et cetera. Sic ergo generamur in praesenti Ecclesia Militante, ut perveniamus ad Triumphantem. Hoc ergo modo illud exponentes, a quatuor describitur mater nostra, scilicet a sublimitate, cum dicit sursum, secundo a nomine, cum dicit Ierusalem, tertio a libertate, cum dicit libera est, quarto a foecunditate, cum dicit mater nostra.* Cf. O. O' Donovan, *The Desire of the Nations* (Cambridge: Cambridge University Press, 1999), 89–92.

[15] John Riches, *Galatians Through the Centuries* (New Malden: Wiley Blackwell, 2013), 233.

[16] Kevin Poole, "The Western Apocalypse Commentary Tradition of the Early Middle Ages," in *A Companion to the Premodern Apocalypse*, ed. Michael A. Ryan, Brill's Companions to the Christian Tradition 64 (Leiden: Brill, 2016), 103–43.

ground by itself. Another recent book[17] lacks much treatment of the second half of the first millennium after Oecumenius (to be dated in the first half of the sixth century as a contemporary of Severus)[18] and Primasius of Hadrumetum in the West (about the same time). The exception to the comparative overlooking of the "Dark Ages" in this *Companion* is Elisabeth Mégier's excellent essay, which is illuminating on Primasius: he accentuated the need for a spiritual understanding beyond the letter, which is precisely the difference between the historical species (the martyrs in New Testament times) and the universal theological genus of "martyrdom."[19] Primasius applied the rules for biblical interpretation of the influential Donatist Tyconius's now-lost Apocalypse commentary, which began with the establishing of the plain sense or letter of Scripture, so as to help form scriptural "figures," which in turn would help believers to read the situation in which the church found itself. Now (following the Tyconian Rule 4) the "Augustinian" mixed church (*corpus permixtum*) ecclesiology would be abandoned around the time of the Gregorian reform, after leaving its mark on the interpretations of Haimo of Auxerre. In the work of Bede and Beatus, however, the idea of "the mixed church" was already coming under pressure.

While Mégier's study provides a detailed account of the texts, there are a few places where more clarity could be sought. The key might as much lie in the interpretation of the last chapters of Revelation.[20] Accordingly, the focus for the rest of this paper will be on Rev 21 in Primasius, Bede, and Beatus. Here we will discover a high ecclesiology that would operate as a beacon of light and encouragement to those in the pilgrim church *in via*.

3 Primasius of Hadrumetum

Bishop Primasius of Hadrumetum (d. 560) was (in)famous for appearing to switch sides under pressure from the Emperor Justinian during the Three Chapters controversy when the century-earlier dyophysite Christologies were outlawed. Isidore of Seville mentions the Apocalypse commentary specifically (*De viris illustribus* 22), so it was not without impact. Primasius[21] was sensitive

---

[17] Konrad Huber, Rainer Klotz, and Christoph Winterer, ed., *Tot sacramenta quot verba: Zur Kommentierung der Apokalypse des Johannes von den Anfängen bis ins 12. Jahrhundert* (Münster: Aschendorff, 2014).

[18] See John Suggit's introduction to *Oecumenius: Commentary on the Apocalypse*, FC 112, trans. John N. Suggit (Washington, DC: Catholic University of America Press, 2008).

[19] Elizabeth Mégier, "Species und genus: Was wird aus den exegetischen Kategorien des Tyconius in den Apokalypsenkommentaren der lateinischen Kirche von Primasius von Hadrumetum bis Rupert von Deutz?" in Huber et al., *Tot sacramenta quot verba* (cf. note 17), 153–94.

[20] These final chapters are not the focus of her study, which emphasizes a trajectory of interpretation of the Apocalypse as a whole over five centuries.

[21] Arthur W. Adams, ed., *Primasius episcopus Hadrumetinus: Commentarius in Apocalypsin*,

to accusations of heresy (not least the Three Chapters controversy) and the ensuing chaos, as well as to the threat of martyrdom in the uncertain times of the disintegration of the Empire; after all, orthodox believers were in danger from marauders (Vandal resistance to Justinian's army). According to Kevin Poole, Primasius was one of the great interpreters of Revelation. His commentary was written around 540 and was a channel for Victorinus of Petovium's commentary, "with its discouragement of millenarianism and its emphasis on the mission of the church in history."[22]

As Poole emphasizes, the vision was upbeat and affirming.

> Primasius believed that they [martyrs] occupy a separate space under the Altar of God. From there, they pray not for God's vengeance upon evildoers, as Victorinus and others believed, but rather for the conversion of sinners. Primasius tells us that God wills not vengeance and death but rather life eternal.[23]

It is perhaps no exaggeration to consider Primasius's approach to be one of contemplative preparation for the soul's ascent into heaven helped by fixing on the vision that John's Apocalypse supplies, whatever else is going on in the world around and its history. However, the frail and wicked human historical context required the consolation and support of spiritual friendships. One might speak of a dialectic between the ascending soul's anagogical reading of the text on the one hand and the tropological or moral interpretation wherein that same soul was inspired to scold the wickedness of the others. Re-using Tyconius's scriptural rules, one can view the species of the corruptible and corrupting church from moral-spiritual high ground, rather than from the lowly viewpoint of one participating in the confusion as a fellow member of a *corpus permixtum* (as per Tyconius). That meant that for Primasius, as the end-times approached and the shadows of the present age grew long, good and evil in the church were in full, embattled opposition. This was a step towards the eleventh-century decision that evil would simply have to be expelled from the church. The special parts, the contemplatives, are not all representative of the church, but can be instructive of the church.

CCSL 92 (Turnhout: Brepols, 1985); Julia Catherine Crick, "Primasius, Commentarius in Apocalypsin ('Commentary on the Apocalypse')," in *Anglo-Saxon Kingdoms*, ed. Claire Breay and Joanna Story (London: British Library, 2018). Johannes Haussleiter, *Leben und Werke des Bischofs Primasius von Hadrumetum: Eine Untersuchung* (Universitäts-Buchdruckerei: Erlangen, 1887) remains useful. See also E. Ann Matter, "The Apocalypse in Early Medieval Exegesis," in *The Apocalypse in the Middle Ages*, ed. Richard K. Emmerson and Bernard McGinn (Ithaca, NY: Cornell University Press, 1992), 38–50.

[22] Douglas Lumsden, *And Then the End Will Come: Early Latin Christian Interpretations of the Opening of the Seven Seals* (London: Routledge, 2001), 8. Chapter 3 is devoted to Primasius. Also, Douglas W. Lumsden, "'Touch No Unclean Thing': Apocalyptic Expressions of Ascetic Spirituality in the Early Middle Ages," *Church History* 66 (1997): 240–51.

[23] Kevin Poole, "Western Apocalypse Commentary Tradition" (cf. note 15), 112.

First, Primasius and what seems particular to him (given than he is a vehicle for Augustine, Tyconius, and Jerome [or Jerome's reworking of Victorinus]), can be viewed early on in his comments on Rev 21:

> From its beginnings the heavenly city descended from heaven, from where throughout the time of this age the grace of God coming down from above through the washing of regeneration in the Holy Spirit sent from heaven, her citizens below increase [*per lavacrum regenerationis in spiritu sancto misso de caelo, subinde cives eius adcrescunt*]. But by God's judgement, which will last of all take place through his son Jesus Christ. So great and so new a clarity will appear from the gift of God that there will remain not a trace of oldness, when bodies too will transition from the old corruption and mortality into incorruption and immortality. For this he promises, saying: "And he will wipe away every tear from their eyes and death will be no more along with sorrow and crying for there will be no more pain." One can be sure that these things pertain to the future life not the present; for now in this life to the extent anyone will be more holy and fuller with holy desires that one will be richer in the eloquence of tears ... these things must be believed rather than explained, especially since it says they are as good as having happened in the past so as there not to be doubt about anything in the future.[24]

Here we can see a "presentist" balanced view in light of the fulness of future hope and past shame that is to be shaken off; one could trace a u-shaped curve from a past salvation through the present trials on to more glorious future salvation.

> *I will freely give to the one who thirsts from the fountain of the water of life;* from this font he drops down now on believers who are on the way, and he will provide abundance on draught for those who will be victorious in the patria, lest pilgrims die in the desert they are rained on, and so that they are made citizens made by the torrents of the delights of God and will be constantly intoxicated. Now either way it is by grace, since the grace of God is eternal life, says the Apostle.[25]

Other insights follow: the bride merits bearing the heavenly image. Christ is the wall of the church, which offers Primasius the chance to quote Isa 26:1-2 and its

---

[24] Primasius, *Commentarius in Apocalypsin* 21 (Adams, ed., CCSL 92, 285.29-286.46): *De caelo quidem ab initio sui descendit, ex quo per huius saeculi tempus gratia dei desuper ueniente per lauacrum regenerationis in spiritu sancto misso de caelo, subinde ciues eius adcrescunt. Sed per iudicium dei, quod erit nouissimum per eius filium Iesum Christum, tanta eius et tam noua de dei munere claritas apparebit, ut nulla remaneant uestigia uetustatis, quando quidem et corpora ad incorruptionem atque immortalitatem noua ex uetere corruptione et mortalitate transibunt. Hinc enim promittit dicens:* Et absterget omnem lacrimam ab oculis eorum, et mors iam non erit, neque luctus atque clamor, sed nec dolor ullus; *quae omnia non huic sed futurae uitae certum est conuenire. Nunc enim in hac uita quanto quis fuerit sanctior, sanctisque desideriis plenior, tanto est in oratione fletus uberior ... Haec credi oportet, non exponi, praesertim quia sic dicit factum esse de praeterito, ut dubitare quemquam non sinat de futuro..*

[25] Primasius, *Comm. Apoc.* 21 (Adams, CCSL 92, 286.49-54): Ego sitienti dabo de fonte uitae aquae gratis. *De hoc fonte inrorat nunc credentes in uia, quem uincentibus ubertim hauriendum praebet in patria, ne peregrini in hac heremo siti deficient conpluuntur, ut ciues facti ex torrente deliciarum die iugiter debrientur. Utrumque autem gratis, quia* gratia dei *inquit apostolus* uita aeterna.

reference to the wall and inner wall of the city. In Christ the apostles merit to be "foundations." Christ illuminates his church.[26]

On Rev 21:14 the discourse on "foundations" leads Primasius to quote Ps 120:1–2: "I lift my eyes up to the hills." These are prophets and apostles, whom the sun of righteousness irradiates, almost as if all the talk of foundations was threatening to suggest that the apostles were nothing special, merely serving as (buried and rightfully obscure) foundations. Well, church servants bear spiritual children whom Christ might choose to adopt; they have merited to be pastors and teachers but they still contend to serve the Lord. On 21:17 Primasius states that the city is occupied partly by angels, partly by pilgrims, making up for the lost numbers of sinners, not, one should note, the fallen angels. When it comes to vv. 18–21, which list all the precious stones, rather than provide his own interpretation he inserts a florilegium of biblical texts that mention jewels.

He is more interested in concluding that the light mentioned in Isaiah (Isa 66:23) is eternal and equated with eternal rest. That the city doors are not closed is sign of security, for "be still and know I am God" (Ps 46:10) means no longer having to watch anxiously at night. Perpetual rest on the sabbath, is as if to say: the light on them from the light and eternal rest will continue for them from rest. This rather suggestive note of a realised eschatology of *rest* is no doubt an attractive and distinctive, even if not a totally original one, being rooted in an already mature monastic tradition. It is the notion of "rest" that arises from his hermeneutic of "contemplation."

4 Bede the Venerable

One of the things that stands in marked contrast from the context of Primasius is that, although Bede (672–745) was a monk, he was a *scholar*-monk with a decent library, thus able to draw on a range of past interpretations, that of Primasius included. His great library at Jarrow stood him in very good stead. Its copy of the Vulgate *Codex Ammatianus* would have been precious. The reasons for Bede's writing the *Commentary on the Apocalypse*[27] as the first commentary he attempted have been well treated by (*inter alios*) Faith Wallis, who argues that Bede consulted Victorinus as well as Tyconius via Primasius, in an effort to fix an eschatology firmly on scriptural foundations.[28] In that sense his interpretation

---

[26] For influences, see Roger Gryson, "Les commentaires patristiques latins de l'Apocalypse," *Revue Théologique de Louvain* 28 (1997): 305–37.

[27] For the text, see Roger Gryson, ed., *Beda Venerabilis. Expositio Apocalypseos*, CCSL 121A, 2001.

[28] Faith Wallis, trans. and ed., *Bede: Commentary on Revelation*, Translated Texts for Historians (Liverpool: Liverpool University Press, 2013), Introduction, 31–35. Still useful is Ansgar Willmes, "Bedas Bibelauslegung," *Archiv für Kulturgeschichte* 44 (1962): 281–314.

incudes also much more doctrine and science than with Primasius, as well as being a resource for piety. In his likewise early work *De temporibus* 22.1.80, Bede insists that the remainder of the sixth age is "known only by God." His was a "New Testament" style eschatology that was not chained to *Anno Mundi* calculations from creation forward.

It seems he must have had some exposure to the more literal approach represented by the Irish heirs of the Antiochene school[29]; its influence on him, however, was not extensive. Instead, recent research has indicated that Bede received a strong stamp of Origen through Gregory the Great. Augustine had used the Donatist Tyconius on the church's being white and black, but twisted it so that the idea was more one of "Isaac versus Ishmael" as per Gal 4, amounting to an "us" (the pilgrim *catholica*) and a "them" (Donatists, Pelagians, Arians, etc.). This means that, while the church was mixed as a body, its progressive sanctification included exclusion and expulsion. This is like Primasius, only that the dividing line runs through parish churches, not between a monastic elite and almost everybody else. Yet Bede was arguably closer to the more liberal vision of Tyconius, whom Bede was not embarrassed to name "teacher." From him Bede accepted the idea of a bipartite church, with the enemy very much within, and not always easy to discern.

In his commentary on Rev 21:6, where the seer writes "and he said to me 'It is done'," Bede excerpted Primasius: This means the prophecy here is about the past not the future, as Augustine believed in *The City of God* 20.7. Indeed "for a thousand years" (Rev 20:3) is part of the remainder of the one thousand years since the incarnation. For Bede the date of the end was not known: yet Revelation itself gives us grounds to believe that Jewish conversion and the appearance of the antichrist will give the church time to get ready, like some sort of alarm clock.

Although part of the reason for writing the commentary was to instruct and correct misapprehension and even combat heresy, one may speak of a new direction with Bede, that of a rhetorical emphasis. As Peter Darby puts it:

> The author voiced his own emotions and made his teachings more personal either through vocative discourse of addressing the reader or through images that allow the reader to reach a more fully developed understanding of the text. A sharp line is drawn in his *De die iudicii* between the present, in which action can be taken to improve the chances of a positive outcome at the end of time, and a post-judgement future in which the opportunity to seek God's forgiveness will have passed, never to return.[30]

---

[29] For an exploration of one facet of the interpretation of the New Jerusalem in the Irish context, see Francis X. Gumerlock's contribution to this volume.

[30] Peter Darby, "Apocalypse and Reform in Bede's De Die Iudicii," in *Apocalypse and Reform from Late Antiquity to the Middle Ages*, ed. Matthew Gabriele and James T. Palmer (London: Routledge, 2019), 77–100. Cf. Stéphane Lebecq, Michel Perrin, and Olivier Szerwiniack, ed., *Bède le Vénérable: Entre tradition et postérité* (Lille: Ceges, 2005), 19–30.

As he comes to comment on Rev 21 Bede wants to take time to put the New Jerusalem in the context of the new heaven and new earth. He follows this up with an interpretation of the New Jerusalem coming from heaven (*caelo*) as meaning *the grace* by which God made her; again, compare Primasius who is more explicit in this interpretation. It contains a slight hint of demythologizing or a wish to avoid any suggestion of a pre-existent church. Rev 21:9 presents her as bride immaculate, in other words betrothed but prior to consummation is the idea. Yet sons are being produced in that she is also "wife": indeed, she continually begets spiritual sons for God. She is fully historical, in motion, even.

On v. 10, speaking of the mountain, Bede comments: "After the fall of Babylon, the holy city, which is the bride of the Lamb, is seen placed on a mountain. For the stone *cut out from the mountain without hands,* broke in pieces the image of worldly glory, and became a great mountain, and filled the whole world."[31] Hence it is the church who is the great stone filling up the world, and this is in some ways reminiscent of (one possible interpretation of) Ephesians. Then moving on to v. 11, which speaks of the city "descending from heaven from God, having the clarity of God," Bede continues: "She will then seem even more fully 'decorous' when through the Spirit who by whom the Groom was conceived and begotten she will have deserved to bear the heavenly image fully."[32] The Spirit prepares the bride, but this training seems to require a prior descent. As for "the wall" in v. 12, it is "the invincible virtue of faith, hope and love." About this wall, Isaiah says (Isa 26:1) that a wall will be placed in her and an inner wall, "that is, the protection of God and the intercession of the saints who journey to it by teaching the hearts of believers." As to the twelve angels that are in the twelve gates, these are "the doctors who follow the vestiges of the faith of the Apostles and the mystery of the word."[33]

The wall is doctrine or the taught faith (*fides quae*): God is conceived of as protecting the church, but the other contribution belongs not to saints above in the church triumphant but the very much alive and active teachers of true doctrine in the footsteps of the apostles. The atmosphere is evangelistic and polemical rather than ecclesiological and irenic. Similarly, at Rev 21:16 the walls (pl.) are the four principal virtues that make up the church raised up by the faith in the Holy

---

[31] Gryson, CCSL 121A, 525.9–11: *Post ruinam Babylonis ciuitas sancta, quae sponsa est agni, supra montem posita uidetur. Lapis enim praecisus de monte sine manibus comminuit simulacrum gloriae mundanae et creuit in montem magnum orbemque impleuit uniuesersum.*

[32] Gryson, CCSL 121A, 525.14–15: DESCENDENTEM DE CAELO A DEO, HABENTEM CLARITATEM DEI. *Tunc enim amplius decora uidebitur, quando per spiritum, quo eius sponsus creditur conceptus et genitus, imaginem plene meruerit portare caelestem.*

[33] Gryson, CCSL 121A, 525.24–30: ET HABEBAT MVRVM MAGNVM ET ALTVM, *id est inexpugnabilem fidei spei caritatis que firmitatem …. de quo Esaias ait: Ponetur in ea murus et antemurale, id est domini protectio et intercessio sanctorum, qui iter faciunt ei docendo ad corda credentium ….* ET IN PORTIS ANGELOS DVODECIM, *doctores scilicet apostolorum uestigia fidei et uerbi mysterio sequentes.*

Trinity (sort of elevated a level), a presaging of the theological virtues enriching and completing the four cardinal virtues, as would be systematised by Aquinas. The city's foundations in plural are the teachers with Christ the foundation of foundations, here drawing on Augustine, *Enarrationes in Psalmos* 86.3.19, and Gregory, *Moralia* 28.13. The doors of the city refer to the patriarchs who as types held the name or figure of the apostles in them. "Through them this city was founded although by the apostles, and as if through doors thrown open to believing nations more widely."[34] The apostles seem to throw open the doors that the patriarchs constructed.

One of the high points of his treatment of Rev 21 is his interpretation of vv. 18–21. In terms of the section on the precious stones Bede seems to allow his imagination free rein. As has been shown by Gryson, there is too little resemblance to Epiphanius's *De gemmis* for that to qualify as a plausible source.[35] A "fantasy world" of spiritual realities seems to be what Bede is aiming to describe or lead the reader into. Gold and glass betoken transparency to each other in the church. For there is nothing counterfeited or concealed in the saints of the church. He adds that the virtues derive their power and character from the Logos. The idea of one stone and many stones here is reminiscent of Origen's doctrine of *epinoiai*. Christian souls are called to reflect their master.

First,[36] jasper indicates the greenness of faith that never withers; second, the fact that sapphire is found in the Red Sea shows that the minds of mortal men are sublimely raised on high by the Lord's passion and through the washing of holy baptism to the heavenly things they should anticipate. Quite often when discussing these jewels he stresses the combination of contrasting colours in each of them. Hence third, it was said of one of these (*carchedonius*) "He was a bright and shining light" (John 5:35). Fourth, emeralds stand for martyrdom, or behind it the virtue that meets suffering by evil spirits; for emeralds are found in Scythis, the home of demons. On the eighth, beryl, the point is that virtues shine more with grace added. On the ninth, topaz, this is "the contemplative life"; although "I have loved your commands above gold and topaz" (Ps 119:27) means that moral obedience to God's will is greater than contemplation. He adds that all these stones were on the breastplate of the high priest of Exod 28, and hence figuratively, of Christ. Towards the end of this section he provides his own summary too:

In jasper the fecundity of faith, in sapphire the height of the heavenly hope, in *carchedon*[37] the form of inner love is signified, in *smaragdus* the strong confession of the same faith

---

[34] Gryson, CCSL 121A, 527.47–50.

[35] Roger Gryson, "Les commentaires patristiques latins de l'Apocalypse (suite et fin)," *Revue théologique de Louvain* 28, no. 4 (1997): 484–502 at 485.

[36] I offer a summary paraphrase of Gryson, CCSL 121A, 533.105–557.354.

[37] This gem seems missing from the detailed treatment prior to the summary.

amidst oppositions, in *sardonix* the humility among the virtues of the saints, in *sardius* the revered bliss of the martyrs is expressed, in *chrysolitus* is confirmed the spiritual preaching accompanied by miracles, in beryl the perfect working of those preaching, in topaz the fervent contemplation of these, moreover in *chrysoprasus* the work of the blessed martyrs and their prize, in *hyacinthus* the heavenly lifting up to the heights of the doctors and on account of weak their humble descent to the human, in *amethystis* is designated the memory of the heavenly kingdom in the mind of the humble ones.[38]

For Bede the Apocalypse is addressed to the whole church as a summons to spiritual improvement, with a message that needs to be heard by all Christians for the sake of their spiritual safety, and not just by the monastic communities, as per Primasius.

5 Beatus of Liébana

What seems to have been most at stake for the Asturian Beatus in his *Commentaria in Apocalypsin* (776–786)[39] was not atypical, just as late antiquity fully gave way to the early Middle Ages. As James Palmer puts it with reference to the early medieval commentators,

> Heresy was perhaps the greatest apocalyptic concern of all …. [A]ll of the earliest Western commentaries on Revelation were composed in the midst of disputes about doctrine, so it is no surprise to find that most subsequent commentators preferred to see Gog and Magog as symbols of heretics – the secret enemies within – rather than as invading foreigners.[40]

John Williams observes that after Beatus wrote *Adversus Elipandum* against the heresy of adoptionism, in 784–786 he reworked his commentary of ten years earlier, so that it was transformed from contemplative reading to the genre of polemic against heretics.[41] One could put this more positively: it was an

---

[38] Gryson, CCSL 121A, 557.344–554 (I have opted not to give a translation of the Latin terms for these gems): *In iaspide ergo fidei uiriditas, in saphiro spei caelestis altitudo, in carchedone flamma caritatis internae figuratur, in smaragdo autem eiusdem fidei fortis inter aduersa confessio, in sardonice sanctorum inter uirtutes humilitas, in sardio reuerendus martyrum cruor exprimitur, in chrysolito uero spiritalis inter miracula praedicatio, in beryllo praedicantium perfecta operatio, in topazio eorundem ardens contemplatio monstratur, porro in chrysopraso beatorum martyrum opus pariter et praemium, in hyacintho doctorum caelestis ad alta subleuatio et propter infirmos humilis ad humana descensio, in amethysto caelestis semper regni in humilium animo memoria designatur.*

[39] Roger Gryson, ed., *Beati Liebanensis Tractatus de Apocalipsin*, CCSL 107B/C (2012).

[40] James Palmer, *The Apocalypse in the Early Middle Ages* (Cambridge: Cambridge University Press, 2013), 233. Also 154: "Yet by incorporating large passages from Isidore on ecclesiastical office, Beatus succeeded in amplifying the ecclesiological interpretations so beloved of his intellectual predecessors and in doing so seems to have set out to create a basis for articulating the importance of the unity of the church."

[41] John Williams, "Purpose and Imagery in the Apocalypse Commentary of Beatus of Liébana," in Emmerson and McGinn, *The Apocalypse in the Middle Ages*, 218. See also Kenneth

affirmation of the essential unity of the church. An awareness of the presence of the enemy within, the doctrinal "other," provoked a response that utilized the last chapters of the Bible. Elisabeth Mégier has shown how the Tyconian *corpus permixtum* had become by the time of Beatus an unbearable tension,[42] even though it was well on its way in Bede even as he thought of it as a necessary tension, wherein it was more about the left and the right of the church fighting politically although the stakes are no less spiritual. For Beatus, lacking Bede's serenity, the church is more a battleground for forces from heaven and hell. To put it bluntly, Beatus believes the end of the world is only a decade away, and that the adoptionist heretic Elipandus was the antichrist. To paraphrase: the time from Adam to Christ adds up to 5227 years. And from the birth of our Lord Jesus Christ to the present era, that is, the year 822, there have been 784 years. If you add from the first man, Adam, to the present time, the year 822, you will have a total of 5987. Therefore, the sixth millennium has fourteen years remaining. With that, the sixth age, and history itself, will end, in 838.

Beatus took over from Tyconius the category of *storiae* to describe the passages in Revelation, which, as is often commented, is a book that provides thematic imagery for the imagination. To enhance this effect Beatus mixes his sources so that they become muddled.[43] So, in Apringius's commentary's first five and last five chapters, Gregory and Isidore were his main influences, yet also Victorinus/Jerome as well as Tyconius through Primasius, but (significantly) not Augustine. His strong conviction that Jerusalem would be saved from the Muslim invasion rather literalizes things. Beatus worked with the *Vetus Latina*, not the Vulgate, but also seems to have been aware of standing in an exegetical tradition of literalist millenarianism that is somewhat heterodox. Augustine (and his views in *City of God* 18.53), gets avoided or played down in Beatus. He drew on Apringius (d. 530, bishop of Pax Iulia, now Beja, in south-eastern Portugal) to receive from the more literal stream of Victorinus/Jerome.

Beatus's work attests by far the greatest amount of Tyconian raw material, but when it comes to Rev 20–21, so much in Beatus is already in Primasius. What I will try to focus on in this last section are some comments where influences are not so easy to spot and there is a *prima facie* case that this *Sondergut* is original to Beatus.

B. Steinhauser, "Narrative and Illumination in the Beatus Apocalypse," *Catholic Historical Review* 81 (1995): 185–210.

[42] See E. Mégier, "Die Historisierung der Apokalypse oder von der globalen geschichtlichen Zeit der Kirche in lateinischen Apokalypsenkommentaren, von Tyconius bis Rupert von Deutz," in *Abendländische Apokalyptik: Kompendium zur Genealogie der Endzeit*, ed. Veronika Wieser et al. (Berlin: Akademie Verlag, 2013), 579–604.

[43] At least a catena tells us its sources, complains Roger Gryson in his introduction to the edition.

For instance, in his comments on the beginning of ch. 21, the contrast with Bede is clear. Beatus takes Rev 21:2 to speak – to paraphrase – of the New Jerusalem not as "grace descending," but as the very church who is always descending in penitence from heaven and God: by imitating the Son of God in penitence she is said to descend in humility, since he, although in the form of God, assumed the form of a slave and humbled himself as far as death (Phil 2:8). For the descent of the Son is his incarnation. This city descends from God by imitating God, that is by following in the tracks of Christ the Son of God, and it says this city-bride is the Lamb's. And it is clear that this is the church: "Here begins the twelfth book concerning the day of judgement and the city of Jerusalem, that is the church."[44] It is very much the church of the present: from the passion of Christ up until the day on which in which she will rise and be crowned with Christ in glory."[45] He describes her as having the radiance of God shining forth from her. The *life* the church lives is that of the world to come (*non presentis seculi, sed futuri*).[46]

All things here are to be understood in a spiritual sense: *omnia haec spiritaliter intellegenda sunt.*[47] The reward for the faithful in his comment on 21:3 will be no less than God himself in a quasi-marital bond. "For God will be the reward of eternal blessedness for the elect/chosen which they, being possessed by him, will possess in eternity."[48]

In terms of the space he gives to the imagery, Beatus is most concerned to communicate, on the basis of Rev 21:10, that it is in the very nature of the church to be penitent, just as Jesus was humble enough to become incarnate: the church is to be that "everyday descending" city.[49] In what immediately follows the importance of Christo-centricity is sounded, not for the first time.[50] The whole humility theme is reinforced in the comment on Rev 21:12: *Habentem murum magnum et altum,* and Gryson helpfully spots the debt to Gregory's *Moralia* here.[51] A verse that mentions a high wall receives an interpretation that concerns self-debasement.

---

[44] Gryson, CCSL 107C, 891: *Incipit liber duodecimus de die iudicii et ciuitate ierusalem id est ecclesia.*; cf. at 901.14: *Celum nouum est ecclesia.*

[45] Gryson, CCSL 107C, 901.1–3: *a Christi passione usque in diem quo resurgat et cum Christo coronetur in gloria.*

[46] Gryson, CCSL 107C, 902.39–40.

[47] Gryson, CCSL 107C, 902.38.

[48] Gryson, CCSL 107C, 903.42–45.

[49] Gryson, CCSL 107C, 907.120–31: *quae semper in penitentia de celo descendet a deo, quia filium dei imitando in penitentia descendere dicitur in humilitate. Sic enim filius dei descendit de celo: cum in forma dei esset, formam serui adsumens humiliauit se usque ad mortem. Descensio filii dei incarnatio eius est. Haec ciuitas cotidie a deo descendet imitando deum, id est sequendo uestigia Christi filii dei, et hanc ciuitatem sponsam dicit agni. Unde manifestum est ipsam esse ecclesiam.*

[50] Gryson, CCSL 107C, 907.132–34: *Quam sic discribit dicens:* Habentem claritatem dei, luminare ... *Lapis pretiossimus Christus est.*

[51] Gryson, CCSL 107C, 907.135–908.140: *Sciendum magnopere est quia tanto unaquaeque anima fit pretiosior ante oculos dei, quanto prae amore Ueritatis dispector fuerit ante oculos*

Conclusion

These readings of the Heavenly Jerusalem provided the collective Christian imagination with much rich sustenance. The emphases on peaceful rest to be realized now and containing a political yet cosmic dimension (Primasius) or on the harnessing of spiritual virtue on the way to an ideal (Bede) or a humble asceticism of the united church to help cleave to true, saving doctrine (Beatus) – all these offer insight into this (at times) delightful chapter of the Apocalypse. The true "Jerusalem" that matters is no longer a place to be visited, and it is the text of Rev 21 that offers a welcome vision alongside the gloomier imagery of judgment towards the end of John's Apocalypse. Nor is Jerusalem something above or beyond the present, for the church has come down and Christians thus possess all they need and can become more aware of that mystery as they contemplate the text of Rev 21. There is something solid and humanly reliable about the church under grace. As ecclesiological readings they do not glorify the church even as they *do* idealize it. Bede might well have read the "slaughtered lamb" in Rev 5:6 as meaning the church, but typological readings make that possible and by no means a usurpation of the place of Christ, as the interpretations of ch. 21 in turn make clear. The foundation and precious stone that gathers all types of "stone" together is Jesus Christ, but the manifestation of that beauty belongs to the church and our three exegetes show no reserve in rejoicing in the grace, virtue, and truth of that ecclesial reality. Jerusalem is neither so much below nor above, although those aspects remain important, but even more so Jerusalem is here and now, itself a present aid in times of trouble.

---

suos. Hinc ad Saul dicitur: Nonne cum paruulus esses in oculis tuis, caput te constitui in tribus Israel? *Ac si aperte diceret: "Magnus mici fuisti, quando despectus eras tibi; mod uero magnus es tibi, despectus sis mici"* (Gregory, *Moral.* 18.59).

Two Early Medieval Hiberno-Latin Texts on the New Jerusalem

Introduction, Transcription, and Translation

Francis X. Gumerlock

Introduction

This contribution introduces two late-antique/early medieval Hiberno-Latin texts[1] on the New Jerusalem and provides Latin transcriptions and the first English translations of them. The first text is a question-and-answer tractate from the eighth century, most likely of Irish provenance. The eleven questions and answers which it contains mainly discuss the various gates and corresponding gemstones of the New Jerusalem, conceived of as a heavenly city in which the Lord Jesus Christ, the evangelists, apostles, prophets, and those dead "who were converted to the Lord" presently dwell.

The second text, in the tenth-century *Catechesis Celtica*, is a portion of a long homily by an unknown Irish abbot and focuses on the gates of the New Jerusalem. In the homily the New Jerusalem is portrayed as a future heavenly city, the abode of all the saints after the last judgment. The abbot informs his hearers about the different apostles stationed as the city's gatekeepers and explains the reasons behind that distribution based on the various apostles' deeds and the geographical locations of the gates. Moral interpretations of the gates are also interspersed throughout the homily.

---

[1] Hiberno-Latin texts refer to texts written in Latin by Irish speaking persons (Ireland in Latin is *Hibernia*), whether they were residing in and writing from Ireland or elsewhere in continental Europe.

1 "Question-and-Answer Tractate on the New Jerusalem"

1.1 Introduction

1.1.1 Manuscript and Editions

The untitled text, which I have designated as a "Question-and-Answer Tractate on the New Jerusalem," was transmitted in a codex in a library in El Escorial, Madrid (MS. Escorial a.II.3). The codex contains 157 folios (hereafter "fols."); and a variety of patristic writings are found on fols. 1–153. Fols. 154–57 did not originally belong to the codex and are written in handwriting (tenth-century Visigothic miniscule) differing from the handwriting on the earlier folios. These last folios contain a portion of the *Vision of Paul* and the "Question-and-Answer Tractate on the New Jerusalem," which is on the recto and verso side of fol. 157.[2] No author of the text is mentioned.

The text of the "Question-and-Answer Tractate" was published in 1909 by G. Antolín and a new edition of it appeared in a 1996 article by Anton Hilhorst.[3] The edition used for my translation, and much of the information on the manuscript and text, I have gathered from Hilhorst's article. Although the "Question-and-Answer Tractate" follows the *explicit* ("It ends here.") of the previous text, and ends with its own *explicit*, Hilhorst believes that the text is not complete, but a fragment of a larger work. One of the reasons for this is its mention of *ipsa civitas* ("that city") in Question 2, which, he says, presupposes that the city had been previously introduced. There also appears to be two *lacunae* in the text, which I have indicated in the translation.

1.1.2 Contents

The text, as we have it, appears to be notes of a short question-and-answer lesson between a teacher and a student or students about the heavenly city.[4] It has a series of eleven questions, which are not enumerated in the manuscript, but are

---

[2] On the relationship of the Vision of Paul (*Visio Pauli*) and Hiberno-Latin literature and the Irish, see Charles Darwin Wright, *The Irish Tradition in Old English Literature*, Cambridge Studies in Anglo-Saxon England 6 (New York: Cambridge University Press, 1993), 106–74.

[3] Guillermo Antolín, "Opúsculos desconocidos de San Jerónimo," *Revista de Archivos, Bibliothecas y Museos* 12 iss. 2 (1908): 207–226; 13 iss. 1 (1909): 60–80, esp. 80; Anton Hilhorst, "The Escorial Fragment on the Heavenly Jerusalem," in *Media Latinitas: A Collection of Essays to Mark the Occasion of the Retirement of L.J. Engels*, ed. Renée. I.A. Nip, Hans van Dijk, Elisabeth M.C. van Houts, Corneille H. Kneepkens, and George A. A. Kortekaas, Instrumenta Patristica 28 (Turnhout: Brepols, 1996), 223–28.

[4] According to Lawrence T. Martin, the question-and-answer format was "a method frequently employed in Irish works of biblical learning." See his "The Verona Homily Collection and its Irish Connections," in *Medieval Sermons and Society: Cloister, City, University*, ed. Jacqueline Hamesse, Beverly M. Kienzle, Debra L. Stoudt, and Anne T. Thayer (Louvain-la-Neuve: Fédération Internationale des Instituts d'Études Médiévales, 1998), 23–33 at 30.

numbered in Hilhorst's edition. I have retained his enumeration of the questions in my translation. The term "New Jerusalem" is not found in the text, but "that city" undoubtedly refers to it. It is possible that a reading of chapters 21 and 22 of the book of Revelation preceded the lesson. For, "that city" echoes the phrase in Rev 21:18, the city's gates seem to refer to Rev 21:12, the recitation of twelve gemstones reflects the list given in Rev 21:19–21 although not exactly and not in the same order, and the trees emitting twelve flowers allude to Rev 22:2.

The city is portrayed as a heavenly city in which Jesus Christ, the apostles, and other holy ones presently reside. The city has thrones and on one of them, the seventh throne, the Lord Jesus Christ sits. This has some affinity with a late eighth- or early ninth-century Hiberno-Latin homily on the seven heavens, in which the Lord Jesus is enthroned in the seventh heaven.[5] The city has twelve gates, as in Ezek 48:30–34 and Rev 21:12–13; and a cherub and seraph have placed names of various gemstones on the gates. These names have some correspondence with, but do not match exactly, the biblical lists of twelve gemstones in Exod 28:17–21; 30:10–14 and Rev 21:19–20. In fact, in the "Question-and-Answer Tractate" the names of the some of the gemstones are barely recognizable, probably due to corruption of the Latin from before the Carolingian reforms in Latin orthography.[6] For comparison, below is a list of the gemstones in the aforementioned biblical texts and the list contained in the "Question-and-Answer Tractate."

Table 1. List of gemstones in "Question-and-Answer Tractate" compared with biblical lists.

Exodus 28:17–21 and 30:10–14	*Revelation 21:19–20*	*"Question-and-Answer Tractate"*
ruby	jasper	sapphire
topaz	sapphire	myxis
emerald	chalcedony	amethyst
turquoise	emerald	emerald
sapphire	sardonyx	beryl
diamond	sardius	jasper
hyacinth	chrysolite	pacta
agate	beryl	chrysoprase
amethyst	topaz	topaz
beryl	chrysoprase	myrmecias
onyx	hyacinth	chalcedony
jasper	amethyst	hyacinth

---

[5] John Carey, "The Reichenau Seven Heavens Homily," in *The End and Beyond: Medieval Irish Eschatology*, 2 vols., ed. John Carey, Emma Nic Cárthaigh, and Caitríona Ó Dochartaigh (Oakville, CT: Celtic Studies Publications, 2014), 1:189–95 at 195.

[6] Hilhorst, "Escorial Fragment" (cf. note 3), 226.

Various groups of people have already entered the heavenly city through various gates: the apostles through one, the evangelists through another, and the prophets through another. This may have been influenced by the Shepherd of Hermas, Vision 3.5 (13), in which various groups enter a large stone building.[7]

Rather than the tree of life, as would be expected based upon Rev 22:2, there are cinnamon and balsam trees in the city, which the Lord planted (cf. Gen 2:8), and which emit twelve flowers, one each month of the year. That there is more than one tree bearing fruit may derive from Ezek 47:7, 12. Its mention of a cinnamon tree bears correlation with 1 Enoch 29.3 and 30.1, in which the seer beholds and smells a cinnamon tree in his other-worldly journey.[8]

1.1.3 Irish Provenance

In this text Hilhorst noticed Irish features such as enumeration, classification, use of apocryphal traditions,[9] and its similarity in form to the Hiberno-Latin text *Quaestiones tam de novo quam de vetere testamentum*. The latter's questions and answers on biblical themes, like the "Question-and-Answer Tractate," are often introduced by the words *Dic mici/mihi* ("Tell me").[10] Since *Quaestiones* was written shortly before AD 750, Hilhorst conjectured that the "Question-and-Answer Tractate" originated in eighth century Irish circles, and I agree with him.[11]

1.1.4 Latin Orthography

The Latin edition often has *mici* for *mihi*, and *que* for *quae*. It also has *abet* for *habet*, *intraberunt* and *introyerunt* for *intrauerunt*, and *profete* for *prophetae*.

---

[7] Herm. Vis. 3.5 (13), in Bart D. Ehrman, *Lost Scriptures: Books that Did Not Make It into the New Testament* (New York: Oxford University Press, 2003), 258.

[8] Richard Laurence, trans., *The Book of Enoch the Prophet* (London: Kegan Paul, Trench & Co., 1883), 36.

[9] These features were distinguished as commonly appearing in early medieval Hiberno-Latin texts by Bernhard Bischoff, "Wendepunkte in der Geschichte der lateinischen Exegese im Frühmittelalter," *Sacris Erudiri* 6 (1954): 189–270. An English translation of Bischoff's article is "Turning Points in the History of Latin Exegesis in the Early Irish Church: A.D. 650–800," in *Biblical Studies: The Medieval Irish Contribution*, ed. Martin McNamara (Dublin: Dominican Publications, 1976), 74–160. Bischoff's conclusions were challenged by some scholars, among others, Michael M. Gorman in "The Myth of Hiberno-Latin Exegesis," *Revue Bénédictine* 110 (2000): 42–85. On enumerative style in early medieval Irish texts, see also Wright, *Irish Tradition*, 49–105.

[10] *Questiones tam de novo quam de vetere testamentum* is edited in CCSL 108B: 187–205.

[11] Hilhorst, "Escorial Fragment" (cf. note 3), 224–25. On the transmission of texts between Spain and Ireland in late antiquity and the early Middle Ages, see Jocelyn N. Hillgarth, "Old Ireland and Visigothic Spain," in *Old Ireland*, ed. Robert McNally (New York: Fordham University Press, 1965), 200–27. On the circulation of apocrypha in the early medieval period, see Brandon W. Hawk, *Preaching Apocrypha in Anglo-Saxon England*, Toronto Anglo-Saxon Series (Toronto: University of Toronto Press, 2018).

1.2 Transcription and Translation

Transcription	Translation
[157r b] 1 Dic mici: In quo trono sedet dominus noster Iesus Christus? Responsum: In septimo trono. 2 Dic mici: ipsa ciuitas quantas abet portas? Responsum: xii. 3 Dic mici nomina illorum. Prima porta dicitur saffira. Secunda porta dicitur mixta. iii porta dicitur metresta. iiii porta dicitur ratan. u porta dicitur mamirella. ui porta dicitur iaspes. uii porta dicitur pacta. uiii porta dicitur gressuspassa. uiiii porta dicitur tupacta. x porta dicitur macimes. xi porta dicitur passa. [157v a] xii porta dicitur iacintus. 4 Editus[18] fuit qui posuit nomina ad ipsas portas. Sanctus Zerubin et Serafin. 5 Dic mihi: Quando ad ipsam ciuitatem confugium fecerunt per quale porta intraberunt? Per porta que dicitur [...] 6 Euangelistas per quale portam intraberunt? Per portam que dicitur mamirella.	1. Tell me, on what throne does our Lord Jesus Christ sit? Answer: On the seventh throne. 2. Tell me, how many gates does that city have? Answer: Twelve.[12] 3. Tell me their names. Answer: The first gate is called "sapphire." The second gate is called "myxis."[13] The third gate is called "amethyst." The fourth gate is called "emerald."[14] The fifth gate is called "beryl." The sixth gate is called "jasper." The seventh gate is called "pacta."[15] The eighth gate is called "chrysoprase." The ninth gate is called "topaz." The tenth gate is called "myrmecias."[16] The eleventh gate is called "chalcedony."[17] The twelfth gate is called "hyacinth." 4. Who was the writer who placed the names on those gates? Answer: The holy cherub and seraph. 5. Tell me, when they [the martyrs?] took flight to that city, through which gate did they enter? Answer: Through the gate which is called ... [lacuna] 6. Through which gate did the evangelists enter? Answer: Through the gate which is called "beryl."

---

[12] Cf. Rev 21:12.

[13] Myxis is a yellowish-red gem among the varieties of jasper stones. See Pliny the Elder, *Natural History* (*Naturalis historia*) 37.37, 116 (David E. Eichholz, trans., *Pliny. Natural History, Books 36–37*, Loeb 419 [Cambridge, MA: Harvard University Press, 1962], 258–59). The "Question-and-Answer Tractate" has *mixta* meaning "mixed." It is possible, therefore, that the author is referring to *sardonyx*, which is a mixture of sardius and onyx. Epiphanius (*De gemmis*, 12) said about *onyx* that its tint is mixed. See Robert P. Blake and Henri de Vis, ed., *Epiphanius. de gemmis* (London: Christophers, 1934), 121–22.

[14] The Latin text has *ratan*, probably referring to a green gem found in Persia, called *tanos* by Pliny, and described among emeralds in his *Natural History* 37.19, 74.

[15] Possibly the gem of all colors called *panchrus* by Pliny in *Natural History* 37.66, 178.

[16] A black stone. See Pliny, *Natural History* 37.63, 174. The "Question-and-Answer Tractate" has *macimes*.

[17] The "Question-and-Answer Tractate" has *passa*, probably meaning *prasius* or "prase," which is a dark green chalcedony. See Pliny, *Natural History* 37.34, 113.

[18] Hilhorst ("Escorial Fragment," 224) conjectured that *Editus* was a corruption of *Quis*.

Transcription	Translation
7 Profete per quale porta intraberunt? Per porta que dicitur pacta.	7. Through which gate did the prophets enter? Answer: Through the gate which is called "pacta."
8 Apostoli per quale porta intraberunt? Per porta que dicitur gressus passa. Per alias uero portas introyerunt qui ad dominum reuerterunt.	8. Through which gate did the apostles enter? Answer: Through the gate which is called "chrysoprase." But through the other gates, those who were converted to the Lord entered.
9 Dic mici: Per quale porta ingressus est dominus noster Iesus Christus in ipsa ciuitate? Per porta que dicitur iaspes.	9. Tell me, through which gate did our Lord Jesus Christ enter into that city? Answer: Through the gate which is called "jasper."
10 Quem tec […]git cinnamus et balsamus.	10. Which …[*lacuna*] cinnamon and balsam?[19]
11 Dic mici: Qualis arbor in anno xii flores emittit? Responsum: Cynnamus et balsamus, quem dominus manum suum[20] plantauit et digitos suos[21] signauit. Et has arbores per singulos menses flores emittunt. EXPLICIT.[22]	11. Tell me, which trees emit twelve flowers per year?[23] Answer: Cinnamon and balsam, which the Lord planted with his own hand and placed a mark[24] with his own finger.

2 "On the Gates of the New Jerusalem"

2.1 Introduction

2.1.1 Manuscript and Editions

From the tenth century is a collection of homiletical material designated by André Wilmart as "Catéchèses celtiques," often referred to as *Catechesis Celtica*. The collection comprises the manuscript: Vatican City, Biblioteca Apostolica Vaticana, Reg. lat. 49. In 1933, Wilmart published about a third of the material in his *Analecta Reginensia*.[25] Jean Rittmueller is editing the entire compilation for the Scriptores Celtigenae sub-series of Corpus Christianorum: Series Latina. She is also preparing an English translation. According to Rittmueller, this

---

[19] The answer seems to be missing as well.
[20] Hilhorst ("Escorial Fragment," 224, n. 5) has "For *manum suum* read *manu sua*."
[21] Hilhorst ("Escorial Fragment," 224, n. 6) has "For *digitos suos* read *digito suo*."
[22] From Hilhorst, "Escorial Fragment," 223–24.
[23] Cf. Rev 22:2.
[24] Lat. *signauit*.
[25] André Wilmart, *Analecta Reginensia: Extraits des manuscrits latins de la reine Christine conservés au Vatican*, Studi e Testi 59 (Vatican City: Biblioteca Apostolica Vaticana, 1933), 29–112.

"miscellany of Latin religious texts ... may have served as a preacher's source book."[26] In this collection, on fols. 32v–35v is a lengthy homily preached by an unknown abbot.[27] Below is a transcription of the Latin text of the last part of that homily, contained on fol. 35r–v of the manuscript and pp. 56–58 in Wilmart's edition. I have used Wilmart's edition for the translation, and have entitled it "On the Gates of the New Jerusalem."[28]

2.1.2 Irish Provenance

Although the manuscript containing the *Catechesis Celtica* is from the tenth century,[29] according to Benjamin Hudson the collection of materials was "for sermons composed, if the extant manuscript is a guide, in the late ninth/early tenth century." Hudson also mentioned that the *Catechesis Celtica*, in its present form, appears to be a product of a scriptorium in a Brythonic-speaking area; and locations in Wales, Cornwall and Brittany have been suggested.[30] According to Rittmueller, half of its fifty-six texts "were copied or adapted from Hiberno-Latin works."[31] The many Irish elements and affiliations of the *Catechesis Celtica* are discussed in a number of publications.[32] Rittmueller studied the specific homily that contains "On the Gates of the New Jerusalem," and showed from its

---

[26] Jean Rittmueller, "Construe Marks, a Contraction Mark, and an Embossed Old Irish Gloss in a Hiberno-Latin Homily on the Octave of Easter," in *Early Medieval Ireland and Europe: Chronology, Contacts, Scholarship. A Festschrift for Dáibhí Ó Cróinín,* ed. Pádraic Moran and Immo Warntjes (Turnhout: Brepols, 2014), 537–76 at 537.

[27] The abbot is described in Irish fashion as *princeps* of the monks. See Martin McNamara, "Sources and Affiliations of the *Catechesis Celtica* (MS Vat. Reg. lat 49)," *Sacris Erudiri* 34 (1994): 185–237 at 213; and Rittmueller, "Construe Marks" (cf. note 26) 546 and 550, where she writes: "*Princeps* frequently replaces *abbas* in Hiberno-Latin texts. It is the Hib. Lat. equivalent of Irish *airchinnech*."

[28] Wilmart, *Analecta Reginensia* (cf. note 25), 56–8.

[29] John Carey, "*In Tenga Bithnua:* From Apocalypse to Homily?" in *The Scriptures and Early Medieval Ireland: Proceedings of the 1993 Conference of the Society for Hiberno-Latin Studies on Early Irish Exegesis and Homiletics,* ed. Thomas O'Loughlin (Turnhout: Brepols, 1999), 51–68 at 64 wrote that the *Catechesis Celtica* is "a compilation of Irish and other materials preserved in a continental manuscript written about the year 900."

[30] Benjamin T. Hudson, "Time is Short: The Eschatology of the Early Gaelic Church," in *Last Things: Death and the Apocalypse in the Middle Ages,* ed. Caroline Walker Bynum and Paul Freedman (Philadelphia: University of Pennsylvania Press, 2000), 101–23 at 109.

[31] Rittmueller, "Construe Marks" (cf. note 26), 537.

[32] Diarmuid Ó Laoghaire, "Irish Elements in the *Catechesis Celtica,*" in *Ireland and Christendom: The Bible and the Missions,* ed. Próinséas Ní Chatháin and Michael Richter (Stuttgart: Klett-Cotta, 1987), 146–64; Martin McNamara, "The Irish Affiliations of the *Catechesis Celtica,*" *Celtica* 21 (1990): 291–334; Jean Rittmueller, "MS Vat. Reg. Lat. 49 Reviewed: A New Description and a Table of Textual Parallels with the *Liber questionum in evangeliis,*" *Sacris Erudiri* 33 (1992–1993): 259–305; Martin McNamara "The Affiliations and Origins of the *Catechesis Celtica*: An Ongoing Quest," in O'Loughlin, *The Scriptures and Early Medieval Ireland* (cf. note 29), 179–203; and McNamara, "Sources and Affiliations" (cf. note 27).

"linguistic, liturgical, ecclesiastical, scholarly, and exegetical expressions" that it is the work of an Irish author.[33]

2.1.3 Contents

The homily was preached on Low Sunday, the Octave of Easter; and its text is John 20:26–31 in which Jesus appeared to Thomas after his resurrection.[34] The portion of the homily translated below begins with a discussion of the significance of the eight days of Easter. It then focuses the majority of its attention on the gates of the New Jerusalem. The eight days of Easter, said the abbot, represent eight time periods. The first six days represent the ages of human history corresponding with the six days of creation, presumably 6,000 years, since the seventh day represents the thousand years in which the last judgment takes place. The eighth day corresponds to the state of eternal life that God will grant to the saints after judgment day, wherein they will dwell in the "highest city of heaven."

The main body of the text explains John's vision of the New Jerusalem in Rev 21. Although clearly a description of New Jerusalem, the city is not called by that name in the homily, but rather is called "the city of heaven" and "the kingdom of heaven." The text focuses more particularly on its gates and the guardians associated with each gate. The colors of the gemstones on the walls of the city are then compared with various actions of the saints. The abbot then gives tropological interpretations of the gates, relating each to various Christian virtues and practices. The three gates on the east represent faith, hope, and love, and the apostle Peter is their key holder. The three southern gates represent virginity, penance, and marriage, and the apostle John has watch over them. The three gates on the west are deeds, words, and thoughts, and the apostle Thomas is their gatekeeper. The northern gates represent baptism, repentance, and martyrdom, and the apostle James is their guardian.

The preacher concludes the sermon with another significance of the eight days of Easter: judgment day. The homily reveals that he believed, based on the Apocalypse of Thomas, that in the seven days preceding the last judgment, the world will experience various signs, culminating with judgment day on the eighth day.

---

[33] Rittmueller, "Construe Marks" (cf. note 26), 539.

[34] McNamara, "Sources and Affiliations" (cf. note 27), 212. The homily's heading is *Secundum Iohannem* or "According to John." Rittmueller, "Construe Marks" (cf. note 26), 538. Brian O'Dwyer Grogan, "The Eschatological Doctrines of the Early Irish Church" (PhD diss., Fordham University, 1973), 292, refers to it as a "homily on Christ's Resurrection."

2.1.4 Sources and Date

The portion of the homily about the New Jerusalem contains quotations from several patristic sources, including Origen (d. 254), the Apocalypse of Thomas (5th c.) and Isidore of Seville (d. 636). It also alludes to the Gospel of the Nazarenes (2nd c.) and *On Hebrew Names* (*De nominibus hebraicis*) by Jerome (d. 419). Interestingly, there are no literary parallels or indications of dependence between this homily and three early medieval Hiberno-Latin Apocalypse commentaries: *Handbook on the Apocalypse of the Apostle John* (late 7th c.), *On the Mysteries of the Apocalypse of John* (ca. 730), and the *Cambridge Gloss on the Apocalypse* (8th c.).[35] However, the Irish illuminated manuscript called the *Book of Armagh*, produced in the year 807, contains a diagram of the New Jerusalem. This diagram contains the walls and gates of the city with their corresponding Hebrew tribe, the names of the apostles, and the names of the gemstones decorating each gate. The diagram was studied in depth by Thomas O'Loughlin, who demonstrated that the diagram was a form of exegesis, which, like glosses and commentaries, "facilitated the reader's access to the sacred text."[36] While it shares with our text the common theme of the New Jerusalem, the diagram stays much closer to the biblical text of Rev 21 (and Ezek 48:30–35) than this homily does.

Concerning the date of the authorship and/or delivery of the homily, the tenth century date of the manuscript, in which the homily is contained, establishes its *terminus ante quem*. *On Church Duties* by Isidore of Seville from the seventh century is cited in the homily, which shows it was delivered after the time of Isidore. It is also likely that the fifth-century Apocalypse of Thomas, quoted in the homily, was not being used among the Irish until the eighth century.[37] Therefore, the homily was probably originally written or delivered in the eighth or ninth century.

---

[35] *Commemoratorium de Apocalypsi Johannis apostoli* (Gryson, CCSL 107:159–229); *De enigmatibus ex Apocalypsi Johannis* (Gryson, CCSL 107:231–95). Both are translated into English in Francis X. Gumerlock, ed., *Early Latin Commentaries on the Apocalypse* (Kalamazoo, MI: Medieval Institute Publications, 2016). The Cambridge *Glossa in Apocalypsin* is edited by Roger Gryson in CCSL 108G, and an English translation is in *The Cambridge Gloss on the Apocalypse*, trans. Colin McAllister, Corpus Christianorum in Translation 36 (Turnhout: Brepols, 2020).

[36] Thomas O'Loughlin, "The Plan of the New Jerusalem in the Book of Armagh," *Cambrian Medieval Celtic Studies* 39 (2000): 23–38 at 26. O'Loughlin discussed other early medieval texts of Irish authors that contain descriptions of the New Jerusalem in "Imagery of the New Jerusalem in the *Periphyseon* and Eriugena's Irish Background," in *History and Eschatology in John Scottus Eriugena and His Time*, ed. Michael Dunne and James McEvoy, Ancient and Medieval Philosophy 30:1 (Leuven: Leuven University Press, 2002), 245–60. These texts include Adomnán's *De locis sanctis*, the *Navigatio sancti Brendani*, and Eriugena's *Periphyseon*.

[37] Martin McNamara, "The (Fifteen) Signs before Doomsday in Irish Tradition," in *Miscellanea Patristica: Reverendissimo Marco Starowieyski septuagenario professori illustrissimo viro amplissimo ac doctissimo oblata*, Warszawskie Studia Teologiczne 20, no. 2 (2007): 223–54 at 233.

2.1.5 Latin Orthography

The Latin transcription has *ebdomadis* for *hebdomadis*, *hostias* and *hostiis* for *ostias* and *ostiis* and once it changes *ostia* to the masculine or neuter *hostio*. *Celorum* is used for *caelorum* one time, *martiria* for *martyria*, *babtismum* for *baptismum*, *sue* for *suae*, *misterio* for *mysterio*, *pulcro* for *pulchro*, *Ebreorum* for *Hebraeorum*, *idest* for *id est*, and sometimes *poenitentia* and *penitentia* for *paenitentia*. Also, in the transcription below I have indicated page numbers from Wilmart's edition and have retained his parentheses and brackets.

2.2 Transcription and Translation

Transcription	Translation
[56] Item isti VIII dies pascae signi(ficant) VIII tempora uitae praesentis a principio mundi usque ad iudicium, quia sub forma ebdomadis constituit deus hunc mundum. Ipsa est VII aetas dies iudicii, in quo fiunt mille anni, dum iudicentur uiui et mortui secundum merita uniuscuiusque. Ipse est VIII dies uita aeterna, quam dabit deus sanctis suis sine fine in summa ciuitate caeli. Ipsa est ci(uitas) quam ostendit angelus Ioh(anni) cum sua quantitate et cum sua altitudine et cum sua cantiditate: quod conuenit sanctis post resurrectionem, quando sedebunt in magnitudine potestatis, in sublimitate meritorum, in claritate sanctitatis et luci aeternitatis.	Again, these eight days of Easter signify the eight periods of the present life from the beginning of the world up to the judgment, since under the form of a week God created this world.[38] The day of judgment is the seventh age, in which are the thousand years,[39] when the living and the dead will be judged according to the merits of each. The eighth day is eternal life, which God will give to his saints without end in the highest city of heaven. This city is that which the angel showed to John with its size and its height and its glory.[40] This [city] is suitable for the saints after the resurrection, when they will sit in the greatness of power, in the loftiness of merits, and in the glory of holiness and eternal light.
Item uidit Iohannes angelum cum arundine aurea uenientem ad ciuitatem coram se et mensus est altitudinem ci(uitatis) et long(itudinem) et latitudinem.	Again, John saw an angel with a golden reed coming to the city before him; and he measured the height of the city and its length and width.[41]
Item uidit XII hostias ci(uitatis), idest III ab oriente et III ab	Again, he saw twelve gates of the city,[42] that is, *three on the east and three on the west and*

---

[38] Cf. Gen 1:1–2:3.

[39] Cf. Rev 20:2–6. The concept that the resurrection of the righteous will take place over a thousand years, saints rising at different times throughout that period based upon their merits, is found in Tertullian, *Against Marcion* (*Adversus Marcionem*) 3.24 (*ANF* 3, 343). It also appears in the Irish *Tidings of Doomsday*. See Hudson, "Time is Short" (cf. note 30), 114.

[40] Cf. Rev 21:9–27.

[41] Cf. Rev 21:15–16.

[42] Cf. Rev 21:12.

Transcription	Translation
occidente et III ad dextera et III ab aquilone;	three on the south[43] and three on the north [Rev 21:13].
uidit XII angelos in hostiis ciui(tatis): angelum in unoquoque hostio;	He saw twelve angels on the gates of the city:[44] an angel on each gate.
et uidit XII Apostolos et XII patriarchas custodientes ciui(tatem): III angelos et III patriarchas et III Apostolos in unaquaque parte ciuitatis, quia hae sunt III familiae quibus commendatum est aperire regnum celorum sanctis omnibus in die iudicii, et quibus iterum commendatum est claudere regnum dei in fine saeculi ad daemones et pec(catores), ut est: QUAECUMQUE ALLIGAVERITIS <et> reliqua.	And he saw the twelve apostles[45] and twelve patriarchs[46] guarding the city: three angels and three patriarchs and three apostles in each part of the city, since these are the three groups to whom it was entrusted to open the kingdom of heaven to all the saints on the day of judgment, and again to whom it was entrusted to close the kingdom of God at the end of the world for demons and sinners, as it is [written]: *Whatsoever things you will have bound*, etc. [Matt 18:18].
Item uidit XII lapides preciosos super muros ciuitatis, et hostia uidit cum multis coloribus, idest alii colores ignite, alii aquati, alii iacinthi, alii rubri, alii candidi, alii porporei. Quibus lapidibus comparantur actus sanctorum, quando per martiria probantur et per plures necessitates: aliis actibus probatis per <candidum> babtismum, aliis per iacintha martiria, aliis per rubra mar(ti)ria ensium persecutor<is> pro amore dei, uel per sanguinem pudoris dando confessionem ductoribus animarum, ut est: CONFITEMINI PECCATA VESTRA ALTERUTRUM.	Again, he saw twelve precious stones upon the walls of the city,[47] that is, some fiery colors, some blue, some hyacinth, some red, some white, and some purple.[48] To these stones are compared the acts of the saints, when they are tested through martyrdom and through lack of many necessities: In some, having been tested[49] in their actions, baptism [is shown] through white; in others martyrdom [is shown] through hyacinth; in others martyrdom for the love of God by the swords of a persecutor [is shown] through red. Or, through [red is shown] the blushing of shame[50] when giving confession to their spiritual directors, as it is [written]: *Confess your sins to one another* [Jas 5:16]."[51]

---

[43] Lat. *dextera*, literally "on the right." Rittmueller, "Construe Marks" (cf. note 26), 540, said that the use of the Latin *dextera* for "south" is the author's rendering of the Old Irish *dess*, which means both "right" and "south."

[44] Cf. Rev 21:12.

[45] Cf. Rev 21:14.

[46] Cf. Ezek 48:30–35.

[47] Cf. Rev 21:14.

[48] Cf. Rev 21:19–20.

[49] Lat. *probatis* or perhaps "approved."

[50] Lat. *sanguinem pudoris*.

[51] Lat. *ductoribus animarum*, meaning "directors of their souls." It refers to the practice of private confession.

Transcription	Translation
Item XII patriarchae quos uidi Iohannes in foribus ciuitatis, hi sunt doctores qui custodiunt ueteris legis [...].[52] Item XII apos(toli) quos uidit Iohannes, hi sunt praeceptores qui seruant nouam legem. Item XII ang(eli) quos uidit Iohannes, hi sunt mi\<ni\>stri et custodes aeclesiae catholicae, ut psalmista dicit: QUONIAM ANGELIS SUIS MANDAVIT DE TE UT CUSTODIANT TE \<et\> reliqua, qui custodiunt angeli caeli animam uniuscuiusque [57] hominis a die natiuitatis sue usque ad diem quando exierit de corpore suo.	Again, the twelve patriarchs whom John saw on the gates of the city, are the teachers who guard the [precepts] of the old law. Again, the twelve apostles whom John saw, these are the lawgivers[53] who keep the new law. Again, the twelve angels whom John saw, these are the ministers[54] and guardians of the Catholic Church, as the psalmist says: *For, concerning you, he entrusted his angels to guard you*, etc. [Ps 91:11], since the angels of heaven guard the souls of each person from the day of his birth up to the day when he leaves his body.[55]
Ibunt igitur peccatores obiam Christo in iudicio ut iudicium pertulerint. Erunt ergo fores regni caelestis clausae obiam illis pro meritis malorum actuum, et proicientur ad poenas perpetuas cum exercitu daemonum, per testimonium apostolorum et patri(archarum) et ang(elorum), et dicetur illis ex ore dei solius: ITE MALEDICTI \<et\> reliqua.	Therefore, in the judgment sinners will go before Christ to suffer punishment. Therefore, the gates of the kingdom of heaven will be closed to them because of the merits of their evil deeds. And they will be cast forth into eternal punishments with the army of demons, through the testimony of the apostles and of the patriarchs and of the angels. And it will be said to them from the mouth of God himself: *Go, accursed ones*, etc. [Matt 25:41].
Sancti uero ascendent cum Christo ad regnum suum et erunt ianuae regni cae[lorum] obiam illis apertae, et duces et custodes erunt illorum illi trini quos praediximus, et uocabit illos uox dei solius in conspectu apostolorum et patriarcharum et angelorum, dicens: VENITE BENEDICTI \<et\> reliqua.	But the saints will ascend with Christ to his kingdom, and the gates of the kingdom of heaven will be opened before them. And these three, whom we have mentioned earlier,[56] will be their guides and guards. And the voice of God himself will call them in the sight of the apostles and of the patriarchs and of the angels, saying: *Come, blessed*, etc. [Matt 25:34].
Item si ad moralitatem six annumerantur istae XII ianuae ciui(tatis), hae sunt III ianuae ab	Again, if these twelve gates of the city are numbered for morality, three of these gates are on the east, that is, faith, hope and love,[57] that is,

---

[52] Wilmart (*Analecta Regensia*, 56, n. 6) notes that *praecepta* should be supplied here.

[53] Lat. *praeceptores*.

[54] Cf. Ps 104:4; Heb 1:7.

[55] This shows the preacher's belief in guardian angels. Cf. Herm. Man. 6.2 (36); Origen, *First Principles* (*De principiis*) 2.10, 7 (*ANF* 4, 296); Vision of Paul (*Visio Pauli*) 7 (Edgard Hennecke, *New Testament Apocrypha*, 2 vols. [Philadelphia: Westminster Press, 1963], 2:761–62).

[56] Apostles, patriarchs, and angels.

[57] Cf. 1 Cor 13:13.

Transcription	Translation
oriente, idest fides, spes, cartias; idest fides trinitatis, sperare bona praemia, dilectio dei et proximi. Ianua caritatis media est inter illas et optima, eo quod illa continentur omnia mandata. Ideo Petrus qui est princeps apostolorum clauicularius est orientatlis portae ciuitatis, quia fides illius fortissimo esse legitur in euangelio, et in ipso maxime reualatur dilectio dei in terra. Item tres dextrales ianuae per quas ueniunt filii benedictionis in ciuitate caeli, idest uirginitas et paenitentia et matrimonium. Ianua uirginitatis ipsarum est excelsissima et optima, quia centenos fructus accipiunt aureum. Et idea Iohannes est dux istarum III ianuarum in parte dextrali, idest in plaga ardoris et lucis et solis, eo quod ipse est heres uirginitatis Christi in terra, et quia ipse est qui ennuntiauit, ardorem lucis solis ueritatis, quando nuntiauit genealogiam domini sui secundum deitatem, dicens: IN PRINCIPIO ERAT VERBUM <et> reliqua. Item ciuitatis III ianuae quae sunt ab occa(su), per quas ueniunt sancti in ciuitate caeli, hae sunt opus et uerbum et cogitatio. Haec est ianua excelsissima et optima earum, idest opus, si fuerit poenitentiale, quia in ipso perficiuntur cogitationes et uerba. Conuenit misterio istas III ianuas esse ad occa(sum) solis in confinio lucis et tenebrarum, quia intraturn in tenebras peccatorum per uerbum et cogita(tionem) et opus, si non sint	the faith of the Trinity, the hope for good rewards, and the love of God and neighbor.[58] The gate of love is in the middle between the other two and is the best, because all of the commandments are contained in it.[59] Therefore, Peter, who is the prince of the apostles, is the key holder of the east gate of the city, since it is read in the Gospel that his faith is the strongest,[60] and in him especially the love of God is revealed on earth. Again, the three southern gates through which the children of blessing come into the city of heaven are virginity and penance and marriage. Of these the gate of virginity yields fruit a hundredfold.[61] And these are they who sing unceasingly a song in heaven around the golden [crowned] Lamb.[62] And for this reason John is the leader of these three gates on the south part [of the city], that is, in the region of the heat and of light, the sun, in that [John] is the heir of the virginity of Christ on earth, and because it is he who announced the region of light, the sun, and the truth when he announced the genealogy of his Lord according to his deity, saying: *In the beginning was the Word*, etc. [John 1:1]. Again, the three gates of the city which are on the west, through which the saints come into the city of heaven, these are work and word and thought.[63] Work is the most excellent and best gate of them because if the work is penitential, then the thoughts and words are perfected in it. The mystery of these three gates applies to the setting of the sun at the border of light and darkness, because one enters the darkness of sins through word and thought and work if these are not illuminated by the lights of the law of God and of doctrine. Again, one enters

---

[58] Cf. Matt 22:37–39.
[59] Cf. Matt 22:40.
[60] Cf. Matt 14:29; 16:16.
[61] Cf. Matt 13:23.
[62] Cf. Rev 14:3–4.
[63] On work, word, and thought as a common Irish triad, see Patrick Sims-Williams, "Thought, Word and Deed: An Irish Triad," *Ériu* 29 (1978): 78–111.

Transcription	Translation
illuminata luminibus legis dei et doctrinae. Item intratur per illa in lucem uitae perpetuae et salutis, si fuerint in sanctitate et perfectione. Ideo Tomas apostolus dux est istarum III ian(uarum) in occidentali parte ciuitatis cuius nomen interpre\<tatur\> abissus scientiae, quia ipsa est scientia [58] profundissima ut custodiat quisque semetipsum in sanctitate uerbi, cogitationis et actus, ut mereatur perpetuam aeternitatem cum angelis. Item tres aliae sinistrales ianuae ciuitatis caeli, idest babtismum, poenitentia, martirium. Ipsa media ianua earum optima est, idest bab(tismum), ut Christus dicit: NISI QUIS RENATUS FUERIT EX AQUA ET SPIRITU SANCTO NON \<et\> reliqua. Item pro babtismo reputatur penitentia, ut est: Lacrimae paenitentiae pro babtismate reputantur. Item martirium pro bab(tismo) reputatur sanctis, ut Orig(enes) dicit: "Babtismum sanguinis solum est quod puriores reddit quam babtismum commune." Item congruum est ut in septentionali parte ciui(tatis) ponerentur istae ianuae, quia ex illa parte ueniunt cogitationes et temptationes daemonum, et in qua fit frigus et tenebrositas, et in qua non currit sol eti(am) aliquo tempore, quia per	through these into the light of perpetual life and salvation if he lives in holiness and perfection. For this reason, the apostle Thomas is the leader of these three gates on the western side of the city, whose name is interpreted "depth"[64] of knowledge, because this [deep knowledge] is the most profound knowledge. And whoever guards himself in holiness of word, thought, and action, merits perpetual eternity with the angels. Again, there are three other northern gates of the city of heaven, that is, baptism, penance, and martyrdom. The middle gate of these is the best, that is, baptism,[65] as Christ says: *Unless one is born again from water and the Holy Spirit, [he will] not,* etc. [John 3:3,5]. Again, penance is reckoned as a baptism, as is [written]: "The tears of penance are reckoned as baptism."[66] Again, martyrdom is regarded by the saints as baptism, as Origen says: "The baptism of blood alone is something that renders people more pure than common baptism."[67] Again, it is fitting that these gates were placed on the north part of the city because from that region come the thoughts and temptations of the demons,[68] and in that [region] it is cold and dark, and in that [region] sometimes even the sun does not run its course, and because through baptism and penance and martyrdom people are separated from the bondage of the devil and from the coldness of unbelief and from the darkness of sins. And for this reason, the apostle James is

---

[64] Jerome, *On Hebrew Names* (*De nominibus hebraicis*), Matthew, Acts. P. de Lagarde, G. Morin, and M. Adriaen, ed., CCSL 72:138, 149.

[65] The homily enumerates three types of baptism: common water baptism, the baptism of tears of penitence, and the baptism of blood in martyrdom.

[66] Isidore of Seville, *On Church Duties* (*De ecclesiasticis officiis*) 16.6. On the baptism of tears in early medieval Anglo-Saxon sources like *The Life of Saint Gregory* (*Vita sancti Gregori Magni*) and the pseudo-Bede *Collectanea*, see Thomas O'Loughlin and Helen Conrad-O'Briain, "The 'baptism of tears' in early Anglo-Saxon sources," *Anglo-Saxon England* 22 (1993): 65–83.

[67] Origen, *Homilies on the Book of Judges* (*Homiliae in Judices*) 7.2.

[68] For the north as the region of the devil, based on Joel 2:20 and Jer 3:12, see Tyconius, *Book of Rules* (*Liber regularum*) 7.4 in William S. Babcock, trans., *Tyconius: Book of Rules* (Atlanta: Scholars Press, 1989), 121–25.

Transcription	Translation
babtismum et penitentiam et martirium separantur homines a iugo diaboli et a frigiditate infidelitatis et tenebris peccatorum. Ideoque Iacobus apostolus dux est istarum III ianuarum in sinistrali parte ciuitatis, cuius nomen interpre<tatur> subplantator, quia istae sunt III ian(uae) per quas maxime superatur diabolus, idest bab(tismum) et penitentia et martirium.	the leader of these three gates on the northern part of the city, whose name is interpreted "supplanter,"[69] because these are the three gates through which the devil is especially overcome, that is, baptism and penance and martyrdom.
His igitur qui habuerit ista III integre et plene non intrabit poenas inferni, et separatus erit ab exercitu daemonum et peccatorum et intrabit in ci(uitate) regni caeli ad Christum, qui uenit ad Apostolos hodie in domu clausa, et intrabit ad exercitus ang(elorum) et archan(gelorum) et patri(archarum) et profe(tarum) et apos(tolorum), et conregnabunt cum gradibus caeli in saecula saeculorum, in conspectu trinitatis in regno amoeno et pulcro et concupito, et in regno candido et claro, et in perpetuo regno sine fine amen.	Therefore, by these the one who will have these three wholly and fully will not enter the punishments of hell, and will be separated from the host of demons and sinners, and will enter into the city of the kingdom of heaven to Christ, who came to the apostles today in a closed house.[70] And he[71] will enter the army of the angels and archangels and patriarchs and prophets and apostles, and will reign together with the ranks of heaven forever and ever in the sight of the Trinity in a kingdom pleasant and beautiful and desirable, and in a kingdom splendid and bright, and in a perpetual kingdom without end. Amen.
Item isti VIII dies pascae in quo resur(rexit) Christus filius dei significant VIII dies post remi(ssionem) paschae in quo iudicabitur totum semen Adae, ut nuntiatur in euangelio	Again, these eight days of Easter, on which Christ, the Son of God, rose again, signify eight days after the passing of Easter,[72] on which the entire seed of Adam will be judged, as it is said in the *Gospel of the Hebrews*.[73] And scholars[74]

---

[69] Cf. Gen 27:36; Jerome, *On Hebrew Names*, Genesis. CCSL 72:67.

[70] Cf. John 20:19.

[71] One who will wholly and fully have baptism, penance, and martyrdom.

[72] Lat. *VIII dies post remi(ssionem) pascae*. Later in this paragraph the author of the homily says that great signs will take place throughout seven of these days and on the eighth the righteous will be summoned to the right hand of God for the day of judgment. This Latin phrase is translated as "eight days after the recurrence [?] of the Passover" in Hennecke, *New Testament Apocrypha* (cf. note 55), 1:150. That the day of judgment will fall at Easter time is also mentioned in MS: Paris, Bibliothèque nationale de France, lat 614A. See John Carey, ed., *Apocrypha Hiberniae II* (Turnhout: Brepols, 2009), 404.

[73] This is not contained in the extant fragments of the second-century *Gospel according to the Hebrews*. See the extant fragments of it in Ehrman, *Lost Scriptures*, 16; and Hennecke, *New Testament Apocrypha* (cf. note 55), 1:163–65. Hennecke (*New Testament Apocrypha*, 1:150–51) has this citation as originating from the *Gospel of the Nazarenes*.

[74] Lat. *sapientes* or "wise people." According to Rittmueller, "Construe Marks" (cf. note 26), 551, "Hiberno-Latin writers often mention *sapiens*, 'a formal term for a scholar (Irish *suí*) used in the Irish annals', a title that describes men expert in 'the Latin language and theological studies.' The context of Homily 26R indicates *sapiens* is to be understood as a biblical scholar."

Transcription	Translation
Ebreorum, et ideo putant sapientes diem iudicii in tempore pascae, eo quod in illo die pascae incipit deus creare creaturas in principio mundi, atque has formauit per VI dies ebdo(madis) usque dum requieuit in septimo die. Item similiter putatur mundus dispergi per VII dies iudicii, et uocari iustos in VIII die, ut sint a dextris dei patris. Item erunt signa magna per VII dies qui numerantur ante diem iudicii: "Haec sunt signa primi diei, idest tonitrua magna" <et> reliqua.[76]	think that the day of judgment [will take place] at Easter time for this reason: because Christ rose again on that day, so also on that day the saints rise again. Again, on the day of Easter God began to create the creatures at the beginning of the world, and formed them throughout six days of a week up to when he rested on the seventh day.[75] Again, similarly the world is thought to be destroyed throughout seven days of judgment, and that on the eighth day the righteous are summoned to the right hand of God the Father. Again, "there will be great signs throughout the seven days"[77] which are counted before the Day of Judgment. "These are the signs of the first day, that is, great peals of thunder, etc."[78]

---

[75] Cf. Gen 2:2. For another Irish text that teaches that God created the world on a Sunday, Jesus rose again on a Sunday, and the resurrection and last judgment will take place on a Sunday, see the apocryphal *Letter of Jesus on Sunday Observance* in Máire Herbert and Martin McNamara, ed., *Irish Biblical Apocrypha: Selected Texts in Translation* (New York: T&T Clark, 1989), 50–54; and "Three Sunday Catecheses" in *Celtic Spirituality,* trans. Oliver Davies with Thomas O'Loughlin (New York: Paulist, 1999), 371–75. Christian of Stablo or Stavelot, also known as Christian Druthmarus, in the ninth century wrote on Matt 24:42 that a writing had been "left to us which [says] that the world was made, the Lord was conceived and died, and in a similar way the world will be destroyed eight days before the Kalends of April [March 25]." *Sic denique nobis scriptum reliquere quod octava Kal. Aprilis fuit mundus factus. Dominus conceptus est et passus, et simili modo erit destructus* (*Exp. Matt.* 55, *PL* 106:1461). Bischoff ("Turning Points" [cf. note 9], 93) noted that the commentaries of Christian of Stablo reveal his "undeniable contacts with the Irish commentaries."

[76] From Wilmart, *Analecta Reginensia,* 56–58.

[77] Apocalypse of Thomas, 4. O'Sullivan, "The Apocalypse of Thomas," in Carey et al, *The End and Beyond* (cf. note 5), 2:567–91 at 580. See also Matthias Geigenfeind, "The Apocalypse of Thomas: A New Translation and Introduction," in *New Testament Apocrypha: More Noncanonical Scriptures,* vol. 2, ed. Tony Burke (Grand Rapids, MI: Eerdmans, 2020), 595. According to McNamara, "The (Fifteen) Signs before Doomsday in Irish Tradition" (cf. note 37), 233, this Apocalypse was present in some form in Ireland by the eighth century. By the eleventh or twelfth century in Ireland these signs developed into fifteen signs of doomsday. See Herbert and McNamara, *Irish Biblical Apocrypha* (cf. note 76), 95; William W. Heist, *The Fifteen Signs Before Doomsday* (East Lansing: Michigan State College Press, 1952), 193–98; and Michael E. Stone, *Signs of the Judgment, Onomastica Sacra and the Generations from Adam* (Chico, CA: Scholars Press, 1981), 4–5.

[78] Apocalypse of Thomas 5. O'Sullivan, "Apocalypse of Thomas" (cf. note 77), 582; Geigenfeind, "Apocalypse of Thomas" (cf. note 77), 596.

3 Concluding Reflections: Irish Curiosity, Creativity, and Classification

The "Question-and-Answer Tractate on the New Jerusalem" and "On the Gates of the New Jerusalem" exhibit curiosity, creativity, and a fondness for classification on the part of their Irish authors. Revelation 21:12 mentions that names were written on the gates of New Jerusalem, but does not specify each gate's name. Perhaps in an effort to fill in what is lacking in the biblical description, the author of the "Question-and-Answer Tractate" supplies names for the various gates. Similarly, the biblical text in Rev 21:14 merely states that the names of the twelve apostles were written on the foundation stones of the city's wall. However, "On the Gates" specifies particular apostles – Peter, John, Thomas, and James – as guardians over certain gates of that city. Also, in their curiosity for additional information about the New Jerusalem, the authors of these texts seem to draw from a well of apocryphal sources at their disposal.[79] The author of the "Question-and-Answer Tractate" may have used 1 Enoch in his description of the city's trees; and perhaps for his description of the "seventh throne" the Vision of Paul or gnostic texts on the seven heavens were influential.[80] "On the Gates" actually quotes from the Apocalypse of Thomas near its end. Both Hiberno-Latin texts on the New Jerusalem may have been influenced by the Shepherd of Hermas. According to Stephen J. Shoemaker, Irish writings of late antiquity and the early Middle Ages provide "numerous examples of continued usage of apocryphal writings."[81]

To say that the Irish were very creative in their eschatology is not an understatement. While eschatology encompasses themes like heaven, hell, life after death, the last judgment, the resurrection, Doomsday, and much more, focusing on early medieval Irish answers to just one question, that of how God will preserve his people in the time of the antichrist, can easily illustrate their eschatological

---

[79] Bischoff, "Turning Points" (cf. note 9), 87–88, mentions "the naturally curious bent of the Irish character" and allowance for apocryphal narratives in their biblical exegesis.

[80] The Vision of Paul (*Visio Pauli*) was contained in the same manuscript as that in which the "Question-and-Answer Tractate on the New Jerusalem" was preserved. See Hilhorst, "Escorial Fragment" (cf. note 3), 223. About Irish texts on the seven heavens being influenced by gnostic texts, which may have come to the Irish through Spanish Priscillianists, see David N. Dumville, "Biblical Apocrypha and the Early Irish: A Preliminary Investigation," *Proceedings of the Royal Irish Academy* 73 (1973): 299–338; Marcel Dando, "Les Gnostiques d'Égypte, les Priscillianistes d'Espagne et l'église primitive d'Irlande," *Cahiers d'études cathares*, 2nd series, 23 (1972): 3–34; and Carey, "The Seven Heavens: Introduction" in Carey et al., *The End and Beyond* (cf. note 5), 1:155–70 at 156–57.

[81] Stephen J. Shoemaker, "Early Christian Apocryphal Literature," in *The Oxford Handbook of Early Christian Studies,* ed. Susan Ashbrook Harvey and David. G. Hunter (New York: Oxford University Press, 2008), 521–48 at 527. On the use of apocryphal writings among the early medieval Irish, see also Martin McNamara, *The Bible and the Apocrypha in the Early Irish Church (A.D. 600–1200)* (Turnhout: Brepols, 2015) and Martin McNamara, *The Apocrypha in the Irish Church* (Dublin: Dublin Institute for Advanced Studies, 1984).

creativity. Far from the usual answers of late antique theologians – God will cut short the days of the antichrist,[82] the saints will hide in deserts and mountains,[83] Enoch and Elijah will protect the saints from his deception[84] – the Irish suggested some amazingly creative future scenarios. Some said that groups of Irish monks will be brought by boat to the island of Paradise where they will take refuge from the antichrist's persecution.[85] Others taught that seven years before judgment day God will mercifully send a great flood so that the sea covers Ireland in a single hour and all of the Irish will perish and thus be spared from the horrors of the antichrist.[86] Such eschatological creativity is also shown in their conceptions of the New Jerusalem set forth in the "Question-and-Answer Tractate" and "On the Gates." In the former, the name of each gate was written by a particular angel and the Lord Jesus Christ entered the city through a specific gate. In the latter, groups of angels, patriarchs, and apostles are not only in charge of opening the gates of the city for the saints, but also for closing them against sinners and demons, as if demons at some point will try to enter the New Jerusalem but be refused access.

Finally, these two Hiberno-Latin texts also show that their authors possessed a fondness for classification. In the "Question-and-Answer Tractate" the twelve gates are each named, and those who have already entered the city through particular gates are specified. The apostles have entered through one, the evangelists through another, and the prophets through still another. In "On the Gates" specific apostles have been assigned for guardianship of specific gates. Also, moral virtues necessary for gaining entry into the New Jerusalem are classified: faith, penitence, love, and for some the virtuous commitment to virginity or the suffering of martyrdom. These moral virtues and actions, especially penitence and virginity, reflect the monastic ideals of the authors of these texts. The New Jerusalem, described by these authors as pleasant, beautiful, desirable, and splendid, is portrayed as the object of the hope of the faithful after death. By adding to the biblical data and giving more precision to New Jerusalem through various classifications, these Irish texts seem to bring greater reality to heaven

---

[82] Victorinus of Petovium, *Fragment on the Olivet Discourse*, in Cuthbert H. Turner, "An Exegetical Fragment of the Third Century," *Journal of Theological Studies* 5 (1904): 218–41 at 228.

[83] Ascension of Isaiah, 4.13 (Hennecke, *New Testament Apocrypha* [cf. note 55], 2:649); Lactantius, *The Divine Institutes* (*Divinarum institutionum libri VII*) 7.17 (ANF 7, 214); Hilary of Poitiers, *Commentary on Matthew* (*In Matt.*) on Matt 24:16 (Daniel H. Williams, ed., FC 125 [Washington, DC: The Catholic University of America Press, 2012], 250).

[84] Caesarius of Arles, *Exposition of the Apocalypse of Saint John* (*Expositio de Apocalypsi Sancti Iohannis*), Homily 10.4 (Roger Gryson, ed., CCSL 105, 171).

[85] *Navigatio Sancti Brendani Abbatis,* 28 in John J. O'Meara, *The Voyage of Saint Brendan: Journey to the Promised Land* (Gerrards Cross: Colin Smythe Limited, 1991), 69; *Life of Brendan of Clonfert* 153, in Charles Plummer, trans., *Lives of Irish Saints*, 2 vols. (Oxford: Clarendon, 1922), 2:76; *The Voyaging of St. Columba's Clerics*, in 2:769, 771, 791; *The Colloquy of the Two Sages*, 251, in 2:631, 641.

[86] *The Colloquy of the Two Sages*, 252, Carey, *The End and Beyond* (cf. note 5), 2:641; Hudson, "Time is Short" (cf. note 30), 104–5.

and the hearing faithful closer to it.[87] In addition, the specification of citizens already abiding in the city and the moral virtues necessary for entry into the city demonstrated to the hearer that entrance was in fact attainable for the faithful. The creative speculations and specifications found in these two texts, traversing well beyond the material found in the biblical text of Rev 21 and manifesting the curiosity of their authors, contribute to our understanding of how the New Jerusalem was perceived by certain Irish teachers in the early Middle Ages.

---

[87] Grogan, "Eschatological Teaching in the Early Irish Church" (cf. note 34), 47.

Imagining the Celestial City

Visual Reception of Patristic Exegetical Traditions in the Carolingian, Beatus, and Anglo-Norman Apocalypses

Ian Boxall

Introduction

In one example it is not possible to present the exact <nature> of the good things of the heavenly city. Wherefore the wide street of the city, on the one hand, he viewed as very extravagant and beautifully colored like gold, and, on the other hand, <it is> clear as crystal, so that for us it is impossible for both <descriptions> to concur in one <image>. The saint saw all these things as he was able. Perfect comprehension of the heavenly city surpasses hearing and sight and thought.[1]

This astute observation by the early seventh-century Greek commentator Andrew of Caesarea, provoked by the textual tension between opaque gold and transparent crystal in Revelation's description of the holy city (Rev 21:21), underscores the challenges faced by all interpreters of the book of Revelation. John of Patmos's lengthy and detailed description of the New Jerusalem taxes the human imagination by its sheer detail and complexity. The New Jerusalem has multiple faces: it is announced as a bride (Rev 21:9), is visualized as a city of massive proportions (Rev 21:10–14), and morphs into an Edenic garden (Rev 22:1–2) with temple features (Rev 21:16; 22:3). Many of its details remain ambiguous. Is the lofty mountain merely the seer's vantage point, or also the terrestrial location to which the celestial city descends? What function is played by the twelve angels positioned at the city gates? Are they guards to prevent hostile intruders (the

---

[1] "Ἐν παράδειγμα τὴν ἀκρίβειαν τῶν τῆς ἄνω πόλεως ἀγαθῶν παραστῆσαι οὐ δύναται. διὸ τὴν πλατεῖαν τῆς πόλεως διὰ μὲν τὸ πολυτελὲς καὶ εὔχρουν ὡς χρυσίον, διὰ δὲ τὸ καθαρὸν ὡς κρύσταλλον ἐθεάσατο· ἅπερ ἀμφότερα ἐν ἑνὶ συνδραμεῖν παρ' ἡμῖν ἀδύνατον. ταῦτα δὲ πάντα ὁ ἅγιος τεθέαται, καθὼς ἠδύνατο· ἡ δὲ ἀκραιφνὴς τῆς ἄνω πόλεως κατανόησις ὑπερβαίνει καὶ ἀκοὴν καὶ ὅρασιν καὶ διάνοιαν. English translation from Andrew of Caesarea, *Commentary on the Apocalypse*, trans. Eugenia Scarvelis Constantinou, FC 123 (Washington, DC: Catholic University of America Press, 2011), 231. Greek text from Josef Schmid, *Studien zur Geschichte des griechischen Apokalypse-Textes: Der Apokalypse-Kommentar des Andreas von Kaisareia*, vol. 1, Münchener theologische Studien 1: Historische Abteilung 1 (München: Zink, 1955).

outsiders of Rev 22:15), or markers of the divine presence within? How is the lofty height of the New Jerusalem – twelve thousand stadia, or some fifteen hundred miles – to be correlated with the disproportionately small size of the city walls (a modest 144 cubits, equivalent to 216 feet)? What should one make of a single tree of life growing on *either* side of the city's river?

Answers to these and many other questions are provided by exegetes of the patristic and early medieval periods. In the process, however, differing patterns of exegesis, whether chiliastic, christological, or ecclesiological, add further layers of textual potential. The commentary genre permits the luxury of expansion and digression to explore this complexity. To take just one example, in his eighth century *Expositio Apocalypseos*, the Venerable Bede elaborates extensively on the properties of the twelve precious stones adorning the city's foundations, their places of origin, and their allegorical meaning for John's readers.[2]

Our interest in this chapter is not primarily in the exegetical tradition preserved in the commentaries, but rather the later visual reception of that early (especially Latin) reception of the text. This chapter will study a select number of images of the New Jerusalem in illuminated manuscripts from the ninth to the thirteenth centuries; specifically, it will consider how Latin patristic and early medieval commentators laid the foundations for these visualizations and what choices had to be made to transform text and commentary into image. Our selection represents three clusters of medieval illuminated Apocalypses. The first cluster comprises the Carolingian exemplars from the ninth century, which are the earliest extant cycles of scenes from the book of Revelation in manuscript form. The second entails the polychromatic Beatus manuscripts from the ninth to the thirteenth centuries. Third, we will consider the Anglo-Norman Apocalypses (produced in large numbers during the thirteenth and fourteenth centuries), especially those manuscripts that were influenced by the commentary of Berengaudus. Unsurprisingly, the influence of the Donatist exegete Tyconius of Carthage (fl. 370–390) looms large over all three, each of which offers a Tyconian ecclesiological reading of the New Jerusalem as signifying not only the eschatological church but also its present state. As Tyconius comments on Rev 21:1–5:

He calls this "Jerusalem" the church, by recapitulating from the passion of Christ up to the day on which she rises and, having triumphed with Christ, she is crowned in glory. He mixes each time together, now the present, now the future, and declares more fully when she is taken with great glory by Christ and is separated from every incursion of evil people.[3]

---

[2] Bede, *Expositio Apocalypseos* 3.37. For an English translation, see Faith Wallis, trans., *Bede. Commentary on Revelation*, Translated Texts for Historians 58 (Liverpool: Liverpool University Press, 2013), 267–77.

[3] *Hanc Ierusalem ecclesiam dicit, recapitulando a Christi passione usque in diem quo resurgat et cum Christo inuicta coronetur in gloria. Miscet utrumque tempus, nunc presens, nunc futurum,*

As will become apparent, despite common or overlapping exegetical sources, visual illuminations depicting the New Jerusalem are far from uniform. The illustrators, or their theological advisers, have had to make decisions about which details to prioritize, how to fill textual gaps, and whether to present the *littera* of the scriptural text or to convey its allegorical potential. Surviving visualizations of the city as *city* range from the architectural to the abstract to the geometric and diagrammatic.[4] Others prioritize specific motifs or narrative moments (e. g., the enthroned Lamb, the river and tree of life) often subdividing the text to create narrative sequences. The exegetical interests and questions of those who produced or commissioned the images, the influence of earlier models, and the specific functions of the manuscripts in question have all contributed to this surprising diversity, as has the new dynamic created by the juxtaposition of biblical text, pictorial image, and commentary excerpts on the same page.[5] Prominent within this dynamic, and emerging explicitly from time to time onto the visual plane, are the patristic voices.

1 Carolingian Illustrations

So how was John's lengthy and detailed vision report concerning the New Jerusalem distilled into accessible visual imagery? We begin with a cluster of illuminations from the Carolingian period, representing the earliest surviving Apocalypse cycles in manuscript form. The oldest is the Trier Apocalypse (Trier, Stadtbibliothek, Cod. 31), probably produced in the region of Tours, France, in the first decade of the ninth century. Peter Klein placed Trier, along with what appears to be a tenth century copy, the Cambrai Apocalypse (Cambrai, Bibliothèque municipale, MS 386), in his Family I of manuscripts, building on James Snyder's proposal that they were based on a late antique Italian prototype from the fifth or sixth centuries. Others remain to be persuaded by aspects of this hypothesis.[6] Whatever the antecedents, both Trier and Cambrai present

---

et cum quanta gloria suscipiatur a Christo et separata sit ab omni malorum incursu plenius declarat. English translation from Francis X. Gumerlock, trans., *Tyconius. Exposition of the Apocalypse,* FC 134 (Washington, DC: Catholic University of America Press, 2017), 181. Latin text from Roger Gryson, ed., *Tyconii Afri Expositio Apocalypseos*, CCSL 107A (Turnhout: Brepols, 2011), 222.

[4] An example of the latter is the twelfth-century Bodleian Haimo Apocalypse (Oxford, Bodleian Library MS Bodl. 352, fol. 13r). Richard K. Emmerson, *Apocalypse Illuminated: The Visual Exegesis of Revelation in Medieval Illuminated Manuscripts* (University Park, PA: The Pennsylvania State University Press, 2018), 87, Fig. 39.

[5] On these challenges, see e. g., Natasha F. H. O'Hear, *Contrasting Images of the Book of Revelation in Late Medieval and Early Modern Art: A Case Study in Visual Exegesis*, Oxford Theological Monographs (Oxford: Oxford University Press, 2011).

[6] James Snyder, "The Reconstruction of an Early Christian Cycle of Illustrations for the Book of Revelation – The Trier Apocalypse," *Vigiliae Christianae* 18 (1964): 146–62; Peter K. Klein,

the narrative of Revelation in seventy-four full-page colored images, with the continuous text of Revelation on the facing pages.

One further Carolingian manuscript will also be considered, as an illustration of the surprisingly diverse approaches to visualizing the New Jerusalem within the same geographical area and time period. The Valenciennes Apocalypse (Bibliothèque municipale de Valenciennes, MS 99), produced in Liège in the first quarter of the ninth century, depicts Revelation in just thirty-eight illustrations.[7] It belongs to Klein's Family II, one stage removed from the Italian prototype, given the reduced number of images and other changes. One proposal is that the Family II manuscripts derive from a Northumbrian model related to the images of Revelation, which, according to Bede, his abbot Benedict Biscop brought back from Rome to adorn the monastic church of St. Peter in Wearmouth (Bede, *Vitae quinque ss. abbatum* 1).[8]

How does Trier confront the challenges of visualizing John's complex description of the New Jerusalem? That it takes an episodic approach, breaking the vision down into several discrete scenes, is only partly due to the format, which pairs scriptural text on one page with a single image on the facing page.[9] The prominence given to the city itself (four images on fols. 69r–71r and 73r) is also a clear reflection of the Carolingian exegetical tradition, derived from Tyconius via Bede and Alcuin, despite the lack of a commentary in the manuscript.[10] This sharply contrasts the New Jerusalem as the faithful church with Babylon as the false church. Trier also contains five images of Babylon as a city to illustrate Rev 17–18 (fols. 56r–60r), together with an additional three presenting her in the more familiar guise of the harlot (fols. 53r–55r).

The first miniature of the New Jerusalem (fol. 69r, illustrating Rev 21:9–12) depicts John standing on a rocky outcrop to the left, accompanied by the interpreting angel who points across to the heavenly city on the right. The city has already descended to earth, where it is firmly established on a masonry foundation. Subsequent images present the angel holding the measuring rod as the

---

"Introduction: The Apocalypse in Medieval Art," in *The Apocalypse in the Middle Ages*, ed. Richard K. Emmerson and Bernard McGinn (Ithaca and London: Cornell University Press, 1992), 159–99 (especially 175–77). For the pros and cons of this hypothesis, see the discussion in Emmerson, *Apocalypse Illuminated* (cf. note 4), 29–30.

[7] It is closely related to Paris Bibliothèque Nationale, nouv. acq. lat. 1132, which may be a tenth-century copy of Valenciennes.

[8] Klein, "The Apocalypse in Medieval Art" (cf. note 6), 177–79.

[9] *Die Trierer Apokalypse: Codex 31 der Stadtbibliothek Trier. Kommentar von Peter K. Klein mit Beiträgen von Richard Laufner und Gunther Franz*, Glanzlichter der Buchkunst 10 (Graz: Akademische Druck- u. Verlagsanstalt, 2001). See also Bianca Kühnel, *From the Earthly to the Heavenly Jerusalem: Representations of the Holy City in Christian Art of the First Millennium*, Römischer Quartalschrift für christliche Altertumskunde und Kirchengeschichte, Supplementheft 42 (Rome, Freiburg and Vienna: Herder, 1987), 124–27; Emmerson, *Apocalypse Illuminated* (cf. note 4), 27–32.

[10] For Alcuin's commentary, see *PL* 100:1087–1156.

angel prepares to measure the city (fol. 70r, illustrating Rev 21:15) and the Lamb and the tree of life in the midst of the city, with the kings of the earth in Frankish costumes bringing their "glory" – symbolized by crossed spheres – towards it on the left (fol. 71r, illustrating Rev 21:22–24; 22:2: Fig. 1). The New Jerusalem is also depicted to the left in fol. 73r, clearly identified by an inscription (*hec ciuitas magna est*) despite the number of towers having been reduced from twelve to six. An additional image of a detail of the New Jerusalem vision, though without the city itself, has an angel holding Christ's cross-staff, inviting an unidentified man to drink from a pond (fol. 74r, illustrating the invitation to the thirsty to receive the water of life at Rev 22:17).[11]

Although often regarded as slavishly literal in its visualization of the text, Trier (or its antique model) prioritizes specific details of the New Jerusalem vision beyond the selection of specific scenes. The city's architectural features are foregrounded, as also in the Cambrai copy, but these are determined less by the text of Revelation, or even by the physical appearance of terrestrial Jerusalem, than perceptions of cities known to the artist.[12] The outer wall is comprised of twelve tall towers, each with a single gate at the base, viewed from the front. There is no attempt to portray the pearl-like gates, the angels at each gate, the names of the twelve tribes, or the foundations bearing the names of the twelve apostles of the Lamb. Despite the flat surface of the frontal perspective, it is combined with a "bird's eye view" perspective causing the remainder of the city wall to appear circular rather than "foursquare" (*civitas in quadro posita est*, Rev 21:16 Vulgate). Such a visualization of the New Jerusalem, shaped by images of known cities, is to be expected in a culture in which, as Mary Carruthers has shown, sense data was transformed into "memory images," – "cognitive fictions" that could be stored away in the memory's treasury for later use. Indeed, on this point, she explicitly cites the Carolingian Alcuin:

So perhaps one of us might have formed in his mind an image of a putative Jerusalem: however greatly different the actuality may be, as his mind has fashioned [its image] for itself so [Jerusalem] will seem to him.... He does not imagine the actual walls and houses and squares of Jerusalem, but whatever he has seen in other cities known to him, these he fashions as being possibly like those in Jerusalem; from known shapes he fashions a thing unknown. (*Liber de animae ratione* 7)[13]

---

[11] For commentaries, see Klein in *Trierer Apokalypse* (cf. note 9), 57–59.

[12] Some see dependence here on earlier archetypes rather than the influence of contemporary architecture. According to van der Meer, Trier's buildings reflect those of the sixth century. Frederick van der Meer, *Apocalypse: Visions from the Book of Revelation in Western Art* (Antwerp: Mercatorfonds, 1978), 97.

[13] English translation from Mary Carruthers, *The Craft of Thought: Meditation, Rhetoric, and the Making of Images, 400–1200*, Cambridge Studies in Medieval Literature 34 (Cambridge: Cambridge University Press, 1998), 119–20.

Fig. 1. Trier Apocalypse, fol. 71r, *The Lamb in the New Jerusalem* (ninth century). Trier, Stadtbibliothek, Cod. 31, fol. 71r. Source: Wissenschaftliche Bibliothek der Stadt Trier / Stadtarchiv Trier. Photo: Anja Runkel; Ru No. 155 2021.

A further non-scriptural detail is the presence of two rectangular gabled buildings inside the city, just visible behind the front towers in fols. 69r and 70r. There are visual similarities with depictions of the seven churches earlier in the manuscript, as well as the temple that John measures in Rev 11:1–2 (fol. 33r), and the heavenly sanctuary opened at Rev 11:19 (fol. 36r). Bianca Kühnel has made the tentative suggestion that they represent two overlapping exegetical traditions, found together in Tyconian exegesis: the eschatological heavenly city, and the New-Jerusalem-as-church.[14] This is possible, given that a single similarly gabled

---

[14] Kühnel, *From the Earthly to the Heavenly Jerusalem* (cf. note 9), 126–27.

building on fol. 72r apparently symbolizes the earthly church to which God's angel is sent at Rev 22:6. Trier thus seeks to convey visually Tyconius's mingling of the church's present and its glorious future in the new Jerusalem vision.

Arguably more intriguing than Trier's New Jerusalem itself is the depiction of the Lamb and the tree of life in the miniature on fol. 71r (replicated in Cambrai), combining Rev 21:22–24 with 22:2. The Lamb, a crossed nimbus around his head, stands at the center of the city, holding the cross of his victory. The tree of life is visualized as a substantial trunk with three large branches, extending heavenwards beyond the city walls and towers. Yet the precise relationship between the Lamb and the tree is unclear. Is the tree located behind the Lamb, as Klein proposes?[15] Or does the tree grow out from the Lamb, such that the two are merged? The exegetical tradition might support the latter interpretation, given that the tree of life is identified with Christ himself in both the Greek (e. g., Oecumenius) and the Latin tradition (e. g., Primasius, Apringius).[16] Most relevant for Trier, given their influence on Carolingian interpretation of Revelation, this christological reading is also attested by Bede.[17]

Equally striking are the twelve fruits borne by the tree, which resemble clusters of grapes. This may suggest an additional Johannine intertext, the discourse on the vine and the branches in John 15:1–10, though such a connection is not immediately evident in the Latin exegetical tradition. However, given the baptismal connection frequently made for the "the water of life" (called a "fountain," *fons*, in the Vulgate of Rev 21:6, and a "river," *fluvium*, at 22:1), a eucharistic interpretation of the fruit would not be inappropriate. This would further underscore the ecclesial dimension of the New Jerusalem vision in these two Carolingian manuscripts.[18]

If Trier and Cambrai emphasize the architectural aspects of the New Jerusalem, spread across several miniatures, the single depiction of the city in Valenciennes (fol. 38r, Fig. 2) is both economical and altogether more abstract, almost diagrammatic.[19] The city is viewed from above, and is depicted as entirely circular, or more specifically, as twelve concentric circles punctuated at the four cardinal points by four sets of three gates (the eastern gates at the top of the page,

---

[15] Klein in *Trierer Apokalypse* (cf. note 9), 58.

[16] Oecumenius, *Commentarius in Apocalypsin* 21:26–22:5; Primasius, *Commentarius in Apocalypsin* 22:2; Apringius, *Tractatus in Apocalypsin* 22:2. An alternative identifies the tree of life as the cross, e. g., Caesarius of Arles: *hoc de cruce domini dixit*. Latin text from Roger Gryson, ed., *Caesarii Arelatensis Expositio de Apocalypsi Sancti Iohannis*, CCSL 105 (Turnhout: Brepols, 2019), 241. Bede is also familiar with this interpretation.

[17] Bede, *Exp. Apoc.* 3.37 (on Rev 22:2).

[18] The baptismal interpretation of Rev 21:6 and 22:1–2 is attested e. g., in Tyconius, Caesarius, and Apringius of Béja. For Bede, the baptismal reference has been superseded by the fruit that sacrament promised.

[19] On Valenciennes, see Kühnel, *From the Earthly to the Heavenly Jerusalem* (cf. note 9), 128–37; Emmerson, *Apocalypse Illuminated* (cf. note 4), 32–36.

Fig. 2. Apocalypse de Valenciennes, fol. 38r, *The Angel Shows John the New Jerusalem* (ninth century). Bibliothèque municipale de Valenciennes, MS 99. ©Médiathèque Simone Veil de Valenciennes.

reflecting the orientation of medieval maps). At the center is the Lamb as the symbol of the divine presence, with an explanatory quotation from Rev 21:23 (*et ciuitas non eget sole neque luna nam claritas dī inluminauit eum & lucerne eius est agnus*). The different colors of the circles, in various hues of green, yellow, and red-brown, perhaps recall the twelve precious stones adorning the city's foundations according to Rev 21:19–20. At the bottom of the page are John and the interpreting angel, viewing the city from outside.

There are good reasons to interpret Valenciennes's circular city as a non-literal indicator of the combination of ecclesiological and eschatological interpretations of the New Jerusalem in Carolingian exegesis. The circle is a symbol of eternity. Kühnel draws attention to the Carolingian exegete Candidus, who saw in it an image of the never-ending church, as well as God's eternal reign.[20] But Carol Heitz has also highlighted a more terrestrial explanation: the visual impact of Christian Jerusalem, and especially the Church of the Holy Sepulchre, which according to Eusebius was specifically constructed as a new Jerusalem over against

---

[20] Kühnel, *From the Earthly to the Heavenly Jerusalem* (cf. note 9), 216–17, n. 84.

the old.²¹ There is a strong visual resemblance to Arculf's sketches of the Holy Sepulchre and especially to the rotunda of the Anastasis, which is portrayed as a series of circles punctuated at the four compass points by the entrance and three apses.²² The Holy Sepulchre had been for Charlemagne, as previously for Constantine, "the meeting point between the heavenly and the earthly realm, between heavenly and earthly Jerusalem."²³

2 Beatus Manuscripts

In striking contrast to the early Carolingian Trier are the vividly-colored Beatus manuscripts, the illustrations of which may have been based on an earlier Spanish or North African prototype.²⁴ Twenty-nine illustrated manuscripts (including fragments) survive from the ninth to the thirteenth centuries, almost all from Spain, containing the illustrated commentary of the eighth-century Asturian monk Beatus of Liébana. Beatus explicitly attests indebtedness to Jerome, Augustine, Ambrose, Fulgentius, Gregory (whom John Williams identifies as Gregory of Elvira), Tyconius, Irenaeus, Apringius of Béja, and Isidore of Seville.²⁵ Tyconius is by far the most significant predecessor, and Beatus is in turn a major source, along with Primasius and Bede, for recent reconstructions of Tyconius's lost commentary.²⁶

The commentary contains the biblical text of Revelation, divided into *storiae* (using a North African form of the *Vetus Latina*), images depicting the relevant *storia*, and *explanationes* or commentary proper, often presenting a spiritualizing interpretation.²⁷ For the most part, the images closely follow the biblical text rather than the exegesis provided in the *explanatio*. If Kenneth

---

²¹ Eusebius, *Vita Constantini* 3.33.

²² Carol Heitz, *L'architecture religieuse carolingienne: les forms et leurs fonctions* (Paris: Picard, 1980), 210–14. See also Kühnel, *From the Earthly to the Heavenly Jerusalem* (cf. note 9), 129–32.

²³ Kühnel, *From the Earthly to the Heavenly Jerusalem* (cf. note 9), 117.

²⁴ On Beatus, see e. g., Klein, "The Apocalypse in Medieval Art" (cf. note 6), 176, 186–88; John Williams, "Purpose and Imagery in the Apocalypse Commentary of Beatus of Liébana," in *The Apocalypse in the Middle Ages*, ed. Emmerson and McGinn (cf. note 6), 217–33; John Williams, *The Illustrated Beatus: A Corpus of the Illustrations of the Commentary on the Apocalypse in Five Volumes* (London: Harvey Miller, 1994–2003); John Williams, *Visions of the End in Medieval Spain: Catalogue of Illustrated Beatus Commentaries on the Apocalypse and Study of the Geneva Beatus*, ed. Therese Martin, Late Antique and Early Medieval Iberia 3 (Amsterdam: Amsterdam University Press, 2017).

²⁵ Williams, *The Illustrated Beatus* (cf. note 24), vol. 1, 19.

²⁶ Kenneth B. Steinhauser, *The Apocalypse Commentary of Tyconius: A History of Its Reception and Influence* (Frankfurt a. M.: Lang, 1987); Gryson, *Tyconii Afri* (cf. note 3).

²⁷ The critical edition of Beatus is Roger Gryson, ed., *Beati Liebanensis Tractatus de Apocalypsin*, CCSL 107B–C (Turnhout: Brepols, 2012).

Steinhauser is correct, this three-fold division between text, image, and commentary closely models Beatus's own hermeneutical method, set out most fully in his anti-adoptionist *Adversus Elipandum*, co-authored in 785 with Bishop Etherius of Osma. Here Beatus presents Scripture as consisting of three parts: "the letter, the metaphor, and the mystical understanding," or the literal, the metaphorical or tropological, and the mystical, corresponding to the human body, soul, and spirit. In the commentary, the *storia* would present the literal meaning, the *pictura* the tropological, and the *explanatio* the mystical.[28]

The Beatus commentary divides the New Jerusalem vision into three *storiae*, each with an accompanying picture, corresponding to Rev 21:1-27 (the city itself), Rev 22:1-5 (the river of life, flowing from God's throne), and Rev 22:6-21 (the final scene of John attempting to worship the angel). Unsurprisingly, the accompanying *explanatio* shares the Tyconian conviction that the New Jerusalem is simultaneously a vision of the ongoing descent of the celestial city in the church and of the final consummation.

The New Jerusalem image from the Morgan Beatus (New York, Pierpont Morgan Library, MS M. 644, fol. 222v) has been chosen to illustrate the Beatus tradition (Fig. 3). Morgan, dated to ca. 940-945, is the oldest surviving manuscript in the largest family of Beatus manuscripts (Branch II, further subdivided into IIa and IIb). It is a representative of the expanded Beatus cycle of the commentary's final edition, which incorporated symbols of the evangelists, genealogical tables, and Jerome's *Commentary on Daniel*.[29] Its scribe and illustrator, a certain Maius, monk of Tábara, describes in a colophon how he has "painted a series of pictures for the wonderful words of its stories so that the wise may fear the coming of the future judgement of the world's end."[30] The "wise" here are probably his monastic readers/viewers.

Morgan's New Jerusalem illumination follows a compositional format that is fairly consistent across the various Beatus manuscripts of both Branches I and II. The city is presented foursquare, in conformity with the biblical text, and viewed from above, as if John were looking down from his lofty mountain vantage point (Rev 21:10, 16).[31] The consequence is a flattened, two-dimensional form,

---

[28] Kenneth B. Steinhauser, "Narrative and Illumination in the Beatus Apocalypse," *The Catholic Historical Review* 81 no. 2 (1995): 185–210.

[29] On the Morgan Beatus, see e.g., John Williams and Barbara A. Shailor, *A Spanish Apocalypse: The Morgan Beatus Manuscript* (New York: George Braziller with The Pierpont Morgan Library, 1991); Williams, *The Illustrated Beatus* (cf. note 24), vol. 2, 21–33. Scholars are divided over whether this third edition was produced by Beatus himself ca. 786, as part of his anti-adoptionist crusade, or is a tenth-century posthumous expansion (Emmerson, *Apocalypse Illuminated* [cf. note 4], 47–48).

[30] Williams, *The Illustrated Beatus* (cf. note 24), vol. 2, 21. There may be evidence for another hand besides Maius towards the end, given the different technique in depicting figures in the Fountain of Life (fol. 223) compared with the Heavenly Jerusalem (fol. 222v).

[31] Alternatively, the view from above is an attempt to convey the city's celestial character. Kühnel, *From the Earthly to the Heavenly Jerusalem* (cf. note 9), 142.

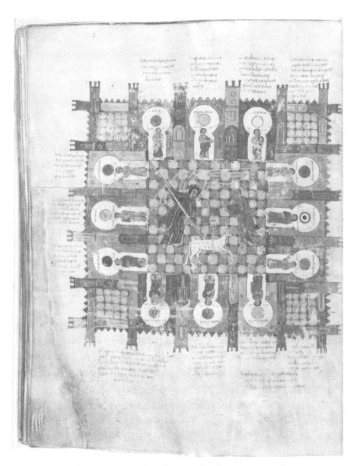

Fig. 3. Morgan Beatus, *The New Jerusalem* (ca. 945). The Morgan Library & Museum, New York, MS M.644, fol. 222v. Purchased by J. P. Morgan (1867–1943) in 1919. Photographic credit: The Morgan Library & Museum, New York.

"wherein the walls seem to have collapsed outward."[32] At the center stands the Lamb, holding a cross-staff, flanked by John and the angel with the measuring rod. The image is richly colored, with shades of orange and yellow conveying the

---

[32] Williams and Shailor, *A Spanish Apocalypse* (cf. note 29), 209. Exceptions which depict the New Jerusalem as rectangular are either conforming the image to the page size, as in the Lorvão Beatus (Lisbon, Arquivo Nacional da Torre do Tombo, fol. 209v) and Geneva Beatus (Bibliothèque de Genève, MS lat. 357, fol. 241), or using a two-page spread, e. g., the Turin Beatus (Turin, Biblioteca Nazionale Universitaria, Segn. I.II.1, fols. 179v–180).

magnificence of this city of pure gold.³³ Its twelve gates have Mozarabic horseshoe arches, an indicator of the Spanish Christian appropriation of Muslim architectural styles.³⁴ The gates, together with the flattened corners of the city, are flanked by crenellated towers, twenty-four in all, in hues of green, blue, orange and red. White is also liberally used for the Lamb, the tracing of the angel's wings, and the interior of the gates. This latter detail probably symbolizes the twelve pearls of which the gates are comprised according to Rev 21:21.

In other details, Morgan departs significantly from the biblical text. According to John's description (Rev 21:12), there are twelve angels at the gates, and the gates themselves are inscribed with the names of the twelve tribes, presumably in the order previously revealed at Rev 7:5–8. Morgan lacks the angels, understandably in light of the variant reading *angulos* ("angles," "corners," or perhaps "alcoves") in place of *angelos* in Beatus's *Vetus Latina* text. Instead, the twelve apostles stand within the gates, identified by their names, Peter given primacy in the top left, followed by his brother Andrew. Over the heads of the apostles are the twelve precious stones, again named, represented by disks of the appropriate color. The colors of the gemstones partially follow those provided by Isidore of Seville in his *Etymologiae*, excerpts from which are copied in the margins of the Morgan image.³⁵

The replacement of the angels and names of the tribes by the twelve apostles and their gemstones is surprising, given John's association of both apostolic names and precious stones with the city's foundations, not its gates (Rev 21:14, 19–20).³⁶ A solution suggests itself in the ecclesiological exegesis of Beatus's commentary, in which the multiple twelves of the city, including the gates, are all correlated with the apostolic foundation of the church. This is initially laid out in the Prologue to Book Two, which draws upon Isidore of Seville's *De ortu et obitu patrum* (*On the Life and Death of the Fathers*) to describe the division of mission territory among the apostles:

> These are the twelve gates of the Heavenly Jerusalem, through which we enter the blessed life. They constitute the first apostolic Church, which we believe to be the foundation stone firmly built on Christ. They are the twelve thrones that are to judge the Twelve Tribes of Israel. This is the Church spread all over the earth.³⁷

---

³³ On the priority of value (tone or brightness) over hue in medieval appreciation of color, and its implications for the Beatus manuscripts, see Elizabeth S. Bolman, "*De coloribus*: The Meanings of Color in Beatus Manuscripts," *Gesta* 38 no. 1 (1999): 22–34.

³⁴ Williams, *Visions of the End in Medieval Spain* (cf. note 24), 52.

³⁵ Hana Šedinová, "The Precious Stones of Heavenly Jerusalem in the Medieval Book Illustration and Their Comparison with the Wall Incrustation in St. Wenceslas Chapel," *Artibus et Historiae* 21/41 (2000): 31–47, especially 33–36.

³⁶ Such mixing and matching of elements of the New Jerusalem's structure in a way that is dissonant with the biblical text has a long exegetical history, especially in relation to the precious stones. E. g., Clement, *Paedagogus* 2.12; Origen, *Homiliae in Ezechielem* 13.3.2.

³⁷ *Hii sunt duodecim portae celestis Ierusalem, per quos ad uitam beatam ingredimur. Hii*

This is reiterated in Beatus's commentary on Rev 21:12, which understands the twelve gates and twelve tribes to symbolize the twelve apostles and twelve prophets respectively (a probable allusion to Eph 2:20). An apostolic interpretation of the gates is no innovation of Beatus but is already attested in Primasius, who also influenced Bede.[38]

Two puzzles remain in the Morgan image: the order of the apostles, and the correlation between apostles and precious stones. The sequence (moving clockwise from top left) and corresponding gemstones are as follows:[39]

Table 1. Order of apostles and correlation between apostles and precious stones in Morgan Beatus.

Top (east?)	Peter	jasper
	Andrew	sapphire
	Judas	chalcedony
Right (south?)	Simon Zelotes	emerald
	Bartholomew	sardonyx
	James[40]	carnelian
Bottom (west?)	John	chrysolite
	Philip	beryl
	Thomas	topaz
Left (north?)	James	chrysoprase
	Matthew	jacinth
	Matthias	amethyst

Correlating precious stones with apostles had previously been attempted in the Greek tradition by Andrew of Caesarea, though the only points of agreement with the Morgan Beatus are the correspondence of Peter with jasper and

---

sunt prima apostolica ecclesia, quam credimus firmissime supra Christum petra fundata. Hii sunt duodecim throni iudicantes duodecim tribus Israel. Haec est ecclesia per uniuersum orbem terrarium dilatata (Book 2, prologue, 3.19–20). English translation from Alessandro Scafi, *Mapping Paradise: A History of Heaven on Earth* (Chicago: University of Chicago Press, 2006), 109. Latin text from Gryson, *Beati Liebanensis* (cf. note 27), vol. 2, 163–64.

[38] Primasius, *Commentarius in Apocalypsin* 21.112–14. "These gates are *the apostles* who by their writings or their labor *first* opened *the gate of the Church* to the nations" (Bede, *Commentary on Revelation*, 263).

[39] A similar correlation is found in the Valladolid Beatus (Valladolid, Biblioteca de la Universidad, MS 433, fol. 182v). The Geneva Beatus (fol. 241) is almost identical, except that Judas and the second James have between transposed, perhaps to have the three "pillars" (Gal 2:9) in a place of primacy (Beatus identifies James the Less, son of Alphaeus, with James the Lord's brother: prologue to Book 2, 3.9).

[40] This James is almost certainly the son of Zebedee since he is located just before John.

Matthias with amethyst.[41] Beatus's commentary offers no such correspondence to explain the image.[42]

Equally puzzling is the order of the twelve apostles. It does not reflect any of the canonical lists of the twelve (Matt 10:2–4; Mark 3:16–19; Luke 6:14–16; Acts 1:13) nor does it follow the western liturgical order, at least as preserved in the Roman canon.[43] Nor does it fit the earlier list of the apostles in the Beatus commentary, nor the locations of their missionary territories in the *mappae mundi* of earlier Beatus manuscripts, marked by the apostles' heads.[44] Peter was assigned Rome, Andrew Achaia, Thomas India, James Spain, John Asia, Matthew Macedonia, Philip Gaul, Bartholomew Lycaonia, Simon the Zealot Egypt, Matthias Judea, and James the Lord's brother Jerusalem. In this earlier list, Paul is added as the twelfth, though strangely through removing Judas (Thaddeus) rather than the replacement Matthias from the list.[45]

None of this explains the positioning of the apostles in the New Jerusalem in Morgan. Not only are both Judas and Matthias included to the exclusion of Paul, but the grouping of three apostles on each of the four walls fails to reflect their direction of mission, irrespective of the orientation of the city.[46] For example, the three apostles at the bottom of the page (John, Philip, and Thomas) are allocated Asia (i.e., western Turkey), Gaul, and India respectively.

What is clear is the ecclesiological interpretation of the twelve offered in the Morgan image and an emphasis on their foundational missionary activity. Early commentators had already made this connection. For Caesarius of Arles, the number and positioning of the gates reflects the dispersal of the church into the four parts of the earth to preach the mystery of the Trinity.[47] A similar interpretation is found in Apringius, one of Beatus's sources, and Bede.[48]

---

[41] These could be deductions from the text, attributing the first and twelfth gemstones to the primary and the newest apostles respectively. Andrew of Caesarea also replaces Judas (Thaddaeus) with Paul.

[42] See Francis X. Gumerlock's contribution on Hiberno-Latin treatment of the configuration elsewhere in this volume.

[43] By contrast, the New Jerusalem diagram in the Book of Armagh, which may possibly have had some influence on the Beatus tradition, follows the order of Matthew. Thomas O'Loughlin, "The Plan of the New Jerusalem in the Book of Armagh," *Cambrian Medieval Celtic Studies* 39 (Summer 2000): 23–38.

[44] The *mappa mundi* in the Morgan Beatus (fols. 33v–34) lacks the apostles' heads. On Beatus maps, see e.g., Scafi, *Mapping Paradise* (cf. note 37), 108–13.

[45] Beatus, *Tract. Apoc.* 2 prologue 3.17–18.

[46] One can probably assume that the top is oriented to the east, following the model of the Beatus maps.

[47] Caesarius, *Expositio de Apocalypsi sancti Iohannis* 19 (Gryson, *Caesarii Arelatensis Expositio*, 237).

[48] Apringius, *Tract. Apoc.* 21:13; Bede, *Exp. Apoc.* 3.17 (on Rev 21:13).

3 Anglo-Norman Apocalypses

Our final cluster of New Jerusalem images represents the Anglo-Norman Apocalypse tradition of the thirteenth and fourteenth centuries.[49] These illuminated Apocalypses fall into two broad groupings: those with excerpts (normally in Latin, though occasionally in Anglo-Norman translation) from the *Expositio super septem visiones libri Apocalypsis* (*Exposition concerning the Seven Visions of the Book of Revelation*) of Berengaudus, and those with an anonymous vernacular commentary in Anglo-Norman or French.[50] Many were commissioned by aristocratic and even royal patrons, thus functioning somewhat differently from earlier manuscripts intended for monastic usage. In particular, they reflect a shift from a communal and oral experience of reading to one that is more private and visual.[51]

Berengaudus's eclectic commentary, influenced *inter alia* by Bede, Ambrose Autpert, and Haimo of Auxerre, is probably the work of a Benedictine monk of the eleventh century, inspired by the church reforms of Pope Gregory VII (1073–1085).[52] Richard Emmerson summarizes the author's exegetical approach: "His exegesis is primarily ecclesiological and prophetic, but it also develops many moral and historical interpretations."[53] Like Bede, Berengaudus divides the biblical text into seven visions, the seventh beginning at the point when the angel shows John the descending city, identified as "the bride of the Lamb" (Rev 21:9). The emphasis in this final vision is primarily on the future eschatological consummation rather than the present reality of the New Jerusalem in the church:

> We arrive, God willing, at the seventh vision to which pertains everything in that time which is the future after the resurrection. And order demands that, the general resurrection having been described, the glory of the saints, which after the resurrection they possess without end, be described, which in this vision is described under the figure of the city of Jerusalem.[54]

---

[49] On the Anglo-Norman corpus, see e.g., Klein, "The Apocalypse in Medieval Art" (cf. note 6), 188–92; Suzanne Lewis, *Reading Images: Narrative Discourse and Reception in the Thirteenth-Century Illuminated Apocalypse* (Cambridge: Cambridge University Press, 1995); O'Hear, *Contrasting Images* (cf. note 5), 11–42; Emmerson, *Apocalypse Illuminated* (cf. note 4), 111–60.

[50] For lists of manuscripts belonging to these two groupings, see Emmerson, *Apocalypse Illuminated* (cf. note 4), 119, 128.

[51] Lewis, *Reading Images* (cf. note 49), 2–6; O'Hear, *Contrasting Images* (cf. note 5), 11–13.

[52] Latin text in *PL* 17:763–970. In favor of a ninth century dating, see Derk Visser, *Apocalypse as Utopian Expectation (800–1500): The Apocalypse of Berengaudus of Ferrières and the Relationship between Exegesis, Liturgy and Iconography,* Studies in the History of Christian Traditions 73 (Leiden: Brill, 1996), 44–103.

[53] Emmerson, *Apocalypse Illuminated* (cf. note 4), 112.

[54] *Septima visio ad quam, Domino donante, pervenimus, tota ad illud tempus quod post resurrectionem futurum est, pertinet. Et ordo poscebat, ut generali resurrectione descripta, gloriam sanctorum, quam post resurrectionem sine fine possidebunt, describeret; quae sub figura civitatis*

Our main examples come from the so-called "Metz" group of the Berengaudus-type manuscripts: the Lambeth (London, Lambeth Palace Library, MS 209), Abingdon (London, British Library, Add. 42555), and Gulbenkian (Lisbon, Museu Gulbenkian, L. A. 139) Apocalypses. In contrast to the latter two, however, which both contain additional images depicting details from the Berengaudus gloss, the Lambeth images are almost entirely shaped by the biblical text.[55] Indeed, given the rather haphazard placement of the Lambeth's commentary excerpts, Natasha O'Hear has made the plausible suggestion that they were added to provide *faux gravitas* to the manuscript, impacting little on the experience of the aristocratic reader.[56] Alternatively, a chaplain may have functioned as translator and interpreter, with the images then serving as memory aids for the viewer to recall instruction received.[57]

The Lambeth Apocalypse was produced ca. 1264–1267 for a female aristocratic patron, either Lady Eleanor de Quincy, Countess of Winchester, or Margaret Ferrers.[58] It contains seventy-eight miniatures depicting scenes from the Apocalypse, together with an additional twenty-eight images at the end, twenty of them depicting the life of John.[59] Its page format is typical: a rectangular image at the top, followed by two columns of text, comprising a short excerpt from the text of Revelation followed by a longer excerpt from the Berengaudus commentary, both in Latin.

Lambeth presents the New Jerusalem vision in narrative sequence over three miniatures: the descent of the New Jerusalem (Rev 21:1–2, fol. 37v); John being shown the city by the angel (Rev 21:9–22, fol. 38r, Fig. 4); the river flowing from God's throne (Rev 22:1–2, fol. 38v). Following a depiction of John's misguided attempt to worship the interpreting angel (fol. 39r, illustrating Rev 22:8), Lambeth has a final image, in which the seer is granted a direct vision of the enthroned Christ (fol. 39v), a fitting end to his apocalyptic journey.[60]

Hierusalem in hac visione describitur. English translation from Lewis, *Reading Images* (cf. note 49), 189. Latin text from *PL* 17:945.

[55] Gulbenkian has 152 miniatures, Abingdon 156. Both Abingdon and Gulbenkian combine excerpts from Berengaudus's commentary with selections from Haimo of Auxerre (in Abingdon's case, in Anglo-Norman translation). Daron Burrows, ed., *Abingdon Apocalypse (British Library, Add. 24555)*, Anglo-Norman Texts 74 (Oxford: Anglo-Norman Text Society, 2017).

[56] O'Hear, *Contrasting Images* (cf. note 5), 21–22.

[57] Nigel Morgan, *The Lambeth Book of Revelation, Manuscript 209 in Lambeth Palace Library: A Critical Study* (London: Harvey Miller Publishers, 1990), 94.

[58] O'Hear, *Contrasting Images* (cf. note 5), 22–25.

[59] Suzanne Lewis believes that John's *vita* was originally intended to precede the Apocalypse miniatures. Lewis, *Reading Images* (cf. note 49), 274.

[60] Natasha O'Hear, "Seeing the Apocalypse: Pre-1700 Visualizations of Revelation," in *The Book of Revelation and Its Interpreters: Short Studies and an Annotated Bibliography*, ed. Ian Boxall and Richard Tresley (Lanham, MD: Rowman & Littlefield, 2016), 85–124, especially 99–102.

Fig. 4. Lambeth Apocalypse, fol. 38r, *John Measuring the New Jerusalem* (late thirteenth century). Lambeth Palace Library, LPL MS 209. ©Trustees of Lambeth Palace Library.

Lambeth's New Jerusalem emphasizes, albeit differently from Trier, Cambrai, and the Beatus manuscripts, the architectural aspects of the city. There is no attempt to emulate its cuboid shape. Rather, it is viewed from the front as a tall, four-story structure, with three empty gates on each story. Nor does it depict the precious stones adorning the New Jerusalem, though touches of green probably signify the jasper of which the city walls are constructed (Rev 21:18). By contrast, the gateways of the three-spired city in the Gulbenkian Apocalypse are richly colored, perhaps conveying "the glory of the saints" of which for Berengaudus the New Jerusalem is a figure, while Abingdon depicts twelve heads, probably representing the apostles rather than the angels or the founders of the twelve tribes, in the city gates (fol. 79v, Fig. 5).

An intriguing symbolic detail found in both Lambeth (fol. 38r, Fig. 4) and Gulbenkian (fol. 74) is the presence of an owl at the foot of the terrestrial foundation on which the celestial city now stands. Its precise significance is uncertain. In medieval bestiaries and illuminated manuscripts, the night owl is generally an anti-Semitic symbol of the Jews, perceived as preferring the darkness to the light. This seems out of place in this image, however. An alternative view, more appropriate to the context, is found in the Aberdeen Bestiary, produced in England ca. 1200: "In a mystic sense, the night-owl signifies Christ. Christ loves the darkness of night because he does not want sinners – who are represented by darkness – to die but to be converted and live" (University of Aberdeen, MS 24, fol. 35v).[61] Its position would then recall the patristic identification of Christ as the mountain on which the city comes to rest.[62]

A final departure from the biblical text concerns the person of John. John is a prominent figure throughout the Berengaudus manuscripts, appearing in various guises as author, protagonist, seer, and guide. This stands in sharp contrast to Berengaudus's *Expositio*, where he is a marginal figure. Often, John appears in the margins of the frame, looking in, providing the point of access for the viewer into the visions and therefore, potentially, a similar transformative experience to the seer of Patmos.[63] However, it is not his visual presence in the New Jerusalem miniatures that is unexpected, given that at this point in Revelation John is participant in a visionary journey. The surprise lies rather in the angel handing John the gold measuring rod (Lambeth fol. 38r; Abingdon fol. 79v; Gulbenkian fol. 74). In the biblical text, only the angel can measure the celestial city, given its vast size (Rev 21:15, 17), in contrast to an earlier passage where John himself is permitted to measure "the temple of God," its altar, and those who worship in it (Rev 11:1). No explicit solution to this transfer of measuring rod from angel

---

[61] Transcription from "Folio 35v – the pelican, continued. De nicticorace; the night owl," The Aberdeen Bestiary, The University of Aberdeen, accessed 25 October, 2022, https://www.abdn.ac.uk/bestiary/ms24/f35v.

[62] E. g., Caesarius, *Exp. Apoc.* 19.

[63] O'Hear, *Contrasting Images* (cf. note 5), 31–34.

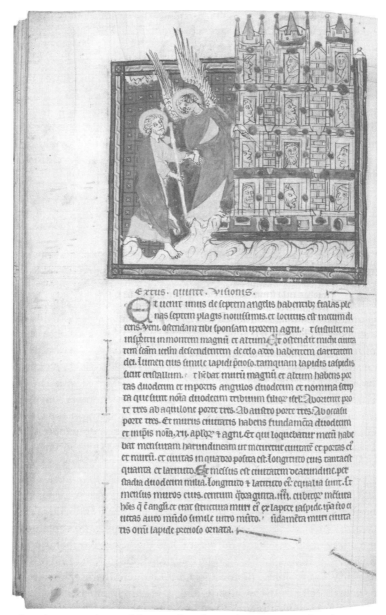

Fig. 5. Abingdon Apocalypse, fol. 79v, *John Shown the New Jerusalem* (ca. 1270–1275). British Library, London. ©The British Library Board (Add. MS 42555).

to seer suggests itself in the exegetical tradition. Nor does Berengaudus's *Expositio* on the New Jerusalem vision, which interprets this angel allegorically as Christ ruling the nations with an iron rod (cf. Rev 12:5; cf. 2:26–28; Ps 2:9), shed immediate light on this detail.

If there is a solution, it probably depends on an ecclesiological reading of the New Jerusalem, which is not entirely expunged by Berengaudus's emphasis on the final consummation in the seventh vision. Berengaudus had interpreted the temple of Rev 11:1 as the church, the altar as the saints, and the worshipers as other members of the church instructed in doctrine. Here it would be appropriate for John to measure the city-as-church, a task entrusted to him by Christ himself in angelic guise.[64]

Conclusion

In these richly diverse pictorial images of the New Jerusalem vision, medieval reception of patristic voices finds visible form as illustrators respond to differing dimensions of the biblical text. No attempt is made to depict the celestial city in a slavishly literal fashion, such as its cuboid shape (though the flattened, two-dimensional Beatus image comes close). Instead, the ecclesiological dimension of Tyconian exegesis is foregrounded, mixing the present effects of Christ's victory with future hopes for its final consummation. The contemporary battle between the false and true churches is played out visually in the Carolingian manuscripts, with their detailed attention to Babylon and the New Jerusalem. The dynamic between the already and the not yet of the church's perfection is conveyed in the juxtaposition of temple and city in Trier and Cambrai and in the circular city of Valenciennes, a symbol of perfection and eternity that nonetheless hints at a partial realization in post-Constantinian Jerusalem and its Church of the Holy Sepulchre.

The Beatus manuscripts do not only emphasize the divine presence in the midst of the city, which is visualized by the Lamb. They also prioritize the apostolic founders of the church over the twelve tribes and the angelic guardians of the city gates (though the omission of the latter may also be explained by the variant reading in Beatus's *Vetus Latina* text). In the Anglo-Norman Apocalypses, the miniatures indicate that the New Jerusalem will be fully accessible only in the eschatological future. John and the angel must content themselves with measuring the visionary city from the outside, and, at least in Lambeth and Gulbenkian, are separated from it by a ravine. Even in the final miniature in the Metz group,

---

[64] Another possibility is that the artist has picked up on two hints that the New Jerusalem, rather than containing a temple, *is* itself a temple: its cuboid shape recalling the holy of holies in Solomon's Temple (Rev 21:16; cf. 1 Kgs 6:20), and the presence of God and the Lamb (Rev 21:22).

which depicts John's direct vision of Christ (Lambeth fol. 39v; Abingdon fol. 82v; Gulbenkian fol. 76v), he "kneels before the Lord enthroned within a barrier of celestial clouds, still filled with longing and desire as he reaches out for what remains beyond his grasp."[65]

A final question presents itself: what role did these diverse images of Revelation's New Jerusalem serve beyond the generic function of creating memory pictures? In all probability, the answer will vary according to the provenance and intended usage of the different manuscripts. Kenneth Steinhauser has proposed that the first edition of Beatus's commentary served the purpose of monastic *lectio divina*, while the expanded version, present in the Morgan Beatus, had a more polemical function in combating adoptionism in Spain.[66] However, even here the intended viewers seem to have been monastic.[67] Revelation had been an important liturgical text in Spain since the Fourth Council of Toledo in 633, when excerpts from the book, including the New Jerusalem vision, were introduced into the Mozarabic liturgy for the Sundays between Easter and Pentecost.[68] This Eastertide context would have underscored the ecclesial dimension of the New Jerusalem as established through the Paschal victory of the Lamb. Still, the Beatus manuscripts seem not to have been composed for liturgical use, given that the commentary's *storiae* diverged from the Mozarabic lectionary division. More probably, they were intended for monastic communal reading in the refectory (certainly marginal glosses in some manuscripts point to such use in a much later period).[69]

The resemblance of the New Jerusalem to a monastic cloister in the Beatus manuscripts has often been noted. This is vividly exemplified by a much later Beatus manuscript which, like the Morgan Beatus, is housed in New York's Pierpont Morgan Library. The Las Huelgas Beatus (New York, Pierpont Morgan Library, MS 429), dated to September 1220, is believed to have been produced for the Cistercian convent of Santa María la Real de Las Huelgas in Castile, perhaps gifted by Queen Berenguela, the widow of Alfonso IX of León. The city gates of the New Jerusalem in Las Huelgas are clearly modelled on its monastic cloister, Las Claustillas. They are rounded, in contrast to the Mozarabic shape in Morgan, and each supported by two pillars with carved capitals.[70]

---

[65] Lewis, *Reading Images* (cf. note 49), 23.
[66] Steinhauser, "Narrative and Illumination" (cf. note 28), 200–202.
[67] The royal Facundus Beatus is a rare, non-monastic exception.
[68] On early liturgical use of Revelation, see e. g., Harald Buchinger, "Die Johannes-Apokalypse im christlichen Gottesdienst: Sondierungen in Liturgie und Ikonographie," in *Ancient Christian Interpretations of "Violent Texts" in the Apocalypse*, ed. Joseph Verheyden, Tobias Nicklas, and Andreas Merkt, Novum Testamentum et Orbis Antiquus/Studien zur Umwelt des Neuen Testaments Band 92 (Göttingen: Vandenhoeck & Ruprecht, 2011), 216–66.
[69] Williams, *Visions of the End in Medieval Spain* (cf. note 24), 26.
[70] Rose Walker, "The Poetics of Defeat: Cistercians and Frontier Gothic at the Abbey of Las Huelgas," in *Spanish Medieval Art: Recent Studies*, ed. Colum Hourihane (Tempe: Arizona

The Cistercians famously viewed the monastic cloister as a paradisiacal space, following St. Bernard, who also linked it with the garden in the Song of Songs.[71]

A monastic context, however, does not apply to the Anglo-Norman Apocalypses considered here. Nonetheless, the prominence of the illuminations, and the limited knowledge of Latin even among elite lay readers, strongly suggests that the former serve to replicate monastic-type meditation for lay viewers by drawing them into the story of what John sees. It is frequently noted that the Apocalypse proper is either prefaced or framed by an illustrated *Life of John,* thus making John's visionary journey a part of his *vita,* his visionary exile functioning as a kind of "rite of passage" allowing him to resume his previous life at Ephesus transformed. Suzanne Lewis has even made the intriguing suggestion that the illustrations afforded the reader a kind of surrogate pilgrimage to the ultimate destination, the New Jerusalem, given the impossibility of actual pilgrimage to the Holy Land following Jerusalem's fall in 1244.[72]

To return to the observation of Andrew of Caesarea with which we began: "Perfect comprehension of the heavenly city surpasses hearing and sight and thought." The limitations of sight, and the thought provoked by visual images, can be amply demonstrated by the visual reception of the New Jerusalem, since artists lacked the luxury of textual expansion and elaboration open to the authors of written commentaries. Yet our selective survey of the visual reception has also revealed how artists can enable aspects of the complexity of patristic and early medieval exegesis to emerge on the page with visual immediacy. Not least among these is the interweaving of present reality with the eschatological future, visualizing a fantastical and currently inaccessible city, which paradoxically is already "coming down out of heaven from God" (Rev 21:2).

Center for Medieval and Renaissance Studies, 2007), 187–213; Williams, *The Illustrated Beatus* (cf. note 24), vol. 5, 38–41; Williams, *Visions of the End in Medieval Spain* (cf. note 24), 64–66.

[71] For more details on Bernard, see Walker, "The Poetics of Defeat" (cf. note 70), 208–9.

[72] Lewis, *Reading Images* (cf. note 49), 25–39.

Part 2

Topical Studies

Heaven on Earth

Some Noteworthy Greek and Roman Parallels to Revelation 21:2

Joseph Verheyden and Mathieu Cuijpers

Introduction

Revelation 21:1–8 forms the concluding section of Rev 19:11–21:8, which is itself framed by "two parallel angelic revelations" in Rev 17:1–19:10 and 21:9–22:9.[1] The source-critical analysis of the section between them has been a matter of debate, as is the relation of 21:1–8 to the following section. The source-critical issue is not really of importance for the topic we wish to deal with. As for the relation to 21:1–8, it seems that modern commentators pass over it in silence. R. H. Charles nuances his firm assertion that the city mentioned in 21:2 "is clearly distinguished from that in 21:9–22:2" when writing, just before, that "[t]his city is either wholly distinct from that described in 21:9–22:2 – the seat of the Millennial Kingdom – or it is that city wholly transformed and hence described καινήν."[2] Charles probably makes too much of the fact that in the new creation death is said to be no more (21:4), whereas the inhabitants of the New Jerusalem need to eat from the tree of life to attain immortality (22:1). Revelation 21:4 speaks on a more general level and in more general terms, but the result is the same: death has no place anymore. Charles's position is silently countered by Gregory K. Beale who writes, "21:9–22:5 is the last and seventh major segment of the book. It primarily recapitulates 21:1–8, and 21:1–8 anticipates it."[3] This is also our position. From such a perspective, one is then probably entitled to say that Rev 21:1–8 introduces a motif that will be described in more detail in the next section, namely, the New Jerusalem descended from heaven. This, verse 2 formulates as follows: "and I saw the holy city the New Jerusalem coming down out of heaven from God, prepared as a bride adorned for her husband" (καὶ τὴν πόλιν τὴν

---

[1] So David E. Aune, *Revelation 17–22*, Word Biblical Commentary 52C (Nashville, TN: Nelson, 1998), 1113.

[2] R. H. Charles, *The Revelation of St. John*, vol. 2, International Critical Commentary (Edinburgh: T&T Clark, 1920), 205.

[3] Gregory K. Beale, *The Book of Revelation*, New International Greek Testament Commentary (Grand Rapids, MI: Eerdmans; Carlisle: Paternoster, 1999), 1039.

ἁγίαν Ἰερουσαλὴμ καινὴν εἶδον καταβαίνουσαν ἐκ τοῦ οὐρανοῦ ἀπὸ τοῦ θεοῦ, ἡτοιμασμένην ὡς νύμφην κεκοσμημένην τῷ ἀνδρὶ αὐτῆς).

The city is named by name, called "new" and "holy," and is emphatically said to (have) come down from heaven from God (see below for the apparent redundancy in naming both heaven and God). Commentators have rightly pointed out in this description and its immediate context a number of allusions to passages from the Old Testament. Isaiah offers several parallels: the newness of it all in Isa 65:16–19 and 66:22; the motif of the disappearing sea in 51:10–11; that of the salvation of the "holy city" of Jerusalem in ch. 52 (esp. v. 1; see also 48:2). Ezekiel does likewise, above all in the motif of the new city in chs. 40–48 but also in 37:27.[4] A special place is given, so it seems, to Isa 62, which refers to Jerusalem as a new city (vv. 1–2) and speaks abundantly of the marriage relationship that Israel will have with its God (vv. 3–5, 10),[5] a theme that is also referred to in 61:10. In addition, the author of Revelation was also inspired by passages that occur earlier in his book: Rev 21:2a reads like a doublet of 3:12b[6] and will itself be repeated shortly after in 21:10,[7] in both instances using the same apparently redundant expression "out of heaven from God."[8] Rev 19:7–8 praises the marriage of the Lamb.[9] The motif of "being made ready," dear to the author,

---

[4] Aune, *Revelation 17–22* (cf. note 1), 1120–22; Beale, *Revelation* (cf. note 3), 1046–47. Beate Kowalski, *Die Rezeption des Propheten Ezechiel in der Offenbarung des Johannes*, Stuttgarter Bibelstudien 52 (Stuttgart: Katholisches Bibelwerk, 2004), esp. 408–22.

[5] In this sense, the combination of city and bride is perhaps less "abrupt" than some have thought; see Wilfrid J. Harrington, *Revelation*, Sacra Pagina 16 (Collegeville, MN: Liturgical Press, 1993), 209.

[6] Though with the not unimportant difference that whereas in 3:12 the author only hears of the message, in 21:2a he also sees it happening. In this sense, 21:2 introduces an extra dimension. Cf. Theodor Zahn, *Die Offenbarung des Johannes*, vol. 2, Kommentar zum Neuen Testament 18 (Leipzig: A. Deichert, 1924), 598. Martin Karrer, *Johannesoffenbarung (Offb. 1,1–5,14)*, Evangelisch-katholischer Kommentar zum Neuen Testament 24.1 (Ostfildern: Patmos; Göttingen: Vandenhoeck & Ruprecht, 2017), 357, rather sees the difference (and a tension) between the two in the fact that 21:1–8 no longer speaks of the temple as a place for encountering God.

[7] Which some have taken as proof "dass der Vf. hier bewusst die Darstellung V. 9 ff. vorwegnimmt"; so Akira Satake, *Die Offenbarung des Johannes*, Kritisch-exegetischer Kommentar über das Neue Testament 16 (Göttingen: Vandenhoeck & Ruprecht, 2008), 399.

[8] The change in preposition makes sense and was probably intended. Cf. Wilhelm Bousset, *Die Offenbarung Johannis*, Kritisch-exegetischer Kommentar über das Neue Testament 16 (Göttingen: Vandenhoeck & Ruprecht, 1896), 509: "ἐκ giebt den Ursprung, ἀπό den Urheber an"; cf. Heinrich Kraft, *Die Offenbarung des Johannes*, Handbuch zum Neuen Testament 16a (Tübingen: Mohr Siebeck, 1974), 263. The motif of descending from heaven is dear to the author and may refer to individuals and to (extraordinary) natural processes; see 10:1; 18:1; 20:1 (thrice an angel); 12:12 (Satan); 13:13 and 20:9 (fire); and 16:21 (hailstones).

[9] The personification of a city as a woman is not uncommon generally and is also very much present in Revelation. Note the possible allusion in v. 2b to Ezek 16:10–14 where the first Jerusalem is said to be adorned by God (cf. Kraft, *Offenbarung* [cf. note 8], 263, limiting the parallel to v. 11). Kraft also points out the apparent tension in the way the bridal imagery had previously been used in Jewish tradition for describing the special bond of sinful Israel with its God and is now transposed to the glorious Jerusalem, but he also offers a plausible explanation when

also occurs several times (8:6; 9:7, 15; 12:6; 16:12), and according to one author, is said of "an event occurring ultimately as a result of God's decree and not human action."[10] The precise meaning of the motif of the new era that is installed remains a matter of dispute, with some commentators arguing that the author indeed thinks of a new creation after the destruction or disappearance of the old one, and others arguing for an ethical renewal of the old.[11] In the same way, commentators remain divided on whether the motif of the descent from heaven points to the pre-existent character of this city or rather to its being created by God.[12] The motif of the heavenly city occurs also in Gal 4:26; Phil 3:20; and Heb 12:22, the first and third of these explicitly calling it Jerusalem.[13]

It is clear that the author is profoundly inspired by the biblical imagery cited in the previous paragraph. We have no intention of disputing this. Rather, our purpose is to show that the motif of the heavenly city, and more specifically that of a heavenly city that can be visited already on earth (see v. 2), is attested also in Greco-Roman literature, be it only sparingly and not without noteworthy variation. Our focus in this essay, then, is not so much on Jerusalem itself, but rather on another city as the model for any such thoughts and feelings about a heavenly city that has or will become accessible to all in this world. That, of course, is the city of Rome.

Many cities have been praised, and highly praised, in ancient literature. Rome, especially imperial Rome, however, is described in grandiose terms in nearly every respect. Ancient authors do not weary of singing the praise of the capital of

---

adding, "Die Apokalyptik nimmt in Kauf, dass das Bild unlogisch wird, wenn die Bezeichnung der Stadt als Braut Gottes auf das himmlische Jerusalem ausgedehnt wird" (Kraft, *Offenbarung*, 263). Hermann Lichtenberger, *Die Apokalypse*, Theologischer Kommentar zum Neuen Testament 23 (Stuttgart: Kohlhammer, 2014), 260, is rather more critical about connecting this previous passage with 21:2b.

[10] Beale, *Revelation* (cf. note 3), 1045.

[11] Cf. Beale, *Revelation* (cf. note 3), 1045. Craig R. Koester emphatically notes, "Significantly, Revelation does not picture God destroying the first heaven and earth": *Revelation: A New Translation with Introduction and Commentary*, Anchor Bible 38A (New Haven, CT: Yale University Press, 2014), 803.

[12] See the references in Koester, *Revelation* (cf. note 11), 804 (largely repeated at 813), who himself sides with the second position, though without offering any new arguments against the *in se* more probable view that the motif indeed suggests a city "prefabricated in heaven"; so the commentaries of Jürgen Roloff, *Die Offenbarung des Johannes*, Zürcher Bibelkommentare, Neues Testament 18 (Zürich: Theologischer Verlag Zürich, 1993); Heinz Giesen, *Die Offenbarung des Johannes*, Regensburger Neues Testament (Regensburg: Pustet, 1997); Edmondo Lupieri, *L'Apocalisse di Giovanni*, Scrittori greci e latini (Milano: Mondadori, 1999), to which one can add Ernest-Bernard Allo, *Saint Jean, L'Apocalypse*, Études bibliques (Paris: Gabalda, 1921), 306: "Jérusalem préexistante". Cf. Kraft, *Offenbarung* (cf. note 8), 263: "Das himmlische Jerusalem, das bei Gott bereit ist."

[13] Note also the interest in the motif in Second Temple Jewish apocrypha (esp. 2 Baruch 4; 4 Ezra 7.26; 10.53; 13.36); cf. Bousset, *Offenbarung* (cf. note 8), 509; Allo, *Apocalypse* (cf. note 12), 307–308; and below n. 42.

the world, and its politicians, and later on its emperors, did everything necessary to make this picture come true. Rome's greatness is based above all on political and military strength; but it is also founded on specific societal and indeed theological views on the origin and destiny of the city. While we cannot and need not review in this essay all the various forms in which this aggrandizing effort took place, it is useful to mention several of the common *topoi* that suggest what Rome was or could be for its inhabitants, its subjects, and its enemies. First, there is the obvious fact that imperial Rome was a metropolis, a cosmopolitan city, with all that such a status entails.[14] Second, Rome's origins and its destiny were said to have been marked out by the gods, demonstrating that Rome is theologically and teleologically grounded. Third, it was said that Rome would never disappear – indeed, that it is eternal.[15] From here, it is a small step to a final characteristic. All cities, including Jerusalem, have their city gods and temples for their divine protectors. In the case of Rome, she is a goddess of her own: *Dea Roma*.[16] Thus is it clear how Rome differed from any other city the world had ever known – at least in the eyes of its admirers.

As stated above, our purpose in this essay is modest. It consists of illustrating from several passages how ancient Greek and Roman authors have connected the motif of an earthly-situated heavenly city with Rome, and in ways that are comparable to how Jerusalem in Rev 21:2 is said to have descended from heaven to earth.

But before proceeding to this, we must first turn to the archetypal text that must be addressed when one speaks of heavenly cities.

---

[14] See the collection of essays in Catherine Edwards and Greg Woolf, ed., *Rome the Cosmopolis* (Cambridge: Cambridge University Press, 2006), drawing attention to what this means for the arts, for society as a whole, and in daily life in general. See also the collection of studies by Robert Turcan, *Ouranopolis. La vocation universaliste de Rome (De Rome à la troisième Rome)* (Paris: CNR – Publisud, 2011), who focuses on political (171–80), social and demographic (119–31, esp. the constant tension there exists between a cosmopolite "optimistic" view of reality and the many negative experiences of the masses), and religious aspects (113–18, 133–43, and 147–69); note the title of the book and see below n. 68, which quotes p. 121.

[15] On the well-known theme of *Roma aeterna*, see, among many others, Turcan, *Ouranopolis* (cf. note 14), 9–34; Stephan Mols, "The Cult of Roma Aeterna in Hadrian's Politics," in *The Representation and Perception of Roman Imperial Power*, ed. Lukas de Blois et al. (Amsterdam: J.C. Gieben, 2003), 458–65; Javier Andrés Pérez, "Aproximación a la iconografía de *Roma aeterna* como vía de transmisión de un mito," in *El futuro del pasado* 1 (2010): 349–63; Benjamin Isaac, *Empire and Ideology in the Graeco-Roman World: Selected Papers* (Cambridge: Cambridge University Press, 2017), 33–44.

[16] On the latter, see, e.g., Ronald Mellor, *Thea Romè: the Worship of Goddess Roma in the Greek World*, Hypomnemata 42 (Göttingen: Vandenhoeck & Ruprecht, 1975); Carla Fayer, *Il culto della dea Roma: origine e diffusione nell' impero* (Pescara: Trimestre, 1976).

1 Plato

That text is found at the very end of the ninth book of Plato's *Republic*. There, Plato has Glaucon dispute the possibility that the ideal state that Socrates proposes can ever be realized. Socrates counters Glaucon's objection by arguing that such a state may well exist in heaven and function as a "paradigm" for any such human project quite apart from whether this state already exists:

> "I understand," he said, "you mean in the state we've been founding and discussing, the one existing in words, since I don't think it exists anywhere on earth." "Well, perhaps there's a model up in heaven for anyone willing to look and if he sees it, found himself on it. But it makes no difference whether it exists anywhere or will do. You see, he'd only involve himself in its affairs, not those of anywhere else." (592a10–b5)[17]

The Greek here is not without problems.[18] The passage has occasionally been cited as a parallel for Rev 21:2,[19] but this fails to take into account an important difference that exists between the two in both content and presentation. Socrates's tentative suggestion (ἴσως) and the hesitation that speaks from his διαφέρει οὐδέν, Glaucon's consent notwithstanding (εἰκός γ', ἔφη, 592b6), stand in sharp contrast with the firm εἶδον in Rev 21:2 and the equally confident ἤκουσα following in v. 3 (both of them repeatedly used before in the book and not to be doubted anymore at this stage). As for the content, Socrates explicitly says that this city is not yet found on earth. It is rather the contrary: it is a paradigm "from heaven," only in the process of being realized to the degree that Socrates hopes

---

[17] Μανθάνω, ἔφη· ἐν ᾗ νῦν διήλθομεν οἰκίζοντες πόλει λέγεις, τῇ ἐν λόγοις κειμένῃ· ἐπεὶ γῆς γε οὐδαμοῦ οἶμαι αὐτὴν εἶναι. Ἀλλ', ἦν δ' ἐγώ, ἐν οὐρανῷ ἴσως παράδειγμα ἀνάκειται τῷ βουλομένῳ ὁρᾶν καὶ ὁρῶντι ἑαυτὸν κατοικίζειν. διαφέρει δὲ οὐδέν, εἴτε που ἔστιν εἴτε ἔσται· τὰ γὰρ ταύτης μόνης ἂν πράξειεν, ἄλλης δὲ οὐδεμιᾶς. John Burnet, ed., *Platonis opera*, vol. 4, Oxford Classical Texts (Oxford: Clarendon, 1902). Transl. Christopher Emlyn-Jones and William Preddy, LCL 276 (Cambridge, MA: Harvard University Press, 2013), 389.

[18] In particular in older literature several conjectures have been proposed for the phrase ὁρῶντι ἑαυτὸν κατοικίζειν, none of which has been retained in more recent editions. Henrik van Herwerden first suggested reading καὶ ὁρῶντι αὐτό (i. e., the model) κατοικίζειν (i. e., that city), but later proposed ὁρῶντι πρὸς (or εἰς) αὐτό. Herbert Richards put forward the reading ἑαυτὸν [αὐτόσε] (or [εἰς αὐτήν]) κατοικίζειν. Benjamin Jowett and Lewis Campbell in turn suggested ἑαυτὸν κατοικίζειν [ἐκεῖ]. See Henrik van Herwerden, "Ad Platonis libros de Republica," in *Mnemosyne* 12 (1884): 319–36, esp. 332; "De locis nonnullis Platonis e libris de Republica," in *Mnemosyne* 19 (1891): 325–40, esp. 339; Herbert Richards, "Critical Notes on the *Republic* of Plato," in *The Classical Review* 8 (1894): 292–94, esp. 294; Benjamin Jowett and Lewis Campbell, *Plato's Republic: The Greek Text* (Oxford: Clarendon, 1894), 438.

[19] Cf. Georg Strecker and Udo Schnelle, in cooperation with Gerald Selig, ed., *Neuer Wettstein: Texte zum Neuen Testament aus Griechentum und Hellenismus*. vol. 2. *Texte zur Briefliteratur und zur Johannesapokalypse* (Berlin – New York: de Gruyter, 1996), 1647 (actually the passage is only referred to, but it is cited in full at Gal 4:26, which is in some respects a more appropriate parallel).

that some at least would wish to have their life steered by its laws.[20] Actually, the city is to be established within oneself.[21] The passage may reflect sound Socratic/ Platonic thinking,[22] but it cannot really be brought into line with what is said in Rev 21:2. However, it seems to have inspired both pagan and Christian authors, the former using the term "heavenly citizen" (οὐρανοπολίτης) in this context, a word that will find some success with other Christian authors as well, together with the noun οὐρανόπολις, on which more below.

First, the Christian attestations. At the end of book 4 of the *Stromateis*, Clement of Alexandria ponders, in a rather personal way, on the possibility of reaching out for a heavenly Jerusalem:

But I shall pray the Spirit of Christ to wing me to my Jerusalem. For the Stoics say that heaven is properly a city, but places here on earth are not cities; for they are called so, but are not. For a city is an important thing, and the people a decorous body, and a multitude of men regulated by law as the church by the word – a city on earth impregnable – free from tyranny; a product of the divine will on earth as in heaven. Images of this city

---

[20] Cf. Torsten J. Andersson, *Polis and Psyche: A Motif in Plato's Republic*, Studia graeca et latina gothoburgensia 30 (Göteborg: Acta Univ. Gothoburgensis, 1971), 200: "Bk IX ends with some of the most famous words of the whole Republic. ... Whether such a city exists anywhere or not, or ever will exist, is of no importance, for he will stick to this one and no other."

[21] Cf. the detailed survey of the meaning of the term "paradigm" in James Adam, *The Republic of Plato*, vol. 2 (Cambridge: Cambridge University Press, 1929), 369–71, and his comment on its importance for Plato's thought and its connections with other similarly important concepts: "The mysterious and haunting phrase ἐν οὐρανῷ παράδειγμα recalls the 'imperial place whence we came', and the whole sentence reminds us once again of that profound and inspiring doctrine ἄνθρωπος οὐράνιον φυτόν, οὐκ ἔγγειον, which, as I have often pointed out, underlies so much of Platonism. The sister-doctrine of Immortality seems also to be implied, and from this point of view the Christian parallels are highly remarkable and significant" (370), with reference to Phil 3:30; Heb 11:16; 12:23; 13:14; 1 Pet 1:4; and 2 Pet 3:13. See *Resp.* 590e; 591e; 605b; 608b. That is also how Philo understands the reference to the city of God and the river in Ps 46:5 in *Somn.* 2.246–50 (cited as a parallel to Rev 21:2–7 as a whole in Strecker, Schnelle and Selig, *Texte zur Briefliteratur und zur Johannesapokalypse*, 1646). This cannot be Jerusalem, Philo adds, for that city does not have a river. The verse must refer to the world as a whole or to the soul of the sage, of which it is said that God wanders in it as in a city (citing Lev 26:12): πόλιν γὰρ θεοῦ καθ' ἕνα μὲν τρόπον τὸν κόσμον καλεῖ, ..., καθ' ἕτερον δὲ τὴν ψυχὴν τοῦ σοφοῦ (247). In the end, it is the second of these two options that carries the day for Philo: ὥστε μὴ ζήτει τὴν τοῦ ὄντος πόλιν ἐν κλίμασι γῆς, ..., ἀλλ' ἐν ψυχῇ ἀπολέμῳ καὶ ὀξυδορκούσῃ τέλος προτεθειμένη τὸν δὲ θεωρητικὸν καὶ εἰρηναῖον βίον (250); cf. Pierre Savinel, ed., *Philon d'Alexandrie: De Somniis I–II*, Les oeuvres de Philon d'Alexandrie 19 (Paris: Cerf, 1962), 222–24.

[22] See, by way of example, the comment, made long ago, by Franz Susemihl, *Die genetische Entwickelung der Platonischen Philosophie*, vol. 2.1 (Leipzig: Teubner, 1857), 249: "Der Sinn kann nämlich nach dem Obigen nur ein hypothetischer sein: gesetzt auch, jener Staat wäre schlechthin zu keiner Zeit auf Erden zu finden, so würde er noch immer die Bedeutung behalten, dass der Philosoph, so gut er könnte, in allen seinen Handlungen so verführe, als lebte er in ihm; und wie es damit auch stehen mag, dass derselbe jenes Urbild von ihm in seiner Seele trägt, hat eben darin seinen Grund, dass ein solches im Weltall selbst einen grossen analogen Staat bildet, sondern dass auf einem vollkommeneren Gestirne, als die Erde ist, des Philosophen Seele einst in einem seligeren Zustand wirklich in einem solchen Staate gelebt und ihn angeschaut und von ihm vermöge der ‚Rückerinnerung' jenes Urbild in sich bewahrt hat."

the poets create with their pen. For the Hyperboreans, and the Arimaspian cities, and the Elysian plains, are commonwealths of just men. And we know Plato's city placed as a pattern in heaven. (4.26.172.2–3)[23]

Clement's wish to fly heavenward (πτερῶσαί, evoking the use of wings) is a commonplace in ancient tragic lyric and usually expresses the escapist desire to flee from worldly sorrows. This is evidenced by his prior quote from Euripides (fr. 911),[24] in which the person speaking ascends heavenward on golden wings to be with Zeus. The lyrical poet Anacreon had already expressed this desire when writing ἀναπέτομαι δὴ πρὸς Ὄλυμπον πτερύγεσσι κούφῃς (fr. 33).[25] This wish to "fly on wings to heaven" reverberates throughout the classical tragedies.[26] It also recurs in Christian literature: for instance, in a similar lyrical way, Gregory of Nazianzus expresses his ardent desire to ascend to heaven on wings and to become οὐρανοφοίτης.[27]

Clement's wish, however, is also more than a reiteration of an ancient theme. He immediately counters Euripides (cf. ἐγὼ δὲ) and clarifies that he wishes for *"Christ's Spirit* to fly me to my Jerusalem" and to ascend to the Heavenly

---

[23] ἐγὼ δὲ εὐξαίμην τὸ πνεῦμα τοῦ Χριστοῦ πτερῶσαί με εἰς τὴν Ἰερουσαλὴμ τὴν ἐμήν· λέγουσι γὰρ καὶ οἱ Στωϊκοὶ τὸν μὲν οὐρανὸν κυρίως πόλιν, τὰ δὲ ἐπὶ γῆς ἐνταῦθα οὐκέτι πόλεις· λέγεσθαι μὲν γάρ, οὐκ εἶναι δέ· σπουδαῖον γὰρ ἡ πόλις καὶ ὁ δῆμος ἀστεῖόν τι σύστημα καὶ πλῆθος ἀνθρώπων ὑπὸ νόμου διοικούμενον, καθάπερ ἡ ἐκκλησία ὑπὸ λόγου, ἀπολιόρκητος ἀτυράννητος πόλις ἐπὶ γῆς, θέλημα θεῖον ἐπὶ γῆς ὡς ἐν οὐρανῷ. Εἰκόνας τῆσδε τῆς πόλεως καὶ οἱ ποιηταὶ κτίζουσι γράφοντες· αἱ γὰρ Ὑπερβόρεοι καὶ Ἀριμάσπειοι πόλεις καὶ τὰ Ἡλύσια πεδία δικαίων πολιτεύματα· ἴσμεν δὲ καὶ τὴν Πλάτωνος πόλιν παράδειγμα ἐν οὐρανῷ κειμένην. Otto Stählin, ed., *Clemens Alexandrinus, zweiter Band: Stromata Buch I–VI*, GCS 15 (Leipzig: Hinrichs, 1906), 324–25. Transl. William Wilson, *The Writings of Clement of Alexandria*, ANF 12.2, 215.

[24] Euripides, fr. 911 (August Nauck, ed., *Tragicorum Graecorum fragmenta* [Leipzig: Teubner, 1889], 655): χρύσεαι δή μοι πτέρυγες περὶ νώτῳ | καὶ τὰ σειρήνων πτερόεντα πέδιλα [ἁρμόζεται], | βάσομαί τ' εἰς αἰθέριον πόλον ἀρθεὶς | Ζηνὶ προσμείξων = Clement, *Stromata* 4.172.1 (Otto Stählin, ed., *Clemens Alexandrinus*, 324, 2.19–23).

[25] Denys L. Page, ed., *Poetae melici Graeci* (Oxford: Clarendon, 1962). This phrase seems to have been taken over in Aristophanes, *Aves* 1372 (Nigel G. Wilson, ed., *Aristophanis Fabulae*, vol. 1, [Oxford: Oxford University Press, 2007]).

[26] Sophocles, *Oedipus Coloneus*, 1079–81 (Francis Storr, ed., *Sophocles*, vol. 1 [Cambridge, MA: Harvard University Press, 1968], 248): εἴθ' ἀελλαία ταχύρρωστος πελειὰς | αἰθερίας νεφέλας κύρσαιμ' ἄνωθ' ἀγώνων | αἰωρήσασα τοὐμὸν ὄμμα; Euripides, *Hippolytus*, 732–734 (James Diggle, ed., *Euripidis fabulae*, vol. 1 [Oxford: Clarendon, 1984]): ἠλιβάτοις ὑπὸ κευθμῶσι γενοίμαν, | ἵνα με πτεροῦσσαν ὄρνιν | θεὸς ἐν ποταναῖς ἀγέλαις θείη; Euripides, *Ion*, 1238 (James Diggle, ed., *Euripidis fabulae*, vol. 2 [Oxford: Clarendon, 1981]): τίνα φυγὰν πτερόεσσαν.

[27] Gregory Nazianzen, *Carmina* II.1.32, Περὶ τοῦ βίου ματαιότητος καὶ ἀπιστίας καὶ κοινοῦ πάντων τέλους (*CPG* 3036.32), lines 1–7 (Christos Simelidis, ed., *Selected Poems of Gregory of Nazianzus*, Hypomnemata 177 [Göttingen: Vandenhoeck & Ruprecht, 2009], 113): Ἤθελον ἠὲ πέλεια τανύπτερος ἠὲ χελιδὼν | ἔμμεναι, ὥς κε φύγοιμι βροτῶν βίον, ἤ τιν' ἔρημον | ναιετάειν θήρεσσιν ὁμέστιος (οἳ γὰρ ἔασι | πιστότεροι μερόπων) καὶ ἡμάτιον βίον ἕλκειν | νηπενθῆ, νήποινον, ἀκηδέα· ἓν τόδ' ἄθηρον | μοῦνον ἔχειν, θεότητος ἴδριν νόον, οὐρανοφοίτην, | ὥς κε γαληνιόωντι βίῳ φάος αἰὲν ἀγείρω.

Jerusalem.²⁸ This wish is grounded, in this order, in Stoic and Platonic thought.²⁹ The Stoics are said to take heaven for the sole true city (τὸν μὲν οὐρανὸν κυρίως πόλιν), playing on associations with Stoic cosmopolitanism, but speaking of οὐρανός rather than κόσμος.³⁰ Plato, who is quoted almost verbatim, seals the argument as he most succinctly defines the function of this city. In this way, Clement restyles Plato's ideal city as the heavenly Jerusalem.³¹

In line with Clement, Origen makes the same reference to Plato in much the same language.³² But now the latter's ideal city is also explicitly contrasted with Moses's very real project of assembling a people devoted to its God.³³

> Would that they had not sinned and broken the law, both earlier when they killed the prophets and also later when they conspired against Jesus! Otherwise we might have an example of a heavenly city such as even Plato attempted to describe, although I doubt whether he was as successful as Moses and his successors when they trained an "elect nation" and a "holy people", devoted to God, by means of doctrines which were free from all superstition. (*Contra Celsum* 5.43)³⁴

---

²⁸ "Spirit joins intelligence to holiness. It is the spirit who wings the believer to the Jerusalem above" (Eric Osborn, *Clement of Alexandria* [Cambridge: Cambridge University Press, 2005], 151).

²⁹ Cf. the general estimation of Plato's influence on Clement in Salvatore R. C. Lilla, *Clement of Alexandria: A Study in Christian Platonism and Gnosticism*, Oxford Theological Monographs (Oxford: Oxford University Press, 1971), 59: "Platonism filtered through Philo and bathed in Middle Platonism."

³⁰ In Stoic philosophy, the οὐρανός is but a part of the κόσμος, which is defined as a σύστημα ἐξ οὐρανοῦ καὶ γῆς καὶ τῶν ἐν τούτοις φύσεων (see Hans von Arnim, ed., *Stoicorum Veterum Fragmenta*, vol. 2 [Stuttgart: Teubner, 1903], 527–29).

³¹ See Eduard Lohse, "Σιών," in *Theologisches Wörterbuch zum Neuen Testament*, vol. 7, ed. Gerhard Friedrich (Stuttgart: Kohlhammer, 1964), 338. Cf. Dietmar Wyrwa, *Die christliche Platonaneignung in den Stromateis des Clemens vol Alexandrien*, Arbeiten zur Kirchengeschichte 53 (Berlin: de Gruyter, 1983), 295–97. Note the term οὐρανόπολις in Clement's *Paedagogus*: Λίθοις δὲ ἁγίοις τὴν ἄνω Ἰερουσαλὴμ τετειχίσθαι παρειλήφαμεν, καὶ τὰς δώδεκα τῆς οὐρανοπόλεως πύλας τιμίοις ἀπεικασμένας λίθοις τὸ περίοπτον τῆς ἀποστολικῆς [φωνῆς] αἰνίττεσθαι χάριτος ἐκδεχόμεθα. (2.12.119.1).

³² In an article on Origen's citations of Plato, Kazimierz Romaniuk points out this curious passage, but fails to identify *Resp.* 9 (592b) as the source of παράδειγμα πόλεως οὐρανίας. See his "Le Platon d'Origène: Les citations *des Lois, du Phédon, du Phèdre* et de *la République* dans *Contre Celse* d'Origène," in *Aegyptus* 41 (1961): 44–73, esp. 50–51. Romaniuk offers some parallels of minor importance, which he seems to have taken over from PG 11.1249, n. 69.

³³ See also Theodoret, who contrasts Plato's never realized ideal city with the Christian view: *Graecarum affectionum curatio*, 5.65 (Pierre Canivet, ed., *Thérapeutique des maladies helléniques*, SC 57 [Paris: Cerf, 1958], 247).

³⁴ Καὶ εἴθε αὐτοῖς μὴ ἡμάρτητο παρανομήσασι καὶ πρότερον μὲν "τοὺς προφήτας" ἀποκτείνασιν ὕστερον δὲ καὶ τῷ Ἰησοῦ ἐπιβουλεύσασιν· ἵν' ἔχωμεν παράδειγμα πόλεως οὐρανίας, ἣν ἐζήτησε μὲν διαγράψαι καὶ Πλάτων οὐκ οἶδα δὲ εἰ τοσοῦτον δεδύνηται, ὅσον Μωϋσῆς ἴσχυσε καὶ οἱ μετ' αὐτόν, "γένος τι ἐκλεκτὸν" καὶ "ἔθνος ἅγιον" καὶ θεῷ ἀνακείμενον ἐντρέφοντες λόγοις καθαροῖς ἀπὸ πάσης δεισιδαιμονίας. *Origène: Contre Celse*, ed. Marcel Borret, SC 147 (Paris: Cerf, 1969), 126. Transl. Henry Chadwick, *Origen: Contra Celsum* (Cambridge: Cambridge University Press, 1953), 298.

Origen has a somewhat ambiguous relationship with Platonism in the *Contra Celsum*, which may in part be explained by the genre and the addressee.³⁵ Also, his view on Plato's theory of ideas is not without its problems.³⁶

The anonymous author of a sixth-century introduction to Platonic philosophy that is usually referred to, with a Latin title, as *Prolegomena philosophiae Platonicae*, demonstrates how, in his opinion, Plato surpasses all other philosophical schools, including the New Academy and its scepticism (2.7–12).³⁷ The author critically discusses six arguments in favor of sceptic epistemology (2.10–11). The fourth argument, he reports, is based principally on some passages from Plato's *Phaedo* (esp. 65b3–5; 66b5–7; 79c2–8) that seemingly deny the possibility of obtaining knowledge (τὴν γνῶσιν) either by sense-perception (τὴν μὲν δι' αἰσθήσεως) or by intellection (τὴν δὲ διὰ νοῦ γινομένην, 2.10.26–27). In his reply to this argument, the anonymous author concedes that the senses (τοῦ πάθους) cannot offer knowledge about the essence (τὴν οὐσίαν). To refute the second part, i.e., that knowledge cannot be obtained by intellection, he refines Plato's statement in 66b5–7 about the contamination of the soul. For Plato (66b5–7) says that "as long as we possess the body, and (as long as) our soul is contaminated by such an evil, we will surely never adequately gain what we desire (i.e., the truth)". The first of Plato's premises is considered insufficient; it is rather a necessary condition for the second premise. It is thus a matter of how much the soul is "mingled" and wedded to the body. On this basis he distinguishes between two types of individuals:

Again, when he [i.e., Plato] says that the soul is incapable of intellection while joined to this wretched body, he does not refer to all men, but only to those whose lives are bound up with matter, whose souls are subject to the body; in another work, he calls them "sown men", because they are rooted in the earth like plants; the pure, however, those whom he calls "citizens of heaven" elsewhere, can behold the intelligible world.³⁸

---

³⁵ Cf. Andrea Villani, "Platon und der Platonismus in Origenes' *Contra Celsum*", in *Origenes der Christ und Origenes der Platoniker*, ed. Balbina Bäbler and Heinz-Günther Nesselrath, Seraphim 2 (Tübingen: Mohr Siebeck, 2018), 109–27 (no mention, however, of *Contra Celsum* 5.43).

³⁶ See Winrich Löhr, "Der platonische Ideenkosmos bei Origenes," in Bäbler and Nesselrath, *Origenes* (cf. note 35), 91–108, arguing that Origen is "*up to date* im Hinblick auf dem zeitgenössischen Schulplatonismus," but more problematic is his "Hypostasierung der platonischen Ideenwelt" (104).

³⁷ Cf. Danielle A. Layne, "The Anonymous Prolegomena to Platonic Philosophy," in *Brill's Companion to the Reception of Plato in Antiquity*, ed. Harold Tarrant et al., Brill's Companions to Classical Reception 13 (Leiden – Boston: Brill, 2018), 538–40.

³⁸ πάλιν ὅταν εἴπῃ ὅτι ἡ ψυχὴ οὐ νοεῖ συνοῦσα τῷ κακῷ τούτῳ, οὐ περὶ πάντων τῶν ἀνθρώπων λέγει τοῦτο, ἀλλὰ περὶ τῶν ἐνύλως ζώντων· ἐκεῖνοι γὰρ καὶ ἡττωμένην ἔχουσι τὴν ψυχὴν ὑπὸ τοῦ σώματος, οὓς καὶ 'σπαρτικοὺς' ἀλλαχοῦ ὀνομάζει, δίκην φυτῶν ἀποβλαστάνοντας· οἱ δὲ καθαροὶ καὶ ὑπ' αὐτοῦ ἀλλαχοῦ οὐρανοπολῖται λεγόμενοι, οὗτοι νοοῦσιν. Leendert G. Westerink, ed. and transl., *Anonymous Prolegomena to Platonic Philosophy* (Amsterdam: North-Holland Publishing Company, 1962), 10, ll. 38–44. See also Leendert G. Westerink, Jean

For the first type of men – the "sown men" – the author probably refers to a passage from the *Sophist* where such people are mentioned (σπαρτοί, 247c5 – "sown men"), and he seems to connect this passage with one from the *Phaedo* when speaking of "being rooted in the earth like plants" (80d5–81c6; 83d1). For the second type – the "citizens of heaven" – the author seems to refer to the famous passage from the *Republic*. These individuals are both capable of and willing to look to the heavenly city as a model for their own soul. They are rightly called οὐρανοπολῖται.

In his commentary on Aristotle's *De anima*, Stephanus of Alexandria deals with much the same question as the anonymous author and answers it in a similar way, referring to the *Phaedo* and to the *Republic*:

> In regard to this Plato says that intellect, when it is in the realm of becoming, can be a citizen of heaven, and act in connection with immaterial things and be contemptuous of the body. For if souls outside the body that indulged the body are always with body, even in tombs, what wonder if also souls in the realm of becoming should act in connection with immaterial things? (563.7–11)[39]

Like the anonymous author, Stephanus did not feel the need to identify the references to Plato, which may indicate that he was indeed thinking of the famous passages in the *Republic* and the *Phaedo*, as is clear for the latter from the motif of the tombs (cf. περὶ τὰ μνήματά τε καὶ τοὺς τάφους, 81c11–d1) and for the former from οὐρανοπολίτης.

As is so often the case, Plato's influence stretched widely and lasted.[40] But what is missing in this specific instance is the motif of a heavenly city that is or will be made accessible on earth. For that, we have to turn to a couple of other passages.

Authors of so-called *Observationes* literature and (older and more recent) commentators of Revelation have been rather uninspired when it comes to citing parallels to Rev 21:2 (or to the doublet in 3:12). G. D. Kypke and J. A. Bengel have

---

Trouillard, and Alain P. Segonds, ed. and transl., *Prolégomènes à la philosophie de Platon* (Paris: Les Belles Lettres, 1990); Miguel Á Spinassi, "Introducción a la filosofía de Platón (Anónimo): Capítulo I," in *Rónai* 8 (2020): 99–125; Anna Motta, *Prolegomeni alla filosofia di Platone*, Classici della filosofia (Rome: Armando, 2016); Layne, "The Anonymous Prolegomena" (cf. note 37), 533–54.

[39] πρὸς τοῦτο δὲ ὁ Πλάτων φησὶν ὅτι δύναται ὁ νοῦς ἐν γενέσει ὢν οὐρανοπολίτης εἶναι καὶ περὶ τὰ ἄυλα ἐνεργεῖν καὶ καταφρονεῖν τοῦ σώματος. εἰ γὰρ αἱ ἐκτὸς ψυχαὶ αἱ φιλοσώματοι ἀεὶ μετὰ σώματός εἰσι καὶ ἐν τάφοις, τί ἄτοπον καὶ τὰς ἐν γενέσει ψυχὰς περὶ τὰ ἄυλα ἐνεργεῖν; (Michael Hayduck, ed., *Ioannis Philoponi in Aristotelis De anima libros commentaria*, Commentaria in Aristotelem Graeca 15 [Berlin: Reimer, 1897], 563). Transl. William Charlton, *"Philoponus": On Aristotle On the Soul 3.1–8*, Ancient Commentators on Aristotle (London: Bloomsbury, 2013), 143–44 (slightly adapted). Cf. Matthias Perkams, *Selbstbewusstsein in der Spätantike. Die neuplatonischen Kommentare zu Aristoteles' "De anima,"* Quellen und Studien zur Philosophie 85 (Berlin: de Gruyter, 2008), 274–75.

[40] For an instance of possibly "inverted" reception of this passage from Plato in the motif of Pisthetairus's "fantasy of a heavenly space" in Aristophanes's *Birds*, see Adi Ophir, *Plato's Invisible Cities: Discourse and Power in the* Republic (London: Routledge, 1991), 30–31.

"nothing to declare."[41] J. J. Wettstein cited Tacitus at v. 1 for the motif of the world coming to an end, but has nothing to offer at v. 2.[42] But there is some evidence that is perhaps worth citing.

2 Vergil and Manilius

A specific form of the theme of the descending/descended city, shaped by political motives, is met in Book 8 of the *Aeneid*, where Vergil speaks of the mythical origins of Rome. Fleeing his son and usurper Jupiter, Saturn "came down from ethereal Olympus" (*ab aetherio venit Saturnus Olympo*, 8.319) and founded a citadel called Saturnia (*hanc Saturnus condidit arcem ... illi fuerat Saturnia nomen*, 8.357–58) on a place that later would become a part of Rome. The tradition is known also to Varro, who says that the Capitoline hill was formerly called the "Saturnian Hill" and that the ancient city on that hill used to be called "Saturnia" (5.42).[43] Ovid, too, recounts that Saturn was expelled by Jupiter from the celestial realms and then received on earth (*Fasti* 1.235–36).[44] The motif, which is also well known in Christian tradition,[45] does not speak of a city that

---

[41] Georg David Kypke, *Observationes sacrae in Novi Foederis libros*, vol. 2 (Bratislava: Johann J. Korn, 1755); Johann Albert Bengel, *Gnomon Novi Testamenti*, 3rd ed. (London: David Nutt and Williams & Norgate, 1862).

[42] *Novum Testamentum Graece*, vol. 2 (Amsterdam: Dommerian, 1752; repr. Graz: Akademische Druck; Univ. Verlagsanstalt, 1962), 840: *Senatus – laetus & spei certus, quippe sumta per Gallias Hispaniasque civilia arma, motu ad bellum Germanis, mox Illyrico, postquam Aegyptum Judaeamque & omnes provincias exercitusque lustraverant, velut expiato terrarum Orbe cepisse finem videbantur* (Tacitus, *Historiae* 4.3). He also adds a passage (in Latin translation) from rabbinic literature that he identifies as *Debarim R. S. XI* on the need for the world to be renewed. A couple of other passages from rabbinic literature are cited at Rev 3:12, but they are not relevant for us. For the few parallels from Second Temple and rabbinic literature dealing with the descent of Jerusalem from heaven, see the evidence and comments in Hermann L. Strack and Paul Billerbeck, *Kommentar zum Neuen Testament aus Talmud und Midrasch*, vol. 3, 3rd ed. (Munich: Beck, 1961), 796 (at Rev 3:12): "Das vom Himmel herniederkommende Jerusalem wird in den Pseudepigraphen selten [references to 4 Ezra 7.26; 13.36; and 10.54; 1 Enoch 90.29 and 2 Baruch 4.3 are said to be irrelevant in this respect], in der älteren rabbinischen Literatur gar nicht u. in den jüngeren kleinen Midraschim auch nur einige Male erwähnt [references to Midrash Vayosha; the Coptic Apocalypse of Elijah; Ma'aserot Daniel]. On the evidence cited in the *Neuer Wettstein*, see above notes 19 and 21. References to 4 Ezra 8.51–55 and Sibylline Oracles 3.767–808 for the whole of Rev 21:2–22:5 in M. Eugene Boring, Klaus Berger, and Carsten Colpe, ed., *Hellenistic Commentary to the New Testament* (Nashville, TN: Abingdon, 1995), 584–85.

[43] Varro, *De lingua Latina* 5.42 (Roland G. Kent, ed. and transl., LCL 333 [Cambridge, MA: Harvard University Press, 1938]).

[44] Ovid, *Fasti* (James G. Frazer, ed. and transl., revised by George P. Goold, LCL 253 [Cambridge, MA: Harvard University Press, 1931]).

[45] Cf. Minucius Felix, *Octavius* 21.4–6; Cyprian, *Idola* 2; Augustine, *De civitate Dei* 7.4; Lactantius, *Institutiones* 5.5.9; Macrobius, *Saturnalia*, 1.7.19–26.

descended from heaven, but of a god whose name was given to a city (citadel) that would later become (part of) Rome. Combined with the motif, also known from Vergil, of Rome as the eternal city (*nec metas rerum nec tempora, Aen.* 1.278-79)[46] and the city that puts an end to the turmoil on earth *and* in heaven (*Aen.* 1.279-82), the topic becomes quite unique and invites readers to see Rome as a city that, in the figure of Saturn, came down from heaven (or at least has a privileged relation with the other sphere) to establish peace on earth and harmony in the universe.[47]

In his own way, the astronomer Manilius also emphasises the heavenly nature of the city of Rome.[48] Rome is not only the "capital of the world" (*rerum maxima*), but also "conjoined with heaven" (*caeloque adiungitur ipsa*, 4.694-95). Related to this harmony between Rome and heaven, which pervades the *Astronomica*,[49] is the divinity of the emperor and, ultimately, his apotheosis.[50] Augustus once "descended from heaven" and, in due time, "will replenish heaven" (*descendit caelo caelumque replebit*, 1.799-800). After his apotheosis, he will even rule heaven and make it grow (4.934-35). Similarly, his predecessor Julius Caesar has already "been given to heaven as a god" (*deum caelo dederit*, 1.926). This imperial ideology has the emperor harmoniously govern heaven and earth. Moreover, Manilius compares the city of Rome directly with a heavenly city (5.734-45).[51] The Roman social classes, mentioned in their traditional terminology, reflect the hierarchy of the celestial bodies in that heavenly city.[52] As Wolfgang Hübner aptly notes in commenting on this passage, Rome is a city on earth with a cosmic foundation.[53]

---

[46] The motif of *Roma aeterna* occurs frequently in ancient literature and seems to be ingrained in the Roman mind; cf. Roland Gregory Austin, ed., *P. Vergili Maronis Aeneidos liber primus* (Oxford: Clarendon, 1971), 106-7. See also above n. 15.

[47] On Roman aspirations to maintain or obtain peace, see Turcan, *Ouranopolis* (cf. note 14), 79-98.

[48] Manilius, *Astronomica* (George P. Goold, ed. and transl., LCL 469 [Cambridge, MA: Harvard University Press, 1977]).

[49] Cf. Katharina Volk, *Manilius and his Intellectual Background* (Oxford: Oxford University Press, 2009), 110-11.

[50] As part of the broader motif of the heavenly journey. On the latter, see Thomas Kuhn-Treichel, "Was leistet Lehrdichtung? Neue Perspektiven auf das Motiv der Himmelsreise in Manilius' *Astronomica*," in *Hermes* 148 (2020): 494-504.

[51] Cf. Dora Liuzzi, *M. Manilio: Astronomica: Libro V*, Testi e studi 9 (Lecce: Congedo, 1997), 164-65.

[52] On the relation between heaven and earth in general in Manilius, see Dunstan Lowe, "Heavenly and Earthly Elements in Manilius' *Astronomica*," in *Ramus* 43 (2014): 45-66.

[53] *Manilius: Astronomica Buch V*, vol. 2, ed. Wolfgang Hübner, Sammlung wissenschaftlicher Commentare (Berlin: de Gruyter, 2010), 444.

3 Athenaeus

A perhaps more appropriate passage for comparison with Rev 21:2 is found in Athenaeus (fl. late second and early third centuries). In the first book of his *Deipnosophistae* (1.20a–b, 1.36 in Kaibel's edition), Athenaeus indulges in praise of Rome's grandeur.[54] The passage is worth citing in full, as parts of it require explanation:

A division. [Athenaeus] refers to Rome as an international community. He also says that you would not be far from the mark if you call the city of Rome an epitome of the inhabited world, since you can see every single city settled in it, many of them in individual neighborhoods, for example golden Alexandria, lovely Antioch, gorgeous Nicomedia, and in addition "the most radiant of all the cities Zeus reveals" [*adesp.com.* fr. 100], by which I mean Athens. One day would not be enough, if I tried to offer a complete list of the cities included in the count of the Romans' heavenly city; indeed, there are so many that all the days in a year would be required. The fact is that whole populations have settled there "en masse," such as the Cappadocians, Scythians, Pontians, and many others.[55]

---

[54] In several respects, the *Deipnosophistae* is a singular work. It has been called both "a sprawling and oddly structured work" (Douglas Olson) and "the most important work of late antiquity" (Douglas Olson citing Charles B. Gulick), and both characterizations are probably correct. See Douglas Olson, ed. and transl., *Athenaeus, The Learned Banqueters. Books I–II.106e*, LCL 204 (Cambridge, MA: Harvard University Press, 2007), ix. The lack of structure plays tricks in the passage that concerns us here (see below). With its references to more than one thousand authors and to ten thousand lines of text, its importance as a treasury of antique authorities and sources is unequalled. More recently, commentators have also started to appreciate the work for its compositional aspects. The book gives the account of a famous dinner party with some twenty intellectuals in the house of the politician and administrator Larensis, owner of a famous library. The narrator is Athenaeus, one of the attendees, who informs one Timocrates about the event. All possible topics are up for discussion, so it seems, with little attention whatsoever for structure, while the guests enjoy food from all over the world. The scene has been likened to Trimalchio's party, but this one is for intellectuals. Perhaps the most interesting thing about the work is that all the time it plays on the tension between the universal and the local. The whole world is served in Larensis's house without the guests having to travel; and in the same way the whole intellectual word is put at their disposal without the guests having to leave the house and its library. Actually, the work most probably relies heavily on Larensis's library. On the latter, see David Braund, "Learning, Luxury and Empire: Athenaeus' Roman Patron," in *Athenaeus and His World: Reading Greek Culture in the Roman World*, ed. David Braund and John Wilkins (Exeter: University of Exeter Press, 2000), 3–22, esp. 19; on the contrast with Trimalchio, see 3–4.

[55] ὅρος. οἰκουμένης δῆμον τὴν Ῥώμην φησί. λέγει δὲ καὶ ὅτι οὐκ ἄν τις σκοποῦ πόρρω τοξεύων λέγοι τὴν Ῥώμην πόλιν ἐπιτομὴν τῆς οἰκουμένης· ἐν ᾗ συνιδεῖν ἔστιν οὕτως πάσας τὰς πόλεις ἱδρυμένας, καὶ κατ' ἰδίαν δὲ τὰς πολλάς, ὡς Ἀλεξανδρέων μὲν τὴν χρυσῆν, Ἀντιοχέων δὲ τὴν καλήν, Νικομηδέων δὲ τὴν περικαλλῆ, προσέτι τε "τὴν λαμπροτάτην πόλεων πασῶν ὁπόσας ὁ Ζεὺς | ἀναφαίνει," τὰς Ἀθήνας λέγω. ἐπιλείποι δ' ἄν με οὐχ ἡμέρα μία ἐξαριθμούμενον τὰς ἐν τῇ Ῥωμαίων οὐρανοπόλει [Ῥώμῃ] ἀριθμουμένας πόλεις, ἀλλὰ πᾶσαι αἱ κατὰ τὸν ἐνιαυτὸν [ἀριθμούμεναι] διὰ τὸ πλῆθος. καὶ γὰρ ὅλα ἔθνη ἀθρόως αὐτόθι συνῴκισται, ὡς τὸ Καππαδοκῶν καὶ Σκυθῶν καὶ Ποντίων καὶ ἄλλων πλειόνων. *Athenaeus. The Learned Banqueters. Books I–II.106e*, ed. Olson. Cf. the old edition by Georg Kaibel,

The passage poses several problems of various sorts. First, there are reasons to think that the text as it came down to us does not represent the original, or not completely. Second, the passage cited does not connect in any way with its context. It is preceded by a long section dealing with artists and itinerant showmen from all possible cities (1.19a–20a) and followed by a section on dancers and dressing for dance (1.20b–21a) that has nothing to do with it. Third, there is the strange word ὅρος at the beginning of the passage, which commentators have tried to emend in several ways.[56] Paul Maas wondered if ὅρος is perhaps a corruption of the name of the authority Athenaeus is citing.[57] If, on the other hand, one accepts the reading ὅρος, it is unclear how it relates to the following. Georg Kaibel proposed to connect ὅρος with οἰκουμένης ("limit of the world").[58] Recent commentators, however, take the word to mean "definition" and consider it as the beginning of an excursus on the phrase οἰκουμένης δῆμον, either by Athenaeus himself or by a scribe.[59] Douglas Olson, in turn, proposes to translate it as "a division." Placed roughly in the middle of Book 1, this notice seems to be a remnant of the original division of the fifteen books into thirty half-books.[60] Fourth and last, it remains unclear who is speaking here, and on whose authority. A few pages earlier Athenaeus referred to the rhetor Polemo, who, according to Galen, praised Rome by calling her "the epitome of the world," as does Athenaeus.[61] Galen is mentioned as one of the interlocutors in the *Deipnosophistae* – a happy coincidence, or a hint as to Athenaeus's source?

Athenaei Naucratitae Deipnosophistarum libri XV, vol. 1, Bibliotheca Scriptorum Graecorum et Romanorum Teubneriana (Leipzig: Teubner, 1887).

[56] Casaubon, Schweighäuser and Dindorf proposed to read ὅτι instead: Isaac Casaubon, ed., *Athenaei Deipnosophistarum libri quindecim* (Heidelberg: Commelin, 1597); Johann Schweighäuser, ed., *Athenaei Naucratitae Deipnosophistarum libri quindecim* (Strasbourg: Societas Bipontina, 1801–1807); Wilhelm Dindorf, ed., *Athenaeus*, vol. 1 (Leipzig: Weidmann, 1827). August Meineke, *Athenaei Deipnosophistae*, vol. 1, (Leipzig: Teubner, 1858), conjectured ὅρα, but failed to convince others.

[57] The notes to his edition of the *Deipnosophistae* have been published posthumously by Robert L. Fowler, "Paul Maas's Athenaeus," *Zeitschrift für Papyrologie und Epigraphik* 172 (2010): 55–64 at 57.

[58] *Deipnosophistarum libri XV*, vol. 1, *in loco*.

[59] Cf. Alexandre M. Desrousseaux, ed., *Athénée de Naucratis: Les deipnosophiste: Livres I et II* (Paris: Les Belles Lettres, 1956), 45, n. 2. See also Claus Friedrich and Thomas Nothers, ed., *Athenaios: Das Gelehrtenmahl: Buch I–VI*, Bibliothek der griechischen Literatur 4 (Stuttgart: Hiersemann, 1998); Lucia Rodríguez-Noriega Guillén, ed., *Ateneo: Banquete de los eruditos: Libros I–II*, Biblioteca clásica Gredos 257 (Madrid: Gredos, 1998).

[60] See on this structure, Kaibel, *Deipnosophistarum libri XV* (cf. note 55), xxi–xxiii.

[61] Galen, *De humero iis modis prolapso quos Hippocrates non vidit*, in Karl G. Kühn, ed., *Claudii Galeni opera omnia*, vol. 18.1 (Leipzig: Knobloch, 1829), 347: ἐν Ῥώμῃ [...] πόλει τοσοῦτον ἀνθρώπων πλῆθος ἐχούσῃ, ὡς ἐπαινεῖσθαι Πολέμωνα τὸν ῥήτορα τῆς οἰκουμένης ἐπιτομὴν αὐτὴν εἰπόντα. The *Suda* merely attributes it to Athenaeus (Ada Adler, ed., *Suidae lexicon*, vol. 4, [Leipzig: Teubner, 1935], 303).

The passage is not the only instance of Athenaeus's praising Rome, but nowhere else does he focus so much on its universal and indeed celestial nature.[62] The city is mentioned by name, as is the case with Jerusalem in Rev 21:2, and, in addition, is given many titles, again not unlike in Rev 21:1 where Jerusalem is called "holy" and compared to a bride. Rome, by contrast, is a truly international community (οἰκουμένης δῆμον), an epitome of the inhabited world (πόλιν ἐπιτομὴν τῆς οἰκουμένης), indeed, the heavenly city of all Romans (ἐν τῇ Ῥωμαίων οὐρανοπόλει).[63]

Unfortunately, not all in the text is equally clear and commentaries on the passage are virtually non-existent. Rome is an οὐρανόπολις. The word has been translated as "the heavenly city," "the universal city," "the ideal city" or simply transliterated as "Uranopolis."[64] Christian Jacob suggested that it might refer to the (Cynic-)Stoic notion of a universal city or community ruled by the same laws, or else to the utopian city Uranopolis founded by one Alexarchus.[65] Perhaps a more obvious suggestion is that Athenaeus uses it as a synonym for a "cosmopolitan" city in which all nations, races, and languages can be seen and heard.[66] In our opinion, the meaning of the word in this context cannot be limited to one of these three options, but rather seems to include, to different degrees, aspects of various sorts, as we will now show.

In fact, the text can be read on two levels, the first of which is the most obvious and therefore probably also the most likely, though the second cannot be ruled out; indeed, the two can be read together. On the first level, Athenaeus describes

---

[62] In 3.8, he calls Rome the "beautiful" city (ἐν τῇ καλῇ Ῥώμῃ) and in 3.53 and 3.94 the "governing" or "queen" city (τῆς βασιλευούσης πόλεως; ἐν Ῥώμῃ τῇ βασιλευούσῃ).

[63] On this threefold characterization, which covers political, demographic, and plainly universalistic dimensions, see the comment by Turcan, *Ouranopolis* (cf. note 14), 121.

[64] The first option in Charles B. Gulick, ed., *Athenaeus, The Deipnosophists. Books I-III.106e*, LCL 204 (Cambridge, MA: Harvard University Press, 1969); Olson, *Banqueters*; and Christian Jacob, *The Web of Athenaeus*, Hellenic Studies 61 (Washington, DC: Center for Hellenic Studies; Cambridge, MA: Harvard University Press, 2013); the second in Rodríguez-Noriega Guillén, *Ateneo* (cf. note 59) ("la universal urbe de los romanos"), Desrousseaux, *Athénée* (cf. note 59) ("la ville-univers des Romains") and Turcan, *Ouranopolis* (cf. note 14) ("ville-univers"); the third in Ernst Wüst, "Uranopolis," in *Paulys Realencyclopädie der classischen Altertumswissenschaft*, vol. 2.17 (Stuttgart: Alfred Druckenmüller, 1961); the last option in Charles D. Yonge, trans., *The Deipnosophists, or, Banquet of the Learned of Athenaeus* (London: Henry G. Bohn, 1854) and in Jacob, *Athenaeus*, as an alternative ("Ouranopolis"). Wüst reads it as a mere *epitheton ornans*, both here in Athenaeus and in Clement (*Paed.* 2.2.119) with reference to Jerusalem (see above n. 31). See Wüst, "Uranopolis," 965–66; Turcan, *Ouranopolis*, 122.

[65] Uranopolis was said to have been founded by Alexarchus in the vicinity of Athos. It had a circumference of almost six kilometers (thirty stadia) and its inhabitants spoke a dialect of Alexarchus's own making. See Demetrius of Scepsis (fr. 46; ed. Richard Gaede [Diss. Greifswald: Universitätsverlag, 1880]); Heraclides Lembus (fr. 5; ed. Karl Müller, *Fragmenta Historicorum Graecorum*, vol. 3 [Paris: Didot, 1853]). Cf. Wüst (cf. note 64), *Uranopolis*.

[66] Similarly, Aelius Aristides, *Orationes* 26.11–12 (Wilhelm Dindorf, ed., *Aristides*, vol. 1 [Leipzig: Reimer, 1829]). Cf. John Wilkins, "Athenaeus the Navigator," in *Journal of Hellenic Studies* 128 (2008): 132–52, esp. 135.

Rome as the capital of the world, a city that compares most favourably to all the great cities of the eastern Mediterranean, four of which are mentioned by name, one of them even honoured with an epithet of its own (Athens), well in the style of the author. He also describes it as a city that generously receives all those who wish to settle within its walls, allocating to each of them quarters of their own. In short, it is a city that seems to encompass the whole world. Athenaeus also seems to invite one to read the passage on a second level, one on which he does not so much deal with Rome as the capital of the world, but rather with the whole Roman empire, which on a smaller scale is reflected in its capital. Taken together, these readings show how city and empire coincide, the former being the latter in miniature, and the latter the former on a larger scale. Rome inhabits the world and the world inhabits Rome.[67]

For Athenaeus, then, Rome is neither a utopian city nor a mythical heavenly city. Yes, it is impressive in every respect. It is grandiose. It is all-encompassing. But it is also very real, is situated on earth, and can be experienced. Taken together these characteristics allow one to rightly call it "heavenly" (he does not say "divine"). Rome is wonderful, unique, and cosmopolitan beyond imagination – home to and model for the whole inhabited world. It is indeed what some might call "heavenly," worthy of the highest claim and praise. Rome may have been built by humans, but the result is of an entirely different status and nature. In Rome, one may feel as if in heaven.[68] Needless to say, this is a highly idealized vision of what historical Rome was for many of its citizens, even at its

---

[67] These comments are inspired by those of Jacob (*Athenaeus*, 109–12), who convincingly argues that this "strange digression," as he calls the passage, is crucial for understanding Athenaeus's whole project. The text offers a synopsis of the world centered on Rome, "a universal city, where the entire oikoumenè is summarized. Rome makes it possible to see all of the world's cities through a synoptic gaze" (109). Praises of imperial Rome were of course not unknown of in the Second Sophistic. However, what we get here is "a condensed world" (110), a world in which the whole of Greek culture is condensed into one. Jacob then goes one step further still and considers the phrase "the epitome of the inhabited world" as "perhaps a reading key to the *Deipnosophists*" (110). Athenaeus allows the reader to travel through time and space, virtually, of course, and without ever leaving the rich library of his host where he probably found much of the material he is citing in his work. In this way, he provides intellectual food along with the material food the companions enjoy at the dinner party that is the setting of the book. "Motionless, the reader can travel, he who lets himself be transported by compilations from the interior of the library" (111). While we can agree with the principle (see also above n. 53), we are slightly more hesitant to align this one little phrase with the purpose of the book as a whole.

[68] See Turcan's comment: "Dans le cas de Rome, ouranopolis suppose l'image d'un empire qu'enveloppe le ciel et qui en reflète pour ainsi dire l'immensité" (*Ouranopolis* [cf. note 14], 121). Turcan then continues in a vein that is more appropriate still when adding, "On songe au Panthéon d'Hadrien, dont la coupole évoque, tel un firmament, l'universalité de l'*Orbis Romanus*. Le texte d'Athénée nous fait passer ainsi de la *ciuitas* ou 'cité' au sens antique du terme ... à la 'cosmopolis' impériale ou cité-empire, miroir du monde qu'elle domine et intègre, au moins politiquement," to conclude with a line from Rutilius Numantianus, "Urbem fecisti quod prius orbis erat" (*De reditu suo*, 1.66). Turcan also catches a glimpse of this cosmic dimension in the phrase "there are so many that all the days in a year would be required."

apogee towards the end of the second century. But that is also true for Revelation's idealized Jerusalem, especially taking into account the historical situation of the city at the time the book was composed.

Some of the aspects of the heavenly Rome just given above can be compared to the description in Rev 21. The first and no doubt most important is that both Rome and the New Jerusalem are said to be heavenly cities, or at least cities that feature characteristics that allow for calling them so, even though they are clearly assumed to be situated on earth. These are not ideal cities in the sense of Plato's heavenly abode; they are larger than life, but they are very much real in that they can be described, seen, and sensed. They really do exist. It is not explicitly said that Athenaeus's Rome descended from heaven, but the epithet suggests a divine origin or destination.[69] The label "heavenly city" plays on the sense of a *Roma aeterna*, a city that was wished by God and shaped with divine aid.[70] Second, Athenaeus grows lyrical about this city, as does John when he describes the brilliance of the New Jerusalem when he watches it descend from heaven. Third, both authors are most serious about what they see and describe. The author of Revelation believes in what he sees, and expects his readers to as well. Likewise, there is no hint of irony or sarcasm in Athenaeus's description. He truly believes Rome is a great capital and that it deserves to be such.

But there are also several differences between the two cities as described in these two sources. None of these, however, can be regarded as problematic or as a sign that Rome was of less importance for Athenaeus and his readers than the New Jerusalem was for John and his. A major difference has to do with who is allowed to reside in the city. If both are said to welcome many nations, Revelation's Jerusalem is more selective, as is noted in 21:27: some well-defined groups will not be allowed to enter, and this has been ordained by divine command.[71] Access will only be reserved to "those who are written in the Lamb's book of life." No such restrictions seem to be upheld in the case of Athenaeus's Rome. This city allows everyone to enter it – citizens from the most cultivated cities of the world as well as barbarians and insignificant people. A second difference is not so explicit but is nevertheless perceptible from the descriptions. Jerusalem is selective in its choice and most restrictive in terms of promoting religious life. The city does not even have a temple anymore. By contrast, Rome, it is implied, allows all nations to continue to worship their own gods. Third, Revelation's Jerusalem as a more splendid appearance than Athenaeus's Rome; in any case, it is described in much more detail than the other. Perhaps this means little; however, it may

---

[69] Turcan too points to the religious dimension of Rome's power and glory; it is ecumenical, cosmic, and marked by its destiny: "En fait, c'est la Ville même que tend à déifier le mot 'ouranopole'" (*Ouranopolis* [cf. note 14], 122).

[70] Cf. what was said above about the pre-existent character of the new Jerusalem.

[71] Cf. Beale, *Revelation* (cf. note 3), 1101, who emphasizes the definitive character of the command and compares v. 27 with v. 8.

also points to a need that was felt on the part of Revelation's author that was not felt at all by the other. The intended audience may explain this difference: the author of Revelation wrote for an audience that had in most cases never seen Jerusalem and might have known of its recent desolation after the war; Athenaeus, by contrast, writes for fellow intellectuals who were well acquainted with the city or perhaps even lived there.[72] That Rome is great and beautiful is common knowledge; that Jerusalem is as well needs to be illustrated. Fourth, Jerusalem is the bride of Christ, but Rome is the capital of the world. This again points to a great difference between them. One is in a position of dependence, the other rules the world. Fifth and finally, and perhaps most tricky, Athenaeus's Rome stands for fame and glory, those qualities being what earn it the epithet "heavenly." By contrast, in the broader context of the three great visions of Rev 17–22, the reader is invited to draw a neat comparison between the New Jerusalem coming down to earth in the third vision and the quite obvious Babylon/Rome imagery in the first vision in Rev 17:1–19:10.[73]

In the end, however, what really counts for our comparison is that both cities are heavenly and that both are to be found on this earth. That is also the focus and the limit of David E. Aune's reference to Athenaeus – to our knowledge the only commentator of Revelation to mention the passage at all – when writing, "Rome is called 'the heavenly city [οὐρανόπολις]' in Athenaeus *Deipn.* 1.20C."[74]

4 Plautus

A rather different parallel can perhaps be added to the previous one. In the prologue to Plautus's *Rudens* (*the Cable*), "une des meilleures réussites de Plaute,"[75] the star Arcturus addresses the audience and begins by presenting himself as a fellow citizen of Jupiter (Prol. 1–2): "In the city of the celestials [*civitas caelitum*] I am a fellow citizen of him who wields sway over all peoples, seas, and lands."[76]

---

[72] Cf. the comment by Zahn, *Offenbarung des Johannes*, vol. 2, 596: "In dieser gläubigen Erwartung liess sich Jo und die apostolische Kirche nicht durch die Tatsache irremachen, dass das Jerusalem ihrer Gegenwart eher den namen Sodom und Ägypten (c. 11,8), verdiente, als den Namen eines himmlischen oder eines neues Jerusalem."

[73] See the synopsis in Aune, *Revelation 17–22* [cf. note 1], 1144–45, and his comment at 1146: "These two extensive textual units use antithetical female imagery: the first (17:1–19:10) focuses on Rome-Babylon under the dominating metaphor of a prostitute, while the second (21:9–22:9) focuses on the eschatological city of God, the New Jerusalem, under the metaphor of the bride, the wife of the Lamb." Whether this also explains why the author does not repeat it anymore after 21:9 (so Satake, *Offenbarung* [cf. note 7], 400) remains to be seen.

[74] Aune, *Revelation 17–22* (cf. note 1), 1121.

[75] Henri Clouard, ed., *Plaute Théâtre*, vol. 5, Classiques Garnier (Paris: Garnier, 1936), 4.

[76] *qui gentis omnis mariaque et terras mouet,* | *eius sum ciuis ciuitate caelitum*: Plautus: *The Little Carthaginian: Pseudolus*: Wolfgang de Melo, ed., *The Rope*, LCL 260 (Cambridge, MA: Harvard University Press, 2012), 406–07.

He continues by praising himself as a most loyal and reliable heavenly body who executes Jupiter's orders to the best of his abilities when sent on his course to inspect human life and is truly shocked by the injustice he encounters on a daily basis.

The phrase *civitas caelitum*, in combination with *civis*, may denote a city or community of citizens, but it may also refer to citizenship or franchise. Some have suggested the translation "City of the Celestials" or "Götterstadt."[77] Others take *civitas* as franchise.[78] Still others propose "community or collective of citizens of heaven" – an understanding that would suit Arcturus's claims of being a co-citizen of Jove.[79]

At first sight, Arcturus does not claim that the city he hails from is situated on earth; quite the contrary, he prides himself on his co-citizenship with the highest god. Yet, perhaps such a link between heaven and earth can be made and was indeed intended if the phrase *civitas caelitum* is taken as a pun on *civitas Caeritum*, the citizenship of the inhabitants of the Etruscan city of Caere (modern-day Cerveteri).[80] On this hypothesis poor Arcturus is supposed to suffer from a speech defect blurring the difference between r and l that is thought occasionally to create a comic effect.[81] Arcturus may well have claimed to belong to the city of the celestials, but what the audience hears him say is that he is a citizen of Caere. The latter was known to have been rewarded with the status of *civitas Romana* for having safeguarded the sacred objects during the attack by the Gauls, even if, notably, the right to vote, the *ius suffragii,* was withheld from it.[82]

---

[77] Cf. Edward A. Sonnenschein, ed., *T. Macci Plauti "Rudens,"* (Oxford: Clarendon, 1968), 83; Friedrich Marx, ed., *Plautus Rudens. Text und Kommentar* (Leipzig: Hirzel, 1928), 53.

[78] Friedrich Leo, ed., *Plauti Comoediae*, vol. 2 (Berlin: Weidmann, 1896), 311.

[79] Cf. Émile Benveniste, "Deux modèles linguistiques de la cité," in *Échanges et communications, I: Mélanges offerts à Claude Lévi-Strauss à l'occasion de son 60ème anniversaire*, Studies in General Anthropology 5.1, ed. Jean Pouillon and Pierre Maranda (Berlin: de Gruyter, 1970), 589–96, esp. 593.

[80] So Walter R. Chalmers, "Plautus 'Rudens' 2," in *Classical Philology* 57 (1962): 240; Michael Fontaine, *Funny Words in Plautine Comedy* (Oxford: Oxford University Press, 2010), 102.

[81] See the same phenomenon, with a similar comic effect, in Cicero, *Epistulae ad familiares* 2.10.1.

[82] See Aulus Gellius, *Noctes atticae* 16.13.7 (Peter K. Marshall, ed., *A. Gellii Noctes Atticae*, Oxford Classical Texts [Oxford: Clarendon, 1990]): *Primos autem municipes sine suffragii iure Caerites esse factos accepimus concessumque illis, ut civitatis Romanae honorem quidem caperent, sed negotiis tamen atque oneribus vacarent pro sacris bello Gallico receptis custoditisque. Hinc 'tabulae Caerites' appellatae versa vice, in quas censores referri iubebant, quos notae causa suffragiis privabant*; Pseudo-Acron, *Scholia in Epistulas* 1.6.62 (Otto Keller, ed., *Pseudoacronis scholia in Horatium vetustiora*, vol. 2 [Leipzig: Teubner, 1904], 235): *Cere oppidum in Italia, quo capta a Gallis urbe sacra translata sunt, pro quo beneficio postea ciuitatem Romanam meruit, ita tamen, ne suffragium ferret.* On the *tabula Caeritum* that honoured the status of the city, see also Pseudo-Asconius, *In Ciceronis Divinationem in Caecilium* 8 (Thomas Stangl, ed., *Ciceronis orationum scholiastae* [Hildesheim: Olms, 1964], 189). See also Michel Humbert, "L'incorporation de Caere dans la 'Civitas Romana,'" in *Mélanges de l'École française de Rome* 84 (1972): 231–68; Fabio Colivicchi, "After the Fall: Caere after 273 B.C.E.," in *Etruscan Studies*

On the one hand, there is the *civitas Romana*, and on the other there are those, like the Caerites, who enjoy this status only partially. In the same way, there are those who claim to belong to the city of the celestials, like Arcturus, and those who like Jupiter really do so. The pun is based on an assumed speech defect of the character; it depends on the audience's knowledge of the status of Caere, the important legal difference between full and partial citizenship, and on the assumption that what is claimed to be a heavenly city is actually a second-class Roman city.

As has been said, this is a parallel of a different sort, created by the genre in which it occurs, and is therefore of far less importance as an attestation than that of Athenaeus. But perhaps it is not completely without value, as it shows the potential for disputing any such claims about heavenly citizenship and the like while also again granting Rome a status that is envied by the rest of the world.

Conclusion

This brief essay has presented a few passages from non-Christian authors that may perhaps be of some help, if not in interpreting the text of Rev 21:2, then at least in putting the scriptural passage in a somewhat broader context. It has not been claimed that the passage from Plato might have been known to, or had any effect on, the author of Revelation. Knowledge of Plautus, Vergil, or Manilius is even more improbable, and Athenaeus wrote a century or so after Revelation was published. But parallels such as these can have value – even when they are of a later date – since our evidence from ancient literature is frequently fragmentary. The passages cited here as "parallels" show how the same or a similar motif can take a different form while also continuing to play on the same features, a fact that can invite a modern reader to look at a familiar old motif from a new or more nuanced perspective.

---

18 (2015): 178–99; Fabio Colivicchi, "A Blurring Frontier: The Territory of Caere in the Fourth and Third Centuries B.C.E.," in *Etruscan Studies* 23 (2020): 107–29.

Stones of Stumbling

The Petrographic Scandal of the New Jerusalem in Origen and His Eastern Inheritors*

T. C. Schmidt

Introduction

Origen of Alexandria (d. ca. AD 255) gives advice to pious readers whenever they might come across something apparently contradictory or immoral in the Scriptures: "if at any time in reading the Scriptures," he says, "you stumble at something which is a fair stone of stumbling or a rock of offense," then you must, he claims, "blame yourself."[1] This done, you may, according to Origen, set about finding an allegorical solution. To many Christians, such stones of stumbling were bestrewn across the pages of Revelation, and particularly so the descriptions of the heavenly throne room in Rev 4 and that of the heavenly city in Rev 21–22. In the one, God is described as sitting on a throne and is likened to stones of jasper and carnelian; in the other, the heavenly city is similarly bedecked with all manner of precious stones. For many readers, however, these earthly stones – somehow present in heaven – were rather scandalous and became Origen's previously mentioned "stone of stumbling" and "rock of offense."

In this contribution, I will examine how Greek, Armenian, Syriac and Arabic Revelation exegetes (sixth–thirteenth centuries) negotiated the challenging petrographic imagery within the text of Revelation. I will show that in their solutions commentators often followed the well-worn path of Origen of Alexandria, even if not all of them were aware of his influence. They, like Origen, resorted to allegorical analysis when confronted with difficult passages in Scripture, as per the stones of Revelation. But more than that, under Origen's instruction, the sealed treasure of these problematic passages, once unlocked by allegory,

---

* This contribution contains extracts and expansions of portions of T. C. Schmidt, *The Book of Revelation and Its Eastern Commentators: Making the New Testament in the Early Christian World* (Cambridge, UK: Cambridge University Press, 2021).

[1] *Philocalia* 1.28, translation modified from George Lewis, trans., *The Philocalia of Origen* (Edinburgh: T&T Clark, 1911), 28. For a similar statement, see *Philocalia* 10.1.

could then be used as lodestones disclosing the way towards more profound and mystical understandings of the text.

In this regard, I begin this contribution by discussing Origen and his treatment of Revelation and of Scripture as a whole; I then describe how Revelation exegetes took up Origen's hermeneutic in their Revelation commentaries; lastly, I show how these exegetes applied such an interpretive lens to the Heavenly Jerusalem and to the stones thereof.

1 Origen's Interpretive Rubric and the Heavenly City

While Origen suggests in his *Commentary on Matthew* (*Commentarium in evangelium Matthaei*) that he may have written an exegetical work on Revelation, it is unfortunate that, were he to have carried this out, no fragments of it have been conclusively identified, even if likely candidates exist.[2] He did, though, lay down several interpretive rubrics that were taken up by later Revelation exegetes. As is commonly known, Origen believed that the Old and New Testaments should be analyzed via a three-tiered process in which every stage leads progressively to deeper or higher levels of meaning. He explains that these three tiers are derived from the body, soul, and spirit of Scripture.[3]

These can be imagined either as a series of escalating steps or as a set of concentrically arranged circles. Each tier is defined by Origen in several ways; most frequently the first level (or outer circle) corresponds to the historical, the literal, or the obvious interpretation of a passage; the second to basic moral and doctrinal interpretive issues; and the third to deep and profound spiritual understanding. At every level Origen held certain expectations of what should and should not be contained within. So, in the first stage of exegesis, Origen took care to explain any obvious inconsistencies, in the second he paid great heed to any moral or doctrinal infelicities, and in the third he anticipated great profundity and sublimity.[4]

---

[2] "But the principal explanations and examinations of these matters must take place when the book itself [Revelation] shall have been proposed for us to explain; now, however, this alone must be explained from that Revelation ...." Translation modified from *The Commentary of Origen on the Gospel of St Matthew*, trans. Ronald E. Heine, Oxford Early Christian Texts (Oxford: Oxford University Press, 2018), 623. For further discussion and for possible fragments of a work by Origen on Revelation, see the anonymous Greek Scholia in *Cassiodorus, St. Gregory the Great, and Anonymous Greek Scholia: Writings on the Apocalypse*, Francis X. Gumerlock, Mark DelCogliano, and T.C. Schmidt, trans., FC 144 (Washington, DC: Catholic University of America Press, 2022), 96–106.

[3] ἐκ σώματος καὶ ψυχῆς καὶ πνεύματος. Origen, *First Principles (De principiis)* 4.2.4. Text from *Origen: On First Principles*, ed. John Behr, Oxford Early Christian Texts (Oxford: Oxford University Press, 2018), 498 lines 102–103.

[4] Henri de Lubac, *Medieval Exegesis: The Four Senses of Scripture*, trans. E.M. Macierowski

It is also well known that in practice Origen did not always clearly distinguish between these levels, especially the final two, nor did he believe that Scripture always contains the first level of meaning.[5] But his programmatic approach to the Old and New Testaments was to take note as to whether any of his expectations were violated, such as whenever contradictions, impossibilities, immoralities, and the like presented themselves to the reader. These would then spur him to venture explanations and harmonizations, usually appealing to allegory in the process. And he often framed this endeavor in terms of an ascent to the second and third higher levels of understanding. Reaching the uppermost, mystical, echelon was the ultimate goal of his scriptural interpretation.

As expected, Origen would go on to use this very method whenever his attention was drawn to the stones of the Heavenly Jerusalem. He writes: "If anyone should want to have suggestions of the deeper truths about the way in which the soul enters into the divine realm…. Let him also read from the Apocalypse of John about the city of God, the Heavenly Jerusalem, and about its foundations." He explains that therein the reader will find "symbols," which point the way "for those who will journey to the divine realm" and that, when these passages are properly apprehended, such pilgrims "will perceive truths of considerable profundity."[6] Elsewhere, Origen again touches upon the stones in Revelation, and provides further directions to the souls who journey to God, explaining that they may arrive at the heavenly city by acquiring the virtues that Origen believes the heavenly stones of Revelation represent, such as "faith, continence," and so forth.[7] In another work, Origen mystically instructs that spiritual sojourners must lament their "exile from Jerusalem" and only then may they, paradoxically, reach the Heavenly Jerusalem, becoming incorporated as "crystal" or a "sapphire" or "whatever other precious stones are mentioned, of the ones that constitute the Jerusalem in heaven."[8]

---

and Mark Sebanc, 3 vols. (Grand Rapids, MI: Eerdmans, 1998), 1:42–150; Schmidt, *The Book of Revelation and Its Eastern Commentators* [cf. initial note above], 32–35.

[5] On Origen not always adhering to three interpretive levels, see Henri de Lubac, *History and Spirit: The Understanding of Scripture According to Origen*, trans. Anne Englund Nash (San Francisco, CA: Ignatius Press, 2007), 159–71. An example of this is when Origen states that the historical meaning is sometimes not present in Scripture, see Origen, *First Principles* 4.2.5; 4.3.4. Interestingly, Augustine believed the opposite of Origen and thought that there always was a basic historical meaning, but not always a higher meaning, see Augustine, *City of God* (*De civitate Dei*) 16.2; 17.3.

[6] Origen, *Against Celsus* (*Contra Celsum*) 6.23. Translation from *Origen: Contra Celsum*, trans. Henry Chadwick (Cambridge: Cambridge University Press, 1965), 336.

[7] Origen, *Homilies on Ezekiel* (*Homiliae in Ezechielem*) 13.3.1–3, translation from *Origen: Homilies 1–14 on Ezekiel*, trans. Thomas P. Scheck, Ancient Christian Writers 62 (New York: Paulist, 2010), 163–164.

[8] Origen, *Homilies on the Psalms* (*Homiliae in Psalmos*), Psalm 67 Homily 2.2, translation from *Origen: Homilies on the Psalms: Codex Monacensis Graecus 314*, trans. Joseph W. Trigg, FC 141 (Washington, DC: Catholic University of America Press, 2020), 161.

2 The Inheritors of Origen and their Revelation Exegesis

Now, this idea of using allegory to interpret difficult scriptural passages would be of great use to many interpreters of Revelation, who deployed just such a hermeneutic not only to resolve the challenges presented by Revelation's heavenly stones, but also, as I will show in this contribution, to turn such stumbling stones into stepping stones leading towards a higher or deeper meaning.

Though no commentator directly references Origen's discussions of the Heavenly Jerusalem and its petrographic imagery, many do make great use of his three-tiered interpretive syllabus, especially Andrew of Caesarea (ca. AD 600). He, writing in Greek, explains in the prologue of his *Commentary on Revelation* that there are "three parts" of Scripture: the body, the soul, and the spirit, just as Origen maintained. For Andrew the first part of Scripture relates to history, the second to the intellect and figurative language, and the third to "future and higher things."[9] Andrew was in fact so taken with this method of understanding that he divided every section of his commentary into three chapters, each of which symbolized one of the three levels of scriptural understanding. Curiously, he does not treat each level explicitly within each subdivision; rather, he seems to want the overall structure of the commentary itself to signal a tripartite understanding of Revelation.

From Andrew, this method of segmenting Revelation was taken up by Arethas of Caesarea (ca. AD 930)[10] and also found its way into Armenian tradition via Nerses of Lambron (ca. AD 1179/80).[11] It further entered into Syriac, Slavonic, and Georgian Revelation manuscripts and commentaries, some of which speak explicitly of a trifold interpretation of Scripture in their prologues.[12] Much like

---

[9] Andrew, *Commentary on the Apocalypse* (*Commentarii in Apocalypsin*), prologue [8], translation from *Andrew of Caesarea: Commentary on the Apocalypse*, trans. Eugenia Scarvelis Constantinou, FC 123 (Washington, DC: Catholic University of America Press, 2011), 52. Greek text is from Josef Schmid, *Studien zur Geschichte des griechischen Apokalypse-Textes: Der Apokalypse-Kommentar des Andreas von Kaisareia*, vol. 1, Münchener theologische Studien 1: Historische Abteilung 1 (München: Zink, 1955). It is important to note that Andrew occasionally confuses his terminology and, like Origen, does not always follow his recommended framework for interpreting Revelation, see Juan Hernández Jr., "Andrew of Caesarea and His Reading of Revelation: Catechesis and Paranesis," in *Die Johannesapokalypse: Kontexte – Konzepte – Rezeption*, ed. Jörg Frey, James A. Kelhoffer, and Franz Tóth, WUNT 287 (Tübingen: Mohr Siebeck, 2012), 765 note 44.

[10] For an edition, see J.A. Cramer, *Catenae graecorum patrum in Novum Testamentum* (Oxford: Oxford University Press, 1844), vol. 8, 176–496.

[11] For a translation, see *Nerses of Lambron: Commentary on the Revelation of Saint John*, trans. Robert W. Thomson, Hebrew University Armenian Studies 9 (Leuven: Peeters, 2007).

[12] For further discussion of several of these commentators, see the appendix in Schmidt, *The Book of Revelation and Its Eastern Commentators* (cf. initial note). Note, that the Syriac source for Andrew's rubric comes from an anonymous Syriac commentator who divided his commentary into 72 chapters, exactly as Andrew did to symbolize Origen's threefold understanding of Scripture. The Syriac commentator, as far as I can tell, does not otherwise use Andrew's

Origen himself, these writers did not always follow their stipulated three step interpretive process, but, again like Origen, they eagerly embraced an allegorical hermeneutic as a means to explaining apparent contradictions and inconsistencies in Revelation. And while other exegetes – such as Oecumenius (ca. AD 550), Dionysius bar Ṣalibi (ca. AD 1171), Būlus al-Būshī (c. AD 1250), and Ibn Kātib Qayṣar (c. AD 1266/7) – do not adapt their commentary to suit Origen's interpretive structure, they still inherited a similar emphasis of solving scriptural conundrums through allegorical analysis so as to spur the reader on towards more profound understanding. And this is especially on display when these exegetes deal with the Heavenly Jersalem.

3 Allegory and the Heavenly City

Consequently, Oecumenius, a sixth century Greek writer, states plainly "there should not be anything deficient in Revelation,"[13] yet he finds that he must defend the text when encountering the stones incorporated into the heavenly city in Rev 21–22. He writes, "But if anyone would wish to quibble about the stones – for one may argue about such a vision – let us be content to say a little more."[14] He then justifies inclusion of the stones in heaven by noting that Moses instructed high priests to wear all sorts of decorative paraphernalia inlaid with stones – a robe, ephod, turban, sash, and even a breastplate – and that this was done because these "communicated in mystical symbolism awe and dread."[15] He goes on to argue that when Revelation speaks about the Heavenly Jerusalem it means to depict "the blessedness of the saints, and their life which will be in God and with God, as is meant by describing it in material and grandiose terms, so leading our mind to consider its spiritual glory and brightness in this present setting."[16]

In similar manner, Dionysius bar Ṣalibi, a twelfth century Syriac polymath and biblical commentator, interprets the twelve stones in Revelation as spiritually representing the twelve tribes of Israel, and the twelve foundations as the twelve apostles. Together, these make up a spiritual body of worshipers, who were foreshadowed by Moses through various "types" (ܛܘܦܣܐ)[17] – doubtlessly referring

---

material. For the Syriac commentator and his commentary, see Stan Larson, "The Earliest Syriac Commentary on the Apocalypse: Transcription, Translation and Importance of Brit. Lib. Ms. Add. 17,127" (PhD diss., University of Birmingham, 1984).

[13] Oecumenius, *Commentary on the Apocalypse* (*Commentarius in Apocalypsin*) 5.1.1 (translation from *Oecumenius: Commentary on the Apocalypse*, trans. John N. Suggit, FC 112 (Washington, DC: Catholic University of America Press, 2006), 79.

[14] Oecumenius, *Comm. Apoc.* 12.3.10 (trans. Suggit, 191).

[15] Oecumenius, *Comm. Apoc.* 12.3.10 (trans. Suggit, 191).

[16] Oecumenius, *Comm. Apoc.* 11.16.3 (trans. Suggit, 186).

[17] Dionysius bar Ṣalibi, *Commentary on the Apocalypse* (*In Apocalypsim*) 28 lines 22–26 (my translation from Jaroslav Sedláček, ed., *Dionysius bar Ṣalibi: In Apocalypsim, Actus et Epistulas*

to the priestly garb mentioned above. Bar Ṣalibi further clarifies that these are all symbols of what today is partially fulfilled in the church, adding that after the final judgment all will be "much more sublime than that which is administered here!"[18]

Oecumenius and bar Ṣalibi thus suggest that Revelation deploys the physicality of the heavenly stones in order to exercise the mind in contemplating future spiritual glory, and that this is the same reason why the vestments of the Jewish high priest were decorated with similar stones – a line of reasoning that quite agrees with Origen's hermeneutic of interpreting potential difficulties as a means of spurring on more profound understanding. Here though, both commentators do not seem to have grasped the deeper criticism of the stones: it is one thing for an earthly priest to wear earthly stones, it is quite another for a heavenly chamber or city to have them. Or, more to the point, should not a symbolic depiction of a heavenly city have worthier symbols than those used to decorate an earthly priest? And, in any case, are we to imagine that the heavenly city will actually possess such physical stones?

4 The Heavenly City and Physical Stones

Nerses of Lambron (ca. AD 1179/80), a twelfth century Armenian writer, realized the root of concern. He states forthrightly that the heavenly stones do not represent "tangible substances in heaven"[19] and offers the following comfort to distressed readers: "If the narration of this book includes corporeal apparitions, forms of beasts, and varieties of colors of precious stones, let it not astonish the hearers. For we find this also done by the prophets in many places."[20] He then goes on to cite the heavenly visions of Isaiah, Ezekiel, and Zechariah, which also describe the heavens with bodily terminology. From these he argues that, because such descriptions in the Old Testament "seem not at all unbelievable to us,"[21] we ought not to be troubled when Revelation contains the same. This is particularly so, he reasons, given that God often reveals mysteries with "bodily form."[22] He justifies this spiritual interpretation of physical objects by asserting that the "hues and colors" attributed to the stones in Revelation indicate that the prophet John

---

Catholicas, CSCO/Scriptores Syri, 53/18 (Syriac), 60/20 (Latin) (Paris: Typographeo Reipublicae, 1909), vol. 18 p. 28.

[18] Dionysius bar Ṣalibi, *Commentary on the Apocalypse* 29 lines 10–11 (my translation from Sedláček, 29).

[19] Nerses, *Commentary on the Apocalypse*, prologue [15] (trans. Thomson, 41).

[20] Nerses, *Commentary,* prologue [14] (trans. Thomson, 40).

[21] Nerses, *Commentary,* prologue [15] (trans. Thomson, 40).

[22] Nerses, *Commentary,* prologue [15] (trans. Thomson, 40).

is speaking of incorporeal things.²³ Nerses's logic is not entirely clear, but he seems to believe that colors cannot physically exist by themselves and so discussions of them must therefore indicate incorporeal things. Either way, though, Nerses concludes that with Revelation "tangible things are all images of the spiritual,"²⁴ thus maintaining the allegorical hermeneutic of Origen that he had embraced in the beginning of this commentary.²⁵

When Ibn Kātib Qayṣar, a thirteenth century Coptic Arabic writer, is confronted with the stones in Rev 4 he also notices a similar "problem" (مسألة) and asks, "what is the benefit (فائدة) of this vision?"²⁶ Ibn Kātib Qayṣar answers that the vision is actually of great benefit since through it "one apprehends the value of divine understanding (الإدراك الإلهي),"²⁷ an "understanding" that Ibn Kātib Qayṣar explains refers to "freedom from the attachment of material objects."²⁸ He then finds three meanings in support of his contention, each in turn communicated by the light, color, and genus of the stones. The first two properties of light and color are not actually stated in the text of Revelation, but he argues for his interpretation by saying that the light "is deduced from the color and the color is deduced from the gem (جَوْهَر)."²⁹ Thus, for Ibn Kātib Qayṣar, from the genus of the stone one can deduce its color, and from its color one can then deduce its light spectrum.

Ibn Kātib Qayṣar goes on to claim that even the genus of the gem "is outside of the literal meaning," and that it therefore "symbolizes the highest and holiest divine things that pertain to understanding."³⁰ The other two properties – light and color – being derived from the genus of the stone, symbolize how one obtains divine understanding wherein, as he says, "the soul is guided by light through the apprehension of the eyes, because first they look and then they understand as the stream of light flows into the vision."³¹ Ibn Kātib Qayṣar here remarkably deploys his time's most up-to-date scientific theory concerning the nature of vision. This theory posited that vision was made possible through the refractive properties of light, which brings visual information into the eyes, an idea championed by Ibn

---

²³ Nerses, *Commentary*, prologue [15] (trans. Thomson, 41).
²⁴ Nerses, *Commentary*, prologue [15] (trans. Thomson, 41).
²⁵ Nerses, *Commentary*, prologue [13]. Nerses, in his prologue, only loosely alludes to a three-step interpretive lens, which appears to relate first to physical vision, then intellectual thought, and finally spiritual understanding. He does however maintain the same Origenian method of segmenting Revelation that Andrew of Caesarea used.
²⁶ Ibn Kātib Qayṣar, *Commentary on the Apocalypse* (19 تفسير سفر الرؤيا). My translation from ed. al-Qummuṣ Armāniyūs Ḥabashī Shattā al-Birmāwī, ed., *Tafsīr Sifr al-Ru'yā li-l-Qiddīs Yūḥannā al-Lahūtī li-Ibn Kātib Qayṣar* (Cairo: Maktabat al-Maḥabbah, 1939), 102).
²⁷ Ibn Kātib Qayṣar, *Commentary* 19 (al-Birmāwī, 102).
²⁸ Ibn Kātib Qayṣar, *Commentary* 19 (al-Birmāwī, 102).
²⁹ Ibn Kātib Qayṣar, *Commentary* 19 (al-Birmāwī, 103).
³⁰ Ibn Kātib Qayṣar, *Commentary* 19 (al-Birmāwī, 103).
³¹ Ibn Kātib Qayṣar, *Commentary* 19 (al-Birmāwī, 103).

al-Haytham (Alhazen or Alhacen), one of the founders of optical studies.[32] But, more importantly, for Ibn Kātib Qayṣar, this guiding light corresponds with the light and color of Revelation's gems, which serve as symbolic thoroughfares to the divine understanding represented by the gem itself. Notably, such a suggestion once again, perhaps unbeknownst to Ibn Kātib Qayṣar, mirrors Origen's interpretive emphasis of turning difficulties into a means of sublime understanding, and all via allegorical analysis.

5 The Passing Away of the Heavens and the Earth

Other interpreters found the materiality of the Heavenly Jerusalem troubling for different reasons. Andrew of Caesarea, for example, first prefaces his remarks by saying that when Revelation speaks of a "new heavens and a new earth, for the old heaven and the old earth had passed away," such "does not mean," in his words, the "non-existence of creation but a renewal for the better."[33] Andrew is here worried that someone might interpret Revelation as claiming that heaven and earth will be annihilated and replaced, so he consequently asserts that in actuality heaven and earth will be renewed. For Andrew then, this apparently rejuvenated physical earth would be the landing point for the Heavenly Jerusalem, which as Andrew puts it, descends from the "bodiless powers above onto human beings."[34] However, despite being generated from or at least descending from bodiless powers, Andrew insists that this heavenly city is not just symbolic, but actually exists and was witnessed by Moses. He writes, "From heaven the saint is taught that this tabernacle is real, of which the type was shown to Moses."[35]

Andrew does not explicitly address whether the New Jerusalem would exist physically. On the one hand he believes that the city descends from "bodiless powers," but on the other he seems to have believed that a type of the same city was physically seen by Moses on earth in order to provide the pattern upon which Moses designed the first tabernacle. And, in addition to this, Andrew also believes that the New Jerusalem would exist in a kind of renewed physical earth. Andrew therefore does not seem to have felt the same qualms over the physicality of the New Jerusalem as other exegetes did, but even so, he still does encounter some problems with the stones and precious metals that make up the heavenly city.

---

[32] A. Mark Smith, "What Is the History of Medieval Optics Really About?" *Proceedings of the American Philosophical Society* 148, no. 2 (2004): 180–94 at 181–82.

[33] Andrew, *Comm. Apoc.* 22.65 [232] (trans. Constantinou, 219).

[34] Andrew, *Comm. Apoc.* 22.65 [233] (trans. Constantinou, 220).

[35] Andrew, *Comm. Apoc.* 22.65 [234] (trans. Constantinou, 220).

6 The Unity of the Heavenly Foundations and the Apostolic Band

One of these issues concerns the twelve precious stones that are associated with the heavenly city's twelve foundations. With these Andrew carefully addresses each stone in turn and attributes each one to an apostle, giving reasons for each assignment. But, afterwards, he worries that his readers will think that individually allotting the twelve stones to the twelve apostles needlessly separates the unity of the apostolic band. That is, by segregating and segmenting out the apostles by stones, one might be led to believe that the apostles were not part of a single unified foundation. Andrew answers the criticism in this way:

Therefore, I pray, please dismiss the complaint about the comparison of these <stones and> thoughts arrayed here as <being> forced. For by the distinctiveness of the virtue of each one of the apostles we did not separate <them> in their communion and solidarity, but through greater distinction of the individuality we were eager to point out their complete identity of content, closely connected to one another like a chain.[36]

In other words, Andrew claims that the twelve separate stones do not mean that the apostles are disassociated from one another and lack spiritual unity, but rather that they are connected to one another like links in a chain.

7 The Impossibilities of the Heavenly Stones

Andrew also notices an apparent contradiction in Rev 21:11, which describes jasper, an opaque stone, as being somehow also transparent. This is a clear impossibility, but Andrew explains that each property of the stone, its opaqueness and its – for lack of a better word – "jasperness," has meaningful symbolic value. The stone's quality as being jasper thus represents the everlasting life given by Christ and its transparency represents the radiance of Christ. And, regarding the impossibility of jasper being transparent, Andrew argues that "it is not possible for one type of example to illustrate [Christ's] various kindnesses to us."[37] The reason here seeming to be that since no single stone can fully symbolize the kindnesses of Christ, so Revelation has combined two contradictory characteristics, in this case "jasperness" and transparency, in an attempt to encompass the sublime profundity that the prophet John beheld.

Andrew elaborates on this reasoning in another related passage on Rev 21:21, where the gold of the heavenly city is also described as being transparent. Here he says, "for us it is impossible for both [descriptions] to concur in one [image]. The saint saw all these things as he was able. Perfect comprehension of the heavenly

---

[36] Andrew, *Comm. Apoc.* 23.67 [247] (trans. modified from Constantinou, 230).
[37] Andrew, *Comm. Apoc.* 23.67 [239] (trans. modified from Constantinou, 224).

city surpasses hearing and sight and thought."³⁸ To put it another way, Andrew reasons that humans are incapable of completely understanding the heavenly city and so John simply describes things as far as he was able to do so. In this regard, Andrew takes up Origen's advice to "blame yourself" when Scripture appears contradictory, only in this instance Andrew blames the human nature that we all share with the prophet John.

Būlus al-Būshī, a thirteenth century Coptic-Arabic commentator, gives a similar answer. He notes that the prophet John "spoke about the glory of the city of God [and] how its radiance is like the radiance of a precious stone and like the pure luster of solid gold."³⁹ But, he cautions, "Verily, the glory of the kingdom of heaven is even greater than this. For the Evangelist found no stone on earth more noble than precious stones or gold with which to compare it."⁴⁰ So, for Būlus al-Būshī, the apparent tension of how something can have both the radiance of a precious stone and the luster of solid gold is blamed on the fact that John could not find any substance on earth completely identical to that which he saw in the heavenly city, so John did the best he could – a line of reasoning quite similar to Andrew's aforementioned solution to the same problem.

8 Why Is God Compared to Less-Precious Stones?

Be that as it may though, a problem with the New Jerusalem still presented itself to perceptive readers, one which Oecumenius well articulates: "Perhaps a reader may be troubled by something here: Why is it that while the holy ranks of the incorporeal beings around God are compared to the more precious stone of the emerald, God himself is compared to the less precious, jasper and carnelian?"⁴¹ Oecumenius's answer anticipates the paths that Nerses and Ibn Kātib Qayṣar traversed above. The importance is not the value or the type of stone, but "the meaning of the colors,"⁴² and in any case, Oecumenius points out, God is often compared to less precious stones elsewhere in Scripture, so one should not take offense when Revelation does the same.⁴³ Regarding jasper, Oecumenius observes that it is green and therefore "signifies God's ability to give life and provide for our needs," since everything ultimately is nourished from "green plants."⁴⁴

---

³⁸ Andrew, *Comm. Apoc.* 23.67 [248] (trans. Constantinou, 231).
³⁹ Būlus al-Būshī, *Commentary on the Apocalypse* (تفسير سفر الرؤيا) 29 (translation modified from Shawqi Talia, "Būlus Al-Būshī's Arabic Commentary on the Apocalypse of St. John: An English Translation and a Commentary" [PhD diss., Catholic University of America, 1987], 253).
⁴⁰ Būlus al-Būshī, *Commentary* 29 (trans. Talia, 253).
⁴¹ Oecumenius, *Comm. Apoc.* 3.5.11 (trans. Suggit, 55).
⁴² Oecumenius, *Comm. Apoc.* 3.5.11 (trans. Suggit, 55).
⁴³ Oecumenius, *Comm. Apoc.* 3.5.12 (trans. Suggit, 55).
⁴⁴ Oecumenius, *Comm. Apoc.* 3.5.5 (trans. Suggit, 53).

Carnelian is blood red and hence for him symbolizes the awful power of God, much like a terrible fire.[45] For Oecumenius then, like several of our other commentators, it is the color of the stones that matters and especially the allegorical meanings of the colors, not the actual stones themselves.

Conclusion

Thus, in these struggles over the existence and purpose of Revelation's heavenly stones, commentators resorted to allegorical solutions often patterned on Origen of Alexandria's hermeneutical rubric laid out centuries earlier. Still though, commentators provide different explanations for the stones, even if they follow somewhat similar Origenian pathways. Nerses and Ibn Kātib Qayṣar adhere to a fully symbolic interpretation, in that they believe that the stones are not representative of any kind of tangible reality in heaven at all, but rather are allegories pointing towards deeper, more mystical meanings. Oecumenius, Dionysius bar Ṣalibi, and Būlus al-Būshī are less specific. They believe that the stones are symbolic insofar as they point towards a deeper spiritual reality, but they do not enlighten us as to whether such stones will actually exist in heaven, albeit perhaps in an immaterial way. Andrew, though, seems to be the most concrete. He appears to think that the New Jerusalem will be an actual city that will dwell on earth, though even he still attributes symbolic meaning to the stones in the heavenly city. In all cases though, the lens of allegorical analysis rendered the heavenly stones not as "fair stones of stumbling" and "rocks of offense," but rather as stepping stones towards sublime and profound understanding, or even lodestones guiding the holder to hidden and mystical illumination – exactly as Origen would have wanted them to become.

---

[45] Oecumenius, *Comm. Apoc.* 3.5.6 (trans. Suggit, 53–54).

The Walls of the New Jerusalem

Jewish Context and Patristic Reception

Mateusz Kusio

Introduction

An outer wall is one of the constitutive elements of an ancient city, performing a number of functions, ranging from the practical, i.e. military and protective, to the ideological, serving as a boundary separating the urban center from the countryside and as a symbol of status. Whilst it is true that both nonwalled cities and fortified nonurban settlements are attested across the ancient Near East and the Mediterranean basin, the link between walls and city status is notable across all those contexts.[1] Euripides (*Cycl.* 115–118) treats the presence of walls and fences as a distinctive marker of human habitation as opposed to wilderness.[2] Vitruvius (*Arch.* 1.5.1–8) sees the construction of city walls as one of the first tasks of urban planning and elaborates on it immediately after dealing with how to find a suitable location for a city.[3]

---

[1] The literature on city walls and fortifications in antiquity is unsurprisingly vast. Aside from excavation reports, several studies about the social and cultural role of walls and gates are noteworthy. On ancient Mesopotamia see Marc Van De Mieroop, *The Ancient Mesopotamian City* (Oxford: Clarendon 1997), 73–76; Frances Pinnock, "'Go. Pace Out the Walls of Uruk'. Ideology and Reality of City Walls in Pre-Classical Mesopotamia," *Scienze dell'antichità* 19, no. 2/3 (2013): 157–67; Natalie N. May, "Gates and Their Functions in Mesopotamia and Ancient Israel" in *Fabric of Cities. Aspects of Urbanism, Urban Topography and Society in Mesopotamia, Greece and Rome*, ed. Natalie N. May and U. Steinert (Leiden: Brill, 2014), 77–121. On Roman walls see Edmund Thomas, *Monumentality and the Roman Empire: Architecture in the Antonine Age* (New York: Oxford University Press, 2007), 108–13; Isobel Pinder, "Augustan City Walls in Roman Italy: Their Character and Meaning" (PhD diss., University of Southampton, 2015). On ancient Palestine see Frank S. Frick, *The City in Ancient Israel*, Society of Biblical Literature Dissertation Series 36 (Missoula: Scholars Press, 1977), 10, 81–84. On the walls of Jerusalem itself in antiquity and the Middle Ages see G. J. Wightman, *The Walls of Jerusalem: From the Canaanites to the Mamluks* (Sydney: Meditarch, 1993).

[2] Euripides, *Cyclops,* David Kovacs, trans., LCL 12 (Cambridge: Harvard University Press, 1994), 70–73.

[3] Vitruvius, *On Architecture, Volume I: Books 1–5*, Frank Granger, trans., LCL 251 (Cambridge: Harvard University Press, 1931), 46–53.

The importance of walls manifests itself in the ancient conceptualizations of ideal cities. In Aristophanes's *Birds* the building of Nephelococcygia begins with constructing a wall in the sky, made of bricks and similar to that of Babylon (550–551).[4] When it is completed, it is wide enough to possibly fit two chariots going in opposite directions, and its height is one hundred stadia (ca. 18 km; 1125–1131). The city does not have any other typical features, such as living quarters or an agora, apart from its fortifications. Their presence is enough for Aristophanes to signal the urban status of Nephelococcygia.[5] On the other hand, Plato (*Leg.* 6.778d–779a) advises against city walls when discussing his vision of an ideal city-state, as they would lure its inhabitants into a false sense of security.[6] Even though rejected, such fortifications function for Plato as a standard, even default aspect of a human settlement which can be discarded only for good reason. (His reasoning is later rebuffed by Aristotle, *Pol.* 7.11, 1330b33–1331a19.[7])

The urbanistic practice of fortifying cities had so strong a grip on ancient imagination that even an idealized city in a world of eschatological peace – which the New Jerusalem was certainly expected to be – was depicted as walled. In none of the surviving texts dealing with that eschatological idea are the walls actively constructed, nor are they used for defense. The exterior of the New Jerusalem is static in nature, intended to be gazed upon and marveled at. This raises a practical question: How did Jewish and early Christian writers and readers understand the function of the walls and, more broadly, of the external appearance of the New Jerusalem? Since it serves no easily discernible practical purpose, why did these authors go to such lengths to describe how it will look like from the outside and what size it will be?

Under the general caption of walls, this paper will discuss the following architectural features of the city: their spatial dimensions, gates (especially their names and positioning), and foundations. All these elements emerge in the sources to be scrutinized.

The first two sections of this paper will be devoted to the most important early Jewish representatives of the New Jerusalem tradition, namely Ezek 48:30–35 and the Aramaic *New Jerusalem Text* from Qumran. The focus will then move to Rev 21 (section 3). The subsequent sections of the contribution will be devoted to the patristic reception of that passage in the exegetical writings

---

[4] Aristophanes. *Birds*, Jeffrey Henderson, trans., LCL 179 (Cambridge: Harvard University Press, 2000), 94–95.

[5] See Jennifer Clarke Kosak, "The Wall in Aristophanes' *Birds*" in *City, Countryside, and the Spatial Organization of Value in Classical Antiquity*, ed. Ralph M. Rosen and Ineke Sluiter (Leiden: Brill, 2006), 173–80.

[6] Plato, *Laws, Volume I: Books 1–6*, R.G. Bury, trans., LCL 187 (Cambridge: Harvard University Press, 1926), 478–81.

[7] Aristotle, *Politics*, H. Rackham, trans., LCL 264 (Cambridge: Harvard University Press, 1932), 588–91.

of Victorinus of Poetovium (with Jerome's recension), Tyconius, Caesarius of Arles, Apringius of Beja, Primasius of Hadrumetum, Oecumenius, Andrew of Caesarea, and finally Bede the Venerable.[8] This assemblage of sources might appear ill-conceived, as the Christian interpreters are interested in the Johannine vision, with little engagement with Ezekiel and, obviously, no knowledge of the Qumran literature. As will become clear, however, they all exhibit significant continuity in how they imagine the walls of the eschatological settlement, while their differences in that regard are telling. The conclusion will show that the walls served primarily ideological functions, such as displaying the character of the eschatological community, as well as acting as a canvass for the authors' christological and ecclesiological ideas.

1 Ezekiel 48:30–35

The prophetic writings of the Hebrew Bible speak about an eschatological city several times. The future Jerusalem is depicted as glorious, resplendent, and secure in Isa 54:11–14; importantly for the present purpose, v. 12 describes its wall: "And I will make your pinnacles of rubies, your gates from crystals and your walls from precious stones."[9] Later, in ch. 60, Isaiah sees the radiant Jerusalem (60:5a) as receiving homage and gifts from the Gentiles who construct its walls and continually enter through its ever open gates (vv. 10–11). The walls of the New Jerusalem are also mentioned in Zech 2:1–5 where, interestingly, the city will be like *pĕrāzôt*, "unwalled hamlets"[10] and the Lord himself will be "a wall of fire around it and glory ... within it"[11] (Zech 2:9 MT; 2:5 in the English translations). Both Deutero-Isaiah and Proto-Zechariah, to which the quoted passages belong, come from the late exilic and early postexilic periods, respectively, dating from the second half of the sixth century BC.

While these passages are certainly noteworthy and will be referred to later, pride of place as the starting point of a sustained speculation about the New Jerusalem belongs to Ezek 48:30–35. The passage and the book as a whole are older than any of the passages mentioned above, stemming most likely from the exilic Babylonian context in the first half of the sixth century BC. Given this

---

[8] The scope of the contribution is limited to the ancient commentaries on Revelation and will not include other early Christian authors of apocalyptic or millenarian persuasion who, though interested in New Jerusalem as a concept, rarely expound its outer architectural features.

[9] וְשַׂמְתִּי כַּדְכֹד שִׁמְשֹׁתַיִךְ וּשְׁעָרַיִךְ לְאַבְנֵי אֶקְדָּח וְכָל־גְּבוּלֵךְ לְאַבְנֵי־חֵפֶץ. All quotations from the Hebrew Bible are according to Karl Elliger and Wilhelm Rudolph, ed., *Biblia Hebraica Stuttgartensia*, 5th ed. (Stuttgart: Deutsche Bibelgesellschaft, 1997). Translations of all ancient texts in this contribution are by the author.

[10] See Frick, *City* (cf. note 1), 93 on this term.

[11] חוֹמַת אֵשׁ סָבִיב וּלְכָבוֹד ... בְּתוֹכָהּ

dating, Ezekiel's prophecy, as well as those of Deutero-Isaiah and Zechariah, arises within a cultural group that has already had a chance to witness Mesopotamian urban architecture.

Ezekiel 48:30–35 concludes a lengthy legal stipulation for the eschatological temple and the tribal division of the land (Ezek 40–48)[12] and serves as the ending of the entire book. The city will be located within the *tĕrûmâ*, the portion set apart for the priests, the Levites, and the Prince (48:9–22).[13] Verse 16 identifies the city as a square with each side measuring 4,500 cubits (around 2.3 km),[14] making it around three times larger in circumference than the walls of Jerusalem in the late Judahite period.[15] The description of the city is not provided immediately but is rather appended at the end of the section about the division of the land, in vv. 30–35:

[30]And these are the city entrances which are on the north side [which is] 4,500 [cubits in] measure. [31]The city gates with the names of the tribes of Israel – three northern gates, one gate of Reuben, one gate of Judah, one gate of Levi. [32]And to the eastern side, [which is] 4,500 [cubits long], three gates – one gate of Joseph, one gate of Benjamin, one gate of Dan. [33]And to the southern side, [which is] 4,500 [cubits in] measure, three gates – one gate of Simeon, one gate of Issachar, one gate of Zebulon. [34]To the western side, [which is] 4,500 [cubits long], their three gates – one gate of Gad, one gate of Asher, one gate of Naphtali. [35]The circumference [of the city will be] 18,000 [cubits], and the name of the city [will be] from [that] day "The Lord is there."[16]

Ezekiel's eschatological city differs markedly from that mentioned by Isaiah or Zechariah, and, for that matter, from that familiar to most of the prophet's later

---

[12] On the theology of the entire section see the classic Jon Douglas Levenson, *Theology of the Program of Restoration of Ezekiel 40–48*, Harvard Semitic Monographs 10 (Missoula: Scholars Press, 1976), as well as the more recent Michael Konkel, "The System of Holiness in Ezekiel's Vision of the New Temple (Ezek 40–48)," in *Purity and the Forming of Religious Traditions in the Ancient Mediterranean World and Ancient Judaism*, ed. Christian Frevel and Christophe Niham (Leiden, Boston: Brill, 2013), 429–455; Wojciech Pikor, *The Land of Israel in the Book of Ezekiel*, The Library of Hebrew Bible/Old Testament Studies 667 (Edinburgh: T&T Clark, 2018), 168–225.

[13] On the variegated use of this term in Ezek 40–48 see Soo J. Kim, "*YHWH Shammah*: The City as Gateway to the Presence of YHWH," *Journal for the Study of the Old Testament* 39, no. 2 (2014): 187–207.

[14] Ezekiel most likely refers to the long cubit (= 518 mm) which he specifies as his preferred measurement in 40:5; 43:13.

[15] Measurement based on Wightman, *Walls of Jerusalem* (cf. note 1), 47. Interestingly, Jer 31:38–40 also envisages a change in the boundaries of Jerusalem but since his topography is ambiguous, the dimensions of the walls are difficult to specify.

[16] וְאֵ֣לֶּה תּוֹצְא֣וֹת הָעִ֗יר מִפְּאַ֥ת צָפ֛וֹן חֲמֵ֥שׁ מֵא֖וֹת וְאַרְבַּ֣עַת אֲלָפִ֣ים מִדָּ֑ה: וְשַׁעֲרֵ֣י הָעִ֗יר עַל־שְׁמוֹת֙ שִׁבְטֵ֣י יִשְׂרָאֵ֔ל שְׁעָרִ֥ים שְׁלוֹשָׁ֖ה צָפ֑וֹנָה שַׁ֣עַר רְאוּבֵ֞ן אֶחָ֗ד שַׁ֤עַר יְהוּדָה֙ אֶחָ֔ד שַׁ֥עַר לֵוִ֖י אֶחָֽד: וְאֶל־פְּאַ֣ת קָדִ֗ימָה חֲמֵ֣שׁ מֵאוֹת֮ וְאַרְבַּ֣עַת אֲלָפִים֒ וּשְׁעָרִ֖ים שְׁלֹשָׁ֑ה וְשַׁ֨עַר יוֹסֵ֜ף אֶחָ֗ד שַׁ֤עַר בִּנְיָמִן֙ אֶחָ֔ד שַׁ֥עַר דָּ֖ן אֶחָֽד: וּפְאַת־נֶ֗גְבָּה חֲמֵ֥שׁ מֵא֛וֹת וְאַרְבַּ֥עַת אֲלָפִ֖ים מִדָּ֑ה וּשְׁעָרִ֣ים שְׁלֹשָׁ֑ה שַׁ֣עַר שִׁמְע֞וֹן אֶחָ֗ד שַׁ֤עַר יִשָּׂשכָר֙ אֶחָ֔ד שַׁ֥עַר זְבוּלֻ֖ן אֶחָֽד: פְּאַת־יָ֗מָּה חֲמֵ֤שׁ מֵאוֹת֙ וְאַרְבַּ֣עַת אֲלָפִ֔ים שַׁעֲרֵיהֶ֖ם שְׁלֹשָׁ֑ה שַׁ֣עַר גָּ֗ד אֶחָ֗ד שַׁ֤עַר אָשֵׁר֙ אֶחָ֔ד שַׁ֥עַר נַפְתָּלִ֖י אֶחָֽד: סָבִ֕יב שְׁמֹנָ֥ה עָשָׂ֖ר אָ֑לֶף וְשֵׁם־הָעִ֥יר מִיּ֖וֹם יְהוָ֥ה שָֽׁמָּה.

readers. It is not identified with Jerusalem, although its name, *YHWH šāmmâ*, is possibly meant to function as a pun. This move is in line with Ezekiel's overall ideology of a complete renewal of the temple and the land. As opposed to the historical Jerusalem, the Ezekielic city is separated from the new temple and most likely functions as a station for pilgrims. Its very name points to God's presence outside of its own boundaries.[17] Furthermore, Ezek 48:30–35 specifies only one detail about the city walls themselves, namely their length, leaving the material they are built from and their other physical aspects undiscussed. This silence stands in marked contrast to later descriptions of the eschatological Jerusalem in which its outward appearance is of prime importance.

The main concern of the passage lies in the sequence of the city gates each of which receives a tribal/patriarchal name. The ordering is different to the list of the tribal territories earlier in the chapter and has its own internal logic. Jacob's children from Leah occupy the northern and southern walls. The northern entrances, which face the temple, belong to Reuben, the tribe of Jacob's firstborn, Judah, the Davidic tribe, and Levi, the tribe tasked with caring for the temple. This grouping possibly reflects the prominence these tribes receive in the design of the wilderness camp in Num 2–3 where the Levites surround the tabernacle, the three tribes under the banner of Judah are facing it and those under Reuben are positioned on its right.[18] The children born of Jacob's servants occupy the western wall of the city, except for Bilhah's son, Dan, whose gate is to the east, south of the gates of Joseph and Benjamin, the children of Rachel. This positioning might be purely due to the writer's need to somehow ascribe the names to the gates and hence without any deeper significance. It is, nevertheless, interesting that it is Dan – whose tribal portion is the northernmost and who, as will be discussed later, is excluded from the Christian visions of New Jerusalem – who shares a wall with Joseph and Benjamin.

Ezekiel's vision of the future city and its walls, while providing a starting point for a robust exegetical tradition to be discussed in the next sections, is in itself restrained, even timid. The settlement is only eighteen kilometers in circumference and its walls are made of a nondescript material. The prophet's attention is centered completely on the new temple for which the city serves as a gateway. Through its entrances, *YHWH šāmmâ* calls out to all Israelite tribes, now resettled in the land, by name.

---

[17] Kim, "*YHWH Shammah*" (cf. note 13), 199–207; Stephen L. Cook, *Ezekiel 38–48: A New Translation with Introduction and Commentary*, Anchor Bible 22B (New Haven: Yale University Press, 2018), 296–97.

[18] Émile Puech, "The Names of the Gates of the *New Jerusalem* (4Q554)," in *Emanuel: Studies in Hebrew Bible, Septuagint, and Dead Sea Scrolls in Honor of Emanuel Tov*, ed. Shalom M. Paul, Robert A. Kraft, Lawrence H. Schiffman, and Weston W. Fields, Vetus Testamentum Supplements 94 (Leiden: Brill, 2003), 1.379–92 at 386; Cook, *Ezekiel 38–48* (cf. note 17), 295.

2 The *New Jerusalem Text* from Qumran

While images of the restored Jerusalem and the temple are popular in Second Temple Jewish literature, only one text provides an architectural description of sufficient scope and detail to merit comparison with Ezek 48, Rev 21 and their later reception.[19] An Aramaic text from Qumran, of which seven fragmentary copies across five caves (1Q32, 2Q24, 4Q554, 4Q554ª, 4Q555, 5Q15, 11Q18, all produced in the Herodian period, between ca. 40 BC and AD 40) were found, contains a detailed description of the eschatological temple and city.[20] The structures are presented during a visionary apocalyptic tour that leads inside the settlement and into the temple.[21] For the sake of simplicity, the text preserved in the aforementioned scrolls will be here referred to as the *New Jerusalem Text* (abbreviated as *NJT*). One should be mindful, however, that it is an etic designation, as the preserved copies are untitled. Very importantly, the depicted city is nowhere in the scroll identified as Jerusalem. This silence possibly reflects the overall skepticism of the Qumran community toward the historical Jerusalem of its day. The text is now commonly understood to be a nonsectarian composition dating from the first quarter of the second century BC.[22] The relationship between the *NJT* and

---

[19] On the idea of the eschatological city in Second Temple literature see Peter Söllner, *Jerusalem, die hochgebaute Stadt. Eschatologisches und Himmlisches Jerusalem im Frühjudentum und im frühen Christentum* (Tübingen: Francke, 1998); Pilchan Lee, *The New Jerusalem in the Book of Revelation*, WUNT² 129 (Tübingen: Mohr Siebeck, 2001), 53–238.

[20] On the publication history of the fragments see Lorenzo DiTommaso, *The Dead Sea New Jerusalem Text*, Texts and Studies in Ancient Judaism 110 (Tübingen: Mohr Siebeck, 2005), 1–7.

[21] This direction of travel is assumed in the reconstructions of DiTommaso, New Jerusalem Text (cf. note 20), 89–95, and Hugo Antonissen, "The Visionary Architecture of the New Jerusalem in Qumran," in *Qumran und Archäologie*, ed. Jörg Frey, Carsten Claußen, and Nadine Kessler, WUNT 278 (Tübingen: Mohr Siebeck, 2011), 439–80 at 440–43. Michael Chyutin, *The New Jerusalem Scroll from Qumran: A Comprehensive Reconstruction* translated by Richard Fiantz, Journal for the Study of Pseudepigrapha Supplement Series 25 (Sheffield: Sheffield Academic Press, 1997), 15–32 construes the tour as beginning with the vision of the operation of the temple and then moving outwards but is rightly criticized by DiTommaso, New Jerusalem Text, 98–100. The text, most likely due to its fragmentary preservation, does not identify the person of the seer; Eibert J.C. Tigchelaar, "The Imaginal Context and the Visionary of the Aramaic *New Jerusalem*," in *Flores Florentino: Dead Sea Scrolls and Other Early Jewish Studies in Honour of Florentino García Martínez*, ed. Anthony T. Hilhorst, Émile Puech, and Eibert J.C. Tigchelaar, Supplements to the Journal for the Study of Judaism 122 (Leiden: Brill, 2007), 257–70 cogently proposes Jacob as the intended visionary. The resolution of this question does not have significant bearing on the present argument.

[22] Magen Broshi, "Visionary Architecture and Town Planning in the Dead Sea Scrolls," in *Time to Prepare the Way in the Wilderness: Papers on the Qumran Scrolls by Fellows of the Institute for Advanced Studies of The Hebrew University, Jerusalem, 1989–1990*, ed. Lawrence H. Schiffman and Devorah Dimant, Studies on the Texts of the Desert of Judah 16 (Leiden, New York, Köln: Brill, 1995), 9–22 at 22; Jörg Frey, "The New Jerusalem Text in Its Historical and Traditio-Historical Context," in *The Dead Sea Scrolls Fifty Years After Their Discovery: Proceedings of the Jerusalem Congress, July 20–25, 1997*, ed. Lawrence H. Schiffman, Emmanuel

the *Temple Scroll* (11QT, the longest preserved scroll from Qumran, which includes a description of the future temple and a legal code closely following, but not identical with the Pentateuch) has been a matter of contention, with most of recent treatments seeing the two as distinct and related only indirectly, if at all, despite some degree of formal resemblance.[23]

The blueprint of the city in the *NJT* is far more extensive and detailed than the one offered in Ezek 48 and it cannot be discussed here fully.[24] Its overall regularity and specific architectural features have alerted commentators to the influence of ancient urban designs on the *NJT*.[25] Consequently, the Qumran text ascribes particular importance to the city ramparts which are described in a passage surviving in 4Q554 1 I, 9–II, 10:

[I, I] [9] ... and he showed me sixteen curtains to the south [10] from the northern corner, and the twelve gates of its building and all of them correspond one [11] to another. And we went for a tour round the city to measure it from the eastern corner which is in the north [12] and from this corner he measured up to the gate which is in the north, stadia: thirty-five. And the name [13] of this gate is called the Gate of Simeon. And from this gate up to the central gate [14] he measured, stadia: thirty-five. And the name of this gate is called the Gate of [15] Levi. And from this gate he measured to the southern gate, stadia: thirty-five. [16] And the name of this gate is called the Gate of Judah. And from this gate he measured up to the eastern [17] corner which is to the south; stadia: thirty-five. And from ... this corner to the west [18] he measured up to the gate, stadia: 25. And the name of this gate is called the Gate

---

Tov, and James C. VanderKam (Jerusalem: Israel Exploration Society, 2000), 800–16 at 810–12; DiTommaso, New Jerusalem *Text* (cf. note 20), 191–94. The second quarter of that century is preferred by Émile Puech, "554–554a–555. 4QJérusalem Nouvelle[a–c] ar," in *Qumrân Grotte 4.XXVII: Textes araméens. Deuxième partie*, ed. Émile Puech, Discoveries in the Judean Desert 37 (Oxford: Clarendon, 2009), 91–102 at 100; Antonissen, "Visionary Architecture" (cf. note 21), 480; Antonissen, "The Banquet Culture in New Jerusalem, an Aramaic Text from Qumran" in *Vision, Narrative, and Wisdom in the Aramaic Texts from Qumran: Essays from the Copenhagen Symposium, 14–15 August, 2017*, ed. Mette Bundvad and Kasper Siegismund, Studies on the Texts of the Desert of Judah 131 (Leiden, Boston: Brill, 2019), 52–77 at 52.

[23] The relationship was first posited by Yigael Yadin, *Introduction*, vol. 1 of *The Temple Scroll* (Jerusalem: Israel Exploration Society, 1983), 71–73, and later accepted by, among others, Michael O. Wise, *A Critical Study of the Temple Scroll from Qumran Cave 11* (Chicago: The Oriental Institute, 1990), 64–86; Broshi, "Visionary Architecture" (cf. note 22), 10–13. Counter-arguments have been brought up by Frey, "New Jerusalem Text" (cf. note 22), 805–7; DiTommaso, New Jerusalem *Text* (cf. note 20), 151–59; Adela Yarbro Collins, "The Dream of a New Jerusalem at Qumran" in *The Scrolls and Christian Origins*, ed. James H. Charlesworth, *The Bible and the Dead Sea Scrolls*, vol. 3 (Waco: Baylor University Press, 2006), 231–54 at 237–48. On the presence of New Jerusalem in other scrolls see DiTommaso, New Jerusalem *Text*, 159–69.

[24] See Chyutin, *New Jerusalem Scroll* (cf. note 21), 70–106 and Antonissen, "Visionary Architecture" (cf. note 21) for detailed studies.

[25] The importance of the so-called Hippodamian regular street grid was first noticed by Jacob Licht, "An Ideal Town Plan from Qumran – The Description of the New Jerusalem," *Israel Exploration Journal* 29, no. 1 (1971): 45–59 at 48 and is regularly referenced by scholars. Cf. DiTommaso, New Jerusalem *Text* (cf. note 20), 102–09 who argues for a plurality of the conceptual antecedents to the urban design found in the text.

of Joseph.[19] And from this he measured up to the central gate, stadia: 25. And the name [20] of this gate is called the Gate of Benjamin and from this he measured up to the gate [21] in the west, stadia: 25. And the name of this gate is called the Gate of Reuben and from this gate [22] he measured up to the western corner, stadia: 25. And from this corner he measured up to [1, II] [1] the gate, stadia thirty-five. And the name of this gate is called the Gate [2] of Issachar. And from this gate he measured up to the central gate, stadia: thirty-five. [3] And the name of this gate is called the Gate of Zebulun. And from this gate he measured up to the gate, [4] stadia: thirty-five. And the name of this gate is called the Gate of Gad. And from this gate he measured up to [5] corner, stadia: thirty-five. And from this corner, which is to the east, he measured up to the gate, stadia: [6] 25. And the name of this gate is called … the Gate of Dan. And from this gate he measured up to [the gate in] [7] the center, stadia: 25. And the name of this gate is called the Gate of Naphtali. And from this [8] gate he measured up to the eastern gate, stadia: 25. And the name of this gate is called [9] the Gate of Asher. And he measured from this gate up to the eastern corner, stadia: [10] 25.[26]

Just as is the case in Ezek 48:30–35, the description of the walls centers on providing its measurements and the names of its twelve gates. However, the *NJT* construes both those aspects in a distinct fashion. While the Ezekielic city is small, in 4Q554 it grows almost ten times, measuring 140 by 100[27] stadia (ca. 26.64 by 18.89 km[28]). The city in the *NJT* is a rectangle rather than a square, with its shorter sides perpendicular to the north–south axis. Another passage, 4Q554 2 II, 13–14, specifies the thickness of the walls as fourteen cubits and their height as forty-nine cubits.

Both Ezekiel and the *NJT* make a point of naming each of the twelve gates after an Israelite tribe, but they differ on the question of sequencing. The list of

---

[26] The text according to Émile Puech, "554. 4QJérusalem Nouvelle^a ar (Pl. V–VI)" in Peuch, *Qumrân Grotte 4. XXVII* (cf. note 22), 103–38. Since the Aramaic text contains numerical ciphers, similar to but distinct from standard Aramaic letters, it cannot be reproduced here. The translation renders those ciphers with digits.

[27] This measurement has the support of the majority of commentators. The reading of the numerical cipher in 4Q554 1 I, 19 as 24 is posited by Söllner, *Jerusalem* (cf. note 19), 121, 131, and, forcefully, by DiTommaso, New Jerusalem *Text* (cf. note 20), 21, 30–31; if accepted, this would result in the city walls measuring 140 by 96 stadia. However, Hugo Antonissen, "Some Aspects of New Jerusalem," in Hilhorst et al., *Flores Florentino* (cf. note 21), 239–55 at 243–47 notices that the ligature at the end of cipher in 1 I, 19 must have the numerical value of three rather than two (*contra* DiTommaso), since a very similar ligature in 4Q554 1 II, 18 must equal three to add up to eighteen, which is the sum in the parallel reading in 5Q15 1 I, 4, which does not use ciphers. As observed by Antonissen, "Visionary Architecture" (cf. note 21), 447, the city's circumference of 480 stadia equals that of Babylon in Herodotus, *Hist.* 1.178 (trans. by A.D. Godley, LCL 117 [Cambridge: Harvard University Press, 1920], 220–23; all the following references to Herodotus are to the Loeb edition) – although there it is a square – and of Nineveh in Diodorus, *Lib.* 2.3.2–3 (ed. and trans. C.H. Oldfather, LCL 279 [Cambridge: Harvard University Press, 1933], 254–57). Chyutin, *New Jerusalem Scroll* (cf. note 21), 142, also observes that the ratio of the lengths of the ramparts equals almost exactly the ratio of a side of a square to its diagonal.

[28] Based on the stadium being equal to 189 meters, as claimed by Puech, "Names" (cf. note 18), 382.

names in 4Q554 is incomplete due to the fragmentary preservation of the scroll but, based on parallel lists in the *Temple Scroll* and the *Reworked Pentateuch* (4Q365ᵃ 2 II), scholars agree on the reconstructed order.

Table 1. City gates in Ezek 48 and the *NJT*
(from the westernmost gate on the northern side, clockwise).

Gate	Ezek 48:31–35	4Q554 1 I, 9–II, 10
1	Reuben	Dan
2	Judah	Naphtali
3	Levi	Asher
4	Joseph	Simeon
5	Benjamin	Levi
6	Dan	Judah
7	Simeon	Joseph
8	Issachar	Benjamin
9	Zebulon	Reuben
10	Gad	Issachar
11	Asher	Zebulon
12	Naphtali	Gad

As noted by Émile Puech, the reordering of the names is most likely significant.[29] The Qumranic New Jerusalem has two very broad streets, perpendicular to each other and crossing at the middle of the city, similar and possibly modelled after the Greco-Roman *cardo* and *decumanus*. The street on the north-south axis is delimited by the gates of Naphtali and Benjamin, the youngest sons of Bilhah and Rachel, respectively, whereas the east–west avenue ends with the gates of Levi and Zebulon, both Leah's children. The presence of Levi on the eastern gate undoubtedly relates to the orientation of the temple, which most likely faced east. Unfortunately, the fragmentary state of the preserved documents makes it impossible to conclusively establish where the temple is situated in relation to the New Jerusalem (the reference in 4Q554 1 II, 17: "which to the north/left of the temple,"[30] is unclear and ambiguous). Some scholars envisage the temple to be located near the main intersection, i.e. at the heart of the city, while others, taking a cue from Ezekiel, move the temple outside of the city fortifications.[31] In either scenario, the Levi gate maintains its significance, since it either allows somebody entering the New Jerusalem to see the front of the temple or leads someone leaving the city towards it.

---

[29] Puech, "Names" (cf. note 18), 390–391.

[30] [מא]ל מקדשא

[31] The former option is preferred by Puech, "Names" (cf. note 18), 390–91 and Antonissen, "Visionary Architecture" (cf. note 21), 451–53. The latter is argued for by Chyutin, *New Jerusalem Scroll* (cf. note 21), 85–88; DiTommaso, New Jerusalem *Text* (cf. note 20), 105–06.

The *NJT* refurbishes the exterior of the apocalyptic city in two distinct ways. Firstly, the gates are no longer the only salient architectural feature of the ramparts, which are depicted as being fortified with 1,432 towers,[32] each 70 cubits tall, grouped in threes located one stadium from the nearest gate or another tower (4Q554 2 II, 15–18).

Secondly, the walls and other elements of the city are depicted as adorned with precious stones.[33] 4Q554 2 II, 14–15 specifies the gemstones used to construct the wall: "and all of it is built from electrum and sapphire, chalcedony (?), and its parapets are golden."[34] That aesthetic motif is absent from Ezek 48:30–35 but harks back to Isa 54:11–12 where sapphires and *kĕdakōd* (a sparkling gemstone, possibly ruby or chalcedony) are used.[35] Within the settlement itself the streets are paved with white stone, marble, and perhaps jasper (5Q15 1 I, 6–7).

A striking parallel is to be detected between this passage in the *NJT* and the only other Second Temple source to speak about the future Jerusalem as made of costly materials (rather than simply as resplendent), namely Tob 13:17. The book of Tobit, narratively set in the eighth or seventh century BC, dates most likely from the beginning of the second century BC, but its text in Hebrew, Aramaic, and Greek continued to evolve well into the common era.[36] Very importantly, 4Q554 2 II, 14–15 exhibits a strong affinity to the Aramaic version of that passage preserved in 4QpapTob[a] (4Q196) 18, 7–8,[37] with significant conceptual overlap with both Greek versions of Tobit.

---

[32] This number is the most plausible reading, but cf. the discussion in DiTommaso, New Jerusalem *Text* (cf. note 20), 60–61.

[33] On the Roman techniques of increasing the city's visibility see Pinder, "City Walls" (cf. note 1), 111–14. However, the use of gemstones and gold for such a purpose must have been unthinkable and practically impossible.

[34] וכלה בניה בחש[מל] וספיר כדכוד ועעיתה זהב

[35] Noteworthily, this Isaianic passage receives a markedly different, spiritual interpretation in the sectarian pesher preserved in 4QpIsa[d] (4Q164) 3–4 where sapphires are read as "the council of the congregation, the priests and the people," while rubies signify "the twelve chiefs of priests"; Frey, "New Jerusalem Text" (cf. note 22), 815; DiTommaso, New Jerusalem *Text* (cf. note 20), 188 n. 70.

[36] Joseph A. Fitzmyer, *Tobit*, Commentaries on Early Jewish Literature (Berlin, New York: De Gruyter, 2003), 50–52.

[37] On the Qumran Tobit fragments see Joseph A. Fitzmyer, "The Aramaic and Hebrew Fragments of Tobit from Qumran Cave 4," *Catholic Biblical Quarterly* 57, no. 4 (1995): 655–75; Devorah Dimant,"Tobit and the Qumran Aramaic Texts," in *Is There a Text in this Cave? Studies in the Textuality of the Dead Sea Scrolls in Honour of George J. Brooke*, ed. Ariel Feldman, Maria Cioată, and Charlotte Hempel, Studies on the Texts of the Desert of Judah 119 (Leiden, Boston: Brill, 2017), 385–406. The overlap is noted by Puech, "554. 4QJérusalem Nouvelle[a] ar" (cf. note 26), 124.

Table 2. The *NJT* and the Aramaic and Greek versions of Tobit.

4Q554 2 II, 14–15	4Q196 18, 7–8	Tobit 13:17 GI	Tobit 13:17 GII
וכלה בניה בחש[מל] ו[ספיר כדכוד ועיתה זהב 5Q15 1 I, 6–7 וכל [שוק]י[א וקריתא ר[ציפין באבן חור ... שש ויהלם][38]	תרעי ירושלם ברקת] ו[ספיר תתבנין ...] מגדלי ירושלם ד[הב תתבנין ועע]יתא ...][39]	ὅτι οἰκοδομηθήσεται Ιερουσαλημ σαπφείρῳ καὶ σμαράγδῳ, καὶ λίθῳ ἐντίμῳ τὰ τείχη σου, καὶ οἱ πύργοι καὶ οἱ προμαχῶνες ἐν χρυσίῳ καθαρῷ, καὶ αἱ πλατεῖαι Ιερουσαλημ βηρύλλῳ καὶ ἄνθρακι καὶ λίθῳ ἐκ Σουφιρ ψηφολογηθήσονται.	... καὶ αἱ θύραι Ιερουσαλημ σαπφείρῳ καὶ σμαράγδῳ οἰκοδομηθήσονται καὶ λίθῳ τιμίῳ πάντα τὰ τείχη σου· οἱ πύργοι Ιερουσαλημ χρυσίῳ οἰκοδομηθήσονται καὶ οἱ προμαχῶνες αὐτῶν χρυσίῳ καθαρῷ· αἱ πλατεῖαι[40] Ιερουσαλημ ἄνθρακι ψηφολογηθήσονται καὶ λίθῳ Σουφιρ.
And all of it is built from amber and sapphire, chalcedony (?), and its parapets are golden And all the streets and the city are paved with white stone ... marble and jasper (?)	The gates of Jerusalem [from] sparkling stone and sapphire, and will be built ... the towers of Jerusalem will be built [from] gold, and its parapets[41]...	And Jerusalem will be built with sapphire and emerald, and its walls with precious stone, and its towers and bastions with pure gold, and the streets of Jerusalem will be cobbled with beryl, chalcedony, and the stone of Ophir.	And the gates of Jerusalem will be built with sapphire and emerald, and with precious stone all of its walls. The towers of Jerusalem will be built with gold, and their bastions with pure gold. And the streets of Jerusalem will be cobbled with chalcedony and the stone of Ophir.

The similarity between the *NJT* and the Aramaic manuscripts of Tobit from Qumran, as well as the Greek versions, is too strong to be regarded as accidental or merely conceptual. Since both texts are nonsectarian, at some point in their

---

[38] Text according to Józef Tadeusz Milik, "15. Description de la Jérusalem nouvelle (Pls. XL et XLI)," in *Les 'petites grottes' de Qumrân. Exploration de la falaise. Les grottes 2Q, 3Q, 5Q, 6Q, 7Q à 10Q. Le rouleau de cuivre*, ed. Józef Tadeusz Milik, Maurice Baillet, and Roland de Vaux, Discoveries in the Judean Desert 3 (Oxford: Clarendon, 1962), 183–93.

[39] The text according to Joseph A. Fitzmyer, "196. 4QpapTobit^a ar (Pls. I–V)," in *Qumran Cave 4.XIV: Parabiblical Texts, Part 2*, ed. Megan Broshi et al., Discoveries in the Judean Desert 19 (Oxford: Clarendon, 1995), 7–41.

[40] The passage from Tobit in both version derived from Alfred Rahlfs, ed., *Septauaginta: Id est Vetus Testamentum graece iuxta LXX interpretes*, rev. ed. Robert Hanhart (Stuttgart: Deutsche Bibelgesellschaft, 2006), 1.1085.

[41] Fitzmyer, "196. 4QpapTobit^a ar" (cf. note 39), 30 translates עעיתא as being a cognate of עע/אע, "wood." However, in view of the overlap with 4Q554 2 II, 15, translating the word as "parapets" appears correct.

compositional phase one must have borrowed its New Jerusalem imagery from the other, even if the direction of that borrowing is difficult or impossible to ascertain. The relationship between the *NJT* and the texts of Tobit merits further study, which, unfortunately, cannot be undertaken here.

To conclude the discussion on the *NJT*, several observations should be made. The basic trajectory of the New Jerusalem tradition as exemplified in this document is to make the walls of the city more glorious and more imposing. Its size increases in comparison to both the earthly Jerusalem and its Ezekielic depiction, most likely in order to underscore the city's significance and to provide ample living space for a large number of inhabitants.[42] The gates still perform their function of recalling the fullness of Israel to its eschatological settlement, at the same time emphasizing its priestly ideology by linking the gate of Levi with the temple. The walls – very much in keeping with ancient urbanism – have a twofold role, ideological and protective. The use of gemstones and precious metals reflects the city's self-understanding as incredibly wealthy and economically powerful. Its sumptuousness is visible to an outside observer and, at the same time, spread evenly across the settlement, likely to reinforce a sense of egalitarianism. The ramparts, however, appear to retain some of their military and defensive function, since they are said to be equipped with towers and parapets.[43] Consequently, the city's fortifications might serve an actual defensive purpose or, if the conflict preceded the revelation of the New Jerusalem, provide a sense of security to alleviate the trauma of war.

3 Revelation 21:9–27

The description of the New Jerusalem in Rev 21 is one of the most extensive within the entire tradition and is most likely the most studied one. The volume of the existing scholarly discussion on this passage obviates the need for a detailed introduction.[44] The vision of the eschatological city is one of the last ones in the

---

[42] The motif of Jerusalem increasing in size is present in Jewish postbiblical traditions, e. g. *Sib. Or.* 5.252 (Johannes Geffcken, ed., *Oracula Sibyllina*, GCS 8 [Leipzig: Hinrichs, 1902], 116) where the walls extend up to Joppa, or *Shir ha-Shirim Rabba* 7.5.3 (Maurice Simon, trans., *Midrash Rabbah: Song of Songs* [London: Soncino, 1939], 286) where they reach Damascus. *Eicha Rabba* 1.1.2 (Abraham Cohen, trans., *Midrash Rabbah. Lamentations* [London: Soncino, 1939], 69) relates Rabbi Samuel's exorbitant estimate of the number of houses in Jerusalem as twenty-four to the power of six.

[43] Fragments 13 and 14 of 4Q554 include a four-empire scheme, akin to and possibly inspired by Daniel 2 and 7, which seems to end with an eschatological confrontation (see 4Q554 13+14, 20: ויבאשון לזרעך, "and they will do violence to your offspring").

[44] See Lee, *New Jerusalem* (cf. note 19), 239–304 for an exhaustive study. For a recent contextual study see Eric J. Gilchrest, *Revelation 21–22 in Light of Jewish and Greco-Roman Utopianism*, Biblical Interpretation Series 118 (Leiden: Brill, 2013).

book, following on from the millennial kingdom (20:4–6), the ultimate defeat of Satan (vv. 7–10), and the last judgment (vv. 11–15). The conclusion of the eschatological combat before the appearance of the heavenly Jerusalem positions it within the final era of peace. The city is part of the completely renewed creation (21:1, 5) and is "prepared like a bride adorned for her husband" (v. 2b), evoking the marital imagery of Isaiah (see Isa 49:18; 61:10) and anticipating its aesthetic splendor.

The passage in Rev 21:9–27 has numerous points of contact with the previously studied texts from Ezekiel and Qumran, displaying both similarity to and divergence from the earlier tradition. For the purposes of this paper, the following aspects alone will be discussed: the size of the city walls, the naming of the gates, and the use of precious stones.

While the *NJT* saw a considerable expansion of the size of the eschatological city in comparison to the Ezekielic prototype, Rev 21 goes beyond any architecturally realistic limits and envisages the city as a cube of the fantastical dimensions of twelve thousand stadia, i. e. around 2,220 kilometers, in each direction (v. 16). The size of the city is in keeping with its heavenly origin, expressed in vv. 2a, 10. Another dimension of the wall, most likely its thickness, is specified in v. 17 at 144 human cubits, equaling almost 64 meters.[45] While this makes the wall quite thick from a human perspective, it is disproportionately thin relative to its own height, making the structure architecturally unfeasible. John bestows numerical significance on the city's measurements, as both 12,000 stadia and 144 cubits are multiples of twelve, the number of the Israelite tribes (v. 12) and of the apostles (v. 14). The wall does not perform any defensive functions, since all of the enemies have been decisively dealt with during the eschatological events of ch. 20.[46] The size of the fortifications signals John's move away from practical urban considerations towards a fully idealized vision of a city that embodies the community that is to settle in it.

Just as in the cities of Ezek 48:30–35 and the *NJT*, the Johannine New Jerusalem can be entered through one of the twelve gates. Each of the four walls has three gates, with each gate being provided with one angel and named after one of the tribes of Israel. The gates are said to be continually open, evoking the imagery

---

[45] David E. Aune, *Revelation 17–22*, World Biblical Commentary 52C (Nashville: Thomas Nelson, 1998) 1162–63; Craig R. Koester, *Revelation: A New Translation with Introduction and Commentary*, Anchor Bible 38B (New Haven: Yale University Press, 2014), 817; cf. Lee, *New Jerusalem* (cf. note 19), 276–79; DiTommaso, New Jerusalem *Text* (cf. note 20), 143 who think that the city measures 12,000 by 12,000 stadia and its wall is 144 cubits tall. This estimation disregards the latter part of 21:16 where the city is explicitly said to be a cube. Should the city be 12,000 stadia tall and its wall measure only 144 cubits, there would be a rather comical discrepancy between the two. It would be at odds with the beginning of 21:12, where the wall is "great and high," as well as other relevant sources, which never distinguish the height of the city from that of its wall.

[46] Lee, *New Jerusalem* (cf. note 19), 277–78.

of Isa 60:10–11. However, unlike the texts studied above, John does not assign names to particular gates. It is also unclear what tribal list the names would be taken from, but most commentators agree that it would be identical to the one included in Rev 7:4–8. The list is peculiar as it contains Joseph as well as his son Manasseh, but leaves out Manasseh's brother Ephraim, as well as Dan,[47] most likely based on their past moral failings.[48] It is difficult to provide a concrete and plausible reason for John's lack of interest in the order of the names of the gates, which is a salient feature of the visions in Ezekiel and the *NJT*. Most likely, John had less interest in emphasizing the names of particular tribes on the city walls or perhaps thought it redundant, having listed them earlier in his prophecy.[49]

The ample architectural use of gemstones and gold in Rev 21:9–27 is a distinctive feature of John's vision. Just as he enlarged the city to gargantuan proportions, he then asks his audience to join him in marveling at its visual opulence. The city's radiance, bestowed upon it by God's indwelling glory, is the first feature noticed by the seer whose mind immediately employs lithic comparisons to "the most precious stone, [to] crystal-clear jasper" (v. 11). Jasper (ἴασπις) is usually red or green in color and opaque, making the adjective "crystal-clear" striking, even paradoxical.[50] John attaches some importance to this stone, as it emerges twice more in his description of the New Jerusalem – both as the material of the walls (v. 18a) and as the first of the foundation stones (v. 19). The city thus becomes more similar to the appearance of Christ himself who is likened to jasper and carnelian in 4:3.

---

[47] The exclusions have generated some debate among commentators; see Christopher R. Smith, "The Portrayal of the Church as the New Israel in the Names and Order of the Tribes in Revelation 7.5–8," *Journal for the Study of the New Testament* 39 (1990): 111–18; Richard Bauckham, "The List of the Tribes in Revelation 7 Again," *Journal for the Study of the New Testament* 42 (1991): 99–115; Christopher R. Smith, "The Tribes of Revelation 7 and the Literary Competence of John the Seer," *Journal of the Evangelical Theological Society* 38, no. 2 (1995): 213–18; Stephen Goranson, "The Exclusion of Ephraim in Rev. 7:4–8 and Essene Polemic against Pharisees," *Dead Sea Discoveries* 2.1 (1995): 80–85; Gert J. Steyn, "The Order of the Twelve Tribes of Israel and its Reception in Revelation 7," in *New Perspectives on the Book of Revelation*, ed. Adela Yarbro Collins, Bibliotheca Ephemeridum Theologicarum Lovaniensium 291 (Leuven: Peeters, 2017), 523–44 at 536–38.

[48] Michael W. Troxell, "The Order and Significance of the Sealed Tribes of Revelation 7:4–8" (Master's diss. Andrews University, 2011), 84–90.

[49] Importantly, none of the gates receives additional significance from its relation to the temple, since no such structure is to be present in John's new Jerusalem (21:22a). Nevertheless, the seer does not dispense with the cult, since God and the Lamb are the temple (21:22b), while the elect will minister (λατρεύσουσιν) to them (22:3). The absence of a temple building in the New Jerusalem should not be read as John's break with Jewish religious practice (however construed), as nowhere in Revelation is the temple cult explicitly criticized; see Eyal Regev, *The Temple in Early Christianity: Experiencing the Sacred*, The Anchor Yale Bible Reference Library (New Haven: Yale University Press, 2019), 242–46.

[50] The most sustained ancient discussion of jasper is to be found in Pliny, *Nat.* 37.37 (trans. D. E. Eichholz, LCL 419 [Cambridge: Harvard University Press, 1962], 248–49; all the following references to Pliny's *Natural History* are based on the Loeb edition).

The statement that the city gates will be "each a single pearl" is unclear. It is possible that John simply thinks that the gates are incrusted with nacre (also known as mother-of-pearl). On the other hand, Craig Koester might be right in claiming that each gate is made of a single gigantic, exorbitantly expensive pearl.[51] Both interpretations would contribute to the overall appearance of the city as opulent. Unlike in the *NJT*, which paid minute attention to the living quarters of the settlement, John's interest in the city's interior is expressed only through statements that the city (v. 18b) and its streets (v. 21b) are made of translucent gold. His focus is primarily on the city's external visuality.

Interestingly, the visionary reveals the names and the order of the precious stones decorating the foundations of the city wall (vv. 19–20), which, from an architectural perspective, would have to be hidden from view. Such a design must have been inspired by the presence of precious stones in the foundations of the Solomonic Temple (1 Kgs 5:17; 7:9–10). John's list of gemstones, far from being a random assortment, has been recognized by interpreters ancient and modern alike to be dependent on the lists of stones in the priestly breastplate (Exod 28:17–20) and the paradisiac coverings of the king of Tyre (Ezek 28:13).[52] The correspondence is not exact, especially since some of the Hebrew lithic nomenclature is unclear, but it is certain that John consciously tried to incorporate Edenic and priestly imagery, which is amplified by other links to the paradise narrative (the tree of life in 22:2) and the role of the temple (its explicit absence in 21:22). In Exod 28:21, the stones are inscribed with the names of the Israelite tribes who inspire their presence in Rev 21:12; the foundations of the wall of the Johannine New Jerusalem, however, bear the names of the twelve apostles.[53] The seer makes the apostolic foundations of the eschatological city as solid and as manifest as possible.

Revelation 21 is an innovative iteration of the New Jerusalem *topos*, which departs from the preexisting patterns but can only really be understood within the larger tradition. John abandons almost any concern for the architectural realism that governed the vision of Ezekiel and was still palpable in the *NJT*. His focus is on representing the city as perfect in every conceivable sense. Thus, its proportions are not only vast but also evoke the number twelve, strongly suggesting completion, perfection, and regularity. While the *NJT*, likely incited by the passages from Isa 54 and Tob 13, begins to emphasize the presence of precious materials in the structure of the eschatological settlement and especially its

---

[51] Koester, *Revelation* (cf. note 45), 819.

[52] See Koester, *Revelation* (cf. note 45), 818 for the comparison of these lists, in their MT and LXX versions, with Rev 21:19–20.

[53] David Mathewson, "A Note on the Foundation Stones in Revelation 21.14, 19–20," *Journal for the Study of the New Testament* 25, no. 4 (2003): 487–98 argues that John draws on Isa 54 and that his interpretation, focused on the community leaders, parallels that are present in 4Q164 (4QpIsa^d) (see also above, n. 35).

walls, Revelation again knows no boundaries to its imagination and envisages a plethora of gemstones as well as gold in immense quantities. Such luxury, as in the Qumran text, conveys the sense of prestige and economic security.[54] John's appropriation of Exod 28:17–20 and Ezek 28:13 makes the New Jerusalem into a reflection of the splendor of the tabernacle and the abundance of the garden of Eden.

Since the end of John's prophecy represents a period of ultimate peace, the walls of the New Jerusalem do not function as a defensive boundary; after all, their gates are continually open and invite the earth's people and their kings to bring offerings to the city (21:24–26). John makes it clear that those not enrolled in the Lamb's book of life will not be granted access to the city (v. 27), but this might be a purely rhetorical assertion since the same group, slightly differently named, is placed in the fiery lake in 21:8. Consequently, the wall most likely was not envisaged to really exclude or defend against any tangible "other." Quite the contrary – since the names of the tribes of Israel and of the apostles both appear on the gates and on the foundations of the walls respectively, John emphasizes the continuity between his audience and the historical and eschatological Israel.

4 Victorinus and Jerome

After the discussion of the three major representatives of the New Jerusalem tradition, the following sections will be devoted the patristic commentaries on Revelation. This selection is by no means meant to be exhaustive of the entirety of Christian speculation about the eschatological city and leaves out important Jewish *comparanda* but will nevertheless be illuminative of how the walls of that city – so richly described by John – continued to play a variety of roles in the exegetical imagination.

The first author to be considered is Victorinus of Poetovium, the author of the first fully preserved commentary on Revelation, dated to the second half of the third century.[55] The original work is preserved in a single significant manuscript, whereas Jerome's late-fourth-century antimillenarian recension was received much more widely.[56] Surprisingly, despite the richness of the source material, Victorinus does not spend much time on the New Jerusalem or its exterior. His commentary on Rev 21 begins with a brief restatement of John's description

---

[54] On the New Jerusalem in Revelation in the context of Roman architecture and economy see Candida R. Moss, Liane M. Feldmann, "The New Jerusalem: Wealth, Ancient Building Projects and Revelation 21–22," *New Testament Studies* 66, no. 3 (2020): 351–66.

[55] Roger Gryson, ed., *Victorini Poetovionensis opera quae supersunt*, CCSL 5 (Turnhout: Brepols, 2017), 5.

[56] On the textual history of both versions see Gryson, *Victorini* (cf. note 55), 10–98.

(5.46–59[57]). Victorinus then, quite curiously, tries to identify the city with a geographical region:

But we should not understand the city just as we know it, for without guidance we are not able to assess anything to be greater than what we hear about or see. Moreover, the city refers to every region of those eastern provinces that were promised to Abraham the patriarch. "Look up," [God] said, "to the sky from the place where you are standing" – that is, "from the great river Euphrates to the river of Egypt" – "all earth that you gaze upon I will give to you and to your offspring" [Gen 15:18]. Then the Holy Spirit said, "He will rule from the sea up to the sea" – that is from the Red Sea, which is in Arabia, up to the Northern Sea which is the Phoenician sea[58] – "and to the ends of the earth" [Ps 72:8] – those are the parts of Greater Syria (5.59–68).[59]

Victorinus treats the dimensions of the Johannine New Jerusalem broadly literally and sees it as a region rather than an urban settlement, most likely so that its twelve-thousand-stadia-long side can be accommodated. The geography is specified by the means of quotations from Gen 15:18 and Ps 72:8 (71:8 in the Vetus Latina and the Vulgate) as the land between the Nile and the Euphrates and between the Red Sea and a northern body of water, perhaps the Mediterranean or the Black Sea.[60]

Victorinus then seamlessly moves on to the discussion of the future kingdom of Christ (5.73–119) where the saints enjoy riches, probably echoing the economic opulence of the Johannine city. Some visual aspects of the New Jerusalem walls are referenced and interpreted in the final section of the commentary (5.120–133). The precious building materials represent both the variety of persons, as well as "the most precious variety of faith of a single person"[61] (5.125–126). In a slight but significant change to John's vision, Victorinus emphasizes the apostolic aspect of the city over against the patriarchal one. The city gates now are said to represent the apostles rather than the Israelite tribes (5.126–127) and the names of Jesus's disciples appear not only on the foundations of the walls but also over the gates (5.130–131). Victorinus in his treatment of the exterior of the New Jerusalem combines a "down to earth" realism, with which he understands

---

[57] The chapter and verse numbering of both Victorinus and Jerome is based on Gryson's edition (cf. note 55).

[58] The manuscript reading seems corrupt and confused at this point; see Gryson, *Victorini* (cf. note 55), 291 for emendation and discussion.

[59] *Sed ciuitas non ita ut nouimus intellegitur; nos enim nihil amplius possumus arbitrari sine duce, quam quod audiuimus et uidimus. Ceterum dicitur ciuitas omnis illa prouinciarum orientalium regio promissa patriarchae Abrahae. Aspice, inquit, "in caelo a loco, in quo modo tu stas," id est "a flumine magno Eufrate usque ad flumen Aegypti; omnem terram quam tu aspicis, tibi dabo illam et semini tuo." Deinde spiritus sanctus ait: "Dominabitur a mari usque ad mare," id est a mari Rubro, quod est Arabiae, usque ad mare Aquilonis, quod est mare Fenicis, "et usque ad fines terrae," – sunt Siriae maioris partes.*

[60] On the geographic location of New Jerusalem in Victorinus's commentary see Konrad Huber's contribution to this volume.

[61] *uarietatem fidei preciosissimam singulorum hominum.*

the city's spatiality, with touches of a more spiritual exegesis. The settlement also becomes, in a sense, ostensibly apostolic, with its walls becoming a way to express that identity.

In 398, Jerome, not willing to dispense wholly with Victorinus's groundbreaking work, but put off by its chiliastic tendency, provided his own recension of the commentary.[62] He considerably transforms Victorinus's interpretation in respect to the visuality of the eschatological city. The recension retains very little of the original, agreeing with it only on the identification of the gates with the apostles (5.113–114). Jerome is more interested in the geometrical shape of the city, which, being a square, reminds him of the square planks Noah was commanded to use to build the ark.[63] Just as the ark withstood the flood, so the saints' constancy and devotion allows them to face persecutions (5.89–92). They are also linked to another Johannine detail, namely the precious stones, which cannot be dissolved by rain (5.94). Jerome's exegesis takes Victorinus's investment in Christian founding figures to a new level as the gates are explicitly ascribed to the apostles while the patriarchs are not mentioned at all. The difficult statement about gates made of pearls (Rev 21:21) is understood by Jerome as meaning that one pearl served to construct three gates on each side of the ramparts. The four pearls can stand for the four so-called cardinal virtues (prudence, fortitude, justice, temperance), which the apostles embody and with which they lead the saints into the city (5.109–117). The fact that the gates remain ever open is taken by Jerome to signify that the apostolic doctrine will never be stifled by error (5.118–119), which allows him to conclude his commentary on a strongly polemical and antiheretical note. Jerome's recension purges Victorinus's New Jerusalem of any earthly realism and identifies it wholesale with the redeemed church, at the same time overwriting the Jewish nature and origin of the New Jerusalem *topos* and of the Johannine subtext.

5 Tyconius

Expositio Apocalypseos by Tyconius, only the second Western Christian exegetical work on Revelation after Victorinus's chiliastic commentary, is a pivotal point in the reception history of the book. The author – a Donatist layman whose literary activity is dated between 370 and 385, with *Expositio* most likely

---

[62] For this dating see Martine Dulaey, ed., *Victorin de Poetovio: Sur l'Apocalypse et autres écrits*, SC 423 (Paris: Cerf, 1997), 28. On Jerome's recension see further Alessandro Capone's contribution to this volume.

[63] This detail is taken from the Old Latin version of Gen 6:14a: *fac ergo tibi arcam ex quadratis lignis* (so Itala). This reading mirrors the LXX which has ποίησον οὖν σεαυτῷ κιβωτὸν ἐκ ξύλων τετραγώνων. The MT has a semantically difficult עֲצֵי־גֹפֶר, likely referring to a tree species. Jerome himself in the Vulgate opts for a different reading: *fac tibi arcam de lignis levigatis*.

his last work[64] – offered a profoundly spiritual reading of the Johannine vision, laying foundations for all its later Latin interpretations.[65] Despite its historic significance, the commentary did not survive completely, but was reconstructed by Roger Gryson.[66]

Tyconius's approach to the external appearance of the New Jerusalem is structured by the guiding thought of the entire commentary, namely that Revelation is a story about the church. This view prefaces the interpretation of Rev 21 in *Expositio* 7.31: "this Jerusalem he calls the church"[67] (see also 7.34).[68] The jasper in 21:11 is identified with Christ himself, surely under the influence of Rev 4:3 and 1 Pet 2:6. In relation to the names of the twelve city gates, Tyconius takes the opportunity – forgone by Victorinus and later Jerome – to engage with their patriarchal association:

He shows the twelve gates to be the twelve patriarchs, from whose shoot the entire nation of Israelites propagated and from among whom, according to the apostle, 'remnants are saved by the election of grace' [Rom 11:5]" (7.36).[69]

The implication of Tyconius's exegesis and especially of his use of Rom 11 is that some descendants of the patriarchs, i.e. Jews, will be saved and thus present in the New Jerusalem. The walls and gates of the city are thus seen as marking some degree of continuity between Israel and the church. Nevertheless, they also later express a specifically Christian notion, as the angels in Rev 21:12 represent the entirety of the faithful, composed of the clergy and laity.

Further exterior aspects of the New Jerusalem also receive spiritual exegesis. The location of the gates, with three of them facing each of the four cardinal directions, is read as the proclamation of the Trinity by the church throughout the whole world (7.37). While describing the walls of the city, Tyconius focuses exclusively on the gold from which they are made, noting its fragility (7.39) and transparency (7.40), which is supposed to characterize the saints. The question of personal character is also raised in relation to the gemstones in Rev 21:19–20, which signify a variety of spiritual gifts bestowed by the Spirit (7.41).

---

[64] On the little that is known about Tyconius's life see Matthew R. Lynskey, *Tyconius' Book of Rules: An Ancient Invitation to Ecclesial Hermeneutics*. Vigiliae Christianae Supplements 167 (Leiden: Brill, 2021), 22–28.

[65] For a study of Tyconius's exegetical resonance see Kenneth B. Steinhauser, *The Apocalypse Commentary of Tyconius: A History of Its Reception and Influence*, Europäische Hochschulschriften 23 (301) (Frankfurt am Main: Peter Lang, 1987).

[66] Roger Gryson, ed., *Tyconii Afri expositio Apocalypseos*, CCSL 107A (Turnhout: Brepols, 2011).

[67] *[h]anc Ierusalem ecclesiam dicit.*

[68] The text and its division follow Gryson's edition.

[69] *Ostendit duodecim portas duodecim esse patriarchas ex quorum stirpe uniuersa Israelitarum gens specialiter propagate est, et ex quibus secundum apostolum "reliquiae per electionem gratiae saluae factae sunt."*

Even though brief in his discussion of the walls of the end-time city, Tyconius transforms them into even more than John intended them to be. While the latter accentuated their immensity, regularity, and opulence, Tyconius provides each of the architectural features with a spiritual meaning and brings them together to represent the entirety of the church. The external aspects of New Jerusalem point both backwards, to its Jewish origin, and forwards, to Christ, represented by jasper. The static outwardness of the eschatological settlement is no longer simply defensive or impressive but tells the whole narrative of salvation.

6 Caesarius of Arles

Caesarius (470–542), the bishop of Arles, preached a series of homilies on the book of Revelation sometime between 510 and 537.[70] Caesarius's reading of Revelation is heavily reliant on Tyconius, as well as the original version of Victorinus's commentary.[71] The exposition of the New Jerusalem is contained in *Homily 19* (the last in the collection) and begins with an unequivocal identification of the city with the church (19.2).[72] Christ is not only the spouse of the church but also its adornment, since he is symbolized by the most precious jewel from Rev 21:11 (19.3). This ecclesiological insight permeates the rest of Caesarius's reading. His interest in the city walls is limited to the equation of the gates to the apostles and the prophets, with the latter replacing the patriarchs originally mentioned by John (19.4). The positioning and number of the gates achieves doctrinal and missionary significance, derived from Tyconius: "And because the city described is the Church spread all over the world, three gates are said to be on each of the four sides of the city, because the mystery of the Trinity is preached in the Church throughout all four corners of the world." (19.5)[73]

The church-oriented interpretation transforms the costly building materials of the New Jerusalem into moral qualities; thus gold symbolizes faith (19.7–8), glass stands for purity (19.8), whereas the gemstones at the foundations of the walls are read as the gifts of the Holy Spirit received by the apostles (19.9). Interestingly, Caesarius shows no interest in interpreting the measurements of the city, possibly to preclude any possibility of understanding John's New Jerusalem as an

---

[70] For this dating see Steinhauser, *Apocalypse Commentary* (cf. note 65), 50–51. On Caesarius more generally see William E. Klingshirn, *Caesarius of Arles: The Making of the Christian Community in Late Antique Gaul* (Cambridge: Cambridge University Press, 1994).

[71] On this dependence see Gryson, *Victorini* (cf. note 55), 22–24.

[72] The text and its division according to Roger Gryson, ed., *Caesarius Arelatensis: Expositio de Apocalypsi sancti Iohannis*, CCSL 105 (Turnhout: Brepols, 2019).

[73] *Et quia ciuitas ista quae describitur ecclesia est toto orbe diffusa, ideo per quattuor partes ciuitatis ternae portae esse dicuntur, quia per totas quattuor mundi partes trinitatis mysterium in ecclesia praedicatur.*

actual, material city. Instead, all of its external appearance is exegeted in an ecclesiological vein. Thus, although Caesarius most likely did not know Jerome's recension of Victorinus, he approaches the first commentary on Revelation with similar caution and willingness to transform the visuality of the eschatological city into moral and doctrinal symbols.

7 Apringius of Beja

A different attitude to the New Jerusalem is offered by Apringius, bishop of the city of Pax Iulia, modern Beja in Portugal. While very little is known about his life, Isidore of Seville (*Vir. ill.* 30) dates him to the reign of Theudis (531–548), a Visigothic Arian king. Apringius's commentary in its only extant manuscript incorporates Jerome's recension of Victorinus and offers original exegesis only on Rev 1–5 and 18–22.

Apringius's exegesis of Rev 21 is quite substantial and exceeds in volume those of Victorinus, Jerome, and Caesarius. His original thinking about the end-time city and its appearance might have been at least one of the reasons he decided to provide his own commentary on the final chapters of the book (or why it was subsequently considered worth preserving). The visuality of the New Jerusalem is first brought up when Apringius comments on Rev 21:11:

> Just as the luster of jasper is not within it, nor is it shone on from outside, but is transparent by nature of its clarity, so this city is described not as being illuminated by the brightness of stars, but as being lit invisibly by God's glory. Therefore, the reddening in the brilliance of the crystal signifies the grace of baptism. (7.304–308)[74]

Apringius makes two theological points about the luster of the city. Firstly, since Rev 21:11 speaks about "crystal-clear jasper," the walls of the city must be translucent and not emit their own light, but rather reflect the light of God's glory. Secondly, the exegete appears to know that jasper can have red coloration and links it to the grace of baptism, likely having in mind the connection between baptism and Christ's blood (see Rev 1:5b).

Unlike his exegetical forerunners, Apringius does not erase the Israelite aspect of the end-time settlement. While Christ must be understood as the door (based on John 10:9), the presence of the patriarchal names on the city gates (Rev 21:12) means that "the entire band of the patriarchs abided in the faith of our Lord Jesus Christ" (7.321–322), thus suggesting some sort of continuity between Israel

---

[74] *Sicut enim splendor lapidis in eo non est, non extrinsecus radiatur, sed est naturae claritate perlucidum, ita ciuitas ille describitur nullo siderum fulgore luminari, sed sola dei inuisibiliter luce lustrari. In crystalli autem candore baptismi in ea significat gratiam rutilare.* The text according to Roger Gryson, ed., *Apringius Pacensis: Tractatus in Apocalypsin fragmenta quae supersunt* in *Commentaria minora in Apocalypsin Iohannis*, CCSL 107 (Turnhout: Brepols, 2003), 31–79.

and the eschatological church. Such relationship can also be garnered from Apringius's later comment on Rev 21:14: "Then the fact that the gates are divided into fours ... signifies the four corners of the world receiving the mystery of the Trinity, and that it is inscribed with the names of the patriarchs, this shows the ancient faith to have come together" (7.341–346).[75]

A highly idiosyncratic feature of Apringius's commentary is his pervasive interest in numerology, most amply applied to the walls of the New Jerusalem and its size. While John's vision attaches some importance to the dimensions of the Heavenly Jerusalem, primarily to symbolize its completion and perfection, the bishop of Pax Julia is eager to see them as figures for more profound theological ideas. This approach is first deployed in relation to Rev 21:13 (7.323–327) where Apringius adds up the twelve corners of the walls (reading *angulos* instead of *angelos*), the twelve gates, and the twelve foundations, and reads the resulting number thirty-six as representing the number of hours Jesus lay in the tomb. Consequently, it is said to convey the centrality of belief in Jesus's incarnation, passion, and resurrection in the faith of the church (7.338–340).

Apringius's numerical method is used with even greater ingenuity when he unravels the significance of the measurements of the walls, which his text of Rev 21:16 must have stated as a very modest twelve stadia rather than twelve thousand. The exegesis of this number is lengthy and complex (7.368–410) and perhaps is best summarized as follows:

12 stadia = 1,000 paces (fullness of generations; see Ps 105:8) + 5 stadia
1 stadium = 143 paces = 100 paces (perfection of the saints) + 40 paces (Decalogue × Gospels) + 3 paces (the Trinity)
5 stadia = 715 paces = 700 paces (seven days of Creation × perfection of the saints) + 15 (fullness of deity in the Lord Jesus Christ? uncertain due to a lacuna)

Likewise, 144 cubits, which Apringius understands as the height rather than the thickness of the wall, is broken down as follows (7.422–440):

144 cubits = 10 × 10 (the Decalogue) + 44 cubits
44 cubits = 10 × 4 (the Gospels) + 4
144 cubits = 6 (days of Creation) × 24 (elders in Rev 4:4 / patriarchs + apostles)

Apringius does not stop at that. Instead, he combines the two measurements for a chronological purpose:

1715 paces × 3 (the assumed conversion rate) + 144 cubits = 5289 cubits

In an unclear and cryptic passage, the commentator states that this number relates to the six thousandth year of the world in which Jesus was born (7.441–454).

---

[75] *Porro quod portae in quatuor diuiduntur... trinitatis mysterium quatuor mundi partes suscepisse significat, et inscripta patriarcharum nomina hoc est fidem ueterum confluxisse demonstrat.*

Apringius pays some attention to the building materials of the walls of the end-time city. In 7.455–459, the jasper of the walls in Rev 21:18, unlike previously, is envisaged to have a green hue and thus represent virginity, evoking Christ's virgin birth. Gold, as it is refined through fire, represents for Apringius the trials endured by the saints (7.460–465). Just like Caesarius in his homily, Apringius sees the gemstones of Rev 21:19–20 as the apostles and the various gifts of the Holy Spirit received by them (7.466–476), while the pearls of the gates in Rev 21:21 all point to Christ who is identified as the single pearl, perhaps under the influence of Matt 13:45–46.

Apringius's approach to the walls of the New Jerusalem stands out from the rest of the exegetical tradition. He appears much more sympathetic to the Jewish origin of the *topos* and to the continuity between the church and Israel that is espoused in Rev 21.[76] At the same time, his understanding of the materials and especially of the dimensions of the end-time city is undoubtedly ecclesiological and, on a deeper level, christological. The meanings Apringius ascribes to gemstones and numbers all come together and are unified in Christ. The visuality of the New Jerusalem is not simply a backdrop for the commentator's doctrinal ideas but becomes a complex embodiment of Christ itself. Jesus is attached to every building in the city and is himself its wall (7.457–459; see also 309–310 for a quotation from Zech 2:5). Within the Arian religious context of Visigothic Spain, the details of the Johannine prophecy allow Apringius to construct and argue for an almost superhuman Christology, as evidenced in a comment in 7.407–410: "And if he ought be believed to be above all flesh, as the apostle said, 'And if we knew Christ according to the flesh, we now do not know him thus' [2 Cor 5:16], then we should not stretch ourselves to consider him to be like a common human."[77] Such a conclusion is only possible after Apringius has reinterpreted each aspect of the walls of the eschatological city as aspects of the life and appearance of Christ himself.

8 Primasius of Hadrumetum

Apringius's commentary on Revelation is roughly contemporary with that penned by Primasius, the bishop of the North African city of Hadrumetum (modern-day Sousse in Tunisia). His work, reliant on Tyconius as well as on

---

[76] On Apringius's attitude towards the Jews see Joop van Banning, "Bemerkungen zur Apringius von Beja-Forschung," *Zeitschrift für antikes Christentum* 3, no. 1 (1999): 113–19 at 117.

[77] *[H]ic supra omnem carnem credendus est, quia dicit apostolus: "Et si nouimus secundum carnem Christum, sed nunc iam non nouimus," ne forte extenderemus nos quasi communem hominem contemplari.*

Augustine, dates to the early 540s.[78] Given these sources, it is unsurprising to find a wide range of overlaps between him and, on the other hand, Caesarius and Apringius. Primasius, like to some extent Tyconius and Apringius, identifies the massive wall of the Johannine New Jerusalem with Christ himself (5.21.102–103).[79] The number of the gates represents the apostles (5.21.135–138) who themselves are shone on by and transmit Christ's splendor: "Thus Christ is the light illuminating and they are the light illuminated" (5.21.150–151).[80] For Primasius, ecclesiology also unlocks the mystery of the regular dimensions of the New Jerusalem, which symbolize the stability of the church's truth (5.21.214–215). Just as other interpreters, Primasius understands the foundation gemstones in Rev 21:19–20 as representing the spiritual qualities of the saints (5.21.268–270).

While those comments are largely in keeping with his exegetical sources, Primasius is the only one to develop Tyconius's point, providing substantial and novel insight into the meaning of the patriarchal names on the gates of the New Jerusalem. The evocation of Israel in the city, that he is otherwise eager to identify with the church and its saints, poses a palpable theological challenge.

We know indeed that from the beginning our Lord has offered to all a passage towards faith through the twelve apostles. The surroundings of that place, however, call us back from this endeavor, when he inserts a mention of the twelve tribes of the sons of Israel, as he wants the twelve patriarchs to be understood first. As we know, it is specifically from their shoot that the entire nation of Israelites propagated. Also, from them, according to apostle Paul, "remnants are saved by the election of grace" [Rom 11:5], adding that "God did not reject his people" [Rom 11:1]. And thus we ought to accept the twelve patriarchs in as many gates, especially as we hear that "It is not you who carry the root, but the root that carries you" [Rom 11:18]. (5.21.112–123)[81]

---

[78] This dating is based primarily on the mention of Primasius and his commentary in Cassiodorus, *Institutiones divinarum et saecularium litterarum* 1.9.4 (ed. Roger Aubrey Baskerville Mynors [Oxford: Clarendon, 1961], 33); see Johannes Haussleiter, *Leben und Werke des Bischofs Primasius von Hadrumetum: Eine Untersuchung* (Erlangen: E.Th. Jacob, 1887), 16. On the reception of Primasius see E. Ann Matter, "Latin Reception of the Apocalypse in the Early Middle Ages," in *The Cambridge Companion to Apocalyptic Literature*, ed. Collin McAllister (Cambridge: Cambridge University Press, 2020), 120–36, esp. 125–31.

[79] The text and its division according to Arthur White Adams, ed., *Primasius Hadrumetinus. Commentarius in Apocalypsin*, CCSL 92 (Turnhout: Brepols, 1985).

[80] *Christus itaque lumen inluminans, illi autem lumen inluminatum.*

[81] *Scimus quidem per duodecim apostolos dominum nostrum uniuersis ad fidem introitum primordialiter praebuisse, huius tamen circumstantia loci ab hac nos intentione reuocauit quando duodecim tribuum filiorum Israhel interposuit mentionem, tamquam duodecim primum patriarchas hic intellegi uolens, ex quorum stirpe nouimus uniuersam israhelitarum gentem specialiter propagatam, et ex quibus, secundum apostolum Paulum: "Reliquiae per electionem gratiae saluae factae sunt," adiungens quoniam "non reppulit deus plebem suam," atque ideo duodecim hic patriarchas in totidem portas debemus accipere, praesertim audientes quod "non tu radicem portas, sed radix te."*

Primasius goes beyond Tyconius's brief remark on Rev 21:12 and makes a singular effort to face and grapple with the question of how much continuity there is between the New Jerusalem and the historical Israel. While he asserts that the city of the saints can only be entered through the apostles, he at the same time feels compelled by the Johannine text to reflect on the patriarchal names on the gates. The seriousness of this issue is readily recognized, as Primasius adduces perhaps the most direct and profound discussion of the relationship between Judaism and Christianity, i.e. Romans 11. The conclusion appears to be that to reject the explicitly Jewish aspect of the visuality of the New Jerusalem would be a sign of insolence and of cutting oneself off from one's own foundations. Consequently, while Primasius is not exactly original in his exegesis of the outer appearance of the Johannine city, his recognition and discussion of its Jewish nature, based on Tyconius's earlier insight, is highly perceptive.

9 Oecumenius

While the exegetical tradition and practice associated with Revelation is continuously attested in the late antique Latin West, the book's canonical status and, consequently, need for exposition were widely contested in the Christian East.[82] The first sustained Greek engagement with John's prophecy comes almost three centuries after Victorinus. Little is known about its author, Oecumenius, and while the dating of the commentary is uncertain, it can be safely assumed to originate in the sixth century.[83]

Despite the contextual differences that separate Oecumenius from his Western counterparts, his exegetical insights overlap with theirs at several points. The New Jerusalem is identified with the gathering of the saints (11.16.2–3),[84] Christ functions as the city's wall and its radiance (11.16.5–6), the gates signify the apostles and the doctrine of the Trinity (11.16.7–8, 10). Since the luxury of the New Jerusalem is meant to denote future spiritual riches (11.16.3), Oecumenius reads particular precious materials in this vein. Thus, jasper, due to its perceived green

---

[82] For the history of the Eastern Christian engagement with and debate over Revelation see a historical overview by Eugenia Scarvelis Constantinou, *Guiding to a Blessed End: Andrew of Caesarea and His Apocalypse Commentary in the Ancient Church* (Washington, DC: Catholic University of America Press, 2013), 14–46.

[83] On the date of Oecumenius see John C. Lamoreaux, "The Provenance of Ecumenius' Commentary on the Apocalypse," *Vigliae Christianae* 52, no.1 (1998): 88–108; *Oecumenius: Commentary on the Apocalypse*, trans. John N. Suggit, FC 112 (Washington, DC: The Catholic University of America Press, 2006), 3–6. On the manuscripts of his commentary see Marc de Groote, ed., *Oecumenii Commentarius in Apocalypsin*, Traditio Exegetica Graeca 8 (Louvain: Peeters, 1999), 9–56.

[84] The text and its division according to de Groote, *Oecumenii Commentarius* (cf. note 83).

color, represents Christ's vivifying power and, because of its crystalline clarity, his purity and sanctity (11.16.5; 12.3.7). Likewise, the gold of the city streets symbolizes the purity of the saints (12.3.8). Oecumenius, like Primasius and unlike Apringius, is uninterested in any sort of numerical speculation based on the exact measurements of the end-time settlement. His exegesis of its dimensions focuses on their equality and immensity which are said to signify that the saints' future rewards are well assured and that their number will not be insignificant, since they will be able to populate so great a structure (12.3.2–3).

Oecumenius stands out at the backdrop of the broader New Jerusalem tradition in his discussions of the Jewish aspect of its visuality. This is first evidenced in his discussion of the patriarchal names: "In appearance, Israel is those born of Jacob the patriarch, but in spirit, it is those following the faith of our father Abraham" (11.16.9).[85] Then, by adducing Paul's statement from Rom 4:12 and the etymology of the word "Israel" as "a mind seeing God" or "having insight," Oecumenius can conclude that the names of the Israelite tribes represent the complete gathering of the faithful (11.16.9–10). Historical Israel is thus wholly supplanted by the Christian saints. The interpretative strategy at work here is different from the lack of interest on the part of Victorinus or Jerome or, on the other hand, from the genuine attempt at theological reconciliation by Tyconius and Primasius. Oecumenius's spiritual understanding of Israel actively erases any memorial to Jewish history from the New Jerusalem.

Similar conclusions are reached in the substantive discussion he devotes to the foundation gemstones of Rev 21:19–20. It begins with a standard identification in which the stones stand for the virtues of the apostles (12.3.9). Oecumenius, however, thinks more clarification is needed and he refers his reader to the description of the priestly breastplate in Exod 28, being the first commentator to expound its relation to Rev 21 explicitly. As a result of comparing the two texts, Oecumenius notes that four of the Johannine gems (chalcedony, sardonyx, chrysoprase, jacinth) do not appear on the breastplate; the same is the case for nacre from which the gates are made. The exegetical conclusion is that just as the stones of the New Jerusalem are altogether more precious than the priestly ones, so are the commandments of the new covenant in comparison to those of the old one (12.3.12). Thus, that which in the original Johannine text serves as an evocation of the past temple, for Oecumenius becomes a vehicle for stark differentiation between the historical Jewish cult and the eschatological city of the saints.

To recapitulate, though his work is a starting point for the Greek exegetical tradition concerning Revelation, Oecumenius already offers a mature interpretative insight on the walls of the New Jerusalem that partly parallels that of

---

[85] Ἰσραήλ ἐστιν μὲν αἰσθητῶς οἱ ἐξ Ἰακὼβ τοῦ πατριάρχου γεννηθέντες, ἔστι δὲ νοητῶς οἱ στοιχοῦντες τῇ πίστει τοῦ πατρὸς ἡμῶν Ἀβραάμ.

Western commentators. At the same time, he is at his most original when he deals with the Jewish aspects of the city's visuality, which, in his mind, in the end only reinforce its explicitly and exclusively Christian character.

10 Andrew of Caesarea

The second late antique Greek commentary on Revelation – one which would go on to become the standard for the Eastern Christian interpretations of this biblical book, comes from Andrew of Caesarea. The commentary dates most likely to the early 610s and builds on the work of Oecumenius, although Andrew rejects his forerunner's Monophysite tendencies.[86]

Andrew's discussion of the New Jerusalem is based on the unspoken – most likely taken to be obvious – assumption that it should be identified with the church. While that insight is shared with other Christian interpreters of Revelation, it permeates Andrew's exegesis more fully. Christ functions as the city's wall and radiance, while the apostles are naturally its gates (23.67 on Rev 21:11, 12).[87] Andrew incorporates, condenses, and develops Oecumenius's supersessionist reading of the patriarchal names:

> The names of the tribes of the spiritual Israel are written on the apostolic entrances, since those of the physical Israel were written on the shoulder of the archpriest of old. And now Scripture through the means of these names further testifies about the apostles' concern for the faithful.[88]

Andrew then proceeds to quote from Paul (2 Cor 11:28; 6:11; 1 Cor 4:15). While noting the priestly antecedent to John's vision, he understands the mention of Jacob's sons as really referring to the church. Likewise, when discussing the positioning of the gates (23.67 on Rev 21:13), Andrew adduces an Old Testament reference to twelve oxen supporting Solomon's Sea (1 Kgs 7:25; 2 Chr 4:4), but immediately overlays it with multiple Christian meanings: the cruciform layout of the gates, the number of the apostles and the Gospels, and the preaching of the Trinity.

---

[86] On the dating of Andrew's commentary and its relationship to Oecumenius, see Constantinou, *Guiding* (cf. note 82), 47–71; Nathan Betz, "The New Jerusalem: A Metaphor for Deification in the Commentaries on Revelation by Oecumenius and Andrew of Caesarea," *Ephemerides Theologicae Lovanienses* 96, no. 1 (2020): 1–39 at 4–9.

[87] The text and its division according to Josef Schmid, *Der Apokalypse-Kommentar des Andreas von Kaisareia: Text*, vol. 1 of *Studien zur Geschichte des griechischen Apokalypse-Text*, Münchener Theologische Studien 1 (München: Karl Zink, 1955).

[88] τὰ δὲ ὀνόματα τῶν φυλῶν τοῦ νοητοῦ Ἰσραὴλ ἐπὶ ταῖς ἀποστολικαῖς εἰσόδοις γέγραπται, ἐπειδὴ καὶ τὰ τοῦ αἰσθητοῦ ἐν τῇ ἐπωμίδι τοῦ πάλαι κατὰ καιρὸν ἀρχιερέως ἐγέγραπτο· καὶ γὰρ ἡ γραφὴ νῦν διὰ τῶν ὀνομάτων τούτων τὴν περὶ τῶν πιστῶν μέριμναν τοῖς ἀποστόλοις προσμαρτυρεῖ.

Further original exegetical insight is visible in 23.67 on Rev 21:16 where Andrew tries to understand the dimensions of the end-time city. He begins with a standard claim that their equality denotes its solidity and stability, but then recalculates 12,000 stadia as 1,714 miles,[89] which he breaks down in a mystical fashion as one thousand (perfection of eternal life), seven hundred (perfect rest), and fourteen (two Sabbaths, one for the body and one for the soul). Andrew is the only commentator apart from Apringius who is interested in this kind of numerical exegesis.

Much of Andrew's engagement with the New Jerusalem is spent on the exegesis of the twelve foundation stones (23.67 on Rev 21:19–20). Again, as is the case with the patriarchal names on the gates, he begins with Oecumenius's insight, stating that the Johannine extension of the list of gemstones from Exod 28 illustrates the superiority of the new covenant over the old one. Having stated that, Andrew focuses his attention on the presence of the apostle's names on the gemstones (Rev 21:14) and offers a comprehensive identification of each precious stone with one of Christ's disciples. The list can be reproduced in a tabulated form (see table 3).

Andrew's knowledge of the gemstones is taken primarily from Epiphanius of Salamis's *De duodecim gemmis*, a late-fourth-century commentary on Exod 28 focused on gathering information about precious stones.[90] Using it as his basis, the bishop of Caesarea through his exegesis of Rev 21:19–20 provides a form of apostolic history and thus pushes the ecclesiological reading of the New Jerusalem to its conceptual limits.

Overall, Andrew certainly displays exegetical ingenuity in his vision of how the New Jerusalem would look. He is aware of its scriptural roots, at the same time offering novel readings of the city's dimensions and precious foundations. All of that, however, is treated ultimately as signs of its ecclesial identity. The Israelite aspect of its visuality is treated as a mere herald of the new covenant, while the opulent outer look of the future city has no real significance beyond evoking the virtues and exploits of the apostles. While all Christian interpreters discussed here would agree that the Johannine city in its walled shape is the church, it is with Andrew that this identification becomes complete.

---

[89] The source of this equation is unknown. If the Byzantine mile (μίλιον) used here is taken to be 1,574 meters, then the side of the Johannine cubic city would measure for Andrew just short of 2,700 km.

[90] See Robert P. Blake, Henri de Vis, ed., *Epiphanius. De Gemmis* (London: Christophers, 1934); Felix Albrecht, Arthur Manukyan, *Epiphanius von Salamis, Über die zwölf Steine im hohepriesterlichen Brustschild (De duodecim gemmis rationalis)*, Gorgias Eastern Christian Studies 37 (Piscataway: Gorgias Press 2014). On Andrew's use of Oecumenius see Constantinou, *Guiding* (cf. note 82), 86–93.

Table 3. The gemstones of the New Jerusalem in Andrew of Caesarea's interpretation.

Gemstone	Properties	Apostle	Reason
ἴασπις (jasper)	green	Peter	Peter's faith leads to green pastures.
σάπφειρος (sapphire)	azure	Paul	Paul was taken into the third heaven and in heaven he has his citizenship.
χαλκηδών (chalcedony)	coal-like	Andrew	Andrew burnt like coal lit by the Spirit.
σμάραγδος (emerald)	green, brilliant when oiled	John	Oil of John's teaching adds luster to the sorrow of sin.
σαρδόνυξ (sardonyx)	like human fingernail	James	James's martyrdom is like the nail which experiences no sensations when injured.
σάρδιος (sardion/carnelian)	red, therapeutic	Philip	Philip's virtue is bright because of the Spirit and heals spiritual wounds.
χρυσόλιθος (chrysolite)	gold	Bartholomew	Bartholomew was glorious.
βήρυλλιος (beryl)	sea-like in color, close to jacinth	Thomas	Thomas travelled overseas to India.
τοπάζιον (topaz)	deep red, secretes a healing lactose substance	Matthew	Matthew was martyred, while his Gospel brings spiritual healing.
χρυσόπρασος (chrysoprase)	deep gold	Thaddeus	Thaddeus proclaimed Christ's kingdom, which is like gold, to Abgar, and was also martyred, signified by ashes.
ὑάκινθος (jacinth)	deep blue	Simon	Simon was zealous for heavenly gifts and wisdom.
ἀμέθυσος (amethyst)	fiery	Matthias	Matthias received the tongue of fire at Pentecost.

11 Bede the Venerable

The last and, chronologically, the latest exegete to be scrutinized is Bede the Venerable (672/673–735). His *Expositio* (also known as *Explanatio*) *Apocalypseos*, dating to the first decade of the eighth century, is most likely the earliest of Bede's many exegetical writings.[91] The commentary is prefaced by a letter to one Eusebius (also known as Hwaetberth), who would become the abbot of Wearmouth and Jarrow; in the letter, Bede discusses and praises the work of Tyconius, thus consciously positioning himself within the Western exegetical tradition relating to Revelation. His commentary also exhibits knowledge of Jerome's recension of Victorinus, as well as Primasius.[92]

Bede offers the most sustained and peculiar treatment of the exterior of the New Jerusalem. Its outer appearance becomes for him the key to the whole vision, which was not necessarily the case for earlier interpreters. This being said, Bede's reading of some of the pertinent Johannine verses is unmistakably based on prior exegetical tradition, much of which has been scrutinized above. The city is the church, the precious jewel in 21:11 is Christ, jasper symbolizes the clarity of the church's virtues (3.37.15–23).[93] Christ also functions as the city's wall, the gates of which are, unsurprisingly, the apostles (3.37.24–32). Moreover, the fact that three gates face each of the cardinal directions is interpreted as the sign of the church proclaiming the Trinity to the four corners of the world (3.37.42–43). The city's dimensions indicate its perfect stability and immovability (3.37.62–82).

Interestingly, Bede, perhaps taking his cue from Tyconius and Primasius, provides a theological framework for understanding the presence of patriarchal names on the city gates: "[John] signifies the memory of the ancient fathers that is implanted in the hearts of the preachers. For this reason, when the high priest entered the tabernacle, he was commanded to carry the remembrance of the fathers in the breastplate" (3.37.36–38).[94] Although the discussion of the Israelite past of the city is not as explicit and loaded in Bede as it was in Tyconius and especially Primasius, the former still makes a significant point. He certainly recognizes John's dependence on the description of the priestly breastplate in Exod 28 (see also 3.37.364–366), which was worn as an explicit memorial of the sons of Jacob (Exod 28:12). Bede, connecting the temple imagery with that of the

---

[91] Peter Kitson, "Lapidary Traditions in Anglo-Saxon England: Part II," *Anglo-Saxon England* 12 (1983): 73–123 at 74; Kevin Poole, "The Western Apocalypse Commentary Tradition of the Early Middle Ages," in *A Companion to Premodern Apocalypse*, ed. Michael A. Ryan (Leiden: Brill, 2016), 103–43 at 130–31.

[92] Poole, "Western Apocalypse Commentary" (cf. note 91), 132 n. 89.

[93] The text according to Roger Gryson, ed., *Bedae Presbyteri Expositio Apocalypseos*, CCSL 121A (Turnhout: Brepols, 2001).

[94] *Memoriam ueterum patrum significat praedicatorum cordibus insitam. Vnde et pontifex tabernaculum ingressus memoriale patrum in rationali pectoris ferre iubetur.*

New Jerusalem, exhorts preachers and perhaps all the faithful to likewise bear the remembrance of Israel.

The most original portion of Bede's commentary – one in which he is, so to say, in his element – is his extensive discussion of the foundation gems in 21:19–21 (3.37.97–379). Here, the lemma incites the interpreter to provide a fully developed lapidological discussion, drawing on a wide range of ancient sources on natural history and with their help bestowing a meaning on each individual stone. The sources and contemporary parallels of Bede's discussion were thoroughly examined by Peter Kitson and do not have to be analyzed anew here.[95] The basic logic of Bede's exegesis is that the stones represent a variety of virtues.

Table 4. The gemstones of the New Jerusalem in Bede's interpretation.

Stone	Color	Personal characteristic
iaspis (jasper)	either green or white with reddish hue	vigor of faith
saphirus (sapphire)	bright blue	pursuit of heavenly things
carchedonius (chalcedony)	like pale fire	humble, interior faith
smaragdus (emerald)	deep green	faith strong in the face of adversity
sardonix (sardonyx)	bright red	humility, purity
sardius (sardion/carnelian)	like pure blood	martyrdom
chrysolitus (chrysolite)	sparkling blue green	wisdom, preaching
beryllus (beryl)	red	wisdom and divine grace
topazius (topaz)	either gold or translucent; reddish	contemplation
chrysoprasus (chrysoprase)	green and gold	charity
hyacinthus (hyacinth/ jacinth)	dark blue	devotion to heaven
amethystus (amethyst)	purple	memory of heaven

Being a consummate commentator, Bede adduces much biblical material to prove that the exegetical links are not haphazard. In this manner, when he posits that the second stone, sapphire, represents the hope of heavenly things, he strengthens his case by quoting from Exod 24:10: "Under his feet was a work

---

[95] See Kitson, "Lapidary Traditions: Part II" (cf. note 91) and his discussion of Bede's sources in "Lapidary Traditions in Anglo-Saxon England: Part I, the Background; the Old English Lapidary," *Anglo-Saxon England* 7 (1978): 9–60. Of special interest is perhaps Bede's use of Epiphanius's *De duodecim gemmis*; see "Lapidary Traditions: Part I," 20–22, and "Lapidary Traditions: Part II," 80–88.

of sapphire stone, clear as the sky" (adduced already by Epiphanius, *De gemmis* 2.27[96]) and Ezek 1:26a: "And above the dome over their heads there was something like a throne, in appearance like sapphire."

Furthermore, Bede exhibits a unique interest in the origins of the stones, e. g. about chalcedony he says: "And that it occurs among the Nasamones, which is a region of Ethiopia, signifies those who, despite the ardent fervor of love, are despised through low repute, as if due to swarthy skin" (3.37.148–150).[97] The reference to the Nasamones – a people on the southern edges of the known world, first noted by Herodotus (*Hist.* 2.32–33) – most likely originates from Pliny the Elder (*Nat.* 37.30.104) who claims chalcedony originates from the regions settled by them. Very soon after, when elaborating on the Scythian origins of emeralds, Bede refers to a tale, first told from Herodotus (*Hist.* 3.116; 4.13, 27) and repeated by Pliny (*Nat.* 4.26; 6.19; 7.2, 60), about a mythical people, the Arimaspi, unsuccessfully trying to snatch those gems from griffins (3.37.163–191). The subsequent discussion of chrysolite takes the gems' sparkling and marine hue as an explanation for its putative Hebrew name *tharsis*, which Bede certainly connects with the standard Hebrew toponym of the most far-flung overseas regions of the known world, *taršīš*.[98] According to Bede, it is fitting for the seventh stone on the list to be associated with water, since both the number seven and water symbolize the Holy Spirit (3.37.213–232). In his discussion of topaz, Bede identifies its place of origin as the Thebaid in Upper Egypt,[99] which allows him to connect the stone's brilliance with the holiness of the life of Egyptian monks (3.37.272–277).

Bede's interpretation of the New Jerusalem and especially of its foundation gemstones is marked by a willingness to leave no visual detail unexplained and no exegetical connection unjustified. To achieve that, he musters the entire interpretative tradition available to him, as well as many ancient sources on lapidology. The reader of the commentary is taken on a guided tour around the city whose every aspect is related to ecclesiology and Christology. Bede decorates his exegesis of Rev 21 with an array of theological, ethnographic, and naturalistic detail that is not, however, a haphazard assemblage but rather a carefully crafted story about the future church.

---

[96] The division of the text according to the division found in Felix Albrecht and Arthur Manukyan, ed., *Epiphanius von Salamis* (cf. note 90).

[97] *Et quod apud Nasamonas, quae est Aethiopiae prouincia, nascitur, indicat eos sub ardente feruore dilectionis fama tamen obscura quasi nigranti cute sordere.*

[98] This connection is made explicitly in Jerome's commentary on Isa 2:16; see Gryson, *Bedae* (cf. note 93), 544. Moreover, Bede might have associated the sound of the Latinized Hebrew name with the Greek θάλασσα, "sea."

[99] On the sources of this identification see Kitson, "Lapidary Traditions: Part II" (cf. note 91), 95–98.

Conclusion

This contribution has attempted to trace the development of the outer appearance of the New Jerusalem across two sets of sources: the first set consisting of Jewish texts composed before (Ezekiel), during (the Qumran *NJT* text), and after (Revelation) the existence of the Second Temple in Jerusalem, and the second set including early Christian readings of one of those texts, namely Revelation.

When viewed diachronically, the texts show how the walls of the New Jerusalem cease to perform any practical function and become purely a vehicle for ideological expression. Ezekiel likely envisages a real city in need of a real wall and the *NJT* requires it to provide protection in a world engulfed by or emerging from eschatological conflict. In both cases, the city gates serve as ways to recall the fullness of Israel. Revelation, on the other hand, dispenses with any architectural realism and describes a wall that displays the city's unrivalled dimensions and affluence. In the course of the Christian reception of the Johannine text, the city's fantastical appearance becomes increasingly a symbol for the church, its doctrine, its history, and its saintly faithful.

Within that framework, several descriptive details gain or lose significance. While Ezekiel's city is nondescript, some luxurious material is introduced in Isa 54, Tobit, and more amply in the *NJT*. It then becomes the defining feature of John's architectural design, later faithfully preserved and expounded on by subsequent interpreters. On the other hand, Ezekiel and the *NJT* both display a strong interest in ascribing specific gates to specific tribes, developing and employing implicit rules as to their particular order. This interest disappears almost completely from Revelation whose author is content for the entrances to merely evoke the patriarchal names. No Christian interpreter is interested in ascribing one to the other in any rigid way. Very importantly, the New Jerusalem in Ezekielic and Qumranic imagination is organized around and oriented towards the new temple. The temple is explicitly absent from (though not disparaged in) John's Jerusalem and paid no attention to by his commentators.[100]

The last two points are evidence of a larger tendency within the tradition as exemplified and discussed in this contribution. The Christian exegetes interested in the New Jerusalem are interested in it as depicted by Revelation, which they treat as the source of the binding and paradigmatic design. Ezekiel, who definitely influenced the author of Revelation and who is considered rightly to be the paramount exemplar of the New Jerusalem tradition within the Hebrew Bible, is absent from the Christian commentaries on Revelation.[101] The other relevant

---

[100] On the absence of the temple in the Johannine New Jerusalem and its later interpretations, see Mark Edward's contribution to this volume.

[101] Some early Christian authors, however, do mention Ezekiel in relation to the New Jerusalem, e.g. Justin, *Dial.* 80.5 (Philippe Bobichon, ed., *Dialogue avec le Tryphon: edition critique* [Fribourg: Academic Press, 2003], 1.406) and Tertullian, *Marc.* 3.24.4 (Ernest Evans,

prophetic passages from Isaiah and Zechariah and especially the description of the breastplate in Exod 28 appear significantly more often, but even they are not present uniformly across all Revelation commentaries. On the one hand, it might be true that they find Ezekiel's mundane description of little use when confronting Revelation. On the other, the replacement of Ezekiel's text by John's as the description of the New Jerusalem might be motivated by the eagerness of some Christian interpreters to tone down, overwrite, or even mute and supplant the Israelite or Jewish aspects of the city's outer appearance. This approach is especially explicit in – although not limited to – the Eastern exegetical tradition, where the historical Israel is seen as not belonging properly to the eschatological city, neither physically nor even through an evocation of patriarchal names, which are taken as denoting the church. This supersessionist tactic is by no means universal and authors such as Tyconius, Primasius, and Bede recognize the issues at stake and find exegetical ways of preserving Israel's symbolic presence.

This study should not be seen as exhaustive of the topic at hand, as several strands of evidence and possible inquiry have been, by necessity, left out. Understanding the notion of the eschatological city within the context of actual urban designs has proven exceedingly fruitful in relation to the *NJT* and should be applied to other depictions of the New Jerusalem, even those seemingly unrealistic ones.[102] Christian texts have taken up most of this contribution, and further study is needed on how Jewish rabbinic texts envisaged the future restoration of Jerusalem and the temple and to what extent their vision might be read as continuous with biblical and Second Temple antecedents. Investigation of other lines of Christian evidence, such as those possibly contained in commentaries on Ezekiel and other prophetic books as well as in mediaeval and later exegesis of Revelation, will certainly yield results relevant to understanding the appearance of the eschatological city. The walls of the New Jerusalem outgrow their intuitive practical functions and become a striking expression of harmony of physical dimensions, of hope for security and wealth, and of identity as the reconstituted Israel or the eschatological church.

---

ed., *Tertullian: Adversus Marcionem* [Oxford: Clarendon, 1972], 246). I thank Dr. Nathan Betz for bringing these passages to my attention.

[102] On the reverse direction of travel – from the vision of the New Jerusalem to actual architecture – see e.g. Maria Cristina Carile, *The Vision of the Palace of the Byzantine Emperors as a Heavenly Jerusalem* (Spoleto: Fondazione Centro italiano di studi sull'alto Medioevo, 2012). On the artistic depictions of the eschatological city see Armin F. Bergmeier's and Ian Boxall's contributions to this volume.

Representing the Heavenly Jerusalem

Encounters with the Divine in Images and Spaces in Late Antiquity

Armin F. Bergmeier

Introduction

During the central Middle Ages, the Heavenly Jerusalem became a geographical place Christians could move towards across time and space. The era of the Crusades unified the earthly city of Jerusalem with the idea of the heavenly place, enabling people to actively seek it and take possession of it. By conflating the heavenly and earthly Jerusalem, the Christians of the Crusader period made it possible to read the progression towards this place as an eschatological countdown towards the future end times.[1] However, in the preceding centuries, the idea of a Heavenly Jerusalem was not tied to the physical site but rather gave expression to the invisible and intangible divine sphere. Exegetical texts tend to cast the Heavenly Jerusalem as an allegory of the divine realm in the present time. Bianca Kühnel has demonstrated in her seminal monograph on the texts and images pertaining to the Heavenly Jerusalem that the physical place in Judea played no role in the book of Revelation and was of little concern for the patristic and early medieval exegesis of this book.[2] Rather, the Heavenly Jerusalem was understood as a concept and used to describe the state of unity between God and his community of believers, that is, the present church (*ecclesia*).[3] The earthly

---

[1] On the awakening of eschatological notions around Jerusalem see Jay Rubenstein, *Armies of Heaven: The First Crusade and the Quest for Apocalypse* (New York: Basic Books, 2011).

[2] Bianca Kühnel, *From the Earthly to the Heavenly Jerusalem: Representations of the Holy City in Christian Art of the First Millennium*, Römische Quartalschrift für christliche Altertumskunde und Kirchengeschichte: Supplementheft 42 (Rome: Herder, 1987), 78. See also Clementina Mazzucco, "La Gerusalemme celeste dell' 'Apocalisse' nei Padri," in *La dimora di Dio con gli uomini (Ap 21,3): Immagini della Gerusalemme celeste dal III al XIV secolo*, ed. Maria Luisa Gatti Perer (Milan: Vita e Pensiero, 1983), 49–76 at 50; Yves Christe, "Apocalypse et interprétation iconographique: Quelques remarques liminaires sur les images du règne de Dieu et de l'église à l'époque paléochrétienne," *Byzantinische Zeitschrift* 67 (1974): 92–100; Yves Christe, *L'Apocalypse de Jean: sens et développements de ses visions synthétiques* (Paris: Picard, 1996).

[3] For the temporality of visions and presentist, non-eschatological readings see Armin F. Bergmeier, *Visionserwartung: Visualisierung und Präsenzerfahrung des Göttlichen in der Spätantike* (Wiesbaden: Reichert, 2017); Armin F. Bergmeier, "Volatile Images: The Empty

church building was the most likely place where this encounter played out, since, as is well-known, the performance of the liturgy, scent, and song were used to enable and enhance the experience of divine presence.[4]

Informed by later medieval concepts, art historians have tried to identify visualizations of the Heavenly Jerusalem in late antique religious imagery.[5] But this endeavor has proven difficult, as Kühnel and others have since demonstrated. Representations of cities with gem-studded golden walls as described in Rev 21 are scant in the pre-Carolingian period. When they appear, they do so on the fringes of larger, more complex motifs, mostly in monumental mosaics in Rome and Ravenna. The earliest extant image that can be securely identified as a depiction of the Heavenly Jerusalem is located on the triumphal arch of Santa Prassede in Rome, which dates from the early ninth century and will be discussed at the end of this essay.

In this contribution, I argue that prior to the Santa Prassede mosaics, no neatly circumscribed iconography existed for the Heavenly Jerusalem. However, when defined as an image of the presence of the divine and the union of God with his community, we can identify most images of theophanic visions as representations of the Heavenly Jerusalem. This realization has been made difficult by the fact that the images of the Heavenly Jerusalem do not conform to modern categories of iconographic motifs; they must instead be regarded as a fluid cluster of intersecting visual cues that evoke otherworldly settings in which Christ is often approached by saints, apostles, and other humans. Due to the concentration of such images alluding to the Heavenly Jerusalem in monumental art in Rome and Ravenna, this contribution focusses on these two sites.

I further argue in this essay that the theophanic ideas came to be materialized in sacred spaces. It was not an exact emulation of the Biblical description of the Heavenly Jerusalem with gem-studded walls that was transposed into physical spaces. Rather, church buildings sought to enable the experience of God's presence through light and through temporary visions. These were in turn created through precious materials so that the place that appeared to be filled with the divine presence could be understood as an image of the heavenly realm on earth, a place that visualized the unity of the people (*ecclesia*) with the divine sphere. In

---

Throne and Its Place in the Byzantine Last Judgment Iconography," in *Cultures of Eschatology: Authority and Empire in Christian, Muslim, and Buddhist Communities*, ed. Veronika Wieser, vol. 1 (Berlin: De Gruyter, 2020), 86–124; Nathan Betz, "The New Jerusalem: A Metaphor for Deification in the Commentaries on Revelation by Oecumenius and Andrew of Caesarea," *Ephemerides Theologicae Lovanienses* 96, no. 1 (2020): 1–39.

[4] On the use of the book of Revelation in liturgical sources, see Harald Buchinger, "Die Johannes-Apokalypse im christlichen Gottesdienst: Sondierungen in Liturgie und Ikonographie," in *Ancient Christian Interpretations of "Violent Texts" in the Apocalypse*, ed. Joseph Verheyden, Tobias Nicklas, and Andreas Merkt (Göttingen: Vandenhoeck & Ruprecht, 2011), 216–66.

[5] See the extensive catalogue in Gatti Perer, *La dimora di Dio con gli uomini* (cf. note 2), 147–250.

order to do this, it was crucial to cordon off a part of the church interior where this unification could be observed. Chancel screens, often mistaken for liminal structures that enable transformation when crossed, actually served as barriers to the divine sphere, a necessary precondition that allowed people to behold this otherwise invisible place.

1 Theophanies and Visions

Kühnel's monograph contains only one discussion of an image of the Heavenly Jerusalem from late antiquity before moving on to Carolingian and Ottonian examples. This single image is the apse mosaic of Santa Pudenziana in Rome, which has frequently but not unanimously been interpreted as a depiction of the Heavenly Jerusalem in its earthly guise.[6] (Fig. 1) In the foreground we see Christ among his apostles and in the background a city with a monumental golden cross. The four apocalyptic beings hover above the scene. Both Kühnel and Wendy Pullan have identified the buildings in the background as specific Constantinian monuments, namely the rotunda of the Holy Sepulchre in Jerusalem and the octagon of the Church of the Nativity in Bethlehem.[7] Fredric Schlatter reads the cityscape as part of Ezekiel's vision of the temple in Jerusalem (Ezek 40–48).[8] But such a clear attribution cannot be conclusively proven; round and octagonal buildings could be found in any major city in late antiquity. A second argument for an identification with Jerusalem is that the exedra behind the figures contains gates, which might be read as stylized city gates. Today, only six doors are visible. Three more might be hidden behind the figures and two might have been lost when the apse mosaic was cut. However those would amount to a maximum of eleven doors (not twelve). The architecture is furthermore lacking towers, which would seem crucial for depictions of city walls. It therefore seems

---

[6] For eschatological interpretations see, for example, Erich Dinkler, *Das Apsismosaik von S. Apollinare in Classe* (Cologne: Westdeutscher Verlag, 1964), 77–87; Ernst Dassmann, "Das Apsismosaik von S. Pudentiana in Rom: Philosophische, imperiale und theologische Aspekte in einem Christusbild am Beginn des 5. Jahrhunderts," *Römische Quartalschrift* 65 (1970): 67–81; Wendy Pullan, "Jerusalem from Alpha to Omega in the Santa Pudenziana Mosaic," in *The Real and the Ideal Jerusalem in Jewish, Christian, and Islamic Art*, ed. Bianca Kühnel (Jerusalem: HaMakor, 1998), 405–17 at 406. For a non-eschatological interpretation see Olaf Steen, "The Proclamation of the Word: A Study of the Apse Mosaic in S. Pudenziana, Rome," *Acta ad Archaeologiam et Artium Historiam Pertinentia* 11 (1999): 85–113. Galit Noga-Banai allows a wide range of possible interpretations ranging from historical to eschatological readings: *Sacred Stimulus: Jerusalem in the Visual Christianization of Rome* (Oxford: Oxford University Press, 2018), 146.
[7] Kühnel, *From the Earthly to the Heavenly Jerusalem* (cf. note 2), 63–71; Pullan, "Jerusalem from Alpha to Omega" (cf. note 6), 405–17.
[8] Fredric W. Schlatter, "Interpreting the Mosaic of Santa Pudenziana," *Vigiliae Christianae* 46, no. 3 (1992): 276–95 at 283.

Fig. 1. Apse mosaic, Santa Pudenziana, Rome.

more likely that the structure is meant to resemble apsed halls, so common in late antiquity, as a prestigious background for the assembly.

But the apse mosaic can still be read as the Heavenly Jerusalem, not as a literal rendering of the biblical city, but as an iteration of the heavenly realm. The mosaic shares an interest in visualizing the encounter with the divine in the present moment with almost all surviving apse decorations from late antiquity. Thomas Mathews has drawn attention to the fact that such images sought to depict the *divine* Christ.[9] Jean-Michel Spieser concurs and adds that these images allowed viewers to enter into the presence of God.[10] I have argued elsewhere for these divine images' indebtedness to the belief in making the divine visible through visions in the here and now.[11] The connection between these images and late antique religious beliefs surrounding the visionary presence of the divine had not been drawn by earlier scholarship. A reason for this might have been that the images that can be subsumed under the category of theophanies or depictions of the Heavenly Jerusalem do not follow art history's desire for clearly circumscribed and relatively stable iconographies. Therefore, these images are difficult

---

[9] Thomas F. Mathews, *The Clash of Gods: A Reinterpretation of Early Christian Art* (Princeton: Princeton University Press, 1993).

[10] Jean-Michel Spieser, "The Representation of Christ in the Apses of Early Christian Churches," *Gesta* 37, no. 1 (1998): 63–73 at 66.

[11] Bergmeier, *Visionserwartung* (cf. note 3).

Fig. 2. Apse mosaic, Sant'Apollinare in Classe, Ravenna.

to subsume under one iconographic category. However, read more loosely, they all share a common interest in expressing the presence of and unity with the divine through a temporary vision.

To illustrate the friction between modern art historical categories and late antique imagery we might study the apse mosaic at Sant'Apollinare in Classe in Ravenna more closely. (Fig. 2) Scholars have long tried to assign a specific iconographical meaning to this image. Erich Dinkler and others since have striven to show that the image represents the Transfiguration, the metamorphosis of the earthly Jesus into the divine Christ on Mount Tabor (Matt 17:1–13).[12]

---

[12] Dinkler, *Das Apsismosaik von Sant'Apollinare in Classe* (cf. note 6), 19–20; Friedrich Wilhelm Deichmann, *Ravenna, Hauptstadt des spätantiken Abendlandes: Band 1: Geschichte und Monumente* (Wiesbaden: Steiner, 1969), 261–67; Claudia Müller, "Das Apsismosaik von S. Apollinare in Classe. Eine Strukturanalyse," *Römische Quartalschrift* 75 (1980): 11–50 at 48; Angelika Michael, *Das Apsismosaik von Sant'Apollinare in Classe: Seine Deutung im Kontext der Liturgie* (Frankfurt am Main: Lang, 2005), 63–74.

Recently, Annie Labatt has echoed this long-established reading.[13] But while we cannot exclude that late antique viewers were reminded of the story of the Transfiguration – they might very well have been – such an oversimplified interpretation would need more visual or textual proof.

The only visual elements in the apse mosaic that actually suggest a Transfiguration are the two busts of Moses and Elijah hovering on clouds above the scene. However, we must be careful about transferring later stages of meaning-making onto earlier images. If we read the image without trying to construct iconographical developments, Sant'Apollinare in Classe appears less like an anomaly and instead fits with the preoccupations exhibited by many other images from that period. Many images of the time depicted the convergence of the heavenly realm and the human sphere through visionary encounters. Moses and Elijah are not just crucially relevant to late antique Christians because they appear during the Transfiguration, but rather the other way around: they were able to appear during this biblical event because they had already ascended to the heavens prior to the moment when these images were made. Of Elijah, the Bible reports that he rose up to heaven after his death (2 Kgs 2). About the body of Moses, the Bible states that he was buried by God in an unknown place (Deut 34:6). This led to the widespread assumption in late antiquity that Moses was possibly already in the kingdom of God. Flavius Josephus, Clement of Alexandria, Ambrose, and other authors record the tradition that Moses's body had ascended to heaven after his death.[14] Moses and Elijah were thus particularly well suited to testifying to and authenticating theophanic apparitions, as they already inhabited the Heavenly Jerusalem in the present time. Their appeal for late antique Jews and Christians lay in the fact that they would not have to wait until the End of Days in order to enter the divine realm. And this is how the apse mosaic should be primarily understood – as a vision of the divine realm.

The other well-known apse mosaic from Ravenna – the one at San Vitale – even spells out its intention to visualize the heavenly sphere in the form of a vision: directly in front of the apse conch with the enthroned Christ, two visionary images from the Hebrew Testament – Moses and the burning bush and Moses on Sinai – are depicted. Although they clearly mark the apse mosaic as a new Christian theophany through the juxtaposition to the older Mosaic visions, this has largely gone unnoticed in scholarship. The reason for this oversight is likely a crucial misunderstanding regarding early medieval theophanic imagery:

---

[13] Annie Montgomery Labatt, *Emerging Iconographies of Medieval Rome: A Laboratory of Images in the Eighth and Ninth Centuries* (Lanham: Lexington Books, 2019), 99–158.

[14] Flavius Josephus, *Antiquitates iudaicae* 4.326; Ambrose, *De Cain et Abel* 1.2.8; Clement of Alexandria, *Stromateis* 23.153.1. See also Johannes Tromp, *The Assumption of Moses: A Critical Edition with Commentary* (Leiden: Brill, 1993), 281–85; James C. VanderKam and William Adler, ed., *The Jewish Apocalyptic Heritage in Early Christianity*, Compendia Rerum Judaicarum ad Novum Testamentum (Minneapolis: Fortress, 1996), 22.

these images expressed presentist – not eschatological – notions of divine apparitions by trying to anticipate experiences in the here and now that were otherwise inaccessible to humans before the Second Coming. And yet it is once we stop looking for apocalyptic visions of the end that we can understand the images within their late antique thought world.

2 Allegorical Cities

Late antique depictions of cities adorned with gems and golden walls are the most common visual pattern identified by scholars as the Heavenly Jerusalem. Among these depictions are the sixth-century depictions on the former triumphal arch at Santa Maria Maggiore, Santi Cosma e Damiano, and San Lorenzo fuori le mura in Rome, and in San Vitale and Sant'Apollinare in Classe in Ravenna. (Fig. 2–5) The mosaics from the chapel of San Venanzio and Santa Prassede in Rome are slightly later, dating to the mid-seventh and early ninth centuries respectively. (Fig. 6 and 15) Most of these examples feature two cities, identified as Jerusalem and Bethlehem. The identificatory inscriptions invite interpretations as the Heavenly Jerusalem, but at the same time caution against any easy identification. We must ask ourselves; can these images be visual shorthand for the Heavenly Jerusalem, and if so, why is there also a Heavenly Bethlehem?

The reason for the popularity of these two city depictions, which often appear in squinches and corners of more complex images, can be gleaned through a brief study of their iconographic tradition. The two depictions of cities in Santa Maria Maggiore are the first datable ones to be accompanied by an identificatory inscription.[15] (Fig. 3 and 7) But they are not the first vignette depictions of cities surrounded by sheep. The well-known iconography of the *traditio legis,* which can be traced back to the second half of the fourth century, usually includes two allegorical cities, for example in the Anagni slab and in the Pola casket.[16] (Fig. 8) Here, they do not bear inscriptions and are not characterized visually as the Heavenly Jerusalem through either gems or golden color. In fact, they appear in the lowest zone of the composition, not at its top where we would expect a Heavenly Jerusalem, which is where it is located in Santa Prassede, the earliest securely attributable image. In the earliest version of the *traditio legis*, the cities are even reduced to mere huts (Fig. 9). Therefore, we need to assume that these two cities were not identified as the Heavenly Jerusalem in the images of the late antique depictions of the *tradito legis.*

---

[15] See Rotraut Wisskirchen and Stefan Heid, "Der Prototyp des Lämmerfrieses in Alt-St. Peter", in *Tessera: Festschrift für Josef Engemann*, ed. Ernst Dassmann and Klaus Thraede (Münster: Aschendorff, 1991), 138–60 at 147.

[16] Armin F. Bergmeier, "The *Traditio Legis* in Late Antiquity and Its Afterlives in the Middle Ages," *Gesta* 56, no. 1 (2017): 27–52.

Fig. 3. Triumphal arch mosaic, Santa Maria Maggiore, Rome.

Fig. 4. Apse and apse wall mosaic, Santi Cosma e Damiano, Rome.

Fig. 5. Jerusalem and Bethlehem, apse wall, San Vitale, Ravenna.

In Santa Maria Maggiore (AD 434), the two cities on the former apse wall likely visually highlight the beginning and the end points of Jesus's life. Here, Bethlehem and Jerusalem perfectly frame the time between Jesus's birth in Bethlehem and his death on Golgotha. A twelfth-century copy of the fourth-century apse decoration of Old St. Peter's in Rome executed in fresco in the church of San Silvestro in Tivoli (Fig. 10) retains the nameless representation of the two allegorical cities. However, most images of the *traditio legis* executed after Santa Maria Maggiore's mosaics bear the inscriptions of Bethlehem and Jerusalem, for example in the Santi Cosma e Damiano mosaics, which date from AD 526–530. (Fig. 11) But images of the concept of the Heavenly Jerusalem – the ecclesia, the union of humans and the divine – they were not.

Fig. 6. Apse wall mosaic, San Venanzio, Lateran baptistery, Rome.

Fig. 7. Detail depicting Jerusalem, triumphal arch, Santa Maria Maggiore, Rome.

Fig. 8. *Traditio Legis*, burial slab (drawing and photograph), Palazzo Bonifacio VIII, Anagni (with kind permission of the Congregazione delle Suore Cistercensi della Carità).

Fig. 9. *Traditio Legis*, niche mosaic, Santa Costanza, Rome.

Fig. 10. Allegorical city, apse fresco, San Silvestro, Tivoli (first half of the twelfth century).

3 Lambs and Sheep

But another element in the *traditio legis* iconography can, in fact, be identified as an allegorical depiction of the Heavenly Jerusalem. If we follow the late antique exegesis of this concept, we should not look for a literal depiction of a city (in any case only a single city) but rather for a depiction of the community of believers, the church. We find this in the sheep, which have long been identified as depictions of the faithful or as a christological image, but to my knowledge, never as signifying the *ecclesia,* the community with God.[17]

Very often we witness sheep or lambs in proximity to theophanic visions. In Sant'Apollinare in Classe they unusually frame the central image of a theophanic cross apparition. In images of the *traditio legis*, they commonly converge towards a central lamb on a mountain. Stefan Heid and Rotraut Wisskirchen have demonstrated that the *Lämmerfries* was a depiction of Isaiah's prophetic description of the pilgrimage of nations towards Mount Zion, that is towards

---

[17] See for example Geir Hellemo, *Adventus Domini: Eschatological Thought in 4th-century Apses and Catecheses,* Supplements to Vigiliae Christianae 5 (Leiden: Brill, 1989), 117–21.

Fig. 11. Detail depicting Bethlehem, apse mosaic, Santi Cosma e Damiano, Rome.

Jerusalem.[18] I have added to this that the entire iconographic scheme of the *traditio legis* with Christ next to Peter and Paul between two palm trees should be read as a translation of Isa 2:2–4 into visual form.[19] Sometimes, as in Santi Cosma e Damiano, the core iconography was enhanced by the addition of further saints who are shown to be present in the heavenly realm. (Fig. 4) What the beholders experienced was a vision of the Heavenly Jerusalem. In several of these examples, the central theophanic image is framed by further theophanic images on the apse walls taken from the prophetic texts, such as the twenty-four elders from Rev 4:4, who were likely meant to signify the community of believers. These are unified with the divine apparition at the center of the composition, together forming the church. The sheep support this meaning, which seems to have been of central importance to late antique Christians. Here, the believers converge towards Zion, represented as the Lamb of God on a small hill. (Fig. 12) Taken together, the representations of community and divine apparition visualize the intellectual concept of the Heavenly Jerusalem.

---

[18] Wisskirchen and Heid, "Der Prototyp des Lämmerfrieses" (cf. note 15).

[19] For the arguments see Bergmeier, "The *Traditio Legis* in Late Antiquity and Its Afterlives" (cf. note 16). For a development of Is 2:2–4 with respect to the Heavenly Jerusalem, see Antti Laato's contribution in the present volume.

Fig. 12. Detail depicting the lamb on the mountain, apse mosaic, Santi Cosma e Damiano, Rome.

My suggestion that the lambs and not the vignettes of heavenly cities should be read as visual shorthand for the Heavenly Jerusalem can also be confirmed in drawings made of the Santa Pudenziana mosaic before it was altered in the course of renovations: a lamb – probably on a mountain – stands at the bottom of the composition. There is no indication of an entire frieze of lambs, although it might have been obscured over time.[20] Geir Hellemo has interpreted the composition as an image of the Trinity, as the sixteenth- and seventeenth-century drawings show a dove just above the lamb.[21] However, this would presuppose that we read the figure of the enthroned Christ as God the Father. Comparisons with other

---

[20] Schlatter suggests that this part was restored in the eighth century because no images survive that show the juxtaposition of lamb and dove. The highly unusual combination of these two animals might indeed be an indication of a later intervention. However, the lamb's position would fit with the general arrangement of iconographical motifs in late antiquity and has an important parallel in the Milan sarcophagus. See Schlatter, "Interpreting the Mosaic of Santa Pudenziana" (cf. note 8), 286.

[21] Hellemo, *Adventus Domini,* (cf. note 17) 121. Alfonso Ciaconio's drawing can be found in the Biblioteca Apostolica Vaticana, Vat. lat. 5407, p. 81. For another one from the seventeenth century, see John Osborne and Amanda Claridge, *The Paper Museum of Cassiano dal Pozzo: Early Christian and Medieval Antiquities*, 2 vols. (London: Harvey Miller, 1997), cat. no. 176.

Fig. 13. Traditio Legis, city-gate-sarcophagus, Sant'Ambrogio, Milan (after Hans Ulrich von Schoenebeck, Der Mailänder Sarkophag und seine Nachfolge [Roma: Pontificio Istituto di Archeologia Cristiana, 1935], fig. 4).

images of Christ among his disciples show that the lamb has no firm place in the iconography of Christ between his disciples. However, Santa Pudenziana is not the only example where a single lamb was added to a theophanic scene; we find a similar addition on the Milan sarcophagus from Sant'Ambrogio, a visual parallel that has rarely been observed. (Fig. 13) The sarcophagus has been dated to the end of the fourth century, and scholars generally believe that it was produced in Rome and then taken to Milan.[22] Here, no dove is depicted, but Christ is shown sitting on a rock or a mountain, which can be identified as Mount Zion in accordance with the *traditio legis* iconography. That image is depicted on the opposite side together with the frieze of lambs emerging from two cities. The standing Christ of the *traditio* scene is similarly shown on Mount Zion, but given that the standing figure takes up more space, the rock had to be reduced in size. Both scenes take place in front of a row of city gates, a common way for structuring the background of sarcophagi. It is possible that the Santa Pudenziana mosaic borrowed from sarcophagi the idea of city gates to structure the background of the scene.

---

[22] Guntram Koch, *Frühchristliche Sarkophage* (Munich: Beck, 2000), 453.

Thus, it is important to not confuse the vignettes of cities, so common in late antique imagery, with depictions of the Heavenly Jerusalem; it is the frieze of lambs converging towards Mount Zion that can be read as signifying the Heavenly Jerusalem, the unity of earthly and heavenly spheres through God's presence in the church. After Santa Maria Maggiore's mosaics the meaning of these symbolic cities as mere points of origin was enhanced by the inscriptions as Jerusalem and Bethlehem. But while they are connected to the concept of the Heavenly Jerusalem, they are not the thing itself.

4   Churches and Screens

A second important way of representing divine presence, the community of the *ecclesia* or the Heavenly Jerusalem was the physical church space itself.[23] While the fact that Christian church buildings were perceived as holy is frequently discussed in scholarship, the fact that the site's holiness enabled the confluence of divine and earthly spheres in the here and now has been less often noted.[24] Late antique and medieval authors frequently describe church buildings as representations of the heavenly sphere.[25] An experience of the church building

---

[23] Géza Jázai, "Jerusalem, Himmlisches," in *Lexikon der christlichen Ikonographie 2: Allgemeine Ikonographie: Fabelwesen – Kynokephalen* (1994), 394–99; Nadja Horsch, *Ad astra gradus: Scala Santa und Sancta Sanctorum in Rom unter Sixtus V. 1585–1590*, Römische Studien der Bibliotheca Hertziana 35 (Munich: Hirmer, 2014), 51.

[24] For an in-depth discussion see Bergmeier, *Visionserwartung* (cf. note 3), 238–60. On the sacredness of place in the Christian tradition see Paul Corby Finney, "Sacred Place Again," in *Sacralidad y Arqueología: Thilo Ulbert zum 65. Geburtstag am 20. Juni 2004 gewidmet*, ed. J.M. Blázquez Martínez and A. González Blanco, Antigüedad y Cristianismo 21 (Murcia: Universidad de Murcia, 2004), 69–74; Carola Jäggi, "Kirche als heiliger Raum," in *Sakralität zwischen Antike und Neuzeit*, ed. Berndt Hamm, Klaus Herbers, and Heidrun Stein-Kecks, Beiträge zur Hagiographie 6 (Stuttgart: Steiner, 2007), 75–89; Miriam Czock, *Gottes Haus: Untersuchungen zur Kirche als heiligem Raum von der Spätantike bis ins Frühmittelalter*, Millenium Studies 38 (Berlin: De Gruyter, 2012).

[25] Pseudo-Dionysius described the earthly liturgy as "an imitation and revelation of the one in heaven" in the sixth century (a characterization of Pseudo-Dionysius' *De coelesti hierarchia* 1.3 in Alexander Golitzin, "Hierarchy versus Anarchy? Dionysius Areopagita, Symeon the New Theologian, Nicetas Stethatos, and Their Common Roots in Ascetical Tradition," St. Vladimir's Theological Quarterly 38, no. 2 [1994], quoted in Kathleen McVey, "Spirit Embodied: The Emergence of Symbolic Interpretations of Early Christian and Byzantine Architecture," in *Architecture as Icon: Perception and Representation of Architecture in Byzantine Art*, ed. Slobodan Ćurčić [New Haven: Yale University Press, 2010], 59). For more examples see McVey, "Spirit Embodied," 39–71; Armin F. Bergmeier, "Vom Kultbild zur Kirche: Veränderte Materialisierungsformen von Heiligkeit in der Spätantike," in *Erzeugung und Zerstörung von Sakralität zwischen Antike und Mittelalter*, ed. Armin Bergmeier, Katharina Palmberger, and Joseph Sanzo (Munich: Propylaeum, 2016), 63–80. See also the introduction to Emilie M. van Opstall, ed., *Sacred Thresholds: The Door of the Sanctuary in Late Antiquity*, Religions in the Graeco-Roman World 185 (Leiden: Brill, 2018), 1–30.

as an image of the heavens was achieved through words, song, images, scent, and light.[26] But churches were also places where the divine presence encountered the community of believers to form a synesthetic experience with the help of architecture and images.

The authors of the New Testament and the apologists reject the idea that Christians should possess sacred spaces and sacred images. The passage in Acts 7:48 refuses any notion of the Christian God dwelling in a structure made by human hands. Clement of Alexandria echoed this attitude towards things made by human hands and emphasized that his use of the term ἐκκλησία referred to the community of believers, *not* to the church building.[27] Such lofty ideas were, however, forgotten by the beginning of the fourth century. Reality squarely contradicted the rhetoric. The speech given by Eusebius on the occasion of the dedication of the church at Tyrus (between AD 316 and 319) is a testament to the Christian quest to overcome the division between heavenly and earthly spheres within architectural spaces. Eusebius describes the church as an image of heaven and of the Heavenly Jerusalem.[28] He stresses that through the building of churches it has become possible to experience and behold the divine presence on earth.[29]

But how did sacred spaces succeed in making visitors believe they had entered a space where the invisible, immaterial divine entity was palpable and even visible? Agostino Colli has unconvincingly argued that only specific, prominent churches served as images of the Heavenly Jerusalem.[30] Jean-Michel Spieser notes that the aim of generating presence was achieved through "a hierarchical organization of sacred space" through the indication of directionality between the entrance and the apse.[31] I think that the division of the space into two intersecting spaces replicating the division between heavenly and earthly spheres played a more important role. Late antique churches visualized the divine presence by dividing their interiors into two parts, using choir screens and templa. The area in front of the screen was designated for the congregation while the area behind the screen was the locus of the numinous. Both parts of a building

---

[26] See Buchinger, "Die Johannes-Apokalypse im christlichen Gottesdienst" (cf. note 4).

[27] Clement of Alexandria, *Stromateis* 7.5.28–29. Similarly, see Minucius Felix, *Octavius* 32.

[28] Eusebius, *Historia ecclesiastica* 10.4.25 and 10.4.70. Similarly, see Eusebius's description of the Church of the Holy Sepulchre as a new Jerusalem in the *Vita Constantini* 3.33.

[29] Eusebius, *Hist. eccl.* 10.4.6. The trope of heaven embodied by sacred spaces and the idea of the macroscopic world finding its place within the microcosm of the church can be found in later authors such as Choricius of Gaza, Paul the Silentiary, Photius, Constantine Rhodius, and Mesarites among others. See for example Ruth Webb, "The Aesthetics of Sacred Space: Narrative, Metaphor, and Motion in 'Ekphraseis' of Church Buildings," *Dumbarton Oaks Papers* 53 (1999): 59–74 at 67–70; Emilie M. van Opstall, "On the Threshold: Paul the Silentiary's Ekphrasis of Hagia Sophia," in van Opstall, *Sacred Thresholds* (cf. note 25), 31–65 at 35.

[30] Agostino Colli, "La tradizione figurativa della Gerusalemme celeste: linee di sviluppo dal sec. III als sec. XIV," in Gatti Perer, *La dimora di Dio con gli uomini* (cf. note 2), 119–46.

[31] Spieser, "The Representation of Christ" (cf. note 10), 66.

communicated with each other visually, but the boundary between them was usually *not* transcended by the members of the congregation. Therefore, contrary to common assumptions, these spaces were not so much liminal spaces, but instead sites for experiencing a divine presence.[32]

The early history of screens is not altogether clear. But it appears that unlike the closed late Byzantine iconostases, chancel screens provided visual access to the space beyond them: while they sometimes bore images on the transversal beams, they were not clad in images from top to bottom. An entry in the *Liber Pontificalis* records that the Lateran church possessed a high screen, a fastigium, reminiscent of a temple façade, which bore silver statues of Christ among his apostles and of Christ between angels.[33] Pier Luigi Tucci has proposed the existence of various other "pergulas" in early medieval Roman churches.[34] A gift of curtains was recorded for Santi Cosma e Damiano's templon screen, and others existed in Santa Maria Maggiore, and San Paolo fuori le mura.[35] Sible de Blaauw and Klára Doležalová have noted that textile gifts mentioned in the *Liber Pontificalis* were sometimes used to veil the ciboria and the templon screens in eighth- and ninth-century churches.[36] Unlike in the thirteenth-century Western churches and late Byzantine churches, these veils were not used to block the view into the sanctuary during mass entirely. Rather, they were used to "conceal the sanctuary when it was not in use" and to open up the sanctuaries "in certain moments and at certain occasions."[37]

Evidence for the attempted *unification* of the earthly and divine spheres through the *division* of church space into two parts can also be found in liturgical writings. The church father Maximus Confessor (580–662) notes that the division

---

[32] Jelena Bogdanović and Katherine Marsengill, "Conclusions: Iconic Perception and Noetic Contemplation of the Sacred," in *Perceptions of the Body and Sacred Space in Late Antiquity and Byzantium*, ed. Jelena Bogdanović (Abingdon: Routledge, 2018), 190–201 at 190.

[33] *Liber Pontificalis* 34.9–11. See, Sible de Blaauw, "Das Fastigium der Lateransbasilika: Schöpferische Innovation, Unikat oder Paradigma?" in *Innovation in der Spätantike*, ed. Beat Brenk (Wiesbaden: Reichert, 1996), 53–65; and Sible de Blaauw, "Imperial Connotations in Roman Church Interiors: The Significance and Effect of the Lateran Fastigium," *Acta ad Archaeologiam et Artium Historiam Pertinentia* 15 = Rasmus Brandt and Olaf Steen, ed., *Imperial Art as Christian Art: Christian Art as Imperial Art* (Rome: Bardi, 2001), 137–46; Josef Engemann, "Der Skulpturenschmuck des Fastigiums Konstantins I. nach dem Liber Pontificalis und der Zufall der Überlieferung," *Rivista di Archeologia Cristiana* 69 (1993): 179–203 at 201–3.

[34] Pier Luigi Tucci, "The Revival of Antiquity in Medieval Rome: The Restoration of the Basilica of SS. Cosma e Damiano in the Twelfth Century," *Memoirs of the American Academy in Rome* 49 (2004): 99–126.

[35] Tucci, "The Revival of Antiquity" (cf. note 24), 120–22.

[36] Sible de Blaauw and Klára Doležalová, "Constructing Liminal Space? Curtains in Late Antique and Early Medieval Churches," in *The Notion of Liminality and Medieval Sacred Space*, ed. Klara Doležalová and Ivan Foletti (Brno: Didot, 2019), 46–66. Elisabetta Scirocco and Vlad Bedros, "Liturgical Screens, East and West: Liminality and Spiritual Experience," in Doležalová and Foletti, *The Notion of Liminality and Medieval Sacred Space*, 68–89.

[37] De Blaauw and Doležalová, "Constructing Liminal Space?" (cf. note 36), 52.

of the church space into two distinct spheres represents the image and the archetype, the visible and the invisible world. He does not characterize this division as a strong separation, but rather as a form of complementarity.[38] Such an understanding of ecclesiastical space is still echoed in late Eastern Roman (Byzantine) sources. Taking his inspiration from Maximus, the fourteenth-century author Symeon of Thessalonica similarly applied the distinction between the invisible heavenly and the visible earthly sphere to the division of the church space, emphasized by the choir screen or templon. According to Symeon, the two parts of the church are "the heavens in the sacred sanctuary and the earth in the divine nave." The sanctuary "typifies the heavenly tabernacle round about God, where the hosts of angels and the repose of the saints are. By means of the chancel screen or the pillars [the templon], it represents the difference between sensible and spiritual realities."[39] Both Maximus and Symeon use Neoplatonist notions of vision. Andrew Louth has noted that it was Maximus who made the connection between Pseudo-Dionysius the Areopagite's idea of a heavenly hierarchy – in which all elements enter into a union with God – and the production of church spaces.[40] Contrary to our modern understanding of hierarchies and contrary to opaque late medieval chancel screens, the hierarchy expressed horizontally and vertically in the decoration of late antique and early medieval sacred spaces was one of inclusion and union, not of division and separation.[41] It is the confluence of these two parts of the whole, of the material and the immaterial, the sanctuary and the nave, that enabled an experience of divine presence – of a Heavenly Jerusalem. The place where the two spheres touch was marked by choir screens and templa, but was also negotiated through the use of images. Almost none of these furnishings have come down to us in their material form.

---

[38] Maximus the Confessor, *Mystagogia* 2: "How and in What Mode the Holy Church is the Image of the Universe, which Subsists in Visible and Invisible Realities. As the second point of his contemplation, the blessed elder said that the holy Church of God is a representation and image of the entire universe, which subsists in visible and invisible realities, because the Church contains the same oneness and diversity as God." Περὶ τοῦ, πῶς, καὶ τίνα τρόπον εἰκών τοῦ ἐξ ὁρατῶν καὶ ἀοράτων οὐσιῶν ὑφεστῶτος κόσμου ἡ ἁγία τοῦ Θεοῦ Ἐκκλησία. Κατὰ δευτέραν δὲ θεωρίας ἐπιβολὴν, τοῦ σύμπαντος κόσμου τοῦ ἐξ ὁρατῶν καὶ ἀοράτων οὐσιῶν ὑφεστῶτος εἶναι τύπον καὶ εἰκόνα, τὴν ἁγίαν τοῦ Θεοῦ Ἐκκλησίαν ἔφασκεν, ὡς τὴν αὐτὴν αὐτῷ καὶ ἕνωσιν καὶ διάκρισιν ἐπιδεχομένην (*PG* 91:668D). English translation from Jonathan J. Armstrong, trans., *Saint Maximus the Confessor. On the Ecclesiastical Mystagogy* (New York: St Vladimir's Seminary, 2019), 55. On the division of church space, see Andrew Louth, *Maximus the Confessor* (London: Routledge, 1996), 72–73.

[39] Symeon of Thessalonica, *Liturgical Commentaries* 16 and 17 (Steven Hawkes-Teeples, ed. and transl., *Symeon of Thessalonica. The Liturgical Commentaries* [Toronto: Pontifical Institute of Mediaeval Studies, 2011], 90–1): Τὸν οὐρανὸν μὲν διὰ τοῦ βήματος, τὰ περίγεια δὲ διὰ τοῦ Θείου ναοῦ.... Καὶ διὰ μὲν τοῦ ἐν τῷ θυσιαστηρίῳ καταπετάσματος τὴν ἐπουράνιον ἐκτυποῖ περὶ τὸν Θεὸν σκηνήν, ἔνθα τῶν ἀγγέλων οἱ δῆμοι καὶ ἡ τῶν ἁγίων ἐστὶν ἀνάπαυσις. διὰ δὲ τῶν κιγκλίδων, ἤτοι τῶν διαστύλων, τὴν διαφορὰν τῶν αἰσθητῶν πρὸς τὰ νοητά.

[40] Louth, *Maximus the Confessor* (cf. note 38), 19 and 28–31.

[41] Louth, *Maximus the Confessor* (cf. note 38), 30.

The Roman church of Santa Prassede, however, retains a mosaic on its triumphal arch visualizing the Heavenly Jerusalem, one of the earliest images that expressed this concept in the guise of a heavenly city.

5 Santa Prassede

Templon screens shared a function with triumphal arches known from early and high medieval churches in the West: they divided the space into a (larger) western part and a (shorter) eastern part. Erected during the pontificate of Pope Pascal I (817–824), the images in the apse and on the apse wall of Santa Prassede have been carefully copied from the church of Santi Cosma e Damiano; the titular saints Cosmas and Damian were simply replaced with Pudentiana and Praxedis. (Fig. 14 and 15) But the mosaic program contains an important addition to its archetype in Santi Cosma e Damiano. The triumphal arch exhibits the oldest extant depiction of the Heavenly Jerusalem as a city inhabited by angels, apostles, and martyrs. Within the golden, gem-studded walls of Jerusalem we see Christ in the center, flanked by the Virgin, John, and Praxedis. They are surrounded by the twelve apostles, including Peter and Paul approaching from the left and right. These in turn are bracketed by two figures who have frequently been identified as Moses, who is carrying a table inscribed with the word *LEGE*, and Isaiah, who is accompanied by an angel. Four additional angels guard the two entrances into the city. On the right side, Peter and Paul are shown yet again, guarding the entrance, while two groups of saints carrying wreaths approach from the right and the left to enter the city.

Scholars generally agree that the depiction shows the Heavenly Jerusalem in accordance with Rev 21.[42] However, the image does not strictly correspond to the biblical description and instead follows the late antique image practice of visually joining theophanic motifs from various biblical sources.[43] The emphasis on the martyrs results from Pascal's efforts to relocate various martyrs' relics from the cemeteries into his church, an act commemorated by the titular inscription.[44] Some scholars have argued that the scene depicts the second coming of Christ, but evidence for such an eschatological reading is scant, particularly given that late antique and early medieval visual culture generally did not express an interest in depicting the future horrors of the Last Judgment, but rather

---

[42] Marchita B. Mauck, "The Mosaic of the Triumphal Arch of S. Prassede: A Liturgical Interpretation," *Speculum* 62, no. 4 (1987): 813–28 at 814.

[43] Rainer Warland, "Review of R. Wisskirchen, *Das Mosaikprogramm von S. Prassede in Rom*," *Byzantinische Zeitschrift* 84, no. 1 (1992): 541–43.

[44] On the inscription, see Ursula Nilgen, "Die große Reliquieninschrift von Santa Prassede. Eine quellenkritische Untersuchung zur Zeno-Kapelle," *Römische Quartalschrift* 69 (1974): 7–29.

Fig. 14. Triumphal arch, apse, and apse wall, Santa Prassede, Rome.

the community with God and the current state of the world under the reign of Christ in the here and now.[45] It appears to have been Pascal's intention to visualize the saints' proximity to the divine sphere at the present moment. The figures of Moses and Elijah support this reading; as we have seen above, their primary role was not to act as a visual marker for identifying the transfiguration iconography, but to bear witness to divine apparitions because they had already risen up to the heavenly realm.[46] Thus, similar to the mosaic in Sant' Apollinare in Classe, the depiction of the Heavenly Jerusalem in Santa Prassede was just that – a representation of the divine realm, not of the historical Transfiguration or of the future Last Judgment.[47]

This is further underlined by a visual detail on the triumphal arch that has thus far gone unnoticed. A row of figures populates the heavenly city in this mosaic – Christ between two processions of apostles approaching from the left and right – that has clear roots in earlier theophanic imagery. The no-longer-extant apse

---

[45] For an overview of this question, see Bergmeier, *Visionserwartung* (cf. note 3).

[46] For interpretations of the image as a transfiguration see Rotraut Wisskirchen, *Das Mosaikprogramm von S. Prassede in Rom. Ikonographie und Ikonologie,* Jahrbuch für Antike und Christentum (Münster: Aschendorf, 1990), 87–93; Labatt, *Emerging Iconographies* (cf. note 13), 138–40.

[47] Mauck, "The Mosaic of the Triumphal Arch" (cf. note 42), 814; Jaś Elsner, "Image and Iconoclasm in Byzantium," *Art History* 11 (1988): 471–91 at 481; Bergmeier, *Visionserwartung* (cf. note 3), 129–36.

Fig. 15. Heavenly Jerusalem, triumphal arch, Santa Prassede, Rome.

mosaics at Sant'Andrea in Catabarbara, Sant'Agata dei Goti and San Lorenzo in Lucina, which are only preserved in modern drawings, all depicted exactly this visual pattern of Christ between his apostles.[48] This iconography is one example of theophanic motifs found in late antique apse decorations, which all show the convergence of figures – saints or lambs – towards the Godhead.[49] Thus, this visual composition was familiar to Roman viewers at the time, lending additional readability and credibility to Pascal's new visual formula for visualizing the Heavenly Jerusalem in the form of a theophanic vision in the present moment.

Conclusion

The Heavenly Jerusalem was a spiritual state of thinking about the presence of God and of achieving unity with the divine. Therefore, when looking for images of this concept, we should not necessarily look for depictions of literal cities; rather, we should look for creative translations of this concept into visual and architectural formulae. The desire to visually imagine the community with God inspired a variety of methods for representing the concept of the Heavenly Jerusalem. It can be found in images depicting lambs converging towards a center. It can be recognized in processions of saints converging towards Christ and in various depictions of theophanic visions. It furthermore found material expression through the division of church spaces and the installation of a choir screen or templon. As noted by Maximus Confessor, this dividing line was less a stark separation than a way to create unity with the divine. The architectural structure thus mimicked what theophanic images likewise sought to evoke. Thus, the concept of the Heavenly Jerusalem – the quest for unity with the divine through a theophanic vision and the experience of divine presence – does not

---

[48] Osborne and Claridge, *The Paper Museum of Cassiano dal Pozzo* (cf. note 21), cat. no. 71, 163–66, 178.

[49] Mathews, *The Clash of Gods* (cf. note 9), 142–76.

appear to have been represented through literal visualizations of the textual description of the heavenly city in the book of Revelation.

Such a literal approach would be reserved for the era of the Crusades, when the Heavenly Jerusalem would become connected to the physical place of Jerusalem. It was then that Jerusalem began to act as a teleological goal for movement across geographies as well as for the progression of time and history. By contrast, in the early ninth-century mosaics in Santa Prassede, we can witness how image makers strove to invent a new visual language for the spatial demarcation between the sanctuary and the nave. It is the oldest known depiction of the Heavenly Jerusalem as an inhabited city. This visual formula was still very much indebted to late antique theophanic imagery and was less closely tied to the biblical text in Rev 21 and 22. It would be the image makers and patrons of subsequent centuries who strove to bring images and text more closely together. During late antiquity, the Heavenly Jerusalem was predominantly accessible in the form of an experience of the divine presence, triggered by intellectual visions and supported by architectural furnishings and images in sacred spaces.

Where Is the New Jerusalem?

Mark Edwards

Introduction

There is no escaping paradox when we try to conceive the afterlife. On the one hand, since the stuff of all our concepts is the imagery that we draw from our sensations, we cannot but imagine the next world and its denizens as corporeal; on the other, since all bodies that we know are perishable, we must either suppose our concepts to be false or postulate bodies of a kind that our experience has not shown us. Again, we have no consciousness of existence that is not spatial – perhaps too no conception of time without space – and it might seem to follow that if we exist after death there must be a place for us; yet a place outside the world is something of which we can make no sense, while a place inside the world should be inhabited by bodies of the kind that we know already. We are apt to think that the difference between a Christian and a Platonist in antiquity was that one affirmed and one mocked the resurrection of the body; by the end of the second century, however, it was evident that neither of these doctrines could be maintained without qualification.[1] To Platonists the survival of the soul without a body to animate, and without any matter to differentiate it, was barely conceivable, unless soul were reduced to intellect; for Christians, the prospect of a literal resurrection from the grave receded with every year that the kingdom was postponed and with every burning or drowning of a martyr's body. Doubts with regard to the future place of souls could not be answered, though they might be aggravated, by appeals to the myths of Plato or the promises of Jesus. Both appeared to teach that the proper element of the soul, whatever its vehicle, was in heaven; at the same time, texts could be cited to prove that the Hades of one and the paradise of the other were somewhere on earth, though not accessible on this side of death.

Christian speculation on the texture of the resurrection body and its location after death has been much canvassed in recent scholarship. It is generally agreed that, of all theological inquiries, eschatology is the one that levies the highest

---

[1] For discussion see below and also Sophie Cartwright, "The Philosophy of the Resurrection in Early Christianity," in *The Routledge Handbook of Early Christian Philosophy*, ed. Mark J. Edwards (London: Routledge, 2021), 153–63.

tax on human ingenuity, since while it cannot dispense with either philosophy or textual exegesis, the philosophy is peculiarly stochastic and the relevant texts peculiarly arcane. Both pagans and Christians faced this difficulty, but for the latter it involved the more radical problem of reconciling a Hebraic acquiescence in divine speech with a Greek desire for immediate vision of the truth. The subject that I consider in this paper, the materiality of the New Jerusalem, is rendered still more obscure by the division of opinion among ancient commentators as to whether it belongs properly to the next world or to the last days of the present one, and this in turn raises a question as to how faithfully the new will resemble the old. The Greek heritage of early Christian commentators may have made it easier for them to envisage a Jerusalem that was not, in the vulgar sense of that term, corporeal; at the same time it predisposed them to think of a city as a place built to endure, whose walls and streets had more than an adventitious relation to the happiness and self-understanding of its citizens. I shall therefore begin by examining the relation between the present and the future Jerusalem in the two Testaments; I shall then go on to sketch the transition in early Christian thought from an intramundane to an postmundane concept of the New Jerusalem, or rather to a double conception of it as a future city and a present commonwealth, consisting of those who are saved but not yet glorified, and thus at once corporeal and spiritual, of this world and the next.

1 God against the City

The Israelites, according to their own account, were a people whom God had chosen for himself in the loins of Abraham, calling him from the great city of Ur to a territory that at that time was largely unsettled. Abraham himself witnessed the destruction of two opulent cities, Sodom and Gomorrah, not having made his home in either (Gen 19); as strangers in Egypt, however, his descendants were compelled to build two great centers for storage, Pithon and Rameses (Exod 1:11). When his descendants entered Canaan, the fortifications of Jericho fell by a miracle (Josh 6:1–27), while Ai was taken by stratagem with great slaughter (Josh 8:20). The capture of Hebron, "annihilating everything as the Lord required," is ascribed in the Bible to Joshua (Josh 10:26–32), Caleb, and Judah (Josh 21:11; Judg 1:10). The narrative does not commemorate the founders of cities, and when we read in Josh 20 that six of the captured cities were to offer asylum to those accused of murder, we are reminded that that the creator of the first city was the first murderer, after he had gone out from the face of the Lord (Gen 4:16–17).

Josephus, writing for Greeks and Romans who held the founders of cities in great reverence, none the less sees Cain's enterprise[2] as the beginning of a career

---

[2] In fact he attributes to him two foundations, one of Nod with his wife alone, and one of Enoch with the reluctant collaboration of his wife and son.

of pillage and bloodshed, on which his descendants were able to improve in each generation as they invented the arts of agriculture and warfare (*Jewish Antiquities* [*Antiquitates iudaicae*] 1.2). Philo passes a similar judgment on Cain and his posterity, explaining that the city represents the creed that a soul forms for itself when estranged from its Maker. The Hebrew prophets were conscious that swords that could be beaten into ploughshares could be beaten again into swords (Mic 4:3; Joel 3:10). The implements that enable Noah to survive the flood were put to evil use by his progeny on the plain of Shinar (Gen 11:2), and the miraculous overthrow of the tower of Babel (11:8) became a model for the prophetic celebrations that broke out whenever an enemy's capital fell or appeared to be on the eve of ruin. In Isaiah, the burden of Damascus follows hard on that of Babylon.[3] The woes denounced on Nineveh by Nahum came to pass (Nah 3:1–19), and it is only in the fairy tale of Jonah that the object of the prophecy is to bring about repentance and divine pardon (Jon 4:10–12). Jonah's Nineveh at least has streets, but the prince of Tyre in Ezekiel's abortive prophecy (Ezek 28:11–19) is a cherub cast out of paradise, a motif foreshadowed in Isaiah's mockery of the Babylonian king as the morning star that has fallen from the height (Isa 14:6).

2 Jerusalem in the Old Testament

Only one city's destruction is predicted with any reluctance by the prophets. Jerusalem appears for the first time in Scripture as Salem, the seat of the peaceable king and priest Melchisedek (Gen 14:18–20). Before it was seized by David, it was known by the name of Jebus, and its inhabitants as Jebusites (Josh 11:3; 12:10). In the account of the siege, the plan of the city is not described, and we have no clue to the location of the watershaft through which David sent a man to penetrate the stronghold of Zion (2 Sam 5:7–8). David creates a new city around the fortress, starting from the Millo (2 Sam 5:9; 1 Chr 11:8), but we hear little of the thoroughfares or the places of public gathering that figure so largely in depictions of Greek and Roman life. A prophet who runs through its streets in search of a good man (Jer 5:1) will be more likely to surprise a blasphemous ceremony (Jer 44:17; cf. 33:1); a woman in search of her lover will be mishandled by the watch (Song 3:2–3). A little more interest is shown in private domiciles: thus the ark, when brought to Jerusalem, is lodged in the houses of Abinadab and Obed-Edom (2 Sam 6:3, 10; 1 Chron 13:13), and a house is erected for David himself by the architects of Hiram, king of Phoenicia. His son Solomon receives a similar present, but only

---

[3] Isaiah 14:16–20 and 17. Lamentation for cities (though not underwritten by the same theology) is a common motif in antiquity: see now Mary R. Bachvarova, "The Destroyed City in Ancient 'World History': From Agade to Troy," in *The Fall of Cities In the Mediterranean: Commemoration in Literature, Folksong, and Liturgy*, ed. Mary R. Bachvarova, Dorota Dutsch, and Ann Suter (Cambridge: Cambridge University Press, 2016), 36–78.

after a house has been created for God to ensure that his tents will not be overshadowed by the king's house of fragrant wood (2 Sam 7:2).

"The temple of the Lord, the temple of the Lord" (Jer 7:4):[4] Jeremiah may scoff, but the structure of this edifice and its internal decorations are described with an amplitude and precision of detail that we do not encounter elsewhere in the Scriptures. For all that the Decalogue says against graven images and for all their insistence that service of the heart is worth more than sacrifice, the prophet and the psalmist alike perceive in its angelomorphic figures a seat and a train for God himself (Isa 6:1; Ps 99:1), and Isaiah declares that God has laid in Zion a precious cornerstone, an immovable foundation for those who believe (Isa 28:16). As Zion is not only the site of the holy place but the citadel of Jerusalem, the temple seems to function as a palladium against an armed adversary: when the psalmist invites us to number the towers of Zion, to ponder her strength and the number of those who dwell there (Ps 48/49:12–13), he is imitating the praise of Uruk in the epic of Gilgamesh,[5] yet the God who inhabited Zion was not to be trampled with the idols of Arpad and Hamath (Isa 36:18), as Sennacherib's ambassador imagined when he taunted the men on its walls from the aqueduct near the upper pool (Isa 36:2; 36:12).

For all that, the Jewish encomia of the temple are qualified, as those of a pagan shrine would not be, by the consciousness that God does not desire sacrifice[6] and that he cannot dwell – though his Name may – in a house that is made with hands.[7] Moreover, even while it stood, the temple was not safe from profanation: Hezekiah took down the brazen serpent Nehushtan, which had become an idol,[8] and one of Josiah's reforms was to demolish the House of Sodomites where the women wove for Asherah within the sacred precincts (2 Kgs 23:6–7). The people of Jerusalem told Jeremiah that they would go on venerating the Queen of Heaven as their kings had done before them (Jer 44:16–25). The temple did not prove to be impenetrable when Jerusalem fell to the Babylonians, and Belshazzar had defiled its sacred vessels before he incurred the public condemnation of God (Dan 5:2). Was it at this time that Ezekiel witnessed the performance of rites to Tammuz at the north gate (Ezek 8:14)? The sanctuary that was subsequently revealed to him in a vision of unusual length was so unlike its copy in the world (completed by the usurper Herod after forty-six years of building) that untutored Jews were forbidden to read these chapters.[9] Perhaps it was never intended for

---

[4] Quotations from the Bible follow the Revised Standard Version, with occasional adaptation where context demands.

[5] *The Epic of Gilgamesh: A New Translation*, trans. Andrew George (Harmondsworth: Penguin Classics, 1999), 2.

[6] Ps 50:12; Hos 6:6; cf. Amos 5:25.

[7] Acts 7:48; Isa 66:1; 1 Kgs 8:27.

[8] 2 Kgs 18:4; cf. 2 Chr 31:1, but the Asherah returns at 2 Kgs 21:3.

[9] See Origen, proem to *Commentary on Song of Songs* (*Commentarius in Canticum*) at Wilhelm A. Baehrens, ed., *Origenes Werke VIII* (Leipzig: Hinrichs, 1925), 62.24–30. Note that

this world, for the spring that issues from its right side, flanked by trees and providing an abode for every beast of the field (Ezek 47:1–12), is surely not to be found on the hither side of paradise.[10] At the same time, Ezekiel is not wholly indifferent to the real topography of the city, whose gates he mentions at 48:31–35.

Zechariah too is not content to prophesy, with Micah and Obadiah before the exile, that all nations will come up to Jerusalem, or even to Zion.[11] At 6:13 he foresees not only the rebuilding of the temple, but the enthronement of its second founder, the high priest Joshua. When the Lord comes to judge and reign, he declares, he will set his feet on the Mount of Olives (14:4); Jerusalem will be sacked by the gathered armies of the world, but then the Lord will disperse her enemies, living waters will flow out from her, and she will be elevated once more "from the Benjamin Gate to the site of the First Gate, from the corner gate and from the tower of Hananel to the wine-presses" (Zech 14:10). Outside the book of Nehemiah – in which the inventory of renovations includes at least ten gates, together with three towers, a pool, three houses and the sepulcher of David[12] – it would be hard to find so dense a list of sites in Jerusalem. Yet the prophet also foresees that when the angel of God measures Israel, he will find it to be so populous, in livestock as in its citizens,[13] that it can no longer be enclosed within a wall (Zech 2:2–5).

On the one hand, then, the rebuilding of the city inspired, in both prophets and historians, a greater interest in the city's topography than was shown by any writer before the exile. On the other hand, the walls with their dozen gates are as permeable as those of Jericho: the temple is still the sole monument that is more than a name, but now it is far from clear that the one that is destined to be the abiding house of God is the one whose stones have been put together by returning Jews with such ingenuous zeal.

3 Jerusalem in Primitive Christianity

The authors who recounted the early ministry of Jesus may have been Jews, but they wrote in Greek, and it was the custom of Greek storytellers (as Auerbach

---

the word *deuterosis* in this passage refers, as ever, to the Jewish midrash, not the four reserved texts (opening of Genesis, opening and close of Ezekiel, Song of Songs) as is commonly assumed by those who are more familiar with Lawson's translation than the original Latin.

[10] See Jon D. Levenson, *Theology of the Program of Restoration of Ezekiel 40–48* (Cambridge, MA: Harvard University Press, 2019), 25–36.

[11] See Zech 14:16ff, echoing Mic 4:1–2, Obad 17, Isa 51:12.

[12] Neh 3: towers of Meah and Hananel (1), Fish Gate (3), Old Gate (6), Valley Gate (13), Dung Gate (14), Gate of Fountain (15), pool of Siloah (15), sepulcher of David (16), door of high priest's house (20), king's house (25), Water Gate (26), great tower and wall of Ophel (27), Horse Gate (28), East Gate (29), Inspection Gate (31), Sheep Gate (32).

[13] Cf. Jon 4:11 on Nineveh.

notes,[14] contrasting the interiority of Hebraic narratives) to assign every action to its local setting. All the canonical gospels make some reference to the temple, Gethsemane, the Mount of Olives, the hill of Calvary and the garden in which Joseph of Arimathea had built his tomb. Toponyms are especially frequent in the Fourth Gospel, where Jesus heals a paralytic man at the Pool of Bethesda near the Sheep Gate (John 5:2), steals from the temple to the Mount of Olives, instructs a blind man to wash in the Pool of Siloam (9:7), and teaches (or rather bemuses) the Jews in Solomon's colonnade (10:23). Retracing the steps of David in his flight from Absalom, Jesus and his disciples cross the brook Kidron to reach the unnamed garden of Gethsemane.[15] At John 18:13 he is led as a prisoner to the home of Annas, and at 18:24 to that of Caiaphas. It is here that Peter betrays him (18:27), and from here that he is led to the Hall of Judgment (18:28), in which Pilate after a fruitless attempt to conciliate the Jews sits down to judge him on the Pavement which is known as Lithostratos or Gabbatha (19:13). The Place of the Skull on which he is executed is named Golgotha rather than Calvary (19:17); he is buried, as in other accounts, by Joseph of Arimathea, whose tomb is conveniently "near at hand" for those who must finish their task before the Passover (19:42).

After the death of Jesus, it seems that Jerusalem contracts once again to be all but coextensive with the temple. The Acts of the Apostles records the healing of a lame man by the "Gate called Beautiful" (Acts 2:3) and the purification of Paul, which Paul undergoes in the temple to deflect the accusation that he is teaching Gentiles not to obey the Law (21:20–26). For all that, he appears to teach nothing less than this in his letter to the Galatians where he intimates that Jerusalem as a place means little to him, as he had been a convert for three years, travelling first to Arabia and then to Damascus,[16] before he "went up" to spend two weeks with Peter (Gal 1:18). Another eleven, or perhaps fourteen, years elapsed before his second journey (2:1),[17] during which time he had found the synagogues inhospitable to his preaching of a crucified Messiah whose resurrection had revealed the hidden import of God's promise to Abraham (Acts 13:32–36; Rom 4:25). In exhorting the Galatians not to fall into legal bondage, he creates a symbolic topography, according to which the metropolis of Judea (where the temple was still standing) corresponds to Mount Sinai, the source of the law and figurative counterpart of Hagar, whereas Sarah, the true bride of Abraham, represents the free Jerusalem that is above (Gal 4:22–26).

---

[14] Erich Auerbach, *Mimesis: the Representation of Reality in Western Literature,* trans. Willard Trask (Princeton: Princeton University Press, 1953), 8.

[15] 2 Sam 15:23; John 18:1. At 2 Kgs 23:6 the Asherah is thrown into the valley of Kidron.

[16] Gal 1:18; we learn more about the topography of Damascus than about that of Jerusalem, both at Acts 9:11–25 and at 2 Cor 11:23.

[17] If this is the one recorded at Acts 11:2 (more consonant with his own narrative than the one recorded in Acts 15, for which Galatians seems to be his preparatory manifesto), the fourteen years must be dated from the time of his conversion, since the visit in Acts 11 coincides with the death of Herod Agrippa in AD 44.

Here, as so often, the Letter to the Hebrews acts as a commentary on the elliptical imagery of the Apostle. We are come, it says, not to the mountain of which Moses himself exclaimed "I tremble with fear," but to Mount Zion, the city of the living God and the heavenly Jerusalem (Heb 12:18–22). This is the home of those who know that in this world they have no abiding city (Heb 13:14), of those whose citizenship, as Paul said, is in heaven (Phil 3:20). To make it doubly clear that this is not the place where the priests perform their useless rituals of exsanguination, the author directs his audience to the altar outside the city – fit in Jewish eyes only for the disposal of the carcass – on which Christ, as the first and last of victims, shed his sanctifying blood (Heb 13:10–12). We do not know whether the author of this document wrote before or after the burning of the temple, and we are equally uncertain as to the date at which John of Patmos received his vision of the judgment of the nations by the Lamb who was crucified before the foundation of the world (Rev 13:8). Only those who accept the crown of martyrdom for his sake are sure of a place in the new Jerusalem (Rev 3:12), the everlasting city that will descend when our heaven and earth have passed away, adorned as a bride for her husband like a new and more faithful Israel (21:2), and radiant with the glory of the God who makes all things new (21:10; 21:5).

The antitype to Christ's "city on a hill which cannot be hidden,"[18] this new Jerusalem remains unknown until it comes down to the realm of mortal vision. No description of the old Jerusalem is so circumstantial, nor of the postexilic city except in Nehemiah, who is linear and prosaic where his Christian imitator is synoptic and fanciful. Whereas Paul and Hebrews, reticent as the prophets of old, spoke only of Sinai yielding to Zion, the seer of the Revelation measures "the city, its gates, and its walls" with a rod of gold: in contrast to the angel of Zechariah he gauges not only its vast extent (twelve thousand stadia in all three dimensions) but the impenetrable thickness of its walls (Rev 21:15–17). Since this amounts to 144 cubits, twelve foundations are required, each corresponding to an apostle (21:14), and only the power of God could have perforated it with twelve gates, each guarded by its own angel and named after a tribe of Israel (21:12–13). The wall is of jasper, the streets of gold; each gate is a single pearl, and each foundation is from a different stone of the twelve that make up the breastplate of the high priest at Exod 28:15–21 (21:18–21). Where God dwells in his fulness, there can be no need of a temple (21:22), just as when the eternal light is present there will be no need, as Isaiah had foretold, of the sun or moon (Rev 21:22; Isa 60:19). The imagery of paradise, which gives a numinous character to the temple in Ezekiel's vision, recurs in the following chapter, where the tree of life, with its monthly yield of twelve fruits, and its leaves that are for the healing of the nations, occupies the banks of the crystalline water issuing from the throne of God (Rev 22:1–2).

---

[18] See Matt 5:14, with Ken M. Campbell, "The New Jerusalem in Matthew 5.14," *Scottish Journal of Theology* 31, no. 4 (1978), 335–63.

4 Jerusalem Above and Below in Early Christian Literature

The passage in Isaiah[19] that foretells that the walls of Jerusalem will be repaired and that God will renew his marriage to Israel is also the one of which Jesus said in the synagogue, "This prophecy has been fulfilled today in your hearing."[20] Some scholars take him to mean that his ministry was already complete, and the kingdom of God already established, when he had taught the blind to see and the lame to walk, releasing sinners from judgment and the righteous from the fetters of their own pride. On this view the notion of a second coming, with the anxiety occasioned by its delay, was a misunderstanding, and the fall of the first Jerusalem should have been construed as a final judgment on every attempt to build a house for God outside our own conscience.[21] It is true that Jesus did not predict any second building of the city; nevertheless, any Christian who believed that the words of the prophets were dictated by the same Spirit who was at work in the evangelists was bound to find some place in his eschatology for the day when all nations would come up to Zion, and for the descent of the Savior on the same Mount of Olives from which he had been taken up into heaven. So long as the visitation of wrath on the temple had not been extended to the whole city, it was possible to imagine that he would return to the very sites where he had once walked. Justin Martyr's *Dialogue with Trypho* (*Dialogus cum Tryphone*), however, was written some years after Hadrian had punished the revolt of Simon bar-Kochba by expelling the Jews from their capital and refounding it, with little tenderness to its ancient monuments, as the colony of Aelia Capitolina. Hence a new expectation had arisen, that "at his second coming" (as Justin writes), "you shall behold him in that same locality of Jerusalem, the one whom you dishonored" (*Dial.* 40).[22] Later in the *Dialogue with Trypho*, he admits that this expectation was not universally entertained:

> "Tell me" [said Trypho], "do you really profess that this locality, Jerusalem, will be rebuilt, and that your people will be gathered together and rejoice with Christ, together with the patriarchs, the prophets and the saints of our own race, including those who became proselytes before the coming of your Christ?" (*Dialogue with Trypho* 80.1)[23]

---

[19] This discussion is necessarily selective. See further Karl Schmidt, "Jerusalem als Urbild und Abbild," *Eranos Jahrbuch* 18 (1950): 207–48 and Guy Stroumsa, *The Making of the Abrahamic Religions in Late Antiquity* (Oxford: Oxford University Press, 2015), 159–73.

[20] Luke 4:21, after quoting Isa 61:1–2 with Isa 58:6.

[21] See Charles. H. Dodd, *The Parables of the Kingdom* (London: Nisbet, 1936).

[22] Miroslav Marcovich, ed., *Iustini Martyris Apologiae pro Christianis; Iustini Martyris Dialogus cum Tryphone* [Berlin: De Gruyter, 2005], 137.22–23). All translations from patristic sources are mine.

[23] Marcovich, 208: Εἰπὲ δὲ μοι, ἀληθῶς ὑμεῖς ἀνοικοδομηθῆναι τὸν τόπον Ἰερουσαλὴμ τοῦτον ὁμολογεῖτε, καὶ συναχθήσεσθαι τὸν λαὸν ὑμῶν καὶ εὐφρανθῆναι σὺν τῷ Χριστῷ, ἅμα τοῖς πατριάρχαις καὶ τοῖς προφήταις καὶ τοῖς ἁγίοις τοῦ ἡμετέρου γένους, ἢ καὶ τῶν

To which Justin replies:

"I have told you before that I and many others do think this, and are entirely of the opinion that this will occur, but I have also intimated that there are many Christians of a pure and pious persuasion who do not hold this view." (*Dialogue with Trypho* 80.2)[24]

The opponents of this prophecy may have included Irenaeus, who foresees a restoration of the temple, but as the work of the antichrist. Quoting Isa 66:13 ("As a mother comforts her child, so I will comfort you over Jerusalem") at *Against Heresies* (*Adversus haereses*) 5.15, he goes on to predict, on the authority of Baruch and Isaiah,[25] that when the new Jerusalem succeeds the old, as the substance succeeds the shadow, it will occupy the same site as the substance succeeding the shadow (*Haer.* 5.35). The new city will be as solid as the one that Justin imagines, but where that is, as it were, a mere antechamber, this will be an everlasting habitation for the elect, in whose creation human masons will have no hand. This scenario for the last days is evidently closer than that of Justin to the Johannine Apocalypse, which Justin may never have read. Irenaeus, having read it closely, envisages a rebuilding of the temple, not by God, but by the antichrist, who will make it his seat as long as he is allowed to deceive the world.

Other contemporaries of Irenaeus and Justin, however, appear to have read the fall of the earthly Jerusalem as a sign that God had chosen another seat for the elect in the last millennium of this world. According to Eusebius of Caesarea and Epiphanius of Cyprus, this was the delusion put about by the female prophets of the sect that came to be known as the Cataphrygians, or sometimes as the Montanists, after the man who organized them as a church. The expected place of descent was the small settlement of Pepuza, to which, with the neighboring Tymion, Montanus gave the name Jerusalem, announcing that all the nations would gather there to worship God (Eusebius, *Ecclesiastical History* [*Historia ecclesiastica*] 5.18.2). Epiphanius adds that the prophetess Quintilla saw Jesus descending in the form of a woman, infusing wisdom into her and proclaiming that the new Jerusalem would be established in Pepuza (*Panarion* 49.1.2–3).[26]

προσηλύτων γενομένων πρὶν ἐλθεῖν ὑμῶν τὸν Χριστόν, προσδοκᾶτε: Justin alternates between aorist and future infinitives, but the sense appears in all cases to be future.

[24] Marcovich, 208: Ὡμολόγησα οὖν σοι καὶ πρότερον ὅτι ἐγὼ μὲν καὶ ἄλλοι πολλοὶ ταῦτα φρονοῦμεν, ὡς καὶ πάντως ἐπίστασθαι τοῦτο γενησόμενον, πολλοὺς δ' αὖ καὶ τῶν τῆς καθαρᾶς καὶ εὐσεβοῦς ὄντων Χριστιανῶν γνώμης τοῦτο μὴ γνωρίζειν ἐσήμανά σοι.

[25] Bar 4:36–37, attributed to Jeremiah; Isa 49:16 ("the walls are ever before me").

[26] Karl Höll, ed., *Epiphanius Werke 2* (Berlin Akademie der Wissenschaften, 1915), 242.2–8). On the possible influence on Quintilla of the figure of Wisdom in Sir 24 see John C. Poirier, "Montanist Pepuza-Jerusalem and the Dwelling Place of Wisdom," *Journal of Early Christian Studies* 7 (1999): 491–507. It should be said that the so-called Quintillianoi, with their female bishops and gnosticizing eulogies of Eve, differ strongly from the Montanists of Eusebius and *Panarion* 48, as Epiphanius seems to concede, not only by placing them in a separate chapter, but by noting that they were also called Artotyrites (Bread-and-Cheesers) because of their singular manner of celebrating the eucharist (Höll 2.243.11–13).

Epiphanius jubilantly declares that in his own day (ca. 376) Pepuza was a wilderness (*Pan.* 48.14).[27] For centuries its location was unknown, but a plausible case has been made by William Tabbernee and Peter Lampe for giving its name to a recent excavation in Turkey,[28] some eighty miles from the ancient Philadelphia, the first church to be promised a share in the New Jerusalem (Rev 3:12).[29]

Momentous as this discovery is, it is fanciful to suggest, as Tabbernee appears to do, that in unearthing the gates and corridors of Pepuza we are plotting the map of the New Jerusalem as it was imagined by the Montanists. Their claim, as reported by the heresiologists, is not that Pepuza, as it existed, was to become the everlasting city but that the New Jerusalem would descend upon it. In that respect, they would seem to have stood against Justin with Irenaeus. We may also wonder whether the eighty miles between Pepuza and Philadelphia would have seemed so small a distance to them as to Tabbernee, and his observation that the two centers occupy the same latitude would surely have meant nothing to the cartographers of this era. Whatever the Montanists of Asia Minor may have hoped for, their dreams were evidently short lived, for their only author whose works have survived to us is Tertullian, who, writing perhaps half a century after the first eruption of the new prophecy, appears to know of no city but Jerusalem as the future abode of the saints. He does not put a metaphorical construction on Micah's oracle that "law will go forth from Zion and the Word of God from Jerusalem";[30] the injunction to Ezekiel to inscribe the letter *tau* (that is, a cross) on the foreheads of all the righteous is understood as an eschatological prophecy:

> For that same Greek letter Tau, which is our T, is a sign of the Cross, which according to [Ezekiel's] prophecy will be on our foreheads in the true and catholic Jerusalem, in which the brothers of Christ, i.e. the sons of God, will render glory to God the Father, as Psalm 21 says in the person of Christ, *I shall declare thy name to my brothers, and in the midst of the church I shall sing a hymn to thee.* (*Against Marcion* 3.22.6)[31]

Determined as he is to unite the two Testaments against Marcion, he intimates that the prophet of Judea in Solomon's time and the architect of his temple was the Holy Spirit (*Marc.* 3.23.2). Of course he envisages no temple in the New

---

[27] Höll, 2.238.20–239.2.

[28] William Tabbernee and Peter Lampe: *Pepouza and Tymion: The Discovery and Archaeological Exploration of a Lost Ancient City and an Imperial Estate* (Berlin: De Gruyter, 2008).

[29] This point is made by William Tabbernee, *Fake Prophecy and Polluted Sacraments: Ecclesiastical and Imperial Reactions to Montanism*, Vigiliae Christianae Supplements 84 (Leiden: Brill, 2007).

[30] Mic 4:2 at *Against Marcion* (*Adversus Marcionem*) 3.21.3 and 3.22.1.

[31] Ernest Evans, ed., *Tertullian: Adversus Marcionem* (Oxford: Clarendon, 1972), 240: *Ipsa est enim littera Graecorum Tau, nostra autem T, species crucis, quam portendebat futuram in frontibus nostris apud veram et catholicam Ierusalem, in qua fratres Christi, filios scilicet dei, gloriam patri relaturos psalmus vigesimus primus canit ex persona ipsius Christi ad patrem:* Enarrabo nomen tuum fratribus meis, in medio ecclesiae hymnum tibi dicam.

Jerusalem, but he holds it to have been proved by a celestial revelation that it will descend not on Phrygia but on Judea:

> There is in our own communion a sermon of the new prophecy which predicts that an image of the city will appear to view as a sign before its manifestation. This was promptly fulfilled in an oriental campaign; for even pagan witnesses agree that for forty days in Judea a city was suspended from heaven each morning, though the form of its walls faded after daybreak, while on other occasions all at once there was nothing. (*Marc.* 3.24.4)[32]

He does not concede to the earthly Jerusalem even the honor that Irenaeus grants it, of being an adumbration of the celestial city.[33] It would also seem (perhaps because they had seers of their own) that exponents of the new prophecy did not feel bound to adhere in all respects to the plan of the Johannine Apocalypse: there is nothing unusual in Tertullian's inference from Rev 20 that the last judgment will be preceded by the reign of the saints for a thousand years on earth,[34] but when he opines that this epoch of waiting for heaven is what is meant by the New Jerusalem, he reads ch 20 as though it followed ch 21:

> We confess that a kingdom on earth is promised to us, before [we enter heaven], in another state, namely that which follows the resurrection, for a thousand years in the city of Jerusalem brought down from heaven by divine operation. The apostle calls this our mother above and, by pronouncing our *politeuma*, that is our citizenship (*municipatus*) to be in the heavens [Gal 4:26; Phil 3:20], assigns it undoubtedly to some heavenly city. (*Marc.* 3.24.3)[35]

In Tertullian's apophthegm, "What has Athens to do with Jerusalem?" (*Prescription against Heretics* [*De praescriptione haereticorum*] 7) the two capitals stand respectively for the church and the academy, for sacred and profane learning. Even had Tertullian supposed the New Jerusalem to be the everlasting home of the elect, he would not have denied its corporeality, since in his view it was heresy to doubt that flesh and blood, in the most literal acceptation of

---

[32] Evans, 246: *[Q]ui apud fidem nostram est novae prophetiae sermo testatur, ut etiam effigiem civitatis ante repraesentationem eius conspectui futuram in signum praedicarit. Denique proxime expunctum est orientali expeditione. Constat enim ethnicis quoque testibus in Iudaea per dies quadrginta matutinis momentis civitatem de caelo pependisse, omni moenorum habitu evanescente de profectu diei, et alias de proximo nullam.*

[33] On Irenaeus see above. On the frequency of such matutinal visions see Basil of Caesarea, *Homilia in Genesim* 4 (*PG* 20:77D–78A).

[34] See Charles Hill, *Regnum Caelorum,* 2nd edition (Grand Rapids: Eerdmans 2001), 140–53 on the eccentricity of Tertullian's chiliasm. According to Praedestinatus, *Against Heresies* 1.26, Tertullian averred that Montanists differ in nothing from psychics except in forbidding second marriages and in not rejecting Montanus' prophecies of impending judgment. No reference is made to the New Jerusalem, let alone Pepuza.

[35] Evans, 246: *Nam et confitemur in terra nobis regnum repromissum, sed ante caelum, sed alio statu, utpote post resurrectionem. in mille annos in civitate divini operis Hierusalem caelo delata, quam et apostolus matrem nostrum designat, et politeuma nostum, id est municipatum, in caelis esse pronuntians alicui utique caelesti civitati eum deputat.*

these terms, will inherit the kingdom.³⁶ The soul itself, in his view, was a body of some kind, as was God, although he hints that to be corporeal is not always to be "from matter" (*The Soul* [*De anima*] 11.2). Origen, his younger contemporary, is renowned as a profligate master of allegoresis, yet few Christians of antiquity based their eschatological teaching so consistently on the plain sense of the text. For him it was simply an axiom that flesh and blood cannot inherit the kingdom of heaven; survival after the physical divorce of soul and body was proved by the Witch of Endor's raising of Samuel and by the parable of the rich man and the beggar.³⁷ Since the gross body could not go down to Hades, and since he could not imagine that any creature could subsist without some form of material envelope, Origen holds that the *eidos* or form of the body clings to the soul after death and furnishes it with the vehicle in which it makes its journey first to the earthly paradise and then through the planetary spheres (*First Principles* [*De principiis*] 2.11.6).³⁸ Elsewhere he seems to hesitate as to whether paradise is in earth or heaven – an uncertainty that mirrors the disputation of contemporary Platonists, just as the celestial itinerary that he grants to the soul is foreshadowed in Numenius and the Gnostics.³⁹ It was not in these sources, however, but in his own commonsensical inference that the body in the afterlife must be of rarer stuff than the one that we now inhabit, that he found the authority for his metaphorical reading of the stones and feasts of the new Jerusalem: "They add that there will be marital relations and begetting of children even after the resurrection, imagining that the earthly city of Jerusalem is to be rebuilt with precious stones embedded in its foundations" (Origen, *Princ.* 2.11.2).⁴⁰

He goes on to say, against those who quote promises that the righteous will eat and drink in Jerusalem, that the true sustenance of the redeemed is the word of God. After Origen's time, this equation of the New Jerusalem with paradise or with heaven seems to have ousted the earlier notion that Jerusalem would be the temporary abode of the saints as they waited for the kingdom. In this there is no mystery – and certainly no warrant for alleging a fear of prophecy or a reaction to Montanism – when we reflect that in the Apocalypse the descent of the

---

³⁶ On 1 Cor 15:50 see Tertullian, *The Resurrection of the Flesh* (*De resurrectione carnis*) 48.

³⁷ See Rowan Greer and Margaret Mitchell, *The "Belly-Myther" of Endor: Interpretations of 1 Kingdoms 28 in the Early Church* (Atlanta: Society of Biblical Literature, 2007).

³⁸ Paul Koetschau, ed., *Origenes Werke V: De Principiis* (Leipzig: Hinrichs, 1899), 190.

³⁹ For discussion and bibliography on these questions, see Ilaria Ramelli, "Origen," in *A History of Mind and Body in Late Antiquity,* ed. Anna Marmodoro and Sophie Cartwright (Oxford: Oxford University Press 2018), 245–66; Mark J. Edwards, "Origen, Plato and the Afterlife," *International Journal of the Platonic Tradition* 15, no. 1 (2021), 1–24.

⁴⁰ Paul Koetschau, *Origenes Werke V,* 184.12–16: *Quibus consequenter addunt etiam nuptiarum conventiones et filiorum procreationem etiam post resurrectionem futuras, fingentes sibimet ipsis Hierusalem urben reaedificandam lapidibus pretiosis in fundamenta eius iaciendis.* See also Origen, *Commentary on the Song of Songs* (Wilhelm Baehrens, *Origenes Werke VIII,* 84.15–17) on the New Jerusalem as the church of the firstfruits.

New Jerusalem supervenes on the thousand-year reign of the elect. It is Origen's adherence to the literal *akolouthia* or order of scriptural prophecy that requires him to give a figurative turn to its symbolism; it is for this reason that he finds an ally in the most dogmatic of ancient opponents of allegory, the Antiochene Theodore of Mopsuestia:

> It is therefore by comparison with this [Jerusalem] that he spoke of that Jerusalem which is above [Gal 4:26], referring in this way to that polity (*conversationem*) which we have in heaven [Phil 3:20] inasmuch as that is the place in which we shall spend our lives when we dwell with Christ ... seeing that the Jews when they dwelt in the locality of Jerusalem deemed themselves to be dwelling with God, and it was there that they strove to pay God their debt of obedience, deeming this to be their proper abode, inasmuch as they could perform no sacrifice or holocaust or any other act prescribed by the law in another place.[41]

Thus heaven is called Jerusalem by analogy, a trope that Theodore found more palatable than allegory. In eschewing the figurative interpretation even as an enhancement of the literal one, he was far from representative of the church, and his Latin contemporary John Cassian spoke for the majority, and for posterity, when he opined that "one and the same Jerusalem can be understood in a fourfold way: historically as the city of the Jews; allegorically as the church of Christ; anagogically as the heavenly city of God, which is the mother of all; and tropologically as the human soul" (*Conferences* 14.8.4).[42]

5 Citizens of the Old and New Jerusalem

Hitherto we have treated the comparison of the old and the new Jerusalem as a comparison of two cities, as we must so long as we use the Greek word *polis*. Greeks might differ as to whether a *polis* was the creation of its architects or its citizens, but the citizenship itself was *politeia* or *politeuma*. In Latin, by contrast, *ciuitas* means both city and citizenship, and there were many who boasted Roman citizenship but had no ancestral connection with the ancient seat of power. Paul was not ashamed to exploit his membership of this earthly commonwealth, which he inherited at no price,[43] but it is nothing to him when

---

[41] *In Epistolas B. Pauli* (Henry B. Swete, ed., [Cambridge: Cambridge University Press, 1880], vol. 1, 83): *Ad comparationem ergo huius illam nominauit quae sursum est Hierusalem; conversationem illam nostram quam in caelis habemus hoc modo indicans, eo quod illo commorabimur simul cum Christo degentes ... quoniam et Iudaei in locis Hierusalem commorantes cum Deo se commorare existimabant; ubi et debitum Deo persoluere servitium properabant, hunc locum competentem esse sibi existimantes, eo quod neque sacrificium neque holocaustum neque aliud aliquid secundum legem alibi perficere poterant.*

[42] Michael Petschenig, ed., *Johannis Cassianai Conlationes XXIIII* (Vienna: Gerold, 1886), 405.

[43] Acts 22:28; cf. Mark J. Edwards, "*Romanitas* and the Church of Rome," in *Approaching Late Antiquity*, ed. Simon C.R. Swain and Mark J. Edwards (Oxford: Oxford University Press, 2004), 187–210, esp. 189.

weighed against the heavenly *politeuma* that Christ purchased with his blood.[44] More than three centuries later, the sack of Rome by her unpaid mercenaries prompted Augustine to write his celebrated apology, *De ciuitate Dei*, conventionally known as the *City of God*. Largely unmoved by the decrepitude of the Eternal City, he envisages the New Jerusalem not as its rival in a future world but as a secret diaspora, chosen from each generation of fallen mortals by the secret counsel of God while the rest of the world pursued its schemes of theft and slaughter. Properly speaking, there is no city in his book; it is the testament of a citizenry without walls:

And it did indeed descend from heaven from its inception, since when throughout this temporal age the grace of God has been coming down from above through the bath of regeneration [Titus 2:5] in the Holy Spirit which was sent from God, and thus its citizens grow in number. But through the judgment of God, which will be delivered in the last days through his Son Jesus Christ, the glory that God imparts to it will be so great and so unprecedented that no trace of the former things[45] will remain. (*City of God* 20.17)[46]

In this, as in much else, he differs less from his Donatist opponents than he would have the world believe. For Tyconius, his avowed mentor,[47] the gates of the New Jerusalem stand not for any sacrament of the visible church, or even for any human witness, but for Christ himself.[48] In an anonymous *Commentary on Matthew (Opus Imperfectum in Matthaeum)*, the church is a new Jerusalem, not simply to be identified with the Donatists communion, for its membership will not be determined before the end of the age:

Therefore just as there was that bodily Jerusalem, which has already been taken by siege prefiguratively (*figuraliter*), so also there is another spiritual Jerusalem, namely the church, which is to be tested at the end of the world and is being tested even now. (Homily 24.4.8)[49]

---

[44] See Acts 20:28; 1 Cor 6:20; Phil 3:20.

[45] In Latin *uestigia uetustatis*, mingling Rev 21:4 with an echo of Vergil, *Eclogues* (*Eclogae*) 4.31 (*priscae uestigia fraudis*).

[46] Bernhart Dombart and Alfons Kalb, ed., *S. Augustini de civitate Dei* (Stuttgart: Teubner, 1993), 444.21–30: *Et de caelo quidem ab initio sui descendit, ex quo per huius saeculi tempus, gratia Dei desuper ueniente per lauacrum regenerationis in Spiritu Sacro misso de caelo, subinde ciues eius adcrescunt. Sed per iudicium Dei, quod erit nouissimum per eius filium Iesum Christum, tanta eius et tam noua de Dei munere claritas apparebit ut nulla remaneant uestigia uestustatis.*

[47] Augustine, *Christian Instruction* (*De doctrina christiana*) 3.30.43–37.56. See further P. Fredricksen, "Tyconius and Augustine on the Apocalypse," in *The Apocalypse in the Middle Ages*, ed. Richard K. Emmerson and Bernard McGinn (Ithaca, NY: Cornell University Press, 1992), 20–37.

[48] Tyconius, *Book of Rules* (*Liber regularum*) 7.2 (Jean-Marc Vercruysse, ed. and trans., *Livre des règles* [Paris: Cerf, 2004], 298).

[49] Jesse A. Hoover, *The Donatist Church in an Apocalyptic Age* (Oxford: Oxford University Press, 2018), 145n.

6 The New Jerusalem Above and Below

The shift in sensibility between the second century and the fourth can be illustrated by a comparison of two versions of the same text, the *Commentary on the Book of Revelation* (*Explanatio in Apocalypsin*) by Victorinus of Petavium, which was later edited and amplified by Jerome.[50] Victorinus, reputedly a martyr under Diocletian, is one of the last of the "chiliasts,"[51] that is those who interpreted Rev 20 as a literal prophecy of a thousand-year reign of the saints on earth before the last judgment (*Commentary* 20.1 [140.2–11]). At the same time, he acknowledges that much of the Apocalypse is allegory, in the proper sense of that term in antiquity, insofar as its true import can be elucidated only by the substitution of wholly different terms, not homonyms or etymologies,[52] for those in which the seer conveys his vision. Thus the gates of the New Jerusalem are metaphorically the apostles (*Commentary* 21.6 [154.12]), and the precious stones that compose its walls are metonymically gifts that the kings of the nations bring in homage (*Commentary* 21.2 [148.2–3]). Jerusalem itself, which will rule the earth for a millennium, is a place, yet not coterminous with the capital of Judea; the name is used neither metaphorically nor metonymically, but synecdochically for the whole of the land that was promised to Abraham, from the Euphrates to the Nile (*Commentary* 21.2 [148.8–18]).

Jerome redacts Victorinus's text by omission as well as by augmentation, and he has nothing to say of the literal fulfilment of this promise. Confessedly excising the chiliasm of the original (Jerome, *Commentary* prol. [14.14]), he locates the New Jerusalem in the next world rather than this. As in Victorinus, so in Jerome its twelve gates represent the apostles (*Commentary* 21.2 [151.9]), whose teaching admits us to the kingdom by inculcating perfection in the cardinal virtues, which are symbolized by the division of these gates into four groups of three (*Commentary* 21.2 [151.4–8]). For Jerome the fruits of the tree of life stand for the graces that are bestowed by the apostles (*Commentary* 21.1 [149.16–17]); in the precious stones that compose the walls of the city, we see those who have given their lives for Christ (*Commentary* 21.1 [149.7]). The exegesis may strike us as arbitrary, but the keys are found in Scripture itself, where a tree by a stream is an emblem of the righteous man,[53] and Christians are exhorted to come together

---

[50] Both edited by Johannes Haussleiter, *Victorini Episcopi Petavionensis Opera*, CSEL 49 (Leipzig: Tempsky, 1916).

[51] Hill, *Regnum Caelorum* (cf. note 34), 35 contrasts Victorinus with his contemporary Methodius, who set an enduring precedent in his rejection of chiliasm. On the chiliasm of their younger contemporary Lactantius see Hill, *Regnum Caelorum*, 38.

[52] For these distinctions see Mark J. Edwards, "Origen, Didymus and Theodore on the Literal Sense," in *Perspectives on Origen and the History of His Reception*, ed. Alfons Fürst (Münster: Aschendorff, 2021).

[53] See Ps 1:3 and Rev 2:8, with Mark J. Edwards, "The Tree of Life in Early Christian Literature," in *The Tree of Life*, ed. Douglas Estes (Leiden: Brill, 2020), 217–35.

as a house of living stones.⁵⁴ So far we may say, his hermeneutic method merely extends that of Victorinus, following his principle of substituting the concrete for the concrete; in contrast to his prototype, however, he can countenance allegoresis of the kind that is often called spiritual, entailing as it does a translation not only from one concrete term to another but from the corporeal to the incorporeal. If he is none the less sparing in his use of this device – the only instance being his identification of the streets of Jerusalem with the souls in which God "walks" as he was anthropomorphically said to have walked in Eden (*Commentary* 21.1 [149.7]) – that is no doubt because he does not wish to be mistaken for an Origenist.⁵⁵ And yet he resembles Origen in juxtaposing paradise with Jerusalem but without expressly equating them, and although he does not affirm in this discussion that Jerusalem will be in any sense a place, we know from his other writings that he was even less ready than Origen to imagine that a disembodied soul can exist alone.

7 An Inconclusive Postscript

It ought to be clear by now that, while I have spoken of a shift in sensibility, which rendered obsolete both the materialistic and the chiliastic understandings of the New Jerusalem, I do not maintain that this shift can be reduced to a single trend in exegesis. A distinction can be drawn, even in the fourth century, between those who place the New Jerusalem solely in the future world and those for whom it exists already in this world as an invisible congregation. For the former it may be a city, for the latter it is a citizenry; the former may wish to deny, while the latter will certainly affirm, that its denizens are beings of flesh and blood. Neither shows any interest in the mapping of Jerusalem, in this world or the next. I shall end, however, with two texts that bear witness to a residual diversity of opinion, one undoubtedly written by Cyril, the bishop who had transformed the earthly Jerusalem into a Christian site of pilgrimage, the other attributed to his contemporary and fellow Palestinian Epiphanius of Salamis, who in his last years waged a truceless war against Cyril's successor. Both are interpretations of Zechariah's prophecy that the Lord will stand on the Mount of Olives. For Cyril's congregation this is a visible locality:

Cyril: Give the sign to us in full view of our eyes, so that we may behold it when we are in the very city. And the prophet replies, saying *On that day his feet shall stand on the Mount of Olives, opposite Jerusalem from the east* [Zech 14:4]. Is there anyone standing in the city who will not see the place? (*Catechetical Oration* 12.11)⁵⁶

---

⁵⁴ See 2 Pet 2:4–8 and Shepherd of Hermas, Vision 3.2[10].4–9
⁵⁵ See further Elizabeth Clark, *The Origenist Controversy* (Princeton: Princeton University Press, 1992).
⁵⁶ PG 33:737A: Ἐγγὺς δὲ ἡμῖν δὸς τὸ σημεῖον ὀφθαλμοφανές, ἵνα καὶ ἐν τῇ πόλει ὄντες τὸν

In pseudo-Epiphanius, however, "on the Mount of Olives" is changed to "from the Mount of Olives" to preclude a literal interpretation:

Epiphanius: What is the descent of Christ from the Mount of Olives but the condescension of the Word of God to us from heaven? What are the branches of the olive? The souls of those who show mercy. (Sermon 6)[57]

Cyril was not a chiliast and does not include Revelation in his canon of the New Testament.[58] Nevertheless, he could hardly be expected to put a spiritual or symbolic construction on the name of a site that was exhibited in his time to wondering visitors from every quarter of Christendom. It is possible, on the other hand, that the putative Epiphanius, conscious of the Emperor Julian's attempt to restore the temple as the center of Jewish worship,[59] deemed it unwise to take this verse in Zechariah more literally than his prophecies that the temple would be restored by the high priest Joshua (Zech 6:13) or that the nations would come up to celebrate the Feast of Tabernacles (14:16). He differs from the allegorists, in the proper sense of that term, in assuming the topography of the higher Jerusalem to be homonymic with that of the lower one; on the other hand, he is wholly at one with previous commentators – with Origen no less than with Theodore, and with Tertullian no less than with Augustine – in his presupposition that even in a celestial afterlife something of the corporeal will remain.

τόπον θεωρήσωμεν. Ὁ δὲ προφήτης πάλιν ἀποκρίνεται, λέγων, καὶ στήσονται οἵ πόδες αὐτοῦ ἐν τῇ ἡμέρᾳ ἐκείνῃ ἐπὶ τὸ ὄρος τῶν ἐλαιῶν, τὸ κατεναντι Ἰερυσαλὴμ ἐξ ἀνατολῶν.

[57] PG 43:505A: Τίς ἡ ἐκ τοῦ ὄρους τῶν ἐλαιῶν Χριστοῦ κατάβασις ἢ πάντως ἡ ἐκ τοῦ οὐρανοῦ τοῦ Θεοῦ Λόγου πρὸς ἡμᾶς συγκατάβασις; Τίνες τῶν ἐλαιῶν οἱ κλάδοι; αἱ τῶν ἐλεημόνων ψυχαί.

[58] It does not appear in his catalogue of New Testament books at *Catechetical Oration* 4.36 (*PG* 33:500C).

[59] On the fears aroused by this project, and the absence of secure evidence for any response by Cyril, see Jan W. Drijvers, *Cyril of Jerusalem: Bishop and City* (Leiden: Brill, 1972), 127–52.

List of Contributors

Armin Bergmeier teaches late antique, Byzantine, and Islamic material culture at the University of Leipzig.

Nathan Betz is a research fellow at the Beyond Canon Centre for Advanced Studies at the University of Regensburg.

Ian Boxall is Senior Tutor and Tutor in Biblical Studies at St Stephen's House, Oxford.

Alessandro Capone is Associate Professor of Ancient Christian Literature at the University of Salento.

Mathieu Cuijpers is a doctoral student in Classical Studies at KU Leuven.

Anthony Dupont is Research Professor in Christian Antiquity at KU Leuven.

Mark Edwards is Tutor in Theology at Christ Church, Oxford, and Lecturer/Associate Professor in Patristics and Professor of Early Christian Studies at the University of Oxford.

Mark W. Elliott is Professor of Divinity and Biblical Criticism at the University of Glasgow and Professorial Fellow at Wycliffe College, University of Toronto.

Francis X. Gumerlock teaches Latin in the Archdiocese of Denver.

Konrad Huber is Professor of New Testament Studies at the Johannes Gutenberg University of Mainz.

Mateusz Kusio is a postdoctoral research fellow at the Centre for Research on Ancient Civilizations at the University of Warsaw.

Anni Maria Laato is Senior Lecturer of Systematic Theology at Åbo Akademi University and Adjunct Professor in Patristics at the University of Helsinki.

Antti Laato is Professor of Old Testament Exegetics and Judaic Studies at Åbo Akademi University.

Johan Leemans is Professor of Christianity in Late Antiquity at KU Leuven.

Tobias Nicklas is Professor of New Testament and Director of the Beyond Canon Centre for Advanced Studies at the University of Regensburg.

T. C. Schmidt is Assistant Professor of New Testament and Early Christianity at Fairfield University.

Martina Vercesi is a postdoctoral researcher in the School of Critical Studies at the University of Glasgow.

Joseph Verheyden is Professor of New Testament Studies at KU Leuven.

Index of References

Biblical books

Genesis
1:1–2:3	162
1:26	27, 30
2:2	168
4:16–17	288
6:14	246
11:2	289
11:8	289
13:14	65
13:14–15	61, 63, 65
13:15	63
14:18–20	289
15:18	61, 63, 65, 245
15:5	63
19	288
27:36	167

Exodus
1:11	288
3:8	128
16:3	110
24:10	259
28	148, 254, 256, 258, 262
28:12	258
28:15–21	293
28:17–20	244
28:17–21	155
28:17–29	243
28:21	243
30:10–14	155

Leviticus
26:12	202

Numbers
2–3	233

Deuteronomy
34:6	268

Joshua
6:1–27	288
8:20	288
10:26–32	288
11:3	289
12:10	289
20	288
21:11	288

Judges
1:10	288

1 Kings
5:17	243
6:20	192
7:9–10	243
7:25	255
8:27	290

2 Kings
2	268
5:7–8	289
5:7–9	110
5:9	289
6:3	289
6:10	289
7:2	290
15:23	292
18:4	290
21:3	290
23:6	292
23:6–7	290

1 Chronicles
11:8	289
13:13	289

2 Chronicles
4:4	255
31:1	290

Nehemiah
3	291

Tobit 240, 261
13	243
13:17	238–239

Job
23:8–9	77

Psalms
1	97
1:3	301
1:5	97
2:9	192
21	296
26:8	110
27:13	110
46:4	114
46:5	202
46:10	145
48	62
48:9	61
48:12–13	290
48:8	110, 114
50	104
50:12	290
50:28	104
60	61
60:8	61
60:8–10	61
64	119
72	11, 63–64
72:8	61, 63, 65, 245
72:16	61
82	17, 26
82:6	28
84:1–2	110
84:10	110
86:1–2	110
91:11	164
99:1	290
104:4	164
105:8	250
119:27	148
120:1–2	145
132:7	66, 111
147	119

Song of Songs
3:2–3	289
3:4	111
6:9	111

Ecclesiasticus
24	295
44:21	63

Isaiah
1–4	77–78
1:7–9	78–79, 86
1:8	75, 79
1:8–9	71, 80–81, 83–84, 91–92
1:9	81
1:10–17	75
1:21–25	75
1:26	117
2:1	75
2:1–4	71–75, 77, 80, 86, 91
2:2–3	78
2:2–4	78, 81–82, 276
2:3	117, 75
2:3–4	75
2:14	78
2:16	260
4:2–6	78
4:2–3	73, 77
4:4	64
4:5	60–61
4:5–6	64
4:6	61
5:1–7	83–84
5:2–7	81
8:16–18	73
11:11	81
14:6	289
14:16–20	289
18:7	73
19–20	61
19:23–25	73
22:1	73
24:21–23	73
25:6	62
25:6–7	62
25:6–8	73
26:1	73, 147
26:1–2	144
26:2–8a	73
28:16	290
30:25–26	73
32:7–8	86
35:9–10	73
36:2	290
36:12	290
36:18	290
48:2	198
49:11	73

49:16	75, 295	*Jeremiah*	
49:17	86, 88	3:12	166
49:18	241	5:1	289
52:1	198	7:4	114, 290
51:1–2	87	31:38–40	232
51:10–11	198	33:1	289
51:11	73	44:16–25	290
51:12	291	44:17	289
52:8	86	51:1	110
54	26, 243, 261	51:6	110
54:1	26		
54:11–12	89–90, 238	*Lamentations*	
54:11–14	23, 231	4:12	139
54:12	86, 89–90, 231		
57:12–14	73	*[1] Baruch*	
58:6	294	4:36–37	295
60:1	61, 117, 290		
60:1–2	86	*Ezekiel*	
60:4	86, 117	1:26	260
60:5	62, 231	5:5	139
60:8	117	8:14	290
60:10	64	16:10–14	198
60:10–11	231, 242	28:11–19	289
60:17	62	28:13	243–244
60:18	86	37:27	198
60:19	293	40:5	232
60:21	73	40–48	86, 198, 232, 265
61:1–2	198, 294	43:13	232
61:6	62	47:1–12	291
61:10	198, 241	47:7	156
62:3–5	198	47:12	128, 156
62:5–6	86	48	234–235, 237
62:10	64, 198	48:30–34	155
62:12	18	48:30–35	161, 163, 230–233, 236, 238, 241
64:10–11	18	48:31–35	237, 291
65	16	48:9–22	232
65:1–2	74		
65:8–9	73	*Daniel*	
65:16–19	198	2	82, 240
65:17	76	2:31–45	61
65:17–18	75	2:45	82
65:17–25	16	5:2	290
65:18	117	7	240
65:19–20	88	7:18	61
66:1	290		
66:8	117	*Hosea*	
66:10–11	86	6:6	290
66:12–13	86		
66:13	295	*Joel*	
66:18–20	73, 91	2:20	166
66:19	116	2:25	62
66:22	198	3:10	289
66:23	73, 145		

Amos
5:25	290
9:14	50

Obadiah
17	291

Jonah
4:10–12	289
4:11	291

Micah
3:12	80
4:1–2	291
4:1–5	80
4:2	296
4:3	289

Nahum
3:1–19	289

Zechariah
	262
2:1–5	231
2:2–5	291
2:5	231, 251
6:13	291, 303
14:4	291, 302
14:10	291
14:16	291, 303

Zephaniah
3:8	86

Matthew
2:16	132
5:4	62
5:5	126
5:6	128–129
5:14	114, 293
10:2–4	186
13:8	25, 95, 97
13:23	97, 165
13:45–46	251
14:29	165
16:16	110, 165
17:1–13	267
18:18	163
19:29	62
22:37–39	165
22:40	165
23:37	114
23:38	75
24:2	87
24:15	119
24:16	67, 170
24:42	168
25:31–46	4
25:34	164
25:41	164
26:29	23, 62, 65
27:52–53	105, 113

Mark
3:16–19	186
4:20	25
10:30	62

Luke
4:21	294
6:14–16	186
16:23	4
16:25	62
17:21	114
20:35–36	17

John
1:1	165
3:3	166
3:5	166
4:21–23	108
5:2	292
5:17	53
5:35	148
9:2	292
10:9	249
10:22–42	119
10:23	292
14:2	4, 14, 25, 30, 65
15:1–10	179
18:1	292
18:13	292
18:24	292
18:27	292
19:13	292
19:17	292
19:42	292
20:19	167
20:26–31	160
28:28	292

Acts
1:13	186
2:3	292
7:48	280, 290
9:11–25	292
11	292

11:2	292	2:20	137
13:32–36	292	4	26, 146
15	292	4:22–26	292
17:24	108	4:26	5, 24, 26, 28, 30, 36, 65, 71, 73–78, 80, 82, 85, 108, 111, 114, 137, 199, 201, 297, 299
20:28	300		
21:20–26	292		
22:28	299		
		4:26–27	116–117

Romans

4:12	254	*Ephesians*	
4:25	292	2:20	185
8:11	114	5:25	116
9–11	78, 83, 91		
10:20	75	*Philippians*	
10:27–29	80	3:20	30, 109–110, 114, 137, 199, 202, 293, 297, 299–300
11	247, 253		
11:1	252		
11:1–5	78, 80		
11:5	81, 247, 252	*Colossians*	
11:18	252	3:1	102–103
11:27–29	78		
12:4–5	127	*1 Thessalonians*	
		4:15–17	60, 100, 102

1 Corinthians

2:9	26	*2 Thessalonians*	
4:15	255	1:10	126–127
6:7	60		
6:20	300	*Titus*	
12:12–31a	127	2:5	300
13:13	164		
15:20–28	61	*Hebrews*	
15:24	104	1:7	164
15:25	15, 61	11:9	4
15:26	36	11:16	4, 202
15:27–28	15	12:12	117
15:41	97	12:18–22	293
15:50	298	12:21–22	5
15:52	60, 100, 102	12:22	24, 36, 108, 118, 199
15:52–53	97	12:22–23	30, 40, 99
		12:22–24	71–74, 85
2 Corinthians		12:23	202
5:16	251	13:10–12	293
6:11	255	13:14	72, 202, 293
6:16	114		
11:23	292	*James*	
11:28	255	5:16	163
12:2–4	4		
12:4	125	*1 Peter*	
		1:3	30
Galatians		1:4	202
1:18	292	1:12	26
2:1	292	2:6	247
2:9	185		

2 Peter		13:13	198
2:4–8	301	14:1–5	60
3:13	202	14:3–4	165
		16:12	63, 199
Revelation		16:21	198
1–5	249	17:1–19:10	197, 214
1:5	249	17–18	176
1:8	19, 36	17–22	214
1:15	66	18–21	145
1:19	36	18–22	249
2:7	36, 41	18:1	198
2:8	301	19	36, 46
2:9	16	19:7	127
2:10	41	19:7–8	198
2:11	36	19:11	59, 69
2:17	36, 41	19:11–21	58
2:18	52	19:11–21:8	197
2:20	134	19–21	46
2:26	36	19–22	59
2:26–28	192	20	17, 36–37, 53, 59, 137, 297, 301
3:1–5	19		
3:5	36	20–21	40, 93, 94, 150
3:12	36, 41, 85, 198, 206–207, 293, 296	20:1–3	46
		20:1–6	76
3:21	36	20:1–15	58
4	217, 223	20:2	126
4:1–11	118	20:2–6	162
4:3	242, 247	20:3	146
4:4	250, 276	20:3–7	102
4:7–8	118	20:4	50, 53, 126, 127
5:6	152	20:4–6	16, 38, 39, 46, 50, 126, 241
6:6–13	52		
6:9–10	133	20:5	59, 102–104
6:11	133	20:5–6	59, 65
7:1–8	59	20:6	104, 127
7:4–8	242	20:6–7	94
7:5–8	184	20:7	59–60, 126
7:16–12:6	52	20:7–9	46
8:6	199	20:9	198
9:7	199	20:11–14	4
9:14	63	20:11–15	126
10:1	198	20:15	46
10:7	51	21	4–5, 9, 17, 19, 24, 26, 31, 36–37, 42, 47, 50, 62, 75, 110, 113, 118, 126, 137, 142, 144, 147, 151–152, 160–161, 171, 213, 230, 234, 240–241, 243–244, 247, 249, 251, 254, 260, 264, 283, 297
11:1	190, 192		
11:1–2	112, 178		
11:7–8	112		
11:8	36, 112		
11:19	178		
12:5	192		
12:6	67, 199		
12:12	198	21–22	27, 35–36, 38, 65, 71, 74, 76, 85–86, 91, 107–108,
12:14	67		
13:8	293		

	110, 114, 117, 120, 155, 217, 221, 286	21:15–17	293
21:1	36, 46, 76, 127, 241	21:15–22:16	4
21:1–22:5	58, 60, 69, 207	21:16	42, 50, 68, 147, 173, 177, 182, 192, 241, 250, 256
21:1–2	4, 188, 28	21:16–18	112
21:1–5	174	21:16–21	98
21:1–6	24	21:17	145, 190
21:1–8	197–198	21:18	44, 130–131, 155, 190, 242–243, 251
21:1–27	182		
21:2	19, 30, 36, 38–39, 42, 46, 59, 61, 63, 85, 127, 140, 151, 194, 197–202, 206, 209, 211, 214, 293	21:18–21	148, 293
		21:19	242
		21:19–20	99, 131, 155, 163, 180, 184, 243, 247, 251–252, 256
21:2–7	202		
21:3	4, 110, 151	21:19–21	155, 259
21:4	36, 50, 197, 300	21:21	130–131, 173, 184, 225, 243, 246, 251
21:5	24, 36, 38, 241, 293		
21:5–8	4	21:21–25	100
21:6	19, 38, 146, 179	21:22	131, 192, 242–243, 293
21:7	17, 19, 36, 38	21:22–23	104
21:8	37–38, 46, 244	21:22–24	177, 179
21:9	127, 147, 173, 187	21:23	50, 180
21:9–10	140	21:23–24	130
21:9–12	176	21:24	47, 133
21:9–22	188	21:24–26	244
21:9–27	46, 162, 240–242	21:25	50
21:9–22:2	197	21:26–27	133
21:9–22:5	197	21:27	37, 129, 213, 244
21:9–22:9	197, 214	22	4–5, 9, 17, 110, 297
21:10	4, 38, 39, 42, 63, 147, 151, 182, 293	22:1	4, 114, 128–129, 179, 197
21:10–11	133	22:1–2	173, 179, 188, 293
21:10–12	104	22:1–5	182
21:10–14	173	22:2	16, 128–129, 155–156, 158, 177, 179, 243
21:10–21	120		
21:11	131, 147, 225, 242–249, 255, 258	22:3	173, 242
		22:3–4	20
21:11–21	29	22:4	133
21:12	42, 130, 147, 151, 155, 157, 162–163, 169, 184–185, 241, 243, 247, 249, 253, 255	22:6	179
		22:6–21	4, 182
		22:8	188
		22:13	16, 38
21:12–13	155, 293	22:14	38
21:13	163, 186, 250, 255	22:15	38, 129, 174
21:14	42, 130, 145, 163, 169, 184, 250, 256, 293	22:17	133, 177
		22:21	133
21:15	177, 190	22:18–19	38
21:15–16	162		

Apocrypha

2 Baruch	23	*Gospel according to the Hebrews*	167
4	199		
4.3	207	*Gospel of the Nazarenes*	161, 167
29.5	65		
		Letter of Jesus on Sunday Observance	168
1 Enoch	169		
10.18–19	50	*Shepherd of Hermas*	57, 123, 169
29.3	156	Vis. 3.5(13)	156
30.1	156	Vis. 3.2(10).4–9	302
90.29	207	Mand. 6.2(36)	164
		Sim. 9.15(92)	29
4 Ezra			
7.26	199, 207	*Visio Pauli*	123–135, 154, 169
8.51–55	207	1–2	125
10.53	199	3–10	125
10.54	207	7	164
13.36	199, 207	11–18	125
		19	125
5 Ezra	57, 123	21	125
		21–22	126–130
6 Ezra	57, 123	21–30	125
		23	130–132
Apocalypse of Peter	123	25–28	132
14	129	29	133–135
		31	125

Apocalypse of Thomas 160–161
4   168
5   168

Ascension of Isaiah 57, 123
4.13   170
6–7   57

Dead Sea Scrolls and Rabbinic Texts

4QpapTob^a (4Q196)	238, 239	4Q554	234, 236, 237, 238, 239, 240
18, 7–8	238		
		1 I, 9–II, 10	235, 237
4QpIsa^d (4Q164)	238, 243	1 I, 19	236
3–4	238	1 II, 17	237
		1 II, 18	236
Debarim R. S. XI	207	2 II, 13–14	236
		2 II, 14–15	238–239
Eicha Rabba		2 II, 15–18	238
1.1.2	240	2 II, 15	239
		13+14, 20	240
New Jerusalem Text	261	4Q554^a	234
1Q32	234	4Q555	234
2Q24	234		

5Q15	234, 236, 238	*Shir ha–Shirim Rabba*	
1 I, 4	236	7.5.3	240
1 I, 6–7	238		
11Q18	234	*Temple Scroll*	
		11QT	235

Reworked Pentateuch
4Q365ª 2 II   237

Ancient Christian and Classical Works

Aelius Aristides

Orationes
26.11–12   211

Ambrose

De Cain et Abel
1.2.8   268

De Nabuthae historia
12.53   93

Ambrosiaster

Commentarius in Epistulam ad Corinthios primam
15.41   97
15.52   102

Fragmenta ex Commentariis in Matthaeum   97, 102, 105
2.9   94
4   97
10   94
12   94
13   102
14   102
15   103–104

Quaestiones veteris et novi testamenti
97   104
97.4   104
109   105
110   97
110.17   97
112   104
112.28   104

Anastasius of Sinai

Hexaemeron
1   14
1.7   14

Andrew of Caesarea

Commenarii in Apocalypsin
Prol. (8)   220
22.65 (232)   224
23.67   29, 255
23.67 (239)   225
23.67 (239–240)   255
23.67 (240)   255
24.67 (240–241)   255
23.67 (242)   256
23.67 (247)   225
23.67 (248)   226
23.67 (249)   173, 194

Apringius of Beja

Tractatus in Apocalypsin
7.304–308   249
7.309–310   251
7.321–322   249
7.323–327   250
7.338–340   250
7.341–346   186, 250
7.368–410   250
7.407–410   251
7.422–440   250
7.441–454   250
7.455–459   251
7.457–459   251
7.460–465   251
7.466–476   251
7.559–560   179

Aristophanes

Aves   206
550–551   230
1372   203

Aristotle

De anima   206

Politeia
7.11   230
1330b33–1331a19   230

Athenaeus

Deipnosophistae   210
1.19a – 20a   210
1.20a–b   209
1.20b–21a   210
3.8   211
3.53   211
3.94   211

Augustine

De civitate Dei   300
7.4   207
11.7   140
16.2   219
17.3   219
18.53   150
20.7   146
20.17   300
24   140

De doctrina christiana
3.30.43–37.56   300

Enarrationes in Psalmos
86.3.19   148

Aulus Gellius

Noctes atticae
16.13.7   215

Basil of Caesarea

Homilia in Genesim
4   297

Beatus of Liébana

Commentaria in Apocalypsin   51, 181
Book 2, prol.   184
Book 2, prol. 3.9   185
Book 2, prol. 3.17–18   186
Book 2, prol. 3.19–20   184–185
Book 12, title   151
Book 12, 2.3   151
Book 12, 2.1   151
Book 12, 2.8   151
Book 12, 2.9   151
Book 12, 2.28–30   151
Book 12, 2.30   151
Book 12, 2.31–32   151–152

Adversus Elipandum
    182

Bede the Venerable

Explanatio Apocalypsis
3.17   186
3.37   29, 174, 179
3.37.9–11   147
3.37.14–15   147
3.37.15–23   258
3.37.24–30   147
3.37.24–32   258
3.37.30–33   185
3.37.36–38   258
3.37.47–50   148
3.37.42–43   258
3.37.62–82   258
3.37.97–379   259
3.37.105–354   148
3.37.148–150   260
3.37.163–191   260
3.37.213–232   260
3.37.272–277   260
3.37.344–354   149
3.37.364–366   258

De temporibus ratione
22.1.80   146

Vitae quinque sanctorum abbatum
1   176

Būlus al-Būshī

Commentary on the Apocalypse
29   226

Caesarius of Arles

Expositio de Apocalypsi Sancti Iohannis
10.4   170
19   186, 190, 248
19.2   248
19.3   248
19.4   248
19.5   248
19.7–8   248
19.8   248
19.9   248

Cassiodorus

Institutiones divinarum et saecularium litterarum
1.9.4   252

Cicero

Epistulae ad familiares
2.10.1   215

Clement of Alexandria

Adumbrationes in epistulas canonicas
1 Pet. 1:3   30

Paedagogus   27
1.6.26   28
1.6.36   28
1.6.45   27–28
1.7.54   28
1.12.98   28
2   28
2.8.65   28
2.12   28, 184
2.12.118   28
2.12.119   28
2.12.119.1   204

Eclogae Propheticae
56–57   30
57.4   27

Protrepticus
12.118   28

Stromata
1.1   30
4   29, 202
4.25.155   29
4.26.169   30
4.26.171   30
4.26.172   30–31
4.26.172.1   203
4.26.172–3   203
6.13–15   30
6.14.116   30
7.7.1   30
7.2.13   28
7.5.28–29   280
7.10.56   30
23.153.1   268

Colloquy of the Two Sages 170

Commemoratorium de Apocalypsi Johannis apostoli 161

Commodian

Carmen apologeticum 48
791–792   48

Instructiones   48, 49
1.44   49
1.45   49
1.46   49

Cyprian

Idola
2   207

Ad Quirinium testimonia adversus Iudaeos
2.16–18   82

Cyril of Jerusalem

Catecheses   116
4.12   88
4.36   303
12.11   302
13.28   116
14.1   116
18.26   108, 116
18.33   116
18.34   116–117

Demetrius of Scepsis
Fragment 46   211

Didache
16   57, 123

Didymus the Blind

De Spiritu Sancto
preface of Jerome's translation 109

Diodorus

Bibliotheca historica
2.3.2–3   236

Dionysius bar Ṣalibi

In Apocalypsim
28.22–26   221
29.10–11   222

Egeria

Itinerarium Egeriae 115, 118
23.9–10   107
25.8   120
42.3   80

46.3	115	*Eclogae propheticae*	74–77, 80, 92
		172–173	75
Epic of Gilgamesh	290	173	74–75

Epiphanius of Cyprus

De duodecim gemmis 256, 259
2.27 260
12 157

De mensuribus et ponderibus
14 79

Panarion
48 295
48.14 296
49.1.2–3 295

Euripides
Cyclops
115–118 229

Fragment 33 203

Fragment 911 203

Hippolytus
732–734 203

Ion
1238 203

Eusebius

Commentarius in Isaiam 73–74, 81–82, 84–87
7 81
15 82
16 82–83, 86
17 83
29–31 81
86–87 81
314 89
321 87
342 89
397–98 88
408 91

Demonstratio evangelica 74–75, 77–80, 86, 92
67 77
67–75 77
68–69 78
70 78
73 78
75 77
131 79

Historia ecclesiastica 72, 76, 83
3 10
3.24.18 10
3.25.2 10
3.28 10
3.28.1–5 66
3.39.1 13
3.39.5 13
3.39.8 13
3.39.11 13
3.39.12 13, 66, 68
3.39.12–13 15
4.26.2 19
4.26.4 22
4.5 79
5 76
5.18.2 295
6.13.9 22, 27
7.24.1–3 66
7.25.1–3 66
7.25.22 10
8–10 82
10.4.6 280
10.4.25 280
10.4.70 280

De laudibus Constantini
9.16 88

De martyribus Palaestinae 76
11 77

Onomasticon 79

Vita Constantini 84–85, 87–88, 91
3.25–40 74
3.25–28 87
3.25–40 85
3.28 119
3.33 71, 84–87, 89, 118, 181, 280
3.34–40 90
3.35–36 90
3.38 88, 90, 91
3.40 87, 89, 91
33 118

Flavius Josephus

Antiquitates judaicae
1.2 289
4.326 268

Galen

De antidotis
2   64

De humero iis modis prolapso quos Hippocrates non vidit
347   210

De simplicium medicamentorum temperamentis ac facultatibus
6.22   64

Gennadius

De ecclesiasticis dogmatibus
55   21

Gregory the Great

Moralia   151
18.59   152
28.13   148

Gregory of Nazianzus

Carmina
II.1.32   203

Gregory of Nyssa

Epistulae
2   108

Herodotus

Historiae
1.178   236
2.32–33   260
3.116   260
4.13   260
4.27   260

Hilary of Poitiers

Commentarius in Evangelium Matthaei
Matt. 24:16   170

Ibn Kātib Qayṣar

Commentary on the Apocalypse
19   223

Irenaeus of Lyons

Demonstration of the Apostolic Teaching 26
26   24, 26
29   24, 26
86   75
94   26

Adversus haereses   14, 75
3.6.1   26
4   22
4.1.1   26
4.6.2   22
4.11.2   25
4.26.1   22
4.34.4   75
5   22, 25–27, 58, 64
5.15   295
5.28–36   58
5.28.3   46
5.30.4–5.35.2   22
5.31.1   12
5.32.1   23, 26, 64–65
5.32.1–2   12
5.32.2   25, 65
5.33–36   108
5.33.1   23
5.33.3   50, 65
5.33.3–4   23, 65–66, 128
5.33.3–5   13
5.33.4   13
5.34.1   23
5.34.3–4   23
5.34.4   23
5.35.1   23, 64
5.35.1–2   12, 23
5.35.2   22–24, 65, 75–76
5.36.1   14, 25, 65
5.36.1–2   25, 65, 96
5.36.2   15, 25
5.36.3   22, 26–27, 65

Isidore of Seville

De ecclesiasticis officiis 161
16.6   166

Etymologiae   184

De ortu et obitu patrum 184

De viris illustribus
22   142
30   249

Jerome

Commentariorum in Ezechielem libri XVI 13
11.36   37, 113
48.30   113

Commentariorum in Isaiam libri XVIII 113
10.17   113
15.7   113
15.10   114

17.2	113	5.94	246
17.8	113–114	5.101–103	301
18.1	113	5.109–112	301
		5.109–117	246

Commentariorum in Matthaeum 96–97, 101, 105

prol.	57	5.110–125	100
prol.	96	5.113	301
2.13.23	96	5.113–114	246
4.26.1–2	96	5.118–119	246
4.27.52–53	105	5.124–125	67
4.28.20	101	5.125	66

Explanatio in Danielem 182

Epistulae

Adversus Iovinianum 95, 96

22.24	111	1.3	95
46	99, 110–111		
46.6	99, 112		

In Lucam homiliae XXXIX ex Graeco Origenis Latine conversae

46.6–7	113	prol.	57
46.7	105, 111, 113		
49.2	95		

De nominibus hebraicis 161, 166–167

58.2	114

De viris illustribus

58.2–3	109	18	37, 66
58.3	108, 114	24	19
60.3	105	61	58
64.20	101	74	57
66	101		
66.3	101	John Cassian	
73	105		
107.13	95	*Collationes*	
108	115	14.8.4	299
108.9	110		
108.31	110	John of Dara	
123.8	95		

On the Resurrection of Bodie

Explanatio in Apocalypsin 95, 96, 101, 103, 105

2.13	13

Justin Martyr

(recension of Victorinus *Explanatio in Apocalypsin*; Gryson's numbering)

Apologia i

prol.	95, 105	53.7	48

Dialogus cum Tryphone 18, 294

prol. 6	67	3.7–4.7	17, 22
prol. 7–13	93	11.4	18
prol. 13	67	11.5	18
prol. 13–15	68	16.2	15
prol. 14–15	301	22.11	18
prol. 16–18	96	24	18
5	94, 100, 103	24.2	17
5.33–35	67	25.1	17
5.33–38	94	25.6	18
5.38–44	103	26.1	17
5.40–44	67, 94	26.3	18
5.44–69	98	33.2	18
5.89–92	98, 246	35.6	12
5.92–93	301, 302	40	294
5.93–108	99		

40.4	66	7.24.15	47
43.1–2	18	7.25	45–46
44.4	18	7.25.1	45
45.4	16	7.26.1	46
46.7	16	7.26.5	46
47	18	7.26.6	46
55.3	78		
63.5	18	*Epitome divinarum institutionum*	
64	18	67.3	47
67.9–10	18		
69.7	16	Liber Pontificalis	281
76.4	17	34.9–11	281
80–81	18, 108		
80.1	11, 16, 294	Lucian of Samosata	
80.1–4	66	*Vera historia*	130
80.1–2	18		
80.2	21, 295	Macrobius	
80.2–3	11	*Saturnalia*	
80.5	11, 16, 66, 261	1.7.19–26	207
81.4	16–17		
82.1–2	16	Manilius	
82.3	16	*Astronomica*	208
85.7	66	1.799–800	208
92.2	15	1.926	208
95.3	18	4.694–95	208
108.2	15	4.934–35	208
108.3	18	5.734–45	208
113.4–5	17		
117.3	16	Maximus the Confessor	
120	18	*Mystagogia*	
122.6	18	2	282
123.6–7	18		
123.9	18	Melito of Sardis	
124.1–2	17	*De Apocalypsi Johannis*	19, 21
124.4	17	Fragment 11	20
140.3	78	New Fragment 2	21
142.2–3	18	2.1	21
		2.18–19	21
Lactantius		*De Pascha*	20, 22
Divinarum institutionum libri VII	44, 46, 47	38–39	20
5.5.9	207	39–43	20
7	46	40–43	20
7.17	170	43	20
7.19	46	44	20
7.20	46	45	19
7.22–23	46	70	21
7.24	128	72	20
7.24–26	45	81–82	20
7.24.2	46	93	20
7.24.5	46	94	20
7.24.6	46–47		
7.24.7–14	46–47		

99	21	*Commentarius in Canticum*	
103	20–21	Prol. 62.24–30	290
104	21	Prol. 84.15–17	298
105	19	Prol. 84.15–85.27	15

Methodius

Symposium 58

Minucius Felix

Observationes 206

Octavius
21.4–6   207
32   280

Nerses of Lambron

Commentary on the Apocalypse
prologue [13]   223
prologue [14]   222
prologue [15]   222, 223

Oecumenius

Commentarius in Apocalypsin
3.5.5   226
3.5.6   227
3.5.11   226
3.5.12   226
5.1.1   221
11.16.2–3   253
11.16.3   221, 253
11.16.5   254
11.16.5–6   253
11.16.7–8   253
11.16.9   254
11.16.9–10   254
11.16.10   253
12.2.12–12.7.11   179
12.3.2–3   254
12.3.7   254
12.3.8   254
12.3.9   254
12.3.10   221
12.3.12   254

Opus imperfectum in Matthaeum 300
24.4.8   300

Origen

Commentarii in evangelium Joannis 58

Commentarium in evangelium Matthaei 218
49   58

Contra Celsum   205
5.43   204
6.23   219

Fragmenta ex commentariis in epistulam i ad Corinthios
16.1.3.16–20   99

Homiliae in Ezechielem
3.1–3   29
13.3.1–3   219
13.3.2   184

Homiliae in Genesim
2.4   99

Homiliae in Psalmos
(Codex Monacensis Graecus 314)
Psalm 67 Homily 2.2 219

Philocalia
1.28   217
10.1   217

De principiis   10
2.10   164
2.11.2   15, 298
2.11.3   10
2.11.6   298
3.6.3   15
4.2.4   218
4.2.5   219
4.3.4   219
7   164

Ovid

Fasti
1.235–36   207

Papias of Hierapolis

Expositions of the Sayings of the Lord 13–15

Passio Perpetuae   2–3, 44
4   2
11–13   2
12.1   44

Philo

De opificio mundi
49–50   98

De plantatione
121–122   98

De somniis
2.246–50   202

De vita Mosis
128   98

Plato

Leges
6.778d–779a   230

Phaedo   206
65b3–5   205
66b5–7   205
79c2–8   205
80d5–81c6   206
81c11–d1   206
83d1   206

Respublica   201–202, 206
book 9   201
590e   202
591e   202
592b   204
592A–B   30
592a10–b5   201
605b   202
608b   202

Sophista
216C   29
247c   206

Plautus

Rudens   214–216
Prol. 1–2   214

Pliny the Elder

Naturalis historia
4.26   260
6.19   260
7.2   260
37.19, 74   157
37.30, 104   260
37.34, 113   157
37.37, 116   157, 242
37.63, 174   157
37.66, 178   157

Praedestinatorum haeresis
1.26   297

Primasius

Commentarius in Apocalypsin
5.21.29–46   144
5.21.49–54   144
5.21.102–103   144, 252
5.21.112–114   185
5.21.112–123   252
5.21.135–138   252
5.21.145–146   145
5.21.150–151   252
5.21.164–165   145
5.21.214–215   252
5.21.217–228   145
5.21.232–292   145
5.21.268–270   252
5.21.331–335   145
5.21.335–343   145
5.22.11–27   179

Pseudo-Acron

Scholia in Epistulas
1.6.62   215

Pseudo-Asconius

In Ciceronis Divinationem in Caecilium
8   215

Pseudo-Bede

Collectanea   166

Pseudo-Cyprian

De montibus Sina et Sion 41–42
4   43
4.3   43
9   42
10   42
10.1   42

Pseudo-Dionysius the Areopagite

De coelesti hierarchia
1.3   279

Pseudo-Epiphanius

In festo Palmarum orationis fragmentum
(Homily 6)   303

Rutilius Numantianus

De reditu suo
1.66   212

324   *Index of References*

Sibyllina Oracula   57, 123
3.767–808   207
5.252   240

Sophocles

Oedipus Coloneus
1079–1081   203

Stephanus of Alexandria

Ioannis Philoponi in Aristotelis De anima libros commentaria
563.7–11   206

Strabo

Geographica
16.2.2   64
Suda   210

Symeon of Thessalonica

Liturgical Commentaries
16   282
17   282

Tacitus

Historiae
4.3   207

Tertullian

De anima
11.2   298

De fuga in persecution
7   37
7.2   38
9.3   38

Adversus Hermogenem
22.5   38

Adversus Marcionem   39
1.29.4   38
2.5.1   38
2.10.6   38
3.21.3   296
3.22.1   296
3.22.6   296
3.23.2   296
3.24   37, 39, 66, 76, 108, 162
3.24.3   297
3.24.3–4   39
3.24.4   261, 297
4.11.9   38

De monogamia
5.2   38

De praescriptione haereticorum
7   297

De pudicitia
19.7–8   38
19.8   38
19.9   38

De resurrectione carnis
48   298
58.3   38

Scorpiace   40
12.1   38
12.8   40

De spe fidelium   37

De spectaculis   38, 40
30.1   38

Theodore of Mopsuestia

In Epistolas B. Pauli 299

Theodoret

Graecarum affectionum curatio
5.65   204

Tyconius

Expositio Apocalypseos   51, 103, 247
7.19–22   53
7.20   103
7.31   54, 247
7.34   247
7.36   247
7.37   247
7.39   247
7.40   247
7.41   247
7.48   54

Liber regularum   52
4   142
5.3   52
5.6   53
7.2   300
7.4   166

Varro

De lingua Latina
5.42   207

Vergilius

Aeneid
1.278–279	208
1.279–282	208
8	207
8.319	207
8.357–358	207

Eclogues
4	5, 50
4.31	300

Victorinus of Petovium

Explanatio in Apocalypsin 58, 93, 95, 244, 301
(Dulaey's numbering unless otherwise indicated)
1.5	66, 68
7	60
12.4	60, 67–68
14.1	60
14.3	58
19	58–60, 64
19–21	100
20.1	58–60, 94, 100, 301
20.2	58–60, 102
21	68
21.1	58–60, 100, 301
21.1–2	245
21.1–3	100
21.2	58, 60–64, 245, 301
21.3	60–61
21.3–5	245
21.4	61–62
21.4–6	61
21.5	58, 62, 65
21.6	29, 60–62, 65, 245, 301

Fragment on the Olivet Discourse 170

Vision of Dorotheus 2, 3

Vitruvius

De architectura
1.5.1–8	229

Medieval works

Adomnan

De locis sanctis   139, 161

Alcuin

Liber de animae ratione
7	177

Berengaudus

Expositio super septem visiones libri Apocalypsis   187–188, 190

Bernard of Clairvaux

De laude novae militiae
5	140

Sermones super Cantica canticorum
55.2	140

Book of Armagh   161, 186

Catechesis Celtica   153, 158–159

Christian of Stablo

Expositio in Matthaeum
55	168

Dante

Divina Commedia   123

De enigmatibus ex Apocalypsi Johannis 161

Eriugena

Periphyseon   161

Gilon of Paris

Monumentum de Bello Sacro 139

Glossa in Apocalypsin
(Cambridge Gloss on the Apocalypse) 161

Life of Brendan of Clonfert
153	170

Navigatio sancti Brendani Abbatis 161
28	170

"On the Gates of the New Jerusalem" 153, 158–171

Peter the Venerable

Sermon 2   139

Prolegomena philosophiae Platonicae 205
2.7–12   205
2.10–11   205
2.10.26–27   205

Quaestiones tam de novo quam de vetere testamentum 156

Question-and-Answer Tractate on the New Jerusalem 154–155, 157, 169, 170

Robert Grossteste

Expositio in epistolam Sancti Pauli ad Galatas
4.35   140

Thomas Aquinas

Super ad Galatas
C4.L8   141

Tidings of Doomsday   162

Urban II apud Robert of Reims

Historia Hierosolymitana 139

Vita sancti Gregori Magni 166

Index of Modern Authors

Adam, James 202
Adams, Arthur White 252
Adkin, Neil 99
Albrecht, Felix 260
Allo, Ernest-Bernard 199
Amat, Jacqueline 44
Andersson, Torsten J. 202
Andrès Pérez, Javier 200
Antolín, Guillermo 154
Antonissen, Hugo 234–237
Auerbach, Erich 291
Aune, David E. 36, 214, 241
Austin, Roland Gregory 208

Bachvarova, Mary R. 289
Barnard, Leslie William 17
Barnes, Timothy D. 40
Bauckham, Richard 242
Beale, Gregory K. 197, 213
Bengel, Johann Albert 206
Berger, Klaus 207
Bergmeier, Armin F. 85, 118, 262–263, 276, 279, 284
Betz, Nathan 5, 32–33, 71, 113, 255
Bidez, Joseph 46
Billerbeck, Paul 207
Bischoff, Bernhard 156, 168
Blake, Robert P. 157
Bockmuehl, Markus 72
Boersma, Hans 17
Bolman, Elizabeth S. 184
Boring, M. Eugene 207
Bousset, Wilhelm 198–199
Bowen, Anthony J. 45
Boxall, Ian 51, 262
Bradshaw, Paul F. 80, 107, 115–116, 118
Brandenburg, Hugo 118
Braun, René 39
Braund, David 209
Bremmer, Jan N. 124
Bitton-Ashkelony, Brouria 108
Broshi, Magen 235
Brox, Norbert 64
Buchheit, Vinzenz 45

Buchinger, Harald 193, 264
Burgess, Richard 76
Burini, Clara 41–43
Burrows, Daron 188

Cacitti, Remo 44
Cain, Andrew 95
Camastra, Palma 52
Cameron, Averil 74, 85, 87
Campbell, Ken M. 293
Campbell, Lewis 201
Capone, Alessandro 68, 246
Carey, John 159, 167, 169
Carile, Maria Cristina 262
Carlson, Stephen C. 14, 23
Carozzi, Claude 124
Carriker, Andrew 74–75
Carruthers, Mary 177
Cartwright, Sophie 287
Casaubon, Isaac 210
Castorina, Emanuele 38
Castrillo Benito, N. 48
Cerbelaud, Dominique 41
Chadwick, Henry 27
Charles, R.H. 197
Chyutin, Michael 234–237
Ciceri, Pier Luigi 48
Claridge, Amanda 277
Coleman, Anthony P. 46
Colli, Agostino 280
Colpe, Carsten 2, 207
Conrad-O'Briain, Helen 166
Constantinou, Eugenia Scarvelis 253, 255
Contreras Molina, Francesco 36
Corke-Webster, James 77
Coüasnon, Charles 90
Cramer, J.A. 220
Cuijpers, Mathieu 29
Cumont, Franz 46
Curti, Carmelo 67–68, 93
Czock, Miriam 279

Daniélou, Jean 24, 38, 41, 43, 45–46
Darby Peter 146

Darwin Wright, Charles 154, 156
Dassmann, Ernst 2, 265
Davies, Oliver 168
de Blaauw, Sible 281
de Groote, Marc 253
de Lubac, Henri 219
de Navascués, Patricio 43
de Santos Otero, Aurelio 133
de Vis, Henri 157
Deferarri, Roy J. 73
Denysenko, Nicholas 119
DePalma Digeser, Elizabeth 44
Desrousseaux, Alexandre M. 211
Dimant, Devorah 238
Dindorf, Wilhelm 210
Dinkler, Erich 265–266
DiTommaso, Lorenzo 234–238, 241
Dochhorn, Jan 47
Doležalová, Klára 281
Donner, Herbert 80
Doutreleau, Louis 76
Drijvers, Jan Willem 108, 115–116, 303
Duensing, Hugo 133
Dulaey, Martine 58–60, 64, 66–68, 93, 96, 100–101, 104–105, 246
Dumville, David N. 169
Dunn, Geoffrey D. 37

Edwards, Catherine 200
Edwards, Mark J. 261, 298, 301
Emmerson, Richard K. 175–176, 182, 187
Engemann, Joseph 2

Fayer, Carla 200
Feldmann, Liane M. 244
Ferrar, William J. 74
Filho, José A. 36
Finney, Paul Corby 279
Fitzmyer, Joseph A. 238–239
Fowler, Robert L. 210
Fredriksen, Paula 51, 300
Freund, Stefan 45, 47
Frey, Jörg 36, 235, 238
Frick, Frank S. 229, 231

Garnsey, Peter D. A. 45
Gatti Perer, Maria Luisa 264
Giesen, Heinz 199
Gilchrest, Eric J. 240
Goranson, Stephen 242
Gorman, Michael M. 156
Goulon, Alain 45
Grant, Robert M. 73

Gryson, Roger 51, 59, 94, 145, 148, 150–151, 161, 181, 185, 244–245, 247–248, 258, 260
Gulick, Charles B. 209, 211
Gumerlock, Francis X. 146, 161, 175, 186

Habermehl, Peter 2
Hahn, Traugott 50
Hall, Stuart G. 74, 85, 87
Harrington, Wilfrid J. 198
Hasitschka, Martin 64–65, 67
Haussleiter, Johannes 252, 301
Hawk, Brandon W. 156
Heck, Eberhard 48
Heffernan, Thomas J. 44
Heid, Stefan 275
Heikel, Ivar A. 74
Hellemo, Geir 275, 277
Hennecke, Edgar 167
Herbert, Máire 168
Hernández, Juan Jr. 220
Hilhorst, Anton 124–125, 128, 154–158, 169
Hill, Charles. E. 9–10, 14, 21, 297, 301
Hillgarth, Jocelyn N. 156
Hirschberger, Veronika 123
Hoeck, Andreas 36
Hofmann, Dagmar 126
Hoheisel, Karl 2
Höll, Karl 295
Hollerich, Michael J. 74
Hoover, Jesse A. 50–51
Huber, Konrad 66, 94, 97, 245
Hübner, Wolfgang 208
Hudson, Benjamin 159
Hvalvik, Reidar 84

Inowlocki, Sabrina 71
Iricinschi, Eduard 92

Jacob, Christian 211–212
Jäggi, Carola 279
Jeremias, Joachim 111
Jiroušková, Lenka 124
Johnson, Aaron P. 71, 74, 77
Jowett, Benjamin 201

Kaibel, Georg 209–210
Kannengiesser, Charles 37, 52
Karrer, Martin 57, 66–67, 198
Kessels, A. H. M. 3
Kim, Soo J. 232
Kitson, Peter 259–260
Klein, Peter 175–177, 179, 181, 187
Klingshirn, William E. 248
Koester, Craig R. 35–36, 199, 241, 243

Konkel, Michael 232
Kovacs, Judith 35–37
Kraft, Heinrich 198–199
Kraus, Thomas J. 129
Kühnel, Bianca 85, 178–179, 182, 263–265
Kuhn-Treichel, Thomas 208
Kypke, Georg David 206

Laato, Antti 72, 83, 117–118, 276
Laato, Anni Maria 37–43, 76, 80, 107, 111
Labahn, Michael 37
Labatt, Annie 268
Lamoreaux, John C. 253
Lampe, Peter 296
Larson, Stan 221
Lashier, Jackson 76
Lawlor, Hugh J. 77
Lee, Pilchan 234, 240–241
Lehnardt, Andreas 45
Lehtipuu, Outi 37
Leppin, Hartmut 64
Letsch-Brunner, Silvia 111
Levenson, Jon Douglas 232
Lewis, G. 217
Lewis, Suzanne 187–188, 194
Licht, Jacob 235
Lichtenberger, Hermann 199
Lightfoot, Joseph Barber 14
Löhr, Winrich 205
Louth, Andrew 76, 282
Lowe, Dunstan 208
Lumsden, Douglas 143
Lupieri, Edmondo 199
Lynskey, Matthew R. 247

Maas, Paul 210
Manukyan, Arthur 260
Margoni-Kögler, Michael 117
Martin, Lawrence T. 154
Mathews, Thomas 266
Mathewson, David 243
Matter, E. Ann 252
May, Natalie N. 229
Mazzucco, Clementina 5, 9, 35–38, 41, 43–44, 46, 94
McGowan, Anne 80, 107, 115–116, 118
McNamara, Martin 159, 168–169
Mégier, Elisabeth 142, 150
Meineke, August 210
Meiser, Martin 35
Mellor, Ronald 200
Mercier, Charles 76
Metzger, Bruce M. 72
Meyer, Heinz 94

Milik, Józef Tadeusz 239
Mols, Stephan 200
Moreschini, Claudio 39
Morlet, Sébastien 74
Moss, Candida R. 244
Mosser, Carl 17
Müller, Karl 130
Mutschler, Bernhard 76

Nautin, Pierre 99
Nicholson, Oliver 45
Nicklas, Tobias 57, 72, 123, 126, 133–134
Nilgen, Ursula 283
Nir, Rivka 72
Noga-Banai, Galit 265

O'Dwyer Grogan, Brian 160
O'Hear, Natasha F. H. 175, 187–188
O'Loughlin, Thomas 161, 166, 168, 186
Olson, Douglas 209–211
Ophir, Adi 206
Osborn, Eric 41, 204
Osborne, John 277
Oulton, John E. L. 77

Palmer, James T. 149
Pani, Giancarlo 59, 66
Patterson, Lloyd G. 27
Pikor, Wojciech 232
Pinder, Isobel 229
Pinnock, Frances 229
Podolak, Pietro 40
Poirier, John C. 295
Pollastri, Alessandra 97, 102, 104
Poole, Kevin 141, 143
Presley, Stephen O. 76
Puech, Émile 235–238
Pullan, Wendy 118, 265

Quacquarelli, Antonio 95

Rahlfs, Alfred 239
Ramelli, Ilaria 298
Rand, Jan A. 36
Regev, Eyal 242
Regn, Gerhard 123
Richards, Herbert 201
Riches, John 141
Rittmueller, Jean 158–159, 167
Robinson, David 51
Rodríguez-Noriega, Guillén 211
Roig Lanzillotta, Lautaro 124
Roloff, Jürgen 199
Romaniuk, Kazimierz 204

Roose, Hanna 127
Rousseau, Adelin 76
Rowland, Christopher 35–37
Rubenstein, Jay 263
Ryan, Jordan J. 85, 87

Satake, Akira 198
Savinel, Pierre 202
Scafi, Alessandro 186
Schlatter, Fredric W. 118, 265, 277
Schmidt, Karl Ludwig 138, 294
Schmidt, T. C. 217, 220
Schnelle, Udo 201–202
Schott, Jeremy M. 45
Schubert, Christoph 48
Schweighäuser, Johann 210
Selig, Gerald 201–202
Seppälä, Serafim 107, 118–119
Shailor, Barbara A. 182
Shalev-Hurvitz, Vered 90
Shoemaker, Stephen J. 169
Silverstein, Theodore 124–125, 128
Simonetti, Manlio 45, 47–48, 66
Sims-Williams, Patrick 165
Skarsaune, Oskar 17, 84
Smith, Christopher R. 76, 242
Snyder, James 175
Söllner, Peter 234, 236
Spieser, Jean-Michel 266, 280
Steen, Olaf 265
Steenberg, Irenaeus M. C. 22
Steinhauser, Kenneth B. 181–182, 193, 247–248
Stemberger, Günter 87, 119
Stettner, Johannes 49
Stevens, Luke J. 13
Stewart, Aubrey 80
Steyn, Gert J. 242
Strack, Hermann L. 207
Strand, Kenneth A. 37
Strecker, Georg 201–202
Stroumsa, Guy 72, 294
Suggit, John 142
Suntrup, Rudolf 94
Susemihl, Franz 202

Tabbernee, William 296
Thomas, Edmund 229
Thraede, Klaus 137
Tibiletti, Carlo 38–39
Tigchelaar, Eibert J. C. 234
Tõniste, Külli 36
Tóth, Franz 131

Trevett, Christine 40
Tucci, Pier Luigi 281
Turcan, Robert 200, 208, 211–213

Ulrich, Jörg 92

van Banning, Joop 251
Van De Mieroop, Marc 229
van der Horst, Pieter Willem 3
van der Meer, Frederick 177
van Herwerden, Henrik 201
Vanni, Ugo 36
van Opstall, Emilie M. 280
van Ruiten, Jacques T. A. G. M. 131
Vercesi, Martina 5
Vercruysse, Jean-Marc 52
Verheyden, Joseph 2–3, 29
Verman, Mark 72
Veronese, Maria 64
Visser, Derk 187
von Arnim, Hans 204
von Harnack, Adolf 9–10, 21, 32
von Tischendorf, Constantin 124

Waitz, G. 139
Walker, Rose 84, 194
Walker, Peter W. L. 75
Wallis, Faith 145, 174
Walter, Matthias 127
Webb, Ruth 280
Wettstein, J. J. 207
Wickham, Chris 138
Wightman, G. J. 229, 232
Wilken, Robert Louis 10, 75, 84–85, 87, 110, 118–119
Wilkinson, John 80, 107
Williams, John 149, 181–182
Willmes, Ansgar 145
Wilmart, André 158–159, 162
Wise, Michael O. 235
Wisskirchen, Rotraut 275, 284
Woolf, Greg 200
Wohlmuth, Josef 36
Wüst, Ernst 211

Yadin, Yigael 235
Yarbro Collins, Adela 235, 242
Yasin, Ann Marie 118
Yonge, Charles D. 211

Zahn, Theodor 198, 214
Zamagni, Claudio 71, 123

Index of Historical Figures
(non-biblical only)

Adomnan Abelard 139, 161
Alcuin 176–177
Alfonso IX of León 193
Ambrose Autpert 187
Ambrose of Milan 93, 181, 268
Ambrosiaster 6, 94–105
Anacreon 203
Anastasius of Sinai 13–14
Andrew of Caesarea 29, 173, 185–186, 194, 220, 223–227, 231, 255–257
Apollinaris of Laodicea 66
Apringius of Beja 150, 179, 181, 186, 231, 249–252, 254, 256
Arculf 181
Arethas of Caesarea 220
Aristophanes 203, 230
Aristotle 206, 230
Aspasius of Carthage 2
Athenaeus 209–214, 216
Augustine of Hippo 32, 50, 54, 138–140, 142, 146, 148, 150, 181, 252, 303
Augustus Caesar 208

Basil of Caeasarea, cf. 297
Basilides (gnostic author), cf. 12
Beatus of Liébana 6, 51, 142, 149–152, 174, 181–186, 190, 192–193
Bede the Venerable 6, 29, 51, 142, 145–149, 152, 174–194 passim, 258–260, 262
Berenguela 193
Bernard of Clairvaux 139–141, 194
Bordeaux pilgrim 80
Būlus al-Būshī 221, 226–227

Caesarius of Arles 51, 170, 179, 186, 231, 248–252
Candidus 180
Cassiodorus 252
Cerinthus 10, 47, 66, 73
Charlemagne 138, 181
Clement of Alexandria 11–12, 20, 22, 27–32, 184, 202–204, 268, 280

Constantine I (the Great) 79, 85, 87, 91, 108, 118, 181
Cyril of Jerusalem 80, 88, 107–109, 115–120, 302–333

David (King) 110, 135, 233, 289, 291–292
Didymus the Blind 109, 301
Dionysius (Ps.) the Areopagite 279, 282
Dionysius bar Ṣalibi 221–222, 227
Dionysius of Alexandria 32, 66, 73

Egeria 80, 107–109, 115–121
Elipandus 150
Epiphanius of Salamis 79, 148, 157, 256, 259–260, 295–296
Epihanius (Ps.) 303
Etherius of Osma 182
Euripides 203, 229
Eusebius of Caesarea 6, 10, 13, 15, 68, 71–92, 118, 180, 280, 295
Eusebius of Cremona 96
Eustochium (daughter of Paula of Bethlehem) 99, 107, 109–111, 113

Fulgentius 181

Galen 64, 210
Gennadius 21
Gregory I "the Great" (pope) 138, 146, 148, 150–151, 181, 218
Gregory of Elvira 181
Gregory of Nazianzus 203
Gregory of Nyssa 115
Gregory VII (pope) 187

Hadrian 15, 79, 294
Haimo of Auxerre 142, 187–188
Hippolytus ("of Rome") 32, 45, 57–58
Hystaspes (Hellenistic magian) 45–46

Ibn al-Haytham 224
Ibn Kātib Qayṣar 221, 223–224, 226–227

Irenaeus of Lyons 10, 11–15, 20, 22–27, 28, 30–32, 46–47, 58, 64–67, 75–76, 181, 295–297
Isidore of Seville 142, 149–150, 161, 181, 184, 249

Jerome 6, 37, 66–68, 93–106 passim, 107–115, 120, 139, 144, 181, 244–254
– Jerome, Revision of Victorinus' *Expl. Apoc.* 67, 93–107, 143–145, 150, 244–246, 258, 301
John Cassian 299
John of Dara 13
Joseph of Arimathea 292
Josephus 268, 288
Julian Africanus 45, 68
Julian (emperor) 303
Julius Caesar 208
Justin Martyr 10, 11–13, 15–19, 20, 22–23, 26, 28, 31, 46–47, 66, 78, 294–296
Justinian (emperor) 142–143

Lactantius 32, 44–49, 53, 66, 68, 301

Manilius 207–208, 216
Marcella of Rome 107, 111–112
Marcion of Sinope 12, 39, 57, 296
Martin I (pope) 138
Maximona of Jerusalem 79
Meletani (ancient sect) 21
Melito of Sardis 11–12, 19–22, 27, 32, 57
Methodius ("of Olympus") 32, 58, 301

Nepos of Arsinoe 32, 66
Nerses of Lambron 220, 222–223, 226–227

Oecumenius 142, 179, 221–222, 226–227, 231, 253–256
Optatus of Carthage 2
Origen 6, 10, 15, 29, 32, 58, 75, 77, 98–100, 106, 146, 148, 161, 184, 204–205, 217–227 passim, 298, 303
– intended commentary on Revelation 58, 218
Ovid 207

Pammachius 95, 101
Pamphilus 77

Papias of Hierapolis 11–15, 19–20, 23, 25, 47, 57, 65–66
Papias's sources 13–15, 23–24, 30
Pascal I (Pope) 283
Patriarch of Jerusalem 138
Paula of Bethlehem 99, 107–115, 120
Paulinus (Jerome's brother) 96, 109, 114
Perpetua (martyr) 2–3, cf. 44
Peter the Venerable 139
Philo 98, 202, 204, 289
Plato 5, 29–30, 197–216 passim, 230, 287
Plautus 214–216
Primasius of Hadrumetum 51, 142–145, 146, 147, 150, 179, 181, 185, 251–254, 258, 262
Ps. Epiphanius of Salamis 302–303

Quintilla (Montanist prophetess) 295

Rachel 233, 237
Robert Grosseteste 140–141

Saturus 2, 44
Sergius (pope) 138
Severus of Antioch 142
Socrates 201–202
Sophocles 202
Stephanus of Alexandria 206

Tertullian 32, 35, 37–41, 46, 54, 66, 75–76, 296, 303
Theodore of Mopsuestia 299–300
Theudis (Visigothic king) 249
Thomas Aquinas 141, 148
Trypho (supposed interlocutor of Justin Martyr), cf. 11, 15–16, cf. 294–295
Tyconius 50–54, 55, 103, 142–145, 150, 174, 176, 178, 181, 192, 231, 246–248, 251, 253–254, 258, 262, 300

Valentinus (gnostic author), cf. 12
Van Eyck, Hubert and Jan 1
Varro 207
Vergil 207–208, 216, cf. 300
Victorinus of Petovium 32, 35, 49, 57–69, 93–106 passim, 143–145, 150, 170, 231, 244–246, 248, 254, 258, 301

Index of Places

Alexandria 13, 27–32, 209, 217
Antioch 57, 209
Armenia 108, 119, 131, 217, 220, 222
Asia (Minor) 12–13, 15, 19, 31, 46, 186, 296
Athens 209, 212, 297
Athos 211

Béja 150, 181, 231, 249–251
Belgium 1
Bethlehem 95–96, 105, 107, 109, 114, 118, 269
Black Sea 245
Britain 108, 114, 190
Brittany 159

Caere 215–216
Caesarea (Cappadocian) 173, 185, 220, 255–257
Caesarea (Maritima) 71, 295
Capitoline hill 207
Cappadocia 208–209
Carthage 33, cf. 35–55, 41, 44, 174
Cîteaux 140
Constantinople 107
Cornwall 159
Cyprus 295

Egypt 20, 64, 66, 110, 115, 124, 186, 260, 288
Ephesus 15, 194
Ethiopia 260
Euphrates 63, 71–72, 131, 139, 245, 253, 301

Flavia Neapolis 15

Gaul 13, 31, 186, *see also* Lyons (Ludgunum)
Gauls 215
Gomorrah 288

Hadrumetum 142–145, 251–253
Hibernia *see* Ireland
Hispania 107, *see also* Spain

Holy Roman empire 138
India 186, 257
Ireland 146, 153–171

Jarrow 145, 258
Judea 18, 66–68, 186, 263, 292, 296–297, 301

Las Claustillas (monastery) 193
Las Huelgas 193
Liège 176
Lycaonia 186
Lyons (Ludgunum) 10, 11, 22–27, 57, 64

Macedonia 186
Mesopotamia 108, 115, 229, 232
Milan 278

Nicomedia 209
Nile 63, 245, 301
North Africa 5, 6, 35–55, 181, 142–145, 174, 251–253

Palestine 15, 64, 76–77, 84, 86, 89, 229
Pax Iulia *see* Béja
Pepuza 295–297
Philadelphia (in Asia Minor) 19, 296
Phrygia 295, 297
Poetovio *see* Petovium
Poetovium 35, 57–69, 93, 244
Pontus 108

Ravenna 264–286 passim
Red Sea 63–64, 148, 245
Roman empire 3, 6, 54, 64, 74, 82–83, 95, 139, 143, 197–216 passim
Rome 12, 15, 31, 95–97, 105, 109, 138–139, 186, 197–216 passim

Samaria 15–16
Santa María la Real de Las Huelgas (monastery) 193
Sardis 11, 19

Sea of the North (Sea of Phoenicia) 63–64,
    see also Black Sea
Sodom 288, 290
Spain 107, 156, 169, 173–194 passim, 251, *see also* Hispania
Syria ("Greater Syria") 63–67, 69, 245, cf. 301

Thebaid, the 260
Tymion 295

Wales 159

Index of Subjects

Abgar 257
Abingdon Apocalypse 188, 190–192
abodes (dwellings of the saints) 1, 4, 14, 25, 30, 67, 153, 213, 296
Abraham 4, 21, 18, 30, 61, 63–65, 87, 105, 132, 245, 254, 288, 292, 301, *see also* inheritance, of Abraham
Abraham's bosom 4, cf. 105
Acherousian Lake 129, 130
Adam 111, 150, 167
adoptionism 149–150, 182, 193
advance (spiritual) 29–30, 33, 65, 139, 143, 164, 167, *see also* ascent (spiritual) and progress (spiritual)
– in the eschaton 14–15, 22–27, 65
Alexandrian exegesis 93, 97, 202–205, 217–227
allegorical interpretation 23, 60–69 passim, 93, 97, 100, 115, 174–175, 192, 217–227 passim, 263, 269–286 passim, 294–302 passim
Alpha and Omega (divine title) 19, 36
altar 134, 143, 190, 192, 293
Anagni slab 269, 274
angel(s)
– allegorically interpreted as Christ 192
– as brides of Christ 140
– as guards of the city 283
– as guide to John the Seer 126, 131, 162, 176, 180, 183, 187–188
– as guide to Paul in Vis. Paul. 129, 134–135
– as messengers 179
– descent of 198
– dwelling with humans in New Jerusalem 138, 140, 145, 166–167
– exultation of in the eschaton 28
– fallen 145
– human becoming like 89, cf. 112
– humans becoming equal to 17, 19, 99, 140
– humans becoming 28
– humans being co-citizens with 140
– humans surpassing 26–27
– in New Jerusalem, cf. 44, 130, 145, 170, 283
– monks enjoying the life of 140

– representing the faithful 247
– revelations from 197
– with golden measuring rod 176–177, 183, 190, cf. 291, cf. 293
Anglo-Norman (language) 187
anti-semitism 190
antichrist 43, 49–50, 58, 60, 94, 102, 146, 150, 169–170, 295
Antiochene exegesis 146, 299
Apocalypse *see* Revelation (Apocalypse)
apostles (the twelve)
– Andrew 184–186, 257
– Bartholomew 185–186, 257
– James the Great, son of Zebedee 160, 166, 169, 185–186, 257
– James the Less, son of Alphaeus 185
– James 160, 166, 169, 185
– John (contested author of Revelation) 4, 12–13, 16, 19, 24, 26, 36, 39, 112, 117, 137, 160, 162, 164–165, 169, 173–194 passim, 213, 222–223, 225–226, 250, 257, 293
– Judas 185–186, *see also* Thaddeus below
– Matthew 185–186, 257
– Matthias 185–186, 257
– Peter 160, 165, 169, 184–186, 257, 276, 283, 292
– Philip 185–186, 257
– Simon Zelotes 185–186, 257
– Thaddeus 186, 257, *see also* Judas above
– Thomas 160, 166, 185, 257
apostles (general) 12, 118, 153–171 passim, 184–186, 224, 250
– as foundation stones of church 89–90, cf. 130, 145
– as founders of the church 184, 192, 221, 225
– as gates of the New Jerusalem 101, 246, 248, 252–253, 255, 258, 301
– as guardians of gates of the New Jerusalem 160, 163, 170, cf. 190
– as guardians of the church 164
– disciples of 14–15, 25
– division of apostolic territories 184
– honored in Church of Holy Sepulchre 88

336   Index of Subjects

- individually associated with precious stones 185, 257
- names written on the [foundation] stones of New Jerusalem 169, 177, 243–244, 256, 293
- represented in artwork 264–265, 281, 283–285
- teaching of (apostolic band, choir, voice), cf. 25, 28, 42, 66, 75, 78, cf. 82, 101, 147–149, cf. 165, 186, 225, 246
- virtues, characteristics, gifts of each 29, 225, 246, 251, 254, 256–257, 301
- way of life of 29

apotheosis (of Roman emperors) 208, see also deification
Arabic language and literature 123, 225, 223, 226
architecture
- as representation of divine presence 263–286 passim
- monastic 193–194
- Mozarabic 184
- of Church of the Holy Sepulchre 85, 88, 90–91, 175
- of New Jerusalem 177, 179, 190, 229–262 passim, 263–286 passim

Arcturus (star) 214–216
Arianism 104, 146, 249, 251
ark of Noah 99, 246
Armenian language and literature 119, 123, 217, 220, 222
art see also names of individual buildings and objects
- monumental 71, 84–91, 118–119, 180–181, 192, 263–286
- visual 1, 173–194, 263–286

ascent (spiritual) 14–15, 25–27, 91, see also advance (spiritual) and progress (spiritual)
ascent (to heaven or God) 143, 164, 202–204, 219, 268
astronomical bodies 29, 40, 49–50, 60–61, 77, 90, 130, 145, 165–166, 214–216, 249, 289, 293, 298

Babylon 147, 176, 192, 230–231, 236, 289–290
- as the false church 176
- Jewish exile in 231, 290
- Rome as 109–110, 214

balsam trees 156, 158
baptism 3, 18, 28, 53, 62, 102–103, 117, 129, cf. 144, 148, 160, 162, 163, 166–167, 179, 249
- baptism of blood 166, see also martyrdom

Bar Kochba Revolt 15, 79, 294
battle (final between Christ and Satan) 43, 46
beast out of the abyss 112
beatitude (state of blessedness or bliss) 28, 33, 149, 151, 184, 221
Beatus Apocalypse(s) 149–152, 174, 181–186, 190, 192–194
- Facundus 193
- Geneva 183, 185
- Las Huelgas 193
- Lorvão 183
- *Mappae mundi* 186
- Morgan 181–186, 193
- Turin 183
- Valladolid 185

Bethlehem (visual representation of with Jerusalem) 269, 271, 276, 279
Bilhah 233, 237
body (human) 144, 164, 256, see also resurrection
- in the present life 30, 98, 100, 140, 205
- location of in the resurrection 109–110, 115, 125–126, 287–288, see also death, location of believers after
- of Christ 87, 127
- of Moses 268
- relation to soul 1, 31, 205–206, 287–288, 298, 302

body (metaphorical), church as 146, 221
- city as 202
book of life 40, 213, 244
breastplate (Jewish high priestly) 148, 221–222, 243, 254, 258, 262, 293
bride of Christ see nuptial imagery
bridegroom, Christ as see nuptial imagery
Brythonic (language) 159

Cain 288–289
Cambrai Apocalypse see Carolingian Apocalypses
Carolingian (visual) exegesis 174–181, 264–265
Carolingian Apocalypses 174–181
- Cambrai 175, 177, 179, 190, 192
- Trier 175–179, 192
- Valenciennes 176, 179–180, 192
Carolingian period 138–139
Cataphrygians 295, see also New Prophecy
Catechesis Celtica 153, 158–159
catechumens 88, 115–117
charity see virtues (itemized)
chiliasm see millennialism

Christology 32, 42, 76, 142, 174, 179, 231, 293
- Arianism *see* Arianism
- Christological interpretation of Torah 92
- Duophysite Christology 142
- Marcionite Christology 39
church
- angelic protectors of 164
- announcement of the Trinity by 247–248
- as bride of Christ *see* nuptial imagery
- as *corpus permixtum* 51, 54, 142–143, 146, 150, 174, 182, 192, 300
- as descendants of Abraham 65
- as heavenly or true Jerusalem 4–5, 19–22, 25, 31, 109–111, 114, 116–118, 178, 187, 222, 246–263 passim, 297, 299–300
- as hermeneutical key of Rev. 53
- as holy 43
- as mother 111, 116, 139–141, cf. 145
- as pre-existent 147
- as supplanting Israel *see* supersessionism
- as the new Israel 18, 20, 247, 251
- construction of 104
- earthly (militant) 116, cf. 120, 140–141, 143, 174, 179
- founded by apostles 66, 192
- heavenly (victorious) 108, 114–115, cf. 120, 140–141, 147, 174, 179
- heavenly Jerusalem as paradigm of 30–32, 53–54, 116–118, 138
- humility of 150
- illumination of by Christ 145
- its union with God 263–265, 285
- Jewish churches in Jerusalem 78–84, 91–92
- Jews in 18, 79–84, 92
- liturgy of *see* liturgy and worship
- millennium as time of the church 52–54
- mission of 143
- of the nations (gentiles) 23, 88, 111, cf. 148
- Old Testament prophecies of 78, 80, 110
- pilgrim church 138–139, 142
- reforms of Pope Gregory VII 187
- relation to Jewish synagogue 79–80, 82
- resurrection of with Christ 52
- role of apostles in *see* apostles
- seven churches of Rev. 178
- spiritual church (vs. carnal) 42–43, 88, 90, 104
- true vs. false churches *see* as *corpus permixtum* above
- under persecution *see* persecution (of Christians)
- unity of 81, 149–150

church art 1, 6, 118, 263–286
- apse and apse wall mosaics 263–286 passim
- burial slabs 274
- frescos 271, 275
- niche mosaics 274
- triumphal arch mosaics 264, 269–270, 273, 283–285
church buildings (architecture)
- apses 118, 181, 265–285 passim
- architecture, naves 286
- chancel screens 265, 279–283, 285
- division/unity of space 281–282, 285
- entrances 280
- hierarchical organization of 279–283
- sanctuaries 281–282, 286
- triumphal arches 264, 269–270, 273, 283–285
church buildings (meaning) 5
- as distinct from the community of believers 280
- as representations of heaven and the Heavenly Jerusalem 279–280
- enabling the experience of God's presence 263–285
- holiness of 116, 279
churches (buildings)
- Church of the Holy Sepulchre (Jerusalem) 71, 84–91, 138, 180–182, 192
- – *Anastasis* chapel 90, 118–120, 181
- – as "a new Jerusalem" 71, 84–91, 180, 280
- – as burial place of Jesus 111
- – as manifestation of the spiritual church 90
- – as new Temple 119
- – built to honor the apostles 88
- – Charlemagne's attitude toward 181
- – connection with the heavenly Jerusalem 88
- – details of Constantine's construction of 87–91
- – *Martyrium* basilica 118–120
- – Rotunda 181, 265
- – sketches of 181
- Church of the Nativity (Bethlehem) 118, 265
- Church on the Mount of Olives (Eleona) (Jerusalem) 118
- Old St. Peter's Basilica (Rome) 271
- San Lorenzo (Lucina) 285
- San Lorenzo fuori le mura (Rome) 269
- San Silvestro (Tivoli) 271

338   Index of Subjects

- San Venanzio (Rome), Lateran Baptistery 269, 272
- San Vitale (Ravenna) 268–269, 271
- Sant'Agata dei Goti (Rome) 285
- Sant'Andrea Catabarbara (Rome) 285
- Sant'Apollinare in Classe (Ravenna) 267–269, 275, 284
- Santa Maria Maggiore (Rome) 269–271, 273, 279, 281
- Santa Prassede (Rome) 264, 269, 283–286
- Santa Pudentiana (Rome) 85, 118, 265–266, 277–278, 283
- Santi Cosma e Damiano (Rome) 269–271, 276–277, 281, 283

churches (decoration of) 120, 263–285 passim
cinnamon trees 156, 158
circumcision 18
- circumcised Jewish-Christian priests in fourth-century Jerusalem 79

cities
- allegorical 269, 271, 275
- earthly 197–216 passim, 229–230, 264, 269–273, 277–279, 285, 288–291
- heavenly, in classical thought 197–216 passim
- ideal (paradigmatic) 201–206

citizenship
- *civitas* 207–217
- heavenly 39, 110, 114, 201–206, 214–215, 257, 288, 293, 297, 299, 300
- *politeia* 299
- *politeuma* 39, 297, 299–300
- political idea of 215–216

city walls, function of in antiquity 229–230, 265
color theory (in stones) 28–29
colors (hues) 28–29, 148–149, 160, 163, 180, 184, 190, 222–224, 226
- black 146, 157, 257
- blue 163, 184, 257, 259
- brown 180
- gold 173, 257, 259
- green 148, 157, 180, 190, 184, 226, 242, 251, 253, 257, 259
- orange 183, 184
- purple 163, 259
- red 157, 180, 184, 227, 242, 249, 257, 259
- white 1, 36, 40, 44, 59, 129, 133, 146, 163, 184, 238–239, 259
- yellow 157, 180, 183, 259

coming of Christ 131, 134
- first 82–83
- predictions of 150
- second 9, 11, 18, 23, 36, 38–39, 46, 58, 61, 67, 69, 75–76, 126, 283, 294

confession
- of sin 163
- of the faith 148, 297

conquerors 36, 40, 49, 101
Constantinian shift 83–85, 91–92
consummation 5, 15, 24, 26, 32–33, 101, 147, 182, 187, 192
contemplation 4, 20, 22, 29, 30, 133, 143, 145, 148–149, 259, 302, *see also* vision(s), vision of God
Coptic (language and literature) 123–125, 207, 223, 226
corporeality and incorporeality, in the eschaton 31, 144, 222, 224–227, 287–288, 303
cosmic week *see* world week
cosmic woman (of Rev.) *see* heavenly woman
covenant, new and old 18, 42, 75, 82, 254, 256

creation
- as beginning point of *Anno Mundi* calculations 146
- days of 160, 250
- new creation 24–25, 36, 49, 76, 126, 133, 147, 197, 199, 224, 241
- of humanity 26, 30
- of the world 65, 160, 168
- old (first) creation 24, 25, 133, 199, 224
- protected from destruction 62, 65

cross, of Christ 42–43, *see also* crucifixion
- artistic depictions of 118, 177, 179, 183, 265, 275
- shape of 255
- represented by the letter *tau* 296

crown(s)
- as reward 62, 94
- believers or church crowned together with Christ 151, 174
- of martyrdom 293
- of virginity 67, 94
- worn by Christ 165

crucifixion (Christ's) 18, 43, 119
- John's vision of crucified lamb 293
- location of 112, 119
- narrative of 113

cynicism 211

death
- abolishment of 36, 49, 144, 197
- ascent of Moses and Elijah to heaven after death 268, cf. 284
- Christ's victory over 85, 88

- Christ's 42, 82, 151, 271
- condition of human body after 287, 298
- life after 1, 108, 125, 132, 169–170
- location of believers after *see* body human, location of in the resurrection
- of martyrs 43–44
- second 40–41
- suspension of 23

Decalogue 67, 94, 98, 250, 290
deification
- of Christian believers 17, 26, 30–31, 33, *see also* union with God/Christ
- of Roman emperors (apotheosis) 208

devil *see* "Satan"
divine presence 174, 180, 192, 263–286 passim
doctors of the church 147, 149
Donatism 50–54, 142–146, 246, 300
double eschaton 32
dove, artistic depictions of 277–278
dragon, flight of heavenly woman from 67, 127
dreams 3, 44, *see also* vision(s)

east (cardinal direction) 302
- (New or heavenly) Jerusalem's location in/orientation to 63–64, 69, 77, 90–91, 237, 245
- eastern orientation of churches 283

Easter, cf. 19–22, 66, 96, 160, 162, 167–168, 193
- eighth day of (octave) 160

Eden 173, 243–244, 302, *see also* paradise
Edict of Milan 74, 76, 83
Egypt, Jerusalem called 112
electrum 238
Eleona *see* churches (buildings), Church on the Mount of Olives
Elijah 60, 100, 170, 268, 284
- at the Transfiguration 268
- presence already in the Heavenly Jerusalem 268, 284

Encaenia see Feast of the Dedication
end of all things 9, 36–37, 46, 100, 146, 150, 163, 182, 268, 300
Enoch 170, 288
epinoiai, Origen's doctrine of 148
Epiphany 117, 119
eternal life 16, 62, 76, 114, 144, 160, 162, 166, 225, 256, *see also* immortality
eucharist 119, 179, 295
evangelists (gospel-writers) 88, 111, 153–158 passim, 170, 182, 294
exchange formula 26

faith (the Christian faith) 3, 10, 29, 89, 101, 137, 147, 249, 250, 252
fasting 132
Father's house 4, 14, 25
Feast of Tabernacles 303
Feast of the Dedication (*Encaenia*) 119
Feast of the Presentation of Jesus in the Temple (*Hypapante*) 119
fecundity, of earth during millennium 23, 47, 49–50, 62, 128
final end
- of divine instruction 29, 31
- of human history 286
- of human life being the vision of God 17
- of mankind's creation 26, 32, 28
- of salvation 19, 33
- of the incarnation 26

final judgment *see* last judgment
flesh
- baptism of 28
- becoming spiritual and immortal 44
- circumcision of 18
- in the eschaton 23, 25, 43–44, 297, 302
- inability to inherit the kingdom of heaven 298
- of Christ 42
- resurrection of 11, 16, 23

flood
- Irish expectation of eschatological flood 170
- of Noah 249, 289

food and drink
- Christ as 27–28, 298
- drinking or eating with Christ in the kingdom 23, 62, 65, 298
- eschatological enjoyment of 128, 131–132, 197, 298
- in Athenaeus's *Deipnosophistae* 209–210

foundations of the church
- apostles as 88–90, 145, 148, 243
- Christ as 184

four apocalyptic creatures ("four living creatures") 118, 265
French (language and literature) 187

Gabriel (archangel) 3
garden 2, 78, 81, 173, 194, 244, 292, *see also* Eden and paradise
gates of Jerusalem
- eastward 160, 162, 164–165, 179, 185–186, 232–233, 235–237
- northward 160, 163, 166–167, 185, 232–233, 235–237, 290

- southward 160, 163, 165, 185, 232–233, 235–237
- westward 160, 162, 165–166, 185, 232–233, 235–237

gentiles 141, 231, *see also* nations
- gentiles, church of the 23, 25, 76, 81–83, 88, 111, 148

Georgian (language) 123, 120
Ghent Altarpiece 1
gift(s)
- of God in the age to come 129, 257
- of nations brought to Jerusalem 47, 91, 133, 177, 231, 301
- of the Holy Spirit 247–248, 251–252

glory
- of Christ 131
- of God illuminating the city 4, 60, 64, 130–131
- of God 23, 130, 249, 293, 296
- of Mount Zion 80
- of Rome 213–214
- of the church 54, 151, 174, 300
- of the coming Jerusalem 72, 131, 162, 174, 221–222, 226, 242, 249
- of the kings brought into the city 1, 47, 133, 177, 244, 301
- of the restored Jerusalem predicted by Hebrew prophets 231
- of the saints 22–24, 26, 30, 33, 38, 102, 134, 140, 174, 187, 190, 257, cf. 288
- of the world 147

gnosticism
- Christians as true gnostics 29–31
- gnostic teaching of a coming Jerusalem 12, 75, 295, 298

gnostic texts 169
God, being all in all 15
gods, humans as 17, 28–30, *see also* deification and union with God/Christ
Gog and Magog 102, 149
gold 28, 45–47, 49–50, 60, 87, 112–113, 120, 130–131, 148, 162, 165, 173, 184, 190, 203, 209, 225–226, 238–239, 242–244, 247–248, 251, 254, 257, 259, 264–265, 269, 283, 293, *see also* New Jerusalem of Rev. (details of)
Golden age 45–48, 50
Golgotha 79, 111, 115–116, 118–119, 271, 292
Gomorrah, Jerusalem or Israel called 78
Gospels, the four 42, 250, 255
grace 28, 60, 87, 133, 139–152 passim, 247, 249, 252, 259, 300–301

grief *see* sorrow
Gulbenkian Apocalypse 188, 190, 192

Hades 4, cf. 110, 287, 298
Hagar 292
Haimo Apocalypse 142, 175, 187–188
Harlot of Rev. 176, 214
healing 140, 257, 292
- from the leaves of tree of life 129, 293
heaven(s)
- ascent of Moses' body to 268
- believers' ascent to 2, 25, 143, 103, 268, 284
- called Jerusalem 299
- Christ's ascent to 139, 294
- dwelling of the just 4, 14, 21, 44, 65–66
- Elijah's ascent to 268
- humas becoming 30
- inheritance of land in 44
- journey to 28, 141
- Paul's journey to 4, 125, 127, 257
- seventh 135, 155, 169
- third 4, 125, 127, 257

heavenly things, hope of as reward 20, 148, 259
heavenly woman of Rev. 67
hell 4, 110, 125–126, 130, 135, 150, 167, 169, *see also* punishment of the wicked
heresy 11–12, 101, 143, 146, 149, 297
Hiberno-Latin texts 153–171
hierarchy
- heavenly 208, 282
- of sacred space 280, 282
- of virtues 132, 134, 136
- social 208

holiness
- of Christ 254
- of Christian sites 91
- of Christians 28, 29, 144, 166
- of church buildings 279
- of earthly Jerusalem 111, 115
- of monastic way of life 260
- of the church 282
- of the New Jerusalem *see* New Jerusalem of Rev (details)

Holy Land, pilgrimage to 107–121, 140, *see also* pilgrimage
Holy of Holies 119, 192, *see also* sanctuary
Holy Spirit 14–15, 63, 105, 144, 147, 248, 251, 260, 296, 300
homilies 41, 115, 153–171, 248, 251
house of God 78, 82–83, 291
hues *see* colors

Hypapante see Feast of the Presentation of Jesus in the Temple

iconography 173–194, 263–286
image and likeness of God 27–28, 30, 33, cf. 144
image
- Adam as image of Christ 111
- church as image of universe 282
- church bearing image of New Jerusalem 116
- Jewish religion as image of Christ and church 20
- New Jerusalem as image of church and God's reign 180
- of afterlife 1
- of the heavenly Jerusalem 173–194, 263–286
- of the heavenly realm 264, 280
- of the presence of the divine 264
- of the Trinity 277
imitation of God (*imitatio dei*) or Christ 30, cf. 140, 151
immortality 16–17, 44, 62, 65, 102, 114, 143–144, 160, 197, 202, *see also* eternal life
imperial ideology 3, 208
incarnation 26–27, 33, 151, 250
incorruptibility 14, 16–17, 23–24, 48–49, 144
inheritance
- of Abraham 61, 63, 65, 301
- of the Jewish remnant on Zion 80, 91
- of the saints 18, 22–23, 26, 65, 126, 140, 298
intellection 205
intelligible world 205
intermediate state 126–130, 134
Irish exegesis 146, 153–171
Israel 251, 253–254, 259, 262, *see also* Jews, Holy Land, and Judea
- meaning of the name 20
- twelve tribes of 161

James ("brother of the Lord") 186
Jebus, early name of Jerusalem, cf. 111, 289
Jeremiah 290, 295
Jerusalem (earthly) 20, 77, 82, 87, 105, 109, 137, 186
- Aelia Capitolina, renamed as 15, 79, 294
- as center, navel, of the earth 139–140
- as metonym for people of Israel 20
- as symbol of heaven 139
- at time of writing of Rev. 213
- called "Jerusalem below" 19, 77, 137–141, 152, 301–302

- Christ's journey to 139
- churches within during late antiquity 107–121
- connection with Heavenly Jerusalem 11–12, 15–19, 107–121, 137–141, 181, 286
- Constantine's restoration of 84–92, 107–121, 192, 265
- crusader interest in 139–140, 263, 286
- destruction foretold 75, 78, 291
- during Second Temple period 234–240
- fall of to Babylonians 290
- fall of to Hadrian 15, 79, 294
- fall of to the Khwarazmians 194
- fall of to Titus 15
- holiness of 111
- in early Christian thought 71–92 passim, 107–121 passim, 291–292
- in the Hebrew Bible 289–291
- Jewish prophecies of gentile pilgrimage toward 275, 291, *see also* pilgrimage
- Jewish prophecies of restoration of 65, 80, 234, 262, 294
- late antique and medieval pilgrimage to 107–121, 139–140, 139, cf. 152, cf. 194, 263, *see also* pilgrimage
- location of Christ's crucifixion 19, 112
- political and ecclesiastical status of in late antiquity 137–141
- restoration of during Christ's millennial reign 11–31 passim, 61, 113, 301
Jerusalem (heavenly) 1, 24, 32, 40, 73, 71–92, 107–121, 137, 203–204, 263–286, 292–293, *see also* New Jerusalem of Rev.
- archetypal, eternal, or pre-existent 24, 30, 72, 77, 120, 199, 224
- as allegory of the divine realm 263–286
- as icon of the earthly church 139, 271
- as intellectual concept describing unity of God and church 263–286
- as post-mortem location of the saints 113–115
- Church of Holy Sepulchre reproduction of 89–91
- connection with earthly Jerusalem *see* Jerusalem (earthly), connection with Heavenly Jerusalem
- connection with ethical life 27–31
- connection with millennial reign 59, 65–66
- Jerusalem above 19–28, 65, 82, 86, 116, 118, 137, 152, 204, 294, 301
- visual and architectural representation of 89–91, 173–194, 263–286

Jerusalem (name), multiple meanings of 109–110, 299
Jewish texts 229–240, 261–262, 288–291
Jews, as people or children of Israel 20, 136
- as vineyard 78–81 passim
- Christian criticism of 15–21, 80–88, 91–92, 141
- early Jewish-Christian identity theorized by Eusebius 84
- Jewish-Christian bishops in Jerusalem 79
- Jewish-Christian church in Jerusalem 78–84, 91–92
- night owl as symbol of 190
- presence of in the New Jerusalem 16, 18, 100, 146, 247, 249–250, 252–253
- salvation of 16, 18, 60, 78–81, 91–92, 100, 146
Joshua (high priest) 291, 303
Joshua (son of Nun) 288
Jupiter (Roman god) 15, 207, 214–216

kingdom
- of Christ 13, 17, 22–23, 26, 61, 100, 164, 245, 257
- of God 16–17, 23, 114, 163, 268, 294
- of heaven 39–40, 43, 160, 163–164, 167, 226, 298
knowledge of God or Christ 28–31, 33, 89, cf. 166, cf. 205, 251

lake of fire 244
lamb
- Christ as 1, 4, 60, 118, 147, 151–152, 165, 177, 179–180, 183–184, 192, 244, 275
- church as lamb of God, the church as 152
- paschal lamb 20, 193
Lambeth Apocalypse 188–190, 192
lambs *see* sheep
land of the living 110, 115
last judgment 4, 9, 24, 34, 46–47, 53–54, 58, 102, 126, 133–134, 137, 146, 152–153, 160, 164, 168–169, 182, 222, 241, 283–284, 294, 297, 301
last supper 62, 65
Lateran church 272, 281
law
- classical civil, cf. 31, cf. 141, 202, 211
- of God (general) 204
- new law 18, 42, 74, 82–83, 117, 164
- Jewish law (Torah) 20, 22, 81, 84, 91–92, 141, 164, 292, 296, 299
Lazarus and the rich man 4, 105
Leah 233, 237

lectio divina 193–194
light 25, 44, 49–50, 60, 77, 101, 117, 144–145, 148, 162, 165–166, 223–224, 249, 252, 264, 293
- ancient theories of, cf. 28–29, 223
- role of in church architecture 264, 280
literalism (in biblical exegesis) 10, 11–19, 21, 22–27, 31–33, 35–41, 44–50, 57–69 passim, 75, 86, 93, 95, 97–98, 107–115, 120, 146, 150, 182, 218, 245, 297–299, 301, 303
liturgy 135, 160, 264, 279, *see also* prayer and worship
- earthly as imitation and revelation of heavenly 279
- heavenly 4, 107–108, 117–118, 279
- Jerusalem as motif in 139
- practice in Jerusalem 107, 115–121, 134–135
- use of Rev. in 193
- use of senses in 279–280
living stones 301
Low Sunday 160

Madaba Map 119
mansions, heavenly *see* abodes
marriage 160, 297
- chastity within 129
- human marriage in next age 49, 298
- Montanist prohibition of second marriage 165
- of Israel to God 198, 294
- of the Lamb 140, 151, 198
- virginity more praiseworthy than 95
martyrdom literature 2, 35, 43–44, 118
martyrdom 40–41, 43–44, 49–50, 54, 142–143, 148, 160, 166–167, 170, 259, 293
martyrs 1, 2, 40, cf. 133, 137, 149, 156–158, 163, 257, 283, 301
- martyrs, rewards of 44, 54, 62, 149
medieval exegesis 137–152, 153–171, 258–260
- visual 173–194, 263–286 passim
memory
- cultural 4, 135
- memory images and aids 177, 188, 193
messianic reign *see* millennial reign
milk and honey 128, 140
millennialism 9–33 passim, 35–55 passim, 57–69 passim, 93–106 passim, 108, 150, 197, 231, 241, 244–246, 295, 297, 301
- criticisms of 93–106 passim, 108, 113, 120, 143
- definition of 9, 37
- roots of teaching 38–39, 66

Index of Subjects

millennium (eschatological) 9–33 passim, 35–55 passim, 57–69, 93–106 passim, 126–128, 135, 139, 198, 299
- literal interpretations of *see* millennialism
- non-literal interpretations of 9–33 passim, 93–106 passim

millennial reign
- of Christ 5, 14–15, 58–59, 127, 245, 284, 301
- of the saints 23, 40, 47, 54, 58–60, 62, 98, 100, cf. 127, 167

monasteries 96, 107, 109, 120, 193
- as paradisical space 194
- New or heavenly Jerusalem resemblance to monastic cloister 120, 136, 192–193

monasticism 118, 132–133, 136, 140, 145, 149, 170, 182, 187, 192
- Cistercian 193–194
- Egyptian 260

monophysitism 255
Montanism *see* New Prophecy
Moses 204, 224, 221, 268, 283
- and the Burning Bush 268
- at the Transfiguration 268, 284
- in the Heavenly Jerusalem 268, 284
- law of 74, 81
- on Mount Sinai 268, 293
- song of 62
- witness of the Heavenly Jerusalem 224

Mount of Olives 118, 291–292, 294, 302–303
Mount Sinai 20, 41–42, 268, 292–293
Mount Tabor 267
Mount Zion
- as gathering place of apostles 80
- Christ/Lamb on 275, 278
- head of Christ's kingdom 139
- heavenly 82, 86
- holy place in Jerusalem 290
- in the *Traditio legis* 278
- Jewish church on 77–80
- made desolate 88
- new 18, 85–86, 88
- on which the 144,000 stand 59–60
- out of which law would go forth 42, 117, 296
- pilgrimage of lambs toward 279
- pilgrimage of nations toward 75, 109–110, 275–276, 279, 291, 294
- place of hope 36
- place of rebellion 36
- prophetically referring to New Jerusalem 61–62, 65, 117
- referring to heavenly city/Jerusalem 72, 77, 82, 110, 117, 139, 293

- referring to the church 80
- representing the New Testament 42
- ruled by gospel 82
- small church located on 79–81
- stronghold in Jerusalem 289
- synagogue located on 79–80
- towers of 290
- worship on by Jewish Christians 78–80

mountain *see also* individually named mountains
- as artistic motif 275, 277–278, 293
- filling the whole earth 61, 82, 147
- new 78
- of God 18, 83, 86
- on which New Jerusalem is visible/situated, cf. 114, 140, 147, 173, 182, 190

Mozarabic culture
- architecture 184, 193
- lectionary 193
- liturgy 193

Muslim architecture 184
Muslim invasion 150

nations 4, 18, 47, 59–60, 64, 74–75, 77, 82–83, 86–88, 111, 129, 139, 148, 185, 192, 211, 213, 275, 291, 293–295, 301, 303, *see also* gentiles

neo-platonism *see* platonism
Nephelococcygia 230
New Jerusalem (Jewish concept of) 229–240, 261–262
New Jerusalem of Rev. (visual representations of) 1–5, 173–194, 263–286
New Jerusalem of Rev. (details of)
- as bride *see* nuptial imagery
- as garden 2, 14, 25, 65, 125–128, 173, 194, 243–244, 298, *see also* Eden and paradise
- as tabernacle 24, 139, 224, 244
- brightness of 61, 126, 130, 167, 221, 225–226, 242, 249, 253, 255, *see also* light of and transparency
- cardinal directions in 160, 162–167, 185, cf. 232–237, 247, 250, 258
- descent from heaven of 19, 24, 30, 42, 49, 58, 61, 65, 75, 77, 109, 126, 131, 138, 144, 147, 151, 176, 182, 187–188, 194, 197–199, 224, 293, 296, 298–299
- dimensions of 4, 49–50, 57–69, 99, 112–113, 131, 162, 173–174, 229–262 passim, 293
- excluded persons 132, 170, 173–174, cf. 244
- foundation(s) of 23, 42, 49, 60, 113, 130–131, 145, 148, 152, 174, 176–177, 180, 184, 219, 221, 225, 229–262 passim, 293, 298

- gates (doors) of 3, 4, 23, 42, 44, 49–50, 60, 99, 100–101, cf. 110, 112–114, 130–134, 145, 147–148, 153–171 passim, 173, 177, 184–186, 229–262 passim, 265, cf. 278, 293, 301
- glory of 4, 22, 24, 47, 54, 60, 64, cf. 72, 131, 133, 162, 177, 179, 187, 190, 221, 226, 231, 241, 249, 293, 300, see also glory
- gold of 60, 112–113, 130, 148, 173, 184, 225, cf. 239–240, 242, 248, 251, 254, cf. 257, 264, cf. 269, cf. 283, 293
- jasper of see precious and semi-precious stones, jasper
- light of 4, 44, 47, 49–50, 60–61, 130–131, 145, 151, 162, 166, 249, 252, 293
- pearl(s) of see pearl
- precious stones of see precious and semi-precious stones
- radiance of see brightness of and light of
- river of water of life in 4, 27–28, 60, 128, cf. 131–132, 174, 177, 188, 293, 301
- shape of 42, 98–99, 112–113, 177, 179–182, 192, 232, cf. 236
- street in 4, 113, 131, 173, cf. 236–239, 243, 254, 288, 293, 302
- sun and moon in 49–50, 60–61, 130–131, 165, 293
- temple absent from 119, 131, 192, 198, 213, 242–243, 293, 296–297
- temple features in 173, 242
- throne in 4, 24, 40, 62, 128, 135, 155, 157, 169, 182, 188, 217, 293
- towers of 130, 177–179, 184, cf. 235, cf. 238, cf. 239–240, 260, cf. 265
- transparency of 60, 131, 147–148, 173, 219, 225, cf. 231, 242, 247–249, 254, 258, 293
- tree of life in (with its fruit and leaves) see tree of life
- twelve "angles" of 184, 250
- twelve angels at gates of, cf. 1, cf. 44, 130, cf. 138, cr. 140, 145, 147, 155, 163–164, 170, 173, 177, 184, 190, 192, 241, 247, 283, 293
- twelve apostles named in 42, 60, 101, 130, 153–171, 177, 184–186, 240–262 passim, 283, 301
- twelve tribes of Israel named in 130, 148, 161, 177, 184–185, 190, 192, 221, 241–245, 254–255, 293
- wall(s) of 4, 6, 23, 28, 44, 99, 104, 112–114, 130–131, 133–134, 144–145, 147, 148–149, 151, 174, 186, 229–262 passim, 264–265, 269, 283, 288, 293–294, 301

New Prophecy 19, 39–41, 295–298, see also Cataphrygians, Priscillianism, and Quintilla
Nimbus 179
Noah 246, 289
Northumbrian Apocalypses 176
numbers, significance of (numerology) 43, 52, 67, 94–96, 130–131, 164, 184, 241–243, 248–256 passim, 260
nuptial imagery 24, 116, 127, 140, 144, 147, 151, 173, 187, 197–198, 214, 241, 248, 293, 294
- angels as brides of Christ 140
- Christ as bridegroom 147
monks as brides of Christ 140
(New) Jerusalem as bride of Christ 19, 24, 127, 136, 140, 144, 147, 151, 173, 187, 197–198, 211, 214, 241, 292, 293

Oceanus 126–127
Olympus 207
Oriental churches 217–227
- attitude toward Rev. 253
Ottonian visual art 265
Ouranopolis (Uranopolis) 29, 211–212
overcomers see conquerors

pain see sorrow
parable of the sower (thirty-, sixty-, hundred-fold production) 14, 25, 95–97, 165
paradise see also Eden 2, 13–14, 25, 65–66, 105, 108, 125–126, 128, 139, 170, 194, 243, 287, 289, 291, 293, 298, 302
- Jerusalem as 108, 139, 173, 293
parousia see coming of Christ
Pascha see Easter
Passion (of Christ) 42–43, 52, 54, 80, 105, 112, 148, 151, 174, 250
Passover 20, 167, 292
Patriarchs 148, 164, 167, 170, 229–262 passim (esp. 232–237), see also New Jerusalem of Rev., twelve tribes of Israel named in
- Asher 232, 236–237
- Benjamin 232–233, 236–237, 291
- Dan 232–233, 236–237, 242
- Ephraim 242
- Gad 232, 236–237
- Issachar 232, 236–237
- Joseph 87, 232–233, 236–237, 242
- Judah 18, 61, 232–233, 235
- Levi 232–233, 235, 237, 240
- Manasseh 61, 242
- Naphtali 232, 236–237
- Reuben 232–233, 236–237

- Simeon 232, 235, 237
- Zebulon 232, 237

Paul (apostle) 26, 83, 89, 91, cf. 123–136 passim, 186, 257, 276, 283, 292, 299

Pax Romana 81–82

pearl 28–29, 60, 99–100, 177, 184, 243, 246, 251, 254

penance 130, 132, 139, 160, 164–167, 170, *see also* penitence and repentance

penitence 170, *see also* repentance and penance

Pentecost 193, 257

perfection
- circle as symbol of 192
- of comprehension of heavenly city 173, 194, 225–226
- of eternal life 256
- of God 25
- of preachers 149
- of rest 256
- of stability and immovability 258
- of the church 192
- of the New Jerusalem 243, 250
- of the saints 22, 26–28, 30–31, 66, 94, 97–98, cf. 111, 165–166, 250, 301

persecution (of Christians) 3, 40, 44, 51, 62, 74, 82, 99, 163, 170

pilgrim church 138, 142, 146

pilgrim narratives 5, 107–121

pilgrimage 107–121, 139, 194, 275, 302

pilgrims 1, 80, 107–121, 133, 144–145, 194, 219, 233

platonism 17, 29, 141, 201–205, 282, 287, 298

Pola casket 269

prayer 18, 30, 82, 116–121 passim, 143, 202, *see also* liturgy and worship

precious and semi-precious stones 6, 23, 28–29, 60, 99–101, 112 – 114, 145, 148–149, 152–171 passim, 174, 180, 184, 185, 190, 217–227, 229–262 passim, 293, 298, 301
- amber 239
- amethyst 149, 155, 157, 185–186, 257, 259
- beryl 148–149, 155, 157, 185, 239, 257, 259
- carnelian 185, 217, 226–227, 242, 257, 259
- chalcedony 155, 157, 185, 238–239, 254, 257, 259–260
- chrysolite 149, 155, 185, 257, 259–260
- chrysoprase 149, 155, 157–158, 185, 254, 257, 259
- coal 257
- emerald 148, 155–157, 185, 226, 239, 257, 259–260

- hyacinth (sometimes "jacinth") 149, 155, 157, 163, 185, 254, 257, 259
- jacinth *see* hyacinth above
- jasper 89, 112–113, 131, 148, 155, 157–158, 185, 190, 217, 225–226, 238–239, 242, 247–249, 251, 253, 257–259, 293
- lapis lazuli 89, 90
- marble 238–239
- myxis 155, 157
- ruby 155, 238
- sapphire 148, 155, 157, 185, 219, 238–239, 257, 259
- sardius (sometimes "sardion") 149, 155, 157, 257, 259
- sardonyx 149, 155, 157, 185, 254, 257, 259
- stone of Ophir 239
- topaz 148–149, 155, 157, 185, 257, 259–260

Priscillianism 169, *see also* New Prophecy

progress (spiritual) *see* advance (spiritual)" and "ascent (spiritual)

promised land 4, 61, 63, 65, 68–69, 110, 125–130, 133, 135, 140

punishment of the wicked 2–5, 38, 46, 97, 126, 164, 167, *see also* hell

purity, of Christ 28
- of the church 51
- of the saints or their lives 11, 17, 28, 30, 97, 129, 132, 136, 166, 205, 248, 254, 295, *see also* virtues itemized, chastity

"Question-and-Answer" literature 153–158, 169–170

Quintillians 295, *see also* New Prophecy

Qumran (community and writings) 84, 230–231, 234–239, 241, 244, 261

recapitulation, exegetical principle 43, 54, 76, 174

relics 137, 283

repentance 18, 129, 160, 289

rest (repose) 16, 137, 145, 152, 256, 282

resurrection 1, 287–288
- Christ as 20
- doctrine of two resurrections 60, 102
- location of 119
- of Christ 52, 82, 87–88, 90, 116, 119, 160, 167–168, 250
- of the flesh 16
- of the just (the "first" resurrection) 13, 23, 26, 38, 46, 49, 52–53, 59–60, 65, 100, 102, 126, 151, 162
- universal (the "final" or "everlasting" resurrection) 16, 24, 46, 60, 102, 134

346 Index of Subjects

return of Christ *see* coming of Christ
Revelation (Apocalypse) (New Testament book), troubled reception of in East 35, 72–73, 253
reward of the just (eschatological) 4–5, 17, 21, 23, 28, 33, 40, 41, 43–44, 54, 62, 65, 97, 151
– threefold reward 14, 25, 30, cf. 62, 65
river of water of life 4, 28, cf. 114, 128–129, 174–175, 179, 182, 188, cf. 202, *see also* rivers of paradise
rivers of paradise 131–133, *see also* river of water of life
Roman Empire 6, 54, 64, 82–83, 138–139, 143, 212
Rome
– as "capital of the world" 208, 212, 214
– as divine (*Dea Roma*) 200, 213
– as eternal (*Roma aeterna*) 200, 208
– as universal 212
– foundation of 73, 208
– heavenly 208, 211–213

sabbath 145, 256
sacramental theology 141, 179, *see also* baptism and eucharist
sacred topography 107–121
salvation 14–15, 18–19, 20–21, 23–26, 28, 40, 78, 87, 139, 144, 150, 166, 198, 247–248, 252, 288
sanctification 29, 139, 146, 293
sanctuary
– heavenly in Rev. 178
– of Ezekiel's temple vision 290
– within church buildings 281–282, 286
Sarcophagi, late antique 278
Sarcophagus of Stilicho, Sant'Ambrogio, Milan 278
Satan 67, 166, 167
– binding of 46, 97–98, 126
– defeat of 36, 241
– release of 59, cf. 98, 102
Saturn (Roman god) 207–208
second advent *see* Coming of Christ
Second Temple *see* temple Jewish
Second Temple texts 199, 207, 229–240, 243, 262
sense perception 173, 194, 205, 223
senses of scripture 182, 218–221
sheep, depiction of saints as in friezes 269, 275–279, 285
silver 87, 88, 126, 182
skepticism (philosophical) 205
Slavonic (language) 220

Sodom, Jerusalem or Israel called 78, 99, 112, 214
Solomon 111, 119, 192, 243, 255, 289, 296, 298–290
Son (hypostasis of Trinity) 14–15, 20, 25–26, 104, 116, 151, 167, 300
Son of Man (divine title) 4, 66
sons of God, humans as 17–19, 23, 26, 33, 147, 296
sorrow, absence of in life to come 16, 36, 49–50, 62, 144, 203
soul(s) 298, *see also* body (human), relation to soul, as a sort of body
– as embodied 205, 287
– attaining image and likeness of God 30
– attaining to divine realm 219, 287, 298
– becoming heaven 30
– contamination of 205
– in the resurrection 1, 46, 256
– interpretation of (the New) Jerusalem 4, 299
– journey to God *see* advance (spiritual), ascent (spiritual), and progress (spiritual)
– of scripture (hermeneutical) 182, 218, 220
– of the dead 125–126
– of the living 164
– of the sage 202
– relation to body 287, 298, 302
– relation to earthly cities 289
– relation to heavenly city 206
– relation to physical vision 223
space (physical) 6, 62, 110, 115, 137, 152, 206, 246, 263–286 passim
stoicism 101, 202, 204, 211
stone cut without hands 82, 147
Sunday, creation of world, resurrection, and last judgment on in Irish tradition 168
– Jerusalem Christians gathering at site of resurrection on 116
– Low Sunday, octave of Easter 160
– Rev. readings of on Sundays between Easter and Pentecost in Mazarabic liturgy 193
supersessionism 18, 19–21, 25–26, 80–84, 91–92, 111, 244–262 passim
Syriac (language) 123, 217, 220–221

tabernacle, heavenly 224, 282
– tabernacle, Jewish 224, 233, 244, 258
telos see final end
temple (Jewish) 78, 80–81, 111, 119, 192, 234, 254, 258–259, 261, 290–291
– area of left unbuilt by Constantine 87, 119
– Babylonian destruction of 290

– Christian expectations of rebuilding of 295
– Julian's intended restoration of 303
– Old Testament prophecies of rebuilding of 89, 232–233, 235, 237, 242, 261, 265, 290–291, 293, 303
– replaced by Church of the Holy Sepulchre 119
– Roman destruction of (A.D. 70) 28, 80, 87, 293, 294
– Second Temple 80, 207, 261, 290, 292
– Solomon's 119, 192, 243, 289–290, 296
temple (metaphorical), Christ as 119
– Christians as 114
– eschatological 232–238, 262
– humans as pillars in 40
– in Rev. 178, 190, 192
theophany *see* visions
Three Chapters controversy 142–143
throne of God/Christ 4, 24, 40, 62, 89, cf. 118, 128, 135, 155, 157, cf. 175, 182, 188, cf. 193, 217, 260, cf. 268, cf. 277, 293
Toledo, Fourth Council of 193
Tower of Babel 289
traditio legis, as visual representation of heavenly Jerusalem 275
– visual depiction of 269–278
Transfiguration (of Jesus) 267–268, 284
tree of life (with its fruit and leaves) 4, 16, 27–28, 41, 60, 128–129, 156, 174, 176, 179, 197, 243, 293, 301
tribulation 67
Trier Apocalypse *see* Carolingian Apocalypses
Trinity 14–15, 25, 147–148, 165, 167, 186, 250
– image of 277
– preached 247–248, 253, 255, 258
trumpet(s) (eschatology) 60, 102
twenty-four elders 250, 276
Tyconian rules (hermeneutics) 52, 142–143, 166, 300
Tyre, king of, precious coverings of 243, cf. 289

union with God/Christ 5, 263–264, 267, 271, 282, 285–286, *see also* deification
Uranopolis *see* Ouranopolis
urban design 240–241, 262
Uruk 290
utopia 133, 211–212

Valenciennes Apocalypse *see* Carolingian Apocalypses

virtue
– life of 5, 28–30, 33, 100
– of the apostles 254, 256
virtues (itemized) 147–148, 151–152, 160, 219, 246, 257, 259
abstinence 95, 132, *see also* continence below
– cardinal 100–101, 246, 301
– celibacy 130, 135
– chastity 129–130, 132, 136
– continence 96, 219
– devotion 134, 136, 246, 259
– faith 18, 60, 62, 77, 103, 140, 147–149, 160, 164–165, 170, 219, 245, 248, 254, 257, 259
– fortitude 100, 246
– hope 87, 130, 141, 144, 147–148, 160, 164–165, 170, 259
– hospitality 132–133
– humility 132, 134, 136, 149, 151–152, 259
– justice 100, 129, 246
– love for God and/or neighbor (charity) 116, 132, 140, 147, 148, 160, 163–165, 170, 259–260
– prudence 100–101, 246
– simplicity (simple-mindedness) 134
– temperance 100, 246
– theological 146–148, 160, 164
– virginity 67, 94–96, 98, 100, cf. 129–130, 136, 160, 165, 170, 251
vision (physical sense), theories of 223–224, 282
vision(s) 2–4, 44, 222, 233–234
– of peace (*visio pacis*), Jerusalem as 137, 140, cf. 152
– theophanic 263–269, 275–276, 278, 282, 284, 286
– vision of God (*visio Dei*) or Christ 4, 14–15, 17–18, 20–23, 25–26, 28–30, 33, 60, 65, 133, 167, 188, 192
visual exegesis 173–194, 263–286
visuality of New Jerusalem 229–262

war
– absence of in consummation 49, 83, cf. 240
– eschatological 102, 112
white garments 2, 40, 44, 133
wife of the Lamb *see* nuptial imagery
wings 30, 202–203
wisdom
– divine 22, 26, 295
– human 257, 259
woman, cities personified as 198
world week 52–53, 160, 162, 168

– eighth day 160, 168
– seventh day 23, 43, 53, 102, 160, 162, 168
– sixth day/millennium 48, 52–53, 250
worship 111, 192, *see also* liturgy and prayer
– in the eschatological Jerusalem 4, 66, 135, 136, 190, 295
– Jewish 77, 78, 79, 81, 88, 91, 303
– John's worship of the angel 183, 188
– Roman 213

Zeus 203, 209